American Women Writers

*A Critical Reference Guide
from Colonial Times to the Present*

A Critical
Reference Guide
from Colonial Times
to the Present

IN FOUR VOLUMES

VOLUME 3 : Li TO R

AMERICAN WOMEN WRITERS

Editor   Lina Mainiero
Associate Editor   Langdon Lynne Faust

Frederick Ungar Publishing Co.
New York

Copyright © 1981 by Frederick Ungar Publishing Co., Inc.
Printed in the United States of America

Designed by Patrick Vitacco

Library of Congress Cataloging in Publication Data

Main entry under title:

American women writers.

   Includes bibliographies.
   1.   American literature—Women authors—History and
criticism.   2.   Women authors, American—Biography.
3.   American literature—Women authors—Bibliography.
I.   Mainiero, Lina.
PS147.A4   016.810′9′9287   78-20945
ISBN 0-8044-3151-5 (v. 1)

CONTENTS: v. 1. A to E.—v. 2. F to LE.—v. 3. Li to R.

Contributors to Volume Three

Adams, Barbara
Aimee Semple McPherson

Alldredge, Betty J.
Katherine Mayo

Anderson, Celia Catlett
Florence Crannell Means
Cornelia Lynde Meigs

Bakerman, Jane S.
Ruth Doan McDougall
Margaret Millar
Toni Morrison

Bannan, Helen M.
Kathleen Anderson McLean
Franc Johnson Newcomb

Barnhart, Jacqueline Baker
Sarah Bayliss Royce

Barr, Marleen S.
Deborah Norris Logan

Benardete, Jane
Elizabeth Palmer Peabody

Ben-Merre, Diana
Helen McCloy

Berke, Jacqueline
Eleanor Hodgman Porter

Bienstock, Beverly Gray
Anita Loos
Shirley MacLaine

Bird, Christiane
Harriet Mulford Stone Lothrop
Alice Duer Miller

Bittker, Anne S.
Mary Margaret MacBride

Blair, Karen J.
Ella Giles Ruddy

Bordin, Ruth
Mary Ashton Rice Livermore

Boyd, Zohara
Sophia Louisa Robbins Little
Josephine Pollard
Martha Remick

Bremer, Sidney H.
Lucy Monroe
Elia Wilkinson Peattie

Brown, Lynda W.
Anne Newport Royall

Buchanan, Harriette Cuttino
  Blair Rice Niles
  Marie Conway Oemler
  Josephine Lyons Scott
    Pinckney
  Lizette Woodworth Reese

Bucknall, Barbara J.
  Phyllis McGinley

Byers, Inzer
  Alma Lutz
  Nellie Neilson
  Martha Laurens Ramsay

Carlin, Sandra
  Louella Oettinger Parsons

Carr, Pat
  Flannery O'Connor

Chew, Martha
  Maria Jane McIntosh

Cohn, Jan
  Mary Roberts Rinehart

Cook, Martha E.
  Katherine Sherwood Bonner
    McDowell
  George Madden Martin
  Mary Noailles Murfree

Cook, Sylvia
  Grace Lumpkin

Crabbe, Katharyn F.
  Ella Farman Pratt

Cutler, Evelyn S.
  Rose Cecil O'Neill

Dame, Enid
  Edna St. Vincent Millay

Darney, Virginia Grant
  Laura Elizabeth Howe
    Richards

Davidson, Cathy N.
  Laura Jean Libbey

Davis, Barbara Kerr
  Ellen Moers

Deegan, Mary Jo
  Helen Merrell Lynd

DeMarr, Mary Jean
  Alice Caldwell Hegan Rice

Deming, Caren J.
  Agnes Eckhardt Nixon
  Irna Phillips

Denniston, Dorothy L.
  Paule Marshall

Eliasberg, Ann Pringle
  Josephine Preston Peabody

Evans, Elizabeth
  Frances Newman
  Margaret Junkin Preston

Ewell, Barbara C.
  Eliza Jane Poitevent Nicholson
  Eliza Lofton Phillips Pugh

Fish, Virginia Kemp
  Annie Marion MacLean

Franklin, Phyllis
Judith Sargent Murray
Elsie Worthington Clews
Parsons

Freibert, Lucy
Jessica Nelson North
MacDonald
Marianne Dwight Orvis

Friedman, Ellen G.
Joyce Carol Oates

Gabbard, Lucina P.
Clare Boothe Luce

Gibbons, Sheila J.
Mary McGrory

Gladstein, Mimi R.
Ayn Rand

Gottfried, Erika
Rose Pesotta

Graham, Theodora R.
Josephine Miles
Harriet Monroe

Greene, Dana
Martha Shepard Lippincott
Lucretia Coffin Mott
Sara Louisa Vickers
Oberholtzer

Hamblen, Abigail Ann
Honoré McCue Willsie
Morrow
Louise Redfield Peattie
Lucy Fitch Perkins

Hannay, Margaret P.
Marabel Morgan

Hardesty, Nancy A.
Phoebe Worrall Palmer
Elizabeth Payson Prentiss

Hardy, Willene S.
Mary Therese McCarthy

Heilbrun, Carolyn G.
A. G. Mojtabai

Healey, Claire
Amy Lowell

Helbig, Alethea K.
Myra Cohn Livingston
Emily Cheney Neville

Henning, Wendy J.
Marie Manning

Hershan, Stella K.
Eleanor Roosevelt Roosevelt

Hill, Vicki Lynn
Theresa Serber Malkiel
Dorothy Myra Page

Hoeveler, Diane Long
Marya Mannes
Jessica Mitford

Holdstein, Deborah H.
Harriet Livermore
Vienna G. Morrell Ramsay
Dora Knowlton Thompson
Ranous
Itti Kinney Reno

Hornstein, Jacqueline
  Sarah Parsons Moorhead
  Sarah Wentworth Apthorp
    Morton
  Sarah Osborn
  Sarah Porter
  Elizabeth Mixer

Johnson, Claudia D.
  Olive Logan
  Clara Morris

Johnson, Robin
  Marianne Craig Moore

Jones, Anne Hudson
  Esther Clayson Pohl Lovejoy
  Kate Campbell Hurd Mead

Kahn, Miriam
  Margaret Mead

Kalechofsky, Roberta
  Cynthia Ozick

Karp, Sheema Hamdani
  Adrienne Cecile Rich

Kaufman, Janet E.
  Mary Ann Webster
    Loughborough
  Judith White Brockenbrough
    McGuire
  Elizabeth Avery Meriwether
  Phoebe Yates Pember
  Sarah Agnes Rice Pryor
  Sallie A. Brock Putnam
  Eliza Moore Chinn McHatton
    Ripley

Keeshen, Kathleen Kearney
  Miriam Ottenberg

Kessler, Carol Farley
  Elizabeth Stuart Phelps

King, Margaret J.
  Elizabeth Linington
  Madalyn Mays Murray O'Hair
  Emily Price Post

Klein, Kathleen G.
  Ruth McKenney
  Anne Nichols

Knapp, Bettina L.
  Anaïs Nin

Koengeter, L. W.
  Adah Isaacs Menken

Kohlstedt, Sally Gregory
  Almira Hart Lincoln Phelps

Koon, Helene
  Anna Cora Mowatt Ritchie
  Elizabeth Robins

Kouidis, Virginia M.
  Mina Loy

Londré, Felicia Hardison
  Jeannette Augustus Marks
  Frances Aymar Mathews
  Adelaide Matthews
  Marguerite Merington
  Lillian Mortimer
  Martha Morton
  Josephina Niggli
  Charlotte Blair Parker
  Lillian Ross

Ludwig, Linda
Margaret Mitchell

McCarthy, Joanne
Betty Bard McDonald
Kathleen Thompson Norris

McCrea, Joan M.
Sylvia Field Porter

McFadden-Gerber, Margaret
Harriet Mann Miller
Louise Dickinson Rich

Madsen, Carole Cornwall
Louisa Lula Greene Richards

Maida, Patricia D.
Lillian O'Donnell

Maio, Kathleen L.
Lenore Glen Offord
Anna Katharine Green Rohlfs

Margolis, Tina
Rochelle Owens

Masteller, Jean Carwile
Annie Nathan Meyer

May, Jill P.
Maud Fuller Petersham

Mayer, Elsie F.
Anne Morrow Lindbergh

Menger, Lucy
Ruth Shick Montgomery
Jane Roberts

Mitchell, Sally
Margaret Mayo
Cora Miranda Baggerly Older
Mary Hayden Green Pike
Rose Porter

Moe, Phyllis
Emily Clark Huntington
Miller

Mollenkott, Virginia Ramey
Grace Livingston Hill Lutz
Sarah Towne Smith Martyn
Marjorie Hope Nicolson

Mortimer, Gail
Katherine Anne Porter

Mossberg, Barbara Antonina
Clarke
Sylvia Plath

Murphy, Maureen
Blanche McManus Mansfield
Mary L. Meany
Asenath Hatch Nicholson
Florence J. O'Connor
Jessie Fremont O'Donnell
Katharine A. O'Keefe
O'Mahoney

Newman, Anne
Julia Mood Peterkin

Nichols, Kathleen L.
Ellen Peck
Harriet Waters Preston

Nochimson, Martha
Carry Amelia Moore Nation
Martha Harrison Robinson

Penn, Patricia E.
Del Martin
Annie Smith Peck

Phillips, Elizabeth
Frances Sargent Locke Osgood

Pogel, Nancy
Constance Mayfield Rourke

Pouncey, Lorene
Vassar Miller

Puk, Francine Shapiro
Victoria Lincoln
Dorothy Rothschild Parker
Frances Gray Patton

Rayson, Ann
Ann Lane Petry

Richmond, Velma Bourgeois
Ruth Painter Randall
Agnes Repplier

Richter, Heddy A.
Olive Higgins Prouty

Roberts, Elizabeth
Fannie W. Rankin
Maggie Roberts

Rosenberg, Julia
Rebecca Rush

Rosinsky, Natalie M.
Anne McCaffrey
Judith Merril
Catherine Lucille Moore

Rowe, Anne
Elizabeth Madox Roberts

Rudnick, Lois R.
Mabel Ganson Dodge Luhan

Ryan, Rosalie Tutela
Jane Erminia Starkweather
Locke

Scanzoni, Letha
Virginia Ramey Mollenkott

Schoen, Carol B.
Penina Moise

Schofield, Ann
Helen Marot

Schwartz, Helen J.
Tillie Olsen
Grace Paley

Shakir, Evelyn
Abigail May Alcott Nieriker

Seaton, Beverly
Alice Lounsberry
Josephine Woempner Clifford
McCrackin
Helen Reimensnyder Martin
Sarah Carter Edgarton Mayo
Helen Alice Matthews Nitsch
Frances Theodora Smith Dana
Parsons
Grace Smith Richmond

Shaffer-Koros, Carole M.
Ruth Putnam

Sharistanian, Janet
Helen Waite Papashvily
Katharine M. Rogers

Sherman, Sarah Way
Louise Chandler Moulton
Mary Alicia Owen

Skaggs, Peggy
Catherine Marshall

Smith, Susan Sutton
Sara Jane Clark Lippincott
Sarah Margaret Fuller,
  Marchesa d'Ossoli
Harriet Jane Hanson Robinson

Snipes, Katherine
Carson Smith McCullers

Sproat, Elaine
Lola Ridge

Staples, Katherine
Caroline E. Rush

Steele, Karen B.
Mary Traill Spence Lowell
  Putnam

Stein, Karen F.
Alice Ruth Moore Dunbar
  Nelson

Stiller, Nikki
Helaine Newstead

Swidler, Arlene Anderson
Sister Madeleva

Sylvander, Carolyn Wedin
Mary Britton Miller
Mary White Ovington

Tebbe, Jennifer L.
Anne O'Hair McCormick

Terris, Virginia R.
Sarah Morgan Bryan Piatt
Jessie Belle Rittenhouse

Thiébaux, Marcelle
Marjorie Kinnan Rawlings

Thomas, Gwendolyn
Pauli Murray

Thompson, Ann
Rosemary Radford Ruether

Thompson, Dorothea Mosley
Mary Simmerson Cunningham
  Logan
Ruth Bryan Owen
Irma von Starkloff Rombauer

Turner, Alberta
Muriel Rukeyser

Uphaus, Suzanne Henning
Marge Piercy

Wahlstrom, Billie J.
Alice Mary Norton
Joanna Russ

Walker, Cynthia L.
Caroline Pafford Miller
Myrtle Reed

Ward, Jean M.
*Bethenia Angelina
Owens-Adair*

Werden, Frieda L.
Kate Millett

White, Barbara A.
*Frances Gray Patton
Marilla M. Ricker*

Wolfson, Rose
Klara Goldzieher Roman

Young, Melanie
Harriet Fanning Read

Zilboorg, Caroline
*Louisa Susannah Cheves
McCord
Dolley Payne Todd Madison
Maria G. Milward
Agnes Woods Mitchell
Mrs. H. J. Moore
Martha Read*

Writers Included, Volumes 1-4

Pen names and pseudonyms are cross-referenced to the article's title in this table of contents.

Dix, Dorothea Lynde
Dix, Dorothy. *See* Gilmer,
  Elizabeth Meriwether
Dixon, Franklin W. *See* Adams,
  Harriet Stratemeyer
Dodge, Mabel. *See* Luhan,
  Mabel Ganson Dodge
Dodge, Mary Abigail
Dodge, Mary Mapes
Dominic, R. B. *See* Lathen,
  Emma
Donovan, Frances R.
Doolittle, Antoinette
Doolittle, Hilda
Dorr, Julia Caroline Ripley
Dorr, Rheta Childe
Dorsey, Anna Hanson
  McKenney
Dorsey, Ella Loraine
Dorsey, Sarah Anna Ellis
Doubleday, Nellie Blanchan
  De Graff
Douglas, Amanda Minnie
Douglas, Ann
Drew, Elizabeth
Drinker, Elizabeth Sandwith
DuBois, Shirley Graham. *See*
  Graham, Shirley
DuJardin, Rosamond Neal
Dunbar, Alice. *See* Nelson,
  Alice Ruth Moore Dunbar
Duncan, Isadora
Duniway, Abigail Scott
Dunlap, Jane. *See* Davis, Adelle
Dupuy, Eliza Ann
Durant, Ariel
Durant, Mrs. Kenneth. *See*
  Taggard, Genevieve
Durrant, Theo. *See* Offord,
  Lenore Glen

Dwight, Marianne. *See* Orvis,
  Marianne Dwight
Dykeman, Wilma

Earle, Alice Morse
Eastman, Crystal
Eastman, Elaine Goodale
Eastman, Mary Henderson
E. B. C. *See* Bayard, Elise Justine
Eberhart, Mignon Good
E. B. W. *See* Wells, Emmeline
  Blanche Woodward
Ecclesiae, Filia. *See* Dorsey,
  Sarah Ann Ellis
Eckstorm, Fannie Hardy
Eddy, Mary Baker Glover
Edgarton, Sarah C. *See* Mayo,
  Sarah Carter Edgarton
Edson, N. I. *See* Denison, Mary
  Andrews
Edwards, Eleanor Lee. *See*
  Victor, Metta Victoria Fuller
Egan, Lesley. *See* Linington,
  Elizabeth
E. H. *See* Tietjens, Eunice
  Hammond
Eiker, Mathilde
E. J. B. *See* Bayard, Elise Justine
Elder, Susan Blanchard
Eliot, Alice C. *See* Jewett,
  Sarah Orne
Ellen Louise. *See* Moulton,
  Louise Chandler
Ellet, Elizabeth Fries Lummis
Elliot, Elisabeth
Elliott, Maude Howe
Elliott, Sarah Barnwell
Ellis, Anne
Ellis, Edith

Florepha. *See* Hall, Sarah Ewing
Flynn, Elizabeth Gurley
Follen, Eliza Lee Cabot
Foote, Mary Hallock
Forbes, Esther
Forbes, Kathryn. *See* McLean,
    Kathryn Anderson
Ford, Harriet
Ford, Sallie Rochester
Forrester, Fanny. *See* Judson,
    Emily Chubbuck
Forten, Charlotte L.
Foster, Hannah Webster
Fox, Helen Morgenthau
Fox, Paula
Francesca. *See* Alexander,
    Francesca
Frank. *See* Whitcher, Frances
    Miriam Berry
Frankau, Pamela
Franken, Rose
Franziska, Mathilde. *See* Anneke,
    Mathilde Franziska Giesler
Freeman, Mary Eleanor Wilkins
Fremantle, Anne Jackson
French, Anne Warner
French, Lucy Virginia Smith
Friedan, Betty
Frings, Ketti
Fuller, Frances. *See* Victor,
    Frances Fuller
Fuller, Margaret. *See* Ossoli,
    Marchesa Sarah Margaret
    Fuller, d'
Fuller, Metta Victoria. *See*
    Victor, Metta Victoria Fuller
Furness, Edith Ellis. *See* Ellis,
    Edith
F. W. R. *See* Rankin, Fannie W.

Gage, Frances Dana Barker
Gale, Zona
Gardener, Helen Hamilton
    Chenoweth
Gardner, Isabella
Gardner, Mary Sewall
Garrigue, Jean
Gary, Dorothy Page. *See* Page,
    Dorothy Myra
Gates, Eleanor
Gates, Susa Young
Gellhorn, Martha
Genêt. *See* Flanner, Janet
George, Jean Craighead
Gerould, Katharine Fullerton
Gerstenberg, Alice
Gestefeld, Ursula Newell
Gibbs, Mary Foster. *See* Gates,
    Susa Young
Gilbert, Fabiola Cabeza de Baca
Gilchrist, Annie Somers
Giles, Ella. *See* Ruddy, Ella Giles
Gill, Sarah Prince
Gilman, Caroline Howard
Gilman, Charlotte Perkins
    Stetson
Gilmer, Elizabeth Meriwether
Giovanni, Nikki
Glasgow, Ellen Anderson
    Gholson
Glaspell, Susan
Godchaux, Elma
Godwin, Gail
Goldman, Emma
Goodale, Elaine. *See* Eastman,
    Elaine Goodale
Goodsell, Willystine
Goodwin, Maud Wilder
Gordon, Caroline

Harris, Bertha

Harris, Corra May White

Harris, Mrs. L. H. *See* Harris,
Corra May White

Harris, Miriam Coles

Harris, Mrs. Sidney S. *See*
Harris, Miriam Coles

Harrison, Constance Cary

Hart, Frances Noyes

Hartwell, Mary. *See*
Catherwood, Mary Hartwell

Hasbrouck, Lydia Sayer

Hastings, Susannah Willard
Johnson

Hatch, Mary R. Platt

Haven, Alice Bradley

Haven, Emily Bradley Neal.
See Haven, Alice Bradley

Hawthorne, Elizabeth Manning

Hawthorne, Hildegarde

Hawthorne, Rose. *See* Lathrop,
Rose Hawthorne

Hay, Elzey. *See* Andrews, Eliza
Frances

Hay, Timothy. *See* Brown,
Margaret Wise

Haydn, H. *See* Read, Martha

Hayes, Henry. *See* Kirk, Ellen
Warner Olney

Hazlett, Helen

H. B. G. *See* Talcott, Hannah
Elizabeth Bradbury Goodwin

H. D. *See* Doolittle, Hilda

Hegan, Alice Caldwell. *See* Rice,
Alice Caldwell Hegan

Heilbrun, Carolyn G.

Helen. *See* Whitman, Sarah
Helen Power

Helfenstein, Ernest. *See* Smith,
Elizabeth Oakes Prince

Hellman, Lillian

Hemingway, Martha. *See*
Gellhorn, Martha

Henderson, Zenna

Henkle, Henrietta. *See*
Buckmaster, Henrietta

Hennissart, Martha. *See* Lathen,
Emma

Henry, Alice

Henry, Marguerite

Hentz, Caroline Lee Whiting

Hermine. *See* Elder, Susan
Blanchard

Herschberger, Ruth

Hewitt, Mary Elizabeth Moore

Heyward, Dorothy Hartzell
Kuhns

Heywood, Martha Spence

H. H. *See* Jackson, Helen Maria
Fiske Hunt

Higgins, Marguerite

Higginson, Ella Rhoads

Higham, Mary R.

Highet, Helen MacInnes

Highsmith, Patricia

Hill, Grace Livingston. *See*
Lutz, Grace Livingston Hill

Hobart, Alice Nourse Tisdale

Hobbes, John Oliver. *See*
Craigie, Pearl Mary Teresa
Richards

Hobson, Laura Keane Zametkin

Hoffman, Malvina

Holden, Roger. *See* Guiney,
Louise Imogen

Holding, Elisabeth Sanxay

Holley, Marietta

Hollingworth, Leta Stetter

Holme, Saxe. *See* Jackson, Helen
Maria Fiske Hunt

Johnson, Diane
Johnson, Georgia Douglas Camp
Johnson, Helen Louise Kendrick
Johnson, Josephine Winslow
Johnson, Mrs. Rossiter. *See*
  Johnson, Helen Louise
  Kendrick
Johnson, Susannah Willard. *See*
  Hastings, Susannah Willard
  Johnson
Johnston, Annie Fellows
Johnston, Mary
Jones, Amanda Theodocia
Jones, Edith. *See* Wharton, Edith
  Newbold Jones
Jones, Gayl
Jones, Mary Harris
Jones, Mother. *See* Jones, Mary
  Harris
Jong, Erica
Jordan, Kate
Josiah Allen's Wife. *See* Holley,
  Marietta
Judd, Cyril. *See* Merril, Judith
Judson, Emily Chubbuck
June, Jennie. *See* Croly, Jane
  Cunningham

Kael, Pauline
Kavanaugh, Cynthia. *See* Daniels,
  Dorothy
Keating, Sally. *See* Wood, Sally
  Sayward Barrell
Keemle, Mary Katherine. *See*
  Field, Kate
Keene, Carolyn. *See* Adams,
  Harriet Stratemeyer
Keith, Agnes Newton
Keller, Helen Adams
Kelley, Edith Summers

Kellogg, Louise
Kelly, Bernice. *See* Harris,
  Bernice Kelly
Kelly, Eleanor Mercein
Kelly, Myra
Kemble, Frances Anne
Kemble, Miss Fanny. *See* Kemble,
  Frances Anne
Kennedy, Rose. *See* Victor,
  Metta Victoria Fuller
Kerr, Jean Collins
Kerr, Sophie. *See* Underwood,
  Sophie Kerr
Keyes, Frances Parkinson
  Wheeler
Kilmer, Aline Murray
Kimbrough, Emily
King, Mrs. Francis. *See* King,
  Louisa Yeomans
King, Grace Elizabeth
King, Louisa Yeomans
King, Sue Petigru. *See* Bowen,
  Sue Petigru
Kingston, Maxine Hong
Kinney, Elizabeth Clementine
  Dodge
Kinzie, Juliette Augusta Magill
Kirby, Georgiana Bruce
Kirk, Ellen Warner Olney
Kirkland, Caroline Matilda
  Stansbury
Knapp, Bettina Liebowitz
Knight, Sarah Kemble
Knowles, Sarah. *See* Bolton,
  Sarah Knowles
Knox, Adeline Trafton
Koch, Adrienne
Kohut, Rebekah Bettelheim
Konigsburg, E. L.
Kroeber, Theodora

Pilbury, Aunt. *See* Winslow, Helen Maria

Pinckney, Josephine Lyons Scott

Pine, Cuyler. *See* Peck, Ellen

Plath, Sylvia

Pocahontas. *See* Smith, Eliza Roxey Snow

Pogson, Sara. *See* Smith, Sarah Pogson

P O. L. *See* Guiney, Louise Imogen

Pollard, Josephine

Porter, Eleanor Hodgman

Porter, Gene Stratton. *See* Stratton-Porter, Gene

Porter, Katherine Anne

Porter, Rose

Porter, Sarah

Porter, Sylvia Field

Post, Emily Price

Pratt, Ella Farman

Prence, Katherine. *See* Mayo, Katherine

Prentiss, Elizabeth Payson

Prescott, Harriett. *See* Spofford, Harriett Elizabeth Prescott

Preston, Harriet Waters

Preston, Margaret Junkin

Prouty, Olive Higgins

Pryor, Sara Agnes Rice

Pugh, Eliza Lofton Phillips

Putnam, Emily James Smith

Putnam, Mary. *See* Jacobi, Mary Putnam

Putnam, Mary Traill Spence Lowell

Putnam, Ruth

Putnam, Sallie A. Brock

Quinn, H. *See* Aldrich, Mildred

Rachel. *See* Dinnies, Anna Peyre Shackelford

Raimond, C. E. *See* Robins, Elizabeth

Ramsay, Martha Laurens

Ramsay, Vienna G. Morrell

Rand, Ayn

Randall, Ruth Painter

Randau, Mrs. Carl. *See* Zugsmith, Leane

Rankin, Fannie W.

Ranous, Dora Knowlton Thompson

Rawlings, Marjorie Kinnan

Ray, John. *See* Carrington, Elaine Stern

Read, Harriette Fanning

Read, Martha

Redfield, Martin. *See* Brown, Alice

Reed, Myrtle

Reese, Lizette Woodworth

Refugitta. *See* Harrison, Constance Cary

Regester, Seeley. *See* Victor, Metta Victoria Fuller

Reid, Christian. *See* Tiernan, Frances Christine Fisher

Remick, Martha

Remitrom, Naillil. *See* Mortimer, Lillian

Reno, Itti Kinney

Repplier, Agnes

Rhoads, Ella. *See* Higginson, Ella Rhoads

Rice, Alice Caldwell Hegan

Rich, Adrienne Cecile

Rich, Barbara. *See* Jackson, Laura Riding

Rich, Louise Dickinson

Richards, Laura Elizabeth Howe
Richards, Louisa Lula Greene
Richmond, Grace Louise Smith
Ricker, Marilla M.
Ridge, Lola
Riding, Laura. *See* Jackson, Laura Riding
Riggs, Mrs. *See* Wiggin, Kate Douglas Smith
Rinehart, Mary Roberts
Rip, Henry. *See* Townsend, Mary Ashley Van Vooris
Rip Van Winkle. *See* Jackson, Helen Maria Fiske Hunt
Ripley, Eliza Moore Chinn McHatton
Ritchie, Anna Cora Ogden Mowatt
Rittenhouse, Jessie Belle
Rivers, Pearl. *See* Nicholson, Eliza Jane Poitevent
Rives, Amélie. *See* Troubetskoy, Amélie Rives
Roberts, Elizabeth Madox
Roberts, Jane
Roberts, Maggie
Robins, Elizabeth
Robinson, Harriet Jane Hanson
Robinson, Martha Harrison
Rodman, Ella. *See* Church, Ella Rodman MacIlvane
Rodman, Maia. *See* Wojciechowska, Maia
Rogers, Adela. *See* St. John, Adela Rogers
Rogers, Katherine M.
Rohlfs, Anna Katherine Green
Roman, Klara Goldzieher
Rombauer, Irma von Starkloff
Roosevelt, Eleanor Roosevelt

Ross, Helaine. *See* Daniels, Dorothy
Ross, Lillian
Rourke, Constance Mayfield
Royall, Anne Newport
Royce, Sarah Bayliss
Ruddy, Ella Giles
Ruether, Rosemary Radford
Rukeyser, Muriel
Rupert, Elinore. *See* Stewart, Elinore Pruitt
Rush, Caroline E.
Rush, Rebecca
Russ, Joanna

Sachs, Marilyn
Sadlier, Anna Theresa
Sadlier, Mary Anne Madden
Sage, Juniper. *See* Brown, Margaret Wise
St. John, Adela Rogers
Salisbury, Charlotte Y.
Salmon, Lucy Maynard
Sandoz, Mari
Sanford, Mollie Dorsey
Sanger, Margaret
Sangster, Margaret Elizabeth Munson
Sapoukhyn, Vera. *See* Seawell, Molly Elliot
Sarton, May
Satir, Virginia M.
Savage, Elizabeth
Sawyer, Caroline Mehetable Fisher
Sawyer, Ruth
Sayer, Lydia. *See* Hasbrouck, Lydia Sayer
Scarborough, Dorothy
Schaeffer, Susan Fromberg

Trask, Kate Nichols
Treadwell, Sophie
Tremaine, Paul. *See* Johnson,
    Georgia Douglas Camp
Trevor, Frances. *See* Tietjens,
    Eunice Hammond
Trilling, Diana
Troubetskoy, Amélie Rives
Trusta, H. *See* Phelps, Elizabeth
    Stuart
Tuchman, Barbara Wertheim
Turell, Jane
Turnbull, Agnes Sligh
Turnbull, Charlotte
Turner, Bessie A.
Turner, Lida Larrimore
Turney, Catherine
Tuthill, Louisa Caroline Huggins
Tuve, Rosemund
Tyler, Anne
Tyler, Martha

Uhnak, Dorothy
Ulanov, Ann Belford
Umsted, Lillie Devereux. *See*
    Blake, Lillie Devereux
Uncle Ben. *See* White, Rhoda
    Elizabeth Waterman
Underwood, Sophie Kerr
Untermeyer, Jean Starr
Upton, Harriet Taylor

Valentine, Jo. *See* Armstrong,
    Charlotte
Valerio, Katherine. *See*
    Washburn, Katharine
    Sedgwick

Van Alstyne, Frances Jane
    Crosby
Vance, Clara. *See* Denison, Mary
    Andrews
Vandegrift, Margaret. *See*
    Janvier, Margaret Thompson
Vanderbilt, Amy
Van Duyn, Mona
Van Rensselaer, Mariana
    Griswold
Van Vorst, Bessie McGinnis
Van Vorst, Mrs. John. *See* Van
    Vorst, Bessie McGinnis
Van Vorst, Marie
Velazquez, Loreta Janeta
Vendler, Helen Hennessy
Vicery, Eliza. *See* Vickery,
    Sukey
Vickery, Sukey
Victor, Frances Fuller
Victor, Metta Victoria Fuller
Vining, Elizabeth Gray
Vorse, Mary Marvin Heaton

Wakoski, Diane
Wald, Lillian D.
Walker, Alice
Walker, Margaret
Walker, Mary Spring
Waller, Mary Ella
Waln, Nora
Walton, Evangeline
Walworth, Jeannette Ritchie
Ward, Elizabeth Stuart Phelps
Ward, Mrs. H. O. *See* Bloomfield-
    Moore, Clara Sophia Jessup
Ward, Mary Jane
Ware, Katharine Augusta Rhodes

Abbreviations of Reference Works

AA   American Authors, 1600–1900: A Biographical Dictionary of American Literature (Eds. S. J. Kunitz and H. Haycraft, 1938).

AW   American Women: Fifteen-Hundred Biographies with Over 1,400 Portraits (2 vols., Eds. F. E. Willard and M. A. Livermore, 1897). This is a revised edition of *A Woman of the Century* (1893).

CA   Contemporary Authors: A Bio-Bibliographical Guide to Current Authors and Their Works (various editors, 1962–present).

CAL   Cyclopaedia of American Literature, Embracing Personal and Critical Notices of Authors and Selections from Their Writings (2 vols., Eds. E. A. Duyckinck and G. L. Duyckinck, 1866).

CB   Current Biography: Who's News and Why (Eds. M. Block, 1940–1943; A. Rothe, 1944–1953; M. D. Candee, 1954–1958; C. Moritz, 1959–present).

DAB   Dictionary of American Biography (10 vols., Eds. A. Johnson and D. Malone; 5 suppls., Eds. E. T. James and J. A. Garraty; 1927–1977).

FPA   The Female Poets of America (Ed. R. W. Griswold, 1849).

HWS   History of Woman Suffrage (Vols. 1–3, Eds. E. C. Stanton, S. B. Anthony, and M. J. Gage; Vol. 4, Eds. S. B. Anthony and I. H. Harper; Vols. 5 and 6, Ed. I. H. Harper; 1881–1922).

LSL   Library of Southern Literature, Compiled under the Direct Supervision of Southern Men of Letters (16 vols., Eds. E. A. Alderman and J. C. Harris; Suppl., Eds. E. A. Alderman, C. A. Smith, and J. C. Metcalf, reprinted 1970).

NAW   Notable American Women, 1607–1950: A Biographical Dictionary (3 vols., Eds. E. T. James, J. W. James, and P. S. Boyer, 1971).

NCAB   National Cyclopedia of American Biography: Being the History of the United States As Illustrated in the Lives of the Founders, Builders, and Defenders of the Republic, and of the Men and Women Who Are Doing the Work and Moulding the Thought of the Present Time (various editors, Vols. 1–57, 1892–1976; Vols. A–M, Permanent Series, 1930–1978).

20thCA *Twentieth Century Authors: A Biographical Dictionary of Modern Literature* (Eds. S. J. Kunitz and H. Haycraft, 1942).

20thCAS *Twentieth Century Authors, First Supplement: A Biographical Dictionary of Modern Literature* (Eds. S. J. Kunitz and V. Colby, 1955).

WA *World Authors, 1950–1970: A Companion Volume to Twentieth Century Authors* (Ed. J. Wakeman, 1975).

Abbreviations of Periodicals

In the bibliographies, periodicals have been abbreviated in conformity with the Modern Language Association master list of abbreviations. Newspapers and magazines not in that list are abbreviated as follows:

AHR   *American Historical Review*
CathW   *Catholic World*
CSM   *Christian Science Monitor*
EngElemR   *English Elementary Review*
JSocHis   *Journal of Social History*
KR   *Kirkus Review*
NewR   *New Republic*
NYHT   *New York Herald Tribune*
NYHTB   *New York Herald Tribune Books*
NYT   *New York Times*
NYTMag   *New York Times Magazine*
NYTBR   *New York Times Book Review*
PW   *Publisher's Weekly*
SatEvePost   *Saturday Evening Post*
ScribM   *Scribner's Magazine*
VV   *Village Voice*
WallStJ   *Wall Street Journal*
WLB   *Wilson Library Bulletin*
WrD   *Writer's Digest*
WSCL   *Wisconsin Studies in Contemporary Literature*

American Women Writers

A Critical Reference Guide
from Colonial Times to the Present

Laura Jean Libbey

B. 22 March 1862, Brooklyn, New York; d. 25 Oct. 1925, New York City
D. of Thomas H. and Elizabeth Nelson Libbey; m. Van Mater Stilwell, 1898

L. was one of this country's most prolific writers of fiction, publishing some eighty volumes in her thirty-year career as a popular novelist. Her fiction provided a formula for female escape literature which persists even into the present. Yet despite her productivity and popularity, L.'s current reputation is negligible and her biography obscure. Most of L.'s novels were printed serially in newspapers, magazines, and the weekly "story papers," and then reprinted in cheap paperbound editions. Few libraries kept these inexpensive copies of her once best-selling books.

The obscurity of her biography is partly owing to L.'s own sense that her private life was not the public's business. We do know that she lived most of her life in Brooklyn, although as an adult she traveled continually in order to promote her books. On most of these journeys, the author was accompanied by her mother, a strict, domineering woman who governed L.'s life and forbade her daughter to marry. L. disobeyed this command only after her mother's death in 1898. True to the heroines in her fiction, the popular novelist gave up her career upon marriage to a respectable husband. Only after nearly a decade of retirement could she be coaxed to work again.

L. was a leading practitioner of the so-called working-girl novel. These books about young, female proletarian protagonists netted the author over fifty thousand dollars a year, hardly a working-class income by any standard. All of the novels preached the same simple and not very original message: A young girl who remains virtuous (i.e., virginal) can ultimately expect to secure not only a husband and happiness, but a fortune too.

Not one of the novels can be singled out from the L. canon since each, invariably, tells the same story, shares the same plot, preaches the same moral, and portrays the same heroes, heroines, villains, and villainesses. The books all include compulsory scenes depicting the harshness of city life, thus echoing a standard theme in much popular fiction of the last decade of the 19th c. Named little Leafy, pretty Guelda, or poor Faynie, the heroine attempts to make her way alone in the cruel city. After having been cast out of her idyllic rural home, often by a wicked stepmother or selfish foster parent, she finds she now must support herself and frequently must support indigent siblings as well. In a backhanded and almost ludicrously sentimentalized fashion, this formulaic plot attests to a changing pattern in the American labor force after the Civil War, when women were finding employment in increasing numbers, frequently in low-paying factory jobs.

But L.'s novels do not focus much on the actual working conditions endured by the female protagonists. Instead, the heroine's energies are devoted to fending off often hostile masculine attentions. Only after a series of victimizations is the heroine finally rescued by the hero, a character both virtuous and prosperous. Their marriage presages happiness ever after and an end to both the threat of assault and the daily grind of a factory job. Although men are always the aggressors in these novels and the heroine's moral character is never even questioned, it is interesting to note that the heroine alone is responsible for maintaining her virtue.

The message of L.'s novels is a conservative one, and certainly one that ran counter to ideas endorsed by a growing number of feminists in late-19th-c. America; but the credo she preached is of interest to the social historian. What Horatio Alger did for American working-class men, L. did for female readers. Alger's heroes worked hard, took advantage of every opportunity, and, against all odds, realized the American dream. L.'s heroines worked hard too. But the 19th-c. business world held few opportunities for women. So real success for L.'s heroines came through successful marriage. L.'s socially conservative fables, however we might object to them, spoke to millions of working-class women who needed a fantasy of their own to take them away from the real grime of the sweatshops, the bookbinderies, and the cotton mills.

WORKS: This is a representative list of Libbey's novels, many of which are not even listed in the Library of Congress catalogues: *A Fatal Wooing* (1883). *All for Love of a Fair Face; or, A Broken Betrothal* (1885). *Madolin Rivers; or, The Little Beauty of Red Oak Seminary: A Love Story* (1885). *A Forbidden Marriage; or, In Love with a Handsome Spendthrift* (1888). *Miss Middleton's Lover; or, Parted on Their Bridal Tour* (1888). *Leonie Locke: The Romance of a Beautiful New York Working Girl* (1889). *Willful Gaynell; or, The Little Beauty of the Passaic Cotton Mills* (1890). *Little Leafy, the Cloakmaker's Beautiful Daughter: A Romantic Story of a Lovely Working Girl in the City of New York* (1891). *A Master Workman's Oath; or, Coralie the*

Unfortunate: A Love Story Portraying the Life, Romance, and Strange Fate of a Beautiful New York Working Girl (1892). *Only a Mechanic's Daughter: A Charming Story of Love and Passion* (1892). *Parted at the Altar* (1893). *A Handsome Engineer's Flirtation; or, How He Won the Hearts of Girls* (190?). *Was She Sweetheart or Wife* (190?). *Wooden Wives: Is It a Story for Philandering Husbands?* (1923).

BIBLIOGRAPHY: Davidson, C. N., and A. E. Davidson, "Carrie's Sisters: The Popular Prototypes for Dreiser's Heroine," *MFS* (Autumn 1977). Noel, M., *Villains Galore: The Heyday of the Popular Story Weekly* (1954). Papashvily, H. W., *All the Happy Endings* (1956).

For articles in reference works, see: *NAW* (article by S. G. Walcutt). *NCAB*, 19.

Other references: *American Mercury* (Sept. 1931). *Historical Society of Michigan Chronicle* (4th quarter 1975).

CATHY N. DAVIDSON

Victoria Lincoln

B. 23 Oct. 1904, Fall River, Massachusetts
D. of Jonathan Thayer and Louise Sears Cobb Lincoln; m. Isaac Watkins, 1927; m. Victor Lowe, 1934

L.'s father was a well-to-do manufacturer of textile machinery. She grew up in a small mill town where she was educated in the public schools before attending Radcliffe. She wrote poetry from a rather early age. L. married Watkins the year she graduated from Radcliffe, but was divorced in 1933. She married Lowe, a philosophy student, the following year and now resides in Baltimore, where he works as a teacher at Johns Hopkins. Since her marriage, she has dedicated herself to her art, producing an impressive number of novels and novellas, as well as volumes of short stories and poems originally published in such magazines as *The New Yorker, Harper's,* and *Cosmopolitan.* She is researching a volume on St. Teresa of Avila.

L.'s most popular novel, *February Hill* (1934), appeared as a motion picture and play, *The Primrose Path.* The dry humor which characterizes the narrative tone counterpoints the outlandish vagaries of the characters. For instance, the Harrises' shanty is described as a "brazen slattern of a place" and "a sort of architectural portrait of Grandma." The bewigged, rouged matriarch lives with her golden-hearted prostitute daughter Minna; her three granddaughters (a virginal, innocent petty thief; a homely, soured mill worker; and a precocious youngster fast following in Minna's footsteps); the moody philosopher brother; and their Harvard-educated, alcoholic father. Despite the burlesque qualities of the narrative, L. prevents the novel from disintegrating into caricature by incorporating her firsthand knowledge of small-town life through an excellent use of local color and dialect. The story has a sparkling vitality, and the simple philosophy of "People must be who they are" is amply suited to the youthful quality of the work.

The biographical novel *Charles* (1962) deals with "how Charles got to be the Dickens of the great middle-period" and is faithful to the facts. Despite her great love and admiration for Dickens, L. describes him as "the near-miss great writer who would have been so much better if he had been capable of understanding what Mary Hogarth tried to tell him about his crippling sentimentality and arrivisme." The characters appear more stylized and distanced than in her other works, but L.'s wry humor is again pervasive.

L. seems most attuned to writing about minority groups and the poor. Although many of her characters border on caricature, she is at her best when writing about children and "innocents." Their simplicity allows the presentation of a moral battlefield upon which to confront various complex issues. The Apache boy in "A Necklace for a Saint," whose "body stiffened at the touch that sought to diminish his one possession, his precious grief," eventually finds his place through a new flexibility born of compassion and humility combined with his innate moral sense. It is this vision of people's suffering combined with their "capacity to ask questions, to find that singular occasional *yes*" that continually finds voice in L.'s writing.

As a writer, L. has been unjustly neglected in recent years, just as her poetry was ignored during her writing career. However, her use of metaphoric language combined with her often humorous and insightful elucidation of the human predicament is not only entertaining, but richly rewarding.

WORKS: *The Swan Island Murders* (1930). *February Hill* (1934; dramatization, 1938; film version, 1940). *Grandmother and the Comet* (1944). *The Wind at My Back* (1946). *Celia Amberley* (1949). *Out from Eden* (1951). *The Wild Honey* (1953). *A Dangerous Innocence* (1958). *Charles* (1962). *Desert Water* (1963). *Everyhow Remarkable* (1967). *A Private Disgrace: Lizzie Borden by Daylight* (1967).

BIBLIOGRAPHY: For articles in reference works, see: *CA, Permanent Series* (1975). *Ohio Authors and Their Books*, Ed. W. Coyle (1962). *20thCAS.*
Other references: *Booklist* (1 June 1958). *KR* (July 1951). *Nation* (23 Nov. 1946). *NY* (26 April 1958). *NYHTB* (20 April 1958). *NYT* (28 Oct. 1934). *WLB* (March 1945).

FRANCINE SHAPIRO PUK

Anne Morrow Lindbergh

B. *22 June 1906, Englewood, New Jersey*
D. *of Dwight and Elizabeth Cutter Morrow; m. Charles A. Lindbergh, 1929*

Born into a family devoted to books and scholarship, L. learned to value education, self-discipline, and personal ambition from an early age. She acquired a sense of history firsthand from traveling with her parents throughout Europe. L. received a B.A. (1928) from Smith College, where she also earned recognition as a writer. With her marriage, the publicity engulfing Lindbergh extended to L., shattering the privacy she had treasured.

After her marriage L. learned to fly and operate radio, studied dead reckoning and celestial navigation, and became the first woman in America to obtain a glider-pilot's license. Between 1931 and 1933 L. assisted her husband in charting the international air routes later used for commercial air travel. For her work as copilot and radio operator in flights exceeding forty thousand miles over five continents, the National Geographic Society awarded her the Hubbard Gold Medal in 1934.

In the midst of these achievements the public curiosity haunting the Lindberghs reached frenzied levels with the kidnapping and murder of their twenty-month-old son in 1932. The tragedy and the prolonged investigation terminated with the conviction of Bruno Richard Hauptman. In December 1935, for protection and privacy, the Lindberghs left the U.S. for England, and later France; when World War II descended on Europe in 1939, the Lindberghs returned to the U.S. Since her husband's death in 1974, L. has continued to occupy the family home in Darien, Connecticut, while maintaining a residence on the Hawaiian island of Maui. Although her duties as celebrity and mother of a large family have drawn heavily on her energy, L. has never abandoned her writing career, producing both fiction and nonfiction throughout her life.

In *Gift from the Sea* (1955), originally conceived as a series of auto-biographical essays, L. presents a microcosm of modern American womanhood as contemplated by a solitary figure in retreat at a seashore. With attention to the effects of marriage on woman's struggle for self-identity, L. traces the stages of marriage from the early self-contained relationship between man and woman, through the middle years weighed down with responsibilities, and finally to the mature marriage characterized by a newly acquired sense of freedom.

With the abandoned argonauta, one of several seashells used to symbolize the different stages of marriage, L. offers her view of the ideal relationship: "the meeting of two whole fully developed people as persons." Recognizing that the many demands of marriage hinder woman's growth, L. advocates as a counterbalance to these demands periods of solitude devoted to creativity. If practiced, such creativity would yield self-knowledge. Having reaffirmed her faith in the power of solitude, L. leaves the seashore, strengthened by her reflections, especially by her awareness of the dynamic nature of life. With her customary modesty, L. acknowledges that her answer to woman's predicament is not definitive, except in her assertion that the desire for self-identity will persist. Moreover, she admits new problems will appear just as certainly as the ebb and flow of the sea continues. With this, her most significant work, L. reveals not only her poetic sensitivity but her insight into the nature of womanhood as well.

L.'s single collection of poetry, *The Unicorn, and Other Poems* (1956), presents the spiritual odyssey of an individual pursuing personal freedom. Throughout the poems, L. identifies the demons obstructing this pursuit, all the while attempting to destroy them. Irregular lyric forms appropriately capture her meandering reflections, just as images drawn from winter effectively support passages dealing with spiritual isolation in contrast to the aerial images signaling hope and joy.

L. returns to the theme of marriage in her novel *Dearly Beloved* (1962). Writing in the tradition of the experimental novel, L. eschews simple narration in favor of the stream-of-consciousness technique as a means of revealing certain basic truths about marriage. Organized around the single event of a family wedding in a structure reminiscent of Virginia Woolf's *Mrs. Dalloway*, the novel examines the different attitudes towards marriage held by the wedding guests. As the minister recites the traditional marriage formula and the guests reveal their innermost thoughts, the contradiction between religious precepts and experienced reality gradually emerges. With remarkable restraint but unabashed candor L. crushes the romantic myth surrounding marriage. In the final pages of the novel marriage is redefined simply as a state offering two people a unique opportunity for human growth; hence, a wedding should be a joyous occasion because it crystallizes this awareness. Although L.'s characters remain wooden with little interaction among them, they function effectively insofar as they represent different points of view in this ideational novel.

L.'s literary themes have their genesis in the five volumes of her letters and diaries. From these pages there emerges the figure of a sensitive individual with a penchant for writing, whose circumstances in life have plunged her into the maelstrom of public activity. The anxiety resulting from these conflicting forces and her determination to assert spiritual independence spill over into L.'s writing, making it all of one piece.

L.'s artistic forte lies in her ability to shape her themes into impressive forms. Since her themes are open-ended, her forms are appropriately organic: the lyric, the stream-of-consciousness novel, the familiar essay. L. manages aesthetic distance by objectifying nature. Seashells, barren trees, the sky, birds, and mountains are favorite images conveying her vision. L.'s astute handling of diverse forms and her instinct for selecting the near-perfect image have contributed to her reputation as a significant modern writer.

WORKS: *North to the Orient* (1935). *Listen! The Wind* (1938). *The Wave of the Future* (1940). *The Steep Ascent* (1944). *Gift from the Sea* (1955). *The Unicorn, and Other Poems: 1935–1955* (1956). *Dearly Beloved: A Theme and Variations* (1962). *Earth Shine* (1966). *Bring Me a Unicorn: Diaries and Letters of Anne Morrow Lindbergh, 1922–1928* (1971). *Hour of Gold, Hour of Lead* (1973). *Locked Rooms and Open Doors: Diaries and Letters of Anne Morrow Lindbergh, 1933–1935* (1974). *The Flower and the Nettle: Diaries and Letters, 1936–1939* (1976). *War Within and Without: Diaries and Letters, 1939–1944* (1980).

BIBLIOGRAPHY: For articles in reference works, see: *CA*, 17–20 (1976). *CB* (Nov. 1940; June 1976). *NCAB*, F. *20thCA*. *20thCAS*.
Other references: *America* (28 Feb. 1968). *NYT* (10 June 1962). *NYTBR* (20 March 1955; 27 Feb. 1972). *SR* (2 April 1955; 12 Jan. 1957).

ELSIE F. MAYER

Elizabeth Linington

B. *11 March 1921, Aurora, Illinois*
Writes under: Anne Blaisdell, Lesley Egan, Elizabeth Linington, Egan O'Neill,
Dell Shannon
D. *of Byron and Ruth Biggam Linington*

L. has lived in California since 1928, graduating from Glendale College (B.A. 1942), where she began her writing career with radio and stage dramas. Her first novel, *The Proud Man* (1955), drew upon her family's 19th-c. Irish immigrant background and was followed by other historical novels, including *The Long Watch* (1956), California Commonwealth Club Gold Medal winner for best historical novel by a California author. She turned to the mystery novel in 1960.

Under two pseudonyms and her own name, L. has created four separate police routine series, each featuring a singular detective protagonist. Lt. Luis Mendoza, dapper, mannered Mexican-American sleuth, first appearing in *Case Pending* (1960) by Dell Shannon, lends class, Hispanic pride, and a sharp intelligence to the Los Angeles police department. Two series are by Lesley Egan: one with Detective Vic Varallo, an Italian rose-fancier of the Glendale police (*A Case for Appeal*, 1961) and a second with a tandem, New England Sergeant Andrew Clock of the Los Angeles police and his confrere, lawyer and amateur detective Jesse Falkenstein, a subtly Jewish character who quotes the Talmud (*Some Avenger, Rise!*, 1966). As Elizabeth Linington, L. created Sergeant Ivor Maddox, a dedicated Welsh bachelor of Hollywood's Wilcox Avenue station (*Greenmask!*, 1965).

A strong point of interest in L.'s writing is her innovation of ethnic types endowed—most notably in the case of the Hispanic Mendoza—with a practical awareness of the pluralistic ethnic sociology of Los Angeles and its intercultural conflicts of race, class, politics, money, mores, and opportunity. The ethnicity of these characters, while not fully developed, actually predates the ethnic revolution of the 1960s.

In their scrutiny and judgments of the problems of the "One Big City," these books can also be considered in a more serious vein as novels of social problems or even modern novels of manners. L.'s detailed documentation of everyday life gives a new twist to more conventional formula approaches to the police-procedural detective-story format. In L.'s view, the detective novel is politically and ethically significant as the "morality play of the 20th century" and as a literary form whose influence and brilliance have both been overlooked and underestimated by critics and writers alike.

L. has been cited as "Queen of the Proceedurals" and has been compared to masters of the genre such as Ed McBain, John Creasey, and Dorothy Uhnak. She admittedly bases her knowledge of police routine and law not on direct experience but on the basic texts used by police departments themselves and, for specific plots, on detective magazines.

Philosophically, she focuses on the theme of the irrationality of violence. Her concern is with the balance of good and evil within the delicate relationship between individual psychology and the social and political order. An L. novel characteristically interweaves three or four distinct plot lines in a pattern that follows the natural outlines of actual police work rather than focusing on the ideal "single case" of crime fiction and drama. L. also omits the customary summing-up scenario, forcing readers to trace the solution of the mystery backwards from the denouement themselves.

L. thus combines the conservatism of the law-and-order school of detective mystery with the style and art of the cerebral school to give her works an unusually broad appeal.

WORKS: *The Proud Man* (1955). *The Anglophile* (1956). *The Long Watch* (1956). *Monsieur Janvier* (1957). *The Kingbreaker* (1958). *Case Pending* (1960). *The Ace of Spades* (1961). *Biography of Elizabeth I* (1961). *A Case for Appeal* (1961). *Nightmare* (1961). *The Borrowed Alibi* (1962). *Extra Kill* (1962). *The Knave of Hearts* (1962). *Against the Evidence* (1963). *Death of a Busybody* (1963). *Double Bluff* (1963). *Mark of Murder* (1964). *My Name is Death* (1964). *Root of All Evil* (1964). *Run to Evil* (1964). *The Death-Bringers* (1965). *Death by Inches* (1965). *Detective's Due* (1965). *Greenmask!* (1965). *Coffin Corner* (1966). *Date with Death* (1966). *Some Avenger, Rise!* (1966). *With a Vengeance* (1966). *Chance to Kill* (1967). *Nameless Ones* (1967). *Something Wrong* (1967). *Rain with Violence* (1968). *Kill with Kindness* (1968). *Policeman's Lot* (1968). *A Serious Investigation* (1968). *Practice to Deceive* (1969). *Crime on Their Hands* (1969). *Schooled to Kill* (1969). *Wine of Violence* (1969). *In the Death of a Man* (1970). *Unexpected Death* (1970). *Whim to Kill* (1970). *The Ringer* (1970). *Malicious Mischief* (1971). *Murder, with Love* (1972). *Paper Chase* (1972). *With Intent to Kill* (1972). *Crime by Chance* (1973). *No Holiday for Crime* (1973). *Spring of Violence* (1973). *Crime File* (1974). *Deuces Wild* (1975). *Scenes of Crime* (1976). *Streets of Death* (1976). *Appearances of Death* (1977). *Blind Search* (1977). *Perchance of Death* (1977). *Cold Trail* (1978). *A Dream Apart* (1978). *Look Back on Death* (1978).

BIBLIOGRAPHY: King, M. J., "Interview with Elizabeth Linington," *Armchair Detective* (forthcoming, 1981–82).
Other references: *Writer* (March 1967).

MARGARET J. KING

Martha Shepard Lippincott

B. Moorestown, New Jersey; d. 10 Aug. 1949, West Philadelphia, Pennsylvania
D. of Jesse and Elizabeth Homes Lippincott

Although born in New Jersey, L. lived most of her life in Pennsylvania. The Quaker experience was an important part of her life, and she was commonly known as the Quaker Poetess. She attended Friends' High School and later Swarthmore College. In 1886 she began writing poetry, and after 1895 she made writing her life's work. In all she wrote 4,444 poems and sacred songs and 836 book reviews, articles, and stories which appeared in religious and secular publications in the U.S., Canada, England, Ireland, and Scotland. Many of her songs appeared in hymnbooks.

L. published only one book of verse, *Visions of Life* (1901). This anthology opens with a series of poems on the stages of female life and the distinct vision of reality which emerges in each stage. Infancy, childhood, maidenhood, womanhood, motherhood, widowhood, and death are examined. Basically, L.'s world view is optimistic; however, she sees that joy and sorrow become more firmly intertwined as one ages. The delights of childhood and the dreams of maidenhood are replaced by the sorrow and the possibly deeper joys that come with marriage and motherhood. Although L. never married, the suffering of married women is a central theme of a number of her poems. Her view is that married life is difficult and that women suffer most in the marital relationship. She admonishes the young to marry only for love, for it is only true love which can sustain husband and wife and draw them closer together.

In a number of long poems, L. explores the horrors of liquor and the suffering it causes both wives and children. She describes the drunken husband who, seeking his own pleasure, squanders his money and, enslaved to liquor, destroys both his marriage and his family. L. hails prohibition as a holy crusade blessed by God to rid the world of alcohol and its pernicious consequences. She urges men to use the vote to support this holy work.

Although the dominant theme of this anthology is the problems and visions of female life, L. also includes a substantial number of nature poems. L.'s other interests are manifest in diverse inclusions such as the autobiographical poem, "The Poet's Faith," and "Frances Willard," a poem dedicated to the female educator. Her concern for her own religious tradition is obvious in the poems "Friends' Ministry" and "Quaker Bonnet."

Although L.'s style is often didactic and saccharine, her poetry is distinctive on a numer of counts. She reflects with great sympathy the full range of emotions and hopes experienced by women throughout their life cycle and points out the intimate connections between social problems and female suffering. Finally, as a member of the Society of Friends, a religious group which historically eschewed artistic expression, L. offers prolific examples of poetry marked by a deep religious faith.

WORKS: *Visions of Life* (1901).

DANA GREENE

Sara Jane Clark Lippincott

B. 23 Sept. 1823, Pompey, New York; d. 20 April 1904, New Rochelle, New York
Wrote under: Sara J. Clarke, Grace Greenwood, Mrs. L. K. Lippincott
D. of Thaddeus and Deborah Baker Clarke; m. Leander K. Lippincott, 1853

The youngest daughter among eleven children of a physician and a great-granddaughter of Jonathan Edwards, L. spent her childhood near Syracuse, New York, and attended school for eight years in Rochester, New York. When she was nineteen, she moved with her family to New Brighton, Pennsylvania.

L.'s first poems appeared in Rochester papers, and in 1844 her verse was published in N. P. Willis's *New Mirror*. Soon she wrote prose and informal letters for the *Mirror* and *Home Journal* under the pseudonym "Grace Greenwood." Later she worked as a journalist and correspondent for *Godey's Lady's Book, Graham's, Sartain's,* the *Saturday Evening Post,* the abolitionist *National Era,* the *New York Times,* and the New York *Tribune.* Throughout her career, because of her Puritan heritage or her own staunch sense of right, L. spoke out strongly for such causes as abolition, woman suffrage, prison reform, and Colorado's right to statehood and against capital punishment.

Her marriage was unhappy. She and Lippincott were coeditors of the early and highly popular juvenile magazine *The Little Pilgrim* (1853–75), but in 1876 Lippincott fled the country and disappeared after being indicted for embezzlement connected with his job at the Department of the Interior.

Greenwood Leaves (1850), L.'s first bestseller, epitomizes mid-19th-c. taste. It combines saccharine and sentimental tales and sketches ("Sly Peeps into the Heart Feminine," "A Spring Flower Faded") with a series of lively informal letters and parodies of Poe, Melville, Longfellow, and other authors. The letters, though often prolix and gushing, give promise of the journalism that would later be L.'s forte.

Haps and Mishaps of a Tour in Europe (1854) was another Greenwood bestseller and was still being reprinted in the 1890s. A lively and often humorous account of her journey alone to England, Scotland, Ireland, France, Germany, and Italy, it records visits to literary and historical sites, prisons, almshouses, and lunatic asylums and meetings with literary, artistic, and political lions. *Haps and Mishaps* mixes sentiment and gush, American chauvinism, and some of the dry Yankee wit later to be fully developed in Twain's *The Innocents Abroad.* As in the first and second series of *Greenwood Leaves,* the most interesting parts are the segments of straight reporting, especially L.'s impressions of people.

Merrie England (1855), like *Bonnie Scotland* (1861) and other juvenile works, first appeared in *The Little Pilgrim.* Linked with sites she visited on her first trip to Europe are "tales" or "historical sketches." Most of the history presented is highly suspect by modern standards and often seems comic in its invention and moralizing: "But the neighbors all shook their heads wisely, and said, 'Mrs. Shakespeare is spoiling that boy; he'll never make the man his father is.' I am sorry to say that, as he grew out of boyhood, the young poet fell into rather wild ways."

Heavy morality, sentimentality, and emphasis on sickbed and deathbed scenes typify many of L.'s tales for children. In *Nelly, the Gypsy Girl* (1863), written for the General Protestant Episcopal Sunday School Union and Church Book Society, the eponymous heroine is no Romany, but a motherless girl who reforms her dissipated father by reading him the parable of the prodigal son. Her father then effects a reconciliation with *his* father, who, "the gout having reached his stomach," dies and leaves him £10,000. Nelly and her father devote their lives to good works (improving the vicarage school and playground, founding a training school for servants) until her father dies.

Much of L.'s best writing is in accounts of her travels in Europe during the 1870s and 1880s written for the *Independent*, after she stopped gushing. Her power and charm continued in letters from Washington, D.C., written through the 1890s and even into the 20th c.

Once-popular books by "Grace Greenwood" have now been largely forgotten, while the works of contemporaries she far outsold in her lifetime (e.g., Thoreau and Melville) have become American classics. L.'s poetry, sentimental tales and sketches, and children's books merit obscurity, but her strong-minded, firsthand reporting still deserves and rewards attention.

WORKS: *Greenwood Leaves* (1850). *History of My Pets* (1851). *Poems* (1851). *Greenwood Leaves, Second Series* (1852). *Recollections of My Childhood, and Other Stories* (1852). *Haps and Mishaps of a Tour in Europe* (1854). *Merrie England* (1855). *A Forest Tragedy* (1856). *Old Wonder-Eyes* (1857). *Stories and Legends of Travel and History* (1857). *Stories from Famous Ballads* (1859). *Bonnie Scotland* (1861). *Nelly, the Gypsy Girl* (1863). *Records of Five Years* (1867). *Stories and Sights of France and Italy* (1867). *Stories of Many Lands* (1867). *New Life in New Lands* (1873). *Heads and Tails: Studies and Stories of My Pets* (1874). *Emma Abbott, Prima Donna* (1878). *Treasures from Fairy Land* (with R. W. Raymond, 1879). *Queen Victoria: Her Girlhood and Womanhood* (1883). *Some of My Pets* (1884). *Stories for Home-Folks, Young and Old* (1884). *Stories and Sketches* (1892).

BIBLIOGRAPHY: Pattee, F. L., *The Feminine Fifties* (1940). Thorp, M. F., *Female Persuasion* (1949).

For articles in reference works, see: *AA. The American Female Poets*, Ed. C. May (1854). *American Literary Manuscripts*, Ed. J. A. Robbins. *AW. CAL. DAB*, VI, 1. *Eminent Women of the Age*, Eds. J. Parton et al. (1869). *FPA. The Female Prose Writers of America*, Ed. J. S. Hart (1857). *HWS. NAW* (article by B. Welter). *NCAB*, 4. *Woman's Record*, Ed. S. J. Hale (1853).

Other references: *AL* (Jan. 1938). *Atlantic* (June 1859; Sept. 1859). *NYT* (21 April 1904).

SUSAN SUTTON SMITH

Sophia Louisa Robbins Little

B. 1799, Newport, Rhode Island; d. Boston, Massachusetts
Wrote under: Sophia Louisa Little
D. of Asher Robbins; m. William Little, Jr., 1824

Biographical information about L. is sparse. Her mother's name and the date of L.'s death are not listed in any of the standard biographical sources.

Allibone's *Critical Dictionary of English Literature and American Authors* (1891) cites two works by L., *Pilgrim's Progress in the Last Days* (1843) and *The Betrothed* (1844), which are not listed in the *National Union Catalog*. It may be that these works are no longer extant, as most of her work was privately printed in limited quantity. L.'s books are therefore extremely rare, and most of them are not circulated by the libraries that hold them.

She was both an abolitionist and a temperance advocate, and her prose works are primarily vehicles for spreading these gospels. *The Branded Hand* (1845) is L.'s tribute to Jonathan Walker, an abolitionist who was branded with the letters "SS" (slave stealer) for aiding slaves to escape from Florida to the West Indies. *Thrice through the Furnace* (1852), another book on abolition, deals with the trials of Gilbert and Marian, Sedley Livingston's mulatto children, who are sold when his wife can no longer stand their resemblance to the Livingston family. They are purchased by Arthur St. Vallery, a cousin who wants Marian for a concubine. Aided by the Freemans, a Quaker family that defies the newly legislated Fugitive Slave Act, Marian and Gilbert escape. Arthur pursues them until he meets Aimee Freeman, who converts him and wins his heart. Marian and Gilbert are reunited with their slave sweethearts, Jasmyn and Cornelia, whom Arthur frees. All three couples marry and live together harmoniously on Arthur's land.

The Reveille (1854) is the story of Jerry Woodliffe, a reformed alcoholic who tries to remain sober despite the evil machinations of the Rum Club, a cabal of saloon keepers who strive to get Jerry publicly drunk to discredit the temperance movement. Some of Jerry's friends, all ex-alcoholics, succumb to rum cake served to them on Election Day by one of the plotters. Others are trapped by spiked "temperance punch." Jerry is lured by a rum-tainted glass of soda, but Mary, his vigilant wife, saves him by demolishing the grog shop. As she smashes the bottles, the other wives cheer her on. The temperance movement is victorious.

L.'s religious poetry is a cycle depicting the life of Jesus. The first part, *The Last Days of Jesus* (1839), was first published by itself. L. then added sections on the Annunciation, Birth, and Resurrection. This work was printed several times, in various stages of completion.

L.'s novels are very thin in both plot and characterization. The sufferings, romances, and narrow escapes are all very trite and predictable. Gilbert and Marian, the uneducated slaves, posture and soliloquize like Hamlet. The Rum Club plotters, who rejoice in names such as Stillworm and Rockheart, are clearly cartoons, not people. These books are interesting period pieces, but they were never literature.

L.'s poetry, however, has considerable merit. It is lyrical and emotional, but not effusive. Her verses have rhyme, meter, dignity, and restraint. L.'s intellect and artistic sense are very much in control here. Although the religious subject matter, epic length, and poetic diction of these pieces are not in keeping with modern tastes, these works are a fine example of 19th-c. popular art.

WORKS: The Last Days of Jesus: A Poem (1839). *The Birth, Last Days, and Resurrection of Jesus: Three Poems* (1841). *Poems* (1841). *Pilgrim's Progress in the Last Days* (1843). *The Betrothed* (1844). *The Branded Hand: A Dramatic Sketch, Commemorative of the Tragedies at the South in the Winter of 1844-5* (1845). *Thrice through the Furnace: A Tale of the Times of the Iron Hoof* (1852). *The Reveille; or, Our Music at Dawn* (1854). *Pentecost* (1869). *Massacre at Fort Griswold and Burning of New London, September 6, 1781: A Poem* (n.d.).

BIBLIOGRAPHY: For articles in reference works, see: *CAL. FPA.*

ZOHARA BOYD

Harriet Livermore

B. 14 April 1788, Concord, New Hampshire; d. 30 March 1868,
Philadelphia, Pennsylvania
D. of Edward St. Loe and Mehitable Harris Livermore

Evangelist and religious author, L. was the third of five children and a descendant of Samuel Livermore, U.S. Senator from New Hampshire. Her father, an attorney, was a justice of the New Hampshire supreme court. Her mother died when she was five.

L. is noted for the zeal and fervor which marked her personality. Even as a child, she demonstrated fits of temper severe enough to concern her family. At eight, L. was sent to a girl's boarding school in Haverhill, Massachusetts, and later attended the Byfield Seminary and the Atkinson (New Hampshire) Academy. Her beauty and conversational abilities were highlighted during a visit to Washington, D.C., when she was twenty; socialites of the city were taken with her intelligence, vivacity, and wit. In 1811, she was engaged to Moses Elliott; his parents, however, forbade the liaison, feeling that a woman of such "excitable and stormy temperament" could not insure his happiness. L. herself noted this turning point: she "fled to the name and form of religion, as a present sanctuary from the sorrows of life." In her view, it would be chastisement for her "wild and irregular" disposition.

L.'s works are entirely religious in nature, and most have seen little public success. They parallel her life in that each grew from her evangelical travels and her personal search for religious creed. Raised in the Episcopal church, she turned to Quakerism, then Congregationalism; later, she became a Baptist, but left formal religion to become the self-named "Pilgrim Stranger." But while her writings are impassioned, effusive, and sincere, they most often are directionless, marred by organizational deficiencies and L.'s increasing personal eccentricity.

One of her more lucid efforts, *A Narration of Religious Experience* (1826), documents her turn to spirituality and evangelism with L.'s own testimony that her escape was prompted by the "sorrows of life" and her unfortunate love affair. The *Narration* is essentially her autobiography to 1826; she realized that people thought her "crazy," but insisted on seeking religious truth by her own means. In 1824, she suffered a breakdown, and afterwards reevaluated for a final time her myriad denominational inclinations. The *Narration* epitomizes the religious attitudes guiding L.'s writing. When she fell ill in 1824, a voice told her: "This is to punish you for your infidelity to your master."

Out of L.'s conviction that Christ's return was imminent came her book, *The Harp of Israel, to Meet the Loud Echo in the Wilds of America* (1835). For this, she journeyed through hazardous territory to Fort Leavenworth, Kansas, to seek out the Indians, although local officials prevented her from spreading the gospel. *The Harp* is a work of subjective evangelism. It depicts L.'s fervor in converting the Indians, identified in her text as the lost tribes of Israel, through inspirational prose and poetry.

A Testimony for the Times (1843) focuses on the conversion and "condition" of the Jewish people and state. While her tract is not wholly anti-Semitic, she indicates that Christ would rule on David's throne over the Israelite tribes, the Jews first having to suffer for their rejection of the gospel. Her Christ was due in 1847. By this time, the marked eccentricities of both woman and writer forced even formerly steadfast supporters to abandon her.

In "Snowbound" (1866), John Greenleaf Whittier described L. as "A woman tropical, intense / In thought and act, in soul and sense / She blended in a like degree / The vixen and the devotee." Although she eloquently spoke and ministered before Congress and her speaking abilities were said to be "glorious," L.'s prose writings, adhering to the idiom of early 19th-c. evangelical writing, are obscure and stylistically inaccessible to the general public. L. had hoped that she would be a role model, inspiring other women to greater participation in the church. But her ever-increasing solitude ironically removed her from those she would have reached; this and the impenetrability and extremism of her writings made her even more the "solitary traveler." Despite an inner strength and conviction, her work is, sadly, a curiosity and not of literary merit.

WORKS: Scriptural Evidence in Favour of Female Testimony in Meetings for Christian Worship in Letters to a Friend (1824). *An Epistle of Love, Addressed to the Youth and Children of Germantown, Pennsylvania, County of Philadelphia* (1826). *A Narration of Religious Experience* (1826). *A Wreath from Jessamine Lawn; or, Free Grace, the Flower That Never Fades* (1831). *The Harp of Israel, to Meet the Loud Echo in the Wilds of America* (1835). *A Letter to John Ross, the Principal Chief of the Cherokee Nation* (1838). *Millenial Tidings* (1839). *The Counsel of God, Immutable and Everlasting* (1841). *Glory of the Lord in the Land of the Living by Redemption of the Purchased Possession* (1842). *A Testimony for the Times* (1843). *Addresses to the Dispersed of Judah* (1849). *Thoughts on Important Subjects* (1864). *The Sparrow* (n.d.).

BIBLIOGRAPHY: Adams, J. Q., *Memoirs*, Vols. 10 and 12 (Ed. C. F. Adams, 1876, 1877). Livermore, S. T., *Harriet Livermore, the "Pilgrim Stranger"* (1884). Thwing, W. E., *The Livermore Family of America* (1902).

For articles in reference works, see: *Career Women of America (1776–1840)*, Ed. E. A. Dexter (1950). *NAW* (article by E. F. Hoxie).

Other references: *NEQ* (March 1945).

DEBORAH H. HOLDSTEIN

Mary Ashton Rice Livermore

B. *19 Dec. 1821, Boston, Massachusetts; d. 23 May 1905, Melrose, Massachusetts*
D. *of Timothy and Zebiah Ashton Rice; m. Daniel Parker Livermore, 1845*

The fourth but first surviving child of an English sea captain's daughter and a workingman of Welsh background, L. was educated in the public and private schools of Boston and at Martha Whiting's Female Seminary of Charlestown, Massachusetts. She taught Latin and French at the seminary, made an unsuccessful attempt to matriculate at Harvard, and spent three years as a tutor on a large Virginia plantation with five hundred slaves, an experience which converted her to strong antislavery views. She returned to Massachusetts as head of a private coeducational school in Doxbury, where she met and married a Universalist minister. They were parents of three daughters, two of whom survived to adulthood.

L. began writing for juveniles in 1844, publishing stories, sketches, and poems in religious periodicals and newspapers. *The Children's Army* (1844) is a collection of such stories—simple fiction with obvious plots detailing the evils of drink. *A Mental Transformation* (1848) is probably autobiographical, describing her own rejection of Baptism for Universalism. In 1857 she moved to Chicago with her husband. He became editor of the *New Covenant*, a Universalist newspaper, for which she acted as associate editor, writing for every section of the paper. L. was the only woman reporter at the 1860 national Republican convention.

During the Civil War, L. volunteered her services to the Sanitary Commission. She headed the Chicago office (with Jane Hoge), made frequent speaking tours, organized the Sanitary Fair of 1863, and collected money and large quantities of supplies for the Union armies, meanwhile writing graphic accounts of her activities for the *New Covenant* and other papers.

After the war she joined the woman suffrage and temperance movements and was president of several associations in both movements. In 1869 she established *The Agitator*, a suffrage paper which merged with the *Woman's Journal* in 1870. She edited the *Journal* for two years, resigning in 1872 to devote herself to lecturing, a career she pursued until 1895. She continued her support of suffrage and temperance causes, using the lecture platform as a forum.

L.'s fame in the 19th c. was based largely on her popularity as a lecturer, and her published lectures constitute an important segment of her work. Her style is conversational, interspersed with humor and homely examples. The "woman question" and her commitment to feminism are central themes, although she also lectured on temperance and historical figures, usually women.

Aside from her lectures, L.'s major works are her autobiographies, which sold very well. She wrote the first of these, *My Story of the War: A Woman's Narrative* (1888), because she felt the postwar literature had neglected the common soldier. Her purpose may have been to give the common soldier his due, but much of the volume's emphasis is on the role played by women in the hospitals, on the field of battle, and at home running the farms and staffing the factories. *The Story of My Life* (1897) fills out her reminiscences with material on her early and later life and adds further material on the Civil War. The memoirs are composed in straightforward narrative style, interspersed with skillful dialogue. In her accounts of her plantation experiences, she reproduces with a good ear the dialect of both blacks and whites in the antebellum South. Her descriptions of plantation life are vivid and surprisingly objective.

L.'s literary contribution was as an editor and journalist; she did not see herself as a major literary figure. She launched the *Woman's Journal*, a major publication of the women's movement, and shepherded it through the crucial first two years. Her emphasis on women's rights brought unfavorable criticism early in her career, but this did not deter her from continuing to say what she felt needed to be said or seemingly interfere with her popularity. With Frances Willard, she edited that formidable biographical compilation, *A Woman of the Century* (1893), which Leslie Shepard has called more than a reference book, rather a major record of the emancipation of American women.

WORKS: *The Children's Army* (1844). *Thrity Years Too Late: A Temperance Story* (1845). *A Mental Transformation* (1848). *Nineteen Pen Pictures* (1863). *What Shall We Do with Our Daughters? and Other Lectures* (1883). *My Story of the War: A Woman's Narrative* (1888). *A Woman of the Century* (edited by Livermore, with F. E. Willard, 1893; revised edition, *American Women*, 1897). *The Story of My Life* (1897).

BIBLIOGRAPHY: Brockell, L. P., and M. C. Vaughan, *Woman's Work in the Civil War* (1867). Hanson, E. R., *Our Women Workers* (1882). Newberry, J. S., *The U.S. Sanitary Commission in the Valley of the Miss.* (1871). Thwing, W. E., *The Livermore Family of America* (1902). Whiting, L., *Women Who Have Ennobled Life* (1915). Wittenmyer, A., *History of the Woman's Crusade* (1882).

For articles in reference works, see: *AA. AW. NAW* (article by R. E. Riegel). *NCAB*, 3.

RUTH BORDIN

Myra Cohn Livingston

B. 17 Aug. 1926, Omaha, Nebraska
D. of Mayer Louis and Gertrude Marks Cohn; m. Richard Roland Livingston, 1952

As a child, L. wrote poetry and plays (which were produced at school) and showed a talent for music, winning a national competition on the French horn. "Whispers" (1946), written while L. was a freshman at Sarah Lawrence College, was her first published poem. After graduation, L. wrote book reviews and did public relations work. She continued to write poetry throughout the growing-up of her three children. Very interested in education, she is poet-in-residence for the Beverly Hills School District.

The collections of L.'s poetry can be divided into two groups, those for the very young and those for children in the middle and late elementary-school grades. Some of the former contain short unrhymed prose poems built around a particular topic; the most highly regarded volumes are *I'm Hiding* (1961), *See What I Found* (1962), and *I'm Waiting* (1966). Others of L.'s books for young children are random collections in varying moods and meters about the oddities and joys of daily life. L. writes simply and directly from the child's point of view about things that please and puzzle the preschooler. The poems are very short, seldom more than eight or ten lines, and are intended to be shared with children in those brief moments when their attention can be caught. On the whole, the poems project a certain charm as they show how children can find magic in simple, everyday things, but they are repetitive, uneven, and sometimes strained. The expression lacks the melody and fun with words that small children most enjoy in their poetry. L.'s poems for the very young mirror the child's world rather than extend it imaginatively.

L.'s later poems, in collections such as *Old Mrs. Twindlytart, and*

Other Rhymes (1967) and *A Crazy Flight, and Other Poems* (1969), continue the refreshing unpretentiousness and honesty of her earlier ones, but they show a changing perspective and increasing attention to broader matters which direct them toward a somewhat older audience. In general, these later poems are longer; forms, subjects, and moods are more varied; and there is less repetition. While these are also inconsistent in quality, they are more melodious, less prosy, and reveal a deftness and adventurousness of expression that the earlier poems lack.

In *When You Are Alone / It Keeps You Capone: An Approach to Creative Writing with Children* (1973), L. presents the philosophy behind her own writing and teaching, along with practical suggestions for helping children express themselves poetically. She maintains that exposing children from their earliest years to good poetry is essential for stimulating them to write well: ". . . the sharing of poetry, wherever one is, in the classroom or library or at home, is intrinsic to the development of the imagination and the humanization of child and adult alike." Her recent articles (*Horn Book*, Dec. 1975 and Feb. 1976) deploring current methods of teaching children to write and the tendency of adults to rate poetry done by children higher than it should be, have resulted in a reexamination of attitudes toward children's writing. A capable poet, an anthologist noted for several collections of poetry by other writers, and a respected critic, L. has become a leading influence in the world of literature for children.

WORKS: *Whispers, and Other Poems* (1958). *Wide Awake, and Other Poems* (1959). *I'm Hiding* (1961). *I Talk to Elephants!* (1962). *See What I Found* (1962). *I'm Not Me* (1963). *Happy Birthday!* (1964). *The Moon and a Star, and Other Poems* (1965). *I'm Waiting* (1966). *Old Mrs. Twindlytart, and Other Rhymes* (1967). *A Tune Beyond Us: A Collection of Poetry* (edited by Livingston, 1968). *A Crazy Flight, and Other Poems* (1969). *Speak Roughly to Your Little Boy: A Collection of Parodies and Burlesques, Together with the Original Poems, Chosen and Annotated for Young People* (edited by Livingston, 1971). *Listen, Children, Listen: An Anthology of Poems for the Very Young* (edited by Livingston, 1972). *The Malibu, and Other Poems* (1972). *Poems of Lewis Carroll* (edited by Livingston, 1973). *What a Wonderful Bird the Frog Are: An Assortment of Humorous Poetry and Verse* (edited by Livingston, 1973). *When You Are Alone / It Keeps You Capone: An Approach to Creative Writing with Children* (1973). *Come Away* (1974). *The Way Things Are, and Other Poems* (1974). *One Little Room, an Everywhere: Poems of Love* (edited by Livingston, 1975). *Four-Way Stop, and Other Poems* (1976). *O Frabjous Day! Poetry for Holidays and Special Occasions* (edited by Livingston, 1977). *Callooh! Callay! Holiday Poems for Young Readers* (edited by Livingston, 1978). *A Lollygag of Limericks* (edited by Livingston, 1978). *O Sliver of Liver: Together with Other Triolets, Cinquains, Haiku, Verses, and a Dash of Poems* (edited by Livingston, 1979).

BIBLIOGRAPHY: Livingston, M. C., in *Somebody Turned on a Tap in These Kids*, N. Larrick (1971). Sutherland, A., and M. H. Arbuthnot, *Children and Books* (1977).

For articles in reference works, see: *Anthology of Children's Literature*, Eds. E. Johnson, E. R. Sickels, and F. C. Sayers (1970). *Books Are by People*, Ed. L. B. Hopkins (1969). *CA*, 1–4 (1967). *Something about the Author*, Ed. A. Commire (1973).

ALETHEA K. HELBIG

Jane Erminia Starkweather Locke

B. *25 April 1805, Worthington, Massachusetts; d. 8 March 1859, Ashburnham, Massachusetts*
Wrote under: Jane E. Locke
D. *of Charles and Deborah Brown Starkweather; m. John Goodwin Locke, 1829*

A deacon's daughter, L. reflects in her work the religious and patriotic idealism nurtured in her childhood home. Her uncle Ezra was a Massachusetts state senator and a member of the Constitutional Convention of 1820, as was L.'s father-in-law, John Locke. She was the youngest of ten children.

L. followed her husband to New York shortly after their marriage. The first of their seven children was born there; three of the children were to die in early childhood, and only one, Grace LeBaron Upham, was to survive to adulthood. The family settled in Lowell (1833) and in Boston (1849). While Locke pursued a career in business and government service, L. cared for the children and pursued her own literary interests.

L.'s first collection of poetry is *Miscellaneous Poems* (1842). In the preface, the author tells us that the poems were written "for the most part . . . to relieve the soul of what would cumber it unuttered. . . ." The poems range in subject from reminiscences of her childhood home to expressions of love and concern for husband and children, and beyond this family circle to acknowledgments of the genial accomplishments of others—mostly contemporaries.

One important aspect of L.'s poetry is the evidence of sincere personal concerns and beliefs pertaining to women. A poem entitled "To an Infant," dated 11 August 1837, commemorates the birth of her first daughter. However, rather than greet the child in cheerful language, L. bemoans the estate which the child inherits: the wearisome toil of woman's daily existence. Despite this pessimistic, recurrent theme, in other poems L. stresses in stronger, more positive language another aspect of woman's existence: motherhood.

Two of the most notable examples of this latter theme can be found in the poems "Mount Holyoke Seminary" and "A Poem Adapted to the Times." In the former, L. compares the glories of the school in Northampton to those of the Propylaea at Athens and says, "To learning's inner temple here / Pass *mothers* of the race. . . ." That L. believes generations of educated women will produce generations of enlightened men, implicit here, is explicit in the latter poem, which also reflects her sympathy with the abolitionist movement: "An influence benign she will exert . . . In childhood hearts, that, hence, *man's* common acts / Will be but deeds of charity and love, / And the forged bands of the dark slave fall off, Spontaneous and uninvoked."

L.'s firm, patriotic vision is set forth in a forty-six-page poem entitled *Boston: A Poem* (1846), dedicated "to the names of Appleton and Lawrence. . . ." In it, L. honors scientists, educators, and working men and women, as well as industrialists, all of whom, she believes, contributed to the economic and academic well-being of the "Athens of America."

In *Rachel; or, The Little Mourner* (1844) L. touches with astute sensitivity the problematic situation of the Christian who must try to reconcile joyful belief in eternal life with very real sorrow and pain at the earthly parting.

The Recalled, in Voices of the Past, and Poems of the Ideal (1854), is a collection of poetry that reflects the more mature mind at work. Rather than a random selection of poetry gathered almost at whim, L. arranges this volume in four sections. "Voices of the Past" commemorates public occasions, historic events, and the achievements of prominent personages and includes "Requiem for Edgar A. Poe," whom L. knew. The poems in "Passages from Life" are autobiographical, but L. is more selective than in *Miscellaneous Poems*. Love filtered through

Christian belief is reflected in personal poems such as "One Thousandth Imitation of an Old Song," written for her husband, and "Proverbs," written to her son.

Throughout all of her work, L. alludes to the "ideal," which is also the subject of the third section, "Poems of the Ideal." "The Sisters of Avon," her most philosophical offering, suggests at least an acquaintance with Hermetic philosophy. The final section, a tribute to Daniel Webster consistent with L.'s political sympathies, was first published separately as *Daniel Webster: A Rhymed Eulogy* (1854).

Between 1850 and 1854, L. worked as a newspaper correspondent for the Boston *Journal* and the *Daily Atlas*.

In the same period, she also worked for the James Monroe Publishing Company, writing prefaces for the English publications which they reproduced in this country. L.'s writing, prose and poetry, is lucid and straightforward. Her poetry is representative of the popular poetry of the 19th c. in general, and of the varied interests of its women in particular.

WORKS: *Miscellaneous Poems* (1842). *Rachael; or, The Little Mourner* (1844). *Boston: A Poem* (1846). *The Recalled, in Voices of the Past, and Poems of the Ideal* (1854). *Daniel Webster: A Rhymed Eulogy* (1854). *Nothing Ever Happens* (1938).

BIBLIOGRAPHY: Baldwin, J. S., *Memories and Traditions* (1909). Locke, J. G., *Book of the Lockes* (1853). Starkweather, C. L., *A Brief Genealogical History of Robert Starkweather of Roxbury and Ipswich* (1904). Upham, G. L., *Contributions of the Old Residents' Historical Association, Lowell, Mass.* (1891).

For articles in reference works, see: *CAL*.

Other references: *Lowell Historical Society* (1940).

ROSALIE TUTELA RYAN

Deborah Norris Logan

B. *19 Oct. 1761, Philadelphia, Pennsylvania; d. 2 Feb. 1839, Philadelphia, Pennsylvania*
D. *of Charles and Mary Parker Norris; m. George Logan, 1781*

Many of the figures who influenced Pennsylvania's early history were members of L.'s family. Distinguished guests were frequently entertained in the Norrises' Quaker household. At the age of fourteen, L. heard the first reading of the Declaration of Independence while standing behind a fence in her own yard. Years later she recalled the scene: "The crowd that assembled at the State House was not great and those among them who joined in the acclamation were not the most sober or reflecting."

L. did not take full advantage of her days at Anthony Benezet's Friends Girls' School; however, she soon developed an extensive self-imposed reading course which formed the foundation of her literary pursuits. She did not abandon her interest after 1781, the year she married Logan, an active Republican politician and, later, U.S. senator.

At Stenton, her husband's ancestral home, L. enjoyed an exceedingly happy marriage and a life-style resembling that of an early American Gertrude Stein. Politicians, artists, and historians who were attracted by Philadelphia's position as a chief American city also habitually sought the company of Stenton's charming hostess. Robert Walsh, the accomplished editor of *The National Gazette* and a member of L.'s circle, described her character: "To the expression of our satisfaction with her muse we add the tribute of admiration due to a strength of intellect, a copiousness of knowledge, an habitual dignity of thought and manner, and a natural justness and refinement of sentiment."

In addition to her own work, L. provided John T. Watson with invaluable information while he was writing his *Annals of Philadelphia* (1830). L. was also the first female member of the Historical Society of Pennsylvania.

Stenton literally supplied L. with the material which formed her great service to history. In the attic, she found the correspondence, in worn and delicate condition, of two of Pennsylvania's greatest early leaders, William Penn and her husband's grandfather James Logan. Like the efficient management of her household, she saw the preservation of these letters as her duty. With her usual humbleness she said, "Not that I consider myself as qualified for such work, but that it has small chance of being performed unless I undertake it." A reluctance to neglect her family responsibilities motivated L. to rise before dawn to accomplish the time-consuming task of deciphering, copying, and editing. The eleven quarto manuscripts which resulted from her meticulous labor were eventually published in two volumes by the Historical Society of Pennsylvania (1870–72).

In addition to a zeal for historical preservation, L. also possessed poetic talent. Although L.'s poetry was comparable to some of the verse admired in her time, it would not excite a modern reader.

Rather, we must look toward her diary as the generator of present-day interest. She described this four-thousand-page, seventeen-volume work, started in 1815 and concluded shortly before her death, as a record of "whatever I shall hear of fact or anecdote that shall appear worthy of preservation. And many things for my own satisfaction likewise that may be irrelevant to others." The text's "worthy" portions include lively anecdotes about such figures as John Adams, Joseph Bonaparte, John C. Calhoun, Benjamin Franklin, Thomas Jefferson, Charles Thomson, and George Washington. Happily, the descriptions of these predictably male luminaries do not overshadow the diarist's feminine perspectives. It is the "irrelevant" material which dominates the diary, showing glimpses of L.'s daily thoughts and actions.

L. expresses her awareness of "the prayers and wishes of thousands of the amiable and excellent women of these states whose voices are never heard but in the domestic privacy of their happy homes." She successfully excluded herself from this group since her voice has survived for over a century in the dual guise of professional chronicler and private individual.

Contemporary readers who consult the information she saved must hold her in esteem; those who read the diary will find it difficult to avoid becoming closely attached to her. In these days when we confront new feminine roles, we can derive much from looking back at a woman who adroitly juxtaposed intellect and emotion—a woman who can touch our hearts and heads.

WORKS: *The Norris House* (1867). *Correspondence of William Penn and James Logan* (2 vols., 1870–72). *Memoir of Dr. George Logan of Stenton* (1899). *Diary 1815–1839* (Ed. M. S. Barr, forthcoming).
    Many of Deborah Norris Logan's published and unpublished works are located in the Historical Society of Pennsylvania.

BIBLIOGRAPHY: Myers, A. C., *Sally Wister's Journal* (1902). Norris, I., *Memoirs of the Historical Society of Pennsylvania*, Vol. 9 (1870). Tolles, F. B., *George Logan of Philadelphia* (1953). Wister, S. B., and A. Irwin, *Worthy Women of Our First Century* (1877).
    For articles in reference works, see: *DAB*, VI, 1. *NAW* (article by F. B. Tolles). *NCAB*, 25.
    Other references: *Journal of the Friends' Historical Society* (Jan. 1905). *Poulson's American Daily Advertiser* (4 Feb. 1839).

MARLEEN S. BARR

Mary Simmerson Cunningham Logan

B. 15 Aug. 1838, Petersburgh, Boone County, Missouri; d. 22 Feb. 1923, Washington, D.C.
Wrote under: Mrs. J. A. Logan
D. of Captain John M. and Elizabeth H. La Fontaine Cunningham; m. John Alexander Logan, 1855

L. was born to parents of Irish-French ancestry. L.'s maternal grandfather, La Fontaine, owned many slaves and large tracts of land in Missouri, and her paternal grandfather was a slave owner in Tennessee. Shortly after her birth, L.'s parents moved to southern Illinois, where her father became registrar of the land office as well as an army officer.

L., the oldest of thirteen children, had little formal education except that provided by itinerant teachers. When L. was fifteen, she studied for a year at St. Vincent's Academy near Morganfield, Kentucky. After graduation, L. returned home to marry a friend of her father's. L. wrote in the preface of her autobiography, "To tell my own story is to tell that of my own famous husband, General John A. Logan. Our marriage was a real partnership for thirty-one happy years."

L. traveled with her husband and assisted him by drawing up the forms for indictments and helping draft briefs. When Logan ran for Congress, L. was by his side throughout the political campaign.

After the Civil War, both General Logan and L. were concerned about the welfare of returning veterans. They were enthusiastic participants in the development of the Grand Army of the Republic (GAR). L. was also closely associated with the women's auxiliary of the GAR: the Women's Relief Corps. The Logans were responsible for the establishment of Memorial Day as a national holiday. In 1868, L. noted that the graves of Confederate soldiers in a cemetery in Richmond, Virginia, were marked by small Confederate flags and flowers. As a Senator, Logan effected passage of legislation to perpetuate Memorial Day as a national holiday.

After the death of Logan, L. was forced to earn a living for herself and her two children. *The Home Magazine* was started especially for her to edit and was successful for seven years. However, L.'s political influence and good works were continued. President Harrison appointed her to the board of the Lady Managers of the Chicago World's Columbian Exposition. In 1919, four years before her death, L. received the Belgian medal of Queen Elizabeth for work during the First World War.

L.'s first book was *The Home Manual* (1889), which bore a direct relationship to L.'s magazine. A compendium of etiquette, nostrums, recipes, stories, and games, its focus was self-improvement and self-help. In one chapter, "Society Small Talk," L. writes, "It is true that the newcomer into society often discovers that his or her greatest difficulty lies in finding just the right thing to say at the right time."

Thirty Years in Washington (1901) and *Reminiscences of a Soldier's Wife* (1913) manifest L.'s pride in the city of Washington and in being the wife of a famous general and statesman. *Thirty Years* is composed of a series of vignettes that describe the many agencies and offices of the national government. L.'s descriptions of her privileged access to behind-the-scenes workings of the government make this work an interesting source of information. That there are inaccuracies in the work does not detract from the general interest provided by rich details and L.'s general enthusiasm.

This same enthusiasm is apparent throughout L.'s best work, the autobiographical *Reminiscences*. L.'s eyewitness narration of the Lincoln–Douglas debates, her husband's political campaigns, and battle scenes of the Civil War provide a moving, personal view of those well-known events.

Using the resources of the Library of Congress from 1902 to 1909, L. and her daughter, Mary Logan Tucker, prepared a compendium of biographies of American women. *The Part Taken by Women in American History* (1912) contains two thousand biographical sketches varying in length and organized under rubrics such as Aboriginal Women, Pioneers, Women of the Revolution, Suffragists, etc. Like many other compendiums of the time, effusive encomiums based on scant factual material abound. However, this work is valuable for its great number of biographies of worthy women.

Throughout her life, L. was accorded equal praise with her husband. However, she lived thirty-seven years longer than he, and forged a career of her own as an editor and writer. L.'s works, especially the autobiography, exhibit her enthusiastic appreciation of the historic times through which she lived.

WORKS: *The Home Manual* (prepared by Logan, 1889). *Thirty Years in Washington* (1901; reissued, with two additional chapters, as *Our National Government*, 1908). *The Part Taken by Women in American History* (1912). *Reminiscences of a Soldier's Wife* (1913).

The Logan family papers are in The Library of Congress.

BIBLIOGRAPHY: Busbey, K. G., "Concerning the Author, Mrs. John. A. Logan," in *The Part Taken by Women in American History* (1912).

For articles in reference works, see: *AW. NCAB*, 4. *NAW* (article by L. M. Young).

Other references: *American Historical Review* (Oct. 1902). *Independent* (14 June 1919). *NYT* (23 Feb. 1923).

DOROTHEA MOSLEY THOMPSON

Olive Logan

B. *22 April 1839, Elmira, New York; d. 27 April 1909, Banstead, England*
Wrote under: Chroniqueuse, Olive Logan, Mrs. Wirt Sikes
D. *of Cornelius Logan and Eliza Akeley; m. Henry A. DeLille, 1857;*
  m. William Wirt Sikes, 1871; m. James O'Neill, 1892

L., the daughter of a theatrical couple, made her stage debut as a child and continued acting in New York City and on tour throughout the U.S. until about 1868. Her career was interrupted in the mid-fifties for eight years during her first marriage. It was not for love of the theater that L. returned briefly to the stage in her own play, *Eveleen*, in 1864. The economic necessity brought on by her divorce from DeLille forced her resumption of one career, acting, that she always despised and one, writing, that she enjoyed. She had also by this time begun to make a name for herself as a feminist lecturer. The exact date of her retirement is uncertain, but she seems to have entirely abandoned acting by 1868, continuing her connection with the theater as playwright only. Three plays, *Surf* (1870), *Newport* (1879)—both mild satires of high society—and *Armadale* (1866), a dramatization of Wilkie Collins's novel, were produced for the stage but not published. Her second marriage in 1872 to William Wirt Sikes lasted until his death in 1883. Her third husband, O'Neill, was twenty years her junior. L.'s literary productivity was particularly intense during those years when she was not being supported by a husband. The poverty and insanity which haunted her for most of her adult life became acute in old age and she died at the age of seventy in an English home for the insane.

L.'s literary career began with lectures, articles, and a lengthy record of "politics, art, fashion, and anecdote" in the Paris of 1862. *Photographs of Paris Life* (1862) was first published under the pseudonym Chroniqueuse. *Chateau Frissac: Home Scenes in France* (1865), L.'s first novel, attacked the evils in the French marriage of convenience. In the melodramatic style, love is temporarily thwarted by inadequate dowries, family disapproval, and arranged alliances. Another short novel followed in 1867; *John Morris' Money* is the story of a family of modest means who take in a widowed aunt, entertain her with four tales of the triumph of romantic love over greed, and finally, at the old woman's death, unexpectedly inherit her secret fortune.

In *Apropos of Women and the Theater* (1869), L. expounded upon a theme which often occupied her: the immorality of Lydia Thompson's "British Blondes," the lavish 1866 production of *The Black Crook*, both of which featured dancers in flesh-colored tights, and the subsequent seminudity which gave respectable actresses bad names. L.'s most impressive and longest work appeared in 1870 under the title *Before the Footlights and Behind the Scenes* and in 1871 as *The Mimic World*. This is one of the most informative but disorganized and often biased accounts of backstage life from the legitimate stage to the circus. It includes biographical sketches and anecdotes, arguments for treating actors with respect, and attacks on stage nudity and the third tier.

Also published in 1870, "The Good Mr. Bagglethorpe," is a cinderella story about a poor, orphaned young actress appearing in "moral dramas" who is seen and loved by the well-heeled, Willie Gentry. To make the union between the two possible, she must be taken from the stage and educated for two years.

L. continued her interest in writing nonfiction with *Get Thee Behind Me, Satan: A Home-born Book of Home-Truths* (1872), a celebration of marriage and the home under attack by free love and loveless "mercantile" marriages. L. also warns women of the dangers in believing that marriage is the only existence that awaits them and in allowing themselves to be treated as commodities. Portraits of several types of unhappy women underscore her thesis: one woman whose family is excessively eager to see her married, one considered only as a beautiful object, and one who is neglected by her husband.

They Met By Chance: A Society Novel (1873), L.'s last major work of published fiction, describes the life of the wealthy aristocrat in 19th-c. New York: the vacation spots, the entertainments, the matchmaking, and the petty games. As in her other novels of high society, much hangs on disguise, mistaken reports of a character's death, coincidence, and intrigue.

The American Abroad (1882) is a derisive comment on the contempt with which Americans are treated in England, necessitating the formation of a special organization to act in behalf of Americans abroad and to help Britishers attempting to immigrate to the U.S.

L.'s strengths lie, not in her imagination and creativity, but in her observations of attitudes and details which help to characterize the 19th-c. life and mind.

WORKS: *Photographs of Paris Life* (1862). *Chateau Frissac: Home Scenes in France* (1865). *John Morris' Money* (1867). *Apropos of Women and the Theater* (1869). *Before the Footlights and Behind the Scenes* (1870; reprinted as *The Mimic World*, 1871). *Get Thee Behind Me, Satan: A Home-born Book of Home-Truths* (1872). *They Met By Chance: A Society Novel* (1873). *The American Abroad* (1882).

BIBLIOGRAPHY: Brown, T. A., *History of the American Stage* (1903). Ireland, J. N., *Records of the New York Stage* (1866–67). Ludlow, N., *Dramatic Life as I Found It* (1913). Winter, W., *The Wallet of Time* (1913).
For articles in reference works, see: *AA. DAB*, VI, 1. *NAW* (article by A. E. Johnson). *NCAB 6*.

CLAUDIA D. JOHNSON

Anita Loos

B. 26 April 1893, Sissons, California
D. of Richard Beers and Minnie Ellen Loos; m. Frank Pallma, Jr., 1915;
m. John Emerson, 1919

When L. was four, her family moved from Sissons (now Mount Shasta), California, to San Francisco's Barbary Coast, where her ne'er-do-well father engaged in a series of journalistic and theatrical schemes. L. became a child actress and the family's chief mainstay for many years. After a period in Los Angeles, where her father managed an early movie house, the family settled in San Diego. By this time a youthful correspondent for the New York *Morning Telegraph*, L. hit upon the idea of writing movie scenarios for the Biograph Company. *The New York Hat* (1912) was her first filmed scenario, and by 1915 she had sold D. W. Griffith over one hundred scripts.

Eager to leave her family behind, L. married in 1915. After one night she deserted her young husband and set out for Hollywood where Biograph quickly offered her a contract. (The marriage was later annulled.) It was L. who wrote the title cards for Griffith's epic, *Intolerance* (1916). Her wisecracking verbal humor seemed ill-suited to the silent screen, however, until the chance success of an early Douglas Fairbanks film proved that audiences were willing to read comic subtitles. For the next few years, L. worked closely with Fairbanks, with Constance Talmadge, and with the suave director John Emerson, whom she married in 1919. In collaboration with Emerson she wrote two books about the motion picture industry, *How to Write Photoplays* (1920) and *Breaking into the Movies* (1921), along with several Broadway plays.

Living in New York, L. became a friend of H. L. Mencken. As a spoof of his taste for dim-witted blondes, she wrote a comic diary which first appeared in *Harper's Bazaar* in 1925. *Gentlemen Prefer Blondes* (1925), featuring the irrepressible Lorelei Lee, was a runaway international success, gaining L. such celebrated admirers as Winston Churchill, George Santayana, Mussolini, and James Joyce.

As one of the first women who dared hike her hemlines and bob her hair, L. came to epitomize the flappers of the 1920s. But despite her earning power, she was not in all respects an independent modern woman. As a self-described pushover for rogues, she remained loyal to her husband even while he dated other women and tried to take credit for L.'s own achievements. When she returned to Hollywood as a highly-paid screenwriter under Irving Thalberg at MGM, she protected Emerson's fragile ego by finding him a sinecure at the studio. Seemingly proud of her financial ineptitude, she turned her entire income over to "Mr. E.", who put everything into his own name in a move that could have left her penniless upon his death. Emerson was ultimately diagnosed as a manic-depressive, and spent the last eighteen years of his life in a sanitarium. In her autobiographical *Kiss Hollywood Good-By* (1974), L. chronicles her strictly platonic relationships with several attractive men, among them "the love of her life," the gambler and con man Wilson Mizner.

L.'s Broadway successes include several musical versions of *Gentlemen Prefer Blondes*, two romantic comedies adapted from the works of

Colette, and *Happy Birthday* (1947), written for her good friend Helen Hayes. Hayes, who had recently starred as Queen Victoria and Harriet Beecher Stowe, was "fed up with being noble," and L. obliged with a comic portrait of a drab librarian who blossoms in a barroom. With Hayes she has published *Twice Over Lightly* (1972), an exuberant tour of New York City, her adopted home.

In three play versions, a sequel, and such later works as *A Mouse Is Born* (1951), L. tried to repeat her triumph with *Gentlemen Prefer Blondes,* but she never again so artfully captured Lorelei's blend of innocence and avarice, nor her highly original gift of gab. Though L.'s later novels seem sadly dated, her gossipy Hollywood memoirs, *A Girl Like I* (1972) and *Kiss Hollywood Good-By,* are delightful souvenirs of a bygone age.

WORKS: *How to Write Photoplays* (with J. Emerson, 1920). *Breaking into the Movies* (with J. Emerson, 1921). *The Whole Town's Talking* (with J. Emerson, 1925). *Gentlemen Prefer Blondes* (1925; dramatized by Loos, with J. Emerson, 1926). *But—Gentlemen Marry Brunettes* (1928). *Happy Birthday* (1947). *A Mouse Is Born* (1951). *Gigi* (dramatization of the story by Colette, 1951; revised, 1956). *Chéri* (dramatization of the novel by Colette, 1959). *No Mother to Guide Her* (1961). *A Girl Like I* (1966). *The King's Mare* (1967). *Twice Over Lightly: New York Then and Now* (with H. Hayes; 1972). *Kiss Hollywood Good-By* (1974). *Cast of Thousands* (1977).

BIBLIOGRAPHY: For articles in reference works, see: *CA,* 21–22 (1969). *CB* (Feb. 1974). *2othCA. 2othCAS.*
Other references: *Atlantic* (Oct. 1966). *Film Comment* (Winter 1970–71). *NewR* (10 Aug. 1974). *NY* (28 Dec. 1946). *NYT* (27 Dec. 1925). *NYTBR* (18 Aug. 1974). *SatR* (24 Sept. 1966).

BEVERLY GRAY BIENSTOCK

Harriet Mulford Stone Lothrop

B. *22 June 1844, New Haven, Connecticut; d. 2 Aug. 1924, Concord, Massachusetts*
Wrote under: Margaret Sidney
D. of Sidney Mason and Harriet Mulford Stone; m. David Lothrop, 1881

L. grew up in a religious New England family whose ancestors included the Reverend Thomas Hooker and several distinguished colonial governors. L.'s father was a respected architect, and it was in deference to his disapproval of women writers that L. adopted the pen name of "Margaret Sidney." The disciplined atmosphere of learning and religion that pervaded L.'s childhood days is reflected in the tight moral tone dominating her many works.

In 1878, L. contributed a short story entitled "Polly Pepper's Chicken Pie" to *Wide Awake*, a children's magazine. Reader response was enthusiastic, and the editor requested that L. provide the magazine with twelve more installments. L. hesitated, unsure of her ability; but she succeeded in completing the requested chapters. They were later compiled into the best-selling children's book, *Five Little Peppers and How They Grew* (1881).

L. followed this first success with *Five Little Peppers Midway* (1890) and then proceeded to write ten more Pepper volumes, ending with *Our Davie Pepper* in 1916. The Pepper series traces the development of five energetic children from their early childhood days in the country, through their adolescent education in the big city, and on to the decisions of their adult lives. Although all the Pepper volumes were greeted with enthusiastic reviews, L.'s first volume remained the most popular, selling over two million copies by the time of her death.

Five Little Peppers and How They Grew opens in a little brown house in the country where five children and their recently widowed mother are struggling to survive through a bitter winter. L., herself from a well-to-do family, always wanted to live in a little brown house, and the picture she presents of impoverished country life is extremely romanticized. Despite their many misfortunes, the Peppers are never downcast and they meet all adversity with an amazing fortitude. They are intent on being good Christians, never giving in to petty emotions such as jealousy or conceit.

This moral tone does not get in the way of the narrative, however. The Pepper adventure is energetic and amusing, filled with mischief and practical joking. L. has a deep-rooted understanding of children and she provides the action as well as the repetition that her audience demands. Her language, although overworked, is effective and sincere. L. claimed that the Peppers lived independently in her imagination for years before she ever wrote about them, and this philosophy gives her narratives a natural fluidity.

In 1881, at the age of thirty-seven, L. married a Boston publisher of children's books, and they moved to Concord, Massachusetts. Here, L. gave birth to her only child, Margaret, and Lothrop bought the historic house, The Wayside, as a surprise for his wife. The Wayside had been the childhood residence of Louisa May Alcott, whose work L.'s so closely resembles. In Massachusetts, L. continued working on the Pepper narratives, as well as writing historical novels such as *A Little Maid of Concord Town* (1898) and *The Judges' Cave* (1900). L. had a strong interest in history and was a careful researcher, but she never succeeded in bringing life to these historical novels. Primarily written for an adult audience, they lack the spark and energy of the Pepper novels, while retaining their didactic overtones.

L. was always active in community life. She combined her interest in history with her interest in children by founding the national society of Children of the American Revolution. She belonged to innumerable clubs—women's, writers', and historical—but showed little interest in the woman suffrage movement. Shortly before her death at the age of eighty, she was still going strong, working on an article about Edgar Allan Poe.

WORKS: Five Little Peppers and How They Grew (1881). *So As By Fire* (1881). *The Pettibone Name* (1882). *Hester, and Other New England Stories* (1886). *The Minute Man* (1886). *A New Departure for Girls* (1886). *Dilly and the Captain* (1887). *How Tom and Dorothy Made and Kept a Christian House* (1888). *Five Little Peppers Midway* (1890). *Rob: A Story for Boys* (1891). *Five Little Peppers Grown Up* (1892). *Old Concord, Her Highways and Byways* (1893). *Whittier with the Children* (1893). *The Old Town Pump* (1895). *The Gingham Bag* (1896). *Phronsie Pepper* (1897). *A Little Maid of Concord Town* (1898). *The Stories Polly Pepper Told* (1899). *An Adirondack Cabin* (1900). *The Adventures of Joel Pepper* (1900). *The Judges' Cave* (1900). *Five Little Peppers Abroad* (1902). *Ben Pepper* (1903). *Sally, Mrs. Tubbs* (1903). *Five Little Peppers and Their Friends* (1904). *The Five Little Peppers at School* (1907). *Five Little Peppers in the Little Brown House* (1907). *A Little Maid from Boston Town* (1910). *Our Davie Pepper* (1916).

BIBLIOGRAPHY: Lothrop, M., *The Wayside: Home of Authors* (1940). Swayne, J. L., *The Story of Concord* (1906).

For articles in reference works, see: *AA. AW. DAB*, VI, 1. *NAW* (article by E. F. Hoxie). *NCAB*, 8.

Other References: *Book News Monthly* (Feb. 1910). *Boston Transcript* (4 Aug. 1924). *PW* (9 Aug. 1924).

CHRISTIANE BIRD

Mary Ann Webster Loughborough

B. 27 Aug. 1836, New York City; d. 27 Aug. 1887, Little Rock, Arkansas
M. James M. Loughborough, 1850s

Little is known about L.'s early life or education, but it is obvious that she was a well-read and intelligent woman. Her marriage to Loughborough in the 1850s brought her to the South, where she spent the rest of her life. When the Civil War began, L. apparently followed her soldier husband from place to place, living for a while in Tennessee and Mississippi.

L. is best known for her only book, *My Cave Life in Vicksburg* (1864), a graphic description of the siege of that city by the Union army in 1863. L. arrived in Vicksburg a few weeks before the assault began. She had been living in Jackson, Mississippi, but moved to Vicksburg in the mistaken belief that it would be safer. "Ah! Vicksburg," she recalls, "our city of refuge, the last to yield thou wilt be; and within thy homes we will not fear the footsteps of the victorious army but rest in safety amid thy hills." General John C. Pemberton, commander of the Confederate defenders, had already ordered women and children out of the city. L., however, chose to remain close to her husband and feared she would not be able to get to Mobile, the closest city of refuge.

The bombardment and siege of Vicksburg began on 17 May 1863. Shells from stationary cannons and gunboats on the river rained on the city, forcing the inhabitants to seek shelter in caves dug into the surrounding hillsides. According to the author, many of these caves were large enough to be divided into several rooms, and when furnished with beds and tables were comfortable, if not exactly fashionable. However, a heavy rain or mortar shell reminded the occupants that they lived under fragile earth.

Remarkably, life inside the caves soon became routine. Cave dwellers learned to distinguish the sounds made by the various types of shells as they exploded and could calmly predict their point of impact, although L. records several near-fatal miscalculations. One night a visiting soldier picked up a guitar and all joined the impromptu party. "How could we sing and laugh amid our suffering fellow beings—amid the shriek of death itself?" she asks. They learned to take amusement when and where it came.

Shells and mortars were not the only problems faced by the cave dwellers of Vicksburg. Food became scarce as the Union army closed trade routes into the city. Fresh meat and vegetables were almost impossible to obtain, so with true ingenuity the cave dwellers found substitutes. Mule, squirrel, and rat replaced beef and pork; and peas, dried, mashed, and baked into bread became the staple diet.

Finally, the city could hold out no longer. With the army on one-quarter rations and no reinforcements in sight, General Pemberton surrendered the city on 4 July 1863. Cautiously, L. and others moved out of their caves. For the first time in forty-seven days, there was no gunfire.

As soon as it was safe, L. moved to St. Louis. Friends there were interested in her description of the siege and urged her to record her experiences for publication. The first edition of *My Cave Life* was published by Appleton and Company in 1864. After the war, L. settled in Little Rock, Arkansas. There in 1883, she founded the *Southern Ladies Journal*, one of the first modern women's magazines. She served as its editor until her death.

My Cave Life in Vicksburg is one of the few complete, firsthand accounts of the siege and life inside the city. Although written shortly after the event, it has the immediacy of a newspaper account and the detail of a daily diary. One of the problems of Civil War historiography is that scholars have tended to focus on the political and military aspects of the conflict while ignoring the effects of the war on the noncombatants. However, recent scholarship is beginning to reverse this trend, and memoirs like *My Cave Life* will be invaluable in this effort.

WORKS: My Cave Life in Vicksburg (1864).

BIBLIOGRAPHY: Hoehling, A. A., *Vicksburg: 47 Days of Siege* (1969). Walker, P. F., *Vicksburg: A People at War* (1960).

JANET E. KAUFMAN

Alice Lounsberry

D. 22 Nov. 1949, New York City
D. of James S. and Sarah W. Lounsberry

While information on the life of L. has proven scarce, many of the references in her works suggest that she was a New Yorker with ties in New England, or at least extensive knowledge of those parts of New England near New York. And since she was a former treasurer of the National Society of Colonial Dames, we can place her in the upper middle class.

While most of her publications are about trees and flowers, we do not know her background for her work as a botanical and horticultural writer. Turn-of-the-century readers called for nature guides in large numbers, and most of the popular flower, tree, and bird guidebooks were written by women. L. and her illustrator, Australian artist Mrs. Ellis Rowan, worked on the books as a team, traveling all over the country together. Her first book, *A Guide to the Wild Flowers* (1899), was the most popular of her guidebooks. Organized by habitat, this work is very similar to other such works of the period, describing the plants and telling a bit about them, particularly where they might be seen. This book is illustrated with sixty-four beautiful colored plates as well as many black-and-white illustrations.

A companion volume, *A Guide to the Trees*, was published the next year and was also illustrated by Mrs. Rowan. The two works were issued in uniform format. Then the next year the two women collaborated on *Southern Wild Flowers and Trees*, in which L. describes their journey, including railway incidents, through the South.

In addition to her guidebooks for adults, L. wrote three books for children, one of them a wild-flower guide. Her *Garden Book for Young People* (1908), illustrated with photographs, is not a book on how to garden but rather a fictionalized account of two orphaned young people who make their home in a suburban town called Nestly. On their own in an old brick house, they strive to improve their property and do so, with the help of many friends and neighbors. The book has little plot, apparently being intended to inspire young readers to garden.

Probably her most important garden book, *Gardens near the Sea* (1910) is a large, handsome work illustrated with photographs and color plates by H. W. Faulkner. It includes practical directions for various seaside locations and descriptions of gardens she had seen. The book includes gardens in New England and on Long Island and shows that she had extensive acquaintance with plant material and a lesser interest in garden design.

L.'s last book, published many years after her garden writings, was a biography of Sir William Phips, a 17th-c. governor of Massachusetts Bay Colony who had an interesting and eventful life. This work is intended for the average reader, and there is no indication of why she chose to write a book about this man, who has not been ignored by other writers.

L's works are not much different from those of other such writers, but she is an example of the many upper-middle-class women, mostly New Yorkers, who put their knowledge of plants to profit when nature study became a popular pastime.

WORKS: *A Guide to the Wild Flowers* (1899). *A Guide to the Trees* (1900). *Southern Wild Flowers and Trees* (1901). *The Wild Flower Book for Young People* (1906). *The Garden Book for Young People* (1908). *Gardens near the Sea* (1910). *Frank and Bessie's Forester* (1912). *Sir William Phips* (1941).

BIBLIOGRAPHY: Samuel, H. J., *Wild Flower Hunter: The Story of Ellis* (1961).
Other references: *NYT* (22 Nov. 1949).

BEVERLY SEATON

Esther Clayson Pohl Lovejoy

B. Nov. 1869, near Seabeck, Washington; d. 17 Aug. 1967, New York City
Wrote under: Esther Pohl Lovejoy
D. of Edward and Annie Quinton Clayson; m. Emil Pohl, 1894; m. George A. Lovejoy, 1913

L. was born in a logging camp. She worked her way through the University of Oregon Medical School, graduating in 1894, the second woman to receive an M.D. from that institution. L. and her first husband, also a physician, practiced together in Portland for several years. In 1898, they joined the gold rush to Alaska and set up practice and a hospital in Skagway, returning in 1900 to Portland. Following the birth of her son the next year, L. continued her practice in Portland and was director of Portland's Health Department from 1907 to 1909. Her son died in 1908; Pohl died in 1911. She divorced her second husband, a Portland businessman, in 1920.

From 1919 until the year of her death, L. served as chairman of the American Women's Hospitals (AWH) executive board, organizing relief efforts in thirty different countries. She helped found the Medical Women's International Association in 1919 and served as its president until 1924. She also served as president of the American Medical Women's Association from 1932 to 1933. In acknowledgment of her outstanding service on behalf of their people, many foreign countries bestowed upon L. their highest honors.

L.'s first book, *The House of the Good Neighbor* (1919), tells of her experiences during World War I at a French *résidence sociale* in Levallois, a suburb of Paris. As a representative of the Medical Women's National Association, L. went to France to find ways American women physicians might aid relief efforts there. Her stay with Marie-Jeanne Bassot, who conducted the social center known affectionately as the "House of the Good Neighbor," allowed L. to observe directly the effects of the war on French women and children. L. tells of the French government's campaign encouraging women to have children as a patriotic duty at a time when eighty thousand French babies were dying each year of starvation or disease and concludes that for women war is worse than death.

Certain Samaritans (1927) tells of the AWH's relief efforts in Europe. Because American women physicians wanted to serve their country and were not accepted for military service by the war department, in 1917 the Medical Women's National Association established the AWH, directed and staffed entirely by women, to bring relief and medical aid to noncombatant populations in war-stricken countries. AWH relief work did not end with the war, however. The book focuses on the Christian exodus from Turkey in 1922 and AWH efforts to help the hundreds of thousands of refugees suffering everything from smallpox to starvation. The story is remarkable and is well told. *Women Physicians and Surgeons* (1939) tells the same story but offers more specific supporting details, including actual letters, reports, records, and minutes of AWH executive meetings. It is of more interest to historians and scholars than to the general reader.

In *Women Doctors of the World* (1957), her last book, L. records the history of women physicians throughout the world. She summarizes the early historical background in her first chapter, relying heavily on the work of Kate Campbell Hurd Mead, and concentrates on the 19th and 20th centuries, thus supplementing Mead's work, *A History of Women in Medicine* (1938). L. traces the careers of the first women physicians in countries around the world; includes the history of the AWH; and concludes with a chapter, "Women Doctors in the Golden Age of Medicine," asserting that women physicians may be responsible for the present golden age of medicine.

L. wrote to provide young women interested in medicine with role models of successful women physicians. She succeeded and made a great contribution to women's history.

WORKS: The House of the Good Neighbor (1919; rev. ed., 1920). *Certain Samaritans* (1927; rev. ed., 1933). *Women Physicians and Surgeons* (1939). *Women Doctors of the World* (1957).

BIBLIOGRAPHY: Burt, O. W., *Physician to the World: Esther Pohl Lovejoy* (1973). Medical Women's International Association Golden Jubilee Souvenir, *Esther Pohl Lovejoy, M.D.* (1970).

Other references: *Journal of the American Medical Women's Association* (Aug. 1967; Sept. 1967). *NYT* (18 Aug. 1967). *Time* (25 Aug. 1967). *Today's Health* (Aug. 1970).

ANNE HUDSON JONES

Amy Lowell

B. *9 Feb. 1874, Brookline, Massachusetts; d. 12 May 1925, Brookline, Massachusetts*
D. *of Augustus and Katherine Bigelow Lawrence Lowell*

L., a descendant of a clan of cultivated New England intellectuals, was raised in a family of devout Episcopalians on a ten-acre estate (Sevenels); the stately brownstone mansion, with its high mansard roof and extravagant gardens, became her home on the death of her parents. Her life of opulence was reinforced by a full staff of servants and her secretary-companion, Ada Russell. L. disapproved of wasting time and money on frivolities, however, claiming she was "an old-fashioned Puritan," who "let each day pass, well ordered in its usefulness."

Following several years of solitary apprenticeship in the atmosphere of the seven-thousand-book–lined library at Sevenels, she became a student of verse, and finally, in 1902, settled into the serious business of being a poet. The image of the social *grand dame* was not easily overcome; however, L. was determined that she be recognized as a hardworking, serious poet. At the time her first serious poem, "Fixed Idea," appeared in *The Atlantic Monthly* (Aug. 1910) her recognition consisted of the admiration accorded the sister of an eminent astronomer and the president of Harvard.

Despite the uncharitable opinions of some of her relatives, the portly, liberated woman, who resembled the director of a girls' school in her mannish coat, stiff collar, and pince-nez, knew what she was about. For more than thirteen years, L. was an ardent and indefatigable campaigner for poetry, and her prominence in both social and literary circles, coupled with her histrionic presence, gave her easy access to poetry societies, publishing offices, and public platforms. As a self-appointed prophet, she felt her mission was to reconstruct the taste of the American public, whom she felt had little comprehension of contemporary poetry.

It was not until her meeting with the Imagists in London in 1913 that L. began to gain some recognition. Despite controversy with writers such as Ford Maddox Ford and Ezra Pound over the reconstructed version of Imagism she imported to America, L. successfully published three Imagist anthologies and continued unwavering in her determination to create a climate conducive to the creation of American poetry.

Together with her poetry, L. published two volumes of critical essays, *Six French Poets* (1915) and *Tendencies in Modern American Poetry* (1917), and numerous reviews, some of which reflected critical misjudgments particularly in the case of Pound, Eliot, and Marianne Moore.

Following the publication of her first volume of poems, *A Dome of Many-Colored Glass* (1912), highly conventional in subject and style, L. was more experimental, studiously noting in each of her prefaces the development of her own poetics, her experimentation with unrhymed cadence, fluctuating rhythm, and most notably "polyphonic verse," a flexible verse form which she first used in *Sword Blades and Poppy Seeds* (1914), and later in *Can Grande's Castle* (1918). Generally, L. was successful when she was on native ground; her lack of success is reflected in departures, such as her "oriental poems."

Occasionally a memorable poem ("Meeting-House Hill," "Patterns," "Lilacs") appears among the six hundred and fifty preserved in published volumes, but L. will not be memorialized for her poetry. She had unlimited faith in her own capacity and a shared concern with other poets for the enterprise of poetry; and until her death she was a tireless and dedicated impresario of modern poetry.

WORKS: *A Dome of Many-Colored Glass* (1912). *Sword Blades and Poppy Seeds* (1914). *Six French Poets* (1915). *Some Imagist Poets: An Annual Anthology* (1915–17). *Men, Women, and Ghosts* (1916). *Tendencies in Modern American Poetry* (1917). *Can Grande's Castle* (1918). *Pictures of the Floating World* (1919). *Fir-Flower Tablets* (translated by Lowell, with F. Ayscough, 1920). *Legends* (1921). *A Critical Fable* (1922). *John Keats* (1925). *What's O'Clock* (1925). *Eastwind* (1926). *Ballads for Sale* (1927). *Selected Poems* (1928). *Poetry and Poets* (1930). *Correspondence of a Friendship* (with F. Ayscough, 1946). *Complete Poetical Works of Amy Lowell* (Ed. L. Untemeyer, 1955).

BIBLIOGRAPHY: Damon, S. F., *Amy Lowell: A Chronicle, with Extracts from Her Correspondence* (1935). Gould, J., *Amy: The World of Amy Lowell and the Imagist Movement* (1963). Healey, C., "Amy Lowell Visits London," *NEQ* (Sept. 1970). Healey, C., "Some Imagist Essays: Amy Lowell," *NEQ* (March 1970). Ruihley, G. R., *The Thorn of a Rose: Amy Lowell Reconsidered* (1963). Scott, W. T., *Exiles and Fabrications* (1961).

For articles in reference works, see: *DAB*, VI, 1. *NAW* (article by W. Berthoff). *NCAB*, 19. *20thCA*. *20thCAS*.

Other references: *JML* 5 (1963). *TQ* 6 (1964).

CLAIRE HEALEY

Mina Loy

B. 27 Dec. 1882, London, England; d. 25 Sept. 1966, Aspen, Colorado
D. of Sigmund and Julia Brian Lowy; m. Stephen Haweis, 1903; m. Arthur Cravan (Fabian Avenarius Lloyd), 1918

L. has always been considered an American modernist poet. Her modernist education began at seventeen with the study of painting in Munich, London, and Paris. She was elected to the Autumn Salon in 1906 and then left Paris for Florence. There she met the Futurists and incorporated their revolutionary theories of painting and literature into her early poetry. Her poems began appearing in the American little magazines in 1914, and she joined the New York avant-garde in 1916. L. shared the Americans' commitment to the rejuvenation of word and image and their search for new poetic forms, derived from modern painting, to depict the movement of consciousness. At the forefront of poetic experiment, L. earned notoriety for her structural innovations and her sexual subject matter. After 1925 she was largely forgotten, partly because she lacked the discipline to develop her early breakthroughs, and also because she gave much of her creative energy to painting.

L. was married twice: in 1903 to Stephen Haweis, an English painter; in 1918 to Dadaist Arthur Cravan. Of her four children, one died in infancy, one in adolescence. She lived in Paris from 1923 to 1936 and in New York from 1936 to 1954; she spent the remainder of her life with her daughters in Aspen, Colorado.

In her poetry, L. explores the self, "a covered entrance to infinity." Her main symbol is the eye; her enduring theme the necessity of persistent, self- and world-defining vision in a chaotic and indifferent universe. In poems written from 1914 to 1917, she analyzes a female self deformed by social mores that limit women to the roles of wife and mistress and make her success in the marriage market dependent on virginity and sexual ignorance. Educated on romantic love stories, the Italian matrons of "At the Door of the House" (1917) and "The Effectual Marriage" (1917) are soon disillusioned with marriage. The semiautobiographical *Anglo-Mongrels and the Rose* (first half, *Little Review*, 1923–24; second half, *Contact Collection of Contemporary Writers*, 1925) details the English version of the domestic drama. "Parturition" (1914) uses irregular typography to convey woman's physical pain and spiritual quest during childbirth. Her central work is the *Love Songs* (Poems I–IV, *Others*, 1915), or *Songs to Joannes* (Poems I–XXXIV, *Others*, 1917), thirty-four poems on the failure of romantic love, using irregular typography and a collage structure. Proto-surrealist images link sexuality and the psyche, and narrative blurs as the speaker is accosted by fragments of love that introduce her to a meaningless universe. L. retreats from nihilism in "Human Cylinders" (1917), "The Black Virginity" (1918), and "The Dead" (1920), where, recognizing the impossibility of attaining absolute answers to the cosmic mystery, she shifts her emphasis to the *act* of vision.

Lunar Baedeker (1923) contains early poems (thirteen *Love Songs* from 1914 and 1915) and new poems. The theme of the unique vision of the artist, who alone shapes chaos into divine Form, dominates the newer poems. L.'s heritage here is Art for Art's Sake as it developed through Baudelaire, Parnassianism, Laforgue, and the English 1890s. "Apology of Genius" (1922) stresses the artist's alienation from philistine society, the supremacy of art, and the importance of artistic craftsmanship. Other poems draw upon this heritage to defend abstract art. The title poem and "Crab-Angel" satirize the dishonest artist who abandons vision and treats art as a circus for self-display.

Lunar Baedeker reflects the development of L.'s imagery. Early poems alternate abstraction and image to depict the movement of consciousness between intellect and intuition. Later poems are series of vivid images, unified by the interplay of sounds (L.'s trademark), that unite abstraction and image in flashes of vision.

Lunar Baedeker & Time-Tables (1958) retraces former ground and includes a few later poems. In poems written during the 1940s and 1950s L. elaborates a minor early subject, the clownish bum who, as "in Hot Cross Bum," sidesteps vision to pursue false Nirvanas. His companions are other denizens of the metropolis who fabricate illusions in order to escape reality.

Since 1944 L. has been rediscovered by poets and critics who find in her, as in Gertrude Stein, Ezra Pound, and William Carlos Williams, elements of modernist poetry that feed the present. An innovative structuring of consciousness, honesty of subject, and deployment of radiant words and images are qualities that made L. a seminal modernist and connect her to the present.

WORKS: *Auto-Facial Constructions* (1919). *Psycho-Democracy* (1920). *Lunar Baedeker* (1923). *Lunar Baedeker & Time-Tables: Selected Poems of Mina Loy* (1958).

BIBLIOGRAPHY: Burke, G. G., in *Americans in Paris, 1920–1939* (Dictionary of Literary Biography, 1980). Burke, G. G., in *Women's Studies* (1980). Fields, K., "The Rhetoric of Artifice—Ezra Pound, T. S. Eliot, Wallace Stevens, Walter Conrad Arensberg, Donald Evans, Mina Loy, and Yvor Winters" (Ph.D. diss., 1967). Kouidis, V. M., *Mina Loy: American Modernist Poet* (1980). Kouidis, V. M., "Rediscovering Our Sources: An Introduction to the Poetry of Mina Loy," *Boundary 2* (Spring 1980).

For articles in reference works, see: *CB* (Oct. 1950).

Other references: *Circle* (1944). *ConL* (Spring-summer 1961). *Dial* (June 1926). *Little Review* (March 1918). *Nation* (May 1961). New York *Evening Sun* (13 Feb. 1917). *SoR* (July 1967).

VIRGINIA M. KOUIDIS

Clare Boothe Luce

B. 10 April 1903, New York City
Writes under: Clare Boothe, Clare Boothe Brokaw, Clare Boothe Luce
D. of William F. and Ann Clare Snyder Boothe; m. George Tuttle Brokaw,
1923; m. Henry R. Luce, 1935

L. has been a playwright, journalist, politician, diplomat, and feminist. She planned a theatrical career, attending Clare Tree Major's School of the Theater, but her direction was changed by a brief stint for the woman suffrage movement and her marriage to George Brokaw in 1923. Six years later when her marriage ended, she turned to journalism, serving in editorial posts for *Vogue* and then *Vanity Fair*. In 1931 she resigned, determined to write plays, and shortly thereafter married Henry Luce, then president of Time Inc.

This second marriage did not interrupt her career. She wrote four plays for Broadway, then devoted herself to journalism and politics. She traveled and wrote for *Life*, campaigned for Wendell Willkie and later for Eisenhower, served two terms as U.S. Congresswoman from Connecticut in the 1940s, and competed for a Republican senatorial nomination in the early 1950s. She lost the last race, but Eisenhower appointed her Ambassador to Italy.

During these years, L. wrote and lectured, not only on politics but also on Catholicism, to which she was converted in mid-life. After the death of Henry Luce, she retired to Hawaii, where she still writes and lectures on such diverse subjects as the women's movement, the Catholic stance on abortion, and conservative Republicanism.

As a writer, L.'s most significant body of work is her plays. The first, *Abide with Me* (1935), is a somber melodrama about a sadistic husband who is finally shot by the faithful family servant. It ran for only thirty-six performances. Fame came with *The Women* (1936), a vitriolic comedy about wealthy ladies of leisure. The play centers on the struggles of a devoted wife to regain her husband while living amidst a jungle of catty women nourished on gossip and the misfortunes of their acquaintances. The play was filmed twice, in 1939 and 1956, and was revived on Broadway in 1973. In the light of the women's liberation movement of the 1960s and 70s, however, the play comes across as false and unworthy.

L. made Broadway again with *Kiss the Boys Good-Bye* (1938), a frivolous comedy about the much-ballyhooed Hollywood search for an unknown actress to play Scarlet O'Hara, which ran for 286 performances. L.'s last play, *Margin for Error*, a satiric melodrama with an anti-Nazi plot, was produced in 1939. All of her plays, except the first, were later filmed.

A review of L.'s journalistic writings reveals her personal development. Her first piece, *Stuffed Shirts* (1931), is a brittle series of sketches lampooning various New York characters, such as the newly rich dowager, the divorcee, and the Wall Street ladies' man. Later L.'s interests became more international. *Europe in the Spring* (1940) is a lively account of her European travels at the time of the great German offensive. After her seven years in politics, she wrote a series of articles for *McCall's* magazine (1947) describing her religious conversion. In 1952 she edited a volume of essays by American and British authors called *Saints for Now*. *Ladies' Home Journal* printed the essay "Growing Old Beautifully" in 1973.

Despite the more mellow works of her later years, L. is remembered best as a playwright with a heavy hand for sensationalism and sentimentality—two qualities with great appeal for audiences of the 1930s. Her plays are infused with social snobbery and a brisk but vituperative wit with which she characterized the wealthy, sophisticated class. It is a great irony that the hostile, unflattering portraits of her own sex, in plays such as *The Women* and *Kiss the Boys Good-Bye*, should overshadow the more constructive efforts of this feminist.

WORKS: *Stuffed Shirts* (1931). *Abide with Me* (1935). *The Women* (1936; film versions: *The Women*, 1939; *The Opposite Sex*, 1956). *Kiss the Boys Good-Bye* (1938; film version, 1941). *Margin for Error* (1940; film version, 1943). *Europe in the Spring* (1940). *Saints for Now* (edited by Luce, 1952).

BIBLIOGRAPHY: Betts, A. P., *Women in Congress* (1945). Gray, J., "Dream of Unfair Women," in *On Second Thought* (1946). Mersand, J., *American Drama 1930–1940* (1941).

For articles in reference works, see: *CA*, 45–48 (1974). *Catholic Authors: Contemporary Biographical Sketches, 1930–1947*, Ed. M. Hoehn (1952). *NCAB*, F. *20thCA*. *20thCAS*.

Other references: *NewR* (11 May 1953). *Newsweek* (26 Nov. 1973). *Woman's Home Companion* (Nov. 1955; Dec. 1955; Jan. 1956).

LUCINA P. GABBARD

Mabel Ganson Dodge Luhan

B. 26 Feb. 1879, Buffalo, New York; d. 13 Aug. 1962, Taos, New Mexico
Wrote under: Mabel Dodge, Mabel Dodge Luhan
D. of Charles and Sarah Ganson; m. Karl Evans, 1900; m. Edwin Dodge,
  1905 (?); m. Maurice Sterne, 1917; m. Antonio Luhan, 1923

The only child of upper-class parents, L. had an economically and socially secure, but emotionally starved, childhood. Tended by nursemaids and kept at a distance by an ineffectual father and a strong-willed, socialite mother, L. felt like an orphan who spent her life in search of a community in which she could be "at home."

L. devoted her life to overcoming her anomie by directing her energies to the discovery and creation of her identity. She identified herself with an enormous variety of aesthetic and political causes; constructed model communities she hoped would define her role and purpose in modern society; collected famous artists and activists whose careers she tried to shape and who, in turn, she hoped would give shape and meaning to her life; spent twenty years in psychoanalysis while dabbling in a number of mind-cure philosophies; and left twenty-four volumes of autobiographical materials that bear witness to the multiple ways in which she sought self-definition.

Although financially independent and sexually liberated, L. was crippled by her belief in woman's cultural subservience. Believing women capable of only "secondary" forms of creativity, she played the role of Muse to men of genius, attempting to achieve an identity by inspiring their creativity. At the same time, she wished to create in her own right, so her relationships with men often turned destructive and self-destructive. She was married four times; only in her last marriage to a full-blooded Pueblo Indian did she achieve any sense of fulfillment. Among the Pueblos, she found a culture in which individual, social, and religious values were integrated by a unifying mythos that was organically related to a land in which she finally felt at home.

L. became a leading symbol of modernism, in fact and fiction. As a spokeswoman for the avant-garde, L. was a published poet, book reviewer, essayist, biographer, and social critic. Her prose styles and subject matter were a melting pot of Americana, ranging from the banality of the Dorothea Dix–type columns she wrote for the Hearst papers to superbly evocative descriptive prose on life in the Southwest.

L.'s major contribution to American literature is her book *Winter in Taos* (1935). While she sought for years to find writers (D. H. Lawrence and Robinson Jeffers were the two most famous) to publicize her southwestern paradise, she wrote its finest testament herself. *Winter in Taos* is a first-rank contribution to American regional literature, a work of intense lyrical beauty and metaphoric power that achieves a richly sustained integration of her emotional life with the landscape surrounding her.

L.'s discovery of the Indians as potential saviors for a declining white civilization led to the writing of her best-known works, *Intimate Memories* (4 vols., 1933–37). Begun in 1924 as part of an ongoing process of psychotherapy, L. presented her fragmented personality as a metaphor for a world she wished would die and be reborn, as she felt she had, through the grace offered by a prewestern tribal culture. Although L. was not a feminist, her self-portrait reveals the destructiveness of the feminine mystique of which she was both perpetrator and victim.

L.'s memoirs are a significant contribution to social, intellectual, and feminist history. In spite of her sometimes unreliable and self-serving observations, she is an insightful eyewitness to childrearing in Victorian America, the fin de siècle world of American expatriates in Europe, the major revolutionary movements of pre–World War I America, and the fascination of postwar intellectuals with "primitives."

WORKS: *Lorenzo in Taos* (1932). *Intimate Memories* (Vol. 1, *Background*, 1933; Vol. 2, *European Experiences*, 1935; Vol. 3, *Movers and Shakers*, 1936; Vol. 4, *Edge of the Taos Desert*, 1937). *Winter in Taos* (1935). *Taos and Its Artists* (1947).

BIBLIOGRAPHY: Crunden, R., *From Self to Society, 1919–1941* (1972). Hahn, E., *Mabel* (1978). Lasch, C., *The New Radicalism in America (1889–1963)* (1967). Rudnick, L. P., "The Unexpurgated Self: A Critical Biography of Mabel Dodge Luhan" (Ph.D. diss., Brown Univ., 1977).
For articles in reference works, see: *20thCA. 20thCAS.*

LOIS P. RUDNICK

Grace Lumpkin

B. 1903 (?), Milledgeville, Georgia

Raised and educated largely in South Carolina, L. later taught school in Georgia and worked as a home demonstration agent for the government, thereby coming into contact with the poverty of many southern farm families. Her sympathy for the poor was expanded by living and working among North Carolina mountain people and watching their migration to the cotton mills. She became a staunch anticapitalist and ardent supporter of industrial unionism.

L. went to New York when she was twenty-five and began to write short stories, becoming involved in liberal and radical politics. Her first story was published in *The New Masses*, and during the 1930s, like many young writers, she became a fellow traveler. During this period she wrote two proletarian novels, both about the southern poor. *A Sign for Cain* (1935) was the subject of a 1953 inquiry by the Senate Permanent Investigating Sub-Committee, at which L. testified that she had been forced to write communist propaganda into that novel, under threat of having her career "broken" by communist book reviewers. L., who lives now in Columbia, South Carolina, is said to be working at present on a new novel, *God and a Garden.*

L.'s first and best novel, *To Make My Bread* (1932), traces the movement of poor southern tenant farmers and sharecroppers from their rural homes to newly industrialized mill towns. It is a compassionate novel that uses the author's intimate knowledge of these people to explore the cultural shock and the disillusion that they encountered in the transition. While in the southern mountains, these people had endured a stable kind of poverty, ameliorated by the natural beauty of their surroundings, the intoxicating rituals of their fundamentalist religion, and the closeness of family and community ties. In the cotton mills, their large families became a burden, especially for the women who were needed as wage earners; their religion became a tool of the bosses who exploited and distorted its ideals of submissiveness; and the natural beauty was replaced by dreary industrial ugliness. L.'s heroine, Bonnie McClure, like many of the other women, is pushed, almost reluctantly, out of her traditional feminine role as childbearer by the economic exigencies of her life: sooner than watch children starve to death she will become a union organizer and strike leader. L.'s sympathies for factory women are strong, but she tends ultimately to see the resolution of their problems in a socialist transformation of society, despite the fact that their sufferings are markedly different in nature from those of their husbands and brothers.

In her second novel, *A Sign for Cain*, L. again attempts to demonstrate that the interests of all the poor are best served by communism, this time by exploring the potential power of a political alliance between black and white sharecroppers in the South. This novel has, as a kind of antiheroine, a rebellious bourgeois woman, Caroline Gault, who, modern and assertive in her sexual morality, is nevertheless condemned for trying to substitute a reactionary code of individualism for collective action. This novel proposes even more directly than the first that women should not seek sexual justice outside the framework of a socialist redistribution of society's resources.

L.'s third novel, *The Wedding* (1939) makes a movement away from political tendentiousness in favor of a rather sympathetic examination of a southern middle-class family in a state of personal crisis. Her last published work, *Full Circle* (1962), is a novel that has enhanced neither her political nor her literary reputation, dealing as it does with what one critic has called the overcultivated soil of international communist conspiracy.

It is in the first two novels that L. makes her most significant contribution to the literature of feminism. Both provide early examples of the continuing dialectical debate between the adherents of solidarity with other movements of oppressed groups and those who believe that no economic or social equality can ever exist without a prior radical revision of the relationships between men and women.

WORKS: *To Make My Bread* (1932; dramatization, *Let Freedom Ring* by A. Bein, 1936). *A Sign for Cain* (1935). *The Wedding* (1939). *Full Circle* (1962).

BIBLIOGRAPHY: Rideout, W. B., *The Radical Novel in the United States, 1900–1954: Some Interrelations of Literature and Society* (1956).
For articles in reference works, see: *20thCA. 20thCAS.*
Other references: *Books* (27 Oct. 1935). *Nation* (19 Oct. 1932). *NewR* (7 Dec. 1932; 23 Oct. 1935). *NYT* (26 Feb. 1939). *SatR* (9 Nov. 1935).

SYLVIA COOK

Alma Lutz

B. 2 March 1890, Jamestown, North Dakota; d. 31 Aug. 1973, Berlin, New York
D. of George and Matilda Bauer Lutz

L. was a free-lance writer, a journalist, and a contributing editor of *Equal Rights,* the official journal of the National Women's Party. She achieved her literary prominence primarily as the biographer of 19th-c. women leaders.

L.'s first work was *Emma Willard: Daughter of Democracy* (1929). For this narrative biography of the early 19th-c. educator, L. focuses particularly on Willard's early pioneering investigatory work to prove women's intellectual capacity and on Willard's achievements through her Troy, New York, school. L. later published a revised edition of this book entitled *Emma Willard, Pioneer Educator of American Women* (1964). This second version gives a tightened, more sharply honed study of Willard's mature thought and practice. L. portrays with sympathetic insight the consistency of Willard's views in the midst of changing circumstance.

In 1940 L. turned to the women's rights movement, publishing *Created Equal: A Biography of Elizabeth Cady Stanton.* L. gives relatively little attention to the formative experiences of Stanton's early life or even to her early career. She centers instead on the post-1860 years of Stanton's life, when she could devote nearly full-time attention to the women's rights cause as publicist, lecturer, and brilliant formulator of policy statements. L. places particular stress on Stanton as a "torchbearer for women," underscoring Stanton's broad-ranging concerns, the clarity of her perspective, and her role as pioneer anticipator of issues.

L. further extended the Stanton story by collaborating with Elizabeth's daughter, Harriot Stanton Blatch in Blatch's memoirs, *Challenging Years* (1940). The memoirs themselves deal largely with the women's-rights efforts of the late 19th and early 20th centuries.

In the work about Stanton, L. reveals a keen appreciation of the importance of the Stanton-Anthony collaboration. In 1959 Lutz published a significant biographical study of that second figure, *Susan B. Anthony: Rebel, Crusader, Humanitarian.* L. thoughtfully appraises the complementary nature of the two women's work and also traces with careful precision the separate line of Anthony's thought and action. She underscores the crucial importance of Anthony's organizing ability and the unflagging involvement which made her eventually the symbol of the woman-suffrage movement.

L.'s final work on 19th-c. women leaders was *Crusade for Freedom* (1968), a study of women's roles in the antislavery campaigns. In this collective biography L. evaluates the work of such varied personalities as the early antislavery writer, Elizabeth Chandler; the educator, Prudence Crandle; and the lecturer-writers, the Grimké sisters. She underscores the significance of the interwoven strands of antislavery efforts and the emerging women's-rights movement. L. sees this same interweaving of concerns reemerging as an important theme of the 1960s.

L. was essentially a narrative biographer, concerned primarily with the broad public record of 19th-c. women leaders. She developed a strong, dramatic style of writing and became a vivid portrayer of reform personalities. Though concerned with the ideas of the women's movement, L. focused primarily on the efforts to translate ideas into reality. She gave relatively little attention to intellectual history itself or to critical appraisal of the broad social context within which the women functioned. She excelled in the presentation of the individual personality and the detailed accounts of women's campaigns, rather than in analytical background studies.

L.'s studies of Willard and of Stanton in particular were pioneering works. The Stanton work was the first significant appraisal of that leader since the general *History of Woman Suffrage*. The Anthony biography and the study of antislavery women presented more familiar material and drew more on well-known sources. The works provided dramatic restatements of these women's roles.

L. wrote perceptively, lucidly, and with fervor about the 19th-c. struggles for women's rights. She had a strong, appreciative sense of what had been achieved, but also a personal concern for the unfinished tasks. In the years between the first and second women's movements, L. kept before the general public the sharply lit images of forceful women leaders of the past.

WORKS: *Emma Willard: Daughter of Democracy* (1929; rev. ed., *Emma Willard, Pioneer Educator of American Women*, 1964). *Mary Baker Eddy Historical House, Swampscott, Massachusetts: The Birthplace of Christian Science* (1935). *Challenging Years: The Memoirs of Harriot Stanton Blatch* (with H. S. Blatch, 1940). *Created Equal: A Biography of Elizabeth Cady Stanton, 1815–1902* (1940). *Mary Baker Eddy Historical House, Rumney Village, New Hampshire: The Rumney Years* (1940). *With Love, Jane: Letters of American*

Women on the War Fronts (1945). *Susan B. Anthony: Rebel, Crusader, Humanitarian* (1959). *Crusade for Freedom: Women of the Antislavery Movement* (1968).

BIBLIOGRAPHY: For articles in reference works, see: *CA*, 45–48 (1974); *Permanent Series* (1975).
   Other references: *AHR* (July 1959; Dec. 1968). *NewR* (29 July 1940). *NEQ* (Dec. 1959). *NYT* (9 June 1919; 1 Sept. 1973). *SatR* (7 March 1959).

INZER BYERS

Grace Livingston Hill Lutz

B. 15 April 1865, Wellsville, New York; d. 23 Feb. 1947, Swarthmore,
   Pennsylvania
Wrote under: Grace Livingston Hill, Grace Livingston Hill-Lutz, Grace
   Livingston, Marcia Macdonald
D. of Charles Montgomery and Marcia Macdonald Livingston; m. Frank Hill,
   1892; m. Flavius J. Lutz, 1916

L.'s mother published four romances under the name of Mrs. C. M. Livingston, but devoted herself primarily to being a preacher's wife. Apparently in order to honor her mother as an individual, L. published three novels under her mother's given name, Marcia Macdonald. L.'s father, a Presbyterian minister, also did some writing, exclusively on theological topics. His influence is reflected in L.'s establishment and direction of a mission Sunday school in Swarthmore. Perhaps the strongest of all family influences was that of L.'s aunt, Isabella Macdonald ("Pansy") Alden, an author who not only encouraged L. to write but persuaded her own publisher to print the youngster's first effort, *The Esseltynes; or, Alpsonso and Marguerite.*

   L.'s first husband, also a Presbyterian minister, died after seven years of marriage. L. was forced to publish enough to support herself and her two daughters. She began with Sunday-school lessons in a column syndicated by ten local newspapers, but soon turned to fiction. By 1904 she was successful enough to build herself a comfortable home in Swarthmore. L.'s second marriage was unhappy and soon led to separation, although L. remained adamant in her opposition to divorce. She was active as a writer until the end of her life, her final novel being completed by her daughter Ruth for posthumous publication.

L. worked in a wide range of genres, specializing in the adventure story and contemporary romance but also including fantasy (her first novel, *A Chautauqua Idyll*, 1887), nonfiction (*The War Romance of the Salvation Army*, 1919), historical romance (*Marcia Schuyler*, 1908), and mystery (*The Mystery of Mary*, 1912). She wrote 107 books, which sold over three million copies during her lifetime.

L. was especially successful at writing fast-paced adventures featuring intelligent and resourceful heroines. A good example is *The Red Signal* (1919), set during World War I. When the German truck farm where young Hilda Lessing works turns out to be swarming with German spy activity, Hilda shows herself to be both brave and lucky as she saves the U.S. from a major disaster and wins a presidential medal. She also wins the reward reserved for all of L.'s finest heroines—marriage with a handsome and affluent young man. Although the historical perspective is simplistic—World War I is explained as the result of Germany's "forgetting God"—and although the plot turns on some very unlikely coincidences, the narrative is compelling enough to have thrilled many a reader.

L.'s most popular books were contemporary romances, such as *Matched Pearls* (1933), *Beauty for Ashes* (1935), and *April Gold* (1936). The most widely read of all, *The Witness* (1917), brought her thousands of letters of gratitude. In it as in most of her books, L. utilizes one-dimensional characterization in which Christian believers are sincere, brave, and altruistic while unbelievers are selfish and corrupt. Paul Courtland is the typical L. hero: rich, handsome, popular, athletic, a Phi Beta Kappa man. A rich girl, who parallels the biblical "scarlet woman" by attempting to seduce Paul away from his faith, possesses a "nasty little chin" with "a Satanic point." She is contrasted with a poor orphan girl who, because of her modesty and integrity, wins the prize of marriage to the hero. L. manifests a lively sense of social justice by having Paul refuse a lucrative management position in a company that exploits its factory workers in unsafe conditions. The novel's theme is the actual presence of Christ in any life devoted to human concern and justice. As one character puts it, "It's heaven or hell, both now and hereafter."

L. knew how to wring human emotion and enlist current events to enliven her novels while she was making fairly overt attempts to convert her readers to Christ. For instance, a 1944 novel, *Time of the Singing of Birds*, features an attractive officer who returns wounded from World

War II. When he eventually marries the most deserving of his Christian girlfriends, an observer comments, "Heavens! If I thought I could have a marriage like that it would be worth-while trying to be a Christian."

Improbable coincidence, avoidance of moral ambiguity, unconscious sexism, and almost exclusive use of stock characters work together to keep L.'s fiction lightweight. But her fast-paced upbeat style has refreshed and relaxed many people. And there can be little doubt that L. provided a shining ideal for younger readers by featuring so many heroines of unshakable standards and determined, triumphant integrity.

WORKS: *A Chautauqua Idyl* (1887). *A Little Servant* (1890). *The Parkerstown Delegate* (1892). *Katharine's Yesterday, and Other Christian Endeavor Stories* (1895). *In the Way* (1897). *Lone Point; a Summer Outing* (1898). *A Daily Rate* (1900). *The Angel of His Presence* (1902). *An Unwilling Guest* (1902). *According to the Pattern* (1903). *The Story of a Whim* (1903). *Because of Stephen* (1904). *The Girl from Montana* (1908). *Marcia Schuyler* (1908). *Phoebe Deane* (1909). *Dawn of the Morning* (1910). *Aunt Crete's Emancipation* (1911). *The Mystery of Mary* (1912). *The Best Man* (1914). *The Man of the Desert* (1914). *Miranda* (1915). *The Finding of Jasper Holt* (1916). *A Voice in the Wilderness* (1916). *The Witness* (1917). *The Enchanted Barn* (1918). *The Red Signal* (1919). *The Search* (1919). *The War Romance of the Salvation Army* (with E. Booth, 1919). *Cloudy Jewel* (1920). *Exit Betty* (1920). *The Tryst* (1921). *The City of Fire* (1922). *The Big Blue Soldier* (1923). *Tomorrow About This Time* (1923). *Re-Creations* (1924). *Ariel Custer* (1925). *Not Under the Law* (1925). *Coming through the Rye* (1926). *A New Name* (1926). *The Honor Girl* (1927). *Job's Niece* (1927). *The White Flower* (1927). *Blue Ruin* (1928). *Crimson Roses* (1928). *Found Treasure* (1928). *Duskin* (1929). *An Interrupted Night* by I. M. Alden (introduction by Lutz, 1929). *Out of the Storm* (1929). *The Prodigal Girl* (1929). *The Gold Shoe* (1930). *Ladybird* (1930). *The White Lady* (1930). *The Chance of a Lifetime* (1931). *Kerry* (1931). *Memories of Yesterday* by I. M. Alden (edited by Lutz, 1931). *Silver Wings* (1931). *Beggarman* (1932). *The Challengers* (1932). *Happiness Hill* (1932). *Her Wedding Garment* (1932). *The House across the Hedge* (1932). *The Story of the Lost Star* (1932). *The Beloved Stranger* (1933). *Matched Pearls* (1933). *The Ransom* (1933). *Amorelle* (1934). *The Christmas Bride* (1934). *Rainbow Cottage* (1934). *Beauty for Ashes* (1935). *The Strange Proposal* (1935). *White Orchids* (1935). *April Gold* (1936). *Mystery Flowers* (1936). *The Substitute Guest* (1936). *Brentwood* (1937). *Daphne Deane* (1937). *Sunrise* (1937). *The Best Birthday* (1938). *The Divided Battle* (1938). *Dwelling* (1938). *Homing* (1938). *The Lost Message* (1938). *Maria* (1938). *Marigold* (1938). *The Minister's Son* (1938). *Patricia* (1939). *The Seventh Hour* (1939). *Stranger within the Gates* (1939). *Head of the House* (1940). *Partners* (1940). *Rose Galbraith* (1940). *Astra* (1941). *By Way of the Silverthorns* (1941). *In Tune with Wedding Bells* (1941). *Crimson Mountain* (1942). *The Girl of the Woods* (1942). *The Street of the City* (1942). *The Sound of the Trumpet* (1943). *The Spice Box* (1943).

Through These Fires (1943). *More than Conquerer* (1944). *Time of the Singing of Birds* (1944). *All through the Night* (1945). *A Girl to Come Home To* (1945). *Bright Arrows* (1946). *Where Two Ways Met* (1947). *Mary Arden* (completed by R. L. Hill, 1948).

BIBLIOGRAPHY: Karr, J., *Grace Livingston Hill: Her Story and Her Writings* (1948).

For articles in reference works, see: *DAB*, Suppl. 4. *NAW* (article on Grace Livingston Hill by P. S. Boyer). *Reader's Encyclopedia of American Literature*, Ed. M. J. Herzberg (1962). *20thCA*. *20thCAS*.

Other references: *Book News Monthly* (Oct. 1915).

VIRGINIA RAMEY MOLLENKOTT

Helen Merrell Lynd

B. 1896, La Grange, Illinois
D. of Edward Tracy and Mabel Waite Merrell; m. Robert S. Lynd, 1921

Raised as a Congregationalist, L. shifted her religious orientation while at Wellesley College (B.A. 1919) to an explanation of the world based on Hegelian dialectics. She earned an M.A. (1922) and a Ph.D. (1944) in history from Columbia University; her teaching career centered around Sarah Lawrence College, where she taught from 1929 to 1964. L. has shared with her husband a rich, full life as wife, mother of their two children, and professional colleague.

Middletown: A Study in Contemporary American Culture (1929) and the companion volume, *Middletown in Transition: A Study in Cultural Conflicts* (1935), written by L. and her husband, are well-documented studies outstanding in their comprehensiveness, accuracy, and interpretation of community life in the U.S. In 1924 and 1925, the Lynds and their research staff lived in the Middletown community and collected information from a variety of sources, as anthropologists study primitive tribes. The study is organized by an analysis of the major activities for community survival: getting a living, making a home, training the young, and engaging in religious practices and community activities. Although ending their first study on a cautious note recognizing the problems resulting from rapid social change, the prosperity and optimism of the community is evident.

The Lynds returned to Middletown during the Depression. Earning a living, staying healthy, and in general surviving the effects of financial collapse make life in 1935 starkly different from what it was in 1925. The ability of the city to recover and retain optimism is still striking though. Class privileges and strain are more apparent in the later study, yet a sense of worker solidarity is lacking. Radical social change did not occur as a result of radical changes in economics. Rather, the community adhered to "the American way," hoping for a better future.

These remarkable community studies provide a systematic view of an American city in times of stability and change. They also set a high standard of sociological expertise making them landmark studies of community development.

In *Field Work in College Education* (1945), L. studies student-teacher interaction and the application of social-science principles in everyday life. *England in the Eighteen-Eighties: Toward a Social Basis for Freedom* (1945) is a sweeping and powerful study, beautifully written, of the interaction between ideas, material changes, and social movements during a period of social ferment. In *On Shame and the Search for Identity* (1958), L. analyzed more contemporary problems arising from the relationship between the individual and society. The 1965 collection, *Toward Discovery*, serves as a brief overview of L.'s writings.

L.'s interests and skills cover a wide range of topics and disciplines. Always dedicated to the holistic approach to human behavior, her work reflects her standards of excellence and consistent probing for new insights into the human experience.

WORKS: *Middletown: A Study in Contemporary American Culture* (1929). *Middletown in Transition: A Study in Cultural Conflicts* (1935). *Field Work in College Education* (1945). *England in the Eighteen-Eighties: Toward a Social Basis for Freedom* (1945). *On Shame and the Search for Identity* (1958). *Toward Discovery* (Ed. B. J. Loewenberg, 1965).

BIBLIOGRAPHY: Loewenberg, B. J., Introduction to *Toward Discovery* (1965).
For articles in reference works, see: *20thCA*. *20thCAS*.

MARY JO DEEGAN

Mary Margaret McBride

B. 16 Nov. 1899, Paris, Missouri; d. 7 April 1976, West Shokan, New York
D. of Thomas Walker and Elizabeth Craig McBride

M., the daughter of a modestly successful farming couple, always knew she would be a journalist. Two relatives whose interest had permanent influence on M. were her maternal grandfather, a Baptist minister, who schooled her in bible readings, and her paternal grandfather, a scholar, who gave her an appreciation of Greek and Latin poetry. The first woman in her family to aspire to a career, she attended the University of Missouri, graduating in two and a half years, and financing her education by working on the Columbus *Times*. Successive feature-writing positions on the Cleveland *Press* and the New York *Mail* catapulted her to a syndicated column, a woman's-page editorship, and extensive magazine free-lance work.

A second and third career for M. emerged from the Depression years when periodicals ceased publication or could no longer pay her prices. She turned to producing books and to conducting a daily program on radio (and ultimately on television), earmarking each media venture with her special vitality, her wide-ranging interests, her candor, and her respect for facts.

Though, on the one hand, M.'s work was characterized by deep-seated religious and moral convictions, plus sincere and un-self-conscious sentimentality, she was at the same time a tough and searching reporter. And though she struggled against and never conquered deep feelings of guilt and insecurity, she numbered among her close friends heads of state and celebrities in diverse fields in the U.S. and abroad. Testaments to her personal popularity and magnetism were the quarter of a million letters she received annually from listeners and a party on her tenth anniversary in radio, held at Madison Square Garden and attended by 125,000 "Mary Margaret" fans.

M.'s newspaper assignments were, for the most part, self-selected. She managed, whether the story involved a parade, a political convention, or a luncheon, to make the reader feel like a ringside spectator by introducing particulars of texture, smell, and other detail. Her acute sensory awareness coupled with searching curiosity and a zealot's concern for the truth contributed to M.'s being one of the most sought-after and highest-paid journalists in the country.

When the magazine market suffered reverses in the late 1920s, M. completed four travel books with coauthor and journalist, Helen Josephy. Though the books sold well because European travel was becoming popular, they have little value today except as social documents. Their preoccupation with where celebrities dined, resided, and shopped, made these books highly palatable to middle America and were a harbinger of M.'s modus operandi and subsequent success in radio and television, but the net result is a sensual, somewhat naive recitation of a time long past.

Several other volumes are autobiographical, nonintellectual, nonliterary, but highly readable. *A Long Way from Missouri* (1959) and its sequel, *Out of the Air* (1960), recount with modesty and pride the events of M.'s life. Both books are replete with names and anecdotes, her successes and her setbacks, all treated honestly and with the utmost simplicity. At a moment of success on a New York paper she was to confess, "but I never felt really secure in my love life or in my job, not for long, even when I had two beaux at once and a byline on front page center."

Her shift in media to radio, and later to television, made no difference in the persona of M., though, for contractual reasons, she assumed initially the "radio name" of Martha Deane. The same buoyancy, frankness, and cozy confidentiality prevailed. Her selection of guests, books, professions, and hobbies were examined like feature stories, utilizing, for the first time, newspaper techniques in radio presentation. To the extent that material was written, she prepared it herself, including the commercials. Products were always personally pretested for acceptability before she agreed to their sponsorship. *Printer's Ink*, authoritative bible of the marketing world, commenting on the slavish acceptance of her listeners, described the response to her program and her merchandising prowess as "the most outstanding example of reliance upon the word of a human being in the commercial field."

With the death in 1954 of her friend and manager, Stella Karn, M. gave up her own program and restricted herself to guest appearances. Six years later she moved permanently to a refurbished barn in West Shokan, New York. Her own assessment of her career was characteristically candid and self-effacing: "I've enjoyed my life and don't regret any of it. But I can see that, taken altogether it is faintly, sometimes even blatantly ridiculous. I wanted to be a great writer, and now I never shall be."

WORKS: Jazz: A Story of Paul Whiteman (with P. Whiteman, 1926). Charm (with A. Williams, 1927). Paris Is a Woman's Town (with H. Josephy, 1929). The Story of Dwight Morrow (1930). London Is a Man's Town (with H. Josephy, 1931). New York Is Everybody's Town (with H. Josephy, 1931). Beer and Skittles: A Friendly Modern Guide to Germany (1932). Here's Martha Deane (1936). How Dear to My Heart (1940). America for Me (1941). Tune in for Elizabeth (1945). How to be a Successful Advertising Woman (edited by McBride, 1948). Harvest of American Cooking (1957). Encyclopedia of Cooking (1959). A Long Way from Missouri (1959). Out of the Air (1960). The Giving Up of Mary Elizabeth (1968).

BIBLIOGRAPHY: For articles in reference works, see: CB (1954; June 1976). Ladies of the Press, I. Ross (1974). Successful Women, I. Taves (1943). Whatever Became of . . . ?, R. Lamparski (1970).
    Other references: American Mercury (Jan. 1949). Life (4 Dec. 1944). NY (19 Dec. 1942). NYT (8 April 1976). SatR (1 March 1947). Scribner's (March 1931).

ANNE S. BITTKER

Anne McCaffrey

B. 1 April 1926, Cambridge, Massachusetts
D. of George Herbert and Anne Dorothy McElroy McCaffrey; m. Wright Johnson

M. was graduated from Radcliffe College and studied voice and drama. She directed opera before abandoning professional ambitions in theater arts and began writing full time in the late 1950s.

In addition to the science fiction for which she is widely recognized, M. has written Gothic mysteries and edited Cooking Out of This World (1973). Having also worked as an advertising copywriter, M. now resides at Bragonhold, Wicklow County, Ireland.

"The Ship Who Sang" (1964) is one of the earliest works in which M. broaches the issue of sexual stereotypes. This story of Helva, one of many severely physically deformed infants whose healthy brains are encapsulated in spaceships to enable them to lead productive lives, emphasizes the humanity of such cyborgs and their "normal" partners rather than their original genders. Thus, the caring relationship which develops between Helva, the "brain" of a spaceship, and her first partner, its "brawn," is predicated upon their mutual love of music rather than their sexual identities. In 1969, this story was anthologized with five others about Helva as *The Ship Who Sang*. *Get off the Unicorn* (1977), a subsequent anthology, contains a further story about Helva, "Honeymoon."

In 1968, "Weyr Search" won the Hugo Award for best short story of the year, while "Dragonrider" won the equivalent Nebula Award. Both of these works were later incorporated into *Dragonflight* (1968), the first volume in the Dragonriders of Pern series for which M. is best known. This series, composed to date of six novels, has received acclaim for its depiction of the telepathic bonding between humans and a dragonlike alien species native to the planet of Pern. M. describes not only the rapport between individual humans and dragons as they fight the life-threatening spores that periodically attack Pern but also the ways in which this rapport permeates the intricate, almost feudal social structure of Pern. *Dragonflight* focuses upon an independent, courageous female protagonist, Lessa, who reappears as a minor character in the later novels.

M.'s concern with women's roles and struggles in Pern's society is most vividly realized in *Dragon Song* (1976) and *Dragon Singer* (1977), both of which center upon Mennolly, a young woman whose ambition to be a harper runs counter to Pern's social norms for women. Like Lessa, Mennolly achieves her goals through perseverance, courage, and quick wit. Because *Dragon Song*, *Dragon Singer*, and *Dragon Drums* (1979) are designed for a juvenile audience, they lack the scope of characterization and development of other novels in the series.

Decision at Doona (1969) is akin to the Dragonriders series in its presentation of the evolving, intricate relationship between humans and another sentient alien species. The Hrrubans, lionlike beings, are as reluctant as Terrans to coexist on the colony planet of Doona. The lifesaving friendship of two of their offspring brings the two species together.

Dinosaur Planet (1978), which also has a woman protagonist whose professional competence and personal integrity are essential plot elements, is the first volume in a new series. It touches again upon the relationships between humans and aliens.

M.'s work has been criticized for occasionally being overly romantic and sentimental. Certainly some of her earlier fiction, such as *Restoree* (1967) and "A Wonderful Talent" (1969), is susceptible to this charge and to the charge of sexual stereotyping. In her other works, however, such flaws are counterbalanced by believable, intriguing portraits of human and alien interaction and by the creation of female protagonists who successfully struggle against discrimination in their societies.

WORKS: Restoree (1967). *Dragonflight* (1968). *Decision at Doona* (1969). *The Ship Who Sang* (1969). *Alchemy and Academe* (edited by McCaffrey, 1970). *Dragonquest* (1971). *Cooking Out of This World* (edited by McCaffrey, 1973). *To Ride Pegasus* (1974). *Dragon Song* (1976). *Dragon Singer* (1977). *Get off the Unicorn* (1977). *Dinosaur Planet* (1978). *The White Dragon* (1978). *Dragon Drums* (1979).

BIBLIOGRAPHY: Friend, B., "Virgin Territory: The Bonds and Boundaries of Women in Science Fiction," in *Many Futures, Many Worlds: Theme and Form in Science Fiction*, Ed. T. Clareson (1977). Sargent, P., ed., *Women of Wonder* (1974). Sargent, P., Introduction to *The New Women of Wonder* (1977).

For articles in reference works, see: *Index to Science Fiction Anthologies and Collections*, Ed. W. Contento (1978).

Other references: *Algol/Starship* (Winter 1978–79).

NATALIE M. ROSINSKY

Mary Therese McCarthy

B. 21 June 1912, Seattle, Washington
D. of Roy Winfield and Theresa Preston McCarthy; m. Harold Johnsrud, 1933;
m. Edmund Wilson, 1938; m. Bowden Broadwater, 1946; m. James Raymond
West, 1961

M. graduated from Vassar in 1933 and then settled in New York City, where she began her writing career. M.'s early book reviews appeared in *The New Republic* and *The Nation*, and in 1937 she became drama editor of the *Partisan Review*. She quickly attracted the attention of the literary establishment, which she often sharply attacked.

Known primarily as a novelist, M. is a very fine expository writer, who covers a wide range of subjects, from theories of the novel to travel observations to art history. Many of her essays are on political subjects. "My Confession" (*On the Contrary*, 1962) tells of her left-wing associations during the 1930s, and other essays discuss the national anticommunist hysteria of the late 1940s and early 1950s. Although liberal herself, M. is unsympathetic toward "liberals" who are ill-informed, careless, or dishonest. Sharply critical of the Vietnamese war protesters who rested their case in a "sterile" and vague "indictment" of American culture, she went to Vietnam in order to oppose America's involvement in the war from an informed point of view.

M.'s prose style is graceful and precise, showing the influence of her classical education. M. dislikes slang and often uses Latinate diction as well as long, balanced structures, but her writing is generally informal. M.'s sentences are often barbed, sometimes given to startling generalizations; but she is usually concrete, meticulous, and reasonable.

M. began writing fiction at the suggestion of her second husband, the critic Edmund Wilson, and published her first story in 1939. She was long admired by a small readership, but *The Group* (1963) was an enormous bestseller and vastly enlarged her public. The novel recreates an era as it follows the lives of eight Vassar girls of the class of 1933 during the seven years after their graduation. It details their experiences with sex, psychiatry, domesticity, and politics; a description of one character's defloration is both funny and shockingly graphic. The book has a unique third-person point of view: The narrative "voice" is that of the Group, sometimes in chorus, sometimes individually. The girls are comic characters by M.'s definition—ineducable, unchanging, and therefore immortal.

M. is an extremely personal writer whose uses of her acquaintances in fiction are often unflattering. *The Oasis* (1949), a prize-winning *conte philosophique* about a utopian experiment, is a case in point; Philip Rahv and Dwight Macdonald were the "originals" of two satiric portraits which expose the dishonesty and pretentiousness of liberals whose high ideals and rhetoric offer no immunity against human frailty. M. is no gentler with herself than with her friends. Some readers have mistaken "Artists in Uniform" for fiction, probably because of the uncomplimentary light it casts upon the author, but it is fact. So, M. says, are two of the short stories about Margaret Sargent, heroine of M.'s first novel, *The Company She Keeps* (1942), which is actually a collection of stories unified by Margaret's quest for self. Other characters based to some extent on M. include Kay (*The Group*), Martha Sinnott (*A Charmed Life*, 1955), and Rosamund Brown (*Birds of America*, 1971). These characters are self-consciously "superior" but at times self-doubting, and relentlessly honest with themselves, believing that if action is sometimes compromised, thought should never be. Although liberal intellectuals, they believe in ritual and ceremony and abhor the common, the cheap, and the ugly.

These characteristics are discernible in the child described in *Memories of a Catholic Girlhood* (1957), M.'s autobiography. A collection of memoirs brought together with an introduction and epilogues, the book derives its unity chiefly from the character of the young Mary and from its themes of education, Catholicism, Jewishness, the quest for superiority, and the difficulty of doing the right thing for the right reason. M., orphaned at six, had a bizarre childhood, and the most striking passages of the book are the ones about the Minneapolis years. The material is Dickensian, but M. treats it with remarkable coolness. There is more bewilderment than anger, and very little that can be called pathos. Indignant, independent of mind, striving to be a "superior girl," the young Mary suffered outrageous abuses until she was taken to live with her maternal grandparents in Seattle in 1923.

Both the child of personal history and the heroines of fiction cultivate the appearance of superiority, but they also hold themselves answerable to rigid moral standards. Margaret Sargent is less anxious about looking ridiculous than about being "hard as nails." When she wakes up in bed with the Man in the Brooks Brothers Shirt, she must carry on from this undignified moment and see the vulgar "love story" to its conclusion. The need for private truth rather than public superiority requires Martha Sinnott to have an abortion rather than bear a child of doubtful paternity.

In *The Company She Keeps*, M. experiments with points of view. Margaret is seen both publicly and privately; she is seen from a distance through the eyes of the Yale man and from close through her own eyes as she undergoes analysis. In *The Groves of Academe* (1952), M.'s academic novel, M. uses the point of view of a character quite the opposite of herself. Henry Mulcahy is a physically and morally repulsive man, and his voice—whining, raging, pleading, gloating—carries much of the narrative. Fired from his previous position amid suspicions of communism, Mulcahy is hired by the liberal President Hoar to teach, temporarily, at Jocelyn College, a "progressive" school. When his term of appointment is up, Mulcahy fights dismissal by the startling device of falsely confessing to membership in the Communist Party, thereby cynically enlisting the support of faculty liberals. The novel moves with relentless logic from Mulcahy's letter of dismissal to the resignation of

Hoar, blackmailed by the triumphant Mulcahy. In conforming to liberal conventions, Hoar and the faculty override their own good sense and powers of observation.

Yet even when not self-deceived, the liberal in M.'s fiction finds moral integrity difficult to achieve. In *Birds of America*, Peter Levi, a nineteen-year-old egalitarian and literary kinsman of Candide, sees that the things he most loves—nature, tradition, art—are threatened by the advance of the thing he believes in most—equality; yet the evils of injustice and poverty persist undiminished. In *Cannibals and Missionaries* (1979) a committee of liberals en route to Iran to investigate the Shah's regime and a tour group of American art collectors are hijacked by an international terrorist group and held in Holland while the collectors are exchanged for their priceless paintings and a farmhouse is turned into an unlikely gallery. Liberals and paintings are then offered in exchange for Holland's withdrawal from NATO and severing of relations with Israel. The novel's moral center is a senator who comes to the recognition that terrorism is a "kid brother" of minority electoral politics; both are equally ineffectual against the inertia of facts. The outcome is grim, but the mode is comic; people and their institutions are impervious to these events, and at the end, the Reverend Mr. Frank Barber, among others, has survived to go on counting his blessings.

M.'s ear is true, and her fiction is rich with the sounds of authentic voices, heightened but not distorted. If her characters are often ridiculous, she tolerates their absurdities even as she exposes them, although she is merciless with self-professed intellectuals who exempt themselves from responsibility to facts. Her most malevolent characters—Henry Mulcahy and Norine Schmittlapp (*The Group*)—thrive in personal and moral squalor with no foothold in truth.

As social critic and moralist, M. has consistently and scrupulously sought truth. Neither hopeful nor sentimental, M.'s messages often fall on unwelcoming ears. Like most satiric writers, she sometimes writes about the topical. But her range is wide, her eye and ear are keen, and her literary commitment is to the durable and universal facts of human life candidly and often caustically recorded.

WORKS: *The Company She Keeps* (1942). *The Oasis* (1949). *Cast a Cold Eye* (1950). *The Groves of Academe* (1952). *A Charmed Life* (1955). *Sights and Spectacles: 1937–1956* (1956). *Venice Observed* (1956). *Memories of a Catholic Girlhood* (1957). *The Stones of Florence* (1959). *On the Contrary: Articles of Belief, 1946–1961* (1961). *The Group* (1963). *Mary McCarthy's Theatre Chronicles, 1937–1962* (1963). *Vietnam* (1967). *Hanoi* (1968). *The*

Writing on the Wall, and Other Literary Essays (1970). *Birds of America* (1971). *Medina* (1972). *The Mask of State: Watergate Portraits* (1974). *The Seventeenth Degree: How It Went, Vietnam, Hanoi, Medina, Sons of the Morning* (1974). *Cannibals and Missionaries* (1979).

BIBLIOGRAPHY: Auchincloss, L., *Pioneers and Caretakers: A Study of Nine American Women Writers* (1965). Goldman, S., *Mary McCarthy: A Bibliography* (1968). Grumbach, D., *The Company She Kept* (1967). Hardwick, E., *A View of My Own: Essays in Literature and Society* (1963). McKenzie, B., *Mary McCarthy* (1966). Mailer, N., *Cannibals and Christians* (1966). Stock, I., *Mary McCarthy* (University of Minnesota Pamphlets on American Writers, No. 72, 1968).

For articles in reference works, see: *CA*, 5–8 (1969). *20thCAS.*

Other references: *Columbia University Forum* 6 (1973). *Esquire* (July 1962). *JAmS* 9 (1975). *Paris Review* (Winter-Spring 1962).

WILLENE S. HARDY

Helen McCloy

B. *6 June 1904, New York City*
Writes under: *Helen Clarkson, H. C. McCloy, Helen McCloy*
D. *of William Conrad and Helen Worrell Clarkson McCloy; m. David Dresser, 1946*

M.'s father was managing editor of the New York *Evening Sun;* her mother wrote short stories under her maiden name. A Quaker, M. studied at the Brooklyn Friends School in New York. At fourteen, she published a literary essay in the Boston *Transcript;* at fifteen, she published verse in the *New York Times.* M. lived in France for eight years, studying at the Sorbonne in 1923 and 1924. M. was Paris correspondent for the Universal News Service (1927–31) and the monthly art magazine *International Studio* (1930–31). She also was London correspondent for the Sunday *New York Times* art section and wrote political sketches for the London *Morning Post* and the *Daily Mail.*

M. returned to the U.S. in 1931 and spent several years writing magazine articles and short stories. In 1938, she published her first mystery novel, *Dance of Death.* She has one daughter. She was divorced in 1961 from her husband, who writes mysteries under the name Brett Halliday.

M. has been rather prolific, writing twenty-eight novels of detection and suspense, many short stories, and newspaper and magazine articles. She won Ellery Queen Mystery Magazine awards for the short stories "Through a Glass, Darkly" (reprinted in *The Singing Diamonds*, 1965) and "Chinoiserie" (reprinted in *20 Great Tales of Murder*, 1951), and the Edgar Award from the Mystery Writers of America for the best mystery criticism. M. was the first woman president of the Mystery Writers of America.

Dance of Death features her detective, Dr. Basil Willing, a psychiatrist and an expert in forensic medicine; he appears in many of what are considered her strongest novels. The social satire in such novels as *Cue for Murder* (1942) and *Two-Thirds of a Ghost* (1956), as well as the fine presentation of New York society in *Alias Basil Willing* (1951) and *Unfinished Crime* (1954), suggests, as Erik Routley has indicated, that M. is one of those mystery writers in whom "there is a good deal of straight novel-writing." Anthony Boucher believes that M. "has always resembled the best British writers of the Sayers-Blake-Allingham school in her ability to combine a warm novel of likeable people with a flawless deductive plot."

M.'s choice of a psychiatrist-detective as hero reveals her interest in psychology, especially in its more paranormal manifestations, as is evident in *Through a Glass, Darkly* (1949), *Who's Calling?* (1942), and *The Slayer and the Slain* (1957). Her interest in the fragile structure upon which an individual's personality is based is shown in *The Changling Conspiracy* (1976), which deals with political kidnapping and brainwashing. This and other recent novels reflect M.'s interest in contemporary affairs; *The Goblin Market* (1943) and *Panic* (1944), which were written during World War II and deal with problems created by the war, suggest that this interest is not new.

In general, critics have preferred M.'s novels of detection to the novels of suspense or terror. M. herself believes that the current popularity of detective stories is related to "some lack in the accepted literary diet." The "moral understanding of common minds which results in sympathy for common lives" and the themes "that mean so much to the common man—love and death"—are missing from modern novels. In her best works, M.'s success in providing interesting characters and themes is matched with her ability in plotting.

WORKS: *Dance of Death* (1938). *The Man in the Moonlight* (1940). *The Deadly Truth* (1941). *Cue for Murder* (1942). *Who's Calling?* (1942). *Do Not Disturb* (1943). *The Goblin Market* (1943). *Panic* (1944). *The One That*

Got Away (1945). *She Walks Alone* (1948). *Through a Glass, Darkly* (1949). *Alias Basil Willing* (1951). *20 Great Tales of Murder* (edited by McCloy, with B. Halliday, 1951). *Unfinished Crime* (1954). *The Long Body* (1955). *Two-Thirds of a Ghost* (1956). *The Slayer and the Slain* (1957). *The Last Day* (1959). *Before I Die* (1963). *The Singing Diamonds* (1965). *The Further Side of Fear* (1967). *Mister Splitfoot* (1968). *A Question of Time* (1971). *A Change of Heart* (1973). *The Sleepwalker* (1974). *Minotaur Country* (1975). *The Changling Conspiracy* (1976). *The Imposter* (1977). *The Smoking Mirror* (1979). *Burn This* (1980).

The papers of Helen McCloy are at the Boston University Library, Boston, Massachusetts.

BIBLIOGRAPHY: Routley, E., *The Puritan Pleasures of the Detective Story* (1972).

For articles in reference works, see: *CA*, 25-28 (1971). *A Catalogue of Crime*, J. Barzun and W. H. Taylor (1971). *Encyclopedia of Mystery and Detection*, Eds. C. Steinbrunner and O. Penzler (1976). *WA*.

Other references: *NYHTB* (28 Nov. 1943; 7 Oct. 1956). *NYT* (27 Feb. 1938; 11 Oct. 1942; 18 June 1950).

DIANA BEN-MERRE

Louisa Susannah Cheves McCord

B. 3 Dec. 1810, Charleston, South Carolina; d. 23 Nov. 1879, Charleston, South Carolina
Wrote under: L. S. M.
D. of Langdon and Mary Elizabeth Dulles Cheves; m. David James McCord, 1840

Although born in South Carolina, M. spent formative years (1819–1829) with her family in Philadelphia, where her father served under Monroe as president of the Bank of the United States. Langdon Cheves early recognized his daughter's intellect and motivation and, despite his strict conception of a woman's role, encouraged her education with her brothers in math and Latin. Inheriting "Lang Syne" from an aunt in 1830, M. skillfully managed the large cotton plantation with its two hundred slaves near Columbia, South Carolina. Her husband, a widower with ten children, was a minor but vigorous political figure, with high if traditional expectations of his wife: beyond her responsibilities for her stepchildren and her own three children, M. became a perceptive participant in her husband's social and political world.

Encouraged by McCord to support the Southern cause while maintaining the conventionally female role in which she ardently believed, M. translated Frederic Basiat's *Sophisms of Protection* (1847) in 1848. Vehemently against protective tariffs and for free trade, the document has sharpness, passion, and wit; M.'s translation is precise yet literal and dull. The work was well received in the South, and M. soon began to publish her own writings.

Later in the same year, *My Dreams*, a collection of abstract and formal poems, appeared. This work suggests the girlhood tensions that probably underlie her staunch support of an essentially conservative and traditional position for women. She quickly followed these pieces with other occasional poems and with frequent articles on economics, finance, slavery, and women's rights. Both her husband's and Basiat's influence is clear in these writings, but their emotional vigor, acute wit, and satire make them compelling reading.

M. was startlingly versatile in her writing. In 1851, when her own son was ten, M. published *Caius Gracchus*, a blank-verse tragedy in five acts, with strong autobiographical elements: The protagonist, Cornelia, strongly influences the development of her able son, Caius. Veiled but clear parallels between the exploitive Senate and the North and between the plebeians, inspired by the orator Caius, and the oppressed South pervade the work. The drama's interest for today's readers lies primarily in the implied identification of M. with her son and the revelation of her sublimated political desires.

After her husband's death in 1855, M. settled in Columbia, South Carolina, and devoted herself to her children and to civic pursuits. She took a brief European tour after her father's death in 1857. During the Civil War she spent much of her time nursing the wounded and encouraging the Confederate troops; in 1861, she was elected president of the Soldier's Relief Association and of the Lady's Clothing Association. During this period, her friend Mary Boykin Chesnut noted in her diary that M. had "the intellect of a man and the perseverance and endurance of a woman." At the end of the war, M. lived in Canada for two years before agreeing to take the oath of allegiance to the federal government.

M. strove ardently with both unusual strength and style to preserve a passing way of life. This position places her firmly within a strict southern tradition, while her energy, sharp perception, and firm character give her a deserved prominence in southern letters.

WORKS: *Sophisms of Protection* by F. Basiat (translated by McCord, 1848). *My Dreams* (1848). *Caius Gracchus* (1851).

BIBLIOGRAPHY: Chesnut, M. B., *A Diary from Dixie* (Eds. M. L. Avary and I. Martin, 1905). Fraser, J. M., *Louisa C. McCord* (1920). Smythe, Louisa McCord, *For Old Lang Syne* (1900). Thorp, M. F., *Female Persuasion* (1949).

For articles in reference works, see: *CAL. The Living Female Writers of the South*, M. T. Tardy (1872). *The Living Writers of the South*, J. W. Davidson (1869). *LSL. NAW* (article by M. F. Thorp). *NCAB*, 9. *The Writers of South Carolina*, G. A. Wauchope (1910).

Other references: *South Carolina Historical and Genealogical Magazine* (Oct. 1933; July 1934).

CAROLINE ZILBOORG

Anne O'Hare McCormick

B. *16 May 1880, Wakefield, England; d. 29 May 1954, New York City*
Wrote under: *Anne O'Hare, Anne O'Hare McCormick*
D. *of Thomas and Teresa Beatrice O'Hare; m. Francis J. McCormick, 1910*

As an infant M. was brought from England to Columbus, Ohio, by her American-born parents. Intellectually influenced by her Catholic mother, a poet and woman's-page editor, M. was educated in private schools in Ohio, graduating from the College of St. Mary of the Springs. Following in her mother's footsteps, she published children's feature articles and soon became an associate editor for her mother's employer, Cleveland's weekly *Catholic Universe Bulletin.*

After her marriage to an engineer and importer, M. resigned her editorship and traveled with her husband on his European business trips. She wrote several impressionistic articles about European countries in the aftermath of World War I for the *New York Times Magazine.*

In 1921, her dispatches from Europe, serious assessments of the rise of fascism in Italy and of the role of Benito Mussolini (a figure then dismissed as a "posturing lout" by most journalists) impressed *Times*

managing editor Carr V. Van Anda. He hired her as a foreign correspondent in 1922. She was the first woman hired as a regular contributor to the *Times* editorial page (1936) and the second woman to receive
a Pulitzer Prize for journalism (in 1937, for her European correspondence).

Through the early 1950s she lectured in major U.S. cities, made radio
broadcasts, and wrote "Abroad," a column based on reportage in Europe,
Asia, and Africa. She also published editorials commenting on the American political scene.

*The Hammer and the Scythe: Communist Russia Enters the Second
Decade* (1928) is based on articles M. originally wrote for the *Times*
while traveling in Russia in the 1920s. M. reports her impressions of the
Russian people, their conditions, and the clash of new and old. *The
Hammer and the Scythe* is among the best of the books written by
American journalists visiting Russia in the 1920s, but *The World at Home*
(1956), one of two collections of M.'s *Times* columns posthumously
edited by her personal friend, Marion Sheehan, better withstands the
passage of time. Like other writers in the 1930s, M. "rediscovered America" in the pieces included in *The World at Home*. Her generalizations
about the nation are convincing, particularly when examined together
with the essays on Franklin Roosevelt. She connects small details that
blend into larger patterns of the nation's character and dramatizes "that
curious community . . . between the mind of the President and the
mind of the people."

For *Vatican Journal* (1957), Sheehan included *Times* pieces on the
struggle between Mussolini's government and Pius XI, America's relations with the Vatican, the Church's persecuted position in Europe
through the World War II era, and finally Roman Catholics' Cold War
engagement in a fundamentally "spiritual" battle against communism for
"domination over the soul." In the articles, M. often uses the first person,
details specifics of the surroundings in which events occur, and recounts
dramatically the scenes observed. Her own point of view is usually
made clear, balanced against a "fair" presentation of the opposition's
perspectives.

M. considered herself above all else a newspaperwoman. Aside from
her book on Russia, she preferred to write "on top of the news while
people were listening." Her reporting of foreign and domestic events was
clear, incisive, and authoritative. It embodied her commitment to moral
absolutes and professional standards of reporting. The body of correspondence (especially, warnings about fascism's rise in Europe), achieve-

ments as an influential political columnist, and eighteen years of service on the editorial board of America's most prestigious newspaper, secure M. an important place in the ranks of American journalists.

WORKS: *The Hammer and the Scythe: Communist Russia Enters the Second Decade* (1928). *The World at Home: Selections from the Writings of Anne O'Hare McCormick* (Ed. M. T. Sheehan, 1956). *Vatican Journal: 1921–1954* (Ed. M. T. Sheehan, 1957).

BIBLIOGRAPHY: Filene, P. G., *Americans and the Soviet Experiment: 1917–1933* (1967). Hohenberg, J., *Foreign Correspondence: The Great Reporters and Their Times* (1964). Marzolf, M., *Up from the Footnote: A History of Women Journalists* (1977). Talese, G., *The Kingdom and the Power* (1966).

For articles in reference works, see: *Catholic Authors: Contemporary Biographical Sketches, 1930–1947*, Ed. M. Hoehn (1952). *Ohio Authors and Their Books*, Ed. W. Coyle (1962). *20thCA. 20thCAS.*

Other references: *CathW* (Oct. 1954). *NYT* (30 May 1954). *SatR* (19 June 1954).

JENNIFER L. TEBBE

Josephine Woempner Clifford McCrackin

B. 25 Nov. 1838, Petershagen, Germany; d. 21 Dec. 1920, Santa Cruz, California
Wrote under: Josephine Clifford, Josephine Clifford McCrackin
D. of Georg and Charlotte Hartman Woempner; m. James Clifford, 1864;
m. Jackson McCrackin, 1882

A journalist and short-story writer associated with western literary figures such as Bret Harte and Ambrose Bierce, M. lived a courageous and romantic life. Born in Germany and brought to St. Louis as a child, she married a cavalry officer who became insane shortly after their marriage. Although she stayed with him longer than seems reasonable, she finally escaped him and left the desert outpost where they were stationed to make her home in California. There she wrote for *Overland, Harper's Magazine,* and other publications that were eager to print firsthand accounts of western life. A happy second marriage introduced her to ranch life. After the destruction of the McCrackins' ranch by fire in 1899 and her husband's death in 1904, M. became involved in the conservation movement. During her last years she worked as a newspaperwoman in the Santa Cruz area.

Perhaps M.'s most famous piece of nonfiction was her letter to the Santa Cruz *Sentinel* (7 March 1900) attacking the depredations of the lumber business on the redwoods, for it served to mobilize public interest in preserving the trees, leading to the creation of what was then called California Redwood Park.

Much of the background and some of the actual experiences in M.'s short stories come from her own adventures in Arizona and Southern California. California is described as a flowery paradise with clean air, sea breezes, and distant mountain scenery to gaze at. Since M. was born into a military family and married into the army as well, she praised the army men and glamorized the army life. While she often sympathized with the Spaniards and Mexicans, who were being bested by the Americans in the battle for land in California, she showed little concern for the Indians, portraying them as "red devils." The plots and characterizations are melodramatic and repetitious. Many of the stories end with a murder or suicide, the motive for the tragedy usually being thwarted love. Her fictional old Southwest was thickly peopled with broken-hearted heroes and heroines, lovers who had betrayed trusts, daughters who had been maneuvered by their parents into marriage to rich men they did not love, and strong-minded women pursued by evil husbands.

Whether they are good or bad, most of M.'s heroines are strong women. The bad ones are very bad; the cruel Mrs. Arnold of "A Woman's Treachery" tortures animals and cheats on her husband, eventually causing his death. Often the women are high-tempered and nervous, flushing easily and flashing their eyes a lot. They work hard and love horses; they suffer nobly under persecution and remain faultlessly faithful to their first loves. Her men are not very individualized. Most of them are either villains, in the form of dissipated, irresponsible husbands, or heroes, in the person of handsome young lieutenants. Physical and moral courage are both needed for one to remain alive (much more so to be successful in any way) in the landscapes of her tales.

While M.'s short stories are not valuable works of literature, they are an interesting source for details of life on the western frontier. Her career in the conservation movement, typical of those who turned so enthusiastically to that movement in the early 20th c., is also of interest. She was active in several conservation groups, seeking to preserve (in fact) the unspoiled natural reserves of her beloved California which she has helped to preserve (in print) through her descriptions of life there in the last thirty years of the 19th c.

WORKS: Overland Tales (1877). *Pen Pictures of Ventura County, California* (1880). *Another Juanita, and Other Stories* (1893). *The Woman Who Lost Him, and Tales of the Army Frontier* (1913).

BIBLIOGRAPHY: Bierce, A., Introduction to *The Woman Who Lost Him, and Tales of the Army Frontier* by J. C. McCrackin (1913). James, G. W., in *The Woman Who Lost Him, and Tales of the Army Frontier* by J. C. McCrackin (1913).

For articles in reference works, see: *AW. CAL. NAW* (article by M. Cross).

Other references: *Overland Monthly* (Sept. 1902).

BEVERLY SEATON

Carson Smith McCullers

B. 19 Feb. 1919, Columbus, Georgia; d. 29 Sept. 1967, Nyack, New York
Wrote under: Carson McCullers, Lula Carson Smith
D. of Lamar and Marguerite Waters Smith; m. Reeves McCullers, 1937;
  divorced 1940; remarried McCullers, 1945

M.'s childhood was remarkable more for imaginative activity than for external events. She knew firsthand the monotony and dreary heat of a small southern town, which later provided settings for her novels. Her family was very supportive of her artistic talents, which gave early promise in both writing and music.

In 1935, M. went to New York City to study music. She lost her tuition money to the Julliard School of Music, however, and took part-time jobs while studying writing at Columbia University. She married a young army corporal, whom she divorced in 1940 but remarried five years later.

Her health, always delicate, deteriorated steadily from a tragic series of paralyzing strokes, breast cancer, and pneumonia. Yet she received visitors, traveled, and worked at her writing while half paralyzed until a final stroke killed her when she was about fifty.

M. received immediate acclaim with her remarkable first novel, *The Heart Is a Lonely Hunter* (1940), written when she was twenty-two. She became one of the most controversial writers in America and had many prominent friends, including Tennessee Williams, W. H. Auden, Louis MacNiece, and Richard Wright.

With *The Heart Is a Lonely Hunter*, M. established the themes that concerned her in all subsequent writings: the spiritual isolation of the individual and the individual's attempt to transcend that loneliness through love. The action centers on a deaf-mute, John Singer, to whom an odd assortment of characters turn as to a being especially wise and benevolent. The adolescent Mick speaks to him passionately of music, although Singer has never heard music. Dr. Copeland, a black physician, confides desperately his dreams for educating his race. Jake Blount, an ineffectual agitator, rants about the workers' revolution. Biff Brannon, quiet observer of men, is fascinated by Singer because of his effect on all the others. But Singer loves another mute: an indolent, retarded Greek named Antonapoulos, who can never respond in kind to the outpourings of communication from Singer's expressive hands. Thus, each man creates a god fashioned after his own need—but such gods fail. When Antonapoulos dies in a mental hospital, Singer commits suicide. His death signals the fading of a dream for each of those who revered him. This novel, like many of M.'s works, is highly symbolic yet rich in concrete detail. A number of allegorical meanings have been suggested for the story, of which M.'s own, concerning fascism, seems least appropriate.

Reflections in a Golden Eye (1941) is technically more polished and controlled than the first novel but more grotesque in character and event. In the static, ingrown environment of a southern army post, Captain Penderton, a latent homosexual, is impotent with his beautiful wife, Leonora, but infatuated with their neighbor, Major Langdon, who is her lover. The catalyst is Private Williams, an inarticulate young man with an affinity for nature and horses, especially Leonora's high-spirited stallion, Firebird. Captain Penderton both loves and hates Private Williams with a repressed sado-masochism reminiscent of D. H. Lawrence's "The Prussian officer." Williams glimpses the naked Leonora through an open door, and thereafter he creeps into the Penderton house at night and crouches reverently beside Leonora's bed simply to watch her sleep. Captain Penderton discovers him there and shoots him. The influence of Freud is unmistakable in this novel; M. was one of the first American writers to deal openly with homosexual impulses. The approach is consistently objective and nonjudgmental, as though reflected in the disinterested eye of nature.

M.'s novella *The Ballad of the Sad Café* (1951) achieves more successfully the mode of archetypal myth she approached in *Reflections in a Golden Eye*. It combines realistic detail with the legendary quality of folk ballad, in a tale of love at once melancholy and sardonically humorous. Surely no more incongruous pair exists in literature than the manlike, independent, cross-eyed Miss Amelia and her self-centered little hunchback, Cousin Lyman. Singlehandedly running an excellent distillery and the only general store, Miss Amelia is the leading citizen of a tiny backwoods community. The townsfolk, like a stupid and malicious Greek chorus, have no recreation but observing her colorful career. Miss Amelia once married a local bad boy but quickly threw him out when he tried to augment their partnership with sexual attentions. The humiliated lover made threats, turned to crime, and landed in the penitentiary. Now, a pathetic, homeless dwarf who claims kinship to Miss Amelia straggles into town. Contrary to all expectations, she takes in the stranger and builds her life around him. She opens a café, which becomes the social hub of the community, and the misshapen Cousin Lyman becomes a strutting little prince in her modest castle. Eventually, however, her despised husband returns from prison. Ironically, the dwarf becomes enamored with Macy, who uses him to harass Miss Amelia. The competition culminates in a public fistfight between Miss Amelia and Macy. Miss Amelia is actually winning when the dwarf leaps savagely upon her back and turns her victory into physical and emotional defeat. The two men vandalize her café and distillery and then get out of town. Miss Amelia becomes a recluse, and the town seems to share in her emotional death. There is nothing to do there now but listen to the melancholy singing of the chain gang.

M. hardly surpassed the skill and originality of *The Ballad of the Sad Café*, but many people prefer her mood piece, *The Member of the Wedding* (1946). It is certainly the most autobiographical of M.'s novels, and may seem closer to everyday experience, although the view of life as painful and frustrating is consistent with her more bizarre creations. The story concerns a motherless adolescent girl's abortive attempt to outgrow her childhood and create a platonic bond of love with a dimly understood adult world. Frankie Addams wants to find the "we" of "me" and thus escape the prison of selfhood; she decides to go away with her brother and his bride at their forthcoming marriage. This preposterous dream is born of endless conversations in the kitchen with Berenice, the black maid who is her only adult companion, and her seven-year-old cousin, John Henry, who represents the relatively untroubled childhood she wishes to discard. The little boy dies unexpectedly at the end of the novel, suggesting not only that childhood passes but that even children are not exempt from tragedy. Frankie, of course, is denied her dream of the perfect threesome on the honeymoon. She does not die of this traumatic rejection, but something rare and fragile is broken. M. converted this novel into an award-winning play, which ran for 501 performances in New York.

M.'s other works include a number of significant short stories ("A Tree, A Rock, A Cloud," sometimes compared in theme to "The Rime of the Ancient Mariner," was chosen for *O. Henry Memorial Prize Stories of 1942*); some poetry for children; another, less successful play (*The Square Root of Wonderful*, 1958, with fifty-five performances on Broadway); and one other novel, written in the veritable shadow of death.

Clock without Hands (1961) concerns a man who faces death from leukemia. The theme is still loneliness and isolation, but it has taken on existential overtones. Though the world is without intrinsic meaning, human life acquires significance through an individual's commitment to action. The protagonist, J. T. Malone, is Everyman, unrelievedly ordinary, who suspects he has never lived on his own terms. In his new and painful awareness, there are few decisions left to make, but he makes one small gesture: He refuses to accept the community's order to bomb the home of a black man who had made a commitment by moving into a white neighborhood. In Malone's aging friend, Judge Clane, M. has revealed with admirable precision that peculiar combination of sentimentality and cruelty which characterizes the old southern variety of white racism.

Gore Vidal once predicted that "of all our Southern writers Carson McCullers is the one most likely to endure" (cited by Oliver Evans). "Her quality of despair is unique and individual," wrote Richard Wright (*NR*, 5 Aug. 1940), "and it seems to me more natural and authentic than that of Faulkner." Some have called her a writer's writer, which presumably implies that she is more appreciated by professionals than by general readers. If this is true, it may merely indicate that people are uncomfortable with her bleak view of the world. She is, at times, perhaps morbidly engrossed in the grotesque and horrible; yet, the emphasis is never on brutality and gore, but rather on symbolic action equal to psychic pain.

In the foreword to *The Square Root of Wonderful*, M. wrote: "I suppose a writer writes out of some inward compulsion to transform his own experiences (much of it unconscious) into the universal and symbolical. . . . Certainly I have always felt alone." She admired, and to some extent emulated, some of the very greatest writers: Tolstoy, Dostoevsky, and Flaubert. M.'s works do not have the psychological insight or concentrated impact of the European masters, but they still cherished Christian redemption as the answer to human failure, which M. cannot do. For her, there is only human love to pit against the indifferent universe—and that love is tragically flawed.

One of the gentle ironies of the relationship between the author and her work is that M. herself, for all her loneliness, had a remarkable capacity for affection and loyalty to her friends. Her fortitude in the face of terrifying physical infirmity is the best symbol for the supremacy, at least briefly, of spirit over mortal matter.

WORKS: *The Heart Is a Lonely Hunter* (1940; film version, 1968). *Reflections in a Golden Eye* (1941; film version, 1967). *The Member of the Wedding* (1946; dramatization, 1951; film version, 1952). *The Ballad of the Sad Café* (1951; dramatization by E. Albee, 1963). *The Square Root of Wonderful* (1958). *Clock without Hands* (1961). *Sweet As a Pickle and Clean As a Pig: Poems* (1964). *The Mortgaged Heart* (Ed. M. G. Smith, 1971).

BIBLIOGRAPHY: Carr, V. S., *The Lonely Hunter, a Biography of Carson McCullers* (1975). Eisinger, C. E., *Fiction of the Forties* (1963). Evans, O., *The Ballad of Carson McCullers* (1966). Schorer, M., in *The Creative Present*, Eds. N. Balakian and C. Simmons (1963).

For articles in reference works, see: *American Writers*, Ed. L. Unger (1972). *CA*, 5–8 (1969); 25–28 (1971). *Contemporary American Novelists*, M. Felheim (1964). *20thCA*. *20thCAS*.

Other references: *CE* (Oct. 1951). *GaR* (12, 1958; Summer 1963). *Jahrbuch fur Amerikastudien* 8 (1963). *Kenyon Review* (Winter 1947). *SAQ* 56 (1957). *WSCL* (1, 1960; Feb. 1962).

KATHERINE SNIPES

Betty Bard MacDonald

B. 26 March 1908, Boulder, Colorado; d. 7 Feb. 1958, Seattle, Washington
Wrote under: Betty MacDonald
D. of Darsie and Elsie Sanderson Bard; m. Robert Eugene Heskett, 1927;
  m. Donald Chauncey MacDonald, 1942

The second of five children, M. lived in Mexico, Idaho, and Montana before her mining-engineer father transferred the family to Seattle. After his death, the children were raised by M.'s mother and paternal grandmother. In 1927, M. abandoned art studies at the University of Washington to marry an insurance salesman, who brought her to a chicken ranch on the Olympic Peninsula. They separated in 1931, eventually divorcing in 1935. M. remained with her two daughters in her mother's home, holding a variety of jobs until her second marriage.

In 1943, at her sister Mary's urging, M. took a day from work to prepare a book outline for a visiting publisher's representative. That book became *The Egg and I* (1945), and her writing career was launched.

M. lived with her husband on Vashon Island, Puget Sound, until they purchased a California ranch in 1955. Stricken with cancer in 1957, she returned to Seattle for treatment and died at the age of forty-nine.

M.'s major books are autobiographical and are written in high humor. *The Egg and I*, her witty account of life on a primitive chicken ranch, achieved immediate popularity; one million copies were sold in the first year of publication. In 1947, Universal International released the movie, starring Fred MacMurray and Claudette Colbert and featuring Marjorie Main and Percy Kilbride as Ma and Pa Kettle.

Much of M.'s charm as author-character lies in her zealous determination to do the right thing. Nevertheless, her homemade bread is a disaster and her autopsies of spraddled chick carcasses futile ("Cause of death: Eggzema"). Amid the humor, M. probes the loneliness of the farm wife, discovering in a fair exhibit of knotted gunnysacks a pathetic symbol of what isolation can do to a woman. Behind her parade of outlandish characters, she offers carefully muted evidence of her crumbling marriage.

The Plague and I (1948) details M.'s battle against tuberculosis at age thirty. Confined in a sanatorium, she sketches other inmates with an artist's precision, barely touching on her own fears. *Anybody Can Do Any-*

thing (1950) encompasses her years as a career woman during the Depression, and *Onions in the Stew* (1955) depicts family life on Vashon Island.

A born humorist with a fine sense of timing, M. knows how to tell a story. Her observations are succinct ("piddocks are clams with some sort of neurosis that makes them afraid to face life"), her caricatures barbed ("a small sharp-cornered woman with a puff of short gray hair like a gone-to-seed dandelion"), and her language friendly and pleasantly earthy. Less generally recognized is her affinity to nature. In M.'s almost lyric descriptions of mountains in the mist, damp green rain forests, and the earth itself, the eye of the art student never deserts her.

M.'s humor is frequently self-deprecatory. Actually quite competent, M. creates an impression of hopeless ineptness, at the same time praising courageous women like her mother and sister. Her ambivalence toward housework and domesticity is striking. She genuinely loves children and displays a gregarious nature, yet one senses in her writing a barely repressed undercurrent of frustration, almost anger, at the subordinate role that wife and mother must play in society.

Critically dismissed as a "regional" and "popular" writer, M. still projects an easy warmth and familiarity that draw her reader close. Though her popularity has waned since the 1950s, M.'s work is worthy of rediscovery; her comments are as pungent, her characters as delightful as ever.

WORKS: *The Egg and I* (1945; film version, 1947). *Mrs. Piggle-Wiggle* (1947). *The Plague and I* (1948). *Mrs. Piggle-Wiggle's Magic* (1949). *Anybody Can Do Anything* (1950). *Nancy and Plum* (1952). *Mrs. Piggle-Wiggle's Farm* (1954). *Onions in the Stew* (1955). *Hello, Mrs. Piggle-Wiggle* (1957). *Who, Me? The Autobiography of Betty MacDonald* (1959).

BIBLIOGRAPHY: Spacks, P. M., *The Female Imagination* (1975).
Other references: *NYT* (8 Feb. 1958). *SatR* (14 May 1955). Tacoma *News Tribune* (28 Aug. 1977).

JOANNE McCARTHY

Jessica Nelson North MacDonald

B. 7 Sept. 1894, Madison, Wisconsin
Writes under: Jessica Nelson North
D. of David Willard and Elizabeth Nelson North; m. R. I. MacDonald, 1921

Early in life M. showed signs of the literary potential that would bring her recognition as poet, novelist, critic, and editor. A precocious child, she memorized and recited poetry from the time she could speak. By the age of five, she read the newspaper and composed rhymes. In her youth M. competed successfully with other young poets, including Edna St. Vincent Millay, in the contests conducted by Mary Mapes Dodge, editor of *St. Nicholas Magazine.*

M. discovered *Poetry Magazine* while a student at Lawrence College, from which she was graduated in 1917. When M. moved to Chicago in 1920, she began to contribute poems to *Poetry;* through the next few decades, she placed poems in such magazines as the *Dial,* the *Forge, Atlantic Monthly,* the *London Mercury, the Double-Dealer, Nation, The New Yorker, Voices,* the *Lyric,* and the *Saturday Evening Post.* In 1927 she was awarded the Reed Poetry prize.

M.'s best poetry is finely crafted, and even the weakest shows inventiveness. Her first volume, *A Prayer Rug* (1923), while evincing control of traditional techniques and forms, reveals modernist influences. As Elizabeth Tietjens pointed out, M. creates images with the best of her peers, but knows that "a single image is not enough to make a poem." M. treats a wide range of everyday topics, and a number of the poems shed light on the complexity of woman's role in society. Her calm ironic voice registers clearly in such poems as "Hunger Inn," "The Marionette," and "The Sleeper."

The poems in *The Long Leash* (1928) demonstrate M.'s growth as a poet. The volume exhibits what Horace Gregory calls her "technique of restraint." The selections focus on the power of the creative woman to capture and examine intensely dramatic male-female relationships. The title poem, considered one of her best, treats the confidence with which reciprocated love enables the creative woman to face life's realities and fulfill her artistic potential. "A Sumerian Cycle" and "Hibernalia" illustrate the breathless emotion M. is capable of producing through understatement. M. succeeds best in the longer poems, where she develops and multiplies dramatic scenes.

M.'s artistic control and keen sensibility appear again in *Dinner Party* (1942), although this volume seems to lack the modernity of her other poetry of that period. She is now preparing a fourth volume of poetry for publication.

Although M. is primarily a poet, she has also produced two successful novels: *Arden Acres* (1935) and *Morning in the Land* (1941). *Arden Acres* draws upon her observations of life in a suburban area outside Chicago during the Depression years. The narrator depicts the lives of the Chapin family, plagued by poverty and shocked by the father's murder. Although the emotional impact of the novel is effective, its real strength lies in the characterization of women from three generations —Gram, Loretta, and Joan—each of whom demonstrates unusual resilience and aptitude for survival.

Morning in the Land, based on the recollections of M.'s father, is a fictional account of an English immigrant family in Wisconsin between 1840 and 1861, when the son is about to leave for service in the Civil War. The novel centers on the frontier achievements of the protagonist, Dick Wentworth, but it also calls attention to the difficulties both Indian and white women endured within the male-oriented social structure.

Throughout the period in which her prose and poetry were being published, M. also gained a reputation as editor and critic. She began by editing the Chicago Art Institute *Bulletin* under the direction of Robert Harshe. Learning on the job, M. prepared catalogues for exhibits and published many articles describing various holdings of the institute. In 1927, she moved to *Poetry*, where over the next twenty years, under the leadership of Harriet Monroe, she helped make *Poetry* the showcase for the best young American and British authors. M. filled various editorial posts and, in later years, served as a member of the advisory committee. During this period she wrote twenty-one articles and fifty book reviews. Her contributions ranged from caustically critical pieces such as "The Wrong-Headed Poets," "The Hungry Generations," and "Quality in Madness," to the gently appreciative tribute commemorating the death of Harriet Monroe. In her criticism, as in her poetry, M. displays a sharp eye for honesty of emotion and perfection of form.

WORKS: *A Prayer Rug* (1923). *The Long Leash* (1928). *Arden Acres* (1935). *Morning in the Land* (1941). *Dinner Party* (1942). *Paintings: An Introduction to Art* (with C. J. Bulliet, 1934). *History of Alpha Delta Pi* (1929).

LUCY FREIBERT

Ruth Doan MacDougall

B. *19 March 1939, Laconia, New Hampshire*
D. *of Daniel and Ernestine Crone Doan; m. Donald K. MacDougall, 1957*

M.'s novels reflect her affection for the New England scenes of her youth; a constant theme is regret and anger over the encroachments of "civilization" on the natural beauties of the countryside. A frequent motif is female friendships between contemporaries or between a girl and an older woman who serves as mentor and confidant. M.'s male characters are drawn in brief, telling strokes; they are vivid but secondary to the women.

The Lilting House (1965) progresses from the point of view of the "wise innocent" to the informed commentary of Celia, the narrator, as a young woman taking charge of her life; Celia's development is the novel's frame. The inner story traces the late maturation of Felicia Polichnowski, an intellectual, imaginative woman married to a laborer. *The Lilting House* contrasts several mother-daughter relationships, Felicia's and Celia's families, and the characters' various abilities to reconcile dream and reality.

One of the decade's most powerful novels, *The Cost of Living* (1971) opens with a massacre in a New England supermarket; the motivation is then provided in a long flashback. As narrated sympathetically but unsentimentally by her lifelong friend, Jane, Polly Hall's attempt to be an ideal daughter, wife, and mother is symbolized by her efforts to restore her old home to perfection. The realism of Polly's struggle with an inadequate budget and other details of daily life is contrasted brilliantly with the almost mythic sense of fate that controls the novel's tone.

One Minus One (1971) is a character study of newly divorced Emily Bean, who fears being a single woman. Her relationships with two roommates—one soon to be married, one desperately wishing to be—and her affairs with two men form the plot, which compares her life with those of her mother and grandmother, employing passages from the grandmother's diary. The novel ends on a note of restrained hope; Emily is simply drifting professionally, but she has confronted her former husband's happy second marriage and has faced the impossibility of averting change.

Both these novels also present fascinating studies of one kind of modern American nomad—high school teachers who move from job to job, seeking the good life. All yearn to put down roots, but most move on, searching for a natural environment that no longer exists and an ideal town that perhaps exists only in imagination. M.'s stark contrasting of their realistic need for decent pay and good working conditions with their more dreamlike goals contributes greatly to the tension of these novels.

The Cheerleader (1973) is a *Bildungsroman* that clearly depicts high school life and mores in the 1950s, often employing references to music and films to enhance the realism of the setting. The characterization of the protagonist, Henrietta Snow, is remarkably lifelike because of M.'s treatment of teenage friendships, sexuality, bondage to dress and behavior codes, and desire for both popularity and recognition. Snowy's maturation, though at times painful, is successful, as symbolized by her rejection of childish alliances in favor of the intellectual stimulation of a good college.

The central characters in *Wife and Mother* (1976) are clearly designed to symbolize two forces in American society, with Carolyn representing intellectual values and conservationist attitudes and John representing single-minded business sense and exploitation of the land. Yet the portrait of Carolyn Ash, who marries only because she is pregnant and who achieves a sense of herself largely because of her friendship with Dee Winkler, one of M.'s best realized characters, is sharply drawn. The novel is a strong, useful metaphor for modern life; its celebration of the simple joys of gardening and of animal and bird watching is all the more effective because of the pervading consciousness that John's ambition dooms the environment Carolyn has learned to love.

M. is an accurate, careful reporter of contemporary middle-class life; her novels are well crafted, serious, and worthy of attention.

WORKS: *The Lilting House* (1965). *The Cost of Living* (1971). *One Minus One* (1971). *The Cheerleader* (1973). *Wife and Mother* (1976).

BIBLIOGRAPHY: *NYT* (13 Jan. 1971; 1 Feb. 1973). *NYTBR* (12 Sept. 1971; 4 Feb. 1973).

JANE S. BAKERMAN

Katherine Sherwood Bonner McDowell

B. 26 Feb. 1849, Holly Springs, Mississippi; d. 22 July 1883, Holly Springs, Mississippi
Given name: Catherine Sherwood Bonner
Wrote under: Sherwood Bonner
D. of Charles and Mary Wilson Bonner; m. Edward McDowell, 1871

As a young teenager, M. experienced the harsh realities of the Civil War, when Union troops occupied Holly Springs and even her family home. M. also suffered personal losses during the war years, with the deaths of her youngest sister in 1863 and her mother in 1865. In 1871, M. married another native of Holly Springs; their only child was born in 1872. The McDowells separated in 1873; finally, M. established residence in Illinois and obtained a divorce in 1881.

In 1873, M. moved to Boston to pursue a career in writing; there Nahum Capen, who had published her first story in 1864, recommended her to Henry W. Longfellow, with whom she worked and established a close friendship. During 1876, M. sent from Europe a number of travel articles for the Memphis *Avalanche* and the Boston *Times*. Her only novel, *Like Unto Like*, was published in 1878.

M. returned to Holly Springs in the fall of 1878 and nursed her father and brother through fatal illnesses with yellow fever. In 1881, as her writing career was gaining momentum, M. learned that she had breast cancer. Until her death, she continued to write and to prepare her short stories, which had appeared in such magazines as *Lippincott's*, *Harper's Weekly*, and *Youth's Companion*, for publication in two volumes, *Dialect Tales* (1883) and *Suwanee River Tales* (1884).

M.'s Gran'Mammy tales present a distinctive element of southern life; M. creates one of the finest literary portraits of the black mammy, who sustained and taught the members of her white family. "Gran'Mammy's Last Gifts" (1875) may well be the first example of black dialect published in a northern magazine. The most successful story of the group is "Coming Home to Roost" (1884), in which M. perceptively treats slave superstition. The child narrator has a significant role in the story's action, for her chance remark causes Aunt Beckey to believe she has been bewitched. The story is humorous, yet suspense builds as Beckey weakens spiritually and physically. She is cured by the brash young medical student, Henry, who is able to deal with the "trickery" on Beckey's level. M.'s detailed and accurate descriptions are effective, as is the realistic attitude of the rest of the white family, who can view Henry's actions only as a "fraud."

M.'s months in Illinois resulted in other examples of regional fiction, such as "On the Nine-Mile" (1882), which tells in lower-class dialect the story of Janey Burridge, a farm girl who is severely crippled shortly before her wedding. Her fiancé rejects her because she cannot carry her share of the workload on his farm. Up to this point, the story is realistic and somber. However, M. succumbs to sentimentality; in the last two paragraphs, Janey reforms the alcoholic father of the child responsible for her injury, marries him, regains her ability to walk, and has a child with him.

M.'s longer works, *Like Unto Like* and "The Valcours," a novella published serially (1881), are set during the Reconstruction period. *Like Unto Like* focuses on the continuing conflict of regional ways of life after the war, primarily in the romance of southerner Blythe Herndon and Roger Ellis, a northern radical. There are weaknesses in *Like Unto Like*, but M. avoids sentimentality, especially when Blythe renounces Roger's love and remains alone at the end of the novel. M. has been praised for her characterization, particularly of women such as Blythe Herndon and the lively Buena Vista Church of "The Valcours."

A study of M.'s fiction does not reveal any sustained development from purely regional to more sophisticated realistic works. Even though she began writing as a teenager, M. wrote for too short a period of time to develop her talents fully. *Like Unto Like* was reviewed favorably, but M. is appreciated today chiefly for her short stories, especially for her realistic use of dialects—lower-class midwestern, southern mountain, and black—and her humor. Many readers also enjoy her characterizations and plots. She is important as a forerunner of later southern women writers like Flannery O'Connor and Eudora Welty.

WORKS: *Like Unto Like* (1878). *Dialect Tales* (1883). *Suwanee River Tales* (1884). *Gran'Mammy* (1927).

BIBLIOGRAPHY: Frank, W. L., *Sherwood Bonner* (1976).
  For articles in reference works, see: *AA. DAB*, VI, 2. *NAW* (article by L. J. Budd).
  Other references: *ALR* (Winter 1972). *MissQ* (Winter 1963–64). *NMW* (Spring 1968; Spring 1969).

MARTHA E. COOK

Phyllis McGinley

B. 21 March 1905, Ontario, Oregon; d. 22 Feb. 1978, New York City
D. of Daniel and Julia McGinley; m. Charles L. Hayden, 1937

Beginning her career as a teacher in New Rochelle, New York, M. wrote poetry in her spare time. Her success in publishing it in magazines enabled her to give up teaching. To keep going, M. held various other positions, including poetry editor for *Town and Country* and copywriter for an advertising agency. According to an interview in *Newsweek*, she started writing in the style of Swinburne, but switched to light verse when she found out that that was what *The New Yorker* wanted from her.

Faithful to the eastern seaboard, although brought up in Colorado and Utah, she hymned New York to begin with and then, when she moved to Westchester County, the suburbs. In a volume of essays, *The Province of the Heart* (1959), she speaks out in favor of the Easterner and praises the village in which she lives for the way the neighbors love one another. A suburban housewife and mother was what she was and what she was happy to be.

Her first volume of verse, *On the Contrary*, was published in 1934. It contains mainly occasional verse—light comments on contemporary events. It was followed by *One More Manhattan* (1937), in which M. developed more of the tone we associate with her—light, astringent, and witty. There are times when M. comes close to Emily Dickinson, but she deliberately avoids total seriousness. *A Pocketful of Wry* (1940) contains a fair amount of political comment. In *Husbands Are Difficult;*

or, The Book of Oliver Ames (1941), M. pokes fun at her husband, but her mockery is very mild and loving. In *Stones from a Glass House* (1946), she comments on the war but refuses to hate. *The Love Letters of Phyllis McGinley* (1954) shows her improving and maturing, and won several awards.

M. won the Pulitzer Prize in 1961 for her volume of collected poetry, *Times Three* (1960), which was prefaced by W. H. Auden. The collection starts with the poems of the 1950s and works backward through the 1940s and 1930s. Some of the most charming poems are about saints and reformers, bearing testimony to her religious convictions as a Catholic but also to her moderation and warmhearted reasonableness. In a second volume of essays, *Sixpence in Her Shoe* (1964), M. writes of the trials and rewards of a wife and mother, a state which she accounted woman's most honorable profession.

A Wreath of Christmas Legends (1967) and *Saint-Watching* (1969) show her more deeply entrenched in the Catholic faith. In *Saint-Watching*, M. deliberately brings out the human side of the saints, whom she treats as people endowed with a special form of genius; it is a delight to read and can be described without irony as heartwarming. M. also wrote a number of children's books, but these do not have the distinction of her writing for adults.

Staunchly traditional, M. believed in lifelong vows and in the special vocation of women to motherhood. She also believed in the reality of sin, but was sure it could be forgiven. For her, manners were morals. Her lightness of touch was always backed by an acute intelligence and the feeling that she had found her proper place. She was probably a happy woman.

WORKS: *Mary's Garden* (1927). *On the Contrary* (1934). *One More Manhattan* (1937). *A Pocketful of Wry* (1940). *Husbands Are Difficult; or, The Book of Oliver Ames* (1941). *The Horse Who Lived Upstairs* (1944). *The Plain Princess* (1945). *Stones from a Glass House* (1946). *All Around the Town* (1948). *A Name for Kitty* (1948). *The Most Wonderful Doll in the World* (1950). *Blunderbus* (1951). *The Horse Who Had His Picture in the Paper* (1951). *A Short Walk from the Station* (1951). *The Make-Believe Twins* (1953). *The Love Letters of Phyllis McGinley* (1954). *The Year without a Santa Claus* (1957). *Merry Christmas, Happy New Year* (1958). *Lucy McLockett* (1959). *The Province of the Heart* (1959). *Sugar and Spice: The ABC of Being a Girl* (1960). *Times Three: Selected Verse from Three Decades with Seventy New Poems* (1960). *Mince Pie and Mistletoe* (1961). *The B Book* (1962). *Boys Are Awful* (1962). *A Girl and Her Room* (1963).

How Mrs. Santa Claus Saved Christmas (1963). *Sixpence in Her Shoe* (1964). *Wonderful Time* (1966). *A Wreath of Christmas Legends* (1967). *Wonders and Surprises* (1968). *Saint-Watching* (1969). *Confessions of a Reluctant Optimist* (1973).

BIBLIOGRAPHY: Auden, W. H., Foreword to *Times Three* by P. McGinley (1960).
    For articles in reference works, see: *CB* (Nov. 1961). *20thCAS.*
    Other references: *Commonweal* (9 Dec. 1960). *Newsweek* (26 Sept. 1960). *SatR* (10 Dec. 1960).

BARBARA J. BUCKNALL

Mary McGrory

B. 22 Aug. 1918, Boston, Massachusetts
D. of Edward and Mary Jacob McGrory

M. inherited a love for books, poetry, and reading from her father, a deputy superintendent at the South Boston Post Office. His death when she was twenty-one was a deep loss. M. attended Boston's Girls Latin School. As a senior she had her heart set on going to Radcliffe, but the scholarship she needed did not come through. Instead, she enrolled at Emmanuel College, a Catholic women's school in Boston. She continued to live at home with her mother after graduation, grading papers at night to earn money for her tuition at secretarial school.

Compared to most eminent journalists, M.'s career got off to a slow start. She began at the Boston *Herald* as a secretary to the book review editor. M. hoped she would get a chance to write and report, but the opportunities were few. She "was allowed to write about dogs," but not encouraged to contribute anything more ambitious. In six years there, however, she did manage to get some book reviews published.

She was twenty-nine when a friendly editor at the Boston *Herald* recommended her to the Washington *Star* as a book reviewer. For seven years, M. wrote three or four book reviews a week, "color commentary" about books in a column called "Reading and Writing," and an occasional "odd feature" and profiles for the *Star*'s Sunday section. Her chance to write for the news side of the paper came in 1954 when Newbold Noyes, editor of the *Star*, sent her to the Army-McCarthy hearings, telling her he wanted her to "give color, humor, and charm to the news columns." His guidance launched M.'s interpretive writing, in which people—their conversations and comments, their posture and facial expressions—personify the issues of the day. The Army-McCarthy hearings stories established M. as an imaginative, observant reporter, and she continued to get plum assignments.

Whereas most news reporters record words and statements, M. records faces. A colleague of hers says she has the ability "to write pictures." Her style is much more personal than that of many writers, but it is every bit as factual. Her facility for shorthand enables her to capture quotes and convey exact moods.

In 1955, the Washington-Baltimore Newspaper Guild honored M. for her "unusually penetrating" coverage of the Army-McCarthy hearings, quite an achievement for the "ancient cub" [reporter], as M. described herself at that time. This organization and others have continued to cite the quality of her work. In 1974, M. became the fourteenth woman to win the Pulitzer Prize for journalism for her commentary on the Watergate scandal.

In 1960 M.'s column was syndicated by United Features Syndicate. It appears four times a week in more than 130 newspapers, and is also carried by the wire services of United Press International and the *New York Times*.

M. belies many stereotypes of newspaper reporters. By her own admission she is not a relentless cross-examiner of public figures, nor is she a cozy compatriot of the powerful. She is not a news "personality." She is a syndicated columnist whose quiet, consistent methods of gathering news yield accurate, illuminating commentary. M. rarely refers to herself in her columns, as many columnists do. She does not use the first person; she does not reminisce about her own contact with those she covers. She writes about encounters and events as if she were invisible at the time they happened. Only the keen observations and often-devastating barbs in her columns indicate that M. was very much present.

BIBLIOGRAPHY: Marzolf, M., *Up from the Footnote: A History of Women Journalists* (1977). McLendon, W., and S. Smith, *Don't Quote Me! Washington Newswomen and the Power Society* (1970).

Other references: *Ms.* (May 1975). Washington *Star* (6 May 1975).

SHEILA J. GIBBONS

Judith White Brockenbrough McGuire

B. 1813, Richmond, Virginia
D. of William Brockenbrough; m. John P. McGuire

M. was the daughter of a member of the Virginia state supreme court. Her early life is obscure. We do know that she married the principal of the Episcopal High School of Alexandria, Virginia. At the beginning of the Civil War, the McGuires lived there with their two sons and several daughters.

M. began her diary, published in 1867 as *The Diary of a Southern Refugee,* in May 1861 with the break up of her family. Rev. McGuire and the boys had enlisted while M. and her daughters were forced to leave Alexandria when federal troops occupied the town. "I am keeping this [diary]," she wrote, "for the members of the family who are too young to remember these days." The days to which she refers seem filled with movement and insecurity. The family traveled south through the Virginia countryside to Richmond. Along the way they stayed with friends and relatives, but, M. recalled, "while [their hospitality] is very gratifying, and delightful, yet we must find some place, however small and humble, to call home." By February 1862 they were in Richmond, trying desperately to find a home. Since Richmond had become the seat of the Confederate government, the city's population had doubled and lodgings were at a premium. After being refused board at several homes, M. was finally offered rooms at three dollars less than her husband's monthly salary.

Finding the Confederate capital too expensive, M. and her daughters were on the move again, settling first in Lynchburg and then in Charlottesville, Virginia. There she hoped to get work in the Treasury Department, signing government notes. But widows and orphans were given preference for government jobs, so the family supported itself by making and selling soap. In November 1863, M. obtained a clerkship in the Army's Commissary Department. Like the other thirty-five refugee women, she worked from 7:00 A.M. to 3:00 P.M. daily and received $125 per month in depreciated Confederate paper money. In addition, she worked evenings as a volunteer nurse in local hospitals.

The diary ends abruptly in May 1865 with the notation that General Joseph E. Johnston had surrendered his army on April 26: "My native land, good night!" We do not know what happened to M. after the war, or whether the family was able to return to Alexandria. The end of her life, like the beginning, is a mystery.

Unlike many of the other Confederate women whose diaries have been published, M. did not move in high social circles. Her diary does not record the comings and goings of the Confederacy's military and social elite. However, *The Diary of A Southern Refugee* is perhaps more valuable than other more widely known diaries because M.'s experiences are more representative of the war's effect on Southern society. It is difficult for modern readers to imagine the constant fear and uncertainty under which most Confederates lived. They not only feared for their own safety at the hands of an enemy they believed was inhuman and for the safety of loved ones in the army, but they wondered where their next meal might come from, or whether they would have homes when the war ended. The refugee experience was far more common than most historians have realized, and M.'s diary allows us to relive part of it.

The tone of the diary varies. At times M. is a dispassionate observer, merely chronicling the events of the war. At other times, she allows the reader to share her emotions. These latter passages are infrequent, as though M. feared to let herself feel too deeply, but when they occur, they are moving and effective. It is unfortunate that *The Diary of a Southern Refugee* has been overlooked for so long.

WORKS: *The Diary of a Southern Refugee during the War* (1867). *General Robert E. Lee, the Christian Soldier . . . Published for the City Missionary Association of the Protestant Episcopal Church of Richmond* (1873).

BIBLIOGRAPHY: K. M. Jones, ed., *Heroines of Dixie* (2 vols., 1955). M. E. Massey, *Refugee Life in the Confederacy* (1964).

JANET E. KAUFMAN

Maria Jane McIntosh

B. 1803, Sunbury, Georgia; d. 25 Feb. 1878, Morristown, New Jersey
Wrote under: Aunt Kitty, Cousin Kate, M. J. McIntosh, Maria J. McIntosh,
  Maria Jane McIntosh
D. of Lachlan McIntosh and Mary Moore Maxwell McIntosh

M. was educated at home, at a coeducational academy in Sunbury, and at Baisden's Bluff Academy in McIntosh County. A descendant of the powerful McIntosh clan in Scotland, M. exhibited in her life a self-reliance akin to the moral independence she sets as a standard for the heroines of her novels. Her father, a lawyer, died when M. was only a few years old, and on the death of her invalid mother in 1823, the young M. took over the management of the family estate. Moving to New York in 1835, M. sold her property and invested in New York securities, only to lose her substantial fortune in the 1837 business crisis.

Setting out to make her living by writing, M. published the first of her series of moralistic children's stories in 1841 and the first of her eight novels in 1843. During her prolific writing career she published twenty-four books, which, popular in England and France as well as in America, eventually made her self-supporting.

Conquest and Self-Conquest (1843), M.'s first novel, traces the lives of Frederic Stanley and his friend from the time they are schoolboys through their early adventures as midshipmen in the navy. Conceived by M. as "a history of the mind," the novel presents parallel incidents contrasting Frederic's control and his friend's lack of control of the "rash passions" that lead to "wrong-doing"—in this case fighting, gambling, and drinking. The abstemious Frederic rescues his lady love from pirates and is rewarded by her hand and a state ceremony in his honor, while his friend, lacking Frederic's self-control, is invalided home. Frederic sums up the novel's moral when he explains to his disappointed friend that what makes the true hero is "not conquest over others . . . but self-conquest." For the most part M.'s subordination of character and plot to her didactic purpose results in a tract-like work that is predictably boring.

Woman, an Enigma (1843) again focuses on development of self-control in a young person, but here M. is concerned with a young woman's purposeful direction of her life. Set in 18th-c. France and

England, the novel traces the life of Louise de La Valliere, a convent-bred seventeen year old who suddenly becomes an heiress and the betrothed of a jaded marquis. She adopts the philosophy that "a wife's best talisman for the preservation of peace and purity lay in her devotion to her husband." The result is disastrous: the pair are embroiled in five years of misunderstandings, intrigues, and separations. Suffering forces Louise into action, led by duty and a sense of right, not by a desire to please her husband. M.'s thesis is that the inconsistencies criticized in women stem from their failure to have a purpose in life other than to please men. This work is as didactic as M.'s first novel, but Louise's development of a purpose in life makes for more interesting reading than does Frederic's abstinence.

Two Lives (1846), the first work M. published under her real name, combines the parallel structure of her first novel with the theme of her second novel: the need for women to be independent of men in the spiritual purpose that guides their everyday life. The lovely Grace Elliot "has no fixed principle but the desire to please," whereas her equally lovely but solemn cousin Isabel adheres to "the unchanging and eternal principles of right." Grace's fiancé leaves her when he realizes that "To *seem* what I wished has been her effort, and how shall I know that her whole life is not seeming." Straitlaced Isabel is an unappealing character, but M.'s insight into her coldness and into Grace's desire to please occasionally cuts through the novel's sentimentality and sermonizing.

Charms and Counter-Charms (1848), the most popular of M.'s novels, traces the development of Evelyn Beresford, a young woman very like Grace Elliot and Louise de La Valliere in that "she is as wax in the hands of those she loves." M. structures the novel on parallels, setting Evelyn's trials with her dashing husband, Euston, an "unbeliever" and a "libertine," against her friend Mary's relationship with the exemplary Everard. The novel focuses on what undoubtedly made it a bestseller: the sado-masochistic relationship between Evelyn and Euston. He repeatedly rejects her for another woman so that, at any sign of unhappiness, he can punish her with coldness. When they are eventually reconciled, Evelyn has become less dependent on his love, but the real change is in Euston. Euston represents an excess of the self-control M. praises in her other novels, and her sympathetic insight into his distaste for emotional intimacy adds psychological realism to her portrayal of his and Evelyn's relationship.

M.'s insight into the emotions of her characters only occasionally transcends her rigid parallelism of plot and characters, her sentimentality, and her didacticism. M.'s thematic variations on self-control in her novels are interesting in the context of her life. What is most interesting about her works, however, is that, although her treatise *Woman in America: Her Work and Her Reward* (1850) asserts that woman's role is to be a mother, her novels preach a different message: the need for women to be guided not by a desire to please men, but by their own sense of right.

WORKS: *Blind Alice; or, Do Right If You Wish to Be Happy* (1841). *Florence Arnott; or, Is She Generous?* (1841). *Jessie Graham; or, Friends Dear, but Truth Dearer* (1841). *Ellen Leslie; or, The Reward of Self-Control* (1842). *Grace and Clara; or, Be Just as Well as Generous* (1842). *Conquest and Self-Conquest; or, Which Makes the Hero?* (1843). *Woman, an Enigma; or, Life and Its Revealings. To Which Is Added Medfield; or, The Monomaniac* (alternative title, *Louise de la Valliere*, 1843). *The Cousins: A Tale of Early Life* (1845). *Praise and Principle; or, For What Shall I Live?* (1845). *Two Lives; or, To Seem and to Be* (1846). *Aunt Kitty's Tales* (1847). *Charms and Counter-Charms* (1848). *Woman in America: Her Work and Her Reward* (1850). *The Christmas Guest; or, Evenings at Donaldson Manor* (1853). *Letter on the Address of the Women of England to Their Sisters of America, in Relation to Slavery* (1853). *The Lofty and the Lowly; or, Good in All and None All-Good* (1853). *Alice Montrose: A Tale* (1855). *Rose and Lillie Stanhope; or, The Power of Conscience* (1855). *Violet; or, The Cross and the Crown* (1856). *Maggie and Emma: A True Story* (1861). *Meta Gray; or, What Makes Home Happy* (1853). *Two Pictures; or, What We Think of Ourselves and What the World Thinks of Us* (1863). *Violetta and I* (1870). *The Children's Mirror: A Treasury of Stories* (1887). *Emily Herbert; or, The Happy Home* (n.d.).

BIBLIOGRAPHY: Baym, N., *Women's Fiction: A Guide to Novels by and about Women in America, 1820–1870* (1978). Forrest, M., *Women of the South Distinguished in Literature* (1861).

For articles in reference works, see: *A Critical Dictionary of English Literature*, Ed. S. A. Allibone (1858). *The Female Prose Writers of English Literature*, J. S. Hart (1852). *The Living Female Writers of the South*, M. T. Tardy (1872). *NAW* (article by M. Hornberger). *The Twentieth Century Biographical Dictionary of Notable Americans*, Ed. R. Johnson (1904). *Woman's Record*, S. J. Hale (1853).

MARTHA CHEW

Ruth McKenney

B. 18 Nov. 1911, Mishawaka, Indiana; d. 25 July 1972, New York City
D. of John Sidney and Marguerite Flynn McKenney; m. Richard Bransten,
1937

M. was raised in Indiana and Ohio, where she began working in a print shop at age fourteen. After attending Ohio State University, she wrote for the Akron *Beacon Journal* and the New York *Post*. She married and raised three children (she adopted the son of her sister Eileen and the novelist Nathanael West after their deaths in an automobile accident). M. wrote short semiautobiographical stories for *The New Yorker*, *Publisher's Weekly*, and other popular magazines, and worked as an editor of *New Masses*. M. and Bransten were ousted from the Communist Party in 1946 for deviating from party doctrine.

Exaggerated and amusing, M.'s best-known work, *My Sister Eileen* (1938), was compiled from short stories originally appearing in *The New Yorker*; it was followed by stage, movie, and musical versions. M. published other accounts of her unusual family in *All about Eileen* (1937), *The McKenneys Carry On* (1937), *The Loud Red Patrick* (1947), *Love Story* (1950), and *Far, Far from Home* (1954), sometimes overlapping stories from one volume to the next. These accounts of her youth have lost much of the charm that was their primary attraction; the sisters' adventures (far more concerned with Ruth than with Eileen) are described from childhood to adulthood in humorous but extravagant, unconnected anecdotes.

The nonfictional *Industrial Valley* (1939) is the cornerstone of M.'s socialist writings, which also include *Browder and Ford: For Peace, Jobs, Socialism* (1940), the unsuccessful novel *Jake Home* (1943), and her articles and column, "Strictly Personal," for *New Masses*. Written in journal form, *Industrial Valley* details the struggle between 1932 and 1936 of the Akron rubber workers to unionize. The details of the Depression, both personal and industrial, are related as though by an omniscient observer, revealing the manipulations and deceptions of the powerful. The stark facts recorded in *Industrial Valley* are more arresting than the fictional portrait of a developing union leader in *Jake Home*. Neither his personality nor his motivations are sufficiently engaging to make the novel convincing.

M.'s final two works move away from previously developed patterns. *Here's England: A Highly Informal Guide* (1950), coauthored with Bransten, is a pleasant, well-informed guide to Britain's historical and tourist attractions. *Mirage* (1956) chronicles the adventures of Remi Sainte-Victor, a Lyon chemist, through his imprisonment in the French Revolution, his release through the intercession of Josephine Bonaparte, and the campaign in Egypt with Napoleon. The novel fails to draw the social, personal, and military elements together to focus on either the bourgeois hero or his Corsican emperor.

Although *My Sister Eileen* is still remembered (chiefly for its filmed version), *Industrial Valley*, M.'s most significant work, better displays her ability to humanize a great drama by the presentations of precise and realistic details. The perspective she achieves in the nonautobiographical view of the Midwest is valuable for its clarity and compassion.

WORKS: *All about Eileen* (1937). *The McKenneys Carry On* (1937). *My Sister Eileen* (1938; dramatization, 1940; film version, 1942; musical, *Wonderful Town*, adapted by L. Berstein). *Industrial Valley* (1939). *Browder and Ford: For Peace, Jobs, Socialism* (1940). *Jake Home* (1943). *The Loud Red Patrick* (1947). *Here's England: A Highly Informal Guide* (with R. Bransten, 1950). *Love Story* (1950). *Far, Far from Home* (1954). *Mirage* (1956).

BIBLIOGRAPHY: For articles in reference works, see: *CA* 37–40 (1973). *20thCA. 20thCAS.*

KATHLEEN G. KLEIN

Shirley MacLaine

B. 24 April 1934, Richmond, Virginia
Given Name: Shirley MacLean Beaty
D. of Ira O. and Kathlyn MacLean Beaty; m. Steve Parker, 1954

Born into what she describes as "a cliché-loving, middle-class Virginia family," M. was raised to be respectable and conventional. M. found an early outlet for her energies in ballet lessons, which she began at age three. By the time M. graduated from high school, she had abundant professional credits as a dancer. She soon headed for New York City, and made her way into the chorus of some hit musicals, among them Rodgers and Hammerstein's *Me and Juliet* (1953).

In 1954, Carol Haney broke an ankle three nights after the Broadway opening of *Pajama Game,* and M. was called upon to replace her. Performing without rehearsal, she emerged a star. Hollywood producer Hal Wallis instantly signed her to a long-term contract, and she played the first of many madcap roles in Hitchcock's *The Trouble with Harry* (1955).

In the next decade, M. played a number of major movie roles, specializing in kooks and good-hearted prostitutes. She received Academy Award nominations for *Some Came Running* (1959), *The Apartment* (1960), and *Irma La Douce* (1963). Her offbeat marital life also generated much comment.

When not before the cameras, M. devoted a great deal of time to travel, exploring life-styles radically different from her own. She toured the deep south with black leaders in the early days of the civil rights movement, and researched her role in *Irma La Douce* by witnessing at close range the working life of a Paris streetwalker. M.'s travels are described in her best-selling book, *Don't Fall Off the Mountain* (1970).

In 1971, a television series for which M. had great hopes turned out to be a commercial and artistic disaster. Alienated from the Hollywood establishment, M. turned from show business to politics, playing an active role in the presidential campaign of Senator McGovern. Her second publication was *McGovern: The Man and His Beliefs* (1972), a collection of writings which she selected and edited. Although the McGovern campaign was unsuccessful, M. retained an interest in public affairs and social action. In the spring of 1973 she was asked to lead the first women's delegation to the People's Republic of China. This six-week trip became the central episode of her second bestseller, *You Can Get There from Here* (1975). Another outgrowth of the trip was a documentary film, *The Other Half of the Sky: A China Memoir* (1974), which M. produced and which received an Academy Award nomination.

After the trip to China, M. returned to her theatrical career with renewed vigor. In 1974 she made her hugely successful Las Vegas debut, and has since had triumphs on stage, screen, and television. For her ballet film, *The Turning Point,* M. was once again honored with an Oscar nomination.

M.'s books are marked far less by her stylistic skills than by a keen eye for detail and a refreshing candor. Genuinely interested in all she surveys, M. is not ashamed to reveal the ambivalence of her personal reactions. This is especially true of her account of the China trip: Her focus is not so much on the fact of China as on the way the impact of the Chinese experience threw a group of American women into total mental confusion. In her unflagging eagerness to probe and evaluate the world around her, M. shows herself to be very different from other writers of show-business memoirs.

WORKS: *Don't Fall Off the Mountain* (1970). *McGovern: The Man and His Beliefs* (edited by MacLaine, 1972). *You Can Get There from Here* (1975).

BIBLIOGRAPHY: *Newsweek* (11 Jan. 1971). *NYRB* (1 May 1975). *NYT* (23 March 1975). *NYTBR* (16 March 1975). *Time* (28 Dec. 1970; 3 March 1975). *TLS* (16 April 1971). *VV* (10 March 1975).

BEVERLY GRAY BIENSTOCK

Annie Marion MacLean

B. *Nova Scotia, Canada; d. May 1934, Pasadena, California*
D. *of Reverend John and Christina MacLean*

M. studied sociology at Acadia College, Nova Scotia, before immigrating to the University of Chicago, where she earned a Ph.D. M.'s dissertation, "The Acadian Element in the Population of Nova Scotia," was completed in 1900. M. taught at Adelphi College from 1906 to 1916 and at the National Training School of the YWCA from 1903 to 1916. She was associated with the University of Chicago from 1903 to 1934 as an extension assistant professor of sociology in what was then termed the Home Study Department. M.'s interests are reflected in the titles of the courses she taught: Rural Life, Introduction to Social Problems of Industry, Social Technology, Modern Immigration, and History of the Social Reform Movement.

As a sociologist, M. was keenly interested in social reforms aimed at improving the condition of women in industry and furthering their organizational efforts. Trade unions represented to her "a rational theory of industrial betterment." Her immersion into the "social worlds" of others was of short term and great variety: hop picker; department store clerk (reflecting her interest in the newly formed Consumers' League of Illinois, an organization designed to use the power of consumers to remedy industrial ills); striker; model factory worker; and finally, sweatshop worker. Her interest in the latter was aroused while serving as a member of New York Governor Roosevelt's Tenement House Commission.

M.'s writing style is straightforward, both descriptive and analytical, and eminently readable. A sense of humor keeps her works from taking on a preaching tone. Her primary interests are reflected in two books: *Wage Earning Women* (1910) and *Women Workers and Society* (1916). The former involved M. as a director of a massive effort sponsored by the national board of the YWCA to study typical conditions of representative industries employing women. About four hundred establishments in more than a score of cities were studied. These included textile, clothing, and printing work in New York and New England; meat packing in Nebraska; hop picking in Oregon; and fruit picking and drying in California.

Wage Earning Women advocated regular investigations by both public and private agencies. M. alludes to the work of private agencies such as the Consumers' League; additionally, she points to the role of social-settlement leaders Jane Addams and Mary McDowell in Chicago and Lillian Wald and Mary Kingsbury Simkhovitch in New York, urging a careful study of working conditions. Among the other concerns of the book were improved and uniform legislation among the states, including "protective" legislation for women and children; employer's welfare work; trade unions; and a variety of residential clubs and hotels for working women, in which the YWCA was a pioneer. M. applauds the Eleanor Clubs of Chicago, which served as neighborhood centers as well as providing living facilities.

M.'s interest in immigration culminated in the publication of *Modern Immigration* (1925), which reflects the concerns of that era over the desirability of assimilation and Americanization. The implicit message is almost one of *noblesse oblige:* helping those less fortunate "lose" their own culture and adopt the "superior" American culture. The book also shows a concern with selecting immigrants so that a polyglot race (with structural weaknesses) would not emerge. M. tempers her stance somewhat by noting that this does not mean "an arrogant trampling under the feet of other strains."

As can be inferred, M. was part of the Chicago Hull House network. Like the other women sociology faculty members (E. Abbott and M. McDowell), she occupied a marginal, peripheral role within the university. In spite of her reputation as a sociologist, M. was relegated to the Home Study Department instead of being part of the regular faculty. Her contributions to the sociology of women and work are major; her forthright and militant efforts to improve the conditions of working women are commendable.

WORKS: *Wage Earning Women* (1910). *Mary Ann's Malady* (1913). *Women Workers and Society* (1916). *Cheero* (1918). *Some Problems of Reconstruction* (1921). *Our Neighbors* (1922). *This Way Lies Happiness* (1923). *Modern Immigration* (1925).

BIBLIOGRAPHY: *American Journal of Sociology* (26, 1921; 40, 1934). *The Journal of the History of Sociology* 1 (1978).

VIRGINIA KEMP FISH

Kathryn Anderson McLean

B. *10 March 1909, San Francisco, California; d. 15 May 1966, San Francisco, California*
Wrote under: Kathryn Forbes
D. *of Leon Ellis and Della Jesser Anderson; m. Robert Edward McLean, 1926*

M. was the scion of 19th-c. California pioneers. Her voluntary publicity work for clubs grew into a professional writing career; she published her first story in 1938. M. stopped publishing in the late 1940s, perhaps weakened by the chronic emphysema that caused her death. In 1946, she divorced her husband, on grounds of extreme mental cruelty.

The American public first met Mama, M.'s most famous character (based on her grandmother), in *Readers' Digest* in 1941. In "Mama and Her Bank Account," Mama supervises the careful division of Papa's paycheck, and she and the children work part-time to prevent any withdrawal from the mythical savings account Mama invented to give the children a sense of security.

Mama's Bank Account (1943) is a collection of sketches depicting Mama raising her family in early 20th-c. San Francisco, told from the point of view of Katrin, the eldest daughter, who aspires to a writing career. The book centers on Mama's relationships with her carpenter husband and five children, her patriarchal Uncle Chris, maiden Aunt Elna, and four sisters. This is an extended family that works, chiefly because of Mama's talents for understanding and mediation. M. etches the character of each family member clearly and well; they perform consistently in the stories, which are pervaded by an atmosphere of optimism and humor. In traumatic times of strikes and illness, Mama's common sense and ability to make things right prevail. Several stories highlight the difficulties of Americanization, but Mama's wisdom transcends cultural and class boundaries, as she helps overcome the anti-immigrant prejudice her daughters face at school. Her warmth and wisdom loom large, approximating closely the traditional American maternal ideal.

Critics and public alike applauded *Mama's Bank Account*, and it became a bestseller. Its emphasis on togetherness held special appeal during World War II, and it was reinterpreted in several media. Playwright John Van Druten noted the dramatic possibilities of *Mama's Bank Account*, and wrote and directed a two-act play based upon it. *I Remember Mama* opened on Broadway in 1944 and ran for 714 performances until 1946.

Despite its sentimentality, the play won both general critical approval and the hearts of audiences. Critical charges of sentimentality increased after the film version (produced and directed by George Stevens, with an all-star cast headed by Irene Dunn) opened in 1948, but audiences continued to appreciate *I Remember Mama* and its celebration of old-fashioned domesticity. Mama's proven popularity and the episodic, open-ended nature of her story seemed ideal material for television; the series was an instant success and ran from July 1949 through March 1957.

Unfortunately, Mama's creator did not share her character's long popularity. M. largely left the work of developing Mama to other writers, publishing only two additional stories about her: "Mama and Dagmar" (1944) and "Mama and the Christmas Tradition" (1945). M. continued to write short stories in a variety of settings but with a consistent emphasis on family values and concern for others.

M.'s second book, *Transfer Point* (1947), returns to Mama's San Francisco, but the family in focus is far from idyllic. Ten-year-old Allie Barton, the protagonist, is a daughter of divorce, her parents torn apart by guilt over the tragic deaths of two older sons. Allie, a bright, independent child, loves both her parents, and tries desperately to find continuity, friendship, and a sense of her own identity that will include the different self she is with each parent. The roomers in Allie's mother's boardinghouse provoke more serious problems than Mama ever faced: suspected child molesting, fraud, and murder. M. presents Allie's situation and point of view with great understanding, but the episodic structure of the novel weakens its force. The novel received mixed reviews; hostile critics and readers perhaps expected only domestic bliss from M.'s pen. The serialized version in *Good Housekeeping* was the last of M.'s published fiction.

M. will be remembered for Mama, which showed her apt characterization and her ability to tap the lode of a memory broader than her own. M.'s embodiment of the maternal ideal hovered on the edge of sentimentality, but she never totally lost her balance. Although the televised version of Mama may have provided historical background for the feminine mystique of the 1950s, M.'s novel *Transfer Point* presented a child growing to a well-adjusted maturity under far different domestic arrangements. M. was rejected by the reading public when she removed the rose-colored lens she had earlier used in viewing the past, but she deserves to be remembered for capturing the drama and humor inherent in various forms of family life.

WORKS: *Mama's Bank Account* (1943; dramatization by J. Van Druten, *I Remember Mama*, 1945; film version, 1948). *Transfer Point* (1947).

BIBLIOGRAPHY: For articles in reference works, see: *American Novelists of Today*, H. R. Warfel (1951). *CB* (1945).

Other references: *Commonweal* (16 April 1943). *NYT* (12 March 1948). *NYTBR* (28 March 1943; 9 Nov. 1947). *NYTMag* (14 Oct. 1945). *SatR* (16 Dec. 1944; 24 Jan. 1948; 13 Oct. 1951). *Theatre Arts* (Dec. 1944).

HELEN M. BANNAN

Aimee Semple McPherson

B. *9 Oct. 1890, Ingersoll, Ontario, Canada; d. 27 Sept. 1944, Oakland, California*
D. *of James Morgan and Mildred Pearce Kennedy; m. Robert Semple, 1908; m. Harold Stewart McPherson, 1912; m. David L. Hutton, 1931*

The only child of a Methodist farmer and a Salvation Army mother, M. was dedicated to God's work in the Salvation Army at age six weeks. At seventeen, she was converted to the Pentecostal mission by Robert Semple, whom she then married. Ordained as a preacher of the Full Gospel Assembly in 1909, M. conducted revivals in small towns in the U.S., and then went to China in 1910, where Semple died. A daughter, Roberta, was born a month later. Returning to the U.S., M. worked in missions with her mother in New York City. A second marriage to McPherson, a bookkeeper, produced a son. Wishing to resume her revival work full time, M. left McPherson, and with her mother and two children began her career as evangelist in 1915.

In a Pentecostal mission in Ontario, M. conducted tent meetings characterized by faith healing, crisis conversions, speaking in tongues, premillennialism, and literal interpretation of the Bible. In 1916, M. began her itinerant career, holding tent revivals from Maine to Florida, accompanied by her astute, business-minded widowed mother. They drove to Los Angeles in their "Gospel Car" in 1918, and founded the Angelus Temple in 1923. The funds were raised by her devout lower-middle-class followers, for whom M. formed a new sect, The Church of the Foursquare Gospel.

From her temple, M. launched a wide variety of highly successful religious and social welfare programs. These included a monthly newsletter, *Bridal Call*, and a weekly, *Bridal Call Four-Square;* a church radio station; a commissary to distribute food and clothing to the poor; a telephone counseling service; prayer vigils; and a Bible College. By 1944, when M. died of an accidental overdose of barbiturates, membership in the four hundred branches of her church was over twenty-two thousand, and her Bible College had graduated three thousand. Since then, the sect has continued to thrive, with two thousand seven hundred churches all over the world.

M. wrote all her own sermons, many songs, most of *Bridal Call*, and two autobiographies besides preaching the scheduled ten sermons a week and going on a number of cross-country tours. M.'s writings, though not deep, were based on a solid knowledge of the Bible and a sure understanding of her uneducated audience. The most famous of M.'s cliché-ridden but inspired sermons is "The Rose of Sharon," delivered in 1931. Dressed in her trademark clerical garb of white dress and blue satin cape, and cradling a bunch of red roses, M. compared the short life of the rose to that of humans. Then, tearing off a rose petal, she made her point: While the petal dies, the attar, if extracted, is a fragrance everlasting. Rose attar, like the blood of Jesus, is a symbol of eternal hope, preserving the soul when the body is sacrificed.

M.'s autobiographies are more imaginative than factual, intended to glorify her early life and omitting baser details. M.'s first book, *This Is That* (1919), describes her conversion and mission in a sentimental but vivid style. The second, *In the Service of the King* (1927), probably ghostwritten, attempts to explain her version of her presumed kidnapping and disappearance in 1926. A few of her sermons were recorded, preserving her compelling voice and simplistic metaphors in such messages as "Three Little Pigs," "From Milkpail to Pulpit," and "The Scarlet Thread." A genius at managing publicity, M. received almost daily press coverage throughout her career.

A charismatic evangelist and a beautiful, youthful-looking woman to the end of her life, M. offered solace and material comfort to all. During the Depression, her commissary predated even President Roosevelt's welfare programs. Her always-optimistic sermons gave hope to the neglected working-class poor, people who craved some color and symbol of affection. As a symbol of fundamentalism in America, M. is said to have inspired Sinclair Lewis's antievangelist novel, *Elmer Gantry*.

WORKS: *This Is That: Personal Experiences, Sermons, and Writings* (1919; rev. and enlarged ed., 1923). *In the Service of the King—the Story of My Life* (1927). *The Holy Spirit* (1931). *Give Me My Own God* (1936). *The Story of My Life* (1936).

BIBLIOGRAPHY: Goben, J. D., *"Aimee"—the Gospel Gold-Digger* (1932). McWilliams, C., in *The Aspirin Age*, Ed. I. Leighton (1949). Mavity, N. B., *Sister Aimee* (1931). Thomas, L., *Storming Heaven: The Lives and Turmoils of Minnie Kennedy and Aimee Semple McPherson* (1970). Thomas, L., *The Vanishing Evangelist: The Aimee Semple McPherson Kidnapping Affair* (1959).

For articles in reference works, see: *NAW* (article by W. G. McLoughlin). *NCAB*, 35.

Other references: *JPC* (Winter 1967).

BARBARA ADAMS

Sister Madeleva

B. 24 May 1877, Cumberland, Wisconsin; d. 25 July 1964, Boston, Massachusetts
Given name: Mary Evaline Wolff
D. of August and Lucy Arntz Wolff

The daughter of a German-born harness maker and a former teacher, M. grew up in a mill town in rural Wisconsin. After a year at the University of Wisconsin, M. transferred to St. Mary's College at Notre Dame, Indiana, from which she graduated in 1909. She received an M.A.

from the University of Notre Dame and a Ph.D. in English from the University of California. By 1908, she had joined the Congregation of the Holy Cross which conducts St. Mary's, taking the name Sister Mary Madeleva, and her entire life was devoted to educating women. From 1934 to 1961, M. served as president of St. Mary's; during this time she was responsible for the founding of the first American Catholic graduate school of theology for the laity. From 1942–48 she was president of the Catholic Poetry Society of America.

Her prose works include essays and addresses on education as well as literary criticism. M.'s best-known study is "Chaucer's Nuns" (1925), in which she interprets details of the portrait of the prioress in the prologue to the *Canterbury Tales* by observing her in the context of religious life.

With the publication of *Knights Errant, and Other Poems* (1923), M. became the first of the modern "nun-poets"—a peculiarly American phenomenon.

Most of M.'s poems are short lyrics, usually under twenty lines. M.'s only leisure, she explained, came in recuperating from illnesses; other moments were snatched between tasks, in walking from building to building, or during nights of insomnia.

Only occasionally do her poems focus on secular themes: her visits to Oxford and the Holy Land, glimpses of nature, or literary interests. "Marginalium," for example, protests the death of the Lady of Shalott. The great bulk of M.'s work deals with religious experience.

M.'s religious poetry is always personal and devotional, never didactic or public. By dealing with her own experience, M. avoids the pious and the platitudinous. Her verse abounds in nature imagery of an amiable sort. "My Windows," from *Penelope, and Other Poems* (1927), describes two "wonder-windows": One lets in "tranquillity and noon . . . magic and the moon"; the other looks on a garden with "a sudden rose, / A poppy's flame. . . ." It is through these windows that the poet sees God. Here as always M.'s theme is constant love and serene beauty; images of horror or despair are absent.

Even the tone of religious longing is usually carefully modulated. In "Petals and Wings," from *Four Girls, and Other Poems* (1941), field flowers—"Silent, at peace, and beautiful"—are contrasted with "wild, unlettered birds, / Song-silver things." The poet's question as to whether "petalled peace" or "wilding flight / Into the sun" is ultimately preferable remains unanswered, except in the hidden mind of God.

The mystical "The King's Secret" (in *Penelope*), generally recognized as M.'s best poem, is unlike almost all her other work. In this poem, her longest, M. abandons her usual reticence and in explicitly erotic language, inspired by and even echoing the Song of Songs, speaks ecstatically of union with "this King Who is God and your Lover." Some critics, presumably not recognizing the biblical precedent, were critical of this breach of nunly decorum, and the poem was not included in *Selected Poems* (1939). In her later published work M. returned to the ascetic restraint of her first volume.

WORKS: *Knights Errant, and Other Poems* (1923). *Chaucer's Nuns, and Other Essays* (1925). *Pearl—A Study in Spiritual Dryness* (1925). *Penelope, and Other Poems* (1927). *A Question of Lovers, and Other Poems* (1935). *The Happy Christmas Wind, and Other Poems* (1936). *Christmas Eve, and Other Poems* (1938). *Gates, and Other Poems* (1938). *Selected Poems* (1939). *Four Girls, and Other Poems* (1941). *Addressed to Youth* (1944). *A Song of Bedlam Inn, and Other Poems* (1946). *Collected Poems* (1947). *A Lost Language, and Other Essays on Chaucer* (1951). *American Twelfth Night, and Other Poems* (1955). *The Four Last Things* (1959). *My First Seventy Years* (1959). *Conversations with Cassandra* (1961). *A Child Asks for a Star* (1964).

BIBLIOGRAPHY: For articles in reference works, see: *CB* (1942; 1964). *NCAB*, 51. *20thCA. 20thCAS.*

Other references: *America* (57, 1937; 58, 1938). *Catholic Library World* (12, 1940). *Commonweal* (63, 1956). *Spirit* (6, 1939; 15, 1948). *Thought* (23, 1948).

ARLENE ANDERSON SWIDLER

Dolley Payne Todd Madison

B. *20 May 1768, New Garden, North Carolina; d. 12 July 1849, Washington, D.C.*
D. *of John and Mary Coles Payne; m. John Todd, 1790; m. James Madison, 1794*

M. grew up on a plantation in a Quaker community in Hanover County, Virginia. She went to the local school with her brothers until the family moved to Philadelphia in 1783. Having freed his slaves in 1779, John Payne suffered financially, and M. did well to marry a Quaker lawyer.

Todd and their youngest child died of yellow fever in 1793; although taken ill, M. survived.

M. settled with her second husband, Madison, on his family estate in Montpelier, Virginia, where she lived until Madison became Secretary of State under Jefferson in 1801. Since the President was a widower whose own daughters were seldom available, M. served as hostess at the White House (a name she coined) during the eight years of Jefferson's administration. M. formally assumed the title "First Lady" when her husband succeeded his friend in 1809.

Renowned as a hostess, M. combined social power with impeccable gentility. She well deserves her reputation as a courageous, independent woman; during the War of 1812, she remained a force of diplomatic calm, even saving Gilbert Stuart's portrait of George Washington during the burning of the Capitol in 1814. She again settled at Montpelier when her husband left public life in early 1817; in 1837, a year after Madison's death, she returned to Washington, where she reassumed her position of social influence with grace and good sense. She personally knew all twelve presidents from Washington through Taylor.

M.'s letters are firmly within the American tradition of "private" writings not intended for publication. Focusing on household matters, fashion, social commitments, and the health of her immediate relations, her letters reveal neither the personal self nor accounts of matters of public moment. The letters do, however, suggest M.'s characteristic prudence, modesty, and loyalty—her 18th-c. sense of decorum. Thus, she writes, in 1809, "it is one of my sources of happiness, never to desire a knowledge of other people's business" and, in 1834, "our sex are ever losers when they stem the torrent of public opinion." In the same vein, M. criticizes Cooper as "too melodramatic" and "too emphatic about the horrible." M.'s passing remark to her sister, "You have heard no doubt, of the terrible duel and death of poor Hamilton," seems particularly remarkable when one realizes that Aaron Burr was not only Vice President under Jefferson but was once M.'s suitor.

M. was a significant figure to the men and women of her own time. She was also a woman privileged in her position, influence, and personal advantages—even in her long, happy marriage to a man who realized that "the saddest slavery of all was that of conscientious southern women." Although her letters seldom reveal her influence and prominence, they deserve more attention than they have recently received. It is unfortunate that Clark's edition is incomplete and his commentary cryptic and confusing.

WORKS: *Life and Letters of Dolley Madison* (Ed. A. C. Clark, 1914).

The papers of Dolley Madison are at the Library of Congress, at the University of Virginia Library, and in the Miscellaneous Collection of the District of Columbia Library.

BIBLIOGRAPHY: Anthony, K., *Dolley Madison: Her Life and Times* (1949). Barnard, E. K., *Dorothy Payne, Quakeress: A Sidelight upon the Career of Dolley Madison* (1909). Brant, I., *James Madison* (1941–1961). Cutts, L. B., *Dolley Madison: Memoirs and Letters of Dolley Madison* (1886). Dean, E. L., *Dolley Madison: The Nation's Hostess* (1928). Gerson, N. B., *The Velvet Glove: A Life of Dolley Madison* (1975). Goodwin, W., *Dolley Madison* (1896).

For articles in reference works, see: *AW. NAW* (article by I. Brant). *NCAB*, 5.

CAROLINE ZILBOORG

Theresa Serber Malkiel

B. 1 May 1874, Bar, Russia; d. 17 Nov. 1949, New York City
M. Leon A. Malkiel, 1900

M. emigrated to the U.S. with her family in 1891. Her political activity began when she became a member of the Russian Workingmen's Club. In 1892, she helped organize the Woman's Infant Cloak Maker's Union, was elected its first president, and served as its delegate to the Knights of Labor. In 1893, she joined the Socialist Labor Party and was a delegate to the first convention of the Socialist Trade and Labor Alliance in New York City. M. split from the Socialist Labor Party in 1899 and joined the Socialist Party, in which she continued to be active for many years. M.'s interest in the relationship between feminism and socialism became central to her political work in 1907 when she helped organize the Women's Progressive Society of Yonkers, New York. When a vacancy occurred in the National Woman's Committee, she was elected a member by the national committee of the Socialist Party.

In addition to extensive labor-union organizing throughout the northeast and midwest, M. was an ardent champion of "women's issues." She wrote of the coming "free woman," whose goals could be realized only within the framework of a socialist future. Similarly, M. disagreed with party members who claimed that feminism detracted from the class struggle; to M., the woman question was an important key to the emancipation of all humanity. Throughout her career, M. wrote extensively in such party-affiliated journals as *Socialist Woman, Progressive Woman,* and *Coming Nation* and such periodicals as New York *Call,* Chicago *Daily Socialist,* and *Daily Forward* (New York). She also edited a woman's column in the *Jewish Daily News* (New York).

Both *Woman of Yesterday and Today* (1915) and *Woman and Freedom* (1915) vigorously argue the implicit relationship and politically necessary connection between feminist and socialist goals. Both works establish the historical connections between the women's rights movement and the entrance of women into the wage-earning labor force. In *Woman of Yesterday and Today,* M. writes a brief history of the changing economic status of American women since the revolutionary war, focusing on how working conditions and experiences create a new self-definition for women and a concomitant desire for expanded rights. In *Woman and Freedom,* M. links this new consciousness with the history of political advancement of all working people. M. also underscores the double oppression of the working woman: "Under the present system the working man has only one master—his employer, the workingwoman must bow to the will of husband as well." Both pamphlets stress the importance of a direct and personal involvement in political activity on the part of American women: "She who would be free must herself strike the blow."

In *Diary of a Shirtwaist Striker* (1910), a fictionalized account of the New York shirtwaist maker's strike, M. dramatizes both the obstacles faced and the triumphs attained through direct and personal political activism. Written from the point of view of a native-born American woman who works not for survival but for extra money, the novel depicts the heroine's conversion, first to the immediate goals of the strike and eventually to the wider goals of the Socialist Party. It provides an excellent introduction to many of the problems that were central to the unionization of women during the early years of the 20th c.: the tensions between native and immigrant workers, the hostility of male trade unions, the class bias of the Women's Trade Union League, and the questions about "woman's place" raised by parents and lovers when their daughters and fiancées were on picket lines. M.'s main focus is on the self-respect, comradeship, and capabilities that develop among young women as a result of their strike experiences. Her heroine becomes a vividly portrayed mouthpiece for M.'s vision of the woman of the future, a woman for whom the goals of feminism and socialism have become inseparable.

The resurgence of attention paid to the connection between issues of sex and class has generated a new interest in M.'s writings. Her tireless investigation of the relationship between a woman's personal and political self-definition will strike many readers as surprisingly modern. *Diary of a Shirtwaist Striker* should prove of invaluable interest to any reader interested in questions about the relationship between social movements and literary representation.

WORKS: *Diary of a Shirtwaist Striker* (1910). *Woman and Freedom* (1915). *Woman of Yesterday and Today* (1915).

BIBLIOGRAPHY: Blake, F., *The Strike in the American Novel* (1972). Buhle, M. J., "Feminism and Socialism in the United States, 1820–1920" (Ph.D. diss., Univ. of Wisconsin, 1974). Dancis, B., "Socialism and Women in the United States, 1900–1917," in *Socialist Revolution* (1976). Hill, V., "Strategy and Breadth: The Socialist-Feminist in American Fiction" (Ph.D. diss., SUNY at Buffalo, 1979). Maglin, N., "Rebel Women Writers, 1894–1925" (Ph.D. diss., Union Graduate School, 1975).

Other references: *Progressive Woman* (May 1909).

VICKI LYNN HILL

Marya Mannes

B. 14 Nov. 1904, New York City
Writes under: Marya Mannes, Sec.
D. of David and Clara Damrosch Mannes; m. Jo Mielziner, 1926;
   m. Richard Blow, 1936; m. Christopher Clarkson, 1948

M. spent her childhood in New York City, where she was privately educated. Along with her parents, a violinist and a pianist, the founders of the Mannes College of Music, and her brother Leopold, co-inventor of the Kodachrome process, M. spent many vacations in Europe; upon her graduation in 1923, she spent a year in England independently studying sculpture and writing. After returning to the U.S., M. worked as a playwright, editor for *Vogue* and *Mademoiselle*, and cultural commentator for the *Reporter*, *McCall's*, the *New York Times*, *Harper's*, and

The New Republic. During World War II, she worked for the OSS and was based briefly in Portugal and Spain. M. has been married and divorced three times. She had one son during her second marriage.

In her first published novel, *Message from a Stranger* (1948), M. explored the notion that the dead resume their conscious identities when the living remember and think about them. The story is narrated by poetess Olivia Baird, the leading character, who dies on the second page of the novel and yet continues to "live" in the minds of her lover, husband, and children, so that she eventually achieves self-understanding.

M.'s first book of essays, *More in Anger* (1958), collected her social criticism previously published in the *Reporter.* M. observes that she is "angry with the progressive blurring of American values, the sapping of American strength, the withering of American courage." Specifically, she attacks the mass media, the advertising establishment, and the "Never-Never Land of the 1950's."

M.'s next published work was, according to her, a "long deep look at the city I loved and hated," *The New York I Know* (1959). *But Will It Sell?* (1964) was another collection of social criticism, exploring the invasion of "the government of money" in every sector of our lives. It contains four essays that outline M.'s opinions on the proper egalitarian relationship between men and women. She also attacks contemporary violence, pop art, and commercial television.

M.'s second novel, *They* (1968), depicts the final days of a group of elderly people ostracized by the new youth-dominated culture. Less a futuristic novel than an opportunity for social criticism, *They* condemns modern music, art, and literature while celebrating the "lost world—the long-discredited 'values' of humanism." These values, according to the main characters, are "Discipline, Grace, and Responsibility"—all qualities that M. feels are missing from modern society.

M.'s autobiography, *Out of My Time* (1971), charts the major events in her life as well as her thoughts on woman's role and quest for identity in a male-dominated society. The major theme is the belief in "spiritual hermaphroditism"—the notion that human beings contain both masculine and feminine qualities that must be accepted and balanced in their personalities.

M.'s most recent work, *Last Rights* (1974), expresses her support for euthanasia and her plea for laws to ensure a dignified death for all.

In 1959, M. published a collection of politically satirical poems, *Subverse: Rhymes for Our Times*, originally published in the *Reporter* under the pseudonym of "Sec." The poems attack the materialism of American society, environmental pollution, television inanities, the medical establishment, politicians, and militaristic imperialism.

M.'s writings have received mixed reviews, and she assesses herself as somewhat of a misfit: "Professionally I appear to fall uneasily between the writers who succeed because they appeal to the mass audience and those who succeed because they appeal to a superior intellectual elite. The big magazines find me too special and controversial to handle, and the critical literary fraternity find me too explicit to be important." This perceptive self-assessment helps explain M.'s minor stature among contemporary essayists and novelists.

WORKS: *Message from a Stranger* (1948). *More in Anger* (1958). *The New York I Know* (1959). *Subverse: Rhymes for Our Times* (1959). *But Will It Sell?* (1964). *They* (1968). *Out of My Time* (1971). *Last Rights* (1974).

BIBLIOGRAPHY: For articles in reference works, see: *CA*, 1–4 (1967). *CB* (1959). *WA*.

DIANE LONG HOEVELER

Marie Manning

B. 22 Jan. 1873, Washington, D.C.; d. 28 Nov. 1945, Washington, D.C.
Wrote under: Beatrice Fairfax, Marie Manning
D. of Michael Charles and Elizabeth Barrett Manning; m. Herman
   Edward Gasch, 1905

The daughter of distinguished English parents, M. was educated in private schools in New York City and London but grew so alarmingly tall and gangling in her teens that her father sent her to a western ranch to build strength and poise. This ranch was later to provide the setting for her most successful novel.

M. started in 1893 as a cub reporter for the New York *World* and by 1897 was working for the more prestigious New York *Evening Journal*, where her famous advice column, "Beatrice Fairfax," first appeared in 1898. The column gained immediate success throughout New York State and soon became a national catchword.

In 1905, M. left a thriving career to marry a real estate dealer and raise their two sons. For nearly twenty-five years M. devoted herself to her family, although she remained active in fighting for women's rights. For financial reasons M. resumed her still-popular column in 1929, and later also worked for International News Service.

M.'s first literary work, a romantic adventure novel, *Lord Alingham, Bankrupt* (1902), was a commercial and critical failure, but her second novel, *Judith of the Plains* (1903), fared better, going into two printings and receiving serious praise from reviewers. Here M. creates a strong heroine, Judith Rodney. The story, set in a Wyoming desert that "lies white and palpitating beneath the noonday glare," follows Judith's battle to save her brother from an unjust death sentence, as well as her courage and fire. At one point, Judith wonders whether in marriage "women were dogs, that men should play with them in idle moods, caress them, and then fling them out for other toys." Only when she knows she is in control of her own life does Judith accept an offer of marriage from the man she loves. The book presents a strong, clear picture of an idealized woman and perceptive descriptions of both characters and setting.

Problems of Love and Marriage (1931) and *Personal Reply* (1943) are collections of letters and answers compiled from M.'s "Beatrice Fairfax" column. The pre-Depression letters deal largely with the love dilemmas of young girls, whereas the post-Depression correspondence comes from men and women who are either contemplating divorce or having affairs. M.'s advice was generally to dry your eyes, roll up your sleeves, believe in yourself, and "dig for a practical solution."

Ladies Now and Then (1944), M.'s autobiography, concentrates on her early days as reporter and columnist for the *Evening Journal* and tells little of her personal life. It provides insight into the struggles and sacrifices of all women journalists who were at that time trying to break out of the "latest society divorce scandal" and into the real world of serious reporting. There are many tongue-in-cheek accounts of M.'s interviews with celebrities from William Jennings Bryan to Eleanor Roosevelt. M. ends her life study reflectively, saying that "as an inconspicuous private who helped to fight the good fight for women" she feels a glow of pride whenever she reads of any woman's accomplishment.

Although most of M.'s work is mediocre as literature, she tried, within the limits of popular fiction, to create women who were strong, sometimes unconventional, and yet beloved.

WORKS: Lord Alingham, Bankrupt (1902). Judith of the Plains (1903). Problems of Love and Marriage (1931). Personal Reply (1943). Ladies Now and Then (1944).

BIBLIOGRAPHY: Ross, I., *Ladies of the Press: The Story of Women in Journalism by an Insider* (1974).
For articles in reference works, see: *CB* (Jan. 1946). *NAW* (article unsigned).
Other references: *NYT* (30 Nov. 1945).

WENDY J. HENNING

Blanche McManus Mansfield

B. *1869 or 1870, East Feliciana, Louisiana*
Wrote under: Blanche McManus, Blanche McManus Mansfield
M. *Milburg Francisco Mansfield, 1898*

M. was educated in New Orleans and studied art in Paris. An illustrator of books and periodicals as well as a writer, M. was published in *The Boys' and Girls' Journal* and *St. Nicholas Magazine;* a dozen color illustrations were commissioned for Rudyard Kipling's *Ballad of East and West* (1899). M. married an author in 1898, moved to New York City, and later lived abroad. Her last address was listed as 9 Rue Falguiere, Paris (1945).

M. specialized in travel books for children and for adults, particularly women. She wrote and illustrated eight of the fifty titles in the "Little Cousin" series published between 1905 and 1911. One of the first examples of informational literature for children, the series was designed to introduce American middle-class children to geography and history by identifying with children in other parts of the world. Well-written and illustrated with drawings and photographs, M.'s "Little Cousin" books emphasized food, dress, and customs as well as manners. They were also a child's travelogues that described selected tourist attractions of each country.

M.'s adult travel books include *Romantic Ireland* written with M. F. Mansfield (1904) and *The American Woman Abroad* (1911). *Romantic Ireland* is more ambitious than a travel book: It discusses 19th- and 20th-c. Irish literature and the accomplishments of the Gaelic League, considers social problems like emigration and the want of industry, and suggests a policy of reconciliation with England.

The American Woman Abroad offers advice on a range of topics involving life abroad: cost, servants, foreign marketing and shopping, women traveling alone, and social conventions. It is of interest to the social historian studying Americans abroad or middle-class European social life before World War I. The advice is practical and realistic. The book concludes with M.'s description of three housekeeping experiences: in a cottage in Kent, in a country house in Normandy, and in a villa on the Mediterranean.

M.'s work as an illustrator influenced her work as a writer; her prose, like her excellent draftsmanship, is clear, economical, and attentive to detail. Although her travel books are not limited to landscape, M.'s painter's eye is responsible for their pictorial quality. Her insights into other cultures reflect a thorough familiarity with the people among whom she lived and wrote.

WORKS: *The Voyages of the Mayflower* (1897). *Bachelor Ballads* (1898). *Romantic Ireland* (with M. F. Mansfield, 1904). *Our Little English Cousin* (1905). *Our Little French Cousin* (1905). *Our Little Dutch Cousin* (1906). *Our Little Scotch Cousin* (1906). *Our Little Arabian Cousin* (1907). *Our Little Hindu Cousin* (1907). *Our Little Egyptian Cousin* (1908). *The American Woman Abroad* (1911). *Our Little Belgian Cousin* (1911).

BIBLIOGRAPHY: For articles in reference works, see: *Biographical Dictionary of Southern Authors*, Ed. L. Knight (1978). *Childhood in Poetry*, Ed. J. M. Shaw, (1967). *Dictionary of American Painters, Sculptors, and Engravers from Colonial Times through 1926*, Ed. M. Fielding (1960).

MAUREEN MURPHY

Jeannette Augustus Marks

B. 16 Aug. 1875, Chattanooga, Tennessee; d. 15 March 1964, Westport, New York
Wrote under: Jeannette Marks
D. of William Dennis and Jeannette Holmes Colwell Marks

M.'s father was president of the Edison Electric Light Company and a professor at the University of Pennsylvania. M. studied in Dresden,

Germany, and spent several summers in Wales before entering Wellesley College, Massachusetts, where she earned a B.A. in 1900 and an M.A. in 1903. M. did postgraduate research in English literature at the Bodleian Library and the British Museum. For thirty-eight years M. taught poetry and drama courses at Mt. Holyoke College, Massachusetts, and she was chairwoman of its English department from 1921 to 1939.

M.'s love of nature and outdoor activity provided the impetus for several early books, such as *Little Busybodies* (1910) and *Holiday with the Birds* (1911), both of which offered children "a wholesome sugar-coating to a goodly array of scientific facts." The love of nature that inspired *Vacation Camping for Girls* (1913) also pervaded the poetry she published in numerous national magazines and in the collection *Widow Pollen* (1921). The romantic sincerity of these saccharine and technically clumsy poems is exemplified by the concluding lines of her long poem "Calendar": "I say the sun is a bee, a big bee, a burning bee, / I *know*!" Other poems, like the four-line "Work," are still more personal: "I told my heart that work must be / The only aim of life for me. / But oh! my heart cried, "Love, love, love!" / And wept bitterly."

Drawing upon the knowledge of Welsh peasant life she had gained while hiking in northern Wales, M. published a collection of stories, *Through Welsh Doorways*, in 1909. Encouraged by playwright Edward Knoblock to try her hand at dramatizing them, M. wrote her first three one-act plays. *The Merry Merry Cuckoo* is a simple dramatic statement about married love that has endured into old age. The husband, David, is dying, but he longs to hear once more the song of the cuckoo. Since it is too early for the cuckoo, his wife, Annie, practices its song and, despite the pastor's and the neighbors' admonitions against deceit, gives him his last happiness. *The Deacon's Hat* is a comedy in which a young woman, suspecting that the deacon has been helping himself to the groceries in her shop, forces him to sit by her fire until the butter he has hidden under his tall Welsh beaver hat begins to melt down onto his face. In *Welsh Honeymoon*, local folklore and superstition play a part in the reconciliation of a quarrelsome middle-aged married couple.

Without M.'s knowledge an acquaintance submitted two of the plays to the 1911 Welsh National Theatre competition. Although the prize had been planned for a full-length play, M.'s one-act plays were awarded first place. They were published in *Three Welsh Plays* (1917) and were also included in a later collection, *The Merry Merry Cuckoo, and Other Welsh Plays* (1927), along with four new one-act sketches: *A Tress of*

Hair, Love Letters, Steppin' Westward, and *Look to the End.* M.'s plays were frequently produced by little theater groups and colleges in the U.S. and Great Britain. M. also gave readings of them for literary and social clubs.

The Sun Chaser (1922), a full-length play, is set in an American frontier village near the Canadian border. The title character had once been a fine young man, a good husband and father. But the grasping village storekeeper has encouraged his weakness for drink to the point where he has lost all sense of responsibility and is obsessed with running after the setting sun each evening. The play builds in bathos until his devoted little daughter, attempting to bring him food, freezes to death in a Christmas-eve blizzard. M.'s motive in writing *The Sun Chaser* may be inferred from her next work, *Genius and Disaster* (1926), a critical examination of the effects of alcohol, opium, and laudanum on the writing of Poe, Coleridge, Swinburne, De Quincey, James Thomson, and Francis Thompson. The work contains some interesting passages of literary analysis, but it is largely unfocused and marred by florid rhetoric and sweeping generalizations.

Thirteen Days (1929) is about the Sacco-Vanzetti trial. *The Family of the Barrett* (1938) is a genealogical study of Elizabeth Barrett Browning. In 1928, M. founded the Laboratory Theatre in Connecticut, and she was its director until 1941. From 1942 to 1947 she was chairwoman of the New York State branch of the National Women's Party.

M. was an outstanding educator and a prolific writer of scholarly criticism, plays, short fiction, poetry, and books for children. Her best works are her one-act plays, which capture the quaint charm of Welsh character and customs.

WORKS: *The Cheerful Cricket* (1907). *The English Pastoral Drama* (1908). *Through Welsh Doorways* (1909). *Little Busybodies: The Life of Crickets, Ants, Bees, Beetles, and Other Busybodies* (with J. Moody, 1910). *The End of a Song* (1911). *Girl's Student Days and After* (1911). *Holiday with the Birds: Their Plumage, Their Song, Nesting, and Daily Habits* (with J. Moody, 1911). *Gallant Little Wales* (1912). *Leviathan* (1913). *Vacation Camping for Girls* (1913). *Yellow Curtains* (1913). *Pandy Post* (1914). *The Doctor* (1915). *Early English Hero Tales* (1915). *Baronet and the Baby* (1916). *Glow Man* (1916). *Three Welsh Plays* (1917). *Children in the Wood Stories* (1919). *Courage* (1919). *Madame France* (1919). *Goeffrey's Window* (1921). *Widow Pollen* (1921). *The Sun Chaser* (1922). *Genius and Disaster: Studies in Drugs and Genius* (1926). *The Merry Merry Cuckoo, and Other Welsh Plays* (1927). *Thirteen Days* (1929). *The Family of the Barrett* (1938). *The Life and Letters of Mary Emma Woolley* (1955).

BIBLIOGRAPHY: Mayorga, M., *Representative Plays by American Authors* (1920).
    For articles in reference works, see: *NCAB*, B. *20thCA*. *20thCAS*.
                                                    FELICIA HARDISON LONDRÉ

Helen Marot

B. 9 June 1865, Philadelphia, Pennsylvania; d. 3 June 1940, New York City
D. of Charles Henry and Hannah Griscom Marot

M. was raised in an old, established Quaker family and educated in Friend's schools in Philadelphia. She worked as a librarian from 1893 to 1899. In 1899, she served as an investigator for the U.S. Industrial Commission and was profoundly moved by the conditions of child and female labor, a concern that made her an activist. She became an investigator for various social-reform groups and also served as executive secretary of the Women's Trade Union League (WTUL) from 1906 to 1913. M. organized working women into trade unions and was herself a member of the Bookkeepers, Stenographers, and Accountants Union of New York. M. resigned from the WTUL in 1913, partly because she felt that working women were not adequately represented in the League's administration. For the next six years, she wrote and edited two books and several journals. She served on the editorial boards of the *Masses* (1916–17) and the *Dial* (1918–19). M. retired in 1920 and spent the next years in either Greenwich Village or West Becket, Massachusetts, where she summered with her close friend and sister reformer Caroline Pratt.

M.'s first book, *A Handbook of Labor Literature* (1899), is an annotated bibliography. The thirty-two topics that M. selected, dealing with cultural, political, and philosophical questions, provide a clue to her broadly based conceptualization of the labor movement.

The themes of feminism, socialism, and liberal reform that were foreshadowed in schematic form in M.'s first book are expounded fully in *American Labor Unions* (1914). M. viewed the trade union as an expression of worker autonomy and independence even from well-intentioned reformers. "The reform movement," M. asserted, "is not co-extensive with democracy but with bureaucracy. The labor unions are group efforts in the direction of democracy." She dismissed the charge of discrimination against women by unions as "hypothetical." Women's problems in industry were rooted in society's casting of women in a primarily domestic role. Yet, M. did admit that women were discouraged from seeking leadership positions within unions.

The Creative Impulse in Industry: A Proposition for Educators (1918) is dedicated to M.'s friend Caroline Pratt. It reflects Pratt's and John Dewey's views on educational reform as well as M.'s own program for industrial reform. She insisted that industry must be an extension of education. Thus, creative people will be attracted to it, and the motive for working will be this creative impulse rather than the possessive instinct. M. condemned both state socialism and scientific management.

M.'s concerns in the articles she wrote for the *Masses*, the *Dial*, and other periodicals echoed the themes articulated in her books. Although expository in form and didactic in style, M.'s writings provide us with an excellent example of the crosscurrents of feminism, socialism, and liberal reform which enlivened the progressive era.

WORKS: *A Handbook of Labor Literature: A Classified and Annotated List of the More Important Books and Pamphlets in the English Language* (1899). *American Labor Unions* (1914). *The Creative Impulse in Industry: A Proposition for Educators* (1918).

BIBLIOGRAPHY: Boone, G., *The Women's Trade Union League in Great Britain and the U.S.A.* (1942). Hall, F. S., *Forty Years, 1902–42: The Work of the New York Child Labor Commission* (1943). Pratt, C., *I Learn from Children* (1948).

For articles in reference works, see: *NAW* (article by S. Cohen).

Other references: *Dial* (19 Sept. 1918).

ANN SCHOFIELD

Catherine Marshall

B. *27 Sept. 1914, Johnson City, Tennessee*
D. *of John Ambrose and Leonora Whitaker Wood; m. Peter Marshall, 1936; m. Leonard Earle LeSourd, 1959*

M.'s father was a pastor of a Presbyterian church in Canton, Mississippi, and later in Keyser, West Virginia. M. earned a B.A. in history from

Agnes Scott College. Her first husband was already a well-known pastor in Atlanta when they were married. In 1937, they moved to the New York Avenue Church in Washington, D.C., and in 1946 Peter became chaplain of the U.S. Senate. After her husband's death in 1949, M. became an editor and writer in order to support herself and her son. Her second husband was editor of *Guideposts,* an inspirational magazine that has published many of M.'s shorter articles. M. was woman's editor of the *Christian Herald* from 1958 to 1960, when she became a roving editor for *Guideposts.*

In 1953, M. was named "Woman of the Year" in the field of literature by the Women's National Press Club. She is a member of Phi Beta Kappa, has served Agnes Scott College as a trustee, and has received honorary doctorates from Cedar Crest College and Taylor University.

M.'s first independent work was editing a few of Marshall's sermons and prayers, which were published as *Mr. Jones, Meet the Master* (1949). *Mr. Jones* stayed on the nonfiction best-seller list for almost a year and led to the contract for her most important work, *A Man Called Peter* (1951), a bestseller for many years.

A Man Called Peter has been categorized as "a biography, an auto-biography-biography, a fairy story with a sad ending, a Horatio Alger novel, a how-to book on successful marriage, and a straight-from-the-shoulder devotional on God." Whatever its genre, this book sold over four million copies during its first twenty years and is still selling well. With M. assisting in production, it was made into a successful movie (1955), and it has been translated into Dutch, printed in a large-print edition, and recorded for the blind.

This "autobiography-biography" is, of course, the story of Peter Marshall, the Scotsman who grew up in poverty, emigrated to America, and became one of the most widely admired preachers of the 20th c. The prose is clear, concise, concrete; and the book is saved from excessive sentiment by its simple sincerity, honesty, and forthrightness.

M.'s novel, *Christy* (1967), features a protagonist whose fortitude grows from her faith, much as Marshall's does in *A Man Called Peter.* Based on the experiences of the author's mother, *Christy* is the story of a nineteen-year-old woman who, in 1912, leaves her comfortable home to spend a year teaching in the Smoky Mountains of Tennessee. The clear style and obvious sincerity that mark all of M.'s works enable this long novel to maintain its charm, even though it sometimes moves very slowly.

M. has also written or edited fourteen other book-length works, including several children's books, and many articles for popular and religious magazines. Her latest publication, *The Helper* (1978), is a series of forty devotionals about the Holy Spirit, which M. says "has been written out of my own spiritual need to speak to those who share my longing for thirst-quenching quaffs of the Living Water." Probably everything M. has ever published could be prefaced by those words.

WORKS: *The Mystery of the Ages* (with P. Marshall, 1944). *Mr. Jones, Meet the Master: Sermons and Prayers of Peter Marshall, D.D.* (edited by Marshall, 1949; rev. ed., 1950). *A Man Called Peter: The Story of Peter Marshall* (1951; film version, 1955). *Let's Keep Christmas* by P. Marshall (introduction by Marshall, 1953). *God Loves You: Our Family's Favorite Stories and Prayers* (with P. Marshall, 1953; rev. ed., 1967). *The Prayers of Peter Marshall* (edited by Marshall, 1954). *Friends with God: Stories and Prayers of the Marshall Family* (1956). *The Heart of Peter Marshall's Faith: Two Inspirational Messages from "Mr. Jones, Meet the Master"* (introduction by Marshall, 1956). *To Live Again* (1957). *The First Easter* (by P. Marshall, edited and introduction by Marshall, 1959). *John Doe, Disciple: Sermons for the Young in Spirit* (by P. Marshall, edited and introduction by Marshall, 1963). *Beyond Ourselves* (1966). *Christy* (1967). *Claiming God's Promises: Selections from "Guideposts" by Catherine Marshall and Others* (1973). *Something More: In Search of a Deeper Faith* (1974). *Adventures in Prayer* (1975). *The Helper* (with P. Marshall, 1978).

BIBLIOGRAPHY: Davis, E. L., *Fathers of America: Our Heritage of Faith* (1958). Hosier, H. K., *Profiles: People Who Are Helping to Change the World* (1977).

For articles in reference works, see: *CA* (1976). *Something about the Author*, Ed. A. Commire (1971).

Other references: *Newsweek* (4 April 1956). *PW* (18 Oct. 1971). *SatR* (10 April 1954).

PEGGY SKAGGS

Paule Marshall

B. 9 April 1929, Brooklyn, New York
D. of Samuel and Ada Burke; m. Kenneth E. Marshall, 1957; m. Nourry Menard, 1970

A first-generation American born of Barbadian parents, M. spent her childhood in Brooklyn. At the age of nine, she visited the native land of her parents and discovered for herself the quality of life peculiar to that tropical island. After writing a series of poems reflecting her impressions, M. began a long period of reading. She graduated Phi Beta Kappa from Brooklyn College (1953) and attended Hunter College (1955) for postgraduate study.

M. has worked in libraries and, as a staff writer for *Our World* magazine, has traveled on assignment to Brazil and the West Indies. She has lectured at several colleges and universities within the U.S. and abroad and has contributed short stories and articles to various magazines and anthologies. M. has been the recipient of several awards and grants.

In her first novel, *Brown Girl, Brownstones* (1959), M. explores the coming of age of Selina Boyce and the struggle for survival of a black immigrant family and community. Divided into four sections, the novel functions on several imaginative levels and devotes some attention to the ramifications of power as experienced by the dawning political consciousness of a small black community.

The plot revolves around Selina's growth and awareness as she watches her parents and others devise plans to acquire property. Conflicting attitudes and personalities change the central question of where to live to the more penetrating question of how to live. We are hurled into a world of violence, turmoil, mechanization, and sameness. As the tensions are resolved, the young heroine travels to the homeland of her parents, searching for a more humanistically oriented way of life. Her "return" symbolizes a rehabilitation of her spirit and psyche, and represents the acknowledgment of historical roots essential to her identity.

M.'s consistent use of imagery and symbolism, and her concise, rhythmic, and passionate style dramatically define and technically underscore themes of rebirth and self-definition. The end result is a picture of a world not blurred by racial bitterness, but sharply focused in its unabashed honesty and deliberate confrontation of Western cultural values.

Her language is strikingly beautiful and powerfully effective, capturing the essence of black language as a weapon of survival and revealing how spoken communication can itself be a form of art. M. adopts and adapts the West Indian dialect, fusing it with biblical and literary allusions to create a language that compels imaginative associations and entertains with the sheer delight of sound.

Soul Clap Hands and Sing (1961), a collection of short stories, borows its title from Yeats's "Sailing to Byzantium." Thematic connections are obvious as we read the accounts of four men of different national origins experiencing the inevitable decline of age.

Caught up in the Western credo of amassing wealth and prestige, the characters have developed a hardened exterior impervious to meaningful human relationships. When the submerged need for love and acceptance emerges, they can only respond by reaching out to the young. That itself remains a selfish motivation, and the implications of their wasted lives are recognized too late. Unable to translate harsh reality into lyrical song, their dying moments sound the notes of lamentation and doom, as Marcia Keiz observes in *Negro American Literature Forum.*

The Chosen Place, the Timeless People (1969) is a massive epic novel recapitulating and expanding upon themes developed in earlier works. The main story line concerns a small group of Americans who travel to the Caribbean island of Bournehills. Sponsored by a philanthropic foundation, they intend to design a project to assist an "underdeveloped" but curiously unified people. Juxtapositions and correspondences give the novel its texture, but the cohesive element is achieved through the paradoxical characterization of the native woman Merle Kinbona. With her, we explore the political, sociological, and psychological dimensions of power not only as it influences racial and sexual roles, but also as it shapes cultural patterns and assumptions.

Never sacrificing art to propaganda, M. sustains full human portraiture within a racially turgid atmosphere and concludes with the vision of a world not solely defined by territorial boundaries or even by cultural distinctions.

M. has exceptional talent born of solid scholarship and careful craftsmanship. By choosing to depict West Indian-American culture, M. makes a valuable contribution toward helping contemporary society understand the multidimensional aspects of the black experience.

WORKS: Brown Girl, Brownstones (1959; dramatization by CBS Television Workshop, 1960). *Soul Clap Hands and Sing* (1961). *The Chosen Place, the Timeless People* (1969).

BIBLIOGRAPHY: For articles in reference works, see: *Black American Writers Past and Present,* T. Rush, C. Myers, and E. Arata (1975). *Contemporary Novelists,* Ed. J. Vinson (1976).

Other references: *CLAJ* 16 (1972). *Encore American and Worldwide News* (23 June 1975). *Journal of Black Studies* 1 (1970). *Negro American Literature Forum* 9 (1975). Trinidad *Guardian* (12 Sept. 1962).

DOROTHY L. DENNISTON

Del Martin

B. 5 May 1921, San Francisco, California

A feminist and lesbian activist since the 1950s, M. studied at Berkeley and San Francisco State, majoring in journalism. She married, had one daughter, and divorced before meeting Phyllis Lyon, her partner since 1953. M.'s pioneering activities in the gay and feminist movements are numerous. In 1955, with Lyon and a few friends, M. founded the Daughters of Bilitis (DOB), one of the first international lesbian organizations, and its publication, *The Ladder*. M. became associated with various church groups in an educational capacity. In 1965, she became secretary of the Council on Religion and the Homosexual and served on the Joint Committee on Homosexuality appointed by Bishop Pike. M. is also a cofounder of Lesbian Mothers and Friends (1971).

M. has been a visible lesbian leader in the feminist movement since its resurgence in the sixties. She was secretary of one of the first chapters of the National Organization for Women (NOW), served on the national board of directors, and has been coordinator of NOW's National Task Force on Battered Women/Household Violence since 1975.

M.'s first two books, *Lesbian/Woman* (1972) and *Lesbian Love and Liberation* (1973), were both written with Phyllis Lyon. They were among the first nonfiction books about lesbianism written by lesbians. *Lesbian/Woman* demonstrates the special problems, myths, and realities of lesbians by presenting cases and life-styles. The topics include lesbian mothers, growing up gay, lesbian sexuality, the interrelationship between lesbianism and feminism, and the negative effect of religion and mental-health establishments upon lesbian self-images. The book is unselfconscious, straightforward, and sensitive in style. It is not well documented, but the authors clearly intended it to be a subjective work and to encourage consciousness-raising. It was written mainly for educators and to help professionals and parents of gays.

M.'s most recent work, *Battered Wives* (1977), the first book published on this subject in the U.S., was very influential in initiating what has become the battered-women movement. It is a source book, presenting a historical discussion of societal attitudes promoting domestic violence, which M. believes are exaggerations of traditional sex roles. Several shocking case histories are presented, demonstrating the failure of "helping" and legal institutions to cope with the problem. M. presents practical suggestions for reform in this area, including institutional changes, a guide to the establishment of community refuges, and suggestions for individual action. The interrelation of domestic violence with other feminist issues is discussed. This book has been criticized for giving only a sociological viewpoint and avoiding the idea that intrapersonal interactions may be influencing factors.

M. has spoken on lesbian and feminist topics at universities, medical and law schools, mental health organizations, community workshops, and local women's groups. Her writings and lectures are a direct extension of her social activism. One of her main objectives is to expose problems and educate about women's issues. She hopes that, through consciousness-raising, research will be stimulated and redirected along lines that are more in accordance with real life.

WORKS: Lesbian/Woman (with P. Lyon, 1972). Lesbian Love and Liberation (with P. Lyon, 1973). Battered Wives (1977).

BIBLIOGRAPHY: Association of Humanistic Psychology Newsletter (Jan. 1973). LJ (Aug. 1972). Off Our Backs (Sept. 1972). Psychiatric News (4 March 1977). Psychology of Women Quarterly (Spring 1978). San Francisco Examiner and Chronicle (10 Sept. 1972). SIECUS Report (May 1973). Social Casework (March 1977). Society (Sept. 1977).

PATRICIA E. PENN

George Madden Martin

B. 3 May 1866, Louisville, Kentucky; d. 30 Nov. 1946, Louisville, Kentucky
Given name: Georgia May Madden
D. of Frank and Anne Louise Mckenzie Madden; m. Attwood Reading
   Martin, 1892

M. received most of her education from private tutors. She taught at Wellseley School for two years before her marriage to Martin, who subsequently became a prominent businessman. M. spent her life in Louisville, though she traveled widely.

In the 1890s, M. became an active member of the women's "Author's

Club" of Louisville, along with writers such as Annie Fellows Johnston, Alice Hegan Rice, and her own sister Eva. M.'s career began in 1895 with the publication of the story "Teckla's Lilies" in *Harper's Weekly*. She remained active as a writer well into the 1930s, publishing nine novels, a children's biography of Shakespeare's early years (*A Warwickshire Lad*, 1916), a collection of short stories (*Children in the Mist*, 1920), and a number of short stories.

Like many novels of the period, *The House of Fulfilment* (1904), *Abbie Ann* (1907), and *Letitia: Nursery Corps, U.S. Army* (1907) were first published serially. M.'s career in fiction virtually ended with the publication of the novel *March On* (1921), which reflected her involvement in political and social issues of World War I. Here she specifically focuses on the character of the "new woman" and the role she should play in preventing war. M.'s only subsequent novel, *Made in America* (1935), demonstrates her knowledge of politics and history.

M. served in a number of elected and appointed offices during the 1920s and 1930s. In 1920, she began a fourteen-year term on the board of the Committee on Interracial Cooperation, of which she was a charter member. That same year, M. published *Children in the Mist*, a collection of stories of black life in the South; here she clearly sympathizes with blacks and implicitly castigates whites for keeping them in a subordinate position.

In the 1930s, M. was chairwoman of the Association of Southern Women for the Prevention of Lynching, which objected to mob violence, advocating the solution of the problem of lynching through the abolishment of segregation and economic repression of blacks. However, the position taken by this organization was consistent with M.'s support of states' rights; it advocated an antilynching law that was designed to punish state officers and county governments that failed to prevent lynchings.

In a series of articles for the *Atlantic Monthly* (1924–1925) M. explored her view of the role of the American woman in politics. M. speaks of her personal experience as a woman, yet ironically she continues to use the masculine pseudonym under which she had always published. These articles demonstrate the paradoxes in M.'s political thinking. She was a strong supporter of the rights of blacks, yet consistently advocated strong states' rights. She was not active in the woman-suffrage movement, but urged greater involvement of women in government, chastising them for seeing the centralized federal government as the traditional southern father figure.

Although M. was well known in her day and her books were usually reviewed favorably, her reputation must derive from her limited skill as a novelist. Her fiction is essentially realistic, with accurate details of daily life. Her simple plots are often too easily resolved; she is better with the episodic novel or short story. However, M. confronts realistic social problems ranging from racial prejudice to the failure of the school system to reach the average child.

Unlike her friend Annie Fellows Johnston, M. wrote primarily for adults; yet her greatest achievement is the creation of a child's perspective on life through an adult narrator who supplies the proper distance. Thus, her best-known work is *Emmy Lou: Her Book and Heart* (1902). Emmy Lou's misconceptions and confusions are both delightful and touching; no reader can forget her failure to understand the purpose of learning letters and numbers, or the well-meaning adults who surround her. Although M.'s subjects have limited appeal, her exploration of the emerging role of the "new woman" in realistic novels such as *Selina* (1914), and *March On* is historically significant.

WORKS: *The Angel of the Tenement* (1897). *Emmy Lou: Her Book and Heart* (1902). *The House of Fulfilment* (1904). *Abbie Ann* (1907). *Letitia: Nursery Corps, U.S. Army* (1907). *Selina* (1914). *Emmy Lou's Road to Grace* (1916). *A Warwickshire Lad* (1916). *Children in the Mist* (1920). *March On* (1921). *Made in America* (1935).

BIBLIOGRAPHY: For articles in reference works, see: *LSL. NAW* (article by T. D. Clark). *NCAB*, 33.
    Other references: *Nation* (31 Dec. 1914). *NYT* (3 Oct. 1920). *Outlook* (1 Oct. 1904).

MARTHA E. COOK

Helen Reimensnyder Martin

B. *18 Oct. 1868, Lancaster, Pennsylvania; d. 29 June 1939, New Canaan, Connecticut*
Wrote under: Helen R. Martin, the author of Unchaperoned
D. of Cornelius and Henrietta Thurman Reimensnyder; m. Frederic C. Martin, 1899

Socialist, feminist, and champion of the oppressed, M. was born to an immigrant German clergyman. She attended Swarthmore and Radcliffe

Colleges and taught school in New York City. After her marriage, she lived with her husband in Harrisburg, Pennsylvania, and had two children, a son and a daughter.

In her first published works, M. wrote about society girls trying to make something of themselves, a theme she later returned to. She first met real success with the publication of *Tillie: A Mennonite Maid* (1904); thereafter, most of her books were set in Pennsylvania Dutch communities and depicted the self-improvement campaigns of Pennsylvania Dutch young women. *Tillie* went into many editions and made M. a writer in demand, especially for the women's magazines, where many of her novels were serialized. As a picture of the Pennsylvania Dutch, M.'s novels are informed but very biased, at times melodramatically so. M. was familiar with the colorful manners of her Mennonite, Amish, and other Pennsylvania Dutch neighbors. She created many positive Pennsylvania Dutch characters, especially her heroines, but her most memorable ones are the men: arrogant, mean, illiterate, miserly, and superstitious. Her fathers are usually brutes, while the bumptious youths, brothers or suitors of the heroine, are self-important boors who get what they deserve. M. was criticized for her description of the Pennsylvania Dutch, but she claimed that she got many letters from them which testified to the truth of her portrayals.

M., a feminist, was active as a campaigner for suffrage. All her novels concern the drive for self-improvement, independence, and success of the heroine. She champions votes for women in her pre-1919 novels, but a more prevalent theme is the financial bondage of women. M. was also a socialist, and her works abound in criticism of capitalism, industrialism, and the way in which established churches uphold the status quo. Many of her clergymen are prissy, self-interested hypocrites. Many of the young, reform-minded clergymen have to leave the church over some social issue. M.'s anger often shows in overdramatization bordering on caricature when she portrays those who enslave the female characters.

There is a good deal of repetition in M.'s books. The typical M. heroine is a sensitive, intelligent girl, with a mild manner masking a strong will, who has to make her own way in the world, and the typical plot centers on the girl's fight for survival. Either the girl is an abused Pennsylvania Dutch daughter/sister/stepdaughter/wife who has to fight the Pennsylvania Dutch establishment, or she is a society girl who has to combat her mother or her husband. In the stories of married women, most often the husband wants to keep the wife silly and self-sacrificing while he torments her with money problems. In most of the novels, the woman eventually strikes out against the oppressor and wins; and those who don't win vow that their children will have it better.

M. was not a very good writer, but the force of her feelings about the place of women makes the reading of her work rewarding. The very popularity of such books in the first thirty years of this century tells us something about American women of the time.

WORKS: *Unchaperoned* (1896). *Warren Hyde* (1897). *The Elusive Hildegard* (1900). *Tillie: A Mennonite Maid* (1904; film version, 1922). *Sabina, a Story of the Amish* (1905). *The Betrothal of Elypholate, & Other Tales* (1907). *His Courtship* (1907). *The Revolt of Anne Royle* (1908). *The Crossways* (1910). *When Half-Gods Go* (1911). *The Fighting Doctor* (1912). *The Parasite* (1913; film version, 1925). *Barnabetta* (1914; dramatization by M. de Forest and M. M. Fiske, *Erstwhile Susan*, 1916; film version, 1919). *Martha of the Mennonite Country* (1915). *Her Husband's Purse* (1916). *Those Fitzenbergers* (1917). *Fanatic or Christian* (1918). *Maggie of Virginsburg* (1918). *The Schoolmaster of Hessville* (1920). *The Marriage of Susan* (1921). *The Church on the Avenue* (1923). *The Snob* (1924; film version, 1924). *Challenged* (1925). *Ye That Judge* (1926). *Sylvia of the Minute* (1927). *The Lie* (1928). *Wings of Healing* (1929). *Tender Talons* (1930). *Yoked with a Lamb, & Other Stories* (1930). *Porcelain and Clay* (1931). *Lucy Anderson* (1932). *From Pillar to Post* (1933). *The Whip Hand* (1934). *Deliverance* (1935). *The House on the Marsh* (1936). *Emmy Untamed* (1937). *Son and Daughter* (1938). *The Ordeal of Minnie Schultz* (1939).

BIBLIOGRAPHY: Overton, G., *The Women Who Make Our Novels* (1922). Seaton, B., in *Pennsylvania Magazine of History & Biography* (Jan. 1980).
    Other references: *NYT* (30 June 1939).

BEVERLY SEATON

Sarah Towne Smith Martyn

B. *15 Aug. 1805, Hopkinton, New Hampshire; d. 22 Nov. 1879, New York City*
Wrote under: Sarah Towne Martyn, Mrs. S. T. Martyn
D. *of Ethan and Bathsheba Sanford Smith; m. Job H. Martyn, 1841*

Both of M.'s parents could trace their ancestry to 17th-c. New England settlers. M.'s father, a scholarly clergyman who had fought in the American Revolution, directed her education in channels that were considered "masculine," including not only various modern languages but also Greek and Hebrew. Although M. had considerable musical talent, she soon became far more interested in some of the causes that consumed her father's attention, especially the temperance and antislavery movements. From 1836 to 1845 she was active in the Female Moral Reform Society of New York, assisting the editor of the organization's journal, the *Advocate of Moral Reform,* until she left the society because of internal dissension.

After her marriage to a clergyman, M. became known to New York literati as a gracious hostess at whose home famous reformers and writers frequently gathered.

In addition to her editorial labors for the *Advocate of Moral Reform,* M. edited the *Olive Plant and Ladies' Temperance Advocate* (1842), the *True Advocate* (1845), the *White Banner* (1846), and the *Ladies' Wreath* (1846–50). M. edited excerpts from the latter for *The Golden Keepsake; or, Ladies' Wreath: A Gift for All Seasons* (1851), a collection that reflects the journal's focus on "literature, industry, and religion." Stories and essays by M. are included. In "The Social Position of Woman," M. describes the female role as giving "tone to the manners and morals of the community" and deplores the idea that woman's contracted sphere of action implies any inferiority. Elsewhere she asserts that the true mission of woman is simply to be a good wife and mother.

Despite M.'s rigidly traditional views of woman's status in society, she demonstrated by her own example that a woman's impact could extend far beyond the domestic sphere. She also depicted strong female characters in her fiction. For instance, in *Allan Cameron; or, The Three Birthdays* (1864), one of the many pious books M. wrote during the 1860s for the American Tract Society, M. depicts a young woman who puts abolitionism into action as soon as she becomes the mistress of her guardian's estates. Not only does Cora free her slaves, but she demonstrates sound economic awareness by presenting each of the males with a plot of land to cultivate so that he can support himself and his family. And in *The English Exile; or, William Tyndale at Home and Abroad* (1867), M. describes the words and actions of the great English reformer and translator through a journal kept from 1521 until Tyndale's martyrdom in 1536 by a female theology student who likes being right where the action is.

That M.'s best-known work, *Women of the Bible* (1868), was preceded by an article of the same title in the *Ladies' Wreath* (1850) indicates a prolonged interest in the topic. M.'s approach to biblical women is highly romanticized; for instance, she asserts that the Book of Ruth is "full of thrilling interest and pathos" and indicates that Ruth herself is a "young and beautiful woman," even though there is not a word in the Old Testament narrative to imply that Ruth is either particularly young or physically beautiful. M.'s warmly appreciative nature is the the greatest strength of her work; for example, she evaluates the ode sung by Samuel's mother, Hannah, as "one of the finest specimens of Hebrew poetry extant." Throughout, M. stresses the marriage and motherhood of biblical women; but 19th-c. women might have been stimulated to additional ambitions by her emphasis on their "rare endowments of mind as well as heart."

WORKS: *The Golden Keepsake; or, Ladies' Wreath: A Gift for All Seasons* (1851). *Allan Cameron; or, The Three Birthdays* (1864). *The Huguenots of France; or, The Times of Henry IV* (1864). *The English Exile; or, William Tyndale at Home and Abroad* (1867). *The Hopes of Hope Castle; or, The Times of Knox and Queen Mary Stuart* (1867). *Margaret, the Pearl of Navarre* (1867). *Netty and Her Sister; or, The Two Paths* (1867). *Daughters of the Cross* (1868). *Women of the Bible* (1868).

BIBLIOGRAPHY: Bittinger, J. Q., *History of Haverhill, N. H.* (1888). Hart, John S., *A Manual of American Literature* (1874).

For articles in reference works, see: *AA. DAB*, VI.

Other references: *New England Historical and Genealogical Register* (April 1847).

VIRGINIA RAMEY MOLLENKOTT

Frances Aymar Mathews

B. ca. *1855, New York City; d. 13 Jan. 1923, New York City*
D. of Daniel A. and Sara Eayres Webb Mathews

M., the daughter of a New York City art dealer, was privately educated. In the 1880s, she began publishing feature articles, playlets, and short stories in periodicals. M.'s first professionally staged work was *Bigamy* (1881), "a society play in five acts." Her next full-length play, *Joan* (1898), was written as a result of a letter from actress Fanny Davenport: "I have seen some of your short stories and believe you are the person to write a play for me. . . . I want a play on Joan of Arc." M. spent two years doing research in the Astor Library, but took dramatic license in giving "Joan Darc" some love interest.

M.'s most successful play was *Pretty Peggy* (1902), in which Grace George starred. This comedy was based upon 18th-c. actress Peg Woffington's early career and romance with David Garrick. Audiences were most delighted by the novelty of a scene in Act 4 in which costumed actors suddenly appeared among the audience in every part of the theater, voicing their opinions of Peg's on-stage performance as Rosalind in *As You Like It.*

My Lady Peggy Goes to Town (1901) is a rambling pseudo–18th-c. novel about a well-born country lass who travels to London to visit her twin brother and, she hopes, to be reconciled with Sir Percy, with whom she has had a lover's quarrel. Forced by circumstances to dress as a young man and to pass for a rival suitor for her own hand, Peggy careers from one adventure to another. After improbably becoming a protégé of Beau Brummell, she is frequently thrust into company with the unsuspecting Sir Percy, whose jealous dislike of his rival prevents her from unmasking. The dialogue prickles with period interjections, while the narrative bristles with typical turn-of-the-century rhetorical devices. One of M.'s last published works was a sequel, *My Lady Peggy Leaves Town* (1913).

For a time, M. published and edited *The Havana* (New York) *Journal.* In January 1923, M.'s scantily clad body was found frozen in a snowdrift not far from her home. It was reported in the *New York Times* that she, a pharmacist's assistant, may have been "stricken with a fit of insanity."

M.'s favorite subjects for narrative fiction as well as for her plays were courtship and marriage in an elegant social milieu. Her usual working procedure was to write her plots out first in the form of novels and then to dramatize them. M.'s strength as a dramatist lay in her ability to write graceful, witty dialogue. However, her plots are contrived, and she provided little depth of characterization.

WORKS: *Bigamy* (with E. Henderson, 1881). *To-night at Eight; Comedies and Comediettas* (1889). *The Scapegrace* (1890). *Six to One* (1890). *The Bracelet* (1895). *Wooing a Widow* (1895). *Joan* (1898). *His Way and Her Will* (1900). *The New Yorkers and Other People* (1900). *My Lady Peggy Goes to Town* (1901). *Pretty Peggy* (1902). *The New Professor* (1903). *Little Tragedy of Tien-Tsin* (1904). *Pamela Congreve* (1904). *Billy Duane* (1905). *Finding a Father for Flossie* (1905). *The Marquise's Millions* (1905). *The Staircase of Surprise* (1905). *Up Yonder* (1905). *Undefiled* (1906). *All for Sweet Charity* (1907). *Allee Same* (1907). *American Hearts* (1907). *The Apartment* (1907). *At the Grand Central* (1907). *Both Sides of the Counter*

(1907). *A Charming Conversationalist* (1907). *The Courier* (1907). *En Voyage* (1907). *The Honeymoon* (1907). *A Knight of the Quill* (1907). *On the Stair-case* (1907). *Paying the Piper* (1907). *War to the Knife* (1907). *A Woman's Forever* (1907). *Flame Dancer* (1908). *If David Knew* (1910). *A Finished Coquette* (1911). *Christmas Honeymoon* (1912). *My Lady Peggy Leaves Town* (1913). *Fanny of the Forty Frocks* (1916).

BIBLIOGRAPHY: *NYT* (23 Jan. 1920; 14 Jan. 1923). *Theatre Magazine* (Oct. 1906).

FELICIA HARDISON LONDRÉ

Adelaide Matthews

B. 1886, Kenduskeag, Maine

All except one of M.'s plays were written with collaborators. Her most famous coauthor was Anne Nichols, whose reputation rests mainly upon her own play *Abie's Irish Rose*. M.'s most frequent collaborator was Martha Stanley, with whom she wrote eight plays between 1919 and 1930. W. C. Duncan and Lucille Sawyer each collaborated once with M.

It is difficult to distinguish what M.'s contribution may have been to these joint efforts. All the plays were written for undiscriminating popular theater audiences. The plays abound with contrived comic business that audiences found hilarious, but is trite and silly in print. Characters are not individuated; each is simply assigned an age, a degree of physical attractiveness, and enough stupidity to keep the situation unresolved until the last act. The most distinctive character type that emerges in a number of the plays is the flighty, middle-aged woman who becomes hysterical at the slightest provocation.

If M.'s plays have any redeeming value for the modern reader, it is their depiction of social mores of the 1920s. In *Puppy Love* (1925), for example, much of the intrigue depends upon a quantity of bootleg gin temporarily stored in a convenient teapot that is unsuspectingly pressed into service. The ensuing merriment causes the ladies to abandon their stand against marriage, and a double ceremony is performed on the spot. There are references to a ukulele used by one of the young suitors, to flappers and petting parties, and to the moving pictures.

Anne Nichols was the producer of *Puppy Love*, which M. wrote with Martha Stanley. M. had collaborated with Nichols as early as 1917 on a farcical comedy entitled *What's Your Number?* It was produced in New York and London in the early 1920s as *Just Married*, and in Berlin in 1929 as *Nearly Married*. This comedy is set on a transatlantic steamer. Robert Adams and Roberta Adams are strangers who are mistakenly assigned to the same stateroom. The error goes undetected until morning, since he entered in the dark after she was asleep. Misunderstandings involving a number of other characters grow out of Roberta's attempts to save her reputation, but all is set right when Robert and Roberta, predictably, fall in love and decide to marry.

M.'s work might best be summed up in the words of the *New York Times* reviewer for her *Nightie Night* (1919), which occasioned "several hours of continuous and unforced laughter. . . . It is made of materials that have been used so often in the last twenty-five years that they are worn through in spots. And yet it is funny."

WORKS: *Nightie Night* (with M. Stanley, 1919). *The Teaser* (with M. Stanley, 1921). *Where Innocence Is Bliss* (with M. Stanley, 1921). *Just Married* (with A. Nichols, 1924). *Puppy Love* (with M. Stanley, 1925). *An Errand for Polly* (with W. C. Duncan, 1926). *The Wasp's Nest* (with M. Stanley, 1927). *Sunset Glow* (with L. Sawyer, 1929). *The First Mrs. Chiverick* (with M. Stanley, 1930; produced, as *Scrambled Wives*, 1920). *Innocent Anne* (with M. Stanley, 1930). *It Never Happens Twice* (1938).

BIBLIOGRAPHY: *NYT* (10 Sept. 1919; 6 Aug. 1920; 28 July 1921; 28 Jan. 1926; 26 Oct. 1927).

FELICIA HARDISON LONDRÉ

Katherine Mayo

B. 24 Jan. 1867, Ridgeway, Pennsylvania; d. 9 Oct. 1940, Bedford Hills, New York
Wrote under: S. Deane, Katherine Mayo, Katherine Prence
D. of James and Harriet Ingraham Mayo

One of three daughters of a mining engineer, M. spent part of her youth in Pennsylvania and part in Cambridge, Massachusetts. In 1899, M. accompanied her father in his search for gold in Dutch Guiana, where she spent much of the next eight years.

M. began her writing career by publishing pop articles and, through the guidance and help of Oswald Garrison Villard, began work at the *Saturday Evening Post* as a research assistant. In 1910, she began a long friendship with M. Moyca Newell, an orphaned heiress in her early twenties. This friendship provided financial security for M., freeing her to write and to pursue her own research interests. The two women traveled together extensively to gather material for books, and built an estate in Bedford Hills, New York, where M. lived until her death from cancer.

In her writing M. became a crusader and spokeswoman for what she termed "voiceless underdogs." In 1917, she lobbied successfully for a state police force in New York, writing about the problem in her first book, *Justice to All* (1917). In 1920, M. defended the overseas activities of the YMCA during World War I in *"That Damn Y." Soldiers What Next!* exposed the American Legion lobby in 1934. M. did not seem concerned with the usual interests of feminists of her generation such as woman suffrage, slum conditions, or settlement houses, but preferred to write about the sexual exploitation of women. Interestingly, she did not deal with the problem in her own country or from her own experience, but rather in her writings about distant places and cultures—especially the Philippines and India.

In *The Isles of Fear* (1925), M. rejects the idea of independence for the Philippines. Although M.'s avowed purpose is to "present accurate information, not to influence judgment," her selection of material reflects her bias. M. presents information about local corruption and usury laws, which reflect the Filipinos' inability to govern themselves, but she focuses much of the work on the sexual exploitation of girls by landowners in the tenant relationship and by male Filipino schoolteachers.

M.'s concern with sexual exploitation becomes most vocal in her sensational novel of child marriage, *Mother India* (1927). The book is journalistic in style; the text is documented by photographs, statistics, and other supplementary material. M.'s generalizations about India are much the same as those about the Philippines—India is not ready for self-rule—but M. ascribes the reason to India's preoccupation with sex. M. does deal to some extent with other political and religious concerns, but the sensational elements are clear in her graphic medical descriptions of the forced marriages of very young girls (ages five to ten) to mature males. M. concluded that such marriages kept women in the lowest possible status. The book was widely read and highly controversial; many rebuttals were written.

M. continued this theme in *Slaves of the Gods* (1929), *Volume Two* (1931), and *The Face of Mother India* (1935). *Mother India*, M.'s most widely read book, is stylistically better than some of the others. Descriptive sections achieve an immediacy through specific detail and fragmented structure. On the whole, however, the work is principally muckraking typical of its era. The preoccupation with sexual exploitation limits its effectiveness.

WORKS: *Justice to All* (1917). *The Standard Bearers* (1918). "*That Damn Y*" (1920). *Mounted Justice: True Stories of the Pennsylvania State Police* (1922). *The Isles of Fear: The Truth about the Philippines* (1925). *Mother India* (1927). *Slaves of the Gods* (1929). *Volume Two* (1931). *Soldiers What Next!* (1934). *The Face of Mother India* (1935). *General Washington's Dilemma* (1938).

The papers of Katherine Mayo are at the Yale University Library, Cambridge, Massachusetts. The Oswald Garrison Villard papers at Harvard University contain several of her letters.

BIBLIOGRAPHY: For articles in reference works, see: *NAW* (article by M. F. Handlin). *NCAB*, 30. *20thCA*.

Other references: *Atlantic* (Summer 1930). *Current History* (Aug. 1930). *Fortune* (March 1929). *Forum* (Fall 1928). *Nation* (12 June 1929). *North American Review* (June 1928).

BETTY J. ALLDREDGE

Margaret Mayo

B. *19 Nov. 1882, near Brownsville, Illinois; d. 25 Feb. 1951, Ossining,*
New York
Given name: *Lillian Clatten (Slatten?)*
M. *Edgar Selwyn*

A midwest farm girl, M. adopted the stage name Margaret Mayo when she went to New York City in search of a career. While still in her teens, M. toured in *Charley's Aunt* and *Secret Service* and, between 1899 and 1903, had a few minor roles on Broadway. Dissatisfied with women's character parts, she adapted Ouida's novel *Under Two Flags* so that she could play Cigarette, but Belasco's competing version opened first. M. spent one season in London and then appeared in a New York company with the popular idol Grace George, who asked M. to dramatize *The Marriage of William Ashe* (produced 1905) for her.

The play's success prompted producers to commission vehicles for other stars. M. collaborated with her playwright husband (from whom she was later divorced) on the book to a musical, *Wall Street Girl* (1908; produced 1912). Her own farce *Baby Mine* (1911; produced 1910) was one of the decade's most successful plays. In 1917 M. and her husband joined Sam Goldfish in a film company; amalgamation produced the corporate name Goldwyn, which Sam took for his own when the partnership dissolved. In 1918, M. headed a unit of the Red Cross "Over There" theater; her own act included a solo dance.

M.'s first original play, *Polly of the Circus* (1908; produced 1907), was a sentimental comedy. Bareback rider Polly is taken to the local minister's house after a fall. Under his influence, she loses her fiery temper and slangy speech, and becomes gentle, literate, good at amusing children, and beloved. She runs back to the circus to protect him from gossip—but, of course, he follows her and love conquers all. In 1917 the play became the Goldwyn Company's first film; reviewers agreed that it fulfilled Goldwyn's promise to elevate the state of the art. A second movie version in 1932 starred Clark Gable as the minister.

Farce, however, and not sentimental romance, was M.'s real talent. *Baby Mine* is typical. Alfred Hardy is absurdly jealous, and his wife Zoie is a chronic (though innocent and featherbrained) liar. Alfred leaves; she decides to get him back by giving birth to a son. She lines up a baby from a foundling home and sends Alfred the telegram—and then the baby's mother changes her mind, so that Zoie and her husband's friend Jimmy Jinks (the role Fatty Arbuckle chose for his return to Broadway in 1927) spend the second act scrambling to beg, steal, borrow, or buy a baby. No mother will make a permanent arrangement— babies appear and disappear—the police press in with kidnapping charges —Alfred clasps his "son" to his bosom and hears a spare baby crying elsewhere—Jinks climbs in the window with yet another—and somehow everything is straightened out two minutes before the final curtain.

Baby Mine played London, Paris, and cities from Singapore to Cape Town; it was filmed in 1928 and made into a musical by Herbert Reynolds and Jerome Kern (*Rock-A-Bye-Baby*, produced 1918). *Commencement Days* (1908), *Twin Beds* (1931; produced 1914), and *Seeing Things* (1920) also display M.'s mastery of traditional farce. The characters are simple and rigid, the situations flirt innocently around the edges of the risqué, and in the climactic scene most of the characters are stowed away in closets, under the bed, behind curtains, and in the laundry basket, so that when the spring is wound up tight they can begin to pop out again.

M. cared little for literature; she said that she had never read a play before she began writing them. Her only nondramatic work, *Trouping for the Troops* (1919), is a slender, sentimental account of her wartime tour. She used an entertainer's skills to put together scripts that would play. *Polly of the Circus* let the producer add as many circus acts as the proscenium and the budget would accommodate; *Wall Street Girl* featured Will Rogers and his vaudeville routine. One reason M.'s plays have not survived is that she tailored them so individually to the performer's talents; she did, for example, three different versions of Sardou's *Cyprienne* for three different actresses. She was often called in to doctor other writers' scripts. Her fast-paced, superficial, mechanical, and highly visual farces were a natural for silent films, but by the 1930s and 1940s the sound remakes already looked creaky and out-of-date.

WORKS: *Polly of the Circus* (1908; rev. ed., 1933; film versions, 1917, 1932). *Commencement Days* (with V. Frame, 1908). *Wall Street Girl* (with E. Selwyn, 1908). *Baby Mine* (1911; rev. ed., 1924; film version, 1928). *Cyprienne (Divorcons)* by V. Sardou (adapted by Mayo, 1932). *Twin Beds* (with E. S. Field, 1931; film versions, 1920, 1942). *Trouping for the Troops* (1919). *The Love Thief* (1926; film version, 1926). *The Poor Simp* (revised by Mayo from the version by Zellah Covington, 1935).

BIBLIOGRAPHY: Zierold, N., *The Moguls* (1969).

Other references: *Green Book* (Oct. 1913). *McClure's* (Sept. 1912). *NYT* (24 Dec. 1907; 10 Sept. 1913; 15 Aug. 1914; 26 Feb. 1951).

SALLY MITCHELL

Sarah Carter Edgarton Mayo

B. *17 March 1819, Shirley, Massachusetts; d. 9 July 1848, Gloucester, Massachusetts*
Wrote under: *Miss Sarah C. Edgarton, Mrs. Sarah C. Edgarton Mayo*
D. *of Joseph and Mehitable Whitcomb Edgarton; m. Amory Dwight Mayo, 1846*

Fortunate in her family, friends, and husband, M. lived a brief but active life, tempering her serious, intellectual nature with a cheerful and loving outlook. M. was educated at her parents' home, a large mansion where, as the tenth of fifteen children, she was surrounded by a happy, busy, intelligent family who encouraged her interest in literature. At age sixteen M. began to write for publication, thereafter leading the life of the professional woman editor/writer. The only formal education M. had was fourteen weeks at Westford Academy, but she could read several languages and wrote with ease. Her family belonged to the Universalist church, which M. joined at age seventeen, for that liberal, intellectually minded denomination was best suited to her. In 1846 she married a young man who was later to become a successful minister and a prolific author. They had one child, a daughter, during their short married life. Mayo's *Selections from the Writings of Mrs. Sarah C. Edgarton Mayo; with a Memoir* (1849) is the chief source of information about M.'s life and work.

During M.'s early years as a professional writer, when apparently she needed to earn money, she wrote quantities of stories and poems, finding a ready market. Many of M.'s short pieces appeared in the *Universalist and Ladies' Repository*, a Boston publication where she served as associate editor from 1839 to 1842, and *The Rose of Sharon*, the Universalist gift annual which she edited from 1840 to 1848. Two children's books, *The Palfreys* (1838) and *Ellen Clifford* (1838), appeared during this time, and M. also published two collections of her short pieces, *Spring Flowers* (1840?) and *The Poetry of Woman* (1841). Her husband later said about this period of her life that "she wrote much more than her own judgment would dictate, and necessarily with great rapidity."

One of M.'s personal interests was botany, and combining her love of flowers with poetry, she published three sentimental flower books. *The*

Flower Vase (1843) is a traditional flower-language book, in which M. presents the symbolic meanings of flowers and some passages of poetry illustrating the sentiments. Books like this on flower language were published by most women editors of the day, including Sarah Josepha Hale. Usually presented as gift books, these volumes were displayed on "centre tables" in many homes where they functioned along with other symbolic possessions to provide that gloss of refinement so desired at that time. M. also published *The Floral Fortune Teller* (1846), an involved game using flower meanings and passages of poetry, and *The Fables of Flora* (1844), a collection of flower fables, some her own, some by Dr. Langhorne.

A good selection of M.'s prose and poetry can be found in the book edited by her husband. A study of her poems shows that her admiration for Wordsworth and Burns did not stop short this side of imitation. Most of her poems, populated by figures such as "Young Rosabelle" and "Leila Gray," concern standard subjects such as nature, religion, family feelings, and death. Although M. occasionally gives an interesting background detail or an insightful character analysis, her short stories are mostly sentimental, mawkish romances with happy, moral endings.

Certainly, M. had no illusions about the quality of her work. In the two years after her marriage, she wrote little and seemed dissatisfied with what she did write. Her husband tells us that she was trying to write "a work in the form of a novel, the spiritual autobiography of a woman from childhood to middle age," but M. left only a few fragments. Such a novel would have been worth reading. However, it is debatable whether M., with her ready gifts but essentially imitative attitude, could ever have written it. One of her prides, said her husband, was the acceptability of her work to everyone. "If she ever wrote a controversial line she sincerely regretted it," he boasted.

WORKS: *Ellen Clifford* (1838). *The Palfreys* (1838). *Spring Flowers* (1840 ?). *The Poetry of Woman* (1841). *The Flower Vase* (1843). *Poems by Mrs. Julia H. Scott, Together with a Brief Memoir* (1843). *The Fables of Flora* (1844). *The Floral Fortune Teller* (1846).

BIBLIOGRAPHY: Douglas, A., *The Feminization of American Culture* (1977). Mayo, A. D., *Selections from the Writings of Mrs. Sarah C. Edgarton Mayo; with a Memoir, by Her Husband* (1849).

For articles in reference works, see: *AA. FPA. NCAB,* 2.

BEVERLY SEATON

Kate Campbell Hurd Mead

B. 6 April 1867, Danville, Quebec, Canada; d. 1 Jan. 1941, Haddam, Connecticut
Wrote under: Kate C. Mead, Kate C. H. Mead, Kate Campbell Hurd-Mead
D. of Edward Payson and Sarah Elizabeth Campbell Hurd; m. William Edward Mead, 1893

Born in Canada, M. moved with her family to Newburyport, Massachusetts, where she graduated from high school in 1883. She received her M.D. from Woman's Medical College of Pennsylvania in 1888 and interned the next year at the New England Hospital for Women and Children in Boston. In 1889–90, she studied in Paris, Stockholm, Berlin, and London.

In 1890, M. became medical director of the Bryn Mawr School in Baltimore and founded the Evening Dispensary for Working Women and Girls of Baltimore City in 1891. After her marriage to Mead, a professor of early English at Wesleyan University, she moved to Middletown, Connecticut, where she set up practice. In 1895, M. was an incorporator of Middlesex County Hospital, where she served as a consulting gynecologist from 1907 to 1925.

M. was active in many women's medical organizations and was president of the Medical Women's National Association (MWNA) from 1922–24. In 1925, M. gave up practice to devote herself to full-time research and writing on the history of women in medicine. She traveled extensively in Europe, Asia, and Africa, gathering information about women in medicine.

Medical Women of America (1933), M.'s first book, was dedicated to the MWNA and was published only after the press received two hundred advance subscriptions. The book was oversubscribed—not because it had a wide audience but because many readers ordered more than one copy. M. records the history of medical women in America from the early midwives who practiced in the colonies to the women physicians who served in various capacities during World War I.

M. traces the careers of the first American women medical students and physicians, relating the achievements of these women in founding dispensaries, hospitals, and medical schools. She shows that women physicians did well as private practitioners, as teachers and professors—when given a chance, as researchers, and even as surgeons. M. insists that medical women fall short of men only in writing about their achievements. As a result, the world does not realize the extent of women physicians' abilities and accomplishments. M.'s book is an attempt to remedy that situation.

A History of Women in Medicine from the Earliest Times to the Beginning of the Nineteenth Century (1938) is M.'s *magnum opus*. The task that M. set for herself was great: to write the most complete history of women in medicine possible. M. spent two years doing research at the British Museum library and several more years consulting original manuscripts in many parts of the world. The result is an impressive compilation of facts presenting the story of women in medicine from 4000 B.C. in Egypt through the end of the 18th c. in Europe. Volume II, still unpublished at M.'s death, was to have continued the story of women in medicine through the 20th c.

This volume demonstrates convincingly that restrictions against women in medicine are relatively recent—a product of the Christian era and the founding of universities in the Middle Ages. From ancient times until about the 13th c., women were active in all aspects of medical care, surgery as well as midwifery. The book is extremely detailed; in fact, it is tedious to read.

M.'s accomplishment in discovering and preserving facts about women in medicine in many countries throughout many centuries is extraordinary. She has restored to medical women their proper heritage.

WORKS: *Medical Women of America: A Short History of the Pioneer Medical Women of America and of a Few of Their Colleagues in England* (1933). *A History of Women in Medicine from the Earliest Times to the Beginning of the Nineteenth Century* (1938).

The papers of Kate Campbell Hurd Mead, including the unpublished manuscript of Volume II of her *History of Women in Medicine,* are at the Schlesinger Library, Radcliffe College.

BIBLIOGRAPHY: For articles in reference works, see: *NAW* (article by G. Miller).

Other references: *Bulletin of the History of Medicine* (July 1941). *Journal of the American Medical Women's Association* (April 1956). *Nation* (28 May 1938). *NYT* (15 May 1938). *Women in Medicine* (April 1941). *YR* (Summer 1938).

ANNE HUDSON JONES

Margaret Mead

B. 16 Dec. 1901, Philadelphia, Pennsylvania; d. 15 Nov. 1978, New York City
D. of Edward Sherwood and Emily Fogg Mead; m. Luther Cressman, 1923;
m. Reo Fortune, 1928; m. Gregory Bateson, 1935

M., the eldest of five children, was born in Philadelphia. Her father, Edward Sherwood Mead, was a professor at the Wharton School of Finance and Commerce. M. respected his loyalty to his work, capacity to listen, and powers of concentration, and from him learned that the most valuable thing one could do was to add to the store of known facts. M.'s mother, Emily Fogg Mead, was a gentle and delicate woman with a determined nature and a professional concern for other people and the state of the world. The most decisive influence in M.'s life was her parental grandmother, a strong and determined woman who lived with the family.

M.'s grandmother informally educated her at home until M. went to Doylestown High School and New Hope School for Girls in Pennsylvania. After a disappointing year at DePauw University, M. transferred to Barnard College, where she studied anthropology under Franz Boas and Ruth Benedict and received her B.A. in 1923. Upon graduation from Barnard, she married Luther Cressman. As a graduate student at Columbia, where she earned her Ph.D. in 1929, M. began her first fieldwork in Samoa in 1925. While traveling home from Samoa, M. met her second husband, Reo Fortune, a New Zealand psychologist and anthropologist. Upon returning to New York, M. was appointed curator of ethnology at the American Museum of Natural History, an appointment which grew into a lifelong position. Later, while doing fieldwork in New Guinea, she met her third husband, Gregory Bateson, a British anthropologist by whom she had one daughter. M. held almost forty positions, including professor of anthropology at Columbia University. She was the recipient of many honorary degrees and some thirty-five awards. M. was president of the World Federation for Mental Health (1956–57) and the American Anthropological Association (1960).

M.'s long and productive career as an author-anthropologist blossomed with the publication of her first and most popular book, *Coming of Age in Samoa* (1928). It has since been translated into seven languages and has reappeared in seven editions. The book is based on M.'s first fieldwork, undertaken at the age of twenty-three, in which she set out to discover whether the problems that trouble American adolescents are due to the biological nature of adolescence or to culturally learned attitudes. Her study of the individual within a culture was unique. M. vividly describes the basic character of Samoan life and how attitudes and behavior are shaped from birth to maturity. The results of her nine months of work showed that much of individual behavior is culturally learned. Stripped of the technical jargon of anthropology, M.'s clear presentations of life in Samoa and her answers to a fascinating anthropological question have reached a wide and enthusiastic audience.

Growing Up in New Guinea (1930), based on M.'s second field trip, is about the Manus people of Peri village in the Admiralty Islands. M.'s focus is on family life and the education of young children. Important themes in the education of Manus children are the teaching of physical adaptation to a precarious environment, the instilling of a respect for property, and a combination of firm discipline and gentle solicitude. Children grow up without any feelings of inferiority or insecurity. Throughout the book, M. draws interesting parallels with modern life.

Sex and Temperament in Three Primitive Societies (1935), which has been translated into twelve languages, was the outcome of fieldwork in three villages in New Guinea. When going into the field in 1931, M.'s original intentions were to study the cultural conditioning of the personalities of the two sexes. After working for two years in three different villages, M. discovered that her findings revealed more about differences in human temperament than about gender. Among the Mountain Arapesh, both men and women are gentle and maternal; among the Mundugumor, both sexes are fierce and virile; and among the Tchambuli, the roles of men and women are reversed from our traditional roles. Thus, gender is only one of the ways in which a society can group its social attitude toward temperament.

Balinese Character: A Photographic Analysis (1942), written with Bateson, was the outcome of rich and extensive fieldwork done from 1936–38. It represents a major leap in the use of photography as a method of ethnographic presentation, stemming from the authors' sensitivity to the inadequacy of verbal presentation in portraying the finer shades of cultural meaning. From a total of twenty-five thousand photographs, over seven hundred were selected and grouped so that details from different scenes are thematically related and explained by captions. This type of presentation was followed nine years later by *Growth and Culture: A Photographic Study of Balinese Childhood* (1951), written with Frances Cooke MacGregor.

In 1949, M. wrote *Male and Female: A Study of the Sexes in a Changing World*. It is based on fourteen years of fieldwork in seven different societies, and was written at a time when traditional roles of male and female were undergoing scrutiny in our society. M. discusses ways in which physical similarities and differences are the basis on which we learn about our own sex and our relationship to the other sex. M. includes a discussion of how societies develop myths to answer the questions about differences between men and women, and about how children grow up to be a member of one or the other group. In the final section M. brings her knowledge back to America and discusses ways in which we can make improvements in our society.

M. returned to Manus twenty-five years after her original journey. The cultural changes that occurred during World War II when Manus was overrun by Americans are recorded in *New Lives for Old: Cultural Transformation—Manus, 1928–1953* (1956). This study of culture contact is based on M.'s belief that Americans have something to contribute to a changing world. Since M. investigates mainly the more superficial changes in Manus, the book is anthropologically less satisfying than her others but is otherwise a remarkable account of the rapid leaps one society made from "stone age" to "civilization." M.'s restudy of the Manus is also the subject of two of her films, *New Lives for Old* (1960) and *Margaret Mead's New Guinea Journal* (1968).

An Anthropologist at Work: Writings of Ruth Benedict (1959) is a biography of M.'s teacher, colleague, and lifelong friend. M. interweaves her own introductory chapters on various stages of Benedict's life and career with selections from Benedict's work, diaries, unpublished poems, and personal letters to Edward Sapir, Franz Boas, and M. The reader gains a deep appreciation of Benedict, a sensitive and emotionally complex woman whose great contribution to anthropology was her theory of culture as a "personality writ large." M. wrote a second book entitled *Ruth Benedict: A Biography* (1974), which is less massive than the first and written mainly for students.

Culture and Commitment: A Study of the Generation Gap, written in 1970 and revised extensively in 1978, is written in the belief that if we know and understand enough, our knowledge will breed optimistic and constructive thinking. M. feels that we are experiencing an irreversible evolutionary change brought about by modern technology, population explosion, and destruction of the natural environment, and that it is a change of which, for the first time in human history, we have a full awareness. M. proposes three categories of generational interaction based on past, present, and future orientations. Our culture is a future-oriented one, in which there has been a reverse in the relationship between the generations. Now the young members set the goals for the older to follow.

M.'s autobiography, *Blackberry Winter: My Earlier Years* (1972), is perhaps her most interesting book, providing the reader with some insight into the person behind the prolific and influential personality. In the first and third sections, M. writes about her family life, first from her early point of view as a granddaughter and then from her later view as a grandmother. The middle section is devoted to her field experiences. *Letters from the Field, 1925–1975* (1977), a collection of letters to family and friends from M.'s various expeditions, is another work that provides insight into the determined, fearless, and energetic person who became the world's most popular anthropologist.

M.'s contributions as an anthropologist have been unparalleled. She taught us about the behavior of other human beings—human beings like ourselves in everything but their culture—and in so doing gave us a better understanding of ourselves within a broad perspective. M. applied the results of her studies in primitive cultures to the questions of the day in our rapidly changing world. With the insight and knowledge she gained as a granddaughter and a grandmother, M. was able to span the gaps between the generations to which she spoke. As a person who watched children from isolated primitive societies grow up into a modern world, M. gained and shared a knowledge of cultural change and continuity. M. was a person who made her home the entire world and who communicated what she learned in such a felicitous, direct, and vivid style that people everywhere have benefited from her insights.

WORKS: *Coming of Age in Samoa: A Psychological Study of Primitive Youth for Western Civilization* (1928). *An Inquiry into the Question of Cultural Stability in Polynesia* (1928). *Growing Up in New Guinea: A Comparative Study of Primitive Education* (1930). *Social Organization of Manu'a* (1930). *The Changing Culture of an Indian Tribe* (1932). *Kinship in the Admiralty Islands* (1934). *Sex and Temperament in Three Primitive Societies* (1935). *Cooperation and Competition among Primitive Peoples* (edited by Mead, 1937). *The Mountain Arapesh* (Vol. 1, *An Importing Culture*, 1938; Vol. 2, *Supernaturalism*, 1940; Vol. 3, *Socio-Economic Life*, 1947; Vol. 4, *Diary of Events in Alitoa*, 1947; Vol. 5, *The Record of Unabelin with Rorschach Analysis*, 1949). *From the South Seas: Studies in Adolescence and Sex in Primitive Societies* (1939). *And Keep Your Powder Dry: An Anthropologist Looks at America* (1942). *Balinese Character: A Photographic Analysis* (with G. Bateson, 1942). *Male and Female: A Study of the Sexes in a Changing*

World (1949). *Growth and Culture: A Photographic Study of Balinese Child-hood* (with F. C. MacGregor, 1951). *The School in American Culture* (1951). *Soviet Attitudes toward Authority* (1951). *Cultural Patterns and Technical Change: A Manual Prepared by the World Federation for Mental Health* (edited by Mead, 1953). *Primitive Heritage: An Anthropological Anthology* (edited by Mead, with N. Calas, 1953). *The Study of Culture at a Distance* (edited by Mead, with R. Metraux, 1953). *Themes in French Culture: A Preface to a Study of French Community* (with R. Metraux, 1954). *Childhood in Contemporary Cultures* (edited by Mead, with M. Wolfenstein, 1955). *New Lives for Old: Cultural Transformation—Manus, 1928–1953* (1956). *An Anthropologist at Work: Writings of Ruth Benedict* (1959). *People and Places* (1959). *The Golden Age of American Anthropology* (edited by Mead, with R. L. Bunzel, 1960). *Anthropology, a Human Science: Selected Papers 1939–1960* (1964). *Continuities in Cultural Evolution* (1964). *American Women* (edited by Mead, with F. B. Kaplan, 1965). *Anthropologists and What They Do* (1965). *Family* (with K. Heyman, 1965). *The Wagon and the Star: A Study of American Community Initiative* (with M. Brown, 1966). *Science and the Concept of Race* (edited by Mead, with T. Dobzhansky, E. Tobach, and R. E. Light, 1968). *The Small Conference: An Innovation in Communication* (with P. Byers, 1968). *Culture and Commitment: A Study of the Generation Gap* (1970; rev. ed., 1978). *A Way of Seeing* (edited by Mead, with R. Metraux, 1970). *A Rap on Race* (with J. Baldwin, 1971). *Blackberry Winter: My Earlier Years* (1972). *To Love or to Perish: The Technological Crisis and the Churches* (edited by Mead et al., 1972). *Twentieth Century Faith: Hope and Survival* (1972). *Ruth Benedict: A Biography* (1974). *World Enough: Rethinking the Future* (with K. Heyman, 1975). *The Atmosphere: Endangered and Endangering* (edited by Mead, with W. W. Kellogg, 1977). *Letters from the Field, 1925–1975* (1977). *Aspects of the Present* (with R. Metraux, 1980).

BIBLIOGRAPHY: Cottler, J., and H. Jaffe, in *More Heroes of Civilization* (1969). Gordan, J., ed., *Margaret Mead: The Complete Bibliography 1925–1975* (1976). Moss, A., *Shaping a New World: Margaret Mead* (1963). Rossi, A. S., *The Feminist Papers from Adams to de Beauvoir* (1973). Stoddard, H., in *Famous American Women* (1970). Yost, E., in *American Women of Science* (1955).

For articles in reference works, see: *Britannica Yearbook of Science and the Future* (1971). *NCAB*, 1. *20thCA*. *20thCAS*.

Other references: *Louisiana Academy of Sciences Proceedings* 31 (1968). *New York Magazine* (13 Aug. 1973). *NY* 97 (1961). *NYTMag* (26 April 1970). *SatR* 4 (1977). *Science* 184 (1974). *Science Year: The World Book Science Annual* (1968).

MIRIAM KAHN

Mary L. Meaney

Most of M.'s works are thinly disguised religious tracts written to inspire loyalty to the faith among young Catholic readers. *Grace Morton; or, The Inheritance* (1864) is one of M.'s more successful treatments of the conflict between apostasy and constancy. Grace Morton and her brother are adopted by Gerald Althorpe after he disowns his son for marrying a Catholic. Grace befriends the disinherited family and converts to Catholicism, although it means breaking her engagement with Powhattan Clifton and being disowned by Althorpe. When Althorpe dies intestate, his son's family gets their fortune and Grace's loyalty is rewarded by a reunion with Powhattan, who accepts her religion. In its attempt to demonstrate that virtue is rewarded, the novel is flawed by a melodramatic plot and weak character development.

M.'s best work, *The Confessors of Connaught; or, The Tenants of a Lord Bishop* (1865), is based on the Partry evictions that took place in Ireland on November 21–23, 1860, on the estate of Lord Plunket, a Protestant Bishop. Catholic tenants were evicted for not sending their children to Bishop Plunket's school. In *The Confessors*, the Protestant curate Reverend Gillman refuses to proselytize and instead works cooperatively with Father Dillon, the parish priest. His wife is M.'s best character. A foil for the Bishop's daughter, Mrs. Gillman is shrewder and stronger than her husband, and unafraid to confront the Bishop over his eviction plan.

Gillman proves too charitable for the Bishop's plan and is replaced by Reverend Robinson and new teachers who contrive to make themselves popular with their pupils; however, the school fails. When the tenants remain steadfast, the Bishop calls in the military to evict them. Word of the eviction spreads and becomes the subject of a debate in Parliament. Even the London *Times* is moved to protest. Contributions, including money raised by Reverend Gillman, help Father Dillon resettle his parishioners.

The Confessors succeeds for several reasons. The historical facts of the Partry evictions help structure the plot; M.'s theme, the triumph of real Christianity over sectarian bigotry, is broader than her narrower Catholicism; Mrs. Gillman is a more developed character than sentimental protagonists like Grace Morton and Elinor Johnston; and finally, the tone of this book is less moralistic and more humane than the tone of M.'s other works. Unfortunately, M.'s later books did not reach the standard of *The Confessors*, and her books are of interest only as examples of pious Catholic literature of the late 19th c.

WORKS: *Grace Morton; or, The Inheritance* (1864). *The Confessors of Connaught; or, The Tenants of a Lord Bishop* (1865). *A Father's Tales of the French Revolution* (1866). *Philip Hartley* (1866). *Ralph Berriens and Other Tales of the French Revolution* (1866). *Silver Grange, a Catholic Tale; and Philippine, a Tale of the Middle Ages* (1866). *Elinor Johnston: Founded on Facts; and Maurice and Genevieve; or, The Orphan Twins of Beance* (1868).

MAUREEN MURPHY

Florence Crannell Means

B. *15 May 1897, Baldwinsville, New York*
D. *of Phillip Wendell and Fannie Eleanor Grout Crannell; m. Carleton Bell Means, 1912*

M.'s upbringing in the household of her Baptist theologian father, a man with "no racial consciousness," contributed to her ambition to sway young people to her own conviction that "folks are folks." From her mother's side of the family M. had heard the tales of the pioneering Grout grandparents, and this provided another subject for her pen. M.'s first books recount the adventures of a Mexican-American teenager in Wisconsin and Minnesota during the 1870s. The second, *A Candle in the Mist* (1931), established M. as a writer of considerable talent. Although M.'s work has focused often on the problems of racial prejudice, she has written books on religious tolerance, family relations, the handicapped, and migrant workers. M.'s writing was encouraged by her husband, an attorney and businessman with whom she wrote *The Silver Fleece* (1950), one of many books dealing with Mexico. Their only child, Eleanor Hull, also writes.

M. lives, as she has for many years, in Boulder, Colorado. Failing eyesight has curtailed both her traveling and writing since her last book, *Smith Valley*, was published in 1973.

A book that focused much attention on M. and won the Childhood

Education Association award in 1945 is *The Moved-Outers,* her tale of a Japanese-American family evacuated from California during World War II. Earlier, M. had dealt sensitively with the problems of assimilation for Japanese in America in *Rainbow Bridge* (1934), and she brought the same understanding to the patient suffering of the fictional Ohara family.

Teresita of the Valley (1943) and *The House under the Hill* (1949) have Mexican-American heroines who in maturing come to value their culture and people, a frequent development with M.'s characters.

In her books with black heroines, M. stressed their successes. Although struggles and heartbreaking insults are there, her characters overcome them. Beginning with *Shuttered Windows* (1938), M. has given her readers a number of ambitious, intelligent black girls whose "similarity to any witty white girl should do more to promote understanding between the two races than any amount of sermonizing," as Jane Cobb put it in her *Atlantic* review of *Great Day in the Morning* (1946).

Among M.'s best books are those which deal with the American Indian. For years, M. "spent as much time as possible among the Hopi and Navajo Indians," and her stories differentiate tribal customs in accurate detail. They are beautifully written, though they have been criticized as perhaps "too unhappy to sustain the interest of the young." In *Tangled Waters* (1936), a Navajo girl fights her family's prejudice against education. *Our Cup Is Broken* (1969), one of M.'s last major books, is less upbeat than many of her stories. A young Hopi woman, hurt by society's taboo against interracial marriage, rejects the white world and returns to an unhappy life in her native village.

M.'s books have been called alternately "too tragic" and "too pat." Her novels occasionally seem contrived in their solutions, but more often conflicts between character and situation are resolved realistically. Long before racial tolerance was a popular or even generally accepted subject for juvenile literature, M. was writing straightforward books about minority groups. M.'s approach, however, is far from radical. Her minority characters are dedicated to American ideals.

WORKS: *Rafael and Consuelo* (with H. Fullen, 1929). *A Candle in the Mist* (1931). *Children of the Great Spirit* (with F. Riggs, 1932). *Ranch and Ring, a Story of the Pioneer West* (1932). *Dusky Day* (1933). *A Bowlful of Stars* (1934). *Rainbow Bridge* (1934). *Penny for Luck* (1935). *Tangled Waters* (1936). *The Singing Wood* (1937). *Shuttered Windows* (1938). *Adella Mary in Old New Mexico* (1939). *Across the Fruited Plain* (1940). *At the End of Nowhere* (1940). *Children of the Promise* (1941). *Whispering Girl* (1941). *Shadow over Wide Ruin* (1942). *Teresita of the Valley* (1943). *Peter of the*

Mesa (1944). *The Moved-Outers* (1945). *Great Day in the Morning* (1946).
Assorted Sisters (1947). *The House under the Hill* (1949). *The Silver Fleece*
(with C. Means, 1950). *Hetty of the Grande Deluxe* (1951). *Carvers' George*
(1952). *Alicia* (1953). *The Rains Will Come* (1954). *Knock at the Door,*
Emmy (1956). *Sagebrush Surgeon* (1956). *Reach for a Star* (1957). *Borrowed*
Brother (1958). *Emmy and the Blue Door* (1959). *Sunlight on the Hopi Mesa:*
The Story of Abigail E. Johnson (1960). *But I Am Sara* (1961). *That Girl*
Andy (1962). *Tolliver* (1963). *It Takes All Kinds* (1964). *Us Maltbys* (1966).
Our Cup Is Broken (1969). *Smith Valley* (1973).

BIBLIOGRAPHY: For articles in reference works, see: *CA*, 1–4 (1967). *Junior*
Book of Authors, Eds. S. J. Kunitz and H. Haycraft (1951).
Other references: *Atlantic* (Dec. 1946). *Best Sellers* (15 Dec. 1963). Boston
Transcript (28 Nov. 1931). *Horn Book* (March 1945; June 1946; June 1969).
LJ (15 Nov. 1954). *NY* (8 Dec. 1945). *NYT* (9 Aug. 1953). *NYTBR* (2 Feb.
1964). *SatR* (13 Nov. 1954; 13 Sept. 1969).

CELIA CATLETT ANDERSON

Cornelia Lynde Meigs

B. 6 Dec. 1884, Rock Island, Illinois; d. 10 Sept. 1973, Hartford County,
  Maryland
Wrote under: Adair Aldon, Cornelia Meigs
D. of Montgomery and Grace Lynde Meigs

The strong sense of family tradition that pervades much of M.'s writing
for young people comes naturally from her own appreciation of kinship and its values. A descendant of Commodore John Rogers of Revolutionary fame, M. grew up in a close-knit family on the Mississippi, where
her father was a government engineer.

Graduating from Bryn Mawr College in 1907, M. taught in Davenport,
Iowa (1912–1913), where she began "to tell stories to the younger children
. . . finding quickly just what sort they liked and what they would have
none of." M.'s first book of short stories, *The Kingdom of the Winding*
Road (1915), resulted from this experience. Novels, two plays (*The*
Steadfast Princess won the Drama League prize in 1915), and four
pseudonymous adventure stories followed during the next two decades.

From 1932 to 1950 M. taught English at Bryn Mawr. M.'s work as a
literary scholar culminated in her editing and contributing to the land-

mark book *A Critical History of Children's Literature* (1953; rev. ed., 1969). Ann Pellowski refers to it as "a definitive survey of the literature," and Frances Sayers says that M.'s section "The Roots of the Past" has the "storyteller's narrative pace, the novelist's eye for endearing detail, and the scholar's control of historic perspective."

These talents are evident in most of the fiction, history, and biography that M. wrote. Her historical romances, beginning with *Master Simon's Garden* (1916), are compelling narratives. This first novel is suitable for an adolescent audience and traces the vicissitudes and final triumph of puritan Master Simon's family and garden ("a symbol of tolerance and understanding" according to Constantine Georgiou) through several generations. The sense of continuity of family ideals is strong, and the many characters are clearly individualized.

Three successful shorter fictions followed the "olden days" adventures of eight-year-old heroines. *The Willow Whistle* (1931) has an exciting plot and convincing descriptions of daily living on the prairie. *Wind in the Chimney* (1934) recounts a young girl's growing love for the Pennsylvania farmhouse where her widowed mother has brought the family from England. *The Covered Bridge* (1936) tells of young Constance's stay on a Vermont farm in the winter of 1788.

Vermont, where M. had a summer home for many years, is the setting for other books, notably *Call of the Mountain* (1940). This story of a young man's determination to make a mountainside farm his true inheritance contains M.'s usual mixture of adventure, courage, and generous actions. Another book that deserves mention, although its story line is not so clear as that of M.'s best work, is *Vanished Island* (1941). Here, M. writes some marvelous chapters about steamboating on the Mississippi of her childhood.

Two of her books on American history, *The Violent Men: A Study of Human Relations in the First American Congress* (1949) and *The Great Design: Men and Events in the United States from 1945 to 1963* (1964), show comprehensive research though perhaps not enough winnowing of significant detail to make them as readable as her biographies.

Invincible Louisa: The Story of the Author of Little Women (1933) won the Newbery Medal in 1934. "A thoroughly readable and satisfactory life," Bertha Miller called this labor of scholarship and love. In her acceptance paper for the prize, M. stated that she read Alcott's letters and journals "over and over again through my growing years" and in times of difficulty for "the stimulation of courage" they brought. Her biography carries this same "stimulation of courage," as does her last major work, *Jane Addams: Pioneer for Social Justice* (1970), another excellent biography of a strong woman.

M.'s young heroines, although brave and sensible, often play a comparatively passive role, but of the two real-life models that M. chose for her biographies, each, like Alcott, "gallantly went her own way and won her own triumph." M.'s talents seem fully realized only in her biographies. However, her books, of whatever type, have, as Bertha Miller notes, "given expression to America's best in thought, feeling and action."

WORKS: *The Kingdom of the Winding Road* (1915). *Master Simon's Garden* (1916). *The Steadfast Princess* (1916). *The Island of Appledore* (1917). *The Pirate of Jasper Peak* (1918). *The Pool of Stars* (1919). *At the Sign of the Heroes* (1920). *The Windy Hill* (1921). *Helga and the White Peacock* (1922). *The Hill of Adventure* (1922). *The New Moon: The Story of Dick Martin's Courage, His Silver Sixpence, and His Friends in the New World* (1924). *Rain on the Roof* (1925). *As the Crow Flies* (1927). *The Trade Wind* (1927). *Clearing Weather* (1928). *The Wonderful Locomotive* (1928). *The Crooked Apple Tree* (1929). *The Willow Whistle* (1931). *Swift Rivers* (1932). *Invincible Louisa: The Story of the Author of Little Women* (1933). *Wind in the Chimney* (1934). *The Covered Bridge* (1936). *Young Americans: How History Looked to Them While It Was in the Making* (1936). *Railroad West* (1937). *The Scarlet Oak* (1938). *Call of the Mountain* (1940). *Mother Makes Christmas* (1940). *Vanished Island* (1941). *Mounted Messenger* (1943). *The Two Arrows* (1949). *The Violent Men: A Study of Human Relations in the First American Congress* (1949). *The Dutch Colt* (1952). *A Critical History of Children's Literature: A Survey of Children's Books in English from Earliest Times to the Present* (edited by Meigs, 1953; rev. ed., 1969). *Fair Wind to Virginia* (1955). *What Makes a College? A History of Bryn Mawr* (1956). *Wild Geese Flying* (1957). *Saint John's Church, Havre de Grace, Md. 1809–1959* (1959). *Mystery at the Red House* (1961). *The Great Design: Men and Events in the United Nations from 1945 to 1963* (1964). *Glimpses of Louisa: A Centennial Sampling of the Best Short Stories* (edited by Meigs, 1968). *Jane Addams: Pioneer for Social Justice* (1970). *Louisa M. Alcott and the American Family Story* (1971).

BIBLIOGRAPHY: Georgiou, C., *Children and Their Literature* (1969). Pellowski, A., *The World of Children's Literature* (1968).

For articles in reference works, see: *CA*, 9–12 (1974); 45–48 (1974). *Junior Book of Authors*, Eds. S. J. Kunitz and H. Haycraft (1934; 1951). *Newbery Medal Books, 1922–1955*, Eds. B. M. Miller and E. W. Field (1955).

Other references: *Horn Book* (Sept. 1944). *LJ* (July 1934). *PW* (30 June 1934; 25 April 1936).

CELIA CATLETT ANDERSON

Adah Isaacs Menken

B. 11 April 1835, Milneburg, Louisiana; d. 10 Aug. 1868, Paris, France
Given name: Adah Bertha Theodore
D. of Auguste and Marie Theodore; m. Alexander Isaac Menken, 1856;
   m. John Carmel Heenan, 1859; m. Robert Henry Newell, 1862;
   m. James Paul Barkley, 1866

M., feminist actress, poet, and essayist, astounded audiences of the 1860s with her near nudity and daring equestrian feats in a theatrical version of Byron's *Mazeppa*. Although M.'s perfect figure and unashamed sexuality were of primary appeal to audiences, the multiple talents of this creative and energetic woman should not be dismissed. She knew French, Spanish, Latin, Greek, and Hebrew, and was a competent sculptor and an expert horsewoman and marksman. A pioneer in vaudeville and burlesque, M. made as much as $5000 a week, much of it lavished on the poets, authors, and journalists who were her favorite companions. Four marriages and multiple dalliances made her notorious. A Hollywood star ahead of her time, she was among the first to employ modern publicity techniques, using photographs, fake biographies, and scandals to fill theater seats. "Notes of My Life" (*New York Times*, 6 Sept. 1868), for example, is pure fiction.

From 1857 to 1859, M. converted to Judaism, published poetry in the Cincinnati *Israelite*, and began her theatrical career. Moving to New York, she associated with Walt Whitman and other Bohemians in Pfaff's famous beerskellar. M. contributed poems and letters to the *New York Clipper*, and in a series of short articles for the *Sunday Mercury*, defended Walt Whitman and Edgar Allan Poe, perceptively prophesying their recognition "in the next century." M. wrote on the affinity of poetry and religion, on politics, and on women. In "Women of the World," she spoke of the need to train women for "other missions than wife and mother."

During a California tour, M. met Bret Harte, Joaquin Miller, Artemus Ward, Charles Warren Stoddard, and possibly Mark Twain. On her European tours she became the associate of Rossetti and other Pre-Raphaelites, had a rather strange affair with Swinburne (he wrote "Laus Veneris" for her), and courted Dickens assiduously. Dickens was kind, but kept M. at a respectable distance. M.'s greatest theatrical success was at Paris; there George Sand befriended her and she indulged in a scandalous affair with the aging Alexander Dumas. M. died suddenly in Paris from complications of a chest "abscess."

Before she died, M. gathered a number of poems into *Infelicia* (1868), dedicated to Dickens. His dictum, that "she is a sensitive poet who, unfortunately, cannot write," is reductionist, but her mind was better than her poetry, which lacks consistent discipline. Whitman gave her courage to adopt the free verse form that suited her passionate and extravagant nature, and his chant and litany techniques are much in evidence. Swinburne's often indecipherable sensuality was also congenial. Her talent for the occasional haunting image, often imbedded in a matrix of forgettable incoherence and private allusion, seems indisputable.

M.'s constant theme was "infelix." She contrasted the gaudy trappings of her external life to her sensitive and intellectual inner nature, and posed as the suffering victim of man and fate in "My Heritage" and elsewhere. Death and sobs figure prominently but always voluptuously intertwined with sensual and throbbingly sexual images. If she took her form from Whitman, certainly her idol Poe gave the pattern for her content. Her affinity to the "fleshly school" of the Pre-Raphaelites and Swinburne is also apparent.

M.'s passion seems undifferentiated—religion, poetry, sex—all seem part of the same intense impulse. Betrayed in love, the persona in "Resurgam" "died with my fingers grasping the white throat of many a prayer." But no one is aware of this death because "who can hear the slow drip of blood from a dead soul?"

The feminist "Judith" is a militant prophet of the "advent of power" for women. She rejects utterly the hypocritical and "slimy" ways of the "enemy Philistines": "Stand back! I am no Magdalene waiting to kiss the hem of your garment." She beheads Holofernes with gusto and obvious sensual enjoyment: ". . . the strong throat all hot and reeking with blood, that will thrill me with wild unspeakable joy as it courses down my bare body and dabbles my cold feet." Despite the racy metaphor, the power desire of "Judith" seems primarily the drive toward intellectual and moral control. For M., "Genius is power," and *Infelicia* is full of poems on intellectual and artistic "aspiration."

M. was perceptive enough to be dissatisfied with the quality of her life and work. The last poem in *Infelicia* moans, "Where is the promise of my years; / Once written on my brow? / Ere errors, agonies and fears, / . . . Where sleeps that promise now?" M. was bright and energetic, but with a streak of bad judgment and superficiality that cheapened the final results of her talent. In the ten brief years of her career, she managed to live ten lifetimes. Glamorous and intelligent, willful and kind, she did almost everything, but nothing supremely well.

WORKS: *Infelicia* (1868).

Adah Isaacs Menken's diary is in Harvard College Library Theatre Collection.

BIBLIOGRAPHY: Edwin, J., *The Life and Times of Adah Isaacs Menken* (1881?). Falk, B., *The Naked Lady* (1934; rev. ed., 1952). Lesser, A., *Enchanting Rebel* (1947). Lewis, P., *Queen of the Plaza* (1964). Newell, R. H., *My Life with Adah Isaacs Menken* (n.d.).

For articles in reference works, see: *NAW*.

L. W. KOENGETER

Marguerite Merington

B. ca. 1860, Stoke Newington, England; d. 19 May 1951, New York City
D. of Richard Whiskin Crawford Merington

Although born in England, M. spent most of her life in America after her father emigrated because of business interests. M. was teaching Greek at the Normal College in New York City when she wrote her most famous work, *Captain Lettarblair*, for the prominent actor E. H. Sothern. The play was produced by Daniel Frohman at the Lyceum Theatre in 1891 and revived during the next two seasons.

Captain Lettarblair Litton of the Irish Fusilliers has been scrimping to pay off a debt to clear the name of his wronged, deceased father. He hopes to marry Fanny Hadden. So strongly does she desire a proposal from him that she contrives to send him a large sum of money as though it came from his estate. However, in order to do so, she must press for payment of an old debt owed to her estate, not realizing that the debtor is Lettarblair himself.

The captain is forced to sell all his possessions, including his mare, and to renounce hope of marrying Fanny. The check that Fanny sends him is stolen from the mail pouch by the villainous Merivale, a rival for Fanny's hand, who leads her to believe that Lettarblair has squandered the money. By such complications is the flimsy plot sustained until the lovers are united in act 3. It is further buoyed up by moments of farcical business, such as the scene in which Lettarblair negotiates a sale through the window of his quarters while his valet tries to hold the door against the collection agent, or the scene in which Fanny is stranded in Lettarblair's room with her skirt caught in the door and the knob fallen off out of reach.

The popularity of *Captain Lettarblair* may be attributed to the performance of Sothern. To the modern reader, the play is belabored and contrived, but it won critical acclaim from the *New York Times*: "Miss M. has a knack of devising pictures which is a valuable theatrical gift, and she writes dialogue with great facility. Some of the Hibernicisms of the hero are delightful." In 1906, it was published in an elaborate book edition with numerous photographs from the production.

Love Finds the Way (1898) was M.'s last professionally produced play and the one M. considered her best. Thereafter, M. turned to writing mostly fairy-tale plays for young children and literary adaptations and historical dramas for high-school students. M.'s sincere dedication to these audiences is evident in her article "The Theatre for Everybody" in *The World's Work* (December 1910): "I regard the stage, rightly employed, as part of a broad general training. To language it is invaluable —and what trade is there, what calling, in which language is not a tool? . . . The theatre was part of the national life of the Greeks in their civilization's heyday—and there are matters in which we have yet to outstrip the wisdom of the Greeks."

Although M.'s children's plays now seem dated, they were popular in their time. *Snow White* (1905), written for the dramatic department of the Hebrew Educational Alliance, drew hundreds of children to each Sunday matinee.

In addition to M.'s several collections of fairy-tale plays and plays for holidays, one collection of particular interest is her *Picture Plays* (1911). These are very short one-act plays based upon famous paintings: *The Last Sitting* (da Vinci's "Mona Lisa"), *A Salon Carré Fantasy* (Titian's "Man with the Glove"), *His Mother's Face* (Watteau's "Une Fête champêtre"), and so forth. *Scribner's* magazine published many of M.'s sonnets, which, she later told an interviewer, one editor liked to call "Merington's 57 Varieties of Love, Life, and Death."

M. had met Elizabeth Bacon Custer, the widow of General George A. Custer, in 1894. They became close friends, and when Mrs. Custer died, M. was her literary executor. M.'s only major nondramatic work was an edition of the letters of General Custer and his wife, published in

1950. At the time of M.'s death, she was working on a book of recollections of the pianist Paderewski.

The success of M.'s fifty-nine-year career as a writer may be attributed to the dedication and sincerity of purpose by which she labored at her craft.

WORKS: *Captain Lettarblair* (1891). *Oh, Belinda* (1892). *Goodbye* (1893). *An Everyday Man* (1895). *Daphne; or, The Pipes of Arcadia* (1896). *Bonnie Prince Charlie* (1897). *Love Finds the Way* (1898). *Old Orchard* (1900). *The Gibson Play* (1901). *Cranford* (1905). *The Lady in the Adjoining Room* (1905). *Snow White* (1905). *The Turn of the Tide* (1905). *Scarlet of the Mounted* (1906). *The Vicar of Wakefield* (1909). *Holiday Plays* (1910). *Picture Plays* (1911). *The Elopers* (1913). *Festival Plays* (1913). *More Fairy-Tale Plays* (1917). *A Dish o' Tea Delayed* (1937). *Booth Episodes* (1944). *The Custer Story: The Life and Intimate Letters of General George A. Custer and His Wife Elizabeth* (1950).

Ten undated plays in typewritten manuscripts are at the New York Public Library.

BIBLIOGRAPHY: *NYT* (23 Oct. 1891; 21 May 1951). *NYTBR* (12 Feb. 1950). *Theatre Magazine* 6 (Oct. 1906).

FELICIA HARDISON LONDRÉ

Elizabeth Avery Meriwether

B. *19 Jan. 1824, Bolivar, Tennessee; d. ?1917, Memphis, Tennessee*
Wrote under: *George Edmunds, Elizabeth Avery Meriwether*
D. *of Nathan and Rebecca Avery; m. Minor Meriwether, 1850*

In her autobiography, M. reveals little about her childhood other than to note that her family moved from Bolivar to Memphis when she was eleven. It is obvious, however, that M. was well educated, for after the death of her parents, she became a teacher. When the Civil War began, her husband, a civil engineer, joined the army, leaving M. in Memphis. The city was occupied by the Union army in 1862, and after several unpleasant encounters with Northern generals, M. decided to seek refuge in Alabama.

While in Tuscaloosa, M. resumed her childhood pastime of writing. She won a competition sponsored by the Selma *Daily Mississippian* offering $500 for the best story dealing with the war. "The Refugee" is based partly on her own experiences traveling through Alabama and Tennessee. Encouraged by this success, M. wrote "The Yankee Spy," which the newspaper planned to publish as a book. However, when the Confederacy fell, these plans were abandoned.

After the war, M. combined writing with an interest in social reform. In 1872, she edited and published a weekly newspaper, *The Tablet*, which lasted for a year. A strong believer in woman suffrage, M. "cast a vote" in the Memphis elections of 1872 and began a correspondence with leading feminists. In 1881, M. joined Elizabeth Cady Stanton and Susan B. Anthony on a speaking tour of New England. There she met Henry George and became a supporter of his "single tax" theory of economics.

M.'s first novel, *The Master of Red Leaf*, was published in 1872. It is basically a description of life on a southern plantation before the Civil War and a justification of secession. Her other works include novels, a play, and several works of popular history. M.'s autobiography, *Recollections of 92 Years*, was published the year before her death.

In many ways, M. can be considered a "professional Confederate." Not only do most of her works deal with the antebellum South, but unlike other postwar southern authors, M. refused to acknowledge that slavery had been a moral or social evil. M.'s fiction is replete with stereotyped black characters—happy, carefree, childlike, and unable to govern themselves without the discipline of slavery.

However, with the end of slavery, M. saw her ordered world turned upside down. "Life in the South," M. wrote, "became one long nightmare; then a miracle happened—for surely the way the South escaped from that frightful nightmare was little short of miraculous." The "miracle" was the Ku Klux Klan. M. writes about the Klan with an insider's knowledge and sympathy, for her husband was a member. She witnessed its night raids, terrorism, and destruction of black property, claiming that the corruption of the carpetbaggers and the insolence of "uppity" blacks justified any actions by disfranchised whites. M. concludes: "No doubt many abuses were committed by the Ku Klux. In large bodies of men some unwise ones, some mean ones will inevitably be found. But considered as a whole the work of the Ku Klux was done in a patriotic spirit for patriotic purposes, and I rejoice to see . . . that History is beginning to do justice to that wonderful secret movement. At the time it was misunderstood; in the North it was reviled. But in truth it accomplished a noble and necessary work in the only way in which that work was then possible."

Despite M.'s obvious prejudices, her works are enjoyable. She had a knack for telling a good story and making her characters real. M.'s descriptions of poor white hill people are charming and convey the spirit of these people.

WORKS: *The Master of Red Leaf* (1872). *The Ku Klux Klan; or, The Carpet-bagger in New Orleans* (1877). *English Tyranny and Irish Suffering* (1881). *Black and White: A Novel* (1883). *The Devil's Dances: A Play* (1886). *The Sowing of Swords* (1910). *Recollections of 92 Years* (1916).

BIBLIOGRAPHY: Horn, S. F., *Invisible Empire: The Story of the Ku Klux Klan* (1939). Patton, J. W., *Unionism and Reconstruction in Tennessee, 1860–1869* (1934).

JANET E. KAUFMAN

Judith Merril

B. 21 Jan. 1923, New York City
Given name: Josephine Judith Grossman
Writes under: Ernest Hamilton, Cyril Judd, Judith Merril, Rose Sharon, Eric Thorstein
D. of Samuel S. and Ethel Hurwitch Grossman; m. Mr. Zissman, 1940; m. Frederick Pohl, 1950; m. Daniel Sugrue, late 1950s

The daughter of Zionist activists, M. was involved in the socialist and Zionist movements as a young woman and was only introduced to science fiction in 1940. During World War II, she joined the New York–based "Futurian Society," a group of science fiction enthusiasts that included such nascent luminaries as Isaac Asimov, Cyril Kornbluth, Frederick Pohl, James Blish, Damon Knight, and Virginia Kidd; M. and her daughter Merril, whose first name the author adopted as her pseudonym, shared a communal household with Kidd, whose husband was also overseas. Encouraged by the "Futurians," M. began to write.

After the termination of her marriage to Frederick Pohl, M. continued her own writing as she raised her daughters, Merril Zissman and Ann Pohl, and with Damon Knight organized the first of the annual Milford Science Fiction Writers' Conferences in 1956. During the 1950s and 1960s, M. became an influential editor and critic of science fiction.

Since the late 1960s, in response to U.S. involvement in Vietnam and the 1968 Democratic Convention in Chicago, M. has lived in Canada as a landed immigrant. Currently, she works for the Canadian Broadcasting Corporation, choosing topics, selecting discussants, and making and editing tapes for radio broadcast. M. is also editing an anthology of contemporary Japanese science fiction.

With "That Only a Mother" (1943), M. began a writing career characterized by attention to the lives of women in possible future societies. It describes, through letters and third-person narration, the ability of one woman to love her daughter, who is physically deformed as a result of atomic radiation, despite widespread social condemnation and infanticide of such mutations. It was later included in *The Science Fiction Hall of Fame*. M.'s first published novel, *Shadow on the Hearth* (1950), explores a related situation, an atomic bomb attack on North America. It is set entirely within one woman's household and told from her point of view. The novel was subsequently dramatized for television as "Atomic Attack."

"Survival Ship" (1951), an experiment in the elimination of gender pronouns, depicts a future society in which women dominate in a spaceship hierarchy. M. returned to this exploration of sex-role behavior and reversal in "Wish Upon a Star" (1958), in which the narrator, a male adolescent aboard the Survival Ship, is socially and vocationally constrained because of his gender. His wish is to be female.

The novella "Daughters of Earth" (1952) is noteworthy for its depiction of mother-daughter relationships in a six-generation dynasty of female space pioneers. Employing letters, diary entries, and third-person narration, it realistically presents women who as equal, contributing members of societies that value their professional abilities nonetheless experience, but usually surmount, personal and professional problems.

In 1956, M. began editing an annual series, *SF: The Year's Greatest Science Fiction and Fantasy*, which in 1960 was renamed *The Year's Best Science Fiction* and in 1968 became *SF 12*. These and other anthologies are characterized by the introduction of such (then) avant-garde writers as Brian Aldiss and Harlan Ellison and by M.'s conviction that science fiction is gradually merging with mainstream literature.

Some historians of science fiction maintain that M.'s most important contributions to the field are as editor and critic (she is the author of such essays as "What Do You Mean: Science? Fiction?" 1971), but this claim must be weighed against the contributions she has made to the "humanization" of science fiction. Emphasizing human interaction and potential rather than technological or scientific innovation, M.'s fiction differs significantly from that of many of her contemporaries, whose works often propagate sexual and racial stereotypes. While the clarity of her insight within individual works into present and possible future societies may be debated—the sex-role reversal in "Survival Ship" is, for example, a simplistic and disheartening depiction of future options— and although some of her fiction sentimentalizes human relationships, as a whole M.'s oeuvre remains impressive in its historical context.

WORKS: *Shadow on the Hearth* (1950). *Shot in the Dark* (edited by Merril, 1950). *Beyond Human Ken* (edited by Merril, 1952). *Gunner Cade* (with C. M. Kornbluth, 1952). *Outpost Mars* (with C. M. Kornbluth, 1952). *Beyond the Barriers of Time and Space* (edited by Merril, 1954). *Galaxy of Ghouls* (edited by Merril, 1955; reissued as *Off the Beaten Orbit*, 1956). *Out of Bounds* (1960). *The Tomorrow People* (1961). *SF: The Best of the Best* (edited by Merril, 1967). *England Swings SF* (edited by Merril, 1968). *The Best of Judith Merril* (Ed. V. Kidd, 1976).

BIBLIOGRAPHY: Kidd, V., Introduction to *The Best of Judith Merril* (1976). Knight, D., *The Futurians* (1977). Podojil, C., "Sisters, Daughters, and Aliens," in *Critical Encounters: Writers and Themes in Science Fiction*, Ed. D. Riley (1978). Sargent, P., "Women in Science Fiction," in *Women of Wonder* (1974).

For articles in reference works, see: *CA*, 13–16 (1975). *Index to Science Fiction Anthologies and Collections*, Ed. W. Contento (1978). *WA*.

Other references: *Algol/Starship* (Winter 1978–1979).

NATALIE M. ROSINSKY

Annie Nathan Meyer

B. 19 Feb. 1867, New York City; d. 23 Sept. 1951, New York City
D. of Robert Weeks and Annie Florance Nathan; m. Alfred Meyer, 1887

Born in New York City, the youngest of four children, M. proudly claimed her heritage in a prominent Jewish family that dated to the revolutionary era. After the 1875 stock-market crash, her family moved to the Midwest, where M. lived until just before her mother's death in 1878, when the three youngest children were sent to New York to live with M.'s grandfather. Later M. lived with her father until her marriage; she spent the rest of her life in New York City.

In 1885 she secretly studied for and passed the entrance examinations for Columbia University's collegiate course for women. At that time women were not allowed to attend Columbia's classes but could be admitted to the collegiate course for women and allowed to study independently for the same examinations taken by men. When her father learned of her activities, he warned, "You'll never marry" because "men hate intelligent wives." Undaunted by his criticism, she decided "to forego all chances of winning a husband." This potential sacrifice, described in her autobiography, *It's Been Fun* (1951), and in her account of the founding of Barnard College, *Barnard Beginnings* (1935), proved unnecessary. She described her husband, Dr. Meyer, as sympathetic to her literary ambitions.

Although M. felt continuation of the Columbia course no longer necessary for her literary ambitions, she did begin campaigning for a women's college affiliate of Columbia that would allow women the full advantages of a collegiate education comparable to that available to Columbia's male students. As an incorporator and trustee of Barnard College, M. continued throughout her life to support the college she had helped found in 1889.

M. also pursued her own literary career, writing novels, plays, and short stories; articles on education, art, and feminism; and frequent letters to the editors of various publications. Her stories and articles appeared in such periodicals as *Bookman, Critic, Harper's Bazaar, North American Review, Putnam's,* and *Century*.

Many of M.'s works deal with the special problems resulting from women's search for new roles in the late 19th and early 20th centuries. After expressing her concern for the improvement of education for women in the late 1880s, she turned to the special problems of the women who entered the professions in *Woman's Work in America* (1891), a collection of essays by prominent women, such as Mary Putnam Jacobi, Frances Willard, and Clara Barton.

In 1892 M. anonymously published *Helen Brent, M.D.,* a novel about the special problems of a woman doctor. The heroine refuses to surrender her career to marriage and insists that she has as much right to ask a man to give up his ambition as he does to demand such a sacrifice from her. Until she can find a man willing to accept a wife who will continue her career, she will forgo marriage. Of all of M.'s works, this one stirred the most controversy among reviewers.

Several of M.'s plays also addressed complexities faced by the new woman. M. did not, however, maintain any consistent prowoman philosophy. In *The Dominant Sex* (1911), she satirizes the club woman who ignores her own child while she campaigns for child-protection legislation. This play also satirizes the tendency of some women to assume that they are the superior sex. Eventually chastened by the knowledge that her husband represents the dominant sex, the club woman gives up her club work and returns to her proper role at home.

The Dominant Sex dramatizes the strong antisuffrage views M. presented in "Woman's Assumption of Sex Superiority" (*North American Review*, Jan. 1904), which rejects both the ideas that women could combine marriage and career and that women represent a morally superior group. Although M. claimed in her autobiography that *Helen Brent, M.D.* and *The Advertising of Kate*—a play about the "delicate adjustment of the claims of sex to the work of the business woman," written in 1914 and produced on Broadway in 1922—were ahead of their times, other works seem very dated in their opposition to the new woman.

Among her approximately twenty-six plays, several addressed other social issues. In *The New Way*, a comedy directed by Jessie Bonstelle at the Longacre Theatre in New York in 1923, M. treated humorously the complexities of marriage and divorce. Her more serious *Black Souls* (1932), directed by James Light in 1932 at the Provincetown Playhouse in New York and including members of Zora Neale Hurston's choral group, dealt with the horrors of the lynching of blacks and the hypocrisy of white attitudes toward blacks.

In addition to numerous published works, M.'s unpublished manuscripts and correspondence reveal both her wide-ranging social interests and her occasionally contradictory convictions about the issues of her day.

WORKS: *Woman's Work in America* (1891). *Helen Brent, M.D.* (1892). *My Park Book* (1898). *Robert Annys, Poor Priest* (1901). *The Dominant Sex: A Play in Three Acts* (1911). *The Dreamer: A Play in Three Acts* (1912). *P's and Q's: A Play in One Act* (1921). *The New Way: A Comedy in Three Acts* (1925). *Black Souls: A Play in Six Scenes* (1932). *Barnard Beginnings* (1935). *It's Been Fun: An Autobiography* (1951).

The papers of Annie Nathan Meyer are at the American Jewish Archives, Cincinnati, Ohio.

BIBLIOGRAPHY: Askowith, D., *Three Outstanding Women: Mary Fels, Rebekah Kohut, and Annie Nathan Meyer* (1941).

For articles in reference works, see: *AW*.

Other references: *Harper's Bazaar* (4 June 1892). *NY* (23 Oct. 1943; 30 Oct. 1943). *NYT* (2 April 1911; 9 May 1922; 31 March 1932; 24 Sept. 1951; 25 Sept. 1951).

JEAN CARWILE MASTELLER

Josephine Miles

B. 11 June 1911, Chicago, Illinois
D. of Reginald Odber and Josephine Lackner Miles

M. is descended from an English business family which came to America on the Mayflower. M.'s mother studied history and education with John Dewey and Colonel Parker at the University of Chicago.

M. attended grammar and high school in Los Angeles and graduated Phi Beta Kappa from the University of California at Los Angeles in 1932. She took graduate degrees from the University of California at Berkeley and joined the Berkeley faculty in 1940. She retired, university professor emerita, in 1978.

M. began writing poems at age eight. In high school, she gained a strong foundation in Latin and Greek poetry, followed in college by rigorous training in literary history. During early graduate study, M. developed her compelling interests in poetic language and form. The metaphysical poets and Yeats led her own early verse in a direction counter to that of a number of her contemporaries. Later, the writing of Neruda and Rilke offered in subject and approach modern alternatives to the more oblique expression of the metaphysical poets. The contemporary poets she has regarded most highly include Eberhart, Rukeyser, Levertov, Dickey, Stafford, Nathan, and Ammons. Those characteristics M. identifies as important in their verse—incisiveness, factualness, simplicity, power, and lyricism—are evident in her own finest poems. M. has received distinguished awards for her poetry and for her literary scholarship.

M.'s approach to what she calls "verse composition" is often determined by "the idea of speech . . . people talking . . . as the material from which poetry is made." In an early poem, "Speaker," the voice admits: "My talking heart talked less of what it knew / Than what it saw." What is known in many of M.'s poems is conveyed obliquely by what is observed in commonplace landscapes. Long a city resident, M. includes in these landscapes the repeated sights of urban life. In "Entry," the quantifiable city where "the small matter is put down already / To depreciation" is contrasted with the country, a place of hints and expectation.

M.'s poetry has not received the critical attention it deserves. It is difficult to generalize about M.'s writing except to note its condensation, craft, unexpected juxtaposition of images, pleasure in "the space and active interplay of talk," and—in recent volumes—willingness to employ more irregular form and an increasingly more direct political and ethical stance. Negative criticism of her work has centered on a miscellaneous quality of a number of the poems, as well as a control which has seemed to some to force a too moderate, reasonable, and civil response. However, longer poems, such as "Two Kinds of Trouble (for Michelangelo)," "Ten Dreamers in a Motel," and "Views from Gettysburg," show M. capable of sustaining and varying form.

M.'s doctoral dissertation, "Wordsworth and the Vocabulary of Emotion," was published in 1942. In this systematic study, M. establishes a historical and quantitative approach to criticism based on a method which she later refined and applied to other poets and eras and to prose style as well. By "counting the number of previously established names of emotion and standard signs of emotion in every poem, group, and in the complete poetical works" of a poet, the literary scholar could, M. demonstrates, formulate a more scientific, evidential basis for analyzing the relationship of thought and feeling in an era and the specific vocabulary a poet considered "poetic." In *Style and Proportion* (1966), by tabulating numerous British and American writers' use of adjectives, nouns, verbs, and connectives, M. recognizes "three styles distinguishable on the basis of structural choice: the predicative, the connective-subordinate, and the adjectival." At times reluctant to acknowledge the prior necessity of such tabulation, some scholars have praised M.'s aesthetic criticism and insight into the social nature of language at the expense of appreciation of the scientific method she employed in describing English poetry from the 16th c. to the present.

WORKS: *Lines at Intersection* (1939). *Poems on Several Occasions* (1941). *Pathetic Fallacy in the Nineteenth Century* (1942). *Wordsworth and the Vocabulary of Emotion* (1942). *Local Measures* (1946). *The Vocabulary of Poetry: Three Studies* (1946). *Criticism: The Foundations of Modern Literary Judgment* (edited by Miles, with M. Schorer and G. McKenzie, 1948; rev. ed., 1958). *The Continuity of English Poetry from the 1540's to the 1940's* (1951). *Prefabrications* (1955). *Eras and Modes in English Poetry* (1957; rev. ed., 1964). *The Poem: A Critical Anthology* (edited by Miles, 1959; rev. and abridged ed., *The Ways of the Poem*, 1969; rev. ed., 1973). *Poems, 1930–1960* (1960). *Renaissance, Eighteenth-Century, and Modern Language in English Poetry: A Tabular View* (1960). *Classic Essays in English* (edited by Miles, 1961; rev. ed., 1965). *Ralph Waldo Emerson* (1964). *Civil Poems* (1966). *Style and Proportion* (1966). *Kinds of Affection* (1967). *Fields of Learning* (1968).

Poetry and Change: Donne, Milton, Wordsworth, and the Equilibrium of the Present (1974). *To All Appearances: New and Selected Poems* (1974). *Coming to Terms* (1980).

BIBLIOGRAPHY: Bogan, L., in *A Poet's Alphabet* (1970). Dickey, J., in *Babel to Byzantium* (1968). Smith, L., in *Rereadings*, Ed. G. Kuzma (1978). For articles in reference works, see: *CA*, 1–4 (1967). *Contemporary Poets*, Ed. R. Murphie (1970). *Contemporary Poets*, Eds. J. Vinson and D. L. Kirkpatrick (1975). *20thCAS.*

Other references: *PrS* (Winter 1958–9). *TLS* (25 April 1975).

THEODORA R. GRAHAM

Margaret Millar

B. 5 Feb. 1915, Kitchener, Ontario, Canada
D. of William and Lavinia Ferrier Sturm; m. Kenneth Millar, 1938

M. studied at the University of Toronto; her early interests were classics, archeology, music, and psychiatry. M.'s husband writes mysteries under the name Ross Macdonald. M. is a former president of the Mystery Writers of America and widely known as an environmentalist. *The Birds and the Beasts Were There* (1967) recounts the difficulties and the pleasures of a major current interest, bird watching.

Primarily known as a mystery writer, M. created two series detectives. Dr. Paul Prye, psychiatrist and witty amateur sleuth, appears in *The Invisible Worm* (1941) and *The Weak-Eyed Bat* (1942), which details Prye's search for a killer and his courtship of clever, brash Nora Shane. Their wedding, in *The Devil Loves Me* (1942), is complicated by a murder and allows for the introduction of the second continuing character, Detective-Inspector Sands.

Sands, unprepossessing but perceptive and humane, is more typical of M.'s characters and appears in two other novels. *Wall of Eyes* (1943) uses an important M. device—characters who are not what or who they seem. The relationship between the Heath sisters, pliant Alice and blind, shrill Kelsey, asks who is prey and who is predator. *The Iron Gates* (1945) finds Sands investigating the disappearance of Lucille Morrow, one of M.'s most successfully complex characters. The novel also features another important M. motif, dream imagery, and a key theme, the evil power of love.

Fire Will Freeze (1944) and *Rose's Last Summer* (1952) are comedy-mysteries. *Fire* provides amusing characters, a measure of terror, and a clever surprise ending. All the early novels employ the "closed circle of suspects" technique.

Psychotic personalities are the focus of *The Cannibal Heart* (1949) and *Beast in View* (cited as best mystery of 1955 by the Mystery Writers of America). In *The Cannibal Heart*, the relative innocence of young Jessie Banner and adolescent Luisa Roma contrasts with the corruption of Janet Wakefield as she attempts to compensate for disappointment in marriage and motherhood. *Beast in View* is the study of Helen Clarvoe, rejected and repressed as a child and dangerous as a woman. Hurtful family impact is a central theme, and the novel employs yet another pattern, the outsider drawn into a turmoil of family entanglements.

Perhaps M.'s best novels are *Vanish in an Instant* (1952) and *The Fiend* (1964). The former compares the relationship between Virginia Barkley, accused of a murder, and her overprotective mother with that between Earl Loftus, who confesses to the killing, and his alcoholic mother. *The Fiend*, compassionate and unsentimental, probes the interactions within and between five families as Charlie Gowen, former child molester, struggles against his interest in little Jessie Brant. The characterizations are vivid, and M. uses a variation of the mother-child theme here, as a childless woman interferes with another's daughter.

The Listening Walls (1959) compares the self-protective instincts of a Mexican hotel maid with those of a pampered California matron. *Beyond This Point Are Monsters* (1970) and *Ask for Me Tomorrow* (1976) have fine Southern California settings, and in each M. provides sensitive examinations of the position of Mexican-Americans within that culture.

How Like an Angel (1962) interweaves two plots—a disappearing husband and the fate of the True Believers, a strange religious cult. The Believers' impact on the elderly Sister Blessing and teenaged Sister Karma are of especial interest, as is the portrait of Charlotte Keating, the seemingly controlled, competent, independent physician of *Do Evil in Return* (1950). The detectives in these novels, Quinn and Easter, are imperfect but decent men doing their best to cope with murder and with love.

Experiment in Springtime (1947), *Wives and Lovers* (1954), and *A Stranger in My Grave* (1960) treat failed marriages. In each, recognition of failure and termination of the marriage symbolize growth toward maturity for at least one partner. *Experiment in Springtime* contrasts the "second youth" of Martha Pearson and Steve Ferris, reunited lovers, with the realistic adolescence of Laura Shaw, who also loves Steve. *A Stranger in My Grave* effectively combines gothic overtones with a search for self-definition as Stevens Pinata discovers factual reasons for Daisy Harker's nightmares.

M. is considered a novelist of skill and power, especially noted for her effective imagery and excellent characterizations.

WORKS: *The Invisible Worm* (1941). *The Weak-Eyed Bat* (1942). *The Devil Loves Me* (1942). *Wall of Eyes* (1943). *Fire Will Freeze* (1944). *The Iron Gates* (1945). *Experiment in Springtime* (1947). *It's All in the Family* (1948). *The Cannibal Heart* (1949). *Do Evil in Return* (1950). *Rose's Last Summer* (1952). *Vanish in an Instant* (1952). *Wives and Lovers* (1954). *Beast in View* (1955). *An Air That Kills* (1957). *The Listening Walls* (1959). *A Stranger in My Grave* (1960). *How Like an Angel* (1962). *The Fiend* (1964). *The Birds and the Beasts Were There* (1967). *Beyond This Point Are Monsters* (1970). *Ask for Me Tomorrow* (1976).

BIBLIOGRAPHY: For articles in reference works, see: *CA*, 13–16 (1975). *Encyclopedia of Mystery and Detection*, Eds. C. Steinbrunner and O. Penzler (1976). *WA*.

Other references: *The Armchair Detective* (Jan. 1970). *NYT* (13 Oct. 1976). *NYTBR* (30 May 1954; 21 June 1964).

JANE S. BAKERMAN

Edna St. Vincent Millay

B. *22 Feb. 1892, Rockland, Maine; d. 19 Oct. 1950, Steepletop, New York*
Wrote under: Nancy Boyd, Edna St. Vincent Millay
D. of Henry and Cora Buzzelle Millay; m. Eugen Boissevain, 1923

M. was the oldest of three daughters. Her father, a schoolteacher and school superintendent, left the household when M. was seven. Her mother supported the family by working as a practical nurse. She also did her utmost to encourage all three girls to develop their creative talents.

M. first received recognition as a poet when her long poem "Renascence" was selected in 1912 for inclusion in *The Lyric Year*. However,

"Renascence" narrowly missed receiving one of the three prizes awarded for the best poems in the volume. Publication of the anthology brought forth a storm of protest. Readers maintained that M.'s youthful statement of despair, rebirth, and affirmation was the strongest in the book.

M.'s success brought her to the attention of Caroline Dow, who made it possible for the poet to attend Vassar College. In 1917, soon after graduation, M. moved to Greenwich Village, where she quickly became a legend.

Several images of M. during this period emerge: the serious artist living on limited funds; the bohemian, careless of health and propriety; the passionate woman involved in brief, intoxicating love affairs. During her Village years, M. published *Renascence, and Other Poems* (1917) and *A Few Figs from Thistles* (1920). The latter, with its famous "candle" quatrain (beginning "My candle burns at both ends; / It shall not last the night") and flippant love poems, captured the imaginations of the "emancipated" youth of the early 1920s. At the same time, M. finished the poems that would appear in *Second April* (1921), and wrote and directed a pacifist verse play, *Aria da Capo* (1920).

In 1922, M. received the Pulitzer Prize for *The Ballad of the Harp-Weaver*, an expanded edition of *Figs* with eight new sonnets. The following year, she married a Dutch businessman. Boissevain's first wife had been Inez Milholland, the famous suffragist, who died in 1916. M., who had admired Milholland at college, dedicated to her a sonnet honoring the women's rights movement.

Eventually, Boissevain gave up his coffee business to manage M.'s highly successful poetry-reading tours, and to superintend Steepletop, their farm in upstate New York. Their marriage lasted twenty-seven years, until Boissevain's death in 1949. During these years, M. produced several books of poems—*The Buck in the Snow* (1928), *Fatal Interview* (1931), *Wine from These Grapes* (1934)—that are more subdued and more contemplative in tone than her earlier work.

In 1927, M. became active in the movement to save Sacco and Vanzetti. She signed petitions, demonstrated, and, in a futile interview, tried to persuade the governor of Massachusetts to grant clemency. Her involvement in this case is reflected in several poems, most notably "Justice Denied in Massachusetts."

Growing increasingly concerned about the spread of fascism throughout Europe and the start of World War II, M. renounced her former pacifism in the late 1930s. In a series of political poems, she argued for American military preparedness and aid to France and England. Unfortunately, these poems are quite poor, relying on jangling rhythms and trite language. Collected in *Make Bright the Arrows* (1940), they drew a barrage of adverse criticism.

M. is particularly interesting because, at a time when modern poetry was abandoning traditional forms, she chose to write ballads, lyrics, and sonnets. Though M.'s later work is somewhat more experimental, she usually stayed within familiar structures, adapting them to her own use. M.'s strongest poems work precisely because of the balance maintained between the emotional intensity of her subjects and the disciplined craftmanship of her forms. As Floyd Dell said, "She learned the molds first, into which she poured her emotions while hot."

Many of her first poems ("Renascence," "God's World") reveal innocence and youthful exuberance. In "Recuerdo," the young lovers, after riding "back and forth all night on the ferry," impulsively give bags of fruit and "all our money but our subway fares" to an old woman newspaper seller. Other early verses, however, exhibit a mocking, skeptical attitude toward life and love. In many of the poems from *A Few Figs from Thistles*, M. creates a bold, unconventional woman persona who is frankly attracted to men and who initiates and terminates love affairs at will. In *Sonnet xi*, for instance, she tells her lover: "I shall forget you presently, my dear, / So make the most of this, your little day." The poem ends with the forthright statement: "Whether or not we find what we are seeking / Is idle, biologically speaking." In another poem, the persona glories in being a "wicked girl" and declares: "if I can't be sorry, why, / I might as well be glad."

A more serious note appears in *Second April* (1921). The skepticism remains, but the lightness is gone. In "Spring," M. states that "Life in itself / Is nothing" and compares the month of April to "an idiot, babbling and strewing flowers." The love poems in this book are somber. *Sonnet xix*, for example, begins: "And you as well must die, beloved dust / And all your beauty stand you in no stead."

Throughout all of M.'s poetry runs the message that life is short and love ephemeral. Human relationships, however sweet, cannot last. The theme of death constantly recurs. The early "Passer Mortuus Est" begins "Death devours all lovely things" and the late "Epitaph for the Race of Man" mourns, "Earth, unhappy planet, born to die."

M. has been criticized for writing only of herself and her love affairs, but many of her poems reflect wider concerns. However, her love poems, far from being sentimental effusions, are central to her vision of life's brevity and impermanence.

The recipient of much acclaim in the 1920s, M. is less popular today. Feminist readers tend to dismiss her work as old-fashioned and conventional. This is unfortunate because M., though no structural innovator, is in many ways close to the feminist-oriented poets of the 1970s. Certainly M.'s use of highly personal material; her fresh, forthright language; and her creation of strong female personae anticipate modern women's poetry. M.'s finest poems, moreover, ensure her position as an important American woman poet.

WORKS: *Renascence, and Other Poems* (1917). *Aria da Capo* (1920). *A Few Figs from Thistles* (1920). *The Lamp and the Bell* (1921). *Second April* (1921). *Two Slatterns and a King* (1921). *The Harp-Weaver, and Other Poems* (1923). *Distressing Dialogues* (1924). *The King's Henchman* (1927). *The Buck in the Snow* (1928). *Poems Selected for Young People* (1929). *Fatal Interview* (1931). *The Princess Marries the Page* (1932). *Wine from These Grapes* (1934). *Flowers of Evil* by Baudelaire (translated by Millay, with George Dillon, 1936). *Conversation at Midnight* (1937). *Huntsman, What Quarry?* (1939). *Make Bright the Arrows* (1940). *Collected Sonnets* (1941). *Invocation to the Muses* (1941). *The Murder of Lidice* (1942). *Collected Lyrics* (1943). *Poem and Prayer for an Invading Army* (1944). *Mine the Harvest* (1954). *Collected Poems* (1956).

BIBLIOGRAPHY: Atkins, E., *Edna St. Vincent Millay and Her Times* (1936). Bogan, L., *Achievements in American Poetry* (1951). Cheney, A., *Millay in the Village* (1975). Dash, J., *A Life of One's Own* (1973). Dell, F., *Homecoming: An Autobiography* (1933). Gould, J., *The Poet and Her Book* (1969). Gray, J., *Edna St. Vincent Millay* (Univ. of Minnesota Pamphlets on American Writers, 1967). Gurko, M., *Restless Spirit* (1962). Sheean, V., *The Indigo Bunting* (1951). Wilson, E., *I Thought of Daisy* (1929). Wilson, E., in *The Shores of Light* (1952).

For articles in reference works, see: *NAW* (article by J. M. Brinnin). *NCAB*, B.

ENID DAME

Alice Duer Miller

B. 28 July 1874, Staten Island, New York; d. 22 Aug. 1942, New York City
D. of James Gore King and Elizabeth Wilson Meads Duer; m. Henry Wise
Miller, 1899

M. was born into a prominent New York family and spent a long, happy girlhood growing up with her two sisters on the family estate in Weehawken, New Jersey. The idyll ended abruptly, however, when M.'s father lost the family fortune in the Baring Bank failure. Undaunted by the crisis, M. worked her way through a mathematics program at Barnard College by selling stories to *Harper's* and *Scribner's* magazines. Upon her graduation in 1899, M. married a Harvard graduate, and they set sail for Costa Rica. Here, M. was frequently left alone while her husband traveled on business, and the stories M. wrote during the companionless hours supported the Millers throughout their Central American stay. Her efforts continued to be the family's main source of income long after their return to New York in 1903.

In 1915, after fifteen years of serious writing, M. published a serial in *Harper's Bazar* entitled *Come Out of the Kitchen* that made her famous overnight. In 1916 it was published in book form and became a bestseller; a dramatized version ran a long season on Broadway; and Famous Players bought the motion picture rights. *Come Out of the Kitchen* centers on four children of an aristocratic family who cannot make ends meet, and therefore rent out the family mansion while their parents are away. The dashing young bachelor who leases the house falls in love with the daughter who is masquerading as a cook. The novel is light, amusing, and fast-moving; primarily concerned with narrative and dialogue, M. makes little use of description or reflection. She creates a safe and sane world where nothing can go seriously wrong, yet this artificial world is deceptively simple. Along with the goodness and light, M. employs a great deal of masterful irony. She puts the rich and proud in their place by highlighting their ridiculous manners and pompous stupidity. As Harvey Higgins writes in a 1927 *New Yorker* profile, M.'s stories "are written as precisely as if they were engraved by a fashionable stationer, but they are full of the devil."

Many of M.'s later novels follow this same pattern. In the best-selling *The Charm School* (1919) and *Gowns by Roberta* (1933), the simple and sincere are again rewarded, whereas the self-seeking and affected are again chastised. Limited in scope, M.'s stories are written to entertain. Only one of M.'s works, *Manslaughter* (1921), breaks through the insulation of upper-class reality. In this ambitious novel, a heroine who has taken unfair advantage of her wealth, beauty, and social position is convicted in a hit-and-run case like any other common criminal. For once M. does not skirt around the ugly, and the result is surprisingly successful. *Manslaughter* is a complex novel inhabited by characters capable of depth. Like *The Charm School* and *Gowns by Roberta*, *Manslaughter* became a popular motion picture.

M. is best remembered for her poetry, although it is inferior in quality to her prose. From 1914 to 1917, she wrote a poetry column for the New York *Tribune* entitled "Are Women People?" which she compiled into a book (1915) and then followed with the sequel *Women Are People* (1917). These heavily ironic poems point out the hypocritical nature of men's arguments against suffrage, and they are often hilarious. M. is most famous, however, for *The White Cliffs* (1940), a serious narrative poem about an American girl and an English soldier during World War II. Written in sentimental verse, *The White Cliffs* is utterly devoid of the social satire that makes M.'s prose come alive. Throughout its dreary fifty-two sections, the poem remains childishly singsong and superficial. Nevertheless, it became an extraordinary bestseller both in the U.S. and abroad, and was read by Lynn Fontanne on NBC radio for the British War Relief. M. agreed with the critics when they attributed the success of *The White Cliffs* to the emotional climate of the 1940s.

M. never let her writing interfere with her personal life. She traveled extensively, was frequently called to Hollywood on assignment for Goldwyn or Paramount, and socialized regularly with prominent figures. M. was happiest when among others, and she often admitted that she had no style and wrote only for money. Yet M.'s stories, although sentimental and simplistic, are solid and clever narratives. Like the charming, aristocratic woman who once worked her way through Barnard and supported her family in Central America, M.'s works are easy to underestimate.

WORKS: *Poems* (with C. Duer, 1896). *The Modern Obstacle* (1903). *Calderon's Prisoner* (1904). *Less Than Kin* (1909). *The Blue Arch* (1910). *The Burglar and the Blizzard* (1914). *Things* (1914). *Are Women People?* (1915). *The Rehearsal* (1915). *Come Out of the Kitchen* (film version, 1916). *Ladies Must Live* (1917). *Women Are People* (1917). *The Happiest Times of Their Lives* (1918). *Wings in the Night* (1918). *The Charm School* (film version, 1919). *The Beauty and the Bolshevist* (1920). *Manslaughter* (film version,

1921). *Are Parents People?* (1924). *Priceless Pearl* (1924). *The Reluctant Princess* (1925). *Instruments of Darkness, and Other Stories* (1926). *The Springboard* (1927). *Welcome Home* (1928). *The Prince Serves His Purpose* (1929). *Forsaking All Others* (1930). *Come Out of the Pantry* (1933). *Gowns by Roberta* (film version, 1933). *Death Sentence* (1934). *Four Little Heiresses* (1935). *The Rising Star* (1935). *And One Was Beautiful* (1937). *Not for Love* (1937). *Barnard College: The Frst Fifty Years* (with S. Myers, 1939). *The White Cliffs* (1940). *I Have Loved England* (1941). *Summer Holiday* (1941). *Cinderella* (1943). *Selected Poems* (1949).

BIBLIOGRAPHY: Miller, H. W., *All Our Lives* (1945). Overton, G. M., *The Women Who Make Our Novels* (1928).
  For articles in reference works, see: *NAW* (article by S. G. Walcutt). *20thCA. 20thCAS.*
  Other references: *NY* (19 Feb. 1927; 9 Aug. 1941). *NYTBR* (29 June 1941).

CHRISTIANE BIRD

Caroline Pafford Miller

B. 26 Aug. 1903, Waycross, Georgia
Wrote under: Caroline Miller
D. of Elias and Levy Zan Pafford; m. William D. Miller, ca. 1921;
  m. Clyde H. Ray

M. was raised near the Georgia backwoods and has spend most of her adult life there. Her knowledge of the area and its people inspired M. to write *Lamb in His Bosom* (1933), which was awarded the Pulitzer Prize, and the first part of *Lebanon* (1944), her only other novel. M. and her first husband, her high-school English teacher, had three children.

Lamb in His Bosom chronicles the life of Cean Carver Smith from her marriage in the mid-19th c. to the Reconstruction era. Cean is a typical Georgia backwoods woman; she endures hard work, infant deaths, fire, snakebite, lonely childbirth, attacking panthers, and the death of a son in the Civil War. An important secondary character is her brother Lias, whose philandering and thirst for adventure are unexampled in the community.

Lebanon is certainly not the equal of *Lamb in His Bosom*. Although the locale is the Georgia backwoods and the interest in the wilderness life remains, the protagonist, Lebanon Fairgale, is a bit too much the complete frontierswoman. She can kill any critter and cure any disease from colic to the Pest, although surgery doesn't seem to be her line. When her rifle accidentally shoots off her lover's hand and when her face is clawed by a "pet" bear, someone else has to do the stitching. These catastrophes would be enough, but in addition Lebanon suffers desertion by her lover, infidelity by her husband, the deaths of her husband, humpback child, and adopted child, and false accusations of sodomy, harlotry, and murder. In the end she marries a preacher.

M. is at her best in the evocation of routine frontier life and in the lyrical, loving depiction of Georgia; indeed, her attempt to move Lebanon out of Georgia into an unidentified wilderness is one of the second novel's major flaws. M. is at her worst in constructing melodramatic, action-packed plots, which she evidently feels her books need. Yet, despite the plot and M.'s prose, which may be too lyrical for the brutal, uneducated lives she describes, *Lamb in His Bosom* is beautiful, peaceful, and satisfying—a poem to the past, particularly to the past of the "frontier" woman.

WORKS: *Lamb in His Bosom* (1933). *Lebanon* (1944).

BIBLIOGRAPHY: For articles in reference works, see: *20thCA. 20thCAS.*
Other references: Boston *Transcript* (20 Sept. 1933). *Literary Digest* (12 May 1934). *NewR* (20 Sept. 1933). *Newsweek* (12 May 1934). *NYT* (8 May 1933; 17 Sept. 1933; 15 Nov. 1933). *PW* (12 May 1934).

CYNTHIA L. WALKER

Emily Clark Huntington Miller

B. *22 Oct. 1833, Brooklyn, Connecticut; d. 2 Nov. 1913, Northfield, Minnesota*
D. *of Thomas and Paulina Clark Huntington; m. John Edwin Miller, 1860*

One of five children, M. attended local schools in Connecticut and completed her education at Oberlin College. M. had three sons who survived to adulthood.

From 1867 to 1871 M. was associate editor of *Little Corporal*, a Chicago juvenile periodical. After her husband acquired control of the magazine in 1871, M. became editor-in-chief, retaining the position until the magazine was absorbed by *St. Nicholas* in 1875. During these years, M.

was also active in the Chautauqua movement, serving as president of the Chautauqua Woman's Club and writing for the *Chautauquan*. In 1874, M. helped found the Women's Christian Temperance Union.

From 1878 to 1891 M. lived in St. Paul, Minnesota. For six years she was president of the Methodist Women's Foreign Missionary Society of Minneapolis. M. was dean of women at Northwestern University (1891–98) and taught English literature there until 1900.

Throughout her career as editor, administrator, and teacher, M. wrote poetry, children's stories, and adult fiction as well as producing numerous articles for leading American magazines.

Many of M.'s children's books first appeared as serials in *Little Corporal*. These stories combine adventure, often in the form of travel, with sufficient piety to make them attractive to the Sunday-school movement. *The Royal Road to Fortune* (1869) illustrates this formula. Jimmy Marvin, a homeless ten-year-old orphan, finds a card bearing the inscription, "The hand of the diligent maketh rich." From then on diligence—not, however, unaided by good fortune—allows him to progress from sweeping crossings to selling newspapers to bootblacking and ultimately to owning his own farm. It is significant that his social advancement occurs as he moves west, journeying from New York to Ohio to Idaho.

Three volumes of the "Kirkwood Library" use variants of the same formula. *Summer Days at Kirkwood* (1877) is a tale of family fun in a country house near a large lake. The story is episodic in structure, and the tone is free of fervent piety. *A Year at Riverside Farm* (1877) attractively describes the sobering of exuberant Barbie Williams, who has grown to dislike the dull routine of farm life. The realistic portrait of the adolescent girl and M.'s familiarity with rural life compensate somewhat for the fact that the girl's adventures are not really very exciting. *Uncle Dick's Legacy* (1877), by contrast, is an adventure tale of two boys traveling in the wilds of Michigan to find the homestead their uncle has left them. Despite the interesting journey, the tale is unsuccessful because the picturesque characters are overdrawn and the boys themselves are colorless creatures.

In *Captain Fritz, His Friends and Adventures* (1877) M. abandoned the child protagonist and scriptural quotations. Captain Fritz, a performing French poodle, narrates his turbulent life from the vantage point of serene old age, describing with some puzzlement the neglect and cruelty he has suffered. The story is clever and warmhearted, teaching kindness without resort to moral asides.

M.'s ventures into adult fiction and drama also put her pen at the service of religion. *The Parish of Fair Haven* (1876) is a faintly disguised tract supporting missionary work. *The Little Lad of Bethlehem Town* (1911), a nativity play in blank verse, attempts to deal with traditional material in a fresh way, but slips into pathos and sentimentality.

M.'s best-known volume of poetry, *From Avalon, and Other Poems* (1896), contains forty lyrics on such conventional subjects as death, religion, love, motherhood, and nature. M.'s tone is often moralistic and her mood melancholy; in her response to nature, however, she occasionally achieves a genuine lyric quality.

M. was a minor writer whose copious output was often merely a vehicle to express religious and social interests. But in a few of M.'s children's books, she successfully combined entertainment with moral instruction.

WORKS: *The Royal Road to Fortune* (1869). *The Parish of Fair Haven* (1876). *What Tommy Did* (1876). *Captain Fritz, His Friends and Adventures* (1877). *The Kirkwood Library* (5 vols., *The Bears Den; Fighting the Enemy, and The House that Johnny Rented; Summer Days at Kirkwood; Uncle Dick's Legacy, and Working and Winning; A Year at Riverside Farm;* 1877). *Little Neighbors* (1878). *Debt and Credit* (1886). *Kathie's Experience* (1886). *What Happened on a Christmas Eve* (1888). *The King's Messengers* (1891). *Helps and Hinderances* (1892). *Girls' Book of Treasures* (1894). *Home Talks about the Word* (1894). *Songs from the Nest. From Avalon, and Other Poems* (1896). *The Little Lad of Bethlehem Town* (1911). *For the Beloved* (n.d.).

BIBLIOGRAPHY: Darling, F. L., *The Rise of Children's Book Reviewing in America, 1865–1881* (1968). *Literary Writings in America: A Bibliography* (1977).

For articles in reference works, see: *AA. AW. NAW* (article by P. R. Messbarger). *NCAB*, 10.

Other references: *PW* (15 Dec. 1877).

PHYLLIS MOE

Harriet Mann Miller

B. 25 June 1831, Auburn, New York; d. 25 Dec. 1918, Los Angeles, California
Wrote under: Harriet M. Miller, Olive Thorne Miller, Olive Thorne
D. of Seth and Mary Holbrook Mann; m. Watts Todd Miller, 1854

Married at twenty-three, after a finishing-school education, M. waited until after her four children were born to publish her first work, a children's essay on china-making, and she was forty-nine when she began the close observation of birds that led to her best work. M. continued writing children's stories and essays to the end of her life.

One of the most popular and influential nature writers of the last century, M. combined an early conservationist sensibility with the careful naturalist's eye for detailed observation and talent for writing. An urbanite herself, M. contributed to the growing tendency in American popular literature to see nature as a healing retreat. Like other nature writers of the period, M. indulged in extreme feats of anthropomorphism, her birds being regularly described as brides and grooms, proud parents, dutiful husbands, rebellious children, etc. Her blatant racism (a chimpanzee in *Four-Handed Folk*, 1897, "does the work of four negro waiters") is painful to encounter.

M.'s children's stories are not particularly noteworthy, although many (such as *Nimpo's Troubles*, 1880, or the Kristy books) show M.'s special concern for children in difficulty. The nature sketches for children, however, showcase M.'s teaching talent. In *The First Book of Birds* (1899) M. uses the juvenile form to further her own purpose—conservation of birds and their environment. She interests youngsters in unusual bird habits, tries to stimulate further study by means of careful lessons in techniques of observation, and thereby hopes to make the killing of birds seem "almost like murder." This book, like *Little Folks in Feathers and Fur, and Others in Neither* (1875), describes the habits of various species in humanly significant details bound to hold a child's interest. Some of M.'s children's books are beautifully illustrated.

M.'s bird studies for adults, beginning with *Bird-Ways* (1885), were mostly researched and written in her later years. Not content with observation of birds in captivity, M. traveled to Colorado, the Carolina coast, the summit of the White Mountains, and outposts in northern

Maine—all this in the late decades of the 19th c. when M. was in her sixties and seventies. M.'s accounts of these travels and the difficulties she encountered—from barbed wire (how to get over in Victorian skirts!) to human nest robbers to litterbugs—provide absorbing reading.

The usual format for M.'s books is anecdotal; chapters describe separate adventures with various species, usually introduced by appropriate poetry and interspersed with allusions and quotations from other writers. M.'s style is urbane, informal, observant, and witty.

M. contributed to the early conservation movement chiefly by observing how birds, in their natural ecosystems, help humans. M. also tried to ascertain the truth in various bird myths—that doves are mournful, that cuckoos rob nests—through careful observation. Hers was a strong voice for wilderness preservation; she frequently notes in detail how human waste and destruction is left from the Maine coast to Pike's Peak.

M. believed that naturalists tend to study specimens with an eye only to classification, while "the soul of the robin has escaped them." Instead, naturalists must observe "the free, unstudied ways of birds who do not notice or are not disturbed by spectators." Such a study, M. maintains, should be taken up especially by women, with their "great patience and quiet manners."

The concern that women should expand their horizons beyond their traditional occupations was carried over into M.'s public lecturing and publication of *The Woman's Club* (1891), a guide and handbook. Such clubs, M. believed, could "broaden and elevate" women. For these forays into territory unfamiliar to women, for her sound nature observations, and most especially for her adventuring—with mosquito netting, notebook and "good ink"—M. deserves reading today.

WORKS: *Little Folks in Feathers and Fur, and Others in Neither* (1875). *Nimpo's Troubles* (1880). *Queer Pets at Marcy's* (1880). *Little People of Asia* (1882). *Bird-Ways* (1885). *In Nesting Time* (1888). *Old Grip, the Crow* (1891). *The Woman's Club* (1891). *Little Brothers of the Air* (1892). *A Bird-Lover in the West* (1894). *Our Home Pets: How to Keep Them Well and Happy* (1894). *Four-Handed Folk* (1897). *The First Book of Birds* (1899). *Upon the Tree Tops* (1899). *The Children's Book of Birds* (1901). *The Second Book of Birds* (1901). *True Bird Stories from My Notebooks* (1903). *Kristy's Queer Christmas* (1904). *With the Birds in Maine* (1904). *Kristy's Surprise Party* (1905). *Kristy's Rainy Day Picnic* (1906). *Harry's Runaway, and What Came of It* (1907). *What Happened to Barbara* (1907). *The Bird Our Brother* (1908). *A Vision of Moses* (1924).

BIBLIOGRAPHY: For articles in reference works, see: *AA. NAW* (article by R. H. Welker). *NCAB*, 9. *Ohio Authors and Their Books*, Ed. W. Coyle (1962).

MARGARET McFADDEN-GERBER

Mary Britton Miller

B. *Aug. 1883, New London, Connecticut; d. 3 April 1975, New York City*
Wrote under: Isabel Bolton, Mary Britton Miller
D. of Charles Phillip and Grace Rumrill Miller

The tragic events of M.'s childhood, which haunted her throughout her long life, are depicted in two books. *In the Days of Thy Youth* (1943), a fictionalized autobiography, and *Under Gemini* (1966), a memoir, describe the sudden deaths of M.'s parents, within an hour of each other, when M. and her twin sister, Grace, were four. Moved with two brothers and a sister to their grandmother's Springfield, Massachusetts, house, and from thence to other relatives, the twins thought, acted, and reacted as one person.

The two books end with another tragedy—the death, by drowning, of twin sister Grace at age fourteen. Of the aborted twinship experience, M. said "Those early years with her are my treasury . . . of swift and accurate response to human behavior, of a queer sense of seeing into and through human beings who accompany me through life."

M. attended boarding school in Cambridge, Massachusetts, and subsequently traveled and did volunteer social work in Greenwich Village. The poetry M. wrote in her free time resulted in her first publications. It was only after her sixtieth birthday that M. turned to the novel form, dictating (because of eye pain from low-grade arthritis) five books between ages sixty-three and eighty-seven.

Some of M.'s poetry is written for a young audience, and is sensitive, quiet, and nature-loving. Sensitive in a different way is *The Crucifixions* (1944), which includes three Easter poems full of the imagery of guns, armaments, and tanks—the new Golgotha—and a resultant prayer for peace.

Adopting the name Isabel Bolton for her change from poetry to fiction, M. followed her autobiographical *In the Days of Thy Youth* with the novel *Do I Wake or Sleep* (1946). Set in spring-saturated New York City in 1939, and told through the intense consciousness of a young Millicent Munroe, the book skillfully compares midwest, New York City, and European sensitivities, moving around the character of a woman whose idiot child is trapped in Nazi Austria. *The Christmas Tree* (1949), published first in part in *The New Yorker*, compares the inescapably self-destructive lives of New Yorkers of three generations with the world going to smash in 1945.

The special insight into aging and age that M. was able to incorporate into her novels is strongly moving in *Many Mansions* (1952), whose protagonist is the eighty-four-year-old New Yorker, Miss Sylvester. On the day that Truman gave approval for development of the H-bomb, she is reviewing a manuscript she has written revealing a long-held secret love affair and child given up for adoption in her youth. The book gives what must be an intensely realistic picture of a day in the life of an elderly, creative, dying person. Memories of the 19th c. and the two world wars of the 20th c. merge and conflict, while physical difficulties and the present day interrupt the mind's sorting.

The *Whirligig of Time* (1971), M.'s last novel, depicts even more skillfully that combination of memory and desire that her elderly characters exude. Before the scheduled reunion of "Old David Hare" and "Old Blanche Willoughby" after over fifty years of separation, each thinks backward in time to childhood. Histories of mistaken marriages, desertion, deception, affairs, and passions come filtered through the years of their aging.

M.'s slim volumes of fiction deserve appreciative readers and scholars. In a 1971 interview, at age eighty-eight, M. described her admiration for Virginia Woolf, Flannery O'Connor, and Joyce Carol Oates. "I care a good deal for style." "When in doubt, delete." I "fear that too many books try to say too much"—these statements by M. could be her literary epitaph. Diana Trilling in 1966 described M.'s talent as "modest" and "deferential," hard to place in U.S. literary history. Perhaps that means, simply, that the literary history needs rewriting to encompass M.

WORKS: *Menagerie* (1928). *Songs of Infancy, and Other Poems* (1928). *Without Sanctuary* (1932). *Intrepid Bird* (1934). *In the Days of Thy Youth* (1943). *The Crucifixions* (1944). *Do I Wake or Sleep* (1946). *The Christmas Tree* (1949). *Many Mansions* (1952). *Give a Guess* (1957). *All Aboard* (1958). *A Handful of Flowers* (1959). *Jungle Journey* (1959). *Listen—the Birds* (1961). *Under Gemini* (1966). *The Whirligig of Time* (1971).

BIBLIOGRAPHY: For articles in reference works, see: *American Novelists of Today*, H. R. Warfel (1976). *CA*, 1–4 (1967); 57–60 (1976). *20thCAS.*
Other references: *NYHTB* (27 March 1949). *NYT* (4 April 1975). *NYTBR* (20 Oct. 1966). *PW* (5 July 1971).

CAROLYN WEDIN SYLVANDER

Vassar Miller

B. 19 July 1924, Houston, Texas
D. of Jesse G. and Vassar Morrison Miller

M. keeps house for herself and her dog in Houston, Texas. For M., born with cerebral palsy, this testifies to an unusual courage and fiercely independent spirit. M.'s stepmother was the most important person in M.'s childhood and early life. She taught M. to read, and enabled her to attend junior and senior high school and to earn B.S. and M.A. degrees from the University of Houston. The Wings Press, in Houston, was founded as a vehicle to publish and distribute M.'s new work.

Adam's Footprint (1956), M.'s first collection of poems, marked the appearance of an accomplished lyric poet. M.'s peculiar voice is heard in the title poem: "My bantam brawn could turn them back / My crooked step wrenched straight to kill / Live pods that then screwed tight and still." Howard Nemerov wrote that M.'s poems were "at their best brilliant works of language." M. is a maker of the short lyric, songs that sing in words that are worked to the utmost, with rich combinations of meanings. In "Love Song Out of Nothing," M. speaks of the "Mirage . . . formed from the crooked heat waves of my thought," minus which the poet is "nothing but a nought." Without her poems, the poet is nothing; and yet even from this nought she sang a strange convoluted love song to her muse. In the poem "Waste of Breath," M. writes of "waging war with paper pistols." In "Spastic Child," she writes of a boy whose "tongue . . . / Is locked so minnows of his wit may never / Leap playing in our waterspouts of words," . . . "his mind, bright bird, forever trapped in silence."

The confessional aspects of M.'s poetry become more pronounced with each new volume. Meditative, religious, rebellious, anguished, angry, subdued, and quiet, M.'s poems are suffused with learned acceptance. With M.'s "small emphasis" and her "weapons of words," but most especially with her "one two three four / clink clank this small change of being," M. sings something rare—songs that bear hearing over and over.

WORKS: *Adam's Footprint* (1956). *Wage War On Silence* (1960). *My Bones Being Wiser* (1963). *Onions and Roses* (1968). *If I Could Sleep Deeply Enough* (1974). *Small Change* (1976). *Approaching Nada* (1977).

BIBLIOGRAPHY: For articles in reference works, see: *WA*.

Other references: Houston *Chronicle* (2 Feb. 1975). *Sam Houston Literary Review* (Nov. 1977). Houston *Post* (26 Jan. 1969). *Kenyon Review* 20 (1958). *NYTBR* (22 Dec. 1968).

LORENE POUNCEY

Kate Millett

B. *14 Sept. 1934, St. Paul, Minnesota*
D. *of James and ? Feely Millett; m. Fumio Yoshimura, 1965*

The second of three daughters, M. attended parochial schools in St. Paul. Her father, a contractor, abandoned the family when M. was fourteen. Her mother took a job selling insurance, and the girls helped support the family. M. was graduated from the University of Minnesota, magna cum laude and Phi Beta Kappa, in 1956. She studied literature for two years at St. Hilda's College, Oxford, and earned first honors.

M. taught briefly at the Women's College of the University of North Carolina, but later resigned her post and went to New York to paint and sculpt. In 1961, M. moved to Japan, where she taught English and sculpted.

On returning to New York in 1963, M. exhibited "pop furniture," such as chairs with human legs. She joined the civil rights and peace movements, and in 1966 became one of the first members of the National Organization for Woman (NOW). Her first book, *Token Learning* (1967), was a pamphlet for NOW, challenging the validity of the curricula at women's colleges.

In 1968, M. was hired to teach at Barnard College, and began work on a Ph.D. in English and comparative literature at Columbia. M.'s activism in the causes of women's liberation and student rights led to her being relieved of her teaching post in December of her first year. However, a speech M. delivered to a women's group at Cornell became the germ of her doctoral thesis.

M.'s thesis may be considered the first major literary criticism of the new wave of feminism. She sets forth the postulate that the oppression of women is essentially political, and then discredits religious, literary, philosophical, and "scentific" constructs erected by male supremacists to justify their advantage. A second section documents the feminist revolution and male chauvinist counterrevolution in the history of ideas, and the third section exposes the phallic supremacism of three modern male literary idols: D. H. Lawrence, Henry Miller, and Norman Mailer. Finally, M. sets up Jean Genet, the French homosexual writer, as master social critic who reverses every status hierarchy in western culture, including that of masculine and feminine.

In March 1970, M. was awarded the doctoral degree with distinction, and in August her thesis was published by Doubleday. It sold 80,000 copies in the first six months of publication. *Sexual Politics* offered the public a major new concept, and many reviewers merely used the title as a springboard for their personal tirades against feminism. The media both praised and lambasted the book and its author, seizing upon them as a reification of "women's lib."

The Prostitution Papers began as a chapter for Vivian Gornick's *Woman in a Sexist Society* (1971). M. edited oral narratives from two prostitutes and a feminist lawyer, and added an essay of her own arguing that prostitution is only one salient example of the ways in which femaleness has been reduced to a commodity. M. called the chapter "a quartet for four voices," and had the four statements printed side by side in columns; but when the chapter was published separately as a book, the experimental layout was abandoned. The 1976 edition includes M.'s firsthand account of the 1975 French prostitutes' revolt.

M.'s experience with spoken language led her to make the film *Three Lives*, and inspired her fourth book. Frankly confessional, *Flying* (1974) was M.'s response to the enforced two-dimensionality of being created as a media feminist and showed M.'s need to bring together disparate private and public selves. M. had originally planned to write a scholarly treatise in defense of homosexuality, but wrote instead a supremely vulnerable book about her own sexuality, her work, her feelings, her friends, and the movement. Using the writing of the book itself as a framework, M. intercuts scenes from other periods of her life, giving the effect of a sculptural assemblage.

Sita (1977) resembles *Flying* stylistically, but it is focused on a narrower theme. M. takes the reader on a *tour de force* of a dissolving romance between herself and an older woman. Again, M. makes sculpture out of confession. She repeatedly reconstructs her theme, each time from a slightly different perspective, building up the paradigm of emotional attitudes toward a single set of facts. More tightly controlled than *Flying*, *Sita* conveys a relentless progressive present that both encompasses and reshapes history.

M.'s capacity for obsession drives her art. For ten years, she sculpted almost nothing but cages, her response to a newsmagazine article about the murder of a sixteen-year-old girl by her female guardian and a group of kids. *The Basement: Meditations on a Human Sacrifice* (1979) is a cage of words. M. verbalizes the bars of the cage—her subjects' poverty, their isolation from societal restraints, their rationalizations and guilts and enjoyment of petty drama—and fills the cage with monologues representing the interior voices of torturer and victim. There is a constant sliding back and forth between M.'s ideas and voice and those of her characters, as the author performs the ritual of becoming them, the self-abasement of taking on their impoverished language and brutal experience. Much of the tension of the book results from M.'s continual refusal to permit herself to explain the deed cleanly away.

A pacifist and international feminist activist, M.'s politics are frequently denigrated and her works sometimes harshly reviewed in the major press. Nevertheless, her influence is pervasive, and a generation of feminist writers has taken her for its model. She has set a standard for powerful feminist criticism, and provoked reevaluation of confessional and journal writing as artistic literary forms.

WORKS: *Token Learning* (1967). *Sexual Politics* (1970). *The Prostitution Papers* (1971; rev. ed., 1976). *Flying* (1974). *Sita* (1977). *The Basement: Meditations on a Human Sacrifice* (1979).

BIBLIOGRAPHY: Chrysalis (1977; 1978). *Harper's* (1970). *Ms.* (1974).

FRIEDA L. WERDEN

Maria G. Milward

Although there is no available biographical information about M., the fact that she twice signed her stories "Mrs." suggests that she was married. Her stories occur in contemporary rural and urban settings and reveal the author's familiarity with the details of both worlds. Accompanying each of M.'s stories is a note of her current residence: Macon, Georgia, in 1839; Savannah, in 1840; other places in Georgia and Alabama later. M.'s stories suggest that she had a broad education in literature and at least a familiarity with science, geography, and history. She seems to have read widely, and her comparisons reveal a knowledge of classical mythology and of the world beyond Georgia and the south.

M.'s work is consistently well-observed and elegantly composed, showing little change between 1839 and 1846. The intelligence behind the tales is quick-witted, humorous, and lively, ranging from satire to sympathy while consistently avoiding the flaws of her sentimental female contemporaries.

M. has a fine eye for detail and characterization. "The Bachelor Beset; or, The Rival Candidates" (*Southern Literary Messenger*, Nov. 1839), a study of a spinster's sudden interest in a confirmed bachelor who finally eludes her by running "off to Texas," is a moving and humorous exploration of Miss Betsey Bud, of whom M. writes: ". . . age seemed to have dried up every avenue to the tender passion in the heart of Miss Betsey; it was believed that the fire of her juvenile days had burnt out, and though its violence had been extreme, all now regarded her as an extinct volcano." M. notes with similar imaginative humor the plants in Mr. Singlesides' garden—stiff boxwood, bachelor's hat, southernwood (or old man) abound, while he allots a separate area for lady slippers, maiden's blush, and heart's ease. Forced to acknowledge Miss Bud, the bachelor "waved his hand with an action somewhat resembling the motions of a dead body under the effects of a galvanic battery."

M. also has an ear for witty and natural conversation. M. even reproduces dialect convincingly in "The Yellow Blossom of Glynn" (*Southern Literary Messenger*, July 1840), a tale of rough rural folk and the misunderstandings that are finally resolved in several marriages.

M. explores a young man's perspective in "The Winter Nights' Club" (*Southern Literary Messenger*, Jan. 1843), in which Reginald Braithwaite finally decides to tolerate no longer the offhand manner of the coquette for whom he thinks he cares. Reevaluating his view of her rival, Hortensia Hurst, he marries her with real love. M.'s understanding of young men also informs "Mrs. Sad's Private Boarding House," in which the pathetic country bumpkin, Edgar Fairchild, comes to the city to seek his fortune and fails.

M. is at her best when writing in the first person from the point of view of a young woman with whose sensibility we sympathize but who, like Jane Austen's heroines, does not see so clearly as the reader until the end of the tale. The narrator of "Country Annals" is a realistic and compelling character whose humor and clear-sightedness obscure the story's simple plot and emphasize the vividness of the local scenes. "Country Annals"—a sustained two-part tale of sixteen chapters and M.'s finest work—may be autobiographical; its young female narrator of modest means lived with a benevolent uncle in rural comfort, observing the surrounding countryfolk and landowners, and finally marrying a wealthy gentleman from the city. Still, M.'s literary skills are such that she is able to explore various characters with affection and penetration and she need not have written directly from her own experience.

M. finally charms the modern reader, who might, however, have difficulty locating her work, for her six stories appear only in the *Southern Literary Messenger*.

CAROLINE ZILBOORG

Agnes Woods Mitchell

B. *Scotland*

In the preface to her only book, *The Smuggler's Son, and Other Tales and Sketches* (1842), M. suggests the only details of her life available today. She defends the settings of her stories and poems as the realistic result of her "Celtic" childhood. Evidently born in Scotland, M. seems to have been conventionally Presbyterian and relatively comfortable. The preface is dated 1842, Jonesboro, Tennessee, and while M. maintains fierce Scottish loyalties, she apparently thinks of herself as an American author writing for an American public, even comparing a beautiful Highland landscape with "Florida's gardens" in "The Bride of Hawthorne Glen."

M. refers to the works in *The Smuggler's Son* as her "first fruits," and the sometimes vivid stories alternating with unremarkable verse substantiate her implied roughness. However, M. takes responsibility for her writing and emphasizes that the book "was written chiefly with a view to the improvement of the young" and that, despite aesthetic defects, it contains "instruction with amusement." M. offers spoiled, misguided, but likeable heroines who reform and generally marry well. In the title tale, Roderick M'Alpine, the son of Caledonian rustics, finally marries the wealthy orphan, Jane Rutherford, after he has shown her the discipline of education. Similarly, in "The Bride of Hawthorne Glen," motherless Mary Warner, spoiled by her good-hearted governess who neglects her religious training, reads light fiction and finally visits a gypsy caravan, losing there her diamond engagement ring. "Ever the child of impulse," Mary does at last reform and is forgiven at the story's conclusion.

M. is also fond of irreligious young men; in "Carra's Rest," William Murray unwisely reads Cartesian philosophy; his sister strives to recover him from "delusion" but fails. She dies of grief, but William vows reform at her funeral. In "Frederick Gordon," the central character, a passionate, frivolous young man, fails the woman who loves him, marrying instead Corinna, who turns out to be poor and then dies. Devastated, Gordon shoots himself, and M. spares us no details in her vivid description of his body "all mangled and bloody."

Although M.'s work lacks technical elegance, she seems to be aware of literary art and sensitive to language. Her tales are clearly structured; M. repeatedly begins with a scene, then introduces a substantial flashback, only returning to the present at the story's end. Her originality stems from her impressive capturing of Scottish dialects, for her characters speak with charming local syntax and vocabulary. Certainly M.'s frequently simple tales and predominately narrative poems are didactic and even moralistic, but their interest for the modern reader lies essentially in their elements of local color.

WORKS: The Smuggler's Son, and Other Tales and Sketches (1842).

CAROLINE ZILBOORG

Margaret Mitchell

B. 11 Nov. 1900, Atlanta, Georgia; d. 11 Aug. 1949, Atlanta, Georgia
D. of Eugene Muse and Maybelle Stephens Mitchell; m. John R. Marsh, 1925

M. lived in Atlanta all her life, as had her parents and grandparents. Both parents were authorities on Georgian and southern history, especially the Civil War. Her brother edited the *Atlantic Historical Bulletin.*

In 1922, M. began working as a professional writer for the *Atlanta Journal,* where she quickly gained a reputation as a talented and disciplined writer with an imaginative and witty style.

M. never completely comprehended the phenomenal success of *Gone with the Wind* (1936), feeling that it had no philosophic merit or moral value. Nor did M. ever completely recover from its success; unlike many novelists who achieve recognition with their first attempt, M. declared that she would never write again—and she didn't.

Gone with the Wind is a highly authentic historical novel. It has been praised for its accurate portrayal of black vernacular and of the period in general. Its four main characters have obtained archetypal stature; like mythic gods and goddesses, they show us how we live and teach us how to survive.

Scarlett O'Hara is the protagonist regardless of what the author has said elsewhere. For it is Scarlett whom we see in the opening pages as a vibrant, young creature with great strength of character. It is Scarlett, after three husbands, three children, and many trials, who has survived at the novel's end. However, this survival has cost Scarlett her dream.

Legend has it that M. wrote the last chapter first, then the first chapter, and thereafter wrote in no particular chronological order. This is particularly significant from a psychological viewpoint. M. is saying—either consciously or unconsciously—that we remain essentially unchanged by the events that touch our external lives—we are slaves to our earliest childhood experiences. In the last pages, Scarlett achieves a single moment of heightened awareness with enough insight to reflect on how little we really know those who are closest to us: ". . . had she ever understood Ashley, she would never have loved him; had she ever understood Rhett, she would never have lost him." But with that, she reverts even further back into her memories where life was once safe and secure.

Scarlett refuses to be controlled either by men or by circumstance. Her ability to assert herself in the face of social adversity wins our hearts and we root for her as she strikes a blow for the liberation of women. Yet the nature of survival is twofold: whereas one may survive in the physical world, there is still the problem of the psyche to contend with. And in this sense Scarlett fails to survive; she never succeeds in transcending adolescent experience. Given M.'s ambiguity toward her characters and the success of her novel, it is not surprising that *Gone with the Wind* has been relegated to the category of juvenile literature.

WORKS: *Gone With the Wind* (1936). *Gone with the Wind Letters, 1936–1949* (Ed. R. Harwell, 1976).

BIBLIOGRAPHY: Farr, F., *Margaret Mitchell of Atlanta* (1965).

Other references: Atlanta *Journal Sunday Magazine* (18 Dec. 1949). *Collier's* (March 1937). *NewR* (16 Sept. 1936). *NYHTB* (5 July 1936). *NYTBR* (5 July 1936). *Pictorial Review* (March 1937). *Red Barrel* (Sept. 1936). *SatR* (4 July 1936).

LINDA LUDWIG

Jessica Mitford

B. *11 Sept. 1917, Batsford Mansion, Gloucestershire, England*
D. *of David and Sydney Bowles Mitford; m. Esmond Romilly, 1936; m. Robert E. Truehaft, 1943*

M. is the daughter of the second baron of Redesdale. Her eccentric siblings include Nancy, the biographer, Diana, the wife of fascist Oswald Mosley, and Unity, disciple of Hitler. After receiving a private education at home, M. ran away with her second cousin, Esmond Romilly, in 1936 to assist the Loyalist cause in Spain. They worked briefly as journalists before returning to England, where M. was a market researcher for an advertising agency. M. and her husband emigrated to the U.S. in 1939, where each took odd jobs while traveling along the eastern seaboard.

M. worked in Washington, D.C., for two years in the Office of Price Administration after Romilly was killed in action during World War II. She married a lawyer in 1943, and became a naturalized U.S. citizen in 1944. After moving to Oakland, California, M. worked as executive secretary for the Civil Rights Congress, where she pressed for the investigation into charges of police brutality. In 1973, M. was appointed distinguished visiting professor in sociology at San Jose State College, where she taught a class on "The American Way" and a seminar on muckracking.

M.'s first book, *Lifeitselfmanship*, was privately published in 1956. Her autobiography, *Daughters and Rebels* (1960), hilariously recounts her childhood and marriage to Romilly.

M.'s first investigative study, *The American Way of Death* (1963), exposed the greed and commercialism of the funeral industry. Relying on extensive research and quotations from the industry's own publications, M. satirically deflated the pretentious hypocrisy of such establishments as Forest Lawn Memorial-Park. Although the book was viciously denounced by the industry, it was used as the basis for a television documentary.

M.'s second investigative study, *The Trial of Dr. Spock, William Sloane Coffin, Jr., Michael Ferber, Mitchell Goodman, and Marcus Raskin* (1969), concluded with the observation that conspiracy laws threatened personal and civil rights: "Does not the cherished concept of due process of law, the foundation of our system of jurisprudence, become merely an elaborate sham to mask what is in reality a convenient device to silence opponents of governmental policies?"

M. next attacked the Famous Writers School in a lengthy article entitled "Let Us Now Appraise Famous Writers" (*Atlantic*, July 1970). M. charged the Westport, Connecticut, school with deception in advertising and criticized writers who allowed the school to use their names.

Kind and Usual Punishment: The Prison Business (1973) exposes the atrocities of the penal system. In a chapter entitled "Clockwork Orange," M. listed the techniques used in prisons to modify behavior and reform "antisocial personalities," including chemotherapy, aversion therapy, neurosurgery, and drugs. M. points out that prisons have become the "happy hunting ground for the researcher." M. condemns lengthy and indeterminate sentences, the parole system, and the use of prisoners in psychological and physiological research, while supporting the idea of a prisoners' union. M. concludes that prisons are "inherently unjust and inhumane," institutions that demean all people in society.

M. published the sequel to her autobiography *Daughters and Rebels* in 1977. *A Fine Old Conflict* traces M.'s involvement with the Communist Party in America. As M. puts it, being fiercely anti-Fascist and antiracist, the Communist Party seemed to her the only practical outlet for her political and social beliefs. Recreating the ambience of the "witch-hunting" 1950s, M. recalls such activities as her trip to Mississippi in 1951 to appeal the conviction of a black rapist and her efforts to raise money for the party by organizing chicken dinners. After defecting from the party after twenty years, M. describes it as "an embattled, pro-scribed (and, to me, occasionally comical) organization." The appendix reprints her previously unavailable spoof of party jargon, *Lifeitselfman-ship.*

In addition to her book-length studies, M. has published extensively in *Life, Esquire, The Nation,* and the San Francisco *Chronicle.* A staunch supporter of civil liberties, M. has often been accused of communist sympathies and "un-American" activities. All M.'s writings, however, re-veal a satirical perspective on the fraud and corruption of organizations that victimize and exploit human beings.

WORKS: *Lifeitselfmanship* (privately published, 1956). *Daughters and Rebels* (1960; published in England as *Hons and Rebels*). *The American Way of Death* (1963). *The Trial of Dr. Spock, William Sloane Coffin, Jr., Michael Ferber, Mitchell Goodman, and Marcus Raskin* (1969). *Kind and Usual Pun-ishment: The Prison Business* (1973). *A Fine Old Conflict* (1977).

BIBLIOGRAPHY: For articles in reference works, see: *CA* (1967). *CB* (1974).
DIANE LONG HOEVELER

Elizabeth Mixer

M., a native of Ashford, Massachusetts, lived and wrote during the sec-ond quarter of the 18th c. She was the daughter of a deacon of the Ashford congregation. Little is known about her life, besides the scant materials presented in her spiritual autobiography. She states that she had a thorough religious education provided by her parents, and indeed she was literate enough to write a clearly stated account of her regeneration.

An Account of Some Spiritual Experiences and Raptures (1736) was prepared for M.'s admittance into the Ashford church. Her confession is characterized by a stylized, hyperbolic recounting of the three visions sent to her by the Lord. In dramatic, elaborate language, M. pictures Christ in the Heavenly City, Christ appearing in glory to her at night in her bedroom, and the glory and horror of the Last Judgment. Her visionary moments replace the more typically Puritan extended struggle for salvation. This change reflects the climate in which M. wrote, the early years of the Great Awakening, the religious movement of the second quarter of the 18th c. that profoundly affected New England religious life.

M.'s spiritual autobiography, devoid of personal references or theological discourse, remains an illuminating document by a woman of an important religious movement in American history.

WORKS: *An Account of Some Spiritual Experiences and Raptures* (1736).

JACQUELINE HORNSTEIN

Ellen Moers

B. 9 Dec. 1928, New York City
D. of Celia Lewis and Robert Lewis; m. Martin Mayer, 1949

M. received a B.A. at Vassar College in 1948, M.A. at Harvard-Radcliffe in 1949, and Ph.D. at Columbia University in 1957. She has taught at Columbia, Barnard College, and Brooklyn College and Graduate School, City University of New York. M. has two sons and lives in New York City. M., who has published a critical book on a certain classification of men, *The Dandy: Brummel to Beerbohm* (1960), and one on an individual man, *Two Dreisers* (1969), is best known for *Literary Women: The Great Writers* (1976). M. assumes the quality of greatness in her subjects and asks intriguingly, "what did it matter that so many of the great writers of modern times have been women? What did it matter to literature?"

While clearly stating that there is no single female tradition, no single literary form to which women are restricted, no such thing as *the* female genius or *the* female sensibility, and no female style in literature, M. presents a fair amount of evidence to support her contention that women writers have drawn confidence (even if not loyalty) from belonging to a literary movement, an "undercurrent, rapid and powerful," apart from the mainstream. Within this undercurrent, the great writers have seemed to emphasize or to be drawn toward some specific themes and literary forms.

Focusing on "heroinism" in the second half of *Literary Women*, M. integrates biographical, social, and historical factors, as well as literary tradition, into the critical discussion of various works. The "traveling heroinism" of Mrs. Radcliffe's Gothic novels, for example, is noteworthy because the traveling is done entirely indoors—the only way, in that writer's time, that the heroine could be brave and free and still maintain her respectability. M.'s presentation of the tradition of "loving heroinism" in women's literature demonstrates "the woman writer's heroic resolve to write herself, as men for centuries had tried to do, the love story from the woman's point of view."

The final chapter of *Literary Women* concerns metaphors in literature by women. The interpretations are, admittedly, generally made from a Freudian viewpoint, but M.'s brief analysis of landscapes, including the Brontë moors and Cather prairies, may have wider implications and applications; her suggestions invite the reader to examine this subject further.

The question that must be raised about a work like *Literary Women* is: Do women writers really need a criticism especially devoted to them and their works? In *Literary Women*, M. answers that question affirmatively, for her approach to these great writers has resulted in a rich addition to the body of literary criticism and, more significantly, to our appreciation of the works of these women. In its combination of so many elements—the writers' works; their social, political and economic milieu; their themes; and their biographies and literary traditions—this book is a model for further feminist criticism.

WORKS: *The Dandy: Brummel to Beerbohm* (1960). *Two Dreisers* (1969). *Literary Women: The Great Writers* (1976).

BIBLIOGRAPHY: *American Scholar* (Autumn 1976). *Book World* (11 April 1976). *Ms.* (July 1976). *NYRB* (1 April 1976). *NYT* (12 March 1976). *NYTBR* (7 March 1976). *SR* (March 1976). *VQR* (Winter 1977).

BARBARA KERR DAVIS

Penina Moise

B. *23 April 1797, Charleston, South Carolina; d. 13 Sept. 1880, Charleston, South Carolina*
D. *of Abraham and Sarah Moise*

M. was the sixth of nine children of parents who had fled to Charleston during the slave insurrections in Santo Domingo. The death of M.'s father forced M. to abandon formal education and help support the family by needlework, but she nevertheless continued to study and write, publishing poems and stories in newspapers and periodicals. Devoutly religious, M. served as superintendent of the religious school of Beth Elohim beginning in 1842. After the Civil War, although ill and nearly blind, M. founded a school for girls and conducted literary salons.

Fancy's Sketch Book (1833) was probably the first published book to which a Jewish woman appended her full name. Primarily a volume of verse, it includes light satires, epigrams, lyrics, and occasional poems commemorating prominent events. Conventional themes of love, death, and nature predominate, but in many instances they are distinguished by charming poignancy, delicate wit, and clever word play. For example, in "The Disconcerted Concert" M. uses the double meaning of musical terms to describe a quarrel among the instruments.

Serious themes are not neglected, and the book reveals a wide range of interests and knowledge, including Greek mythology, the Bible, Shakespeare, music, art, and history. Women are generally presented in terms of love or motherhood, but in one instance M. writes movingly of the women who donated their wedding rings to support Koscivszko's efforts to liberate Poland.

Hymns Written for the Use of Congregation Beth Elohim, first published in 1842 and enlarged in three subsequent editions, is primarily the work of M. The art of hymn writing, which requires decided meter with little variation, simple language that conveys an immediate sense of emotion, and above all sincere devoutness, brought out M.'s talents to the fullest—her hymns are still included in modern hymnals. In writing the lyrics, M. often added images that echoed many parts of the service, and her dramatic images greatly enhance the effectiveness of the prayer.

Although the bulk of M.'s writings still lies buried in the numerous newspapers and periodicals to which she contributed, a selection of her poems and hymns was collected in *Secular and Religious Works of Penina Moise* (1911). Some of the verses from the earlier volumes were included, but the collection is notable for works on specifically Jewish subjects and a number of previously uncollected poems dealing with political and social issues. The refusal by the British House of Lords to grant constitutional rights to Jews became for M. "that dark deformity from Freedom's code," and when the Jews of Damascus were being persecuted, she reproached the rest of the world that could "the suppliants scorn / From whose inspired relics revelation was born."

Limited by poverty, by social tradition, by illness, and by blindness, M. nevertheless produced a substantial body of poems and hymns. Much of M.'s work reveals an excessive concern for the poetic diction and conventions of her time, but several of her satiric pieces can still delight readers. M.'s poems on serious subjects reveal an unusual awareness of social and moral problems. Her hymns, expressing a deep, sincere faith in God's mercy, continue to evoke a solemn piety. All contemporary accounts of M. emphasize her cheerfulness, good humor, and wit, despite the hardships under which she lived. The mark of suffering which found no voice in her poetry was expressed only in the lines M. wrote for her epitaph: "Lay no flowers on my grave. They are for those who live in the sun, and I have always lived in the shadow."

WORKS: *Fancy's Sketch Book* (1833). *Hymns Written for the Use of Congregation Beth Elohim* (1842). *Secular and Religious Works of Penina Moise* (1911).

BIBLIOGRAPHY: Elzas, B. A., *The Jews of South Carolina* (1905). Moise, H., *The Moise Family of South Carolina* (1961). Reznikoff, C., and U. Z. Engleman, *The Jews of Charleston* (1950).

For articles in reference works, see: *AA. DAB,* VI, 2. *NAW* (article by C. Reznikoff).

Other references: *American Jew's Annual* (1885–86). *American Jewish Yearbook* (1905–06). *Critic* (28 Dec. 1889). *Southern Jewish Historical Society* (1978).

CAROL B. SCHOEN

A. G. Mojtabai

B. 8 June 1937, Brooklyn, New York
D. of Robert and Naomi Alpher; m. Fathollah Mojtabai, 1960

M. had no formal literary training. When very young, M. began dissecting on her own, developing an intense interest in biology. Early in her schooling, M. was tracked for science; while in high school, she interned for two summers at the Jackson Memorial Laboratory.

M. received a B.A. from Antioch College in 1958, concentrating on philosophy and mathematics. She married later, and lived in Iran, where her two children were born. The marriage ended in divorce.

Returning to the U.S., M. lectured in philosophy at Hunter College, receiving an M.A. in philosophy from Columbia in 1968. She worked as a librarian at the Graduate School of Business at Columbia from 1968 to 1970 and received an M.S. in library service in 1970. Thereafter, M. worked for six years as a librarian at the City College of New York. From 1976 to 1978, M. was a Fellow of the Radcliffe Institute for Independent Study, and she is at present Briggs-Copeland lecturer in English at Harvard.

Mundome (1974), M.'s first novel, is a series of reflections or reveries on a few recurring themes. Richard Henken, the narrator, is an archivist, a specialist in "fugitive and ephemeral materials" in a mouldering public library. He spends his time outside of work caring for Meg, his mentally disturbed sister, who deteriorates as the book progresses. Richard is sane, sober, and responsible; Meg is everything Richard is not. The novel has two settings—inner and outer—which fuse at the end, and only one main character, or perhaps two main characters who fuse at the end. There are two equally cogent ways of reading the book; M. claims to have written it both ways, and has preserved all the ambiguities. Her aim is to produce vertigo in the reader—"a sense of radical dislocation." The book was praised for its poetic imagery and lapidary precision, and faulted for its lack of sensuality and lyricism.

The 400 Eels of Sigmund Freud (1976) is a complementary exploration. As Robert Morris noted in the St. Louis *Globe-Democrat*, "If *Mundome* plumbs the elusive recesses of dark psyches to show how two people lose themselves in the labyrinths of madness, *Eels* unfolds with the same sort of quiet horror to reveal how an entire enlightened community crumbles despite its principles of logic and reason." The book describes a summer educational experiment with high school students who live in a mansion called the Four Winds at the edge of the sea. They are told the story of the 400 eels which the young Freud dissected; this monumental dissection is the measure of the man lost to science when he turned to "other" things. Yet for lack of attention to these "other" things, the community at the Four Winds is lost. The book was praised for the high luster of its writing, and both praised and faulted for its meticulous clarity.

M.'s vision of the world is rather bleak. Her refusal to flesh out her books with details of dress, food, and conversation, and her lack of narrative breadth have led some reviewers to claim that M. is not really a novelist.

M.'s literary method is dissection—presenting a character, then trimming away layer after layer of deceptive appearance. M. rarely amplifies a social context; instead, she cuts the individual away from the traditional social underpinnings. Characteristically, there are no seduction scenes; instead we are offered gropings, failures, fantasies, people in juxtaposition rather than in connection.

WORKS: *Mundome* (1974). *The 400 Eels of Sigmund Freud* (1976). *A Stopping Place* (1979).

BIBLIOGRAPHY: *Critique* (Dec. 1978).

CAROLYN G. HEILBRUN

Virginia Ramey Mollenkott

B. 28 Jan. 1932, Philadelphia, Pennsylvania
D. of Robert and May Lotz Ramey; m. Friedrich Mollenkott, 1954

M. had a Christian upbringing and education, receiving a B.A. from Bob Jones University in 1953. A year later, she married a schoolteacher, and a son was born in 1958. The marriage ended in divorce in 1973. M. earned an M.A. from Temple University (1955) and a Ph.D. from New York University (1964). She has chaired several English departments.

M. is known for writings on English literature (especially the 17th c.), religion, education, feminism, and social justice. All of her writings may be subsumed under the theme of *oneness*, which M. variously describes as an "organic wholeness" and a "transcendental integrative vision." The emphasis is on seeing God in all things and serving God in all activities, integration of the human personality around a unifying center, and awareness of humanity's interdependence.

In her first book, *Adamant and Stone Chips* (1967), M. strives to awaken other Christians to the exhilaration and joy of her "Christian humanist" approach. Rather than being fearful and suspicious of human culture, "the Christian humanist takes . . . a positive approach to academics, aesthetics, and human relationships." Using examples from literature, M. illustrates what such a view has meant in earlier times and can mean for today. In *Adam among the Television Trees: An Anthology of Verse by Contemporary Christian Poets* (1971), M. continues her examination of this field.

In Search of Balance (1969) is a personal account of M.'s attempts to deal with questionings, doubts, paradox, freedom, and responsibility. The book amplifies "balance" themes that are found throughout M.'s writings: the counterpoint of now and then, the "dialectic of faith," the distinction between ultimate categories and human categories, and the need for self-awareness.

In *Women, Men, and the Bible* (1977), M. calls for male-female equality through mutual submission and mutual service, stressing that "Christian equality is never a matter of jockeying for the dominant position." The theme of neighbor love and social justice is examined further in *Is the Homosexual My Neighbor?* (1978), where the emphasis is on respecting the dignity and worth of one of society's most oppressed groups.

Equality, compassion, social justice, oneness—all are viewed by M. as grounded in redemptive grace, as "Christ impaled but with forgiving love / impaling his impalers."

Speech, Silence, Action! (1980), a spiritual autobiography, features M.'s analysis of inclusive God-language and other issues with which she has come to be identified in recent years.

Critics have acknowledged M. as an important literary scholar, noted especially for her work on Milton, and also as an articulate Christian humanist and an influential evangelical feminist.

WORKS: *Adamant and Stone Chips: A Christian Humanist Approach to Knowledge* (1967). *In Search of Balance* (1969). *Adam among the Television Trees: An Anthology of Verse by Contemporary Christian Poets* (1971).

Women, Men, and the Bible (1977). *Is the Homosexual My Neighbor?* (with L. Scanzoni, 1978). *Jeremy Taylor's Holy Living* (edited by Mollenkott, 1979). *Speech, Silence, Action!* (1980).

BIBLIOGRAPHY: Hearn, V., ed., *Our Struggle to Serve: The Stories of Fifteen Evangelical Women* (1979). Sims, J. H., "The Bible and Milton," in *A Milton Encyclopedia*, Ed. W. B. Hunter et al. (1978).

For articles in reference works, see: *CA*, 33–36 (1973).

Other references: *The Other Side* (May-June 1976). *Union Seminary Quarterly Review* (Winter 1977). *Christianity and Literature* (Winter 1979).

LETHA SCANZONI

Harriet Monroe

B. 23 Dec. 1860, Chicago, Illinois; d. 26 Sept. 1936, Arequipa, Peru
D. of Henry Stantan and Martha Mitchell Monroe

Poet, editor, and journalist, M. was an influential force in the publication of modern poetry in the U.S. and an important figure in the Chicago Renaissance. Both her parents had moved to the growing city shortly before their marriage in 1855: her father, who became a prominent lawyer, from western New York and her mother from Ohio. Decidedly more erudite and socially ambitious than his beautiful but uneducated wife, Monroe inspired in his daughter a keen interest in literature, painting, music, and the theater; and much of her early education was acquired from reading in his substantial library.

The tensions in her parents' marriage, increased after 1871 by her father's business reverses, contributed along with frail health to M.'s reserved, nervous character as a girl. At the Georgetown Visitation Convent in Washington, D.C. (1877–79), she outgrew her former reticence, forming lifelong friendships with several affluent classmates and discovering the satisfactions of an independent, critical mind. She also blossomed into an aspiring poet.

During the 1880s involvement in the Fortnightly, a literary women's club, and publication of occasional art and drama reviews provided M. entrée into the world of Chicago's writers and journalists, among them Margaret Sullivan and Eugene Field, who became her friends and sponsors. While she had several opportunities to marry, she chose not to.

M. spent the winter of 1888–89 with her sister Lucy in New York as an art, drama, and music correspondent for the Chicago *Tribune*. At E. C. Stedman's Sunday evenings, she tasted the culture of the New York art and literary scene, meeting such luminaries as W. D. Howells and Joseph Pulitzer. Yet, despite her growing knowledge of contemporary art and theater, she considered journalism always second to her poetry and worked during her free time that winter on the verse play *Valeria*.

On her return to Chicago she was commissioned by a group of businessmen to write a cantata for the dedication ceremony of Louis Sullivan's new Auditorium in 1889. After a visit to London and northern France in 1890, she established herself as a free-lance art and music reviewer and, from 1909 to 1914, worked as art critic for the *Tribune*. Her most public success as a poet came in 1892: the performance of her "Columbian Ode," a long poem composed (with music for lyric passages by G. W. Chadwick) for the World's Columbian Exposition in Chicago. *Valeria, and Other Poems* appeared in a private edition in 1891 and a memoir of her brother-in-law, the Chicago architect John Wellborn Root, in 1896.

M. traveled extensively in the U.S., Europe, and Asia. On her return from a P.E.N. congress in Buenos Aires in 1936, she traveled to Peru intending to view the Inca ruins at Machu Picchu. During a stop at Arequipa, however, she died and was buried in the Andean village.

Although M.'s poetry never gained the wide audience and critical notice she hoped for, she continued thoughout her life to write occasional verse, competent but largely conventional in sentiment and language. Among her more interesting poems are short lyrics about the deserts and mountains of the American southwest; longer descriptions of foreign locations she visited—among them, Constantinople, Peking, the Parthenon; and a few ironic observations of modern society like "The Hotel."

M.'s most distinguished and lasting achievement was the founding of *Poetry: A Magazine of Verse* in October 1912 and editing the monthly for twenty-four years. In June 1911, at the suggestion of her friend H. C. Chatfield-Taylor, M., then fifty-one, began the arduous task of soliciting subscriptions of fifty dollars a year for five years from 100 Chicago business leaders and professionals to establish a magazine "which shall give the poets a chance to be heard." To develop a public "interested in poetry as art" became her persistent aim.

The circular and personal letter she sent to many poets, established and unknown, discovered through ardent research—and through Elkin

Mathews's fortuitous presentation to her in London in 1910 of two of Ezra Pound's early books—drew favorable response to her ambitious venture. It also stimulated a flow of letters from Pound, who became the magazine's unpaid foreign correspondent with the second issue. Along with Alice Corbin Henderson, her associate editor, Pound influenced M. to include in *Poetry*'s early years the writing of Yeats, Lawrence, Frost, William Carlos Williams, his own work, and in 1915, Eliot's "The Love Song of J. Alfred Prufrock."

Ellen Williams locates the great years of *Poetry* in 1914 and 1915, when M. opened the publication to controversy over Imagism, experimental verse, and the poet's relation to his audience. In general, M.'s preference for democratic and more accessible American poetry led her to espouse Lindsay, Masters, and many lesser poets. But the contribution she made, despite criticism and financial difficulties, in gaining recognition for poets in the U.S., in articulating modern standards in opposition to those of the powerful established outlets, and in calling attention to new writing and ideas in editorials and reviews was invaluable.

WORKS: *Valeria, and Other Poems* (1891). *The Columbian Ode* (1893). *John Wellborn Root: A Study of His Life and Work* (1896). *The Dance of the Seasons* (1911). *You and I* (1914). *The New Poetry: An Anthology* (edited by Monroe, with A. C. Henderson, 1917; rev. ed., 1932). *The Difference, and Other Poems* (1924). *Poets and Their Art* (1926). *A Book of Poems for Every Mood* (edited by Monroe, with M. D. Zabel, 1933). *Chosen Poems: A Selection from My Books of Verse* (1935). *A Poet's Life: Seventy Years in a Changing World* (1938).

Manuscripts, diaries, letters, and personal papers are located in the Harriet Monroe Collection, University of Chicago Library.

BIBLIOGRAPHY: Cahill, D. J., *Harriet Monroe* (1973). Duffey, B., *The Chicago Renaissance in American Letters* (1956). Hoffman, F. J., et al., *The Little Magazine* (1947). Redle, K. G., "Amy Lowell and Harriet Monroe: Their Correspondence" (Ph.D. diss., Northwestern Univ., 1968). Williams, E., *Harriet Monroe and the Poetry Renaissance: The First Ten Years of Poetry, 1912–22* (1977).

For articles in reference works, see: *DAB*, Suppl. 2; *NAW* (article by M. D. Zabel); *20thCA*.

Other references: *JML* 5 (1976). *Illinois Quarterly* 37 (1975). *Poetry* (Jan. 1961).

THEODORA R. GRAHAM

Lucy Monroe

B. *March 1865, Chicago, Illinois; d. 5 Sept. 1950, Chicago, Illinois*
Wrote under: Lucy Monroe, Lucy Calhoun
D. *of Henry Stanton and Martha Mitchell Monroe; m. William James*
   Calhoun, 1904

M. was the third of four children. Her upper-middle-class parents—a fashion-conscious, self-educated woman and a lawyer fond of horses and books—saw that she was well educated, despite their dwindling family income.

M. and her sister Harriet (later founding editor of *Poetry*) became close, traveling together, sharing interests in the arts, competing as journalists, and joining forces in Chicago's emerging artistic community.

M. wrote newspaper and magazine columns in 1890–96. In 1898–1905 she was an editorial reader for Herbert S. Stone, who published *The Awakening* on M.'s recommendation. She also participated actively in the professional Contributors' Club, named and helped found The Little Room, Chicago's preeminent artistic salon, and played in Anna Morgan's little-theater productions.

M. married a Chicago lawyer who became Taft's minister to China in 1909–13. In 1916, widowed and childless, M. went to France as a wartime nurse, then returned to China as unofficial "first lady" of the Peking diplomatic corps. Forced home by political unrest in 1941, she lived quietly with her younger brother.

M.'s first journalistic endeavors, as art critic for the Chicago *Herald* in 1890–91, did not gain much local attention; but her informed and clear prose earned M. a commission as the first Chicago correspondent for New York's journal of literature and art, *The Critic*.

M. was hailed as "an accomplished littérateuse" whose "Chicago Letter" signaled eastern recognition of her native city as a literary center. From March 1893, one hundred twenty-five weekly installments of M.'s "Chicago Letter" appeared, then nine more after September 1895.

The first seventy "Chicago Letter" installments were M.'s best. They were unified by an implicit theme—the coherence of Chicago's cultural development. As a set, they achieved a rhythmic, narrative structure by tracing the gradual preparation, full-blown celebration, diminishing echoes, and final fiery destruction of the World's Fair Columbian Exposition.

Within that framework, M. embedded commentaries on World's Fair buildings, novels about Chicago, lectures and academic congresses, art exhibits, libraries and museums, little theater, and World's Fair memoirs —all as unfolding events in Chicago's cultural history.

After a five-week break in August 1894, M. began to emphasize her personal interests—especially in paintings, drama, and publishing houses —instead of trying to embody a common cultural motif. Many letters lacked any primary subject, and the separate installments became fragmented by brief notations.

Particularly in her later letters, however, M. frequently took an argumentative stance, berating the Chicago Woman's Club for its near exclusion of a black woman, promoting efforts by Hull House and other civic groups to make art accessible to the poor, and criticizing the *Woman's Bible* for feminist excess and tastelessness.

Generally, M.'s work is more important as historical document than as aesthetic creation. The "Chicago Letter" attests to—and discusses significant facets of—Chicago's self-conscious rise as a cultural center in the 1890s. It also contains frequent commentaries on women's increasing leadership, written from the occasionally feminist perspective of a cultivated society woman.

WORKS: "Chicago Letter," *The Critic*, NS 19–25 (18 March 1893–27 June 1896), passim. "My Chinese House," *House Beautiful*, 57 (Feb. 1925), 133–35.
Correspondence by and memorabilia concerning Lucy Monroe (Calhoun) are included in the personal papers of Harriet Monroe, Regenstein Library, University of Chicago.

BIBLIOGRAPHY: *MidAmerica*, 5 (1978).

SIDNEY H. BREMER

Ruth Shick Montgomery

B. *1912, Sumner, Illinois*
Wrote under: Ruth Montgomery
D. *of Ira Whitmer and Bertha Judy Shick; m. Robert H. Montgomery, 1935*

Little in M.'s Methodist upbringing, marriage, or career as a reporter presaged her later development of psychic abilities or the psychic messages she would disseminate to millions.

M. studied journalism at Baylor and Purdue Universities, subsequently working for the Waco *News-Tribune*, the Louisville *Herald-Post*, the Detroit *News*, the Chicago *Tribune*, and the New York *Daily News*. In 1956, M. became special Washington, D.C., correspondent for International News Service, and later syndicated columnist for Capital Letter King Features, Hearst Headline Service (1958–1968). M. has received many awards for her newspaper work.

M.'s first literary brush with psychic affairs occurred in the mid-1950s when she researched and wrote a series of newspaper articles debunking fraudulent mediums. Her next foray into the field was as a believer with the best-selling *A Gift of Prophecy: The Phenomenal Jeanne Dixon* (1965).

M. herself developed psychic abilities at about this time. First via automatic handwriting and then automatic typewriting, M. began to communicate with "Lily and the group"—beings who claimed to be spirits of the dead and M.'s guides. To prove their veracity, the guides dictated much information previously unknown to M., which she was later able to verify.

From 1960 to 1969, M. worked with her guides to produce *A Search for the Truth* (1967) and *Here and Hereafter* (1968). The first treats M.'s own spiritual progress, and the second karma and reincarnation. In 1969, satisfied that death is not the end of individuality and busy with other projects, M. abandoned automatic typewriting. Early in 1971, however, on discovering that Arthur Ford, her recently deceased friend and a world-famous medium, had become one of her guides, M. recommenced taking spirit dictation. The new communications, now from "Lily, Art and the group" provided the basis for *A World Beyond* (1970), *Companions Along the Way* (1974), *A World Before* (1976), and *Strangers among Us* (1979). These books discuss, respectively, the circumstances of life after death, M.'s previous incarnations, the past history of the world, and the near future prospects of humanity.

The cosmology presented by M. posits God as creating the universe and, to help Him enjoy His universe, also creating trillions of souls, all with free will and creative abilities. Some of these souls chose to remain God's worshipful companions while others entered the bodies of terrestrial animals and became trapped and debased. God then formed the human body as a vehicle more suitable to housing incarnate souls. Souls reincarnate repeatedly for the purpose of expiating past sins, learning, and progressing toward reunion with God.

Strangers among Us warns of an approaching cataclysm. The guides have informed M. that at the close of this century, the earth's axis and its magnetic poles will shift, killing most of the human race. A period of chaos will ensue, to be followed by an era of unprecedented peace and brotherhood. Scientists from other planets are now assembling to observe the axis shift, but will keep themselves hidden. Advanced souls are also assembling to assist those living at the time of the axis shift. Many of these advanced souls have returned or will return to life as "walk-ins" who take over living bodies when the souls born into those bodies wish to leave and agree to such a transfer. The guides say that the walk-ins will reveal themselves as the cataclysm nears.

Few people have done as much as M. to bring widespread recognition of the genuineness of psychic occurrences and to reestablish belief in life after death. The volume and consistency of her writings are convincing. On leaving Schoolhouse Earth through the doorway of death, we continue to learn and grow in the company of those we love. M.'s is no small accomplishment. She has brought comfort and hope to millions.

WORKS: *Once There Was a Nun: Mary McCarran's Years as Sister Mary Mercy* (1962). *Mrs. LBJ* (1964). *A Gift of Prophecy: The Phenomenal Jeanne Dixon* (1965). *Flowers at the White House* (1967). *A Search for the Truth* (1967). *Here and Hereafter* (1968). *Hail to the Chiefs* (1970). *A World Beyond* (1970). *Born to Heal* (1973). *Companions Along the Way* (1974). *A World Before* (1976). *Strangers among Us* (1979).

BIBLIOGRAPHY: Smith, S., *Confessions of a Psychic* (1971). Smith, S., *The Conversion of a Psychic* (1978).

For articles in reference works, see: *CA*, 4 (1967).

LUCY MENGER

Catherine Lucille Moore

B. 25 Jan. 1911, Indianapolis, Indiana
Writes under: Paul Edmonds, Keith Hammond, Hudson Hastings, Kalvin
   Kent, Henry Kuttner, C. H. Liddell, C. L. Moore, Lawrence O'Donnell,
   Lewis Padgett, Woodrow Wilson Smith, etc.
D. of Otto Newman and Maude Jones Moore; m. Henry Kuttner, 1940;
   m. Thomas Reggie, 1963

M. attended Indiana University for a year and a half but was forced by
the Depression to take a job in an Indianapolis bank. She produced her
first published works in her spare time. In 1938, M. met science fiction and
fantasy writer Henry Kuttner; from 1940, when she and Kuttner married,
until his death in 1958, they collaborated, in varying degrees, on almost
everything they wrote.

M. earned B.A. (1956) and M.A. (1963) degrees in English from the
University of Southern California; after Kuttner's death, for four years
she taught his writing course at U.S.C. She completed a screenplay for
Rappacini's Daughter which they had been writing and later wrote scripts
for television. M. lives in Los Angeles with her second husband. Although M. has published no new science fiction or fantasy in some twenty
years, at a 1976 convention she did announce her intentions to return
to this field.

"Shambleau" (1933), M.'s first published short story, innovatively emphasizes characterization, imagery, and human sexuality in its depiction
of an Earth adventurer, Northwest Smith, and his encounter with a Me-
dusa-like alien. Smith, a conventional hero whose illegal exploits are never
immoral, figures in a series of stories which subsequently appeared in
Weird Tales: these include "Black Thirst" (1934), "Scarlet Dream"
(1934), and "Dust of Gods" (1934).

In 1934, M. began a parallel series of stories, featuring Jirel of Joiry,
an independent warrior queen of the 15th c. In "Black God's Kiss"
(1934), Jirel braves the horrors of a supernatural, evil-ridden dimension
to find a weapon to overthrow her castle's conquerer. In subsequent
stories ("Black God's Shadow," 1934; "Julhi," 1935; "Jirel Meets Magic,"
1935; "The Cold Gray God," 1935; and "The Dark Land," 1936) Jirel
continues to triumphantly battle the supernatural. "Quest of the Star

Stone" (1937), on which M. and Kuttner collaborated through correspondence, was of special interest to fans of both series; in it, Northwest Smith is magically transported back to the 15th c. to confront Jirel.

It is difficult to determine which stories written after M.'s marriage are exclusively or predominantly hers and which Kuttner's because both writers, singly and in collaboration, used a total of seventeen pseudonyms. One story, however, written under her own name, is clearly M.'s work. "No Woman Born" (1944), the tale of a dancer caught in a theater fire whose severe burns force her rescuers to transfer her brain into a metal body, highlights M.'s glowing imagery and subtle questions about the nature of humanity. It is one of the first science fiction treatments of cyborgs (creatures part human and part machine) to emphasize characterization rather than technology.

Two of M. and Kuttner's collaborations have been included in *The Science Fiction Hall of Fame.* "Mimsy Were the Borogroves" (1943), written under the pseudonym Lewis Padgett, plays with conventional notions of childhood and maturity. Two Earth children transport themselves into a future dimension by deciphering the puzzles and games that a time-traveling future scientist has lost. "Vintage Season" (1946), published under the name of Lawrence O'Donnell, is a novella about time travelers from the future whose vacations are spent witnessing crucial events in Earth's history. Its action centers upon the characters and personalities of these voyeurs and the reactions of their landlord, a contemporary young man who gradually realizes their origin and motivations. Although these dilettantes might avert disaster in his time, they choose not to.

In addition to their numerous short stories, M. and Kuttner collaborated on one notable novel, *Fury* (1947), set on Venus and describing the aftermath of a failed utopia. The science fiction and the four mystery novels they wrote between 1948 and 1958 are not of the same caliber as their earlier creations.

M.'s lasting contributions to the fields of science fiction and fantasy include not only her own works but also the models that she and Kuttner set for contemporary and future writers. Depth of characterization and setting, attention to the nuances of human motivation and interaction, recognition of the myths that shape human experience, and incorporation of sophisticated mainstream literary techniques (such as the use of a central intelligence in "No Woman Born") are the innovations one may credit to M. Feminist critics have recently begun to praise M. for her strong heroine, Jirel of Joiry, at the same time that they "excuse" or ignore her other works, but such criticism does not recognize the full significance of her oeuvre.

WORKS: *Fury* (with H. Kuttner, 1947). *Judgment Night* (1952). *Northwest of Earth* (1952). *"Shambleau," and Others* (1953). *Doomsday Morning* (1957). *Jirel of Joiry* (1969). *The Best of C. L. Moore* (1975).

BIBLIOGRAPHY: del Ray, L., in *The Best of C. L. Moore* (1975). Gunn, J., in *Voices for the Future: Essays on Major Science Fiction Writers*, Ed. T. Clareson (1976). Knight, D., *In Search of Wonder: Essays on Modern Science Fiction* (1956). Moskowitz, S., *Seekers of Tomorrow* (1966). Rosinsky, N. M., in *Selected Proceedings of the 1978 Science Fiction Research Association National Conference* (1979). Sargent, P., "Women and Science Fiction," in *Women of Wonder* (1974).

For articles in reference works, see: *Index to Science Fiction Anthologies and Collections*, Ed. W. Contento (1978).

NATALIE M. ROSINSKY

Mrs. H. J. Moore

The settings of M.'s works suggest a protestant New England or Middle Atlantic background. M.'s three substantial novels, published within five years, hint at a short but productive period of creativity.

In her first book, *Anna Clayton* (1855), M. has a clear thesis to prove, but she grows more subtle and skillful in her later novels. One imagines that the Protestant cause rather than a dedication to art was the goad for M.'s first work, but even by the end of *Anna Clayton* M.'s aesthetic sensitivity increases. Although her work is always rough, M. reveals a developing artistry that rewards the modern reader in brief passages of acute observation, in a few vivid if sentimental characters (especially servants and children), and in carefully transcribed conversation and snips of amusing dialect.

In *Anna Clayton*, M. focuses on Anna's unfortunate marriage to an English Catholic, Sir Charles Duncan. In rural America, the couple have two children, whom the materialistic Father Bernaldi arranges to kidnap. The plot revolves around the rather naively conceived "lucre-loving priests," who incarcerate the children in order to gain Sir Charles's inheritance, and Anna's first and persevering lover, Robert Graham, who was prevented from marrying her because of Squire Clayton's initial greed and who returns to rescue the children. Both children finally return to their mother, whom Graham marries, and learn true worship from the long-suffering Anna. Throughout this overplotted, sentimental novel, M. uses her characters to glorify motherhood, vilify aristocratic Europe, and attack the Roman church. The novel's strengths are its passion, the suspense that derives from the earnestness of M.'s complex story, and the charmingly ignorant servant Ralph, whose devotion to Myrtie, his "birdie," engages even the sophisticated reader.

The plot of *The Golden Legacy* (1857) is simpler, and M. reveals here a greater sensitivity to character. An orphan, Lonny Brown, is adopted by the farmers Joseph and Henny Atherton because of the concern of their young niece, Nettie. Nettie's aunt Lottie, a model of charity, owes her character to her mother's "legacy," a famed inscription: "Whatsoever ye would that others should do unto you, do ye even so to them." Lottie marries Melville Thornton, who finally discovers that he is Lonny's long-lost father. The novel lacks the suspense of *Anna Clayton*, but it is both less naive and less sentimental. The townspeople, such as the petty minister, Mr. Flint, and the greedy Mrs. Wormwood, provide amusing comic relief, testifying to M.'s increasing versatility.

Wild Nell (1860) has a yet simpler plot, as M. insists that religion and education conquer wildness and stresses the moral for mothers. The crazy fortune-teller, Esther Cram, after nursing the injured son, Walter Everson, of her former lover, gives her child, Nell, to be educated by Dr. and Mrs. Jepson. Nell becomes a beautiful, cultivated young woman while her mother reforms. Nell and Walter fall in love, but when the heroine confesses "I AM WILD NELL," Everson and his mother reject her because of her poverty and lack of social breeding. Augustus Murray, Everson's friend, falls in love with Nell who soon returns his affection. The novel's strengths lie in its local scenery and dialect (Dr. Jepson's constant "Gim-i-ni" and the child Nell's "les run" are well observed) and in Nell's rejection of Everson when he wants her back, an unusual turn in sentimental fiction.

WORKS: *Anna Clayton; or, The Mother's Trial* (1855). *The Golden Legacy: A Story of Life's Phases* (1857). *Wild Nell, the White Mountain Girl* (1860).

CAROLINE ZILBOORG

Marianne Craig Moore

B. 15 Nov. 1887, Kirkwood, Missouri; d. 5 Feb. 1972, New York City
Wrote under: Marianne Moore
D. of John Milton and Mary Warner Moore

M. was raised by her mother and grandfather, a Presbyterian minister. M. was seven when her grandfather died, and her mother moved the two children to Carlisle, Pennsylvania. She became an English teacher in the Metzger Institute, where M. was educated before entering Bryn Mawr college (B.A. 1909). In college M. specialized in biology and histology, but also submitted poetry to the campus literary magazine.

For four years after graduating from the Carlisle Commercial College in 1910, M. taught stenography, typing, and bookkeeping at the U.S. Indian School in Carlisle.

M.'s publishing career began in 1915 when the *Egoist*, a London journal dedicated to the new Imagist movement in poetry, accepted "To the Soul of Progress," a short satire on war. The same year, *Poetry* published M. for the first time in a U.S. magazine of general circulation.

In Greenwich Village, where M. lived with her mother, she became part of a literary group that included poets William Carlos Williams, Wallace Stevens, and Alfred Krembourg. *Poems* (1921) was published without M.'s knowledge by her admirers in England. M. added several poems, including the long *Marriage* (issued first as a pamphlet in 1923), before the collection was published in the U.S. as *Observations* (1924). It won the $2,000 Dial Award for "distinguished service to American letters," and M. was asked to become acting editor of the *Dial*, where she worked from 1926 until the magazine ceased publication in 1929. Thereafter, her vocation was solely poetry and writing.

M. was the recipient of many honorary degrees and awards, including the Bollingen and Pulitzer prizes for her *Collected Poems* (1951). In 1955, M. was elected to the American Academy of Arts and Letters.

Observations shows clearly M.'s celebrated innovations in prosody, formal structuring of verse, and poetic vision of animals and of man. In "The Fish," M.'s sharp powers of close observation enable M. to render vividly the world of the ocean. That poem also reveals M.'s intense interest in design and pattern, indicated by the distinctive forms of typography, and her new emphasis on the whole stanza as a formal unit, rather than on the line. In the first few lines of "Poetry," M. tells us that she, too, dislikes poetry, but that by reading it, one may discover "the genuine." This poem includes M.'s famous description of poetry as seeing real toads in imaginary gardens.

In his introduction to M.'s *Selected Poems* (1935), T. S. Eliot linked her with the Imagist poets, yet pointed out unique characteristics of her work. He acknowledges her as the greatest master of *light* rhyme, admiring her intricate forms and patterns. Eliot recognizes M.'s work as being part of a small number of durable poems from our time.

In "The Mind Is an Enchanted Thing" (from *Nevertheless*, 1944), M. argues, through her own intricate form of syllabics, that contemplation of art has the power to transform spiritual dejection into spiritual joy. The most emotional of all M.'s poems is "In Distrust of Merits." It has been called the best poem to come out of World War II; the theme is the tragedy of war, and the poem reflects M.'s profound hope that contagion, so effective in sickness, may also become effective in creating trust.

M.'s major scholarly work, on which she spent nine years, is a translation of the fables of La Fontaine (1954). The fables are all slyly satirical and entertaining in their striking wisdom and new typographical forms. M.'s criticism, collected in *Predilections* (1955), is eclectic; her topics include Louise Bogan, D. H. Lawrence, Sir Francis Bacon, Ezra Pound, Henry James, and Anna Pavlova. She also wrote a play, *The Absentee: A Comedy in Four Acts* (1962), based on the 1812 Irish novel by Maria Edgeworth. M.'s most popular book, *A Marianne Moore Reader* (1961), includes selections from her best prose and poems.

M.'s main literary contribution is the development of the artful flexibility of direct language in poems. She is remembered as a genius of invention in poetry, for humane wit and intellectual energy, and as a loved and gracious literary artist.

WORKS: *Poems* (1921). *Marriage* (1923). *Observations* (1924). *Selected Poems* (1935). *The Pangolin, and Other Verse* (1936). *What Are Years* (1941). *Nevertheless* (1944). *Rock Crystal, a Christmas Tale* by A. Stifter (translated by Moore, with A. Mayer, 1945). *A Face* (1949). *Collected Poems* (1951). *The Fables of La Fontaine* (translated by Moore, 1954). *Gedichte* (1954). *Predilections* (1955). *Like a Bulwark* (1956). *Idiosyncrasy & Technique: Two Lectures* (1958). *Letters from and to the Ford Motor Company* (1958). *O to Be a Dragon* (1959). *A Marianne Moore Reader* (1961). *The Absentee: A Comedy in Four Acts* (1962). *Puss in Boots, the Sleeping Beauty, and Cinderella* by Charles Perrault (translated by Moore, 1963). *The Arctic Ox* (1964). *Poetry and Criticism* (1965). *Tell Me, Tell Me; Granite, Steel, and*

Other Topics (1966). *The Complete Poems of Marianne Moore* (1967). *The Accented Syllable* (1969).

BIBLIOGRAPHY: Engle, B. F., *Marianne Moore* (1964). Garrigue, J., *Marianne Moore* (University of Minnesota Pamphlets on American Writers, No. 50, 1965). Hall, D., *Marianne Moore: The Cage and the Animal* (1970). Jennings, E., in *American Poetry*, Ed. I. Ehrenpreis (1965). Nitchie, G. W., *Marianne Moore: An Introduction to the Poetry* (1969). Sheehy, E. P., and K. A. Lohf, *The Achievement of Marianne Moore: A Bibliography, 1907–1957* (1958). Thérèse, Sister Mary, *Marianne Moore: A Critical Essay* (1969). Tomlinson, C., ed., *Marianne Moore: A Collection of Critical Essays* (1969). Watts, E. S., *The Poetry of American Women from 1632 to 1945* (1977).

For articles in reference works, see: *CA*, 33 (1973) *CB* (Dec. 1952; April 1968). *20thCA. 20thCAS.*

Other references: *CE* (Feb. 1953). *Harper's* (May 1977). *Quarterly Review of Literature* (4, 1948; 16, 1969).

ROBIN JOHNSON

Sarah Parsons Moorhead

M. lived during the tumultuous Great Awakening, the religious revival of the 1740s which shook New England. M.'s one slender published work, *To the Reverend James Davenport on His Departure from Boston by Way of a Dream* (1742), is an extended poetic comment on the controversy that occurred in Boston over Davenport's theological opinions and religious practices.

Davenport, deeply affected by the religious zeal of the 1740s, deserted his congregation of Southold, Long Island, and began itinerant preaching. He attacked the piety and sincerity of local ministers, creating internal dissension in many congregations. M. comments sharply on his behavior and admonishes backsliding and bickering Bostonians. Her public criticism of the clergy is significant because it was published contemporaneously with the events discussed in the poem. That is, a woman writer had been accepted as a critic of current events as early as 1742.

Stylistically, M. mimics the poetical taste of the day. Paradoxically, although her subject is religious, M. speaks with the voice of a distressed sentimental lover. M. also employs the technique of a dream vision. She interjects a femine feeling through florid description, creating an elaborate tapestry quality. Perhaps M. recognized that using such sugared language would make her severe criticism acceptable to the public. Her style and subject matter thus appear as a strange but well-presented mixture of the religious and the secular, the pious and the sentimental.

M.'s criticism, perhaps influenced by Charles Chauncy, the conservative minister of the First Church of Boston, focuses on the extremist elements of the Great Awakening and on a prevalent religious hypocrisy. She also discusses free grace. Dealing with a major problem among the Puritans—the difficulty of differentiating between moral action and faith—M. depicts the good-deeds churchgoers, who salve their conscience while actually remaining "immers'd in the black Gulph of sin, / . . . Pleas'd with the fancy'd Freedom of their Will." She believed that salvation can be secured only through the gift of free grace.

The poem also emphasizes the breakdown of morale in the Congregationalist churches—a result of continued quarreling over theological differences, notably among the ministers. M. admonishes the New England churches to remain united against external opposition if they are to survive. She restates this notion in a short poetic postscript published with the longer Davenport verse.

M.'s two poems have historical importance as well as poetic merit. They indicate a general easing of social and religious restraints among New England's Puritans, which allowed women a wider range of subjects and an emergent, if limited, public voice in the New England colonies.

WORKS: *To the Reverend James Davenport on His Departure from Boston by Way of a Dream: With a Line to the Scoffers at Religion Who Make an Ill Improvement of His Naming Out Our Worthy Ministers* (1742).

BIBLIOGRAPHY: Benedict, A., *A History and Genealogy of the Davenport Family* (1851).

JACQUELINE HORNSTEIN

Marabel Morgan

B. 25 June 1937, Crestline, Ohio
M. Charles Morgan, 1964

M. recalls that "I never saw a happy marriage when I was young. I grew up amid a lot of fighting. My father left when I was 3, and then my mother married a policeman who adopted me. I adored him." The family was poor, despite the long hours M.'s father worked. Until her father's death, M.'s parents were "in the throes of divorce. . . . I was being wrenched between one parent and the other . . . I had packed and unpacked my few belongings at least a dozen times."

As a beautician, M. earned enough money to study home economics for one year at Ohio State University. After a conversion experience, M. worked with Campus Crusade for one year at the University of Miami, where she met and married a law student. Entering marriage with high expectations, M. was quickly disappointed. She found herself tense, nagging, and resentful, repeating the unhappiness of her childhood home. Her four principles for pleasing husbands were developed in an attempt to save her own marriage—accept him, admire him, adapt to him, appreciate him.

M. first shared her principles with friends, and then began teaching "Total Woman" classes and hiring other women to help her teach. When M. was urged to write up her classes, her editors warned her to keep the writing at a fifth-grade level, which was no problem, she says, since "I'm a two-syllable person." M.'s writing in *Total Woman* (1973) and its sequel *Total Joy* (1976) is breezy, simple, and directed at women like herself—full-time homemakers whose husbands are quite affluent.

The principle of adapting is the most controversial part of M.'s books. She concludes: "God planned for the woman to be under her husband's rule." In a recent interview, M. admitted that the *ideal* is for the husband and wife to discuss decisions and make them together. But if the attempt at compromise fails, the only two alternatives she sees are for the wife to go the husband's way, or for them to split up. The wife usually gets her own way, however, by submitting and using ancient "feminine wiles"; and the rewards for adapting are usually material. *Total Joy* reflects the criticism of the materialism of *Total Woman*, concentrating more on affection and less on presents.

M. was among the first to tell Evangelicals that sexuality and godliness are not incompatible, which may explain why her book was the number-one bestseller of 1947. M. presents two principles: Sex is necessary for a man, and he will get it elsewhere if he doesn't get it at home; and sex is as "clean and pure as eating cottage cheese." M.'s advice (to meet the husband at the door dressed in a "costume" or to put suggestive notes in his lunch box, for example) may seem silly and immature, but by playing these games, with the encouragements of other "gals" in the class, some women are apparently able to develop a more positive attitude toward their own sexuality.

The primary weaknesses of M.'s books are her logical fallacies and her encouragement of materialism and manipulation. M.'s strengths lie in her stress on self-acceptance, hints for efficient home management, positive attitude toward sexuality, and apparently genuine love for her family and faith in God.

WORKS: *Total Woman* (1973). *Total Joy* (1976).

BIBLIOGRAPHY: *Christian Century* (8 Dec. 1976). *National Review* (25 April 1975). *NYT* (28 Sept. 1975). *Time* (14 March 1977). *Wittenburg Door* (Aug.–Sept. 1975).

MARGARET P. HANNAY

Clara Morris

B. *17 March 1847, Toronto, Canada; d. 20 Nov. 1925, New Canaan, Connecticut*
Wrote under: Mrs. Clara Morris Harriott, Clara Morris
D. of Charles La Montagne and Sarah Jane Proctor; m. Frederic C. Harriott, 1874

M. lived with her seamstress mother in boardinghouses. At thirteen, she became a dancer's apprentice in a Cleveland musical company, and advanced after seven years to Augustin Daly's Fifth Avenue Theater in New York. M. then moved to A. N. Palmer's Union Square Company, where she remained for most of her thirty years in the theater as the unchallenged queen of the emotional school of acting. In 1890, chronic poor health forced M. to relinquish regular acting jobs for occasional appearances, lectures, and writing.

M.'s marriage was an unhappy one. In her last years, her considerable fortune exhausted, M. battled poverty and arthritis. Several benefits staged for M. by her fellow actors failed to save her house from creditors.

In a desperate effort to keep herself alive, M. wrote eight books in eight years. *Little Jim Crow* (1899) is a children's book of sketches of real-life waifs. *Life on the Stage* (1901) is both an account of M.'s early childhood and rise to stardom and a defense of the profession. Three volumes appeared in 1902: *A Pasteboard Crown* is a novel about a star's hopeless love for a married man. *A Silent Singer* is another collection of real-life sketches, primarily about old age and death. *Stage Confidences* contains advice for the aspiring actress.

In 1904, M. published *Left in Charge*, a novel of the Ohio frontier of her youth. Many details are autobiographical: A woman alone with her daughter tries to scrape together a living and escape discovery by her bigomist husband. Another short sketch of frontier life, *The Trouble Woman* appeared the same year. It is about a woman who loses husband, children, and farm to the harshness of 19th-c. rural life.

The Life of a Star (1906) is a series of character sketches of people M. knew: a Mormon leader, the pacifist L. Q. C. Lanar, Dion Boucicault, and others.

No element of melodrama is missing from *The New East Lynne* (1908). A wronged wife, disfigured by an accident, returns incognito to be her own children's governess.

The literary strengths and weaknesses of M.'s work derive from the domestic tragedies in which she appeared as an actress—stock melodramatic characters and stories and rapidly moving plots. Despite the superficiality of much of her work, M. learned to tell a story and to reveal the problems of women in her time: the constant "neurasthenia," the double sexual standard, the plight of the woman alone, and the burden of urban and rural poverty.

WORKS: *Little Jim Crow, and Other Stories of Children* (1899). *Life on the Stage* (1901). *A Pasteboard Crown* (1902). *Stage Confidences* (1902). *A Silent Singer* (1902). *Left in Charge* (1904). *The Trouble Woman* (1904). *The Life of a Star* (1906). *The New East Lynne* (1908).

BIBLIOGRAPHY: Ayres, A., *Acting and Actors* (1894). Holcomb, W., *Famous American Actors of To-Day* (1896). Strang, L. C., *Players and Plays of the Last Quarter Century* (1902). Towse, J. R., *Sixty Years of the Theatre:*

An Old Critic's Memories (1916). Wilson, G. B., A History of American Acting (1966). Winter, W., The Wallet of Time (1913).

CLAUDIA D. JOHNSON

Toni Morrison

B. 18 Feb. 1931, Lorain, Ohio
D. of George and Ramah Willis Wofford

The daughter of working-class parents, M. reflects her midwestern background in her novels. Educated at Howard and Cornell, M. has taught at several universities. A senior editor at Random House, she also teaches part-time at Harvard. M. has been married and divorced. She has two sons. M. has been identified by some as the only contemporary black feminist American novelist.

M.'s first novel, The Bluest Eye (1970), depicts the failed maturation of Pecola Breedlove, a black child of the 1940s who believes herself ugly as measured against white American standards of beauty. Pecola's symbol of beauty and acceptance is her intense desire for blue eyes; her search for them leads her into the hands of a charlatan sorcerer. The novel is set into two frames—the school primer, which provides misleading standards of family life, and the perceptions of Claudia Mac-Teer, Pecola's friend, who narrates the story. M. contrasts the two girls' families, providing detailed and powerful flashbacks into the histories of both Breedlove parents. The reader understands clearly that unloved, unvalued human beings cannot love wisely, for Pecola is raped by her father and hence driven into madness and total social isolation. Another important theme is the difficulty of life for southern blacks who move north. Generally well received by critics, the novel was taken as indication of M.'s power and potential as a writer.

In Sula (1973), M. explores the maturation and long friendship of Sula Peace and Nel Wright Greene, as well as the history and values of the Bottom, the black settlement in imaginary Medallion, Ohio. Sula and Nel are revealed as the products of their family backgrounds, and the book stresses the various mother-daughter relationships. Highly episodic and violent, Sula depicts a wide range of the girls' experiences—sexual awakening, black and female social roles, shared responsibility for a playmate's death, an affair between Sula and Nel's husband—and reveals that, could their separate, damaged personalities be merged, the result would be a balanced, effective woman. Thus, the real tragedy is identified when Nel realizes that her great loss is the failure of her friendship with Sula.

M.'s early novels are spare. Two of her greatest stylistic successes are her use of foreshadowing (often connected with extensive nature symbolism) and her realistic dialogue. With *Song of Solomon* (1977), however, M. has made a conscious effort to "write it all out," and the result is a longer, more flowing novel.

Song of Solomon retains some themes of M.'s earlier works. The development and destruction of a friendship is again depicted, and again, the friends would be more nearly whole were they to share one another's traits. This is another maturation novel, and the central character, Macon "Milkman" Dead, Jr., slowly learns to see himself not only as an individual but also as the product of his family history. The central image is Milkman's desire to fly, cleverly associated with both the maturation and family motifs. Flashbacks are used very successfully, allowing the reader to share the mystery and excitement of Macon's search for identity. The novel is panoramic, telling the stories of four generations through stunning characterization and the vivid portraits of two black communities.

In *Song of Solomon*, as in all her work, M.'s key theme is the effect of the presence or the absence of love, an examination of love as a liberating and nurturing (or destructive) force. In exploring various kinds of love, M. makes clear that the capacity for genuine love must be achieved through personal growth that includes evaluation, acceptance, or even rejection of learned patterns for loving.

As an editor, M. stresses high-quality writing and urges women to value their experiences enough to write effectively about them. In conceiving and editing *The Black Book* (by Middleton Harris, et al., 1974), M. has helped provide a journalistic, pictorial, personal "scrapbook" of black American life from its beginnings. Her dedication to this project is in keeping with her desire to produce—and help others produce—true, valid portraits of black Americans and their lives.

WORKS: *The Bluest Eye* (1970). *Sula* (1973). *Song of Solomon* (1977).

BIBLIOGRAPHY: *Book World, Washington Post* (3 Feb. 1974). *Critique* 19(1977). *Essence* (Dec. 1976). *Nation* (6 July 1974). *NY* (23 Jan. 1971).

JANE S. BAKERMAN

Honoré McCue Willsie Morrow

B. *1880, Ottumwa, Iowa; d. 12 April 1940, New Haven, Connecticut*
Wrote under: Honoré Willsie Morrow
D. of William Dunbar and Lilly Bryant Head McCue; m. Henry Elmer
Willsie, 1901; m. William Morrow, 1923

M. grew up in the Midwest, although her family had ties in the East. Her parental grandfather was a Methodist circuit rider who served for fifty-three years in the West Virginia coal mining regions. Her mother's father was a friend of Daniel Webster.

After her graduation from the University of Wisconsin, M. married a construction engineer; they were divorced in 1922. By that time, M.'s writing career was launched. Stories and articles growing out of a visit to an Arizona mining camp had appeared in *Colliers* and *Harper's Weekly*. M. had also written on such subjects as immigration, divorce, and the U.S. Reclamation Service, and had produced six novels. From 1914 to 1919, M. was editor of the *Delineator*, a woman's magazine.

M.'s second husband, a publisher, died in 1931. The next year, M. moved to England, where she lived in a 16th-c. cottage on the Devon coast. She died of influenza while on a visit to her sister in Connecticut. M. was survived by three children.

M.'s early fiction shows her pleasure in and knowledge of the Southwest; her desert settings have been praised for their authenticity. Later, M. was to write of historical events with similar vividness and enthusiasm. An excellent example of her historical fiction is *We Must March* (1925), a dramatized account of the lives and labor of Marcus and Narcissa Whitman, missionaries to the Indians of the Far West, and their part in securing Oregon Territory.

Several of M.'s best-known novels deal with Lincoln and the Civil War. *Forever Free* (1927), *With Malice Toward None* (1928), and *The Last Full Measure* (1930) were published as a trilogy under the title *Great Captain*, with a preface by William Lyon Phelps. "Honoré Morrow," Phelps wrote, "is at once an eminent research scholar and an eminent literary artist. She loves the truth and knows how to tell it." Sherwin Lawrence Cook of the Boston *Transcript* asserted that "she has made a more serious and enlightened study of (Lincoln) than any previous writer of fiction," and went on to say that her portrayal of Lincoln was "without question the best."

M. wrote two notable nonfiction books about generally unpopular figures. *The Father of Little Women* (1927) deals sympathetically with Bronson Alcott, whom M. obviously admired as an intellectual and spiritual giant ahead of his time. Genuinely religious herself, M. writes of him from an almost mystical point of view, and is in complete accord with his views on education. *Mary Todd Lincoln* (1928), M.'s account of Lincoln's unhappy, much-maligned wife, is sensitive, compassionate, and admiring.

M.'s style is conversational, lucid, and only occasionally dramatic and "literary." It gives evidence of a warm sympathy with all kinds of people, plus a real pleasure in living.

WORKS: *Heart of the Desert* (1913). *Still Jim* (1915). *Lydia of the Pines* (1916). *Benefits Forgot* (1917). *The Forbidden Trail* (1919). *The Enchanted Canyon* (1920). *Judith of the Godless Valley* (1922). *The Exile of the Lariat* (1923). *The Devonshers* (1924). *We Must March* (1925). *On to Oregon!* (1926). *The Father of Little Women* (1927). *Forever Free* (1927). *Mary Todd Lincoln* (1928). *With Malice Toward None* (1928). *Splendor of God* (1929). *The Last Full Measure* (1930). *Tiger! Tiger!* (1930). *Black Daniel* (1931). *Beyond the Blue Sierra* (1932). *Argonaut* (1933). *Yonder Sails the Mayflower* (1934). *Let the King Beware* (1935). *Demon Daughter* (1939).

BIBLIOGRAPHY: For articles in reference works, see: *20thCA*.
Other references: *NYT* (13 April 1949).

ABIGAIL ANN HAMBLEN

Lillian Mortimer

D. 19 Dec. 1946, Petersburg, Michigan
Wrote under: Lillian Mortimer, Naillil Remitrom
M. J. L. Veronee

M.'s date of birth is unknown, but she was acting in her own plays by 1895. M. began producing her plays and achieved her greatest success with *No Mother to Guide Her* (1905). For a number of years, M. played the comic soubrette Bunco in that melodrama. M. evidently had a repertoire of *lazzi* to use whenever her stage directions indicated "funny business," and she must have been able to put across lines such as this: "Christopher Columbus! Burglars! I thought dere was somethin' crooked about dat guy. De oder one didn't want to do it. Hully gee—what'll I do? Guess I'll have to take my trusty and go after dem. Dey're comin' back." *No Mother to Guide Her* was revived in 1933 for thirteen performances with a cast of fifteen midgets.

The popularity of *No Mother to Guide Her* can scarcely be comprehended by the reader of the published text. The dialogue is little more than a framework on which to hang innumerable bits of comic business, scuffles, pratfalls, abductions, faintings, fisticuffs, knife fights, and revolver shots. The stage directions at the ends of the acts illustrate the genre: At the end of act 2, "they fight. Livingstone gets the better of the knife fight—stabs Jake and throws him off. Livingstone starts for Jake again with knife, to give him another thrust, and as he does so, Bunco enters from R., shoots him; he staggers. During all this action there is a terrible storm raging."

In 1915, M. left the popular-priced melodrama theater circuit to become a headliner in vaudeville. In an interview about her plans for the future, M. said, "I shall write again—when I get time . . . I've got enough scenarios to keep me busy for the next year if I should make plays of all the plots that I have in mind; but I'm always waiting for a little 'leisure,' and then along comes a new contract, and I jump to the road again." Although M. remained on the Keith Circuit for twenty years, she found leisure time during the 1920s to write three to five full-length "comedy-dramas" each year. Most were published for use by amateur theater groups.

In these plays, M. frequently used ethnic characters for the secondary roles—Irish, German, and Jewish "types," country folk, and blacks. In *Mammy's Lil' Wild Rose* (1924), M. specified that Mammy be "made up with minstrel black (not mulatto) and mammy wig." *Headstrong Joan* (1927) includes a courtship between the lovable middle-aged Irish maid Honora and Abie, a "typical Jewish peddler," who wears a paper collar and his derby pulled down to make his ears stand out. This subplot spoofs the long-running Broadway hit *Abie's Irish Rose*. The various dialects M. used provide a counterpoint to the bright, slangy speech of the lively young couples.

The plot formula that M. found most useful set up a confrontation between two young couples. The more attractive pair is virtuous and romantically idealized. The other two, motivated by greed or jealousy, create obstacles for the innocent lovers. But the lovers are so young and appealing that the plotters finally repent and accept the ethics and values that will enable them to live happily ever after.

The photograph of M. in the New York *Dramatic Mirror* (12 May 1915) is of a self-assured middle-aged woman, flamboyantly dressed. She stands with hand on hip and chin tilted back, archly gazing from heavy-lidded eyes. It is hardly the image one would expect of the author of more than forty moral dramas that reaffirm the values of girlish innocence and of decency and noble self-abnegation for young men.

WORKS: *No Mother to Guide Her* (1905). *A Man's Broken Promise* (1906). *The City Feller* (1922). *Little Miss Jack* (1922). *The Path Across the Hill* (1923). *The Road to the City* (1923). *Yimmie Yonson's Yob* (1923). *Mammy's Lil' Wild Rose* (1924). *That's One on Bill* (1924). *An Adopted Cinderella* (1926). *The Bride Breezes In* (1926). *Mary's Castle in the Air* (1926). *Nancy Anna Brown's Folks* (1926). *Ruling the Roost* (1926). *Headstrong Joan* (1927). *He's My Pal* (1927). *Nora, Wake Up!* (1927). *The Winding Road* (1927). *His Irish Dream Girl* (1928). *Love's Magic* (1928). *Paying the Fiddler* (1928). *Two Brides* (1928). *The Open Window* (192–?, by Naillil Remitrom, pseud.). *Manhattan Honeymoon* (1929). *The Gate to Happiness* (1930). *The Wild-Oats Boy* (1930). *Jimmy, Be Careful!* (1931). *Mother in the Shadow* (1936).

BIBLIOGRAPHY: Leverton, G. H., ed., *America's Lost Plays* (Vol. 8, 1940). Mantle, B., ed., *The Best Plays of 1933–34* (1934).

Other references: New York *Dramatic Mirror* (12 May 1915). *NYT* (26 Dec. 1933; 20 Dec. 1946).

FELICIA HARDISON LONDRÉ

Martha Morton

B. *10 Oct. 1865, New York City; d. 18 Feb. 1925, New York City*
M. *Hermann Conheim*

M.'s family included two playwrights and several novelists and journalists. Her mother encouraged M. to write poems and short stories, some of which were published in magazines. Since the stories were mostly in dialogue, M. was persuaded to try writing a play. Unable to interest any managers in her first effort, *Hélène*, she mounted it at her own expense, for one performance, in 1888. The *New York Times* called it "a lugu-

brious and ill-made though not wholly ineffective drama," but actress
Clara Morris revived it in 1889 for a two-year run that returned fifty
thousand dollars to the novice playwright.

M.'s second produced play, *The Merchant*, won the New York *World*
Play Contest. M. described the prejudice she had to face while directing a
rehearsal: "The men shook their heads. They said the drama was going
to the dogs. Then they crept in through the stage door and watched
that 'green girl' direct the rehearsal and one of them came up to me and
said, 'Are you going to make a business out of this?' . . . I looked him
straight in the eyes and answered fervently, 'God help me, I must!' Then
he put out a friendly hand, crushed my fingers into splinters and gave me
the comforting assurance that a woman would have to do twice the
work of a man to get one-half the credit."

Because women were barred from membership in the American
Dramatists' Club, M. organized the Society of Dramatic Authors. Thirty
women constituted its charter membership, but male playwrights were
also invited to join. In 1907, the older group proposed consolidation,
and the result was the Society of American Dramatists and Composers.

By 1910, M. was called "America's pioneer woman playwright," "the
first successful woman playwright," and "the dean of women playwrights." She wrote about thirty-five forgotten plays, fourteen of which
were professionally produced in New York City between 1888 and
1911.

M.'s most successful plays were written for the popular comedian
William H. Crane: *Brother John* (1893), *His Wife's Father* (1895), *A
Fool of Fortune* (1896), and *The Senator Keeps House* (1911). These
were considered "good and clean, not too subtle and not too obvious."
M.'s favorite subjects were marital adjustments, ups and downs in
the business world, and the foibles of high society. *A Bachelor's Romance* (1896) showed members of the frivolous social élite redeemed by
exposure to rural life. M.'s plays pleased audiences despite the critics' continual readiness to point out their hackneyed qualities.

M. traveled widely in Europe, and was well read in French and German literature. Her most ambitious work was an adaptation of Leopold
Kampf's *On the Eve* (1909), about revolutionary unrest in Russia. For
the part of the heroine, M. sent for German actress Hedwig Reicher,
who made a personal triumph of her first English-speaking role. Of that
character, M. said: "Woman is the tragic element in the social body. . . .
The chief woman figure in *On the Eve* symbolizes the woman of today,
the universal woman seeking her work and finding it." Critics called

this play "a collection of antiquated theatrical effects," but M.'s professionalism afforded her a degree of prestige attained by few other women playwrights.

WORKS: *Hélène* (1888). *The Triumph of Love: The Merchant* (1891). *Geoffrey Middleton* (1892). *Brother John* (1893). *His Wife's Father* (1895, produced in London as *The Sleeping Partner*, 1897). *A Bachelor's Romance* (1896). *A Fool of Fortune* (1896). *The Diplomat* (1902). *Her Lord and Master* (1902). *A Four Leaf Clover* (1905). *The Truth Tellers* (1905). *The Movers* (1907). *On the Eve* (1909). *The Senator Keeps House* (1911).

BIBLIOGRAPHY: *Bookman* (Aug. 1909). *Green Book Magazine* (May 1912). *Theatre Magazine* (10, 1909; 18, 1913). *World To-Day* (July 1908).

FELICIA HARDISON LONDRÉ

Sarah Wentworth Apthorp Morton

B. *Aug. 1759, Boston, Massachusetts; d. 14 May 1846, Quincy, Massachusetts*
Wrote under: Constantia, Sarah Wentworth Apthorp Morton, Philenia
D. of James and Sarah Wentworth Apthorp; m. Perez Morton, 1781

M. was the scion of two influential, wealthy early New England families. She had a thorough education, evidenced in the literary quality of her verses. When the revolution started, M.'s family was accused of Tory loyalties, but she expressed strong patriot sentiments in her post-revolutionary verse. In 1781, M. married a Harvard graduate, a patriot lawyer during the revolution and a prominent figure in state government in the Republic's early years. During their early married life, M. and her husband headed Boston's socialites and remained leading figures in Massachusetts' social and political life. Five of their six children lived to maturity, but all died before M.

In 1788, Perez had an affair with M.'s sister Frances, ending in her sister's suicide. This affair appeared fictively in the first American novel, *The Power of Sympathy; or, The Triumph of Nature* (1789), by William Mill Brown.

M. and her husband led the fight for repeal of Massachusetts's antitheater laws in 1793, subscribing to Boston's first theater. M. supported the earliest American abolitionist groups. In later life she was a patron to young writers.

M.'s subject matter is wide-ranging. Her earliest poems are sentimental plaints or elegies filled with neoclassic devices. Her post-1800 works are mainly occasional poems. Themes throughout focus primarily on moral and political issues.

In much of her work, M. speaks through a languishing, affected female persona, whose sentimental sufferings are suffused with the soft glow of flowery diction. M.'s interest in sentimental neoclassicism also appears in "Ode to Mrs. Warren," a notable example of one early American female poet praising another. In her concern for female attitudes and behavior, M. was a "Sappho," the woman's poet.

However, M. was also an "American" poet, for she wrote verse about the new nation's ideological issues. Her best works in this vein demonstrate a well-developed social and moral conscience, independent thought, and notable poetic scope.

M.'s poem "Beacon Hill" (*Columbian Centinal*, 4 Dec. 1790), written in neat neoclassic couplets, celebrates the sacred, solemn events which transpired on Boston Hill during the revolution. With revisions and enlargements, this poem reappeared as *Beacon Hill: A Local Poem, Historic and Descriptive, Book I* (1797). Here M. tries to revitalize and mythologize the revolutionary era. The poem's introductory section reviews early events: Warren's death, Bunker Hill, Washington's camp at Cambridge. The central section discusses the "natural, moral, and political history" of the colonies. Book One closes with a shepherd-soldier figure defending "his hereditary farm," while the prophetic Columbian muse bears the message of "Equal Freedom" around the earth. Although thoroughly nationalistic in this work, M. also presents a critique of southern slavery.

M.'s "sister" poems, *Ouâbi; or, The Virtues of Nature: An Indian Tale in Four Cantos* (1790) and *The Virtues of Society: A Tale Founded on Fact* (1799), show further interest in moral and social issues. They exemplify her mixed vision of the sentimental-domestic and historical-heroic. *Ouâbi*, perhaps the first American "Indian" poem, discusses a contemporary problem: the survival of simple American virtues beset by luxury and sophistication. *The Virtues of Society*, a spin-off of the failed epic *Beacon Hill*, is a romantic tale based on an incident in the American Revolution.

My Mind and Its Thoughts, in Sketches, Fragments, and Essays (1823) is M.'s only work to appear under her real name. It consists of numerous aphorisms, short essays, and poems—some previously published and re-written, others new to print. Her "Apology" explains that she made the collection to ease her distress (her son had recently died). The book is a curious mixture of the public and private, the patriotic and senti-mental, summarizing M.'s life's interests.

M. was quite popular in the 1790s, but she outlived the vogue for her neoclassical style and post-revolution themes. Her last book was praised nostalgically, not for innate achievement. Her reputation as a poet died with her.

WORKS: Ouâbi; or, The Virtues of Nature: An Indian Tale in Four Cantos (1970). Beacon Hill: A Local Poem, Historic and Descriptive, Book I (1797). The Virtues of Society: A Tale Founded on Fact (1799). My Mind and Its Thoughts, in Sketches, Fragments, and Essays (1823).

BIBLIOGRAPHY: Evans, C., American Bibliography (1912). Field, V. B., Constantia: A Study of the Life and Works of Judith Sargent Murray (1931). Otis, W. B., American Verse, 1625–1807: A History (1909). Pearce, R. H., The Savages of America (rev. ed., 1953). Pendleton, E., and Milton Ellis, Philenia: Life and Works of Sarah Wentworth Morton (1931). Watts, E. S., The Poetry of American Women from 1632 to 1943 (1977).

For articles in reference works, see: AA. CAL. DAB, VII, 1. NAW (article by O. E. Winslow).

JACQUELINE HORNSTEIN

Lucretia Coffin Mott

B. 3 Jan. 1793, Nantucket Island, Massachusetts; d. 11 Nov. 1880, Roadside, Pennsylvania
D. of Thomas and Anna Folger Coffin; m. James Mott, 1811

Born to a hearty, seafaring Quaker family, M. was sent to a Friends' school in New York, where she subsequently served as an assistant teacher. There she met her husband, with whom she had six children. M. was designated a minister of the Society of Friends in 1821. During the Great Separation of the Society in 1827, she allied herself with the lib-eral Hicksite faction. Within the next decade she became a vocal abolitionist who helped found the Philadelphia Female Anti-Slavery Society. Within the abolitionist movement, M. backed the radical faction of William Lloyd Garrison, which urged immediate emancipation of the slaves.

The diary in which M. recorded her experiences at the 1840 World's Anti-Slavery Convention in London, where, because of her sex, she was denied recognition as a delegate of the U.S., has been edited by Frederick B. Tolles (*Slavery and "The Woman Question,"* 1952). M. describes the political wrangling among abolitionists and Quakers, her meeting with English female reformers, her conversations with Elizabeth Cady Stanton, and her travels throughout the British Isles. M.'s friendship with Stanton, begun at the convention, resulted in a decision to call the first women's rights convention in 1848 at Seneca Falls, New York.

A preacher and reformer, M.'s literary corpus consists almost entirely of recorded sermons and discourses. Her appeal to reason and moral principle, powerful delivery, and personal presence gave M.'s words great impact. Her preaching was shot through with the liberal religious belief that practical righteousness was more important than theological speculation. In *A Sermon to the Medical Students* (1849), M. laid out her self-proclaimed heretical view that true religion is not mysterious, but is based on the universal and self-evident conviction that the kingdom of God is within. Humanity is not depraved, and does not need to be brought to righteousness by the atonement of Christ. The work of the present age is to reveal the nobility, and hence the divinity, of humanity through works of reform.

In response to a lecture by Richard Henry Dana, M. delivered her logical and powerful *Discourse on Woman* (1849), in which she shows that the present position of woman is neither her natural nor original one. Her equality with man is established by God, but she is everywhere in subjection to man. Woman's natural ability is illustrated historically in the lives of great women, but society promotes her inferiority. Woman, like the slave, has no liberty. She is subject to laws she does not make, excluded from a pulpit that disciplines her, and bound by a marriage contract that degrades her. She asks for no favors, but for the right to be acknowledged as a moral, responsible being. Her high destiny, to be helpmeet to man, will be achieved only through the removal of all political, professional, economic, legal and religious hindrances to her development.

As president of the Equal Rights Association in the 1860s, M. continued to work for the extension of rights to women and freedmen. When the women's rights movement split in 1869, she joined neither the

National nor the American Women's Suffrage Association. Five sermons and discourses delivered during this period reflect her interest not only in the plight of women and blacks but in the peace, temperance, and antisectarian movements as well.

In *A Sermon at Yardleyville* (1858), M. affirms the divinity of human instincts and claims that the attempt to create greater equality among people is characteristic of the work of the real Christian. In *A Sermon at Bristol* (1860), she urges Christians to be nonconformists like Jesus, and women to reject sectarianism, which sets limits on the divinity within them. M. maintains in *Discourse at the Friends' Meeting, N.Y.* (1866) that human progress is really moral progress and that skepticism and critical thinking are religious duties. In *Discourse at the Second Unitarian Church* (1867), M. urges that religion be carried into all of life's transactions. She denounces sectarianism in her "Remarks" to the Free Religious Association (1867), and in her *Sermon on the Religious Aspects of the Age* (1869), M. states that the work of reform in the present age is an indication of the growth of the Christian spirit and a new reverence for humanity.

"Truth for authority, rather than authority for truth" was M.'s central concern. In her preaching and speaking M. attempted to uncover truth. Through her personal involvement in a myriad of reform movements she tried to live truth and help realize it in her own time. In her home, where M. offered hospitality to hundreds of fellow reformers and society's most oppressed, she helped sustain truth and those who sought it.

WORKS: *Discourse on Woman* (1849). *A Sermon to the Medical Students* (1849). *A Sermon at Yardleyville* (1858). *A Sermon at Bristol* (1860). *Discourse at the Friends' Meeting, N.Y.* (1866). *Discourse at the Second Unitarian Church, Brooklyn* (1867). *Sermon on the Religious Aspects of the Age* (1869). *Life and Letters of James and Lucretia Mott* (Ed. A. D. Hallowell, 1884). *Slavery and "The Woman Questions": Lucretia Mott's Diary of her Visit to Great Britain to Attend the World's Anti-Slavery Convention of 1840* (Ed. F. B. Tolles, 1952). *Lucretia Mott: Complete Sermons and Speeches* (Ed. D. Greene, 1980).

The letters of Lucretia Mott are in the Friends Historical Library, Swarthmore College, and the Sophia Smith Collection, Smith College Library.

BIBLIOGRAPHY: Bacon, M., *Valiant Friend: The Life of Lucretia Mott* (1980). Cromwell, O., *Lucretia Mott* (1958).

For articles in reference works, see: *AW. DAB*, VI, 1. *HWS*, 1. *NAW* (article by F. B. Tolles). *NCAB*, 2.

Other references: *American Scholar* (Spring 1951). *Bulletin of the Historical Society of Montgomery County, Pa.* (April 1948).

DANA GREENE

Louise Chandler Moulton

B. *10 April 1835, Pomfret, Connecticut; d. 10 Aug. 1908, Boston, Massachusetts*
Wrote under: Ellen Louise Chandler, Louisa Chandler, A Lady, Ellen Louise,
  Louise Chandler Moulton
D. *of Lucius Lemuel and Louisa Rebecca Clark Chandler; m. William Upham*
  Moulton, 1855

M. was born on a farm outside a town settled by her Puritan ancestors. Her parents were wealthy, conscientious Calvinists. M.'s childhood was solitary and circumscribed, but reasonably happy. Precocious, M. published her first verses at fifteen. When she entered Emma Willard's Female Seminary in Troy, New York, fellow students knew her as "Ellen Louise," editor of *The Book of the Boudoir* (1853) and author of *This, That, and the Other*, a collection of sentimental stories and sketches which appeared in 1854 and sold 20,000 copies.

Soon after M.'s graduation in 1855, she married the editor and publisher of *The True Flag*, a Boston literary journal. Members of the city's literary society, the Moultons entertained Whittier, Longfellow, Holmes, and Emerson. In 1870, M. became the Boston literary correspondent for the New York *Tribune*. She began contributing stories to magazines such as *Harper's, Galaxy,* and *Scribner's;* her poem "May-Flowers" achieved great popularity after appearing in the *Atlantic*. Other works during this period include *June Clifford* (1855), a novel; *Some Women's Hearts* (1874), short stories; and *Bed-Time Stories* (1873), the first in a series of children's books.

After an initial trip to Europe in 1876, M. divided her life between the two continents. Her overwhelming success in London literary society began in 1877 with a letter of introduction to Lord Houghton (Richard Monckton Milnes) from "the Byron of Oregon," Joaquin Miller. From this time, M. was firmly established in European artistic circles.

Although she had published an earlier volume of poetry in America, *Swallow-Flights* (1877) brought M. her first wave of extravagant praise. Professor William Minto compared her to Sir Philip Sidney; other critics mentioned the lyric poets of the 16th and 17th centuries. *In the Garden of Dreams* (1890) and *At the Wind's Will* (1899) confirmed her reputation. Critics rated her love poetry close to Mrs. Browning's and considered her sonnets second only to Christina Rossetti's. During these years, M. also brought out two delightful volumes of Irvingesque travel sketches and a book of social advice culled from her newspaper column in *Our Continent*.

Certainly any assessment of M.'s achievements must cite her "genius for friendship." Her correspondence, now in the Library of Congress, fills fifty-two volumes; its index is a virtual directory of late Victorian authors. M.'s library, bequeathed to the Boston Public Library, comprised nine hundred books, many of them rare editions and autographed presentation copies. However, M.'s greatest legacy stemmed from her critical astuteness and sympathy. As a European literary correspondent for the Boston *Sunday Herald* and the New York *Independent* during the 1880s and 1890s, M. gained recognition in the U.S. for the Pre-Raphaelites, Décadents, and French Symbolist poets.

Like many late Victorians, M. wrote in traditional forms such as the sonnet, the French ballade, triolet, and rondel. She was known for her polished metrics, sensuous imagery, and meticulous workmanship. While critics appreciated her spontaneity, rarely do her emotions burst their poetic form; poise is all. However, M.'s meditations on love and approaching death hint at deep feeling below the restrained surface. One poem concludes with the lines: "This brief delusion that we call our life / Where all we can accomplish is to die." In another, "Help Thou My Unbelief," she quietly pleads for protection from the contented but godless life. Doubt, although painful, is less dreadful.

Frequently the melancholy, minor note in her poetry is more subtle: "Roses that briefly live / Joy is your dower; / Blest be the fates that give one perfect hour. / And, though too soon you die, / In your dust glows, / Something the passerby / Knows was a rose." Clichés, along with M.'s nostalgia for the lost "Arcady" of childhood and rural life, tend to date her work.

Upon her death, M.'s reputation reached its crest. According to Whiting, she "had left a place in American letters unfilled and that no successor is in evidence will hardly be disputed." M. lamented half-seriously that she seemed to have only two themes: love and death. But, as her biographer Lilian Whiting commented, these are surely two of the very greatest. As a poet, her contribution was small, but worth noting. As a critic and literary publicist, she played a valuable role in American letters. As a woman, her social success and "feminine" artistry reveal a great deal about late Victorian expectations.

WORKS: The Waverly Garland: A Present for All Seasons (edited by Moulton, 1853). The Book of the Boudoir; or, A Momento of Friendship (edited by Moulton, 1853). This, That, and the Other (1854). June Clifford: A Tale (1855). My Third Book (1859). Evaline, Madelon, and Other Poems (1861). Bed-Time Stories (1873). Some Women's Hearts (1874). More Bed-Time Stories (1875). Jessie's Neighbor, and Other Stories (1877). Swallow-Flights (American title, Poems, 1877). New Bed-Time Stories (1880). Random Rambles (1881). Poems (1882). Firelight Stories (1883). Garden Secrets by Philip Bourke Marston (edited, with biographical sketch, by Moulton, 1887). Ourselves and Our Neighbors (1887). Education for the Girls (1888). Miss Eyre from Boston (1889). A Ghost at His Fireside (1890). In the Garden of Dreams (1890). Stories Told at Twilight (1890). A Last Harvest by Philip Bourke Marston (edited, with biographical sketch by Moulton, 1891). Collected Poems of Philip Bourke Marston (edited by Moulton, 1892). Arthur O'Shaugnessy, His Life and His Work (1894). In Childhood's Country (1896). Lazy Tours in Spain and Elsewhere (1896). Against Wind and Tide (1899). At the Wind's Will (1899). Four of Them (1899). The American University Course (State Registered): Second Month Conduct of Life (1900). Jessie's Neighbor (1900). Her Baby Brother (1901). Introduction to the Value of Love and Its Compiler Frederick Lawrence Knowles (1906). Poems and Sonnets of Louise Chandler Moulton (Ed. H. P. Spofford, 1908).

The papers of Louise Chandler Moulton are at the Library of Congress and the American Antiquarian Society.

BIBLIOGRAPHY: Howe, J. W., Representative Women of New England (1904). Spofford, H. P., A Little Book of Friends (1916). Spofford, H. P., Our Famous Women (1884). Whiting, L., Louis Chandler Moulton, Poet and Friend (1910). Winslow, H. M., Literary Boston of Today (1902).

For articles in reference works, see: AW. CAL. DAB, VII, 1. Female Prose Writers of America (1857). NAW (article by L. M. Young). NCAB, 3.

Other references: Boston Transcript (12 Aug. 1908). Poet-Lore (Winter 1908).

SARAH WAY SHERMAN

Mary Noailles Murfree

B. 24 Jan. 1850, Murfreesboro, Tennessee; d. 31 July 1922, Murfreesboro,
   Tennessee
Wrote under: Charles Egbert Craddock, R. Emmet Dembury
D. of William Law and Fanny Dickinson Murfree

Born at the family plantation, M. was the daughter of a lawyer and author and a mother whose love of music greatly influenced the family.
Illness at the age of four left M. with permanent lameness.

In 1855, M. spent the first of fifteen summers at Beersheba Springs in
the Cumberland Mountains, which she fictionalized as New Helvetia
Springs. Soon the family moved to Nashville, where M. and her sister
Fanny were educated at the Nashville Female Academy. After the Civil
War, which the Murfrees spent in Nashville, M. continued her education
at Chegary Institute in Philadelphia, a French finishing school.

M.'s writing career began in earnest with the publication of "The
Dancin' Party at Harrison's Cove" in the *Atlantic Monthly* (May 1878)
under the pseudonym Charles Egbert Craddock. M.'s mountain fiction
was very well received; by 1885, when *The Prophet of the Great Smoky
Mountains* was being serialized, her popularity had led to increased speculation about the author's identity, and the sensation following its revelation gained M. invaluable publicity.

Although the modern reader may find M.'s decorous mountain fiction more romantic than realistic, and may be bored by the lack of in-
dividualization in her characters, contemporary readers were fascinated
by the minute detail, often gleaned through research, with which M.
portrayed people and their activities. The dominant feature of M.'s earlier
work is the mountains themselves. The juxtaposition of florid prose with
dialect is probably its weakest trait.

In spite of M.'s desire for realism, her characters tend to be stereotypes.
Most of the young "mountain-flower" girls, such as Cynthia Ware in
"Drifting Down Lost Creek" and Clarsie Giles in "The 'Harnt' That
Walks Chilhowee," are almost indistinguishable. " 'Harnt,' " probably M.'s
best-known work, is notable for its theme of the superiority of mountain
life.

M.'s greatest achievement is her first volume of stories, *In the Tennessee Mountains* (1884), with its emphasis on the picturesque details of

regional life. M.'s stories appealed to the awareness of sectional differences which had been heightened by the Civil War, as the popularity of this volume indicates.

Except for M.'s first novel, *Where the Battle Was Fought* (1884), based on personal experiences during the Civil War, M.'s work through the late 1890s focuses on mountain places and themes. When the popularity of local-color writing waned, M. turned to historical subjects in undistinguished novels such as *The Story of Old Fort Loudon* (1899) and *The Amulet* (1906). By 1910, M.'s public appeal had diminished to the point that Houghton-Mifflin rejected a proffered novel and collection of stories.

M. has been favorably compared to local colorists such as Bret Harte, Sarah Orne Jewett, and fellow southerner George Washington Cable. Her reputation is based on her mountain stories and novels; the body of her work is flawed by M.'s tendency to repeat characters and plots. However, *In the Tennessee Mountains* remains an important contribution to regional literature in the late 19th c.

WORKS: *In the Tennessee Mountains* (1884). *Where the Battle Was Fought* (1884). *The Prophet of the Great Smoky Mountains* (1885). *In the "Stranger People's" Country* (1891). *The Mystery of Witch-Face Mountain, and Other Stories* (1895). *The Phantoms of the Foot-Bridge, and Other Stories* (1895). *The Story of Old Fort Loudon* (1899). *A Spectre of Power* (1903). *The Amulet* (1906). *The Fair Mississippian* (1908). *The Raid of the Guerilla, and Other Stories* (1912). *The Story of Duciehurst* (1914).

BIBLIOGRAPHY: Cary, R., *Mary Noailles Murfree* (1967). Parks, E. W., *Charles Egbert Craddock (Mary Noailles Murfree)* (1941). Wright, N., Introduction to *In the Tennessee Mountains* (1970).

For articles in reference works, see: *AW. CAL. DAB*, VII, 1. *NAW* (article by E. W. Parks).

Other references: *ALR* (Autumn 1974). *Appalachian Journal* (Winter 1976). *MissQ* (Spring 1978).

MARTHA E. COOK

Judith Sargent Murray

B. 1 May 1751, Gloucester, Massachusetts; d. 6 July 1820, Natchez, Mississippi
Wrote under: Constantia, Honoria, Honoria-Martesia, Judith Sargent,
Judith Stevens
D. of Winthrop and Judith Saunders Sargent; m. John Stevens, 1769;
m. John Murray, 1788

M. was the oldest child of a well-to-do merchant who was active during the Revolution on the colonists' side. M. was better educated than most women of her time, because her father permitted her to study with a brother who was preparing for Harvard. She spent most of her life in Gloucester, where she was married twice: to a sea captain and, two years after his death, to Murray, founder of the American Universalist Church. Two children were born of the second marriage, a son who died shortly after birth and a daughter who survived her mother. Financial difficulties marked the final years of both marriages.

In 1798, M. collected many of her writings into a three-volume work called *The Gleaner*. These volumes include one series of essays that appeared originally from 1792 to 1794 in the *Massachusetts Magazine*, additional essays previously unpublished, and two plays—*Virtue Triumphant* and *The Traveller Returned*, produced with little success at the Federal Street Theatre in Boston. There remain uncollected a number of essays and poems published in periodicals and a catechism for children, which was published as a book under the name of Judith Stevens. In addition, M. edited Murray's letters and autobiography.

M. is best known for her periodical essay series, "The Gleaner." These essays purport to be written by Mr. Vigilius, a well-off, philanthropic man of reason and sensibility who has adopted the pen name of the Gleaner to write about moral, religious, political and family matters. M. reveals her liberal religious views, federalism, cultural nationalism, concern for the special problems of bringing up daughters, and commitment to education, about which she had modern views. Much of the interest, however, centers less on discussions of general issues than on the Gleaner's accounts of his family. Because the story of his daughter is so fully developed, this series has been referred to as a novel of sensibility. In a subplot there is, in contrast with traditions of 18th-c. sensibility, an unusually realistic cameo view of women's experience.

M. is also known for her feminist statement "On the Equality of the Sexes," which she claimed to have written in 1779, before Wollstonecraft's *Vindication of the Rights of Woman* appeared, although it was not published until 1790 in the *Massachusetts Magazine*. Concerned here with arguing the intellectual equality of women, M. went on in the later Gleaner essays to elaborate her defense of women's abilities.

M.'s essay series has attracted some scholarly attention in the past, and her plays, which combine American settings and sentiments with traditions of the Restoration stage, read surprisingly well and are of historic interest. Recently, her essays have attracted attention because of M.'s feminist defense of women's intellectual potential and her insistence on the importance of education and economic independence for women. M.'s work reflects an acceptance of the literary and intellectual traditions of her time and the strength of mind to reject tradition when she believed it incorrect or unfair.

WORKS: Some Deductions from the System Promulgated (1782). *The Gleaner* (3 vols., 1798). *Letters and Sketches of Sermons*, by John Murray (3 vols., edited by Murray, 1812–13). *Records of the Life of the Rev. John Murray, Written by Himself, with a Continuation by Mrs. Judith Sargent Murray* (edited by Murray, 1816).

BIBLIOGRAPHY: Benson, M. S., *Women in Eighteenth Century America* (1935). Field, V. B., *Constantia: A Study of the Life and Works of Judith Sargent Murray* (1933). Hanson, E. R., *Our Women Workers* (1882).

For articles in reference works, see: *DAB*, VII, 1. *NAW* (article by J. W. James).

Other references: *AL* 12 (1940). *AQ* 28 (1976). *EAL* (9, 1975; 11, 1976–77). *SP* 24 (1927).

PHYLLIS FRANKLIN

Pauli Murray

B. 20 Nov. 1910, Baltimore, Maryland
D. of William Henry and Agnes Georgianna Fitzgerald Murray

Orphaned at the age of three, M. was raised by her mother's sister, an elementary school teacher in a small black school. M. attended her aunt's classes and learned to read and write at an early age.

M. received a B.A. from Hunter College in New York. In 1938, she applied to the graduate school of the University of North Carolina but was denied admission to the white institution. During this period, M. wrote prose and poetry under the guidance of Stephen Vincent Benét. M. suspended her literary work to serve as special field secretary for the Workers Defense League. After Benét's death in 1943 she resumed her efforts to write the epic poem which he had urged her to write about blacks in America. She finished the first version of "Dark Testament" during the Harlem riot of 1943.

In 1944, M. was graduated with honors from Howard University Law School in Washington, D.C. As a woman, she was denied admission to Harvard Law School in 1944 and 1946, but received an M.A. in 1945 from the University of California Law School at Berkeley and a Ph.D. from Yale in 1965. From 1948 to 1960, she was in private practice in New York. In 1960 and 1961, M. was senior lecturer on constitutional and administrative law at the Ghana School of Law. While in Accra, she joined Leslie Rubin in the writing of *The Constitution and Government of Ghana* (1961). M. has practiced law, taught law and political science, and served on numerous national committees.

Dark Testament, and Other Poems (1970) includes poems originally published in several magazines. The longest and best is "Dark Testament." Part 1 of "Dark Testament" questions the possibility of hope but ends on a note of determination, saying ". . . let the dream linger on." M. contends that universal brotherhood must be the goal of humanity. Part 2 contains poems dealing with specific historical events: a Detroit riot, the lynching of Mack Parker, and the death of Franklin Roosevelt. The third part focuses upon the universal human predicament and has no racial emphasis. Neither has the fourth part, which takes images from nature for poems dealing with love, friendship, death, and loneliness.

Proud Shoes: The Story of an American Family (1956) is the story of M.'s ancestors. Asserting that "true emancipation lies in the acceptance of the whole past, in deriving strength from all my roots, in facing up to the degradation as well as the dignity of my ancestors," M. traces the family back to great-grandparents who were slaves. But the major portion of *Proud Shoes* is devoted to her greatest source of pride, her grandfather, who taught M. that she ought to cherish "courage, honor, and discipline."

Though she knew her parents only briefly during early childhood, M. found great sources of pride in her mother's family. *Proud Shoes* does more than account for the pride that has made M. such a successful black woman. It analyzes miscegenation as a social phenomenon and examines its bearing on race relations. It attacks stereotypes of the black family as broken and matriarchal. Thus, it is a valuable social document as well as an interesting biography of an American family.

Though M. has chosen to make her social contribution primarily though service rather than literature, her small oeuvre is significant. Her legal writing establishes her as a scholar, *Proud Shoes* proves her a capable biographer, and *Dark Testament* reveals a talented poet whose lines combine the skills of both biographer and lawyer—precision of language and vision—with the compression of poetic forms to achieve powerful effects.

WORKS: *All for Mr. Davis* (with M. Kempton, 1942). *States Law on Race and Color* (1950). *Proud Shoes: The Story of an American Family* (1956). *The Constitution and Government of Ghana* (with L. Rubin, 1961). *Dark Testament, and Other Poems* (1970).

BIBLIOGRAPHY: Diamonstein, B., *Open Secrets* (1972).

For articles in reference works, see: *Black American Writers Past and Present*, T. G. Rush, C. F. Myers, and E. S. Arata (Vol. 2, 1975).

Other references: *Afro-American* (20 Jan. 1968).

GWENDOLYN THOMAS

Carry Amelia Moore Nation

B. 25 Nov. 1846, Garrard County, Kentucky; d. 2 June 1911 Leavenworth, Kansas
Wrote under: Carry A. Nation
D. of George and Mary Campbell Moore; m. Dr. Charles Gloyd, 1867; m. David Nation, 1877

Born into the antebellum American "paradise" of faithful slaves and bountiful nature, as N. describes it, this American symbol of rampant morality is perhaps our real Scarlett O'Hara, stripped of all romantic distortion. Complete with a noble, upright father, a mother sporadically deranged by the illusion that she was Queen Victoria, and a faithful mammy with a grip on reality, N. emerged from the fancies of childhood and the Civil War, like Scarlett O'Hara, with God as her witness—

but it was not physical hunger she vowed never to endure again. Instead, N. was determined never to suffer the deprivation of love, which her first husband's addiction to drink had brought her.

N.'s autobiography, *The Use and Need of the Life of Carry A. Nation* (1908), her one contribution to American letters, chronicles N.'s mission to defend love and life in the American family from the demon rum. The book is not a simple autobiography, for N.'s material is not limited to the exposition of her life. Rather, the autobiography is an encyclopedic work that places itself somewhere beyond confession. Aside from the details of N.'s life, it contains pictures of social conditions in the South before and after the Civil War, and the contemporary medical wisdom on the effects of alcohol and tobacco upon the human constitution. It contains tirades on the abuses of alcohol and tobacco, which outline the philosophical bases of N.'s crusade. It also contains discourses on Christianity, Judaism, the Masons, upper-class education of the time, and the position of women in society.

The book is permeated by a religious hysteria, but the reader will find that N.'s autobiography bristles with the unexpected. Despite N.'s fundamentalist foundation for her crusade, for example, she reveals a profound reverence for sexual love and a desire for openness about sexuality. N. is prudishly hostile to the exposure of the undraped female figure in public, but she expresses unexpected disapproval that children are not told the truth about procreation, and that men do not pay sexual attention to their wives, perversely giving themselves freely to prostitutes whom, N. claims with modern insight, they hate and who hate them in return.

Despite the fact that N. is a true believer of the most single-minded sort, she expresses paradoxical respect and affection for both Jews and Catholics as individuals and in groups. She does not appear to have hopes of saving them as reasonably virtuous pagans, but actually grants them another window in her Father's mansion.

Finally, N. is completely cognizant of the insanity others attribute to her. However, when N. finishes cataloguing the alcohol-induced human misery she has experienced, witnessed, and learned of, her extreme actions to destroy the bane of her existence do not seem insane. They appear, rather, to be lacking in modern insights into the social and chemical roots of alcoholism.

The autobiography exhibits two main qualities. It is a portal leading to increased appreciation of the complex social and moral 19th-c. American climate. It is also a work that in recounting N.'s thoughts about society and her suffering for her cause has such a contemporary ring that it rescues N. from the burlesque stereotype that has wrongly portrayed her as an undistilled essence of harridan.

WORKS: *The Use and Need of the Life of Carry A. Nation* (1908).

BIBLIOGRAPHY: Asbury, H., *Carry Nation* (1909). Beals, D., *Cyclone Carry: The Story of Carry Nation* (1962).
For articles in reference works, see: *DAB*, VII, 1. *NAW* (article by P. R. Messbarger).
Other references: *Les Idees* (Jan.–June 1939). *SHQ* (April 1960).

MARTHA NOCHIMSON

Nellie Neilson

B. *5 April 1873, Philadelphia, Pennsylvania; d. 26 May 1947, South Hadley, Massachusetts*
D. *of William George and Mary Louise Cunningham Neilson*

The first woman to serve as president of the American Historical Association (1943), N. was an outstanding authority on medieval English agrarian economy. Her major concern was the influence of local custom on the development of English common law and on the development of the agrarian economy, especially in Kent. Much of N.'s work was in the form of scholarly articles. A charter member of the Medieval Academy of America, she was for years the sole woman fellow and served eventually as president of the society.

Economic Conditions on the Manors of Ramsey Abbey (1898) was N.'s doctoral dissertation. In this work, N. seeks to give a "full, connected statement" of conditions on a set of church manors during the 12th and 13th centuries. She provides a comparative study of conditions in the two centuries, concluding that there was "an appreciable steady depression in the condition of the villeins" over that period. The decline is particularly evident in the rapid evolution of *precariae*, or boon work.

Another major work was *Customary Rents* (1910), one of two monographs in the second volume of *Oxford Studies in Social and Legal History*. As Paul Vinogradoff noted in his introduction, N. approaches her subject as a student of records. She focuses on three sets of obligations of the typical villein: rents arising from manorial customs, rents originally royal in character, and church rents. Both the latter two had become manorialized in a sense, but they still retained something of their public character. For the study of manorial rents, N. contended, the best sources are the custumals of the church manors and the records kept by manorial officers.

N. traces the complex relationships of five different rents, determined according to origin. As to the royal rents, N. notes that it is difficult to determine the original principle of assessment, in part because the superimposed manor "confused the old arrangements of the vill." Furthermore, since manorial, royal, and church rents were all received by the lord in one capacity or another, few distinctions were noted in the records. The guides N. provides form a basis for classifying and comparing various kinds of rents.

In 1920, N. edited *A Terrier of Fleet, Lincolnshire*, and in 1928 she edited *A Cartulary and Terrier of the Priory of Bilsington, Kent*. The introductory monograph for the latter was a study of customs of the forests and marshes of Kent, based on extensive manuscript research.

Of a quite different nature is *Medieval Agrarian Economy* (1936). This work, part of the *Berkshire Studies in European History*, was designed for use in college classes in general European history.

N. notices the greatest difference between medieval life and modern life in the prominence of agriculture in daily medieval affairs and the closeness to nature. She deals with three levels of life: the village settlement itself, the people and their conditions of life and interrelationships, and the relation of the village to two outside agencies: the government and the church. The general focus is on the pattern of life customary in England and France during the 12th and 13th centuries, with much briefer reference to conditions in central Europe. N. stresses the role of customary law as the moderating force on arbitrary will. As her focus is on the village, her primary concern is how the outside agencies are encountered there.

A thorough and painstaking scholar, N. won the respect of medievalists in both Great Britain and the U.S. She was an indefatigable researcher, and the variety of approaches she used and the effective comparisons drawn give her work strength and depth. N.'s skill in combining the roles of scholar and teacher is part of her hallmark.

WORKS: *Economic Conditions on the Manors of Ramsey Abbey* (1898). *Customary Rents* (in Oxford Studies in Social and Legal History, Vol. 2, 1910). *A Terrier of Fleet, Lincolnshire, from a Manuscript in the British Museum* (edited by Neilson, 1920). *The Cartulary and Terrier of the Priory of Bilsington, Kent* (edited by Neilson, 1928). *Year Books of Edward IV* (edited by Neilson, 1931). *Medieval Agrarian Economy* (1936).

BIBLIOGRAPHY: Ausubel, H., *Historians and Their Craft: A Study of the Presidential Addresses of the American Historical Association, 1884–1945* (1950).

For articles in reference works, see: *NCAB*, 36.

Other references: *AHR* (Jan. 1929; Oct. 1947). *Mount Holyoke Alumnae Quarterly* (Feb. 1948).

INZER BYERS

Alice Ruth Moore Dunbar Nelson

B. *19 July 1875, New Orleans, Louisiana; d. 18 Sept. 1935, Philadelphia, Pennsylvania*
Wrote under: Alice Dunbar, Alice Dunbar-Nelson, Alice Ruth Moore
D. *of Joseph and Patricia Wright Moore; m. Paul Laurence Dunbar, 1889; m. Robert John Nelson, 1916*

The younger of two daughters of middle-class working parents, N. attended public schools and Straight College, New Orleans. After graduation, she began to teach and to submit poetry to the Boston *Monthly Review*.

One of these poems and the accompanying photograph of N. attracted Dunbar, then a young poet. He wrote N., conversationally raising literary issues, and enclosed a copy of his "Phyllis." This began a friendship that led to marriage.

N. separated from Dunbar after a quarrel in 1902, and returned to teaching—she had taught kindergarten at Victoria Earle Matthews's White Rose Mission in New York—becoming head of the English Department at Howard High School in Wilmington, Delaware. She retained this position for eighteen years until she was fired for defying an order to abstain from political activity.

During World War I, N. became involved in organizing black women on behalf of the U.S. Council of National Defense. N. was the first black woman to serve on Delaware's Republican State Committee.

N. became associate editor of the *Wilmington Advocate,* a weekly newspaper published by her second husband and dedicated to the achievement of equal rights for blacks. She also wrote a weekly column for the Washington, D.C., *Eagle* and contributed occasional pieces to the *American Methodist Episcopal Church Review.* Her later years were devoted to social work, especially with delinquent black girls, and to the cause of world peace.

N.'s reply to Dunbar's first letter to her set forth her views on the literary use of "the Negro problem:" "I haven't much liking for those writers that wedge the Negro problem and social equality and long dissertations on the Negro in general into their stories. It is too much like a quinine pill in jelly. . . . Somehow when I start a story I always think of my folk characters as simple human beings, not of types of a race or an idea, and I seem to be on more friendly terms with them." N.'s letter also mentioned the forthcoming publication of her first book, *Violets, and Other Tales* (1895). In accord with her philosophy, the book presents "simple human beings" caught in universal dilemmas such as poverty and love betrayed.

While many of the twelve poems and seventeen tales and sketches in *Violets, and Other Tales* are romantic and slight, they give evidence of a fresh, lively style. Noteworthy in this collection for their sprightliness and originality are the humorous "In Unconsciousness," a mock-epic inspired by a tooth extraction, and "The Woman," a lively meditation on the independent woman. This piece decries "this wholesale marrying of girls in their teens, this rushing into an unknown plane of life to avoid work," and reassures readers that an independent, intelligent woman, a lawyer or doctor, does not lose her ability to love when she gains a vocation.

During the period of her marriage to Dunbar, N. published her second collection, *The Goodness of St. Rocque, and Other Stories* (1899), fourteen local-color stories of New Orleans life. These are crisply written sketches, portraying struggling, heroic characters trapped in difficulties. Most have a surprise twist at their conclusions.

While teaching at Howard High School, N. edited two collections of poems and prose for oratory students, *Masterpieces of Negro Eloquence* (1914) and *The Dunbar Speaker and Entertainer* (1920). Included in the latter are several pieces by N., many of them (such as the one-act play *Mine Eyes Have Seen*) expressing conventional patriotic sentiments and racial pride. The short lyric "I Sit and Sew," while sharing the conventional patriotism of the others, is also a statement of a woman chafing at the limited range of appropriate female activity; it has an intensity, freshness, and power which the other pieces lack.

N. was a pioneer in the black short-story tradition. Her second volume shows an increase in power, which promised further development, had she continued to write in this genre. Instead, N., an energetic woman of diversified talents, devoted her later life to journalism and political and social activism.

WORKS: *Violets, and Other Tales* (1895). *The Goodness of St. Rocque, and Other Stories* (1899). *Masterpieces of Negro Eloquence* (edited by Nelson, 1914). *The Dunbar Speaker and Entertainer* (edited by Nelson, 1920).

BIBLIOGRAPHY: Bernikow, L. *The World Split Open: Four Centuries of Women Poets in England and America* (1974). Brawley, B., *Paul Laurence Dunbar* (1936). Brown, H. Q., *Homespun Heroines, and Other Women of Distinction* (1926). Kerlin, R. T., *Negro Poets and Their Poems* (1935). Loggins, V., *The Negro Author* (1931). Martin, J., ed., *A Singer in the Dawn* (1975). Whiteman, M., *A Century of Fiction by American Negroes, 1853–1952: A Descriptive Bibliography* (1955).

For articles in reference works, see: *NAW* (article by N. A. Ford).

Other references: *Delaware History* 17 (Fall–Winter 1976).

KAREN F. STEIN

Emily Cheney Neville

B. 28 Dec. 1919, Manchester, Connecticut
D. of Howell and Anne Bunce Cheney; m. Glenn Neville, 1948

N. is the youngest child of the large, close-knit family she describes in her autobiographical novel, *Traveler from a Small Kingdom* (1968). N. played and went to school only with siblings and cousins until she was ten. She attended Oxford School in Hartford and graduated from Bryn Mawr with a degree in economics.

After working briefly for the New York *Daily News* as an office girl, N. took a position with the New York *Daily Mirror* writing a profile column. She married a newspaperman with the Hearst Corporation, and retired from journalism to raise her family, doing only occasional writing until all five children were in school.

N.'s books have been full-length realistic novels intended for later elementary and teenage readers. Her first book, *It's Like This, Cat* (1963), developed out of an imaginary scene in which a boy argues with his father over a cat. N. expanded a short piece in the *Mirror* into the novel, which later won the Newbery Award and is regarded as N.'s strongest book. Flimsy in plot, *Cat*'s strong points are its genuine, contemporary dialogue and warm insights into the inner feelings of young adolescents.

For slightly younger children, *Berries Goodman* (1965) is about the adjustments a New York City family must make when they move to Olcott Corners, a suburban community fifty miles out. Accustomed to a heterogeneous environment, nine-year-old Berries, Gentile, is perplexed and disturbed by anti-Semitic sentiment directed toward his new friend, Sidney Fine, the only Jewish boy in Berries's school. Eventually adults and circumstances come between the two and end their relationship. The story describes with sensitivity and perceptiveness the feelings of children caught up in adult tensions, which they regard as irrational but which they are powerless to combat. Well-drawn children offset the stereotyped adults and thin and contrived plot.

The Seventeenth-Street Gang (1966) is an amusing account of the sidewalk adventures of a group of children around Stuyvesant Park, the part of Manhattan in which N.'s own children grew up.

Slower moving, *Traveler from a Small Kingdom* (1968) is a fictionalized autobiography important for evaluating and understanding N.'s work. It tells of the middle years in the childhood of little Emily Cheney, a scrawny, often sickly, but still active and imaginative child. Her "small green kingdom" is "The Place," where a dozen Cheney families live in the mill town of South Manchester, Connecticut. Mrs. Goodall, English governess of Emily and her older sister, comes through as a strong, strict, and affectionate personality, while lively details of family gatherings, walks, domestic animals, and games with an assortment of mischievous and inventive cousins recreate the Cheney realm and a way of life that vanished with the Great Depression.

Less convincing are *Fogarty* (1969) and *Garden of Broken Glass* (1975), written for teenage readers. Both present interesting and sympathetic protagonists but suffer from limp plots, made-to-order incidents, and unbelievable conclusions. While it bravely tackles an important contemporary problem, *Garden of Broken Glass* lacks conviction as a novel because N. seems more concerned with the sociology of alcoholism than with telling a good story well.

N. has said about her work: "My writing is probably an outgrowth of my childhood in a large clannish New England family, mingled with my own quite different experiences raising five children in New York City." Concerned with showing young people the world as it is, she feels that "the job for a writer of junior novels . . . [is] to shine the flashlight on good things, and on bad things. It is not our job to preach that this is right and that is wrong. It is ours to show how and when and why Wrong can be so overwhelmingly attractive at a given moment —and how Right can be found in some very unlikely corners."

N. feels that plot in books for young people is less important than character; her strong point is her ability to create lively, sympathetic protagonists whose feelings, speech, and actions reflect well the concerns and behavior of modern youth. N.'s books are less overtly didactic and sociological than many recent books which deal with contemporary social problems and family relations.

WORKS: *It's Like This, Cat* (1963). *Berries Goodman* (1965). *The Seventeenth-Street Gang* (1966). *Traveler from a Small Kingdom* (1968). *Fogarty* (1969). *Garden of Broken Glass* (1975).

BIBLIOGRAPHY: For articles in reference works, see: *More Books about More People*, L. E. Hopkins (1974). *Newbery and Caldecott Medal Books*, Ed. L. Kingman (1965). *Something about the Author*, Ed. A. Commire (1971). *Third Book of Junior Authors*, Eds. D. De Montreville and D. Hill (1972).

ALETHEA K. HELBIG

Franc Johnson Newcomb

B. 30 March 1887, Jacksonville, Wisconsin; d. 25 July 1970, Albuquerque, New Mexico
Wrote under: Franc J. Newcomb, Franc Johnson Newcomb
D. of Frank Lewis and Priscilla Taft Woodward Johnson; m. Arthur J. Newcomb, 1914

N. was the daughter of an architect and a teacher who both died before her teens. After graduating from Tomah High School in 1904, N. taught locally for five years, studying summers to complete her education degree in 1913. Joining the Indian Service in 1911, N. taught Menominees until her health demanded a transfer from Wisconsin.

In 1912, N. taught Navajos at the Fort Defiance, Arizona, boarding school, where she met her husband, a trader. They established a trading post in a remote Navajo community in northwestern New Mexico. After N. moved to Albuquerque in 1935 to educate her two daughters, she wrote and worked to establish a visiting-nurse service and day nursery there and the Museum of Navaho Ceremonial Art in Santa Fe.

When fire destroyed their trading post in 1936, N.'s husband's alcoholism became acute, straining N. to the breaking point. After their divorce in 1946, N. resumed writing. N.'s first book, *Sandpaintings of the Navajo Shooting Chant* (1937), discusses the origin myth and action, and forty-four of the six hundred sand paintings a friendly medicine man, Hosteen Klah, allowed N. to reproduce. N.'s section of *A Study of Navajo Symbolism* (1956) explains the meanings of materials she saw used in Navajo rituals.

Respect for Navajo lifeways dominates N.'s descriptions of the hogan in two of many articles published in *New Mexico* magazine (Nov. 1934 and Jan. 1940). In *Navajo Omens and Taboos* (1940), N. explains both the ritual reasoning and pragmatic logic behind over two hundred Navajo customs governing all phases of life, from sex roles to luck signs.

N.'s collections of Navajo folklore include histories of Navajo emergence into their "Fifth World" (*Navajo Folk Tales*, 1967); myths recounting the gods' gifts of ceremonies ("Origin Legend of the Navajo Eagle Chant," *Journal of American Folklore*, Jan.–March 1940); and tales explaining animal traits (*Navajo Bird Tales*, 1970). N.'s composite versions gathered from several storytellers have limited value for folklorists, but general readers appreciate the graceful language.

In her poetry based on Navajo materials, N. uses formal meter and rhyme, producing an odd effect of cultural contrast between structure and content. For example, "Nilth-Chizzie" (*New Mexico Magazine*, Oct. 1936) relates Navajo beliefs concerning the ghostliness of the little whirlwind in the form of a sonnet.

N.'s best work is her nonfiction prose blending history, autobiography, and folklore. In "The Price of a Horse" (*New Mexico Quarterly Review*, May 1943), N. lets readers connect a diary entry about discovering a mass burial, a government report of a military incident, and Grandma Klah's story of an Army massacre of fifty-eight Navajos suspected of stealing a horse. In her biography, *Hosteen Klah* (1964), N. fuses these sources, producing a personalized history of changing Navajo culture through compelling portraits of Klah, his mother, and his great-grandfather, Chief Narbona.

Navaho Neighbors (1966) is a collection of reservation memories. The power of Navajo women in their matrilineal society emerges as N. humorously describes a woman divorcing her fat husband by narrowing her hogan door, and poignantly tells of a niece bearing a child to give her aunt, whose children had died. Lack of chronological order reinforces N.'s emphasis upon the continuity of personal ties and tradition in this isolated community.

Although some historians and anthropologists resented N. as an amateur, N. Scott Momaday applauded her realistic portrayals of Navajo life. To N., Navajos were people, not objects for study. This basic assumption permeates N.'s works, enhancing their value as a record of the personal dimension of intercultural communication.

WORKS: *Sandpaintings of the Navajo Shooting Chant* (with G. A. Reichard, 1937). *Navajo Omens and Taboos* (1940). *Hosteen Klah, Navaho Medicine Man and Sandpainter* (1964). *Navaho Neighbors* (1966). *Navajo Folk Tales* (1967). *Navajo Bird Tales Told by Hosteen Clah Chee* (1970).

The papers of Franc Johnson Newcomb, including an unpublished paper, "Autobiography of Franc Johnson Newcomb," are at the Maxwell Museum of Anthropology, University of New Mexico, Albuquerque.

BIBLIOGRAPHY: American Association of University Women, Albuquerque Branch, *Women in New Mexico* (1976).

Other references: *American Anthropologist* (Dec. 1957; April 1965; Dec. 1967; Feb. 1969). *Journal of American History* (Dec. 1967). *New Mexico Quarterly Review* (Aug. 1940). *NYTBR* (8 Jan. 1967). Sante Fe *New Mexican* (31 Mar. 1968). *El Palacio* (5–12 Jan. 1938).

HELEN M. BANNAN

Frances Newman

B. 13 Dec. 1883, Atlanta, Georgia; d. 22 Oct. 1928, New York City
D. of William Truslow and Frances Percy Alexander Newman

Except for travel abroad and brief stays in the East, N. lived in her native Atlanta, Georgia. Her formal schooling included one year in the Carnegie Library School. N. has been a professional librarian at Florida State College for Women, the Atlanta Carnegie Library, and the Georgia

School of Technology Library. She began her writing career as a reviewer for the Atlanta newspapers.

N.'s one published short story, "Rachel and Her Children" (*American Mercury*, 1924), won the O. Henry Memorial Award. "Atlanta Biltmore," her only other story, remains unpublished.

The Short Story's Mutations (1924) was described in a publicity flyer as "sixteen illustrative stories . . . woven into ten chapters like episodes in a well-told biography." Beginning with Petronius and ending with Morand, N. selected stories that were mutations (not evolutions), believing that the presence of a genius could produce a new species that would have lasting effect on what came after it. Thus her book is an anthology illustrating N.'s theory of the short story. Her sixty pages of commentary remain useful and impressive, reflecting her sensitivity to fiction and her irritation towards those who "would like to confine brief fictions in an inflexible form."

N.'s extensive criticism remains uncollected. By 1915, she was writing brilliant reviews for the Atlanta *Constitution and Journal*. Book reviews also appeared in the *Bookman* and *The New York Times*. Twelve of N.'s best critical articles and three episodes from what eventually became the novel *The Hard-Boiled Virgin* (1926) were published in the *Reviewer*, a Richmond journal.

N.'s caustic wit and candor did little to endear her to those she criticized. Repeatedly, she said that her own country did not find convictions very important; it was not a century of beliefs and disbeliefs, but of tastes and distastes. N. was convinced that writers of novels must *brood* over ideas before putting them into words, and "that American writing will probably not be very much better until American critics are better."

The Hard-Boiled Virgin was an instant success, the title alone assuring its *succés de scandale*. N. traced much of her own life in Katharine Faraday, who was also the youngest and least attractive in a handsome family. Trained in southern mores, Katharine met proper young men but lost them when their courtship (passion) violated her expectations (love). Unable to achieve a proper marriage, she turned writer, traveler, and littérateur. The daring exploits of a properly bred southern girl made the book appealing to the public. Structured in short chapters (each a paragraph), the novel contains no dialogue. The long, complex sentences reveal N.'s serious preoccupation with style. Her extraordinary gifts of wit, comic irony, and psychological insight delineate the inner self of Katharine Faraday.

N.'s second novel, *Dead Lovers Are Faithful Lovers* (1928), has little dialogue. Although slightly flawed by an overabundance of "yellow crêpe de chine negliges," "blue-plumed yellow velvet hats," and operatic allusions, the novel nevertheless superbly presents its *ménage à trois:* Charlton Cunningham, a young lawyer who rose to railroad president; his wife Evelyn Page, whose mother "told her that a wife's love always grows and a husband's always lessens"; and Isabel Ramsey, the spinster librarian whom Cunningham began to court after twelve married years. N. included the daring subjects of sexual sensations, miscegenation, adultery, and divorce. Social nuances were rendered faithfully, but equally significant was the presence of the "new woman" apparent in Isabel's thoughts.

N. was an interesting woman, slightly out of place in Atlanta in the 1920s, and a distinguished stylist. With the shift in taste that came with the Depression years, her style fell from fashion. Generally, her published work has been little read since the 1920s. Her first novel, *The Goldfish Bowl*, remains unpublished, and readers are forever cheated of the stories and books left unwritten save for their tantalizing titles: *Eminent Virgins, So-Called, History of Sophistication,* "Mr. Pringle's Deceased Wife's Sisters," and *There's a Certain Elegance about Celibacy.*

WORKS: *The Short Story's Mutations* (1924). *The Hard-Boiled Virgin* (1926). *Dead Lovers Are Faithful Lovers* (1928). *Moralités Légendaires* by J. Laforgue (translated by Newman, 1928). *Frances Newman's Letters* (Ed. H. Baugh, 1929).

BIBLIOGRAPHY: Cabell, J., *Some of Us: An Essay in Epitaphs* (1930). Clark, E., *Innocence Abroad* (1931). Ramsey, W., *Jules Laforgue and the Ironic Inheritance* (1953).

Other references: *GaR* 14 (1960). *London Magazine* (1966).

ELIZABETH EVANS

Helaine Newstead

B. 22 April 1906, New York City
D. of Nathan and Sarah Newstead

An only child of moderately well-off Jewish parents, N. spent her formative years preparing for a career as a pianist. N. attended Hunter

College, to which she returned as a tutor upon her graduation in 1928, and received her Ph.D. from Columbia University in 1937. At Columbia, N. met her mentor, Roger Sherman Loomis, who inspired her research into Arthurian legend.

N. teaches at the City University of New York's Graduate Center. Her attachment to this institution, and to scholarly organizations and causes, has been great: she has been chairman of the Arthurian Romance group of the Modern Language Association (1956–57) and president of the Medieval Club of New York (1950–52) as well as chairman of the English Department both at Hunter College and at CUNY (1962–69). Among N.'s recent honors are an honorary doctorate from the University of Wales (1969), Fellow of the Medieval Academy (1976), and election to the Presidency of the International Arthurian Society (1972–75).

N. has published over seventy-five articles and book reviews, many of them in the *Journal of Romance Philology* and *PMLA*. N.'s major work is probably her doctoral thesis, *Bran the Blessed in Arthurian Romance* (1939). Here, N. painstakingly traces many elements of the French Grail romances to their Celtic antecedents; thus, she argues for the "existence of a Welsh stage in the transmission of Celtic material," restores creative credit to medieval Wales, and illuminates the process of myth making and the accretion of legendary detail.

The unobtrusive style of N.'s writing is somewhat warmer in the introduction to her anthology, *Chaucer and His Contemporaries* (1968). This work includes essays on the black death and medieval technology; it is refreshing in its relation of the literature to the life of the period. N.'s no-nonsense approach both to scholarship and to human behavior may be seen in her learned articles as well. In a study of Chrétien de Troyes's *Le Comte du Graal*, for example, N. contends that Perceval does indeed have more than a spiritual relationship with a lady in great distress who comes to his bed. N.'s subject matter may be obscure and her style flatly academic, but her arguments appeal finally to what we know of real life. Thus, N. is as a scholar both down-to-earth and erudite.

WORKS: *Bran the Blessed in Arthurian Romance* (1939; rev. ed., 1966). *Chaucer and His Contemporaries: Essays in Medieval Literature and Thought* (edited by Newstead, 1968).

BIBLIOGRAPHY: *NY* (March 1957).

NIKKI STILLER

Anne Nichols

B. 26 Nov. 1896 (?, 1891?), Dales Mills, Georgia; d. 15 Sept. 1966
D. of George and Julia Bates Nichols; m. Henry Duffy, 1914

Playwright, producer, director, and actress, N. began performing at age fifteen and continued to be active in the performing arts into the 1950s. Married to a theatrical producer, and mother of one son, N. toured with vaudeville and traveling acting companies, frequently writing scripts for their use. Her writing versatility extended from vaudeville sketches, full-length plays, and musicals to film scenarios and radio adaptations. N. produced both her own works and others', and she acted on stage and in films.

The themes and emphasis of N.'s many plays can be identified easily through their titles: *Just Married* (1921) and *Heart's Desire* (1916), written with Adelaide Matthews, *Her Weekend* (later titled *Pre Engagement*, 1936), and *Marry in Haste* (1921). The varieties of farcical complications which either separate lovers and honeymooners or inadvertently join complete strangers are reused from one play to the next. Mistaken identities, improbable coincidences, quarreling lovers, ticket mix-ups, and unimportant but closely guarded secrets fill each work. The lighthearted activities invariably end in happy marriage, with particular emphasis on the now-fulfilled proprieties. Social obligations are met, families are united, and proper engagements or marriages are planned.

N.'s best-known work is *Abie's Irish Rose* (1922), which has been periodically revived. It was filmed in 1928 and formed the basis for a television situation comedy (*Bridget Loves Bernie*) in the 1970s. Well received by the general audiences in its New York and international appearances, the play was panned initially by the *New York Times*. Replete with Jewish dialect and Irish brogue, it calls upon mechanical devices to present every cliché ever offered by disapproving parents about the marriage of their children. In doubling the traditional means of reconciliation (twins instead of just a single child), the play's final scene is a triumph of sentimentality.

In her various theatrical activities, N. seldom varied from the trite limits of the well-made farce; nevertheless, her popular success indicates a clear awareness of the public taste and a smooth, competent ability to meet it. N. entertains without making demands on her audience's intelligence or attitudes.

WORKS: *Heart's Desire* (with A. Matthews, 1916). *The Man from Wicklow* (1917). *The Happy Cavalier* (1918). *A Little Bit Old Fashioned* (1918). *Her Gilded Cage* (1919). *Linger Longer Letty* (1919). *Seven Miles to Arden* (1919). *Springtime in Mayo* (1919). *Down Limerick Way* (1920). *Just Married* (with A. Matthews, 1921). *Love Dreams* (with W. Jensen, 1921). *Marry in Haste* (1921). *Abie's Irish Rose* (1922; film version, 1928; revised version, by Nichols and J. Lynn, 1954). *Her Weekend* (alternate title, *Pre Engagement*, 1936).

KATHLEEN G. KLEIN

Asenath Hatch Nicholson

B. *24 Feb. 1792, Chelsea, Vermont*
Wrote under: *A. Nicholson, Asenath Nicholson*
D. *of Michael and Martha Hatch; m. Norman Nicholson*

N.'s parents were descendants of New England Puritans. Their example of broad charity and religious tolerance inculcated those virtues in their daughter, who said of her clergyman father: "He hung no Quakers, nor put any man in a corner of the church because he had a coloured skin. He rebuked sin in high places with fearlessness."

N. was trained as a schoolteacher before she married a New York merchant. About 1832, N. opened a Temperance Boardinghouse based on the principles of Sylvester Graham in the old Five Points section of New York, the city's worst slum. Her rules and their rationale are the subject of *Nature's Own Book* (1835). It is a book of crotchets; N. was a vegetarian who objected to tobacco, alcohol, coffee, and even tea, which she argued was capable of giving its users the delirium tremens.

After N. was widowed, she set off for Ireland in 1844 on a self-appointed mission to bring the Bible to the Irish poor. For fifteen months, N. walked through Ireland distributing tracts supplied by the Hibernian Bible Society. Everywhere she scolded against dirt, drink, and tobacco, but her compassion and generosity won N. the acceptance of the Irish country people; others disapproved of her genuine concern for the poor and her outspokenness on matters that outraged her principles.

N. narrates her adventures in *Ireland's Welcome to the Stranger* (1847), a book valuable for its remarkable picture of 19th-c. Irish country life. It is unique among Irish travel books of the time because N. lived among the poor and recorded details of daily life. Although the book is full of N.'s eccentricities, it is marked by vivid writing and by her efforts to help the people she met.

N.'s wish to serve the Irish poor was fulfilled by the end of the decade. Even before she left Ireland in August 1845, the first signs of the potato blight had appeared. With aid from American charitable organizations, N. arrived in Dublin again in 1847 to establish her own soup kitchen. She worked with the Dublin Central Relief Committee until July 1847, when she went to Belfast. N. spent the following winter in the west of Ireland in those areas most devastated by famine, organizing relief for the poor.

Lights and Shades of Ireland (1847) is the journal of N.'s famine experience. Her portraits of the leaders of the Dublin Quakers in the Central Relief Committee, her description of the rural relief officers who worked courageously among the dying, and her vignettes of individual human suffering make the book an important document.

N. left Ireland in 1848 but continued to live in Europe until 1852. In 1850, she was an American delegate to the Peace Conference in Frankfurt. Her last book, *Loose Papers* (1853), a series of sketches, was published after N. returned to the U.S.

N. wished to be remembered for her work as an educator, a missionary, a reformer, and a humanitarian. However, Irish social historians value her for *Ireland's Welcome to the Stranger*, a book that Sean O'Faolain and Frank O'Connor considered one of the two or three most valuable records of Ireland on the eve of the Great Famine, and for *Lights and Shades of Ireland*, a documentary of one woman's efforts to ease human suffering.

WORKS: *Nature's Own Book* (1835; rev. ed., 1846). *Ireland's Welcome to the Stranger; or, Excusions through Ireland, in 1844 and 1845, for the Purpose of Personally Investigating the Condition of the Poor* (1847). *Lights and Shades of Ireland* (1847; rev. ed., 1850; American title, *Annals of the Famine in Ireland*, 1847). *Loose Papers; or, Facts Gathered during Eight Years Residence in Ireland, Scotland, England, France and Germany* (1853). *The Bible in Ireland* (Ed. A. Sheppard, 1925).

BIBLIOGRAPHY: Sheppard, A., Preface to *The Bible in Ireland* (1925). Gwynn, S., "Bible Christian," in *Saints and Scholars* (1929).
  Other references: *Dublin Magazine* (1934).

MAUREEN MURPHY

Eliza Jane Poitevent Nicholson

B. *11 March 1848, Pearlington, Mississippi; d. 15 Feb. 1896, New Orleans,*
  Louisiana
Wrote under: Pearl Rivers
D. *of Captain William James and Mary Amelia Russ Poitevent;*
  m. Alva Morris Holbrook, 1872; m. George Nicholson, 1878

N. was raised by an aunt near the Louisiana-Mississippi border. She entertained herself by roaming the piney woods along the Pearl River, developing in her youth an affectionate regard for nature.

In 1867, N. began submitting the poems she had been writing since age fourteen to newspapers and magazines. Her first published poem appeared in the New Orleans literary sheet *The South* in 1868. Soon poems by "Pearl Rivers" appeared in the New York *Home Journal*, the New York *Ledger*, and the New Orleans *Times* and *Daily Picayune*.

In 1868, N. met A. M. Holbrook, owner and editor of the *Daily Picayune*. He offered her a job as literary editor for $25 a week. Over the strenuous objections of her family, N. accepted, becoming New Orleans' first female journalist. Her lively prose and intelligent selections markedly improved the paper's literary section. In 1872, she married Holbrook, divorced and forty years her senior. (His angry ex-wife returned from New York a month after the wedding and proceeded to attack N. with a pistol and a bottle of rum. The subsequent trial was covered in scandalous detail by the *Daily Picayune*.)

When Holbrook died, four years later, N. assumed ownership and management of the *Picayune*, which was eighty thousand dollars in debt. At twenty-seven, she thus became the first woman ever to own and operate a metropolitan daily paper. With the assistance of a loyal staff, including the part owner and business manager, George Nicholson, whom she married in 1878, N. transformed the *Picayune* into a profitable paper and the first general-interest daily in the South. N.'s most significant innovations were directed at women. She introduced a society column, personal notes, fashion news, home and medical advice columns, children's pages, and plentiful illustrations. N. also employed talented writers, including several women. N.'s own poetry and prose also appeared, including columns of personal and imaginative commentary.

N. was largely responsible for the founding of the New Orleans

Society for the Prevention of Cruelty to Animals in 1888, and she helped gain public support for the night schools instituted by Sophie B. Wright. In 1884, N. became president of the Women's National Press Association and was the first honorary member of the New York Women's Press Club.

N. died of influenza, eleven days after her husband. Their two sons inherited the paper she had shaped, maintaining its ownership and character into the twentieth century.

In N.'s only volume of poetry, *Lyrics* (1873), the theme is almost without exception nature and seasonal change. N.'s rhymed quatrains are characterized by personifications of the months and seasons and by fairylike perspectives of plants and animals. Occasionally, she writes of feminine heartbreak. Technically pedestrian, N.'s poems reveal a delight in nature and an eye for authentic detail. To N., poetry was a "gift of song," intended to cheer and please her audience.

Two later poems, "Hagar" and "Leah," published first in *Cosmopolitan* in 1893 and 1894, suggest a richer dimension of N.'s talent. Long dramatic poems in blank verse, they are uneven but vivid and insightful evocations of their heroines' bitterness and jealousy as overlooked women. "Hagar" is the stronger of the two poems, with an effective use of meter and imagery.

Although her early pastoral poetry is slight, N.'s later poems reflect an ability to dramatize emotion effectively. But it is N.'s journalistic ability that distinguishes her. Her columns are filled with a sure, lively prose, whose mark was entertaining dialogue and reflective commentary. Her paper stands as a model of innovative and responsible publishing. A remarkable and sensitive woman, N. is said to have possessed little confidence in her abilities. Nevertheless, her strong sense of duty and courage often substituted for self-confidence and forged the means by which her creativity and discriminating intelligence were expressed.

WORKS: *Lyrics* (1873). *Four Poems by Pearl Rivers* (1900). *Two Poems by Pearl Rivers* (1900?).

The papers of Eliza Jane Poitevent Nicholson are at the Howard-Tilton Library, Tulane University, New Orleans, Louisiana.

BIBLIOGRAPHY: Dabney, T. E., *One Hundred Great Years* (1944). DeMenil, A. N., *The Literature of the Louisiana Territory* (1904). Farr, E. S., *Pearl Rivers* (1951). Gill, H. M., *The South in Prose and Poetry* (1916). Harrison, J. H., *Pearl Rivers, Publisher of the Picayune* (1932). Maynard, I. P., "Poitevent Genealogy" (Tulane archives, 1967). Mount, M., *Some Notables of New Orleans* (1896). Ross, I., *Ladies of the Press* (1936). Rutherford, M. L., *The South in History and Literature* (1907).

For articles in reference works, see: *DAB*, VII, 1. *Dictionary of American Authors*, Ed. O. F. Adams (1904). *Living Female Writers of the South*, Ed. M. T. Tardy (1872). *The Living Writers of the South*, J. W. Davidson (1869). *NAW* (article by W. Wiegand). *NCAB*, 1.

Other references: *Louisiana Historical Society* (Oct. 1923). New Orleans *Daily Picayune* (16 Feb. 1896). New Orleans *Times-Democrat* (16 Feb. 1896). *Teachers' Outlook* (Feb. 1901).

BARBARA C. EWELL

Marjorie Hope Nicolson

B. 18 Feb. 1894, Yonkers, New York
D. of Charles Butler and Lissie Hope Morris Nicolson

The daughter of a newspaper editor, N. spent most of her adult life in an academic environment, studying at Michigan, Yale, and Johns Hopkins, and teaching at Minnesota, Goucher, Smith, Columbia, and Claremont. She was a member of the Institute for Advanced Studies at Princeton from 1963 to 1968, and now resides in White Plains, New York.

N. earned many honors during her long and distinguished career and blazed many new trails for academic women. As the first woman president of the United Chapters of Phi Beta Kappa (1940), she explained that most academic women had not been able to distinguish themselves because it was hard to be "both scholars and ladies," in that women scholars "have no wives to look after social contacts and to perform the drudgery for them." She was the first woman to be elected president of the Modern Language Association, the first woman to receive Yale's John Addison Porter Prize for original work, and the first woman to hold a full professorship on Columbia University's graduate faculty.

N. was fascinated with the impact on the literary imagination made by science and philosophy, especially in the 17th and 18th centuries. As early as 1935, N.'s lifelong interest surfaced in a study of *The Microscope and English Imagination*, in which she describes how the invention of the microscope had stimulated both serious and satiric themes in literature, even influencing the remarkable technique of Swift's *Gulliver's Travels*.

Several of her best volumes focus on the way scientific advances alter aesthetic judgments and hence modify literary treatments. For instance, *A World in the Moon* (1937) describes the changing attitudes toward the moon brought about by the telescope; *Mountain Gloom and Mountain Glory* (1959) describes humanity's shift from abhorrence of mountains as reflecting sin's disruption to attraction to mountains as symbols of the infinite; and *Breaking of the Circle* (1950) describes the dislocating insecurity caused by the Copernican Revolution as reflected in the works of John Donne and his contemporaries. Although this latter was her most influential book, it also caused considerable scholarly controversy because many argued that N. had overestimated the importance of scientific theory to people who were accustomed to finding their security not in science but in religion. *Newton Demands the Muse* (1946), a study of how Newtonian optics affected 18th-c. poets, merited the Rose Mary Crawshay Prize of the British Academy.

It is not surprising that a woman so interested in science and literature should turn her attention to John Milton, who was similarly attracted to the advanced scientific thought of his day. Accordingly, Nicolson edited a volume of Milton's major poems and published *A Reader's Guide to Milton* (1963), which has proved popular on many campuses.

This Long Disease, My Life: Alexander Pope and the Sciences (1968), written with G. S. Rousseau, after N.'s retirement, includes a detailed medical history of the poet, a study of five medical themes or episodes in his work, an extensive section on Pope and astronomy, and a concluding section on Pope's interest in the other sciences of his day, especially geology.

In addition to her books, N. was a frequent contributor to periodicals. She edited *American Scholar* from 1940 to 1944 and served on the editorial board of the *Journal of the History of Ideas* for many years. Her work is never academic in the "dry-as-dust" sense; it pulsates with the fascination, wry wit, and human involvement she feels toward her subject. It is N.'s flair for making her point memorably that ensures her a continuing influence among lovers of literature.

WORKS: *The Art of Deception* (1926). *Conway Letters* (1930). *The Microscope and English Imagination* (1935). *A World in the Moon* (1937). *Newton Demands the Muse* (1946). *Voyages to the Moon* (1948). *Breaking of the Circle* (1950; rev. ed., 1960). *Science and Imagination* (1956). *Mountain Gloom and Mountain Glory* (1959). *Milton: Major Poems* (edited by Nicolson, 1962). *A Reader's Guide to Milton* (1963). *Pepys' Diary and the New*

Science (1965). *This Long Disease, My Life: Alexander Pope and the Sciences* (with G. S. Rousseau, 1968).

BIBLIOGRAPHY: *CA* (1964). *CB* (1940).

VIRGINIA RAMEY MOLLENKOTT

Abigail May Alcott Nieriker

B. 26 July 1840, Concord, Massachusetts; d. 29 Dec. 1879, outside Paris, France
D. of Amos Bronson and Abigail May Alcott; m. Ernst Nieriker

Fiercely independent and determined to make her own mark in life, N. would be put out to discover that she is remembered today not as an accomplished artist but as the blonde and graceful "Amy" of her sister Louisa's *Little Women*. By the time N., "the lucky child," was growing up, Alcott family fortunes were brightening. Louisa could afford to provide her with the best art training that Boston had to offer and later to help subsidize her studies in London, Paris, and Rome.

In the spring of 1877, N. achieved her first major success as an artist when a small still-life was accepted by the same Paris salon that rejected two paintings by her friend Mary Cassatt. It was strong proof, crowed N., "that Lu does not monopolize all the Alcott talent." She would exhibit again at the 1879 salon.

At thirty-eight, N. married a Swiss businessman and amateur musician sixteen years her junior. Less than two years later, she died at her home near Paris shortly after giving birth to a daughter, Louisa, whom she bequeathed to the care of her sister. Back in Massachusetts, the Concord Art Center, established at N.'s instigation, remained as a memorial to the young woman her neighbor Daniel Chester French recalled was "full of the joy of living."

Though not primarily a writer, N. wrote occasional personal essays and one delightful book, *Studying Art Abroad, and How To Do It Cheaply* (1879). This high-spirited guide, intended for American women artists of limited means, is a charming mixture of pragmatism and romanticism. Pack cheap underclothes, later "invaluable as paint rags," N. recommends, and in Warwick, "board at the baker's for an absurdly low price instead of following all the world to the Warwick Arms." The ruined castle of Kenilworth, on the other hand, with its "crumbling walls and winding stairs," inspires N. to soaring flights of historical fancy.

Studying Art Abroad is sprightly social history, imbued throughout with the author's strong, essentially feminist sense of self. In some ways it corrects, in others confirms, the picture of the American girl abroad as given in *Daisy Miller*, published the same year.

This work by Bronson Alcott's youngest child adds a new dimension to our understanding of Concord's transcendental community; and for those interested in Louisa Alcott, it is of special value. In its expansiveness and sense of adventure, as well as in the rich experience it draws on, *Studying Art Abroad* demonstrates N.'s escape from the code of selflessness that governed Louisa's life, and documents the fantasies that Louisa had to put aside.

Finally, however, N.'s deepest appeal is not so much to scholars as to the generations of women who have shared her childhood. As Amy March, N. has become a part of American folklore.

WORKS: *Studying Art Abroad and How To Do It Cheaply* (1879).

BIBLIOGRAPHY: Ticknor, C., *May Alcott: A Memoir* (1928).

EVELYN SHAKIR

Josephina Niggli

B. 13 July 1910, Monterrey, Mexico
D. of Frederick Ferdinand and Goldie Morgan Niggli

N.'s father, of Swiss and Alsatian ancestry, left Texas in 1893 to manage a cement plant in the village of Hidalgo, Mexico; her mother was a concert violinist from Virginia. In 1913 and in 1925, when revolutions broke out in Mexico, the family fled to San Antonio, Texas, where N. had her only formal schooling. She graduated from Main Avenue High School in 1925 and from Incarnate Word College in 1931.

N. studied playwrighting at the University of North Carolina, a center for the development of regional and folk drama. She wrote a three-act play, *Singing Valley*, for her thesis, and received her M.A. degree in drama in 1937. N.'s work with Professor Frederick H. Koch's Carolina

Playmakers was a major influence on her writing. Koch himself edited an anthology of her work, *Mexican Folk Plays*, in 1938. Since then, N. has lived in North Carolina, except for sojourns with Bristol University and the Bristol Old Vic in England and with the Abbey Theatre in Dublin. N. has taught English and radio scriptwriting at the University of North Carolina, and she established a drama department at Western Carolina University in Cullowhee.

N.'s one-act plays of Mexican folk life have long been favorites of discerning high-school drama groups. These plays enliven a small cast and simple scenic requirements with abundant stage action, sound effects, and opportunities for characterization. N.'s special skill is her ability to blend closely observed local color and customs with universally understood emotions and humor. Although written in the 1930s, her plays have not become dated.

In *This Bull Ate Nutmeg* (1937), N. drew upon her childhood memories of a one-man sideshow attraction and of mock bullfights. The play includes folk music, a romantic rivalry, and a climactic backyard bullfight, underscored by the cheers and laughter of village spectators.

This is Villa! (1939) is a portrait of the murderous Pancho Villa. N. created an incident that reveals his sentimental and childlike side as well as his cruelty. Despite momentary lapses into swashbuckling melodrama, the play, like all N.'s dramatic and narrative fiction, has a convincing documentary quality.

N.'s most frequently performed play is *Sunday Costs Five Pesos* (1939). In her book *New Pointers on Playwriting* (1945), N. commented: "My *Sunday Costs Five Pesos* has made me more money than a best-selling novel, primarily because it is presented again and again in contests."

N.'s first narrative fiction work, *Mexican Village* (1945), a collection of ten stories of daily life in the village of Hidalgo, using recurrent characters, was uniformly praised by critics. *Step Down, Elder Brother* (1947) is set among the aristocracy in Monterrey. N. again studied the impact of social and historical change in Mexico in *Farewell, Mama Carlotta* (1950) and *Miracle for Mexico* (1964). If her writing is occasionally criticized as "excessively romantic," that is also its strength, for it ensnares the reader with the devices of good storytelling and vividly conveys N.'s warm affection for the people of northern Mexico.

WORKS: *Mexican Silhouettes* (1931). *Tooth or Shave* (1936). *Singing Valley* (1937). *This Bull Ate Nutmeg* (1937). *Mexican Folk Plays* (1938). *Sunday Costs Five Pesos* (1939). *This is Villa!* (1939). *Miracle at Blaise* (1944).

Mexican Village (1945). *New Pointers on Playwriting* (1945). *Pointers on Radio Writing* (1946). *Step Down, Elder Brother* (1947). *Farewell, Mama Carlotta* (1950). *Miracle for Mexico* (1964).

BIBLIOGRAPHY: Spearman, W., *The Carolina Playmakers: The First Fifty Years* (1970).
For articles in reference works, see: *American Novelists of Today*, H. R. Warfel (1951). *CB* (1949). *National Playwrights Directory*, Ed. P. J. Kaye (1977).
Other references: *NYT* (21 Jan. 1939).

FELICIA HARDISON LONDRÉ

Blair Rice Niles

B. 15 June 1880, Coles Ferry, Virginia; d. 13 April 1959, New York City
Wrote under: Mary Blair Beebe, Blair Niles
D. of Henry Crenshaw and Marie Gordon Pryor Rice; m. C. William Beebe, 1902; m. Robert L. Niles, Jr., 1913

Exposure to the black tenants of her father's plantation gave N. a sensitivity to alien cultures. Her marriage to a naturalist opened the world of exploration and scientific observation for N. Her first publications were articles and a book, *Our Search for a Wilderness* (1910), drawn from their travels in the South Pacific and South America. N.'s second husband, whom she married after her divorce from Beebe, accompanied her on subsequent explorations and provided the photographs that enhance many of her books.

N.'s next books, *Casual Wanderings in Ecuador* (1923), *Colombia, Land of Miracles* (1924), and *Black Haiti* (1926), are travel books that do more than merely chronicle explorations. Before making her trips, N. always carefully researched the history of her destination. Therefore, each journey becomes for her not only the immediate physical reality, but also the visualization of events both momentous and ordinary in the lives of people of many generations, nationalities, and races. In her research, N. always preferred to work from the diaries and journals of lesser figures, because she felt the major historical personages did not give as true a picture of the impact of historical events on the human mind and heart. Her detailing of history is always interesting, but her real power is in her description of the activities of living people.

N.'s most significant work grew out of her trip in 1927 to the penal colony in French Guiana. She was the first woman ever allowed to make a study of the prison, and her husband took the first photographs made there. *Condemned to Devil's Island* (1928) is the fictional biography of a prisoner. N. gives the reader not only a complete account of life in the penal colony, but also sympathetically treats the effects of such punishment on the spirit as well as the body. The success of this book prompted N. to write the sequel *Free* (1930). N.'s position in both books is that the inhumanity of the prison system either destroys or warps the inmates, and fails to rehabilitate them to a society that has arbitrarily classified them as criminals.

N.'s observations of sexual mores in the prison prompted her to write *Strange Brother* (1931), a novel treating the homosexual subculture of New York with unusual sympathy and perception. This was followed by *Light Again* (1933), a fictionalized study of an insane asylum.

In 1934, N. returned to the history of Central and South America for the material of her novel *Maria Paluna*. This is the moving story of an Indian woman whose life spanned the century of the Spanish conquest of Guatemala. In her life with the Spanish, her love for one of the conquistadores, and her growth as a defender and promulgator of the Indian culture, Paluna convincingly portrays what happened in Guatemala during the 16th c. N. wrote other novels that are fictional accounts of historical events; while good, they do not have the power of *Maria Paluna*.

In 1939, N. published *The James* as one of the "Growing Rivers of America" series. She gives personal and historical accounts of life along the banks of the Virginia river. N.'s research into the life of George Washington for this work resulted in her biography, *Martha's Husband* (1951), which treated Washington from a personal rather than a political or military perspective.

N.'s interest was always in human personality. For their time, N.'s works are exceptionally daring and enlightened. Her genuine sympathy for the people and cultures she studied provides unusual perceptions about the truths of life in those times and places. N. journeys in space and time, and makes both come alive for the reader.

WORKS: *Our Search for a Wilderness* (with C. W. Beebe, 1910). *Casual Wanderings in Ecuador* (1923). *Colombia, Land of Miracles* (1924). *Black Haiti: A Biography of Africa's Eldest Daughter* (1926). *Condemned to Devil's Island: The Biography of an Unknown Convict* (1928; film version, 1939).

Free (1930). *Strange Brother* (1931). *Light Again, a Novel* (1933). *Maria Paluna, a Novel* (1934). *Day of Immense Sun* (1936). *A Journey in Time: Peruvian Pageant* (1937). *The James* (1939; rev. and enlarged ed., *The James from Iron Gate to the Sea,* 1945). *East by Day* (1941). *Passengers to Mexico: The Last Invasion of the Americas* (1943). *Journeys in Time: From the Halls of Montezuma to Patagonia's Plains: A Treasury, Garnered from Four Centuries of Writers (1519–1942)* (1946). *Martha's Husband: An Informal Portrait of George Washington* (1951).

BIBLIOGRAPHY: For articles in reference works, see: *American Novelists of Today,* H. R. Warfel, (1951). *NCAB,* 45.
  Other references: *NYHTB* (29 Dec. 1946). *NYTBR* (6 May 1934; 14 June 1936; 4 April 1943).

HARRIETTE CUTTINO BUCHANAN

Anaïs Nin

B. 21 Feb. 1903, Paris, France; d. 14 Jan. 1977, Los Angeles, California
D. of Joaquin and Rosa Culmell Nin; m. Hugh P. Guiler, 1923

N. was the eldest of three children of a Spanish composer and concert pianist and a French-Danish mother. N. began keeping a diary after her father's desertion. N.'s departure with her mother and brothers for New York, her return to Paris, and her home in Louveciennes in the outskirts of Paris were all delineated. Purposely omitted was her marriage to Guiler, a bank and financial consultant who was also known as the engraver and filmmaker Ian Hugo.

  D. H. Lawrence: An Unprofessional Study (1932) marked N.'s entrée into "creative criticism." N. was an enemy of naturalism, realism, positivism, and rationalism, which she felt distorted reality; what was of import for her was the catalytic effect of Lawrence's work on the reader's senses and imagination. To know Lawrence, she maintained, was to take a fantastic voyage: to "flow" forward with his characters and situations, to follow their feelings as manifested in impulses and gestures.

  N.'s feelings of timidity and inadequacy became so disruptive that in 1932 she consulted the psychiatrist René Allendy, who encouraged her to begin *The House of Incest* (1936). "It is the seed of all my work," N.

wrote, "the poem from which the novels were born." Affinities with Lawrence, Joyce, Woolf, and the surrealists were evident in her reliance upon dream sequences and in her use of stream-of-consciousness style.

Dr. Otto Rank's attitude to the problem of creativity was more to N.'s liking, and she became his patient in 1933. When he moved his offices to New York in 1934, he invited N. to practice as a lay analyst. Although successful, N. understood that her mission in life was artistic and not therapeutic. She returned to France, where she lived until the outbreak of World War II. Her friends included Miller, Artaud, Brancusi, Supervielle, Orloff, Durrell, Breton, Dali, Barnes, Young, Varèse, Varda, and many more.

In New York, artistic and financial setbacks encouraged N. to print her own works: *Winter of Artifice* (1939) and *Under a Glass Bell* (1947). To probe her heroine's dream world in *Winter of Artifice*, N. chose the anti-novel technique, with its pastiches, repetitions, omissions, and ellipses, instead of the structured characters and plot of the psychological novel. After twenty years of separation, Djuna is reunited with her father, whom she idolized. Valescure, in the south of France, is the idyllic setting for their meeting. Moments of ecstasy, when Djuna perceives herself as her father's "mystical bride," give way to periods of depression, when she realizes that her Prince Charming is an illusion, that in reality he is superficial, luxury-loving, and lives for externals only. *Under a Glass Bell* is a collection of thirteen short stories considered among the best of N.'s fictional works.

Cities of the Interior (1959), a "continuous novel," includes six short works: *Ladders to Fire* (1946), *Children of the Albatross* (1947), *The Four-Chambered Heart* (1950), *A Spy in the House of Love* (1954), *Solar Barque* (1958), and *Seduction of the Minotaur* (1961). Labeled "space fiction," *Cities of the Interior* is centered in the unconscious, upon clusters of visual configurations. In this inner space, characters confront, respond, act, and react to each other like multiple satellites. N.'s deepening psychological acumen and intuitive faculties, her heightened powers of observation are brought into play in the recording of minute vibrations in nuanced and counterpuntal relationships.

Ladders to Fire focuses on Lilian, a jazz pianist, a "woman at war with herself." Her hypertense, excitable nature is associated with the instrument she plays. *Children of the Albatross* deals with the private world of children, its arcane rituals and innocent cruelties. *The Four-Chambered Heart* focuses on Djuna and a handsome Peruvian guitar player named Rango, who live out their passionate encounter on a houseboat on the Seine. *A Spy in the House of Love* is set in New York, not Paris. For the first time, the protagonists deal with questions of freedom and guilt, as they develop a new set of values. *Solar Barque* and *Seduction of the Minotaur* take place where the sun "painted everything with gold." In a hedonistic realm, Lilian learns that escape is no longer possible, that she must seek out the minotaur within her own labyrinth (psyche) and face these sides of her personality with strength and vigor.

Collages (1964), a combination of portraits, short stories, and a novella, abounds in alchemical symbolism that adds dimension, beauty, and a mystical quality to the narratives.

The Diary of Anaïs Nin (7 vols., 1966–78) is a "woman's journey of self-discovery," which Henry Miller placed "beside the revelations of St. Augustine, Petronius, Abélard, Rousseau, Proust." The *Diary* is a historical document in that it reports and deals with events chronologically. It is of psychological import because it analyzes inner scapes (dreams, reveries, motivations) and a variety of approaches to the unconscious; it is of aesthetic significance because it introduces readers to the world of the novelist, poet, musician, painter, and the artistic trends of the day: cubism, realism, surrealism, op, pop, and minimal art. The *Diary* is a quest: that of the artist attempting to understand the creative factor within herself; of the woman experiencing her multidimensional selves as she works toward inner growth and fulfillment.

The sixth volume (1955–1966) focuses on N.'s decision to publish her *Diary*, to reveal her innermost thoughts and to remain strong enough to stand the ridicule and the hurt of an unfeeling public. N., who leans heavily on her unconscious to lead the way in the workaday world, made her decision following a dream. It begins: "I opened my front door and was struck by mortal radiation."

It was with her *Diary*, that N. won an international reputation. She was called upon to lecture throughout North America at universities, poetry centers, and clubs. N. synthesized and elaborated her earlier statements of her artistic credo—*Realism and Reality* (1946)—in *The Novel of the Future* (1968), in which she endorses the dictum of C. G. Jung: "Proceed from the Dream Outward."

N.'s writings express an inner need; truth shaped and fashioned into an art form. Thought, feeling, and dream are captured in metaphors, images, and alliterations, which are interwoven in complex designs. The techniques of free association and reverie enable her to penetrate the inner being, evoke a mood, and arouse sensations in an impressionistic and pointilliste manner. N.'s work offers readers perpetual transmutations of matter and spirit. Hers is a very personal, authentic, and innovative talent, unique in her time.

WORKS: *D. H. Lawrence: An Unprofessional Study* (1932). *The House of Incest* (1936). *Winter of Artifice* (1939). *Under a Glass Bell* (1944). *Ladders to Fire* (1946). *Realism and Reality* (1946). *Children of the Albatross* (1947). *On Writing* (1947). *The Four-Chambered Heart* (1950). *A Spy in the House of Love* (1954). *Solar Barque* (1958). *Cities of the Interior* (1959). *Seduction of the Minotaur* (1961). *Collages* (1964). *The Diary of Anaïs Nin* (7 vols., 1966–78). *The Novel of the Future* (1968). *A Woman Speaks: The Lectures, Seminars, and Interviews of Anaïs Nin* (1975). *In Favor of the Sensitive Man, and Other Essays* (1976). *Delta of Venus: Erotica* (1977). *Waste of Timelessness, and other Early Stories* (1977). *Linotte: The Early Diary of Anaïs Nin* (1978).

BIBLIOGRAPHY: Evans, O., *Anaïs Nin* (1968). Franklin, V. B., and D. Schneider, *Anaïs Nin: An Introduction* (1979). Harms, V., ed., *Celebration with Anaïs Nin* (1973). Hinz, J. E., *The Mirror and the Garden* (1971). Hinz, J. E., *The World of Anaïs Nin* (1978). Knapp, B. L., *Anaïs Nin* (1979). Spencer, S., *Collage of Dreams* (1977).

BETTINA L. KNAPP

Helen Alice Matthews Nitsch

D. 28 Oct. 1889, Plainfield, New Jersey
Wrote under: Catherine Owen

N. was a late-19th-c. authority on homemaking. From internal evidence in N.'s works, we can deduce that she was a well-educated woman of the upper middle class, who had probably attended one of the popular cooking schools of the time.

N. published articles in *Good Housekeeping, Harper's Bazar,* and other magazines and wrote specialized cookbooks, but she was best known for her general cookbook *Culture and Cooking; or, Art in the Kitchen* (1881), which was reissued in 1885 in an expanded version as *Catherine Owen's New Cook Book.* N. makes the point that cooking is an art, and as such is not to be despised by refined women. These books make interesting reading, providing as much entertainment as sociological enlightenment.

We can get an interesting glimpse of the eating habits of the genteel American family from N.'s fiction; whether or not it is her subject, food and cooking always take first place in N.'s books. *Ten Dollars Enough: Keeping House Well on Ten Dollars a Week; How It Has Been Done; How It May Be Done Again* (1887) was serialized in *Good Housekeeping* and went through many editions. Its name alludes to another American bestseller of the period, the fictional account of a successful back-to-the-land experience by Edmund Morris, *Ten Acres Enough* (1863). N.'s purpose is to show that a sensible woman can manage a home of her own on a moderate income. Newlyweds Harry and Molly Bishop live in a boardinghouse, the common refuge of many American young couples who were not well-to-do. Molly convinces her husband to rent a small house for the winter and, putting to good use what she has learned in cooking school, proves she can keep house on ten dollars a week. At the end of the story, Molly is pregnant and gets her own home. Harry, a spoiled son of snobbish parents who disdain Molly because of her plebeian origins, hardly appears in the story except to represent the man who must not be disturbed by housekeeping problems.

The financial independence of women is the subject of the sequel, *Molly Bishop's Family* (1888). The family business fails, Harry dies, and Molly must become the sole support of her three children. Molly shows herself to be a clever businesswoman, able to provide well for her family.

The same theme—financial independence for women—is found in *Gentle Breadwinners* (1888). Dorothy and May Fortesque are left penniless on the death of their father, after having been brought up to a life of useless accomplishment. "Oh, what a humiliation it is to think . . . that we two girls, brought up with all the advantages, are not fit to earn a dollar! Oh, if I ever have daughters they shall learn to do one thing well," exclaims Dorothy, the older and more sensible sister. After an unprofitable dressmaking venture, Dorothy builds a successful business baking cakes and sending them to the women's exchange in New York. (In all her books, N. emphasizes the importance of cooking and plays down sewing, the normal mainstay of many "distressed gentlewomen.") In the course of the story, we meet a brilliant, needy widow who fails where Dorothy succeeds because she is not careful. The difference between them is put this way: "Dorothy thought women's work should be just as much a matter of business as a man's, and look for no more favor." Finally, the heroine is rewarded by marriage to an artist.

N.'s cookbooks are probably of interest only to historians of the domestic arts, but her three novels, intended to help young women in their everyday lives, as homemakers or wage earners, are interesting social statements. It is hard today to identify with a society in which a woman can bake a fancy cake, crate it, put it on the train, see it safely delivered the same day to the market, and make a profit on the business, but the basic impulse behind N.'s work is timeless: Women are only well provided for if they can provide for themselves.

WORKS: *Culture and Cooking; or, Art in the Kitchen* (1881; rev. ed., *Catherine Owen's New Cook Book*, 1885). *A Key to Cooking* (1886). *Perfect Bread* (1886). *Six Cups of Coffee* (1886). *Lessons in Candy Making* (1887). *Ten Dollars Enough: Keeping House Well on Ten Dollars a Week; How It Has Been Done; How It May Be Done Again* (1887). *Gentle Breadwinners* (1888). *Molly Bishop's Family* (1888). *Choice Cookery* (1889). *Progressive Housekeeping* (1889).

BIBLIOGRAPHY: Plainfield *Constitution* (7 Nov. 1889).

BEVERLY SEATON

Agnes Eckhardt Nixon

B. 10 Dec. 1927, Chicago, Illinois
D. of Harry J. and Agnes Dalton Eckhardt; m. Robert Nixon, 1951

N. was raised in a devout Catholic household. As a child, N. was an avid reader of comic strips, and she created stories about the characters whose pictures she cut from the funny papers. N. attended St. Mary's College in South Bend, Indiana, and Northwestern University, where she earned a B.A. in drama. N. has four grown children.

N. entered radio to avoid a career in her father's funeral-garment business. She began writing dialogue for *Women in White* (1938–1942), Irna Phillips's popular daytime serial. Also under Phillips, N. has written for the television serial *The Guiding Light* (1952–). As a free-lance teleplay writer, N. has written scripts for *Studio One, Robert Montgomery Presents, Somerset Maugham Theater, Philco Theater, and Hallmark Hall of Fame*. N. later rescued *Another World* (1964–) from flagging audience ratings by updating its characters and themes.

As a result of her success with *Another World*, ABC asked N. to create her own daytime serial. *One Life to Live* (1968–) was the first truly interracial television serial, using black characters in more than token roles. Miscegenation was a central theme until the supposedly white Carla Benari proved to be of the same race as black physician Price Trainor.

In 1970, N. introduced the "fact-in-fiction" format as a way of dealing convincingly with drug abuse. A fictional character, Cathy Craig, aged seventeen, was introduced to a drug therapy session involving actual residents of New York's Odyssey House. The residents were taped on location while they tried to persuade Cathy to give up drugs. This realistic, responsible approach to social issues became N.'s hallmark.

Current social problems, particularly those confronting the generations, also have been central to N.'s most successful creation, *All My Children* (1970–). The program stresses the need for a sense of family and home in the face of such contemporary trials as abortion, the Vietnam war, male sterility, child abuse, uterine cancer, and venereal disease. Other contemporary themes include ecology, mental health, the danger of carbon monoxide poisoning in the home, the readjustment problems of a returned prisoner of war, and the peace movement.

All My Children's stock soap opera characters are interesting because they are modern, likeable, and often funny. Female characters provide most of the dramatic interest. Two villains, Phoebe Tyler and Erica Kane Brent, are humorously overdrawn. N. consciously exploits the opportunity provided by the serial format to create sympathetic "heavies" by allowing viewers to see them in their complexity. In addition to realism and humor, *All My Children* is distinguished by a fast-moving plot, an optimistic outlook, and a contemporary appearance.

With characteristic originality, excellence, and willingness to experiment, N. has been writing one or more daily serials without interruption for nearly twenty-five years. As "Queen of the Soapers" Irna Phillips's successor, N. has been called the "Crown Princess of the Soaps" and "First Lady of Soap Opera."

WORKS: *The Guiding Light* (1952–). *Another World* (1964–). *One Life to Live* (1968–). *All My Children* (1970–).

BIBLIOGRAPHY: Edmondson, M., and D. Rounds, *From Mary Noble to Mary Hartman: The Complete Soap Opera Book* (1976). Soares, M., *The Soap Opera Book* (1978). Stedman, R., *The Serials: Suspense and Drama by Installment* (1977). Wakefield, D., *All Her Children* (1976).
Other references: *Journal of the Academy of Television Arts and Sciences*

(Winter 1972). Los Angeles *Times* (7 May 1978). *McCall's* (May 1970). *NYT* (7 July 1968; 11 Dec. 1969; 20 Oct. 1975). *Television Quarterly* (Fall 1970). *TV Guide* (3 May 1975).

CAREN J. DEMING

Kathleen Thompson Norris

B. *16 July 1880, San Francisco, California; d. 18 Jan. 1966, San Francisco, California*
Wrote under: Jane Ireland, Kathleen Norris
D. *of James Alden and Josephine E. Moroney Thompson; m. Charles Gilman Norris, 1909*

The second of six children, N. grew up in rural Mill Valley, where her father, a San Francisco bank manager, commuted daily by ferry. In 1899, both parents died within a month, leaving the children to shift for themselves. N. worked as clerk, bookkeeper, librarian, and newspaper reporter to help support the family. While covering a skating party, she met her future husband, a writer. She followed him to New York City when he became arts editor for the *American* magazine.

N. published fiction in the New York *Telegram*, winning fifty dollars for the best story of the week. Her husband encouraged N. to send out others, and the *Atlantic* accepted "The Tide-Marsh" and "What Happened to Alanna" in 1910. N. began *Mother* (1911) for another story contest, but it grew too long; it was enlarged to become a popular novel.

For the next half century, despite crippling arthritis, N. wrote ninety books, numerous stories and magazine serials, a newspaper column, and a radio soap opera. A pacifist, she campaigned vigorously against capital punishment and foreign involvement.

Much of N.'s writing is rooted in her own life and California background. Typical is *Little Ships* (1921), centering on a large nouveau-riche Irish-Catholic family and its less fortunate relatives, including a fine old peasant grandmother. Although the book is marred by sentimentality and prejudice, N. creates deft characterization and effective dramatic tension in her family scenes.

Certain People of Importance (1922) is considered N.'s most ambitious work. In this impressive family chronicle spanning more than a century, descendants of Forty-niner Reuben Crabtree invent a "first family" history not in the least based on fact. Scandals and intrigues worthy of any soap opera are plentiful, yet no one lifts an eyebrow. Although N. denies a "knowledge of those dark forces which fascinate modern writers," the novel's true subject seems to be human greed, hypocrisy, and deceit.

One of the book's strengths is its precise attention to forgotten detail —fashions, furnishings, eating habits, and amusements. N. writes sympathetically of independent young women who chafe under the restrictions of parents or brother. She also offers a grim reminder of the risks of pregnancy, childbirth, and poverty. This, N.'s most realistic book, was not well received.

Through a Glass Darkly (1957) is noteworthy only because its first half depicts a Utopia where war does not exist, the government feeds anyone who needs it, and people take care of each other. Those who die on earth "arrive" in Foxcrossing to live happily. But the protagonist, who longs to "go back" to our world to help suffering children, loses her life trying to rescue hurricane victims and is reincarnated in the book's second half. The story moves disappointingly into N.'s familiar formula of a working girl's struggle to survive. The Utopian world is forgotten.

N. also published two sometimes conflicting autobiographies, *Noon* (1925) and *Family Gathering* (1959). Many of her books remain in print, but most of these are frothy romances with pink-and-gold heroines and contrived endings. These characters seem suspended in an eternal 1910, regardless of the real year. N.'s best writing shows more depth: family warmth, sincerity, and pettiness; condemnation of the self-centered rich; and vivid accounts of early California. She portrays men and women of another generation, almost another world, meeting life however they can—with love, with humor, with desperation.

WORKS: *Mother* (1911). *The Rich Mrs. Burgoyne* (1912). *Poor, Dear Margaret Kirby* (1913). *Saturday's Child* (1914). *The Treasure* (1914). *The Story of Julia Page* (1915). *The Heart of Rachael* (1916). *Martie, the Unconquered* (1917). *Undertow* (1917). *Josselyn's Wife* (1918). *Sisters* (1919). *Harriet and the Piper* (1920). *The Beloved Woman* (1921). *Little Ships* (1921). *Certain People of Importance* (1922). *Lucretia Lombard* (1922). *Butterfly* (1923). *Uneducating Mary* (1923). *The Callahans and the Murphys* (1924). *Rose of the World* (1924). *Noon* (1925). *The Black Flemings* (also published as *Gabrielle*, 1926). *Hildegarde* (1926). *The Kelly Kid* (1926). *Barberry Bush* (1927). *The Fun of Being a Mother* (1927). *My Best Girl* (1927). *The*

Sea Gull (1927). *Beauty and the Beast* (1928). *The Foolish Virgin* (1928). *Home* (1928). *What Price Peace?* (1928). *Mother and Son* (1929). *Red Silence* (1929). *Storm House* (1929). *Beauty in Letters* (1930). *The Lucky Lawrences* (1930). *Margaret Yorke* (1930). *Passion Flower* (1930). *Belle-Mère* (1931). *Hands Full of Living: Talks with American Women* (1931). *The Love of Julie Borel* (1931). *My San Francisco* (1932). *Second-Hand Wife* (1932). *Treehaven* (1932). *Younger Sister* (1932). *The Angel in the House* (1933). *My California* (1933). *Walls of Gold* (1933). *Wife for Sale* (1933). *Maiden Voyage* (1934). *Manhattan Love Song* (1934). *Three Men and Diana* (1934). *Victoria: A Play* (1934). *Beauty's Daughter* (1935). *Shining Windows* (1935). *Woman in Love* (1935). *The American Flaggs* (1936). *Secret Marriage* (1936). *Bread into Roses* (1937). *You Can't Have Everything* (1937). *Baker's Dozen* (1938). *Heartbroken Melody* (1938). *Lost Sunrise* (1939). *Mystery House* (1939). *The Runaway* (1939). *The Secret of the Marshbanks* (1940). *The World Is like That* (1940). *These I Like Best* (1941). *The Venables* (1941). *An Apple for Eve* (1942). *Come Back to Me, Beloved* (1942). *Dina Cashman* (1942). *One Nation Indivisible* (1942). *Star-Spangled Christmas* (1942). *Corner of Heaven* (1943). *Love Calls the Tune* (1944). *Burned Fingers* (1945). *Motionless Shadows* (1945). *Mink Coat* (1946). *Over at the Crowleys'* (1946). *The Secrets of Hillyard House* (1947). *High Holiday* (1949). *Morning Light* (1950). *Shadow Marriage* (1952). *The Best of Kathleen Norris* (1955). *Miss Harriet Townshend* (1955). *Through a Glass Darkly* (1957). *Family Gathering* (1959).

BIBLIOGRAPHY: Kilmer, J., *Literature in the Making: By Some of Its Makers* (1917). Woollcott, A., *While Rome Burns* (1934).

For articles in reference works, see: *Catholic Authors: Contemporary Biographical Sketches 1930–1947*, Ed. M. Hoehn (1948). *20thCA. 20thCAS.*

Other references: *Bookman* (Sept. 1922). *NR* (11 Oct. 1922). *NYT* (19 Jan. 1966). *NYTBR* (6 Feb. 1955).

JOANNE McCARTHY

Alice Mary Norton

B. ca. 1915, Cleveland, Ohio
Writes under: Andre Norton, Andrew North
D. of Adalbert Freely and Daisy Bertha Stemm Norton

N.'s choice of profession was encouraged by her high school teacher of creative writing; while editing the high school newspaper and annual, N. wrote her first book, *Ralestone Luck* (1938).

Although considered a science fiction author for juvenile readers, N. has written in various genres. A considerable part of her work takes its impetus from the past, not the future. N. has written pirate tales, Civil War stories, historical romances, fantasies, and even a murder mystery, *Murder for Sale* (1954).

Typical of N.'s early work is *Huon of the Horn* (1951), set in the time of Charlemagne. Other early works are *Scarface* (1948), about the exploits of Justin Blade and the pirate Isle of Tortuga; *Follow the Drum* (1942), about colonial Maryland; *Yankee Privateer* (1955), a historical adventure about privateering; and several other works of historical fiction.

It was not until 1952 that N. published her first science fiction novel, *Star Man's Son* (reissued as *Daybreak, 2250 A.D.*, 1954). Many of N.'s science fiction novels feature an adolescent male and are strictly adventure stories. *Night of Masks* (1964) is typical; it is an adventure story that takes place on the planet Dis, which is lit by a red sun. Only with special goggles can one see in its infrared light. Here Nik Kolherne, an orphan outcast with a severely disfigured face, is sent on an adventure with Vannie, a younger boy wanted by several warring interests. Kolherne agrees to kidnap the boy and takes him to Dis in exchange for plastic surgery on his face and a chance at a normal life. While on Dis, however, he rescues the boy, and in the end Kolherne has a new face as well as an understanding of the responsibilities that accompany manhood.

To even the most familiar and routine fast-moving adventures, N. brings added dimensions by varying the ethnicity of her characters in a genre in which white male heroes are the norm. American Indian heroes are featured in several of N.'s novels: *The Beast Master* (1959), *The Sioux Spaceman* (1960), and *The Defiant Agents* (1962). These heroes are often exiled from Earth and thrust out to survive on an alien planet. Other novels such as *Star Man's Son* have mutant heroes in ethnically varied worlds.

In recent years, N. has been writing both adult and adolescent novels with female protagonists. N.'s Witch World series is one of her most interesting series and one which utilizes strong women.

N. is a writer who thinks about her craft. As a former librarian, she has encouraged present librarians to think seriously about science fiction. She pays attention to the details of alien ways and settings, drawing clear, striking, interesting portraits. This attention to detail, to the establishing of the human in the nonhuman, makes N.'s writing good, even in the most traditional of her adventure tales. She is one of the most widely read of all science-fiction writers.

WORKS: *The Prince Commands: Being Sundry Adventures of Michael Karl, Sometime Crown Prince & Pretender to the Throne of Morvania* (1934). *Ralestone Luck* (1938). *Follow the Drum: Being the Ventures and Misadventures of One Johanna Lovell, Sometime Lady of Catkept Manor in Kent County of Lord Baltimore's Proprietary of Maryland, in the Gracious Reign of King Charles the Second* (1942). *The Sword Is Drawn* (1944). *Rogue Reynard: Being a Tale of the Fortunes and Misfortune and Divers Misdeeds of That Great Villain, Baron Reynard, the Fox, and How He Was Served with King Lion's Justice* (1947). *Scarface: Being the Story of One Justin Blade, Late of the Pirate Isle of Tortuga, and How Fate Did Justly Deal with Him, to His Great Profit* (1948). *Sword in Sheath* (1949). *Bullard of the Space Patrol* (edited by Norton, 1951). *Huon of the Horn; Being a Tale of That Duke of Bordeaux Who Came to Sorrow at the Hands of Charlemagne and Yet Won the Favor of Oberon, the Elf King, to His Lasting Fame and Great Glory* (1951). *Star Man's Son* (1952; reissued as *Daybreak, 2250 A.D.*, 1954). *Island of the Lost* (1953). *Space Service* (edited by Norton, 1953). *Star Rangers* (1953; reissued as *The Lost Planet*, 1974). *At Swords' Points* (1954). *Murder for Sale* (with A. Weston, pseudonym for G. Hogarth, 1954). *Space Pioneers* (edited by Norton, 1954). *The Stars Are Ours!* (1954). *Sargasso of Space* (1955). *Star Guard* (1955). *Yankee Privateer* (1955). *Crossroads of Time* (1956). *Plague Ship* (1956). *Space Police* (edited by Norton, 1956). *Stand to Horse* (1956). *Star Born* (1957). *Sea Siege* (1957). *Star Gate* (1958). *The Time Traders* (1958). *The Beast Master* (1959). *Secret of the Lost Races* (1959). *Galactic Derelict* (1959). *Voodoo Planet* (1959). *Storm over Warlock* (1960). *Sioux Spaceman* (1960). *Shadow Hawk* (1960). *Catseye* (1961). *Ride Proud, Rebel!* (1961). *Star Hunter* (1961). *The Defiant Agents* (1962). *Eye of Monster* (1962). *Lord of Thunder* (1962). *Rebel Spurs* (1962). *Judgement on Janus* (1963). *Key out of Time* (1963). *Witch World* (1963). *Night of Masks* (1964). *Ordeal in Otherwhere* (1964). *Web of the Witch World* (1964). *Quest Crosstime* (1965). *Steel Magic* (1965). *Three against the Witch World* (1965). *X Factor* (1965). *The Year of the Unicorn* (1965). *Moon of Three Rings* (1966). *Victory on Janus* (1966). *Award Science Fiction Reader* (edited by Norton, 1967). *Octagon Magic* (1967). *Operation Time Search* (1967). *Warlock of the Witch World* (1967). *Dark Piper* (1968). *Fur Magic* (1968). *Sorceress of the Witch World* (1968). *The Zero Stone* (1968). *Postmarked the Stars* (1969). *Uncharted Stars* (1969). *Dread Companion* (1970). *Ice Crown* (1970). *Android at Arms* (1971). *Exiles of the Stars* (1971). *High Sorcery* (1971). *Breed to Come* (1972). *Crystal Gryphon* (1972). *Dragon Magic* (1972). *Garan the Eternal* (1972). *Plague Ship* (1972). *Spell of the Witch World* (1972). *Gates of Tomorrow: An Introduction to Science Fiction* (edited by Norton, with E. Donaldy, 1973). *Here Abide Monsters* (1973). *Iron Cage* (1974). *Lavender-Green Magic* (1974). *Outside* (1974). *The Book of Andre Norton* (1975). *The Day of the Ness* (with M. Gilbert, 1975). *Forerunner Foray* (1975). *Knave of Dreams* (1975). *Merlin's Mirror* (1975).

No Night without Stars (1975). *The White Jade Fox* (1975). *Red Hart Magic* (1976). *Star Ka'at* (with D. Madlee, 1976). *Wraiths of Time* (1976). *The Opal-Eyed Fan* (1977). *Trey of Swords* (1977). *Velvet Shadows* (1977). *Perilous Dream* (1978). *Quag Keep* (1978). *Secret of the Lost Race* (1978). *Yurth Burden* (1978).

BIBLIOGRAPHY: Elwood, R., ed., *The Many Worlds of Andre Norton* (1974). Turner, D. G., *The First Editions of Andre Norton* (1974).

BILLIE J. WAHLSTROM

Joyce Carol Oates

B. 16 June 1938, Lockport, New York
D. of Frederick J. and Caroline Bush Oates; m. Raymond J. Smith, 1961

One of three children, O. was born into an Irish-Catholic working-class family in a rural area near Millerport, New York, the "Eden County" country of many of her stories and novels. O., who attended a one-room schoolhouse, graduated Syracuse University, phi beta kappa, in 1960 with a B.A. in English, and earned an M.A. from the University of Wisconsin in 1961.

O. taught English for six years at the University of Detroit. She was in Detroit during the race riots, an event she documents in *them* (1969). Winner of many awards, O. has been elected to the National Academy and Institute of Arts and Letters.

From 1967 to 1977, O. and her husband taught literature at the University of Windsor, Ontario. They now live in Princeton, where they publish *Ontario Review* and run the Ontario Review Press and where O. is writer-in-residence at Princeton University.

In O.'s fiction, the individual is always viewed in the perspective of the larger world. O.'s protagonists strain to escape the world in which they live, but they do not succeed, except in madness or death. As O. drives her characters into a recognition of the boundaries of the real, the ideal is collapsed into the actual, the hope for freedom is converted into a hope for initiation, and the isolated self is confronted with its otherness.

With Shuddering Fall (1964) begins with idealized, romantic characters—a godlike, paternal figure, Herz; his virginal, religious daughter,

Karen; and the violent rebel, Shar. The novel relates the story of Karen's initiation, which is effected not by a complete submission to an authoritarian order represented by her father, but by a rejection of the rootless freedom represented by Shar. Once Karen leaves her father for Shar, the connections that have tied her to a particular identity are severed— the past she has left behind holds her identity. After enduring rape, violent beatings, and the suicide of Shar, Karen returns to her father, ready to reclaim her identity. The encounter with freedom brings a recognition of the values of family, place, and history.

A Garden of Earthly Delights (1967), *Expensive People* (1968), and *them* constitute a trilogy exploring rural, suburban, and urban America. *A Garden of Earthly Delights* focuses on the condition of alienation, a condition O. views as rooted in the circumstances of American history and intensified by the American ideals of autonomy and self-sufficiency. As in *them* and in *Wonderland* (1971), the Depression dislodges the characters from their paternal roots. Clara, the daughter of a migrant laborer who was forced from his land, maniacally and successfully plots to marry a man for his money and land to bequeath to her son a name that wields power. Ironically, rather than accept the world his mother has usurped for him, her son is possessed by a sense of alienation so intense that he finally commits suicide.

Matricide is the solution that Richard, child-hero of *Expensive People* (1968), finds for his mother's narcissistic assertion of freedom that denies him love and recognition. O. portrays affluent suburbia as an antithetical "paradise" into which one is admitted by virtue of greed; the dominant metaphor of the novel is gluttony, which stands not only for excessive material acquisition but for an inflated sense of self that leads to a denial of the world.

In *them*, based on the life of one of her students, O. describes the struggles of two poor urban adolescents to escape an environment that constantly erupts in violence. They attempt to live up to the American idea of freedom, but inevitably come up short against the unpredictable, which is portrayed not so much as a result of sociological upheavals but as an insistent and pervasive rhythm of life. In a universe of caprice and chance, the individual who longs for freedom is the most vulnerable. In the novel, the search for freedom is slowly converted into a search for association, connectedness, and roots.

Wonderland (1971) takes its form and much of its imagery from Lewis Carroll's Alice stories. After escaping his father's gunfire, Jesse undergoes a series of harrowing experiences that cause him to retreat into himself. At the end, he awakens, coming into full, human consciousness by virtue of an act of rescue and love; his emergence from his solipsistic nightmare is earned by an extension of the self to the other.

Although O. has not overtly associated herself with the women's movement, *Do With Me What You Will* (1973) attests to her sympathy with its cause. Elena, the novel's heroine, who tries to avoid reality by an almost psychotic passivity, finally reenters time and history when she leaves her husband and escapes with a lover. For O., the mask of passivity is as narcissistic as the mask of megalomania: The world must be confronted, not avoided or overcome.

O.'s later fiction demonstrates her increasing interest in the novel as an aesthetic object. In these works, form *is* theme. The monistic absolutists who populate the world of *The Assassins: A Book of Hours* (1975) are revealed through their streams of consciousness. Each consciousness is isolated from the others in a separate section of the novel, just as each character is isolated from the living totality of being by virtue of a stubborn adherence to a personal version of reality. A character's refusal to accommodate to the pluralistic universe is a surrender to Thanatos, an "assassination" of reality.

In *Childwold* (1976), O. artfully manipulates the characters' voices so that the very sequence imitates the novel's thematic preoccupations. As the shifting voices represent successive generations, so the novel focuses on the vulnerability of all things human to the transforming assaults of time.

The hero of *Son of the Morning* (1978) is a pentecostal preacher who believes that he is equal to the presence of God. On the other hand, *Unholy Loves* (1979) follows a number of academicians through a series of emotional traumas that finally purge them of their individual delusions. Although not all the characters survive the loss of their delusions, those who do, confront life with renewed vigor and maturity.

In *Bellefleur* (1980), a best-selling novel, O. employs the gothic to create a haunting fictional world perched between the fantastic and the real. Indeed, O. has woven a shimmering tapestry made of odd and contradictory threads: A hermaphrodite birth, a vulture who devours an infant, a dwarf with "powers," and a vampire are harmoniously woven into a history of the powerful Bellefleur family whose significance is not only historical but sociological, psychological, and mythic.

O. is a much anthologized short-story writer. A favorite of anthologists is the haunting "Where Are You Going, Where Have You Been" from *The Wheel of Love* (1970). It concerns an encounter between

Arnold Friend, a demon-lover figure, and the adolescent Connie. The same volume contains the powerful "The Region of Ice," the film version of which won an Academy Award in 1977. The short-story volume *Marriages and Infidelities* (1972) contains a number of "revisions"—literary marriages and infidelities—of renowned works by Kafka, Thoreau, James, Joyce, and others.

All of O.'s fiction affirms that humanity is located in a universe that it cannot avoid, transcend, or control, and from which there is no separation or redemption. She is a writer obsessed with reconciling an age convinced that the isolated self is the final authority of reality and value to experiential plurality and human reciprocity, to time, history, and the manifest world.

Although O.'s fiction has received a good deal of critical attention, much of it intelligent and probing, some critics have tended to catalogue the novels' violent events, ignoring the careful structure of the works and the moral vision that informs them.

WORKS: By the North Gate (1963). *With Shuddering Fall* (1964). *Upon the Sweeping Flood* (1966). *A Garden of Earthly Delights* (1967). *Expensive People* (1968). *Women in Love, and Other Poems* (1968). *them* (1969). *Anonymous Sins, and Other Poems* (1969). *The Wheel of Love, and Other Stories* (1970). *Love and Its Derangements, and Other Poems* (1970). *Wonderland* (1971). *Marriages and Infidelities* (1972). *The Edge of Impossibility: Tragic Forms in Literature* (1972). *Do With Me What You Will* (1973). *Angel Fire* (1973). *Dreaming America* (1973). *The Goddess and Other Women* (1974). *The Hungry Ghosts: Seven Allusive Comedies* (1974). *Where Are You Going, Where Have You Been?: Stories of Young America* (1974). *New Heaven, New Earth: The Visionary Experience in Literature* (1974). *The Assassins: A Book of Hours* (1975). *The Poisoned Kiss, and Other Stories* (1975). *The Seduction, and Other Stories* (1975). *The Fabulous Beasts* (1975). *Childwold* (1976). *The Triumph of the Spider Monkey: The First Person Confession of the Maniac Bobby Gotteson, as Told to Joyce Carol Oates* (1976). *Crossing the Border: Fifteen Tales* (1977). *Son of the Morning* (1978). *All the Good People I've Left Behind* (1978). *Women Whose Lives Are Food, Men Whose Lives Are Money* (1978). *Unholy Loves* (1979). *Bellefleur* (1980).

BIBLIOGRAPHY: Bellamy, J. D., ed., *The New Fiction: Interviews with Innovative American Writers* (1974). Creighton, J. V., *Joyce Carol Oates* (1979). Friedman, E. G., *Joyce Carol Oates* (1980). Friedman, E. G., "The Journey from the 'I' to the 'Eye': Joyce Carol Oates' *Wonderland*," in *Studies in American Fiction* (1980). Wagner, L. W., ed., *Critical Essays on Joyce Carol Oates* (1979). Waller, G. F., *Dreaming America: Obsession and Transcendence in the Fiction of Joyce Carol Oates* (1978).

Other references: *AL* (43, 1971; 49, 1977). *Commonweal* (5 Dec. 1969). *Critique* 15 (1973). *NYTBR* (28 Sept. 1969). *Paris Review* 74 (1978). *Soundings* 58 (1975). *Spirit* 39 (1972). *Studies in the Novel* 7 (1975).

ELLEN G. FRIEDMAN

Sara Louisa Vickers Oberholtzer

B. 20 May 1841, Uwchlan, Pennsylvania; d. 2 Feb. 1930, Germantown,
Pennsylvania
D. of Paxson and Ann Lewis Vickers; m. John Oberholtzer, 1862

The oldest of nine children, O. was raised in a Quaker family and attended Friends' Boarding School and later Millersville State Normal School. In 1862, she married a Philadelphia merchant. They had two sons.

O. was a poet, novelist, and advocate of school savings banks. She supported numerous social and philanthropic activities and participated in the temperance movement.

Violet Lee, and Other Poems (1873) is a collection of simple, unpretentious poems which treat themes of nature and ordinary life. *Come for Arbutus, and Other Wild Bloom* (1882) contains poems on the sentiments of joy and sorrow as well as commemorative poems on Lucretia Mott and Henry Wadsworth Longfellow. The volume is dedicated to John Greenleaf Whittier. The hymns, memorial poems, and seasonal poetry in *Daisies of Verse* (1886) are more somber than those in *Souveniers of Occasions* (1892), which are dedicated to her sons as the "joy-giving, living poems of my heart and life." In *Here and There: Songs of Land and Sea That Come to Me* (1927), human sentiment is explored in its relation to land and sea. In this last, more highly focused collection of poems, O. includes hymns and songs, poems translated from German, and a commemorative tribute to Frances Willard.

O.'s only novel, *Hope's Heart Bells* (1884), is a story of 19th-c. Quaker life in Chester County, Pennsylvania. The lives and loves of two young women provide the forum for a discussion of ideal love and marriage. Both Hope Willis, a trusting, patient, pure Quaker, and her cousin Nellie, a noble, energetic, and intellectual woman, reject the convention and sham of contemporary married life and the materialism which pervades society. Hope ultimately marries Gus Osborn, a childhood friend and son of her mother's former sweetheart. Nellie, a doctor, marries a man who will allow her to work and will regard her as an equal. These are marriages of strength and purity that God, not man, has sealed.

In 1888, O. began to promote the establishment of school savings banks, a program to inculcate thrift in public school children. Under this program, involved teachers collected money weekly from students for deposit in local savings banks. O. was both National and World Women's Christian Temperance Union Superintendent of School Savings Banks, and for sixteen years she edited and personally published *Thrift Tidings* (1907–23), a magazine for school savings bank advocates. In this publication and several pamphlets, the most famous of which was *School Savings Banks* (1914), O. explained the history and value of the banks, published testimonials to their success, provided statistics on their development in the U.S. and abroad, and delineated various methods of collecting monies, tabulating deposits, and banking savings.

O.'s advocacy of school savings banks as well as her prolific output of sentimental poetry ensure her a place as a diverse, miscellaneous writer. O.'s most important artistic achievement was her novel, *Hope's Heart Bells*, in which she not only portrays the uniqueness of 19th-c. Quaker life but creates two strong female characters who by their rejection of contemporary mores exemplify the highest values of the Quaker tradition.

WORKS: *Violet Lee, and Other Poems* (1873). *Come for Arbutus, and Other Wild Bloom* (1882). *Hope's Heart Bells* (1884). *Daisies of Verse* (1886). *Souvenirs of Occasions* (1892). *Letters From Europe* (1895). *School Savings Banks* (1914). *Here and There: Songs of Land and Sea That Come to Me* (1927).

BIBLIOGRAPHY: Albig, W. E., *A History of School Savings Banking* (1928). Other references: *NYT* (4 Feb. 1930).

DANA GREENE

Flannery O'Connor

B. *25 March 1925, Savannah, Georgia; d. 3 Aug. 1964, Milledgeville, Georgia*
Given name: Mary Flannery O'Connor
D. *of Edward Flannery and Regina Cline O'Connor*

O. was the only child of parents whose Georgia manners and Catholic background influenced O. deeply. O. was sent to parochial schools. She remembered as one of the strongest impressions of her childhood the time Pathé News sent a photographer to document her pet chicken that could walk either backward or forward. O. commented that it was an experience that marked her for life, one that initiated her search for birds with deformities. This became another lifelong concern: a preoccupation with the maimed or grotesque.

O. began writing at an early age and listed as her chief hobby in her high school yearbook "Collecting rejection slips." At this time, she also considered herself a cartoonist. After graduation with a B.A. in English in 1945, O. attended the Writers' Workshop at the University of Iowa, from which she received an M.F.A. in 1947. "The Geranium" was accepted by *Accent* in 1946. Publication of other stories followed, and O.'s first novel, *Wise Blood,* triggered by the stories from the Iowa thesis, appeared in 1952.

Described by O. as "a comic novel," *Wise Blood* is the story of Haze Motes, a religious fanatic in an electric blue suit who preaches that "there was no Fall because there was nothing to fall from and no Redemption because there was no Fall and no Judgment because there wasn't the first two. Nothing matters but that Jesus was a liar." In his insistence that "there's only one truth and that is that there's no truth," Motes ricochets from a pseudo-blind prophet and his libidinous daughter, to the company of the moronic Enoch Emery, the one with "wise blood," to a final resting place with a rapacious landlady who plots to marry him. In his desperate quest for meaning, Motes mutilates himself with broken glass in his shoes, blinds himself with lye, and finally dies in a squad car on the way back to the landlady's bed. His physical humiliations and self-flagellations are enacted without hope of redemption; at the end of the novel, he has become a new and distorted Christ who can offer no salvation, even to himself.

Although the book was received with mixed reviews and an uneasy feeling that the cast of characters was too grotesque even for a public used to Faulkner's southern Gothics, the critics were aware that a new talent had indeed appeared. But in 1950, O. had learned that she, like her father, had lupus. She moved back to Milledgeville to a farm where she could raise herds of peacocks and have time to write. She received a *Kenyon Review* Fellowship in 1953, and published her first book of short stories, *A Good Man Is Hard to Find*, in 1955.

The title story of this book is described by O. as "the story of a family of six which, on its way driving to Florida, gets wiped out by an escaped convict who calls himself the Misfit." The Misfit is another Haze Motes, who also equates himself with Jesus and who realizes he is damned if Jesus did what He is said to have done and doomed to an absurd life in which there is "no pleasure but meanness" if Jesus didn't. The climactic killing is that of the Grandmother, who had been insisting that the Misfit is a good man and wouldn't shoot a lady. As the Misfit struggles with his despair over not knowing the truth about Jesus, the Grandmother reaches out to him and murmurs, "Why you're one of my babies. You're one of my own children." With which the Misfit flinches back, shoots her three times in the chest, and concludes that "It's no real pleasure in life."

Motes and the Misfit, as well as a myriad of O.'s protagonists, are psychic cripples with what Hawthorne called "ice in the blood." They have become consumed with an image of Christ, and hence have lost all human feelings. O. commented in a 1960 lecture that "while the South is hardly Christ-centered, it is most certainly Christ-haunted."

The character in "Good Country People" who is preoccupied with religion in order to deny it is a one-legged spinster Ph.D., O.'s most obvious caricature. The lumpish young maid entices a young Bible salesman into a loft with plans to seduce him and instead has her wooden leg stolen by him. The Bible salesman, Manley Pointer, is thus one of the conmen who appear in O.'s fiction with as much regularity as her mad prophets. In "The Life You Save May Be Your Own," the con man, who steals an old woman's car by marrying her daughter, is named Tom T. Shiftlet—or possibly Aaron Sparks or George Speeds—since the identity of these opportunists shifts with equal regularity.

This lack of a secure identity for the characters is also apparent in O.'s use of the double. In countless stories, the protagonist is not only a distorted double for Christ but also has another character who is his own double. In some cases the double can even be an animal, generally a pig, but in "The Displaced Person," the double of the displaced person/Christ figure is a peacock. This story also demonstrates O.'s most skillful use of dramatic irony, and the reader anticipates helplessly as the survivor of a Nazi concentration camp becomes an obsession to the Georgia locals and is finally crushed, literally beneath a tractor, by another collection of good country people.

In 1959, O. received a Ford Foundation grant for creative writing, and in 1960 her second novel, *The Violent Bear It Away*, appeared. The fanatics are back, and this book contains three: old Tarwater, a mad prophet; young Tarwater, his grandson with an obsession to rid himself of Jesus by baptizing his idiot second cousin, Bishop; and his atheist uncle Rayber, who is equally obsessed by preventing the baptism. The violent clashes between the Tarwaters and Rayber become a struggle for young Tarwater's soul, and Rayber loses when the boy drowns Bishop and flees. Young Tarwater tries, with the desperation of a Motes, to convince himself that all old Tarwater had told him was false. But as he flees the murder of Bishop, he is picked up, drugged, and seduced by a man in a lavender car—which the old man had warned him was possible. The book ends as Tarwater gives in to his terrible destiny of prophecy, becoming as mad as his grandfather.

The title story of *Everything That Rises Must Converge* (1965) has as its central conflict the struggle between children and their parents, most often the mother, that appears in some of O.'s best work. The best story in the collection, "Revelation," shows O.'s child-parent conflict at its finest. This story presents another of the maimed and ugly daughters, this time characterized by ferocious acne, and another of those good country people, Mrs. Turpin, so complacent about their own virtue that they become almost evil in their selfishness. In the final story, "Parker's Back," the last story O. wrote before she died, the ubiquitous reversed Christ appears as a tattoo on Parker's back.

In 1972, *The Complete Stories* appeared and received the National Book Award. This book included all the previously published stories as well as those from O.'s Iowa thesis never before published. In the latter group is a slight but hilarious little satire of a lady writer, Miss Willerton, who vicariously enters her own fictional world and falls in love with her own fictional protagonist. But Miss Willerton is very obviously a hack who must fictionalize to escape, while O. herself insisted that a writer dare not escape, but must instead see truly and completely.

The Habit of Being (1979), O.'s selected letters, presents a composite portrait of a writer who constantly emphasized this necessity of seeing. When one newspaper put her in the "realistic school," O. wrote to reject that label, insisting, "I am interested in making up a good case for distortion, as I am coming to believe it is the only way to make people see." The letters, edited by her longtime friend Sally Fitzgerald, offer brilliant glimpses of O.'s personality while they provide invaluable insights into her methods and fiction. She says, "I have to write to discover what I am doing," and at the same time admits that she knows what she is doing is completely unconventional. She acknowledges that her work springs from "the peculiarity or aloneness" of her experience, and yet confesses that she "laughs and laughs" when she rereads her own comic stories.

To call O.'s stories of death and destruction comic seems a contradiction in terms, but as she says blithely in the introduction to *Wise Blood*, "all comic novels that are any good must be about matters of life and death." O. will simply not allow identification with a single character, even when that character is so blatantly O. herself. With her sharp cartoonist's eye, O. has etched the outlines of her characters in stone, and they stonily resist all empathy. O. consistently utilizes the dramatic point of view in which she presents her characters as though on a stage, and the reader is never allowed to see the innermost thoughts of the character's head—or heart.

This lack of heart thus becomes central to O.'s themes, and the single-minded self-centeredness of the characters who are concerned only with their own salvation makes those characters essentially grotesque. As O. said: "whenever I'm asked why Southern writers particularly have a penchant for writing about freaks, I say it is because we are still able to recognize one." In creating her gallery of freaks, O. has eschewed not only the heroic but the normal.

O. insisted that she herself never released her determined hold on Catholicism, but her doomed and maimed characters constantly question God and Christ and the dual possibility of salvation and eternal damnation. In her most significant stories, O. creates protagonists who are vicious yet comic, Antichrists who destroy others and mutilate themselves in a perverted attempt to atone for some sort of original sin. But throughout their agony, there is the nagging doubt that perhaps there is no original sin and thus no redemption from it, that perhaps all suffering is absurd.

But suffer they must, and thus O.'s comedy is essentially violent. In 1963 she said, "I have found that violence is strangely capable of returning my characters to reality and preparing them to accept their moment of grace. Their heads are so hard that almost nothing else will do the work." Thus, O.'s deadly serious comedy illustrates a terrible sort of existentialism in which existence not only precedes but precludes essence.

The fact that her comic characters must suffer mentally and physically gives O.'s fiction overtones of tragedy, and it is perhaps significant that O. read *Oedipus Rex* just before completing the blinding episode in *Wise Blood*. Yet in the final analysis, O.'s work is more comic than tragicomic. Her comedy is not merely that of technique, but of vision; ultimately, the fiction becomes positive despite all its horrors and doubts. There is basically a maturation in the stories, an essential growing up in which the dreadful children do learn from their equally dreadful mothers and perhaps become equipped to cope and accept a moment of grace. In the southern ability to recognize a freak, there is the implicit idea of what a whole man must be, and ultimately this Swiftian view of man as capable of reforming—once his freakishness and his grotesqueness are revealed to him—breaks through the clouds of O.'s bleak fiction to show the pale light of hope.

WORKS: Wise Blood (1952). *A Good Man Is Hard to Find* (1955). *The Violent Bear It Away* (1960). *Everything That Rises Must Converge* (1965). *Mystery and Manners* (Ed. S. and R. Fitzgerald, 1969). *The Complete Stories* (1972). *The Habit of Being* (Ed. by S. Fitzgerald, 1979).

BIBLIOGRAPHY: Drake, R., *Flannery O'Connor* (1966). Driskell, L. V., and J. Brittain, *The Eternal Crossroads* (1971). Eggenschwiter, D., *The Christian Humanism of Flannery O'Connor* (1972). Feeley, K., *Flannery O'Connor* (1972). Friedman, M. J., and L. A. Lawson, eds., *The Added Dimension* (1966). Golden, R. E., *Flannery O'Connor and Caroline Gordon: A Reference Guide* (1977). Hendin, J., *The World of Flannery O'Connor* (1970). Hyman, S. E., *Flannery O'Connor* (1966). Martin, C. W., *The True Country* (1969). May, J. R., *The Pruning Word* (1976). McFarland, D. T., *Flannery O'Connor* (1976). Muller, G. H., *Nightmares and Visions* (1972). Reiter, R. E., ed., *Flannery O'Connor* (1968). Walters, D., *Flannery O'Connor* (1973).

Other references: *Bulletin of Bibliography* (1967). *Critique* (Fall 1958). *Esprit* (Winter 1964). *Flannery O'Connor Bulletin.*

PAT CARR

Florence J. O'Connor

The frontispiece of *The Heroine of the Confederacy* (1864) is a portrait of O.: a profile of a young woman with dark hair, an aquiline nose, and a broad forehead. O., who identified with Louisiana's Creole Catholics, viewed the Civil War as based on matters other than differences over slavery or the sovereignty of the Union; rather, it was a conflict between Anglo-Saxon Protestant and Catholic sensibilities.

O.'s strongly partisan novel romanticizing the Confederate cause was published in London during the Civil War and reprinted in New Orleans in 1869. O. attempted to provide a Southern answer to Harriet Beecher Stowe, who served as the model for Madame N. "She was one of that style of wealthy, ill-dressed, ill-bred Northern aristocrat who fills our hotels during the winter, and who, through courtesy, are invited to the homes of our planters, and then returns to the North to write of Legrees and Uncle Toms."

The novel opens in Rosale, a sugar plantation south of New Orleans, when secession has started but before Louisiana secedes. Natalie de Villerie, ward of Judge de Brevil, is about to be engaged to Lieutenant Clarence Belden, but she is loyal to the South: "I would sever my very heart strings if I thought they bound me to an individual of Northern principles." Belden pleads with Natalie to leave the South, but she breaks with him, joins other Southern women in war efforts, and becomes the first woman in New Orleans to give her jewels to the Confederate cause. A mark of character in O.'s women is their capacity for self-denial and restraint; however, as the novel progresses Natalie becomes more spirited.

The tide of battle turns after Shiloh, and the Union army marches south to take New Orleans. Natalie refuses to lower the rebel flag, wraps it around her, and is shot but not seriously injured. Natalie leaves New Orleans for Mississippi and then Virginia, where as Soeur Secessia, a nursing sister in Richmond Hospital, she discovers Belden among the wounded. They are briefly reunited before he dies. Under various disguises, Natalie performs a number of heroic acts for her cause. Count Bernharnais, fighting for the South, loves Natalie, who is unable to return his love because her heart, like her beloved Rosale, is "in ruins." Perhaps, when the war is over, she can return his love.

The novel is flawed by O.'s intention to publicize the Southern cause to an English audience; however, O.'s portrait of Natalie as a young woman whose character is strengthened by the war and her picture of the response of Southern women to the Confederate cause is a corrective to the stereotype of the Southern belle.

WORKS: *The Heroine of the Confederacy; or, Truth and Justice* (1864).

BIBLIOGRAPHY: Knight, L., ed., *Biographical Dictionary of Southern Authors* (1978).

MAUREEN MURPHY

Jessie Fremont O'Donnell

B. 1860, Lowville, New York; d. 1897
D. of John O'Donnell

O. was educated at the Lowville Academy and at Temple Grove Seminary in Saratoga Springs, where she graduated with highest honors and with the designation of class poet and orator.

O.'s first poems were published in the Boston *Transcript*. Her first volume of poetry, *Heart Lyrics*, was published in New York in 1887; she edited *Love Poems of Three Centuries* in 1890. O. was also a prose writer. "A Soul from Pudge's Corners" was issued serially in the *Ladies' Home Journal*, and "Horseback Sketches" appeared in *Outing* in 1891–92 and enjoyed an enthusiastic reception.

The nature poems in *Heart Lyrics* reveal a gift for imagery. "A White Easter" uses the metaphor of an ice storm on Easter morning to represent the purity of the Resurrection. The theme of the romantic "Night Blooming Cereus" is the manifestation of God in nature. O. uses conventional nature symbolism: hills press in on the poet in "Shut In," spring is renewal in "An Easter Hymn," and autumn is death in "When His Heart Died."

The poems in *Heart Lyrics* frequently have death as their theme. The pantheistic "A Sister's Thought in March" pictures O.'s dead younger sister in the flowers of the following spring. Death appears suddenly in "The Smitten Riviera" to break the idyllic tranquility with an earthquake; "The New Year's Gift" is, ironically, death. O. offers two consolations to death: In "The Sweetest Joy of Heaven" the poet imagines that in death she can help those she loved on earth, and art transcends death in "Immortality." O.'s religious poems suggest a traditional Catholic sensibility.

"Two Women" deals with the important theme of a woman's choice between domestic life and intellectual life; the woman who "chose valley's shelter, safe retreat / life centered in home" is contrasted with the woman who "chose the weary heights, her soul too true / to yield her life into a lesser one." The poem may be autobiographical.

O. wrote best of the world around her; her nature lyrics and "Horseback Sketches" are the work of a modest talent, but reveal a sense of craft and a skill with figurative language.

WORKS: *Heart Lyrics* (1887). *Love Poems of Three Centuries 1590–1900* (edited by O'Donnell, 1890).

BIBLIOGRAPHY: For articles in reference works, see: *AW*.

MAUREEN MURPHY

Lillian O'Donnell

B. 15 March 1926, Trieste, Italy
D. of Zoltan D. and Maria Busutti Udvardy; m. J. Leonard O'Donnell, 1954

O. is a New Yorker; she grew up in the city, where she attended parochial and public schools, pursued a career in the theater, married, and continues to live in the city. With a minor role in *Pal Joey*, O. became involved in Broadway productions as an actress and dancer. Later, she appeared in television productions, and then moved on to direct summer stock, becoming one of the first women managers. After her marriage, O. left the theater and decided to try writing novels.

O.'s early mystery stories reflect a gothic dimension in exotic settings, country-estate motifs, and genteel characters. *Death Schuss* (1963), for example, takes place in Canada at the height of the ski season amid the luxurious environs of an heiress's home. This unlucky young lady becomes the victim in this murder puzzle which is fraught with romantic entanglements and glamour. These early works are too filled with cliches to be unique.

The turning point in O.'s literary career occurred when she cast off the trappings of the mystery cum gothic style and moved into the real world of the police thriller to create Norah Mulcahaney of the New York City Police Department as her serial heroine. Norah Mulcahaney is a credible character. O. gives her heroine ethnic roots and a strong moral fiber. Norah is also appropriately attractive: tall and slim, with long dark tresses. Norah makes her first appearance in *The Phone Calls* (1972); she is just learning the ropes in the department when she is assigned to the case of a psychopathic killer who preys on women. In *Don't Wear Your Wedding Ring* (1973), Detective Mulcahaney becomes more self-assured; this time she is in pursuit of a female prostitution ring. "The chase" as well as the nature of the crime lives up to the tradition of the thriller as Norah eludes a murderous gang. Her relationship with Sgt. Joe Capretto develops in this case; the reader perceives a match is in the making. (Ultimately Norah marries Joe, but she neither retires nor loses her individuality; they do not become a "crime team.")

The crimes which O. chooses for her heroine are usually crimes against women, such as rape (*Dial 577 R-A-P-E,* 1974). Norah Mulcahaney meets all challenges with conviction—she is a feminist who is concerned with the plight of other women (other policewomen in *No Business Being a Cop,* 1978).

O. learned about the inner workings of the police world through observation and careful research. Amid growing concern for the victims of crime, O. chose another dimension to investigate and a different kind of heroine. Mici Anhalt, an investigator for the New York City Victim/Witness Project, makes her debut in *Aftershock* (1977). A combination social worker and detective, she often experiences personal danger. She too is attractive; though a liberated thirtyish female, she has the youthfulness and enthusiasm of a teenager.

In both *Aftershock* and *Falling Star* (1979), Mici does her sleuthing by assignment and under less than optimum conditions. She experiences on-the-job harassment and departmental jealousies, not to mention the perils of attack from malevolent assailants. But, like Norah Mulcahaney, she endures, proving that a resilient female can make her own way in a tough world.

O.'s novels have achieved success not because her characters are profound or unusual, or because her plots are mind-boggling or aesthetically interesting. Hard-core realism, neither sweetened by gingery femininity nor leavened by blood or brutality, is O.'s metier. Her unadorned literary style is honest and appropriate to the street crimes she depicts.

WORKS: *Death on the Grass* (1959). *Death Blanks the Screen* (1960). *Death Schuss* (1963). *Murder Under the Sun* (1964). *Death of a Player* (1964). *The Babes in the Woods* (1965). *The Sleeping Beauty Murders* (1967). *The Tachi Tree* (1968). *The Face of the Crime* (1968). *Dive into Darkness* (1971). *The Phone Calls* (1972). *Don't Wear Your Wedding Ring* (1973). *Dial 577 R-A-P-E* (1974). *The Baby Merchants* (1975). *Leisure Dying* (1976). *Aftershock* (1977). *No Business Being a Cop* (1978). *Falling Star* (1979).

BIBLIOGRAPHY: Booklist (15 July 1977). *KR* (1 July 1979). *LJ* (Aug 1973). *Ms.* (Oct. 1974). *NYTBR* (8 Aug. 1976). *SatR* (29 Jan. 1972).

PATRICIA D. MAIDA

Marie Conway Oemler

B. *29 May 1879, Savannah, Georgia; d. 6 June 1932, Charleston, South Carolina*
Wrote under: Mrs. Marie Oemler
D. *of Richard Hoban and Helena Browne Conway; m. John Norton Oemler,*
1910

O. was born, grew up, and married in Savannah. Her first publications were poems and short stories, which appeared in popular magazines of the day from 1907 through 1917, when O. turned from short works to the novel.

Slippy McGee: Sometimes Known as the Butterfly Man (1917) seemed unremarkable at first, but went through repeated printings. This was O.'s most popular novel, and it contains the elements which constitute both the popular appeal and the more serious aspect of O.'s writing. O.'s success was in part attributable to her ability to exploit the popular taste for sensationalism, sentimentality, and conventional morality.

The sensational element in *Slippy McGee* is found in the seamy background of the title character. The metamorphosis of Slippy McGee, formerly a successful "cracksman," or burglar, into respectable John Flint is brought about by Father de Rancé, the Catholic priest in the small town of Appleboro, South Carolina. When Flint reverts to McGee in order to retrieve some sexually suggestive letters that the heroine, in an adolescent fit of passion, had written to a former sweetheart, suspense is added to sensationalism. The love story between the heroine and the town's crusading young lawyer provides the sentimentality. When this ideally perfect romance is threatened by blackmail, Flint's burglary and heroic denial of his love for Mary Virginia permit its happy consummation, but O. alleviates the sentimentality by mixing praise and gently satiric condemnation in her comments about the South and southerners. She also quietly crusades for reform of the deplorable working conditions in southern factories and mills. This mixture of popular convention and serious comment is present in varying degrees in most of O.'s novels.

O. deliberately appealed to the popular taste for sensationalism when she wrote some of her more exciting adventure scenes. There are: ghosts, secret chambers, and a near rape (in *A Woman Named Smith*, 1919); forced marriage, adultery, and reconciliation (in *The Purple Heights*, 1920); a mysterious "brotherhood" that plots the assassination at Sarajevo, sexual assault, kidnapping, and near torture (in *Two Shall Be Born*, 1922); kidnapping, wife abuse, and a dramatic jungle rescue (in *His Wife-in-Law*, 1925); and a labor riot and divorce (in *Sheaves: A Comedy of Manners*, 1928). At the same time, these and all of her novels contain romances which obey standard conventions of sentimentality and morality.

O.'s most serious work is her historical, biographical novel, *The Holy Lover* (1927), about John Wesley's career as a missionary at Savannah, Georgia. Quoting liberally from his personal diary, O. dramatizes the dissent created in the colony by his demand for rigid adherence to a strict moral and spiritual code. Although critics regarded this as a hopeful departure in her career, O. later reverted to her tried-and-true formula for popular fictions.

As a writer of the fiction that women read to fill their leisure hours, O. was quite successful. The novels that contain a strong suspense plot read more easily today than those which rely more heavily on conventional romances, but even the latter are enlivened by occasional flashes of humor and adventure.

WORKS: *Slippy McGee: Sometimes Known as the Butterfly Man* (1917). *A Woman Named Smith* (1919). *The Purple Heights* (1920). *Where the Young Child Was, and Other Christmas Stories* (1921). *Two Shall Be Born* (1922). *His Wife-in-Law* (1925). *Shepherds* (1926). *The Holy Lover* (1927).

Sheaves: A Comedy of Manners (1928). *Johnny Reb: A Story of South Carolina* (1929). *Flower of Thorn* (1931).

BIBLIOGRAPHY: Overton, G., *The Women Who Make Our Novels* (1928). Wynn, W. T., *Southern Literature: Selections and Biographies* (1932).
  For articles in reference works, see: *20thCA*.
  Other references: *NYTBR* (29 April 1917; 30 Nov. 1919; 24 Oct. 1920). *SatR* (14 March 1925; 24 April 1926).
                                                 HARRIETTE CUTTINO BUCHANAN

Lenore Glen Offord

B. 24 Oct. 1905, Spokane, Washington
Writes under: Theo Durrant, Lenore Glen Offord
D. of Robert and Catherine Grippen Glen; m. Harold R. Offord, 1929

O.'s father was a newspaperman and her mother a piano teacher. O. attended Mills College, where she graduated cum laude in 1925 with a degree in English. The next year, she attended the University of California at Berkeley. O. experimented with writing short stories, dancing, dramatics, and running a rental library before producing her first novel, *Murder on Russian Hill* (1938).

This mystery novel was well received by the critics. But before returning to detection, O. would produce two nonmysteries: *Cloth of Silver* (1939), a romance with backbone (in which the heroine seeks wifely independence), and *Angels Unaware* (1940), a comedy of manners.

In 1941, O. returned to mystery with *The Nine Dark Hours*. The next year she produced a second mystery featuring the heroine of *Murder on Russian Hill*, Coco Hastings. This novel, *Clues to Burn*, is both a detective novel and a spoof of the formula.

Skeleton Key (1943) introduced Georgine Wyeth and her soon-to-be-husband, Todd McKinnon, a crime "faction" writer, as amateur sleuths. All of O.'s remaining mysteries, with the exception of *My True Love Lies* (1947), feature the McKinnons. O.'s last published mystery novel, *Walking Shadow* (1959), involves McKinnon's investigation of a murder/ impersonation plot at the Ashland (Oregon) Shakespeare Festival. This unusual locale was inspired by the participation of O.'s daughter, Judith, in the festival. *Enchanted August* (1956), O.'s only novel for young adults, also focuses on the Ashland Festival.

O.'s mystery fiction is noted for its humor and characterization. Her light touch and humanity, plus a keen sense for domestic terror, have caused O. to be labeled "a respectable member of the re-treaded Had-I-But-Known School." Critics at once recognized the essential female character of her mysteries, and yet were self-conscious in their praise. It is as though they found it somehow surprising that a "feminine" mystery writer should show such skill and good sense. O.'s mystery novels are both skillful and female in their use of women as focal characters, their compassionate (often reluctant) sleuths, and their effective use of suspense within a realistically drawn domestic setting.

Over the years, O. has written several accounts of actual crimes. In 1957, she collaborated with Joseph Henry Jackson in producing *The Girl in the Belfry*, about a 19th-c. murder.

Besides mystery fiction and true crime writing, O. has served the mystery genre as one of its most respected critics. Since 1950, O. has been the mystery critic for the San Francisco *Chronicle*, and is largely responsible for that paper receiving the Mystery Writers of America Edgar award for best criticism in 1951. She has also been active in the Mystery Writers of America. O. was given "titular investiture" into The Baker Street Irregulars (the American Sherlock Holmes society) as "The Old Russian Woman." She was the first woman so honored.

In recent years, O. has continued her critical career and has produced some mystery-oriented light verse, including the often-reprinted "Memoirs of a Mystery Critic." Although O. has not produced a new novel for many years, she remains one of America's most charming and distinguished mysterywomen.

WORKS: Murder on Russian Hill (English title, *Murder before Breakfast*, 1938). *Cloth of Silver* (1939). *Angels Unaware* (English title, *Distinguished Guests*, 1940). *The Nine Dark Hours* (1941). *Clues to Burn* (1942). *Skeleton Key* (1943). *The Glass Mask* (1944). *My True Love Lies* (English title, *And Turned to Clay*, 1947). *The Smiling Tiger* (1949). *The Marble Forest* by T. Durrant (collectively written, 1951; film version, *Macabre*, 1958). *Enchanted August* (1956). *The Girl in the Belfry* (with J. H. Jackson, 1957). *Walking Shadow* (1959).

BIBLIOGRAPHY: For articles in reference works, see: *Catholic Authors*, Ed. M. Hoehn (1948).

KATHLEEN L. MAIO

Madalyn Mays Murray O'Hair

B. *13 April 1919, Pittsburgh, Pennsylvania*
D. *of Irwin and Lena Scholle Mays; m. William J. Murray, mid-1940s;*
  m. Richard Franklin O'Hair, 1965

O.'s unorthodox ideology first came to public attention in 1963 with the renowned "Murray Case" (*Murray v. Curlett*) in the U.S. Supreme Court. O. brought and won suit against the Baltimore public schools on behalf of her eldest son, charging that the required prayer in the classroom—"sectarian opening exercises"—violated the constitutional guarantee of religious freedom.

Over the past twenty years, O. has become one of the most controversial figures in American public life. Calling herself an "individual anarchist," she has devoted her career to a public campaign of exposing the "unconstitutional partnership" between church and state, showing how these two establishments are not separate as the law requires but hopelessly intermingled. The symbiosis of religious and political life has, from her viewpoint as a leading atheist spokeswoman, disastrous consequences for the solution of secular social problems and for the ability of the individual to operate in a "free" society without pressures from dominant religious groups. Her life's work is a critical exploration and exposé of religion—"its origins, its evolution, its political interventions in diverse nations, its wealth, its insanity"—and the effects of "irrational and superstitious" religious beliefs on individuals and society.

Drawing upon a wide and varied background, including academic degrees in philosophy, law, and social work in addition to military service with the Women's Army Corps in World War II (1943–46), O.'s infamy as social activist and writer is the result of her work in founding American Atheists, Inc., the American Atheist Center, the Freethought Society of America, the Society of Separationists, and Other Americans.

O. is the author of an entire canon of volumes dealing with the history, philosophy, and practice of atheism published by the American Atheist Press. These works deal with the past and present impact of organized religion on national economic and political issues. A long-running radio broadcast, *The American Atheist*, is a series of essays on this subject. In addition, O. edits the monthly news magazine *The American Atheist*. The Atheist Center and Press were established because their goals and values were at such marked variance with those of other organizations, both secular and religious, that O. felt the need for a separate forum in which atheist ideas could be voiced.

O.'s self-made career as an atheist separationist, like the careers of the more radical feminist writers, is an interesting case because she goes so far beyond the conventionally accepted position for women writers, the guardianship of agreed-upon standards of public morality. In speaking out against religion and God, O. openly challenges the historical model of female activism.

O.'s standing as an author is based on the polemic, with its mixed reputation in literary circles as an "applied" form in the tradition of social action, persuasion, high emotion, and the definition and pursuit of the public good. In her works, all of these traits are well developed.

WORKS: Why I Am an Atheist (1965). What on Earth Is an Atheist? (1966). The American Atheist (1967). An Atheist Epic: Bill Murray, the Bible, and the Baltimore Board of Education (1968; rev. ed., 1970). The Atheist World (1969). An Atheist Speaks (1970). Let Us Prey: An Atheist Looks at Church Wealth (1970). An Atheist Believes (1971). Understanding Atheism (1971). Atheism: Its Viewpoint (1972). Atheist Magazines: A Sampling, 1927–70 (introduction by O'Hair, 1972). The Atheist Viewpoint (29 vols., edited by O'Hair, 1972). Letters from Atheists (1972). Letters from Christians (1973). Freedom under Seige: The Impact of Organized Religion on Your Liberty and Your Pocketbook (1974). Religious Factors in the War in Vietnam (1975). An Atheist Looks at Gods (1979).

BIBLIOGRAPHY: For articles in reference works, see: CA (1974). CB (1977). Other references: Newsweek (1 Dec. 1975; 19 Sept. 1977). NYTMag (16 May 1976; 13 June 1976). Washington Post (18 Feb. 1970).

MARGARET J. KING

Cora Miranda Baggerly Older

B. 1875, Clyde, New York; d. 26 Sept. 1968, Los Gatos, California
Wrote under: Mrs. Fremont Older
D. of Peter and Margaret Baggerly; m. Fremont Older, 1893

O. was a Syracuse University student on vacation when she met and married her journalist husband, who was soon fighting both corporations and labor as editor of the San Francisco *Bulletin* and later of the *Call*. In her early married years, O. wrote reviews, society news, and celebrity interviews for her husband's paper. Her first novels were fictionalized versions of muckraking journalism. When the family moved to a ranch in the Santa Clara foothills in 1915, O. took charge of managing the property and its staff of paroled convicts.

O. wrote in three distinct genres. O.'s early novels were social melodramas that reflected current events. In *The Socialist and the Prince* (1903), Paul Stryne whips up resentment of cheap Chinese labor into a string of workingmen's clubs, a paramilitary organization, and an enormous political influence, but ultimately loses all for a beautiful, self-willed society girl who flirts with socialism. *The Giants* (1905) plays off the free children of the West against the railroad-monopoly capital of the East. *Esther Damon* (1911) is mildly utopian. The hero, a Civil War veteran reduced to alcoholism through wartime pain and postwar bitterness, reforms and begins a cooperative community. His protegée wins her way back to a place in society after she has been ruined by her parents' excessive Methodism and has had an illegitimate child.

During this period, O. also wrote magazine articles on social questions, including a long account of the San Francisco graft prosecutions for *McClure's*. Her novels were, for the most part, condemned as too sensational, stark, and evident of purpose. Turning away from fiction, O. wrote plays (none of which have been published), and in the 1930s "authorized" and highly laudatory biographies of William Randolph Hearst (who was her husband's employer) and his father George.

O.'s last works took up the matter of California in a more sophisticated fashion. *Savages and Saints* (1936), a novel, two collections of short stories, and a book about San Francisco combine carefully researched history with fictionalized versions of the lives and legends of Hispanic and Anglo pioneers.

O.'s style was not far removed from that of the dime novel. She wrote a spare, journalistic prose, with short simple sentences and abrupt paragraphs; she aroused emotion with predictable confrontations, duels, and love scenes played out on cliffs beside the sea during a thunderstorm. Yet although she shared the western naturalist's admiration for the successful—even brutal—man, she also wrote about women who took action instead of simply being acted upon. Flirtatious, dependent, clinging women are assigned to the villainous role; happy women generally earn a place of their own before marrying. Many of the stories in *California Missions and their Romances* (1938) and *Love Stories of Old*

California (1940) tell of women who endured enormous hardship to keep the flames of religion and civilization alive in an unwelcoming land.

WORKS: *The Socialist and the Prince* (1903). *The Giants* (1905). *Esther Damon* (1911). *George Hearst, California Pioneer* (with F. Older, 1933). *Savages and Saints* (1936). *William Randolph Hearst, American* (1936). *California Missions and their Romances* (1938). *Love Stories of Old California* (1940). *San Francisco: Magic City* (1961).

The diary of Cora Miranda Baggerly Older is in the Bancroft Library, Berkeley, California.

BIBLIOGRAPHY: Older, F., *My Own Story* (1926).

Other references: *Bancroftiana* 59 (1974). *NYT* (29 Sept. 1965). *Time* (27 April 1936).

SALLY MITCHELL

Tillie Olsen

B. *14 Jan. 1913, Omaha, Nebraska*
D. *of Samuel and Ida Beber Lerner; m. Jack Olsen, 1936*

O. has been active on behalf of political, union, and feminist causes since her youth. As a member of the Young Communist League, she was jailed in Kansas City for her efforts to organize packinghouse workers. In 1932, ill with pleurisy, O. began work on a proletarian novel, *Yonnondio*, a chapter of which was enthusiastically received after publication in the *Partisan Review* in 1934. O. worked on the novel while continuing her political activities—in the San Francisco warehouse strike of 1934 and the Spanish Civil War. Married in 1936 to a printer and union man, O. put aside her writing as she assumed her responsibilities as wife, mother of four daughters, and wage earner. Writing again in the 1950s, O. won the O. Henry Award for the best American short story of 1961 for "Tell Me a Riddle," the title story of her first book. The *Yonnondio* manuscript, rediscovered by O.'s husband, was published in 1974 without rewriting or additions. Since that time O. has been active teaching writing and women's studies and helping to rediscover and reprint the works of women writers.

In *Silences* (1978), O. eloquently describes the loss to literature that occurs when great or potentially great writers are stunted by circum-stances—especially of class, race, or sex—which often deny them the continuity and calm so conducive to creation. For women especially, O. argues, the discontinuity comes from the need and desire to nurture as well as the physical responsibilities for daily living. O.'s own experience and the excellence of her slender work lend credence to her argument.

A powerful motive for O.'s writing is to give a voice to the inarticu-late, to those that are silenced. She is unsurpassed in her power to make readers understand and empathize with the lives of people they have seen but have never known in their essential humanity. The elderly couple of "Tell Me a Riddle," in facing the wife's death from cancer, reevaluate their lives and affirm their idealism and love, despite years of bickering and betrayal which have divided them. As revolutionaries, Eva and David had fought and suffered for "that joyous certainty, that sense of matter-ing, of moving and being moved, of being one and indivisible with the great of the past, with all that freed, ennobled." But in America, David has compromised his ideals, without achieving material success, and Eva has had to bury within herself her idealism and love of beauty as she responded to their poverty and the needs of their seven children. Eva's fatal illness, kept secret from her, leads to a series of visits to children and grandchildren. Finally, aware of impending death, Eva can open herself again to beauty and idealism. Her delirious affirmations force David to confront his own betrayals and accept the burden of love imposed by his dying wife.

"Hey Sailor, What Ship?" is the tragedy of an aging seaman. With his friend Lennie, Whitey has fought for brotherhood in early union bat-tles, but the old spirit is dying, and drink and age are decaying him. Lennie's family is Whitey's only haven of love and the old values, but he realizes that his behavior embarrasses the oldest child, and he leaves. An-other story about Lennie's family, "O Yes," chronicles the separation of two "best friends"—one white, one black—as they enter junior high school and respond to the "sorting" pressures exerted by their race and class. The mothers try to help, but when the white girl asks, "Oh why is it like it is and why do I have to care?" the mother silently responds, ". . . caring asks doing. It is a long baptism into the seas of humankind, my daughter. Better immersion than to live untouched."

Yonnondio: From the Thirties (1974) testifies to O.'s early and con-tinuing commitment to give voice to the silent. Named after Walt Whitman's lament for the American Indians, the novel chronicles the struggles and aspirations of the Holbrook family. The vows of Anna and

Jim to work for a decent life and a better chance for their children are "vows that life will never let them keep," whether Jim works in a coal mine, on a tenant farm, or in sewer construction or packinghouse work. Illness, squalor, and despair poison the parents' relationship and warp or maim their five children, but the urge to live and to fight nevertheless survives.

O.'s ability to create and explain character, to involve and move the reader, is coupled with an ear for everyday cadences and the lyricism of unvoiced aspirations. She portrays the victories of the human spirit—not grand in the absolute height achieved, but inspiring because of the awesomeness of the forces to be battled.

WORKS: Tell Me a Riddle (1961). Yonnondio: From the Thirties (1974). Silences (1978).

BIBLIOGRAPHY: AN&Q (1975). Ms. (Sept. 1974). NYT (31 March 1974). Ramparts (June 1973). SSF (Fall 1963).

HELEN J. SCHWARTZ

Katharine A. O'Keeffe O'Mahoney

B. 1855, Kilkenny, Ireland; d. 2 Jan. 1918, Lawrence, Massachusetts
Wrote under: Katharine A. O'Keeffe, Katherine A. O'Keeffe
D. of Patrick and Rose O'Keeffe; m. Daniel J. O'Mahoney, 1895

O. could qualify as one of the famous Irish women about whom she lectured and wrote. Her parents emigrated to Lawrence, Massachusetts, when O. was a child. After a parochial education, O. graduated at the top of her class from Lawrence High School in 1873. In 1875, O. was the first Irish Catholic to be appointed to the Lawrence faculty; she taught history and speech.

O. first became prominent as a lecturer during Fanny Parnell's visit to Boston at the time of the Irish Land League. She continued to lecture on a variety of topics—historical, literary, and Irish—throughout New England. In 1892, O. delivered the Memorial Day oration in Newburyport,

Massachusetts; that summer she lectured at the Catholic Summer School in New London, Connecticut.

When the Catholics of Lawrence moved to establish a Catholic paper in New England, *The New England Catholic Herald* (1880), O. was elected to its board. A correspondent for the Boston-based *Sacred Heart Review* and an associate member of the New England Woman's Press Association, O. also owned and published a Catholic Sunday paper, *The Catholic Register*. Later, O. was active in the Ladies Auxiliary of the Ancient Order of Hibernians, serving as its first president in 1904.

O.'s early writing includes a local history, *Sketches of Catholicity in Lawrence and Vicinity* (1882), and two dramatic entertainments: *Moore's Anniversary: A Musical Allegory* (1887), a frame for a program of Thomas Moore's songs presented at the Moore Centennial Celebration in Lawrence in 1879, and a similar program for Henry Wadsworth Longfellow, *A Longfellow Night: A Short Sketch of the Poet's Life with Songs and Recitations from His Works for the Use of Catholic Schools and Catholic Literary Societies* (1898).

Famous Irishwomen (1907), a collection of O.'s lectures, begins with the disclaimer that the chapters are not original research but retellings. This is true of most of O.'s Irish entries; however, when she turns to contemporary Irish-American women like Eleanor Donnelly, Louise Imogen Guiney, and Katherine Conway, O.'s acccount becomes an invaluable description of prominent Irish-American women from the point of view of a sympathetic contemporary. She also provides important information about Irish women in earlier American history: women who fought in the American Revolution and in the Civil War, founders of Irish or Irish-American religious orders, and writers, educators, and philanthropists.

Like most Irish-Americans, O. identified Catholic with Irish: "We Americans of Irish-blood—millions of us—have kept that sublime Faith of our Fathers." She exhorted her Irish-American listeners and readers to be conscious of their Irish past, to be steadfast in their faith, and to be anti-English. O.'s sentimental and filiopiestic style lends itself better to the lecture hall than to the printed page; however, by her own example and by illustration, O. provided a range of role models of active Irish women for young Irish-Americans.

WORKS: *Sketches of Catholicity in Lawrence and Vicinity* (1882). *Moore's Anniversary: A Musical Allegory* (1887). *A Longfellow Night: A Short Sketch of the Poet's Life with Songs and Recitations from His Works for the*

Use of Catholic Schools and Catholic Literary Societies (1898). *Famous Irish-women* (1907).

BIBLIOGRAPHY: For articles in reference works, see: *AW. The Poets of Ireland,* Ed. D. J. O'Donoghue (1912).

MAUREEN MURPHY

Rose Cecil O'Neill

B. 25 June 1874, Wilkes-Barre, Pennsylvania; d. 6 April 1944, Springfield, Missouri
Wrote under: Rose O'Neill, Rose Cecil O'Neill, Mrs. H. L. Wilson
D. of William Patrick and Alice Asenath Cecelia Smith O'Neill;
  m. Gray Latham, 1896; m. Harry Leon Wilson, 1902

O. was educated in parochial schools in Omaha, Nebraska. Her professional career began at thirteen, when she won a children's drawing contest sponsored by the Omaha *World-Herald,* which then engaged her to do a weekly cartoon series. O. later moved to New York City, where her work found a ready market. At nineteen, she was a nationally known illustrator and later was also a regular contributor of stories and poems to women's magazines. In 1896, she married Gray Latham, whom she divorced in 1901. The next year she married Wilson, the novelist and playwright; that marriage ended in 1907.

O. is best remembered for the Kewpies, sentimentalized "little cupids" whose illustrated adventures in verse appeared first in the 1909 Christmas issue of the *Ladies' Home Journal* and later in other magazines and in several books. In 1913, O. patented the design, and Kewpie dolls and other Kewpie-decorated articles earned a fortune in royalties.

The first of four novels, *The Loves of Edwy* (1904), shows O.'s characteristic charm, humor, and tenderness; it reveals much about her own childhood and youth in a large, needy family. *The Lady in the White Veil* (1909) is a farcical mystery story in which a stolen Titian portrait is repeatedly recovered and lost anew. In spite of prodigious energy and O.'s unremitting mirth, it soon becomes tedious. *Garda* (1929) presents a fantasy world both beautiful and bizarre. Garda and her twin brother,

Narcissus, symbolize a single mystical being represented as body and soul, the one joyously sensual, the other sensitive and suffering. They are in conflict over and ultimately reconciled by a common passion. *The Goblin Woman* (1930) is unsuccessful in attempting to combine a theme of sin and redemption with a milieu of contemporary sophistication.

The Master-Mistress (1922) is a collection of poems, varying in quality from excellent to trivial, on many moods and aspects of natural and supernatural love. Like all O.'s works, it is illustrated by the author.

In spite of substantial critical appreciation, none of the works for adults had a second edition. Their conspicuous merits were overwhelmed by excesses of whimsy and sentimentality. O.'s Irish forebears were given both credit and blame for qualities in her writing described as "Celtic." A modern reader will find much wit, originality, and beauty of language and atmosphere in O.'s works.

WORKS: *The Loves of Edwy* (1904). *The Lady in the White Veil* (1909). *The Kewpies and Dotty Darling* (1912). *The Kewpies: Their Book: Verse and Pictures* (1913). *Kewpie Kutouts* (1914). *The Master-Mistress* (1922). *The Kewpies and the Runaway Baby* (1928). *Garda* (1929). *The Goblin Woman* (1930).

BIBLIOGRAPHY: Brooks, V. W., *Days of the Phoenix* (1957). Kummer, G., *Harry Leon Wilson* (1963). McCanse, R. A., *Titans and Kewpies: The Life and Art of Rose O'Neill* (1968). Wood, C., *Poets of America* (1925).

Other references: *Independent* (15 Sept. 1904). *International Studio* (March 1922). *NY* (24 Nov. 1934).

EVELYN S. CUTLER

Marianne Dwight Orvis

B. *4 April 1816, Boston, Massachusetts; d. 12 Dec. 1901, Boston, Massachusetts*
Wrote under: *Marianne Dwight*
D. *of John and Mary Corey Dwight; m. John Orvis, 1846*

O., the second of four children, lived the first twenty-eight years of her life at the family home in Boston. After receiving a strong liberal arts education, she worked for some time as an assistant and later as a preceptress in Mr. Bailey's High School for Young Ladies in Boston. In 1844, O. and her family moved to the Brook Farm community.

In her first weeks at the farm, O. tried various occupations. She finally chose to teach drawing and assist her brother in teaching Latin. To increase the income of the farm, O. devoted much of her time to painting lampshades, fans, and pictures of wild flowers. In her later years at the farm, O. spent most of her energy in the school, where she had been elected chief of the teachers' group.

O. contributed much to the life of the community through her artistic ability, her devotion to the school, and her belief in association, but her real legacy is her correspondence, published in 1928 as *Letters from Brook Farm, 1844–1847*. A few of the letters were directed to her brother Frank, who worked for an architect in Boston, but most were written to Anna Q. T. Parsons of Boston, a reader of characters and the founder of the Boston Women's Associative Union, or Women's Exchange.

As the editor of the correspondence points out, it represents "the only considerable body of letters now in existence which were written on the spot by a member of the Brook Farm community with the definite intention of describing the life of the place." Although they cover the years from 1844 to 1847 only, the letters give an enthusiastic first-hand account of Brook Farm as it passed from its early structure to an adaptation of a Fourierist phalanx.

The letters reveal their author as a joyful, sensitive, yet realistic person, and they show life at the farm as physically, mentally, and culturally vigorous. A typical early letter (27 April 1844) describes the freedom of interpersonal relations among the young: "we had company come in (up in our room) . . . and were drawn into playing whist and talking till *eleven o'clock*, which in these working days, is as late an hour as I like to keep. Evening before last went into the Pine Woods about sunset. . . . We threw ourselves upon our backs, Dora, Frederick and I, and whilst the rest walked on, and finally walked home, we staid (imprudent children) and talked till about nine o'clock when the dampness warned us home."

A letter written later in the same year (30 August 1844) states: "Women must become producers of marketable articles; women must make money and earn their support independently of man. . . . Raise woman to be the equal of man, and what intellectual developments may we not expect? How the whole aspect of society will be changed!" This serious, feminist tone pervades the remaining letters.

O. records with enthusiasm the visits of people like Margaret Fuller,

Theodore Parker, Ralph Waldo Emerson, Robert Owen, Albert Brisbane, and W. H. Channing. One group of letters written in October 1845 stands as the only explicit record of the period during which Channing led a core group of the community through a deeply spiritual phase.

Channing also served as the presiding minister at the marriage of John and Marianne Orvis on Christmas Eve 1846. After leaving Brook Farm, the Orvises settled in Jamaica Plain, Boston, where their two children were born.

Although O. was not a literary person in the strict sense of the term, her *Letters from Brook Farm, 1844–1847* contains some of the most delightful feminist writing of the first half of the 19th c. The volume also serves as one of the most important documents of the Brook Farm community.

WORKS: *Letters from Brook Farm, 1844–1847* (Ed. A. L. Reed, 1928).

BIBLIOGRAPHY: Codman, J. T., *Brook Farm: Historical and Personal Memoirs* (1894). Cook, T. W., *John Sullivan Dwight, Brook-Farmer, Editor, and Critic of Music: A Biography* (1898). Curtis, E. R., *A Season in Utopia: The Story of Brook Farm* (1961). Orvis, F. W., *A History of the Orvis Family in America* (1922). Swift, L., *Brook Farm: Its Members, Scholars, and Visitors* (1961).

Other references: *Independent* (1 Sept. 1928). *Times* (London) *Literary Supplement* (4 Oct. 1928). *NYTBR* (26 Aug. 1928).

LUCY FREIBERT

Sarah Osborn

B. 22 Feb. 1714, London, England; d. 2 Aug. 1796, Newport, Rhode Island
Wrote under: Sarah Osborn
D. of Benjamin and Susanna Haggar; m. Samuel Wheaton, 1731;
*   m. Henry Osborn, 1742*

O. emigrated to America with her family in 1722. They first settled in Boston, Massachusetts, and later moved to Newport, Rhode Island, where O. spent the remainder of her life. In Newport, O. met and married a seaman, who was lost at sea in November 1733. O. cared for their child alone, sometimes through great hardships, until she remarried.

O. was admitted to the Congregationalist church in Newport in 1737, an event of great significance to a Puritan in the early part of the 18th c. O.'s spiritual autobiography, *The Nature, Certainty, and Evidence of True Christianity* (1755), was evidently written in retrospect over a ten-year period from 1743 to 1753. It was originally couched in terms of a letter from one friend to another "in great Concern of Soul." This fifteen-page work reappeared in later editions and reprints in 1793, and apparently was expanded by or with the help of her minister, Samuel Hopkins, as *Memoirs of the Life of Mrs. Sarah Osborn* (1799). The *Life* was meant as an example of piety for a younger generation.

O.'s work is characterized by foreshadowings of the sentimental, moralistic fiction of the late 18th and early 19th centuries. The work is replete with tear-stained emotion and signs of O.'s sensibility. O.'s moments of doubt are linked to hysterics and excessive agitation. She relates that she could neither eat nor sleep for a week after Satan had suggested to her that the state of her soul was hopeless. Typically, O. weeps when asking her minister for church admittance, a change from the austere intellectualizing of earlier spiritual autobiographies by New England women.

O.'s writing evidences a notable stylistic as well as contextual change from earlier spiritual autobiographies. In her conscious attempt to tell a life story, O. increases the cast of characters to include not only the self, the savior, and the devil, but also family, friends, ministers, and various incidental personages. She includes a variety of incidents and events to carry the story forward. Thus, while the narrative still focuses on her saving experience, it is broadened to contain plot, action, and dialogue. There is even an echo of the English novel of sentiment.

O. shows an ambitious desire to create a lengthy, complex story. As such, her memoirs have importance. Although the content often appears unexceptional or repetitive to the modern reader, it stands out as an early attempt by a woman writer to use available, socially acceptable materials to fabricate a readable and entertaining story.

WORKS: *The Nature, Certainty, and Evidence of True Christianity* (1755). *Memoirs of the Life of Mrs. Sarah Osborn* (Ed. S. Hopkins, 1799).

JACQUELINE HORNSTEIN

Frances Sargent Locke Osgood

B. 18 June 1811, Boston, Massachusetts; d. 12 May 1850, New York City
Wrote under: Ellen, Florence, Kate Carol, Frances Sargent Osgood
D. of Joseph and Mary Ingersoll Foster Locke; m. Samuel Stillman Osgood,
  1835

O. was the daughter of a Boston merchant. She was educated primarily at home. O.'s parents encouraged her to write, and she also benefited especially from the influence of a half-sister, Anna Maria Foster Wells, and an older brother, Andrew Aitchison Locke, both of whom became writers. O. began publishing verse at the age of fourteen in the first American children's monthly, *Juvenile Miscellany*.

O. lived in England (1835–40) with her husband, an artist; her success there in turn commended her to readers at home. O. was estranged from her husband in 1844, but they were reconciled, even though there was much gossip about her literary "romance" with Edgar Allan Poe.

The major subject of O.'s poetry and prose sketches is the relationship between men and women. Love—passionate, spiritual, seductive, secret, instant, eternal, consummated, holy, pious, true, false, forbidden, self-denying, transforming, transcendent, destructive—receives such a variety of expression that it cloys the appetite.

Although O. is adept in the traditional forms—songs, sonnets, ballads, rhymed narratives, and dramatic blank verse—her meters often lack the force or tension of the inevitable line; her rhymes are conventional, so that blank verse is her best measure. O. frequently runs symbol and abstraction together. The poems are customarily straightforward; emotions are often stated directly.

More interesting are O.'s verses about children. Several of the poems describe O.'s own daughters: one of them sleeping with "beautiful abandonment" on a downy carpet; Fanny smiling for the first time; May trying to lift the sun's rays, or inquisitively playing with a watch. The best of these poems is "A Sketch," which describes two little, careless girls—their straw bonnets flung among the leaves—as, silent with delight, they make garlands for one another, and think of nothing but their own sweet play.

It is also in poems about children and their fate that O. reveals a view of life she rarely allowed herself to express. In "The Daughter of

Herodias," O. imagines Salomé, a light and blooming child, without trouble or care, suddenly bewildered and terror-struck as her revengeful mother snares her in an unspeakable woe. The change in Salomé's character is dramatically realized: "Now, reckless, in her grief she goes / A woman stern and wild." Chilled with fear, the once thoughtless girl curses her fatal grace.

During a period of literary nationalism, as well as an age of sentiment, O. was the most popular and most admired of American women poets. There is little of excruciating or evil design in O.'s work; she wished "to live in blessed illusion." As a writer, she idealizes almost every image and sentiment that engages her attention. But O. deserves the appreciation she enjoyed for her verses about children.

WORKS: *Philosophical Enigmas* (183?). *A Wreath of Wild Flowers from New England* (1838, reissued as *Poems*, 1846). *The Casket of Fate* (1839). *Flower Gift* (1840, reissued as *The Poetry of Flowers and the Flowers of Poetry*, 1841, reissued again as *The Floral Offering*, 1847). *The Rose: Sketches in Verse* (1842). *The Snow-drop* (1842?). *Puss in Boots, and the Marquis of Carabas* (1844). *The Flower Alphabet in Gold and Colors* (1845). *The Cries of New York* (1846). *A Letter About Lions* (1849). *Poems* (1849, reissued as *Osgood's Poetical Works*, 1880).

BIBLIOGRAPHY: Hewitt, M. E., ed., *The Memorial: Written by Friends of the Late Mrs. Osgood* (1851). Griswold, R. W., ed., *The Literati* by E. A. Poe (1850). Mabbott, T. O., *Collected Works of Edgar Allan Poe, Poems I* (1969). Moss, S. P., *Poe's Literary Battles* (1963). Quinn, A. H., *Edgar Allan Poe: A Critical Biography* (1941).

For articles in reference works, see: *American Female Poets*, C. May (1848). *FPA. NAW* (article by J. G. Varnet). *The Poets and Poetry of America*, Ed. R. W. Griswold (1847).

Other references: *Godey's* (March 1846; Sept. 1846). *Graham's* (Jan. 1843). *Southern Literary Messenger* (Aug. 1849).

ELIZABETH PHILLIPS

Sarah Margaret Fuller, Marchesa d'Ossoli

B. 23 May 1810, Cambridgeport, Massachusetts; d. 19 July 1850, off Fire
  Island, New York
Wrote under: Margaret Fuller, S. M. Fuller, S. Margaret Fuller, J.
D. of Timothy and Margaret Crane Fuller; m. Giovanni Angelo, Marchese
  d'Ossoli, 1850

O.'s father was a lawyer and politician; her mother bore nine children, seven of whom survived infancy. Having hoped for a son, Fuller gave his oldest child a masculine education. Pushed by her father's ambitions and by her own growing sense that she could achieve greatness, O. read Horace, Ovid, and Virgil in the original at seven and continued reading widely in her father's library until she first attended school at fourteen. Two unhappy years at school in Groton, Massachusetts, made clear the social problems caused by what she herself considered her lack of a normal childhood. Back in Cambridge, she studied French, German, Italian, Greek, and philosophy, and made friends with future Transcendentalists Frederick Henry Hedge and James Freeman Clarke. In 1833, O.'s father retired from public life and moved his family to a farm at Groton, forty miles from Boston. For two years, O. took care of the house and of her younger brothers and sisters while teaching four of the children five to eight hours a day. She also continued her ambitious "self-culture," reading widely in history, literature, philosophy, and religion.

When O.'s father died in 1835, she became breadwinner and head of the family. She taught at Bronson Alcott's school in Boston (1836–37) and the Greene Street School in Providence, Rhode Island (1837–39). In 1839, she moved her family to Jamaica Plain and began her "Conversations" in Boston and Cambridge, which continued until 1844.

In 1836, O. had begun her friendship with Ralph Waldo Emerson. A passage from Emerson's 1837 journal typifies the mixture of affection and exasperation she could arouse: "Margaret Fuller left us yesterday morning. Among many things that will make her visit valuable and memorable, this is not the least that she gave me five or six lessons in German pronunciation never by my offer and rather against my will, each time, so that now spite of myself I shall always have to thank her for a great convenience—which she foresaw." From July 1840 until July 1842, at the urging of Emerson and other Transcendentalist friends, O. edited the *Dial*.

In 1843, O. accompanied James and Sarah Clarke on a trip to Illinois and Michigan. In December 1844, she went to New York City as a correspondent for Horace Greeley's *Daily-Tribune*. In part because of an unfortunate romantic involvement with James Nathan, O. sailed in August 1846 for Europe and subsequently traveled in England, Scotland, and France, still acting as a *Tribune* correspondent. In Rome, in 1847, she met her future husband, the Marchese d'Ossoli. Her son Angelo was born in September 1848. Ossoli supported the Roman Republic, and the family stayed in Rome throughout the French siege. O. directed a hospital and cared for the wounded. After the Republic fell, the family went to Florence and then sailed for America. All three were drowned when their ship broke up in a storm off Fire Island.

O. began writing with translations of Eckermann's *Conversations with Goethe* (1839) and the *Correspondence of Fräulein Günderode and Bettina von Arnim* (1842); some unhappy attempts at fiction; and rhapsodic, sentimental verse of little merit. Her first successful and original work, *Summer on the Lakes* (1844), used the frame of her western visit with the Clarkes for a mixture of realistic reporting, autobiography, historical and philosophical musings, and literary criticism. The result resembles Thoreau's later *A Week on the Concord and Merrimack Rivers* (1849).

Using a journal she had kept on the trip, O. provides fresh and perceptive comments on places and people from Chicago and the prairie settlements of Illinois to Milwaukee and Mackinaw. Whatever is rhapsodic or overly Romantic in her approach to the West usually succumbs before her own observations and her commonsense good will. O. admires the spirit of the new land, even as she recognizes the cruelty with which the native American has been forced from his country. She mourns the vanished romance and vanishing beauties, but admires the new democracy: "In the West, people are not respected merely because they are old in years. . . . There are no banks of established respectability in which to bury talent there; no napkin of precedent in which to wrap it. What cannot be made to pass current, is not esteemed coin of the realm."

O. pities the loneliness of the settlers, particularly the women, whose training she feels has made them less able to bear solitude. She observes that the desire to be fashionable can only slow progress toward adjustment and enjoyment. Educational methods "copied from the education of some English Lady Augusta, are as ill-suited to the daughter of an Illinois farmer, as satin shoes to climb the Indian mounds."

O. herself adapted admirably. In Pawpaw Grove, Illinois, she slept on the supper table in a barroom "from which its drinking visitors could be ejected only at a late hour." She captures the incongruities and cruelties of the western scene in vignettes—the daughter of a famous "Indian fighter" playing the piano at the window of a boarding house in Milwaukee as Indians pass by selling baskets of berries; two thousand Chippewas and Ottawas encamped at Mackinaw to receive their annual payments from the American government—or in a single sentence: "Whenever the hog comes, the rattlesnake disappears." Horace Greeley admired the book enough to offer O. a job on his *Tribune,* and Evert Duyckinck wrote in his diary for 1844 that *Summer on the Lakes* was the only genuinely American book he had seen published.

Papers on Literature and Art (1846) collected O.'s critical pieces, but the only other book she wrote was *Woman in the Nineteenth Century* (1845), a revision and amplification of her July 1843 *Dial* article, "The Great Lawsuit—Man *versus* Men; Woman *versus* Women." O.'s Transcendental tract endorses above all the idea that the powers of each individual should be developed through his or her apprehension of an ideal. Her insistence on the godlike possibilities of *all* humans differs little from the same radical idealism in the writings of Emerson and Thoreau, but O. emphasizes that the fullest possible development of man will not come without the fullest possible development of woman. O. feels also that woman has so far been given fewer chances to realize her possibilities: "the idea of Man, however imperfectly brought out, has been far more so than that of Woman; that she, the other half of the same thought, other chamber of the heart of life, needs now to take her turn in the full pulsation, and that improvement in the daughters will best aid in the reformation of the sons of this age."

O. says that women must not wait for help from men, continuing their old, bad habits of dependence, but must help themselves; self-reliance and independence are the best ways of aiding themselves and their sisters. The capacity for economic independence is prerequisite to moral and mental freedom, and the freedom to choose celibacy over a degrading or unequal and merely convenient marriage is essential. Late in her book she makes her famous statement that women should be able to do anything for which their individual powers and talents fit them —"let them be sea-captains if they will."

Woman in the Nineteenth Century thus mixes Transcendental idealism and insistence on an economic basis for equality; it discusses prostitution and property rights for women along with the true ends and aims of the ideal marriage. O.'s broad social sympathies lead her to point out that the degradation of white women in 19th c. America equals that of red and black men and women. But, she says, what women want is not "poetic incense," not "life-long sway," "not money, not notoriety, not the old badges of authority which men have appropriated to themselves," but "the freedom, the religious, the intelligent freedom of the universe to use its means, to learn its secret, as far as Nature has enabled them, with God alone for their guide and judge." O. is radical because she argues that "Man" encompasses both man and woman, and that both should be allowed equal opportunity to develop.

The myths that have grown up around O.'s brief life and her relatively small oeuvre make her contributions difficult to assess. Some contemporary and many later critics have maintained that the genius she displayed in conversation, whether natural or guided, never became fully evident in her writings: "Ultimately she should be remembered for what she was rather than what she did" (Blanchard). The *Dial* has always been seen as central to the Transcendentalist movement; some contend that the magazine reflects O. more than it does "the generality of Transcendentalist thought" (Rosenthal). O.'s writings for the *Dial* and the *Tribune* gave her a chance to introduce European culture to America, to promote American literature, and to diffuse her social ideals while contrasting them with harsh reality. With Poe she must be considered America's first major literary critic, but her reporting gives evidence of a livelier, more supple prose that might have matured given time. Undoubtedly, she contributed much to American Romanticism and the feminist movement.

WORKS: *Conversations with Goethe* by J. P. Eckermann (translated by Ossoli, 1839). *Correspondence of Fraulein Günderode and Bettina von Arnim* (translated by Ossoli, 1842). *Summer on the Lakes* (1844). *Woman in the Nineteenth Century* (1845). *Papers on Literature and Art* (2 vols., 1846). *Memoirs of Margaret Fuller Ossoli* (Eds. R. W. Emerson, W. H. Channing, and J. F. Clarke; 2 vols., 1852). *At Home and Abroad* (Ed. A. B. Fuller, 1856). *Art, Literature, and the Drama* (Ed. A. B. Fuller, 1860). *Life Without and Life Within* (ed. A. B. Fuller, 1860). *Margaret and her Friends* (Ed. C. W. H. Dall, 1895). *Love-Letters of Margaret Fuller, 1845–1846* (1903). *The Writings of Margaret Fuller* (Ed. M. Wade, 1941).

The papers of Margaret Fuller, Marchesa d'Ossoli, are at the Boston Public Library and the Houghton Library, Harvard.

BIBLIOGRAPHY: Blanchard, P., *Margaret Fuller: From Transcendentalism to Romanticism* (1978). Boller, P. F., *American Transcendentalism 1830–1860: An Intellectual Inquiry* (1974). Brown, A. W., *Margaret Fuller* (1964). Buell, L., *Literary Transcendentalism: Style and Vision in the American Renaissance* (1973). Cooke, G. W., *An Historical and Bibliographical Introduction to Accompany the Dial* (2 vols., 1961). Deiss, J. J., *The Roman Years of Margaret Fuller* (1969). Durning, R. E., *Margaret Fuller, Citizen of the World* (1969). Emerson, R. W., *The Journals and Miscellaneous Notebooks of Ralph Waldo Emerson* (Eds. W. H. Gilman et al.; 14 vols. to date, 1960–   ). Hawthorne, N., *The American Notebooks* (Ed. C. M. Simpson, 1972). Miller P., *The American Transcendentalists* (1957). Miller, P., *The Transendentalists* (1950). Myerson, J., *Margaret Fuller: A Descriptive Bibliography* (1978). Myerson, J., *Margaret Fuller: A Secondary Bibliography* (1977). Rosenthal, B., in *ELN* 8 (Sept. 1970). Stern, M. B., *The Life of Margaret Fuller* (1942). Swift, L., *Brook Farm* (1900). Thoreau, H. D., *The Correspondence of Henry David Thoreau* (Eds. W. Harding and C. Bode, 1958). Wade, M., *Margaret Fuller: Whetstone of Genius* (1940). Wilson, E., *Margaret Fuller: Bluestocking, Romantic, Revolutionary* (1977).

For articles in reference works, see: *AA. The Female Prose Writers of America*, Ed. J. S. Hart (1855). *NAW* (article by W. Berthoff).

Other references: *SAQ* 72 (Autumn 1973).

SUSAN SUTTON SMITH

Miriam Ottenberg

B. 7 Oct. 1914, Washington, D.C.
D. of Louis and Nettie Podell Ottenberg

O. spent two years at Goucher College near Baltimore before transferring to the University of Wisconsin, where she received a B.A. in journalism in 1935. Her first job after college was writing copy for a Chicago advertising agency. A year later, O. became a reporter in the women's department for the now-defunct Akron *Times-Press*.

In 1937, O. joined the *Evening Star*, a Washington daily. Within her first two years on the job, O. launched her first full-fledged newspaper investigation. She broke page-one stories and exposés consistently over the years. By 1947, O.'s specialization was the investigation of crime and the conditions that foster it.

According to the *Star*, O. probed "phoney marriage counselors, a multi-state abortion ring, high food prices, juvenile crime, sex psychopaths and dope addicts." In 1958, the Washington law enforcement community honored O. with a testimonial reception and a plaque crediting her contributions.

When O.'s "Buyer Beware" series broke in the *Star* in November 1959, it presented three months of painstaking investigation. Alerting Congress to the shabby practices of unscrupulous used-car dealers and finance companies, the articles led to wide-ranging legislation outlawing the unethical practices revealed. Her work on the seven-part series brought O. a Pulitzer Prize for journalism in 1960. Only four women had won the award since its inception more than forty years before.

In 1963, another page-one scoop was printed not only by the *Star* but by most other major U.S. newspapers as well. Here, O. introduced the public to an evil underworld empire called the "Cosa Nostra"—"Our Thing"—better known then as the "Mafia." Newspapers across the country ran her story on Joseph Valachi's testimony, significant because it was the first time an insider was willing to talk and confirm the group's existence.

O.'s newspaper copy, always direct and crisp, is lucid, logical, and highly readable. She speaks with authority, and her writing, which focuses on how the individual is affected, makes what might be an impersonal situation personally interesting to the reader.

The Federal Investigators (1962) employs the same combination of vibrant language and swiftly moving action. O. presents vignettes of seventeen federal investigatory agencies, each dedicated to the safety and security of the American public. Tales of high excitement and intrigue illustrate the individual organizations, ranging from the Federal Bureau of Investigation to the Postal Inspection Service.

Retiring on disability in 1974 after a thirty-four-year career with the Washington *Star*, O. in her "semi-retirement" has been working harder than ever as a writer and lecturer. In 1978, O.'s study of her own disease, multiple sclerosis, was published. She used well-learned investigative reporting techniques for a three-year inquiry that included over a hundred interviews with victims of the disease and innumerable medical experts. *The Pursuit of Hope* has been hailed as the first comprehensive book on the disease.

WORKS: *The Federal Investigators* (1962). *The Pursuit of Hope* (1978).

BIBLIOGRAPHY: Hohenberg, J., *The New Front Page* (1966). Marzolf, M., *Up from the Footnote* (1977).

For articles in reference works, see: *CA*, 5–8 (1969). *Foremost Women in Communication* (1970).

Other references: *NYT* (3 May 1960). Washington *Star* (2 May 1960). *Wisconsin Alumnus* (July 1960).

KATHLEEN KEARNEY KEESHEN

Mary White Ovington

B. *11 April 1865, Brooklyn, New York; d. 15 July 1951, Newton, Massachusetts*
D. *of Theodore Tweedy and Louise Vetcham Ovington*

The daughter of a well-to-do New York family, O. was raised by abolitionists and radicals. O.'s education at Radcliffe College (1891–93) was followed by two years in society, after which O. worked as registrar at the Pratt Institute, and then opened the Greenpoint Settlement of the Pratt Institute Neighborhood Association, where she served as headworker from 1895 to 1903.

O.'s fifty years of work in the cause of full equality for black Americans began with *Half a Man: The Status of the Negro in New York* (1911). Begun by O. while she was a Greenwich House fellow in 1904–05, the interviews and research in New York and in the South continued for seven years. Meanwhile, O. had also convinced Henry Phipps to build The Tuskegee in New York City as an experiment in model housing for blacks; had caused a national sensation as the central white female participant in the 1908 interracial Cosmopolitan Club dinner at Peck's Restaurant; had cofounded the Lincoln Settlement for Negroes with Verina Morton-Jones, a black physician; and had been the leading figure in the founding of the National Association for the Advancement of Colored People (NAACP) in 1909.

Work with the NAACP was to consume O.'s energies for the rest of her life. O. was dubbed "Fighting Saint," "Saint Mary," and "Mother of the New Emancipation" by people in and out of that organization. Able to get along with almost everyone, O. was described by co-workers as sensitive, modest, shy, retiring, but fearless and unshakable wherever she encountered injustice, poverty, or exploitation.

O.'s major writing can be grouped into sociological study, children's books, fiction, drama, and biography/autobiography. *Half a Man* is a highly readable and insightful sociological study of what was in 1911 a nearly invisible minority populace. It gives a thorough picture of the differences between white and black women's roles early in the 20th c., and provides a rare early depiction of the peculiar burdens and strengths of the American black woman.

O. wrote two books and helped edit another to fill the gap she perceived in literature for black children. *Hazel* (1913), a novel for girls, was dramatized and performed at the YWCA in Brooklyn in 1916. *Zeke: A School Boy at Tolliver* (1931), was written for boys. With Myron Thomas Pritchard, O. compiled *The Upward Path: A Reader for Colored Children* (1920), an excellent collection of stories and poems by black writers.

Notable in O.'s fiction is a short story, "The White Brute," printed in *The Masses* in 1915 and also in her autobiography. Based on actual incident, the story seeks to realistically reverse the image of the "black brute" so often touted in the South as excuse for lynching. Dialogue and description are effectively done. *The Shadow* (1920) combines O.'s interests in race problems and the labor movement.

Of O.'s two plays, *The Awakening* (1923) and *Phillis Wheatley* (1932), the latter, shorter play remains the less dated. *The Awakening* is primarily a propaganda piece for the NAACP. *Phillis Wheatley* is based on letters of the 18th-c. black poet to her friend Obour Tanner, and on the biographical notes prefacing editions of Wheatley's poems.

O.'s other two long books, *Portraits in Color* (1927) and *The Walls Came Tumbling Down* (1947), show again the clear, appealing writing style evident in *Half a Man*. *Portraits in Color* depicts the life and work of twenty black men and women. *The Walls Came Tumbling Down* is O.'s autobiography, concentrating not so much on the inward person as on O.'s political activities. It provides an excellent personalized picture of the early days of the NAACP and the people, black and white, who helped push down walls of discrimination and exploitation.

WORKS: *Half a Man: The Status of the Negro in New York* (1911). *Hazel* (1913). *The Shadow* (1920). *The Upward Path: A Reader for Colored Children* (edited by Ovington, with M. T. Pritchard, 1920). *The Awakening: A Play* (1923). *Portraits in Color* (1927). *Zeke: A School Boy at Tolliver* (1931). *Phillis Wheatley: A Play* (1932). *The Walls Came Tumbling Down* (1947).

Most of the papers of Mary White Ovington are in the NAACP papers, Library of Congress Manuscript Division.

BIBLIOGRAPHY: Archer, L., *Black Images in the American Theatre: NAACP Protest Campaigns—Stage, Screen, Radio, and Television* (1973). Hughes, L., *Fight for Freedom: The Story of the NAACP* (1962). Kellogg, C. F., Introduction to *Half a Man* by Ovington (1969). Kellogg, C. F., *NAACP: A History of the National Organization for the Advancement of Colored People* (1967). Ross, B. J., *J. E. Spingarn and the Rise of the NAACP, 1911–1939* (1972).

CAROLYN WEDIN SYLVANDER

Mary Alicia Owen

B. 29 Dec. 1858, St. Joseph, Missouri; d. 5 Jan. 1935, St. Joseph, Missouri
Wrote under: Mary Alicia Owen, Julia Scott
D. of James Alfred and Agnes Jeannette Cargill Owen

The daughter of a midwestern lawyer and financial writer, O. was educated in private schools and at Vassar College. She began her career by submitting verses, reviews, and travel sketches to a weekly newspaper in St. Joseph; eventually she became its literary editor. Under the pseudonym "Julia Scott," O. published short stories in *Peterson's Magazine*, *Overland Monthly*, *Century*, and *Frank Leslie's Illustrated Newspaper*. However, O.'s most important work stemmed from her lifelong study of folklore.

O.'s native Missouri sheltered four groups that deeply influenced each other: the native Musquakie (Sacs) Indians, the French and English settlers, and the transplanted African slaves. Raised among these disparate peoples, O. began collecting folklore, customs, and mythology. In 1888, she announced her findings on the voodoo magic practiced by ex-slaves; in 1891, she presented a paper on the Missouri-Negro tradition before the International Folk-Lore Congress in London. In 1893, with the encouragement of folklorist Charles Godfrey Leland, O. published *VooDoo Tales*.

O. cast this book in a form similar to Joel Chandler Harris's *Uncle Remus:* Five old slave women gather around the cabin fire to share their tales with little "Tow Head," the plantation owner's daughter. "Big Angie" carries her eagle-bone whistle with her missal, her "saint's toe on her bosom and the fetish known as a 'luck-ball' under her right arm." Rendered in dialect appropriate to each speaker, the exploits of Wood-peckeh, Ole Rabbit, and Blue Jay have the flavor of true oral tradition. Although the form of *VooDoo Tales* suffers from the effort to combine serious research with literary entertainment, O.'s materials are compelling and accurate and the plots, language, and imagery are fresh.

O. describes gypsy tribes in *The Daughter of Alouette* (1896). The Musquakie Indians, who granted O. tribal membership in 1892, are described in a paper presented before the British Association at Toronto in 1897. O. later expanded this paper into a monograph, published by the English Folk-Lore Society in 1904. Accompanying the text is a catalogue of O.'s extensive collection of Musquakie artifacts.

Folk-Lore of the Musquakie Indians (1904) is a formal anthropological description of the tribe during a critical "clash of cultures." After carefully surveying their myths and yearly festivals, O. introduces the catalogue of her collection. Although she rejects the merely picturesque or aesthetically pleasing artifact in favor of the sacred or ceremonial, O. also recognizes that "to the wild man surrounded by civilization and making a stand against it, everything that pertains to his free and savage past has become a ceremonial object."

Among O.'s other works are *The Sacred Council Hills* (1909), a "folk-lore drama" portraying the Indian's plight, and *Home Life of Squaws*, of which no extant copy has been located.

O.'s writing, like the cultures it described, was influenced by many different traditions: regional humor, pastoral romanticism, the reform spirit, and the pioneering research of other folklorists. Although *VooDoo Tales* retains considerable charm, O.'s books are most interesting for their eclectic blend of literature and science. In an age when specialization was less narrow, O. synthesized several elements of late-19th-c. thought. A member of numerous scientific societies, she based her work on professional, firsthand observations; her conclusions were guided by deep respect for the people of the Mississippi Valley and their ways of life.

WORKS: *VooDoo Tales, as Told among the Negroes of the Southwest, Collected from Original Sources by Mary Alicia Owen* (1893; English title, *Old Rabbit, the Voodoo, and Other Sorcerors*; reissued as *Ole Rabbit's Plantation Stories*, 1898). *The Daughter of Alouette* (1896). *Oracles and Witches* (1902). *Folk-Lore of the Musquakie Indians of North America* (1904). *The Sacred Council Hills: A Folk-Lore Drama* (1909). *Home Life of Squaws* (n.d.). *Messiah Beliefs of the American Indians* (n.d.). *Rain Gods of the American Indians* (n.d.).

BIBLIOGRAPHY: Dorsen, R. M., *The British Folklorists* (1968). Hartland, E. S., Preface to *Folk-Lore of the Musquakie Indians* by M. A. Owen (1904). Leland, C. G., Preface to *VooDoo Tales* by M. A. Owen (1893).

For articles in reference works see: *AW. Dictionary of American Authors Deceased before 1950*, Ed. W. S. Wallace (1951). *NCAB*, 13.

SARAH W. SHERMAN

Ruth Bryan Owen

B. 2 Oct. 1885, Jacksonville, Illinois; d. 26 July 1954, Copenhagen, Denmark
D. of William Jennings and Mary Baird Bryan; m. William H. Leavitt, 1909;
m. Major Reginald A. Owen, 1910; m. Captain Borge Rohde, 1936

O., Congresswoman, Minister to Denmark, lecturer, and author, was the eldest daughter of William Jennings Bryan. She was educated in public schools and at the University of Nebraska.

Forced by the illness of her second husband to support her family of four children, O. lectured on the Chatauqua circuit and taught public speaking at the University of Miami. On the death of her husband, O. went into politics; she was elected to Congress from 1929–1933. Appointed Minister to Denmark in 1933, O. was the first woman ever to serve as minister to a foreign country.

Forced to tender her resignation as Minister in 1936 when she married a captain of the Danish Royal Guards, O. returned to the U.S., where she became the best-known and best-paid platform speaker in the nation, and was a director of the American Platform Guild from its formation. Active in numerous political and world peace organizations, O. was appointed in 1949 as an alternate delegate to the United Nations' General Assembly.

O.'s books reflect the many changes in her career. *Elements of Public Speaking* (1931) stressed her avowed conviction that no one is born with a silver tongue and that oratory is an acquired art. O. stresses the necessity for simplicity and clarity. She quotes her father's teaching of his art:

"The purpose of speaking is to convince. To convince, you must make the people understand. . . ."

A Greenland Diary (1935) is an account of O.'s travels. Mutual admiration between O. and the peoples of Greenland sets the tone of this work.

O.'s children's books exhibit the same deceptively simple style. There is no wasted verbiage in the telling of the story of O.'s trip around Denmark just before her appointment as Minister. *Denmark Caravan* (1936) sparkles with O.'s warmth and camaraderie with the people she encountered. *The Castle in the Silver Wood* (1939), a collection of thirteen fairy tales, is equally charming for young and old. Many of the stories concern soldiers on their way home from the wars who meet witches or magical objects that test their courage. All the tales have happy endings, and no one in these fairy tales is really wicked.

O.'s increasing concern for world peace after World War II was the obvious impetus for *Look Forward, Warrior* (1942). O. based her system for peace on the Declaration of Independence and the Constitution. Although some have criticized the fuzziness of O.'s proposal, the main outlines of her work have found duplication in the actual documents of the United Nations Charter.

Like her father, O. believed that political work is visible proof of concern for one's fellow humanity. This sensible, sensitive love for her fellow human beings is most pronounced in O.'s children's books and travel works.

WORKS: *Elements of Public Speaking* (1931). *Leaves from a Greenland Diary* (1935). *Denmark Caravan* (1936). *The Castle in the Silver Wood, and Other Scandinavian Fairy Tales* (1939). *Picture Tales from Scandinavia* (1939). *Look Forward, Warrior* (1942). *Caribbean Caravel* (1949).

BIBLIOGRAPHY: Chamberlin, H., *A Minority of Members: Women in the U.S. Congress* (1973).

For articles in reference works, see: *American Women*, Ed. D. Howes (Vol. 3, 1974). CB (1944, 1955). DAB, Suppl. 5. NCAB, A.

Other references: *Literary Digest* (22 Sept. 1935). *Newsweek* (28 Sept. 1935). NYT (27 July 1954). *Woman's Home Companion* (Oct. 1933).

DOROTHEA MOSLEY THOMPSON

Rochelle Owens

B. 2 April 1936, Brooklyn, New York
D. of Maxwell Bass and Molly Adler Bass; m. George Economou, 1962

The daughter of a postal inspector, O. graduated from Lafayette High School and then attended the Herbert Berghof Studio. O. then moved to Greenwich Village and held numerous clerical positions; while on the job, she wrote poetry. O. also attended the New School and traveled extensively.

In 1967, O. received wide critical attention for her play *Futz* (1962; revised version, 1968), which established her career as a playwright. The same year, *Futz* received an Obie committee citation as one of the distinguished new plays of 1966–67. In 1973, *The Karl Marx Play* was nominated for an Obie. In addition to her theater pieces, O. is the author of six books of poetry.

Futz opened at the Tyrone Guthrie Workshop, Minnesota Theatre Company, in 1965. It is a violent and controversial tragicomedy, dealing with a simple farmer, Cy Futz, who is emotionally and sexually in love with his pig Amanda. He lives with her in domestic bliss until "the world" invades their privacy.

Majorie Satz, a promiscuous townswoman, seduces Futz and participates in his lovemaking with Amanda. Later, shamed by her actions, she denounces him to the town. Oscar Loop and Ann Fox inadvertently discover Futz and Amanda cavorting together. Oscar becomes mad, beats Ann to death, and blames his violence on what he has seen. The community rises up against Futz. The sheriff places him in protective custody, but Futz cannot escape his fate. Ned Satz enters Futz's cell and stabs him to death.

The emotional center is Futz's relationship to Amanda. Futz is an instinctual being, and his affection for his sow is contrasted to the brutal and bitter relationships among the other characters. Futz says, "I like Amanda because she is good," and, ironically, Futz is the only character in the piece to display a sensitive and deep emotional life. Thus, Futz's murder at the end tragically symbolizes the destructive force of society's rigid, puritanical, and repressive codes. *Futz* is characterized by O.'s crude and passionately intense poetry. She employs words for their alliterative and associative impact, and her images are surreal and shocking.

By working outside the conventions of stage realism, O. underlines the idea that *Futz* is a modern morality fable. Above all, the inventiveness of her story and the raw power of her language make *Futz* an arresting and vibrant theater composition.

In *Homo* (1968), O. explores the unconscious sexual, racial, and economic fantasies of men and women. Each scene depicts a master/slave relationship in which one individual or group is manipulated, threatened, and humiliated by another. This dream, O. suggests, is the root of people's primordial drives.

In *The Karl Marx Play* (1974), the characters do not relate to each other through the story and dialogue but through the subject and theme. At each moment and in each segment the same images and ideas recur. Thus, the piece is "a play with music whose story is told as much by its imagery and tonal 'meanings' as it is by its plot."

O. focuses on Marx's painful physical debilities, his financial dependence on Engels, his rejection of his Jewish heritage, his lust for his wife, and his emotional need to complete his writings. Through this technique, therefore, we do not see the journey of Marx through his life, but the critical threads which constitute the fabric of his existence in the mid-1850s.

O.'s aim in this piece is to create "a theatrical experiencing of the extreme humanness of Karl Marx." She sacrifices a complex portrait of Marx to a theatrical concept. Thus, despite the play's verbal and musical richness, the text lacks the immediacy and power of O.'s other works.

All O.'s plays are characterized by a fluid and free use of language and time. O. is a poet of the stage. Her dramatic imagination and verbal creativity mark O. as a notable postmodern writer.

WORKS: *Not Be Essence That Cannot Be* (1961). *Futz* (1962; revised version, *Futz and What Came After*, 1968). *Homo* (1968). *Salt and Core* (1968). *I Am the Babe of Joseph Stalin's Daughter* (1971). *Spontaneous Combustion: Eight New American Plays* (edited by Owens, 1972). *Poems from Joe's Garage* (1973). *The Karl Marx Play, and Others* (1974). *The Widow and the Colonel* (1977). *The Joe Chronicles II* (1977).

BIBLIOGRAPHY: Brustein, R., *The Third Theatre* (1969). Kerr, W., *God on the Gymnasium Floor* (1969). Novick, J., *Beyond Broadway* (1968). Poggi, J., *Theatre in America: The Impact of Economic Forces, 1870–1967* (1968).

For articles in reference works, see: *Contemporary Dramatists*, Ed. J. Vinson (1977). *Notable Names in the American Theatre*, Ed. R. D. McGill (1976).

TINA MARGOLIS

Bethenia Angelina Owens-Adair

B. 7 Feb. 1840, Van Buren County, Missouri; d. 11 Sept. 1926, Astoria, Oregon
D. of Thomas and Sarah Damron Owens; m. Legrand Hill, 1854; m. Colonel
John Adair, 1884

O.'s pioneer experience began in 1843 when her parents left Missouri with their three children for the first great migration to the Pacific Northwest. No formal schooling was available until O. was twelve and a young teacher boarding with the Owens family offered a three-month school, but O. was inspired to value education.

At the age of fourteen, O. married Hill, a farmhand previously employed by her father. Hill's idleness and business failures, coupled with his temper and harshness with their son, convinced O. to leave him after four years of marriage. O. obtained a divorce in 1859 and resumed her maiden name.

Supporting herself by sewing, nursing, and taking in laundry, O. attended schools in Roseburg and Astoria and became qualified to teach. In 1867, she established a successful millinery business in Roseburg, and sent her son to the University of California at Berkeley in 1870. In 1871, she made the local arrangements for Susan B. Anthony's lecture in Roseburg and became a subscription agent and contributor to Abigail Scott Duniway's women's rights paper, *The New Northwest*.

In 1872, O. sold her millinery shop and enrolled in the Eclectic Medical College in Philadelphia. She returned to Oregon in a year with her M.D. degree and was ridiculed by orthodox doctors who were critical of her "bogus degree." Specializing in women's and children's complaints, O. built a substantial practice in Portland but was eager to obtain more medical knowledge.

O. was accepted by the University of Michigan Medical School in 1878 and received her degree in 1880. She followed this with a summer of hospital and clinical work in Chicago, six months study as a resident physician in Michigan, and a tour of European hospitals. O. returned to Portland in 1881 and established a specialized practice in eye and ear diseases. She later served as a country doctor in Oregon and Washington.

In 1884, O. married Adair, a West Point graduate, farmer, and land developer whom she had known during childhood. Their only child was born in 1887, and died within three days. Later, the Adairs adopted two children. O. had adopted a daughter in 1875.

Following her retirement in 1905, O. intended to "write a book on medicine from a woman's standpoint." However, she decided to make her first attempt at "book-making" a volume of her life experiences, biographical sketches of pioneers, letters received from friends, and her own articles, letters, and speeches. The first one hundred pages of *Dr. Owens Adair: Some of Her Life Experiences* (1906) were devoted to what O. described as the "short, plain, truthful story of my own life . . . purposefully stripped of the sentiment, love, and romance with which my nature has always been super-charged." O. sought to assist in the preservation of the history of Oregon and to show, through her own life story, the labor and struggle of pioneer woman. Local reviewers praised her work and noted that they saw "no view to self-praise or egotism" in O.'s "close personal history."

In 1922, O. published a sixty-four-page volume entitled *A Souvenir: Dr. Owens-Adair to Her Friends*. At the age of eighty-two, her sentimentality was evident as she presented "a pretty little booklet" to preserve "some of the beautiful reviews of the first child of my brain" and congratulations received from friends on her eighty-second birthday.

O. was the pioneer advocate in the Pacific Northwest for eugenic sterilization. Believing that "every child has the right to be born mentally and physically fit," she proposed bills in the Oregon and Washington legislatures to require that: "Criminals, epileptics, insane and all feeble-minded persons committed to any state institution . . . shall be sterilized, except such as in the judgment of a legally appointed board of examiners . . . are exempted." Her two 1922 publications on eugenic sterilization are examples of the major arguments she made in her seventeen-year battle for sterilization laws. O. influenced the passage of a sterilization law in Washington in 1909 and the later passage of a law in Oregon—laws that she believed were humanitarian in nature.

Although O. never wrote the woman's medical book that she had considered at retirement, she lectured and wrote articles on causes that were vital to her—temperance, woman suffrage, the values of vigorous exercise and physical culture for women, the proper raising of children, and the influence of heredity and habit—and was recognized as a straightforward and intelligent writer.

The marker at O.'s grave reads: "Only the enterprising and the brave are actuated to become pioneers." O. had dedicated herself to a life of action and enterprise, dreaming of the "new woman" whom she had described in an address to the 1896 Women's Congress: "She will be cleansed of the dross of dependence, and the prejudice of past ages."

WORKS: Dr. Owens-Adair: Some of Her Life Experiences (1906). Human Sterilization: Its Social and Legislative Aspects (1922). A Souvenir: Dr. Owens-Adair to Her Friends, Christmas, 1922 (1922). The Eugenic Marriage Law and Human Sterilization: The Situation in Oregon: A Statement (1922).

BIBLIOGRAPHY: Evans, E., et al., History of the Pacific Northwest II (1889). Gaston, J., The Centennial History of Oregon IV (1912). Gray, D., "Professional Women in the West," in Women of the West (1976). Fred Lockley, in With Her Own Wings, Ed. H. K. Smith (1948). Miller, H. M., Woman Doctor of the West: Bethenia Owens-Adair (1960). Ross, N. W., Westward the Women (1944).
    Other references: The New Northwest (1871–87).

JEAN M. WARD

Cynthia Ozick

B. New York City
D. of William and Celia Ozick; m. Bernard Hallote

O. was educated at New York University (B.A., 1949) and at Ohio State University (M.A., 1950). She lives with her husband, a lawyer, and their daughter in New Rochelle, New York.

Trust (1966), O.'s first novel, is narrated by the illegitimate daughter of Allegra Vand and her former lover. Allegra's lover and her two husbands each represent a distinct social milieu and a historical posture of the years from the 1920s to the 1960s. Trust contains some fine witty, aphoristic dialogue, but at times the interminable repartee contributes little to characterization. Another stylistic weakness is O.'s propensity for images, such as the "refrigerator died out into silence," and extended descriptions of minute movements. These shortcomings are offset by the psychological and social reality of the characters, by some hilarious scenes, and by O.'s ability to render a zeitgeist without nostalgia. O. is justly compared with Henry James for her ability to convey the density of the social scene and the modus operandi of society: money, status, and class.

In *The Pagan Rabbi, and Other Stories* (1971), O. controls the vice of overwriting and develops her virtues. A number of these stories demonstrate O.'s characteristic use of luxurious imagery and fascination with the fantastical. Chief among O.'s abiding themes are the conflict between nature and history, and between paganism and Judaism.

"Envy; Or, Yiddish in America" has become the most popular story of the collection. It is a story of complicated intentions and meanings, built on a slender plot concerning one writer's envy of another. Edelshtein, a forty-year-old American from Kiev, is a failed Yiddish poet consumed with envy for Ostrover, a writer whose sodomistic fiction about his Polish village has won him acclaim as a "modern" writer. Both write in Yiddish, and Edelshtein has convinced himself that Ostrover's success has been due to his translator. The problem, in its wider context, is one of translating a "dying" language into a living medium, of finding a bridge between past and present. The literary problem is of only superficial interest; O. finds greater significance in the relationship of Judaism to history and to the world.

Bloodshed, and Three Novellas (1976) contains four stories and an important preface in which O. expresses her concern that the English language is an inadequate medium for Jewish culture. In "Usurpation (Other People's Stories)," O. succumbs to a weakness for contrivance that all but buries her concern for whether Jewish genius and religiosity are best served by the "magic" of storytelling. "A Mercenary," however, is O. at her best, in control of complex subtleties and the ability to express the psychological, social, and historical aspects of character.

In much of O.'s literary criticism, as in her fiction, her interest is attracted by a subject's social milieu or personal relationships—in "Mrs. Virginia Woolf" (*Commentary*, Aug. 1973), for instance, by Bloomsbury and Woolf's marriage. O.'s objective is often to analyze an issue or attitude. In the essay on Woolf, she makes an important distinction between classical feminism, which "asserts a claim on the larger world," and "present-day liberation," which "shifts to separtism." Classical feminism, O. feels, addresses moral and intellectual problems, not differences of gender.

O.'s career as a short-story writer marks a stage in the development of the form. O. has reinvested the short story with some of the dimensions and virtues of the novel—social density and philosophical earnestness and intensity. O. has reintroduced the prospect of the writer's commitment to values and ideas as well as to form and esthetic. O. believes that "a story ought to judge and interpret the world," and in "Envy" she does this with verve.

WORKS: *Trust* (1966). *The Pagan Rabbi, and Other Stories* (1971). *Bloodshed, and Three Novellas* (1976).

BIBLIOGRAPHY: *Commentary* (June 1976). *Discussion* 62 (1976). *Moment* (April 1976). *NYRB* (1 April 1976). *Playboy* (June 1976). *Present Tense* (Spring 1972).

ROBERTA KALECHOFSKY

Dorothy Myra Page

B. ca. 1899, Newport News, Virginia
Given name: Dorothy Gary
Wrote under: Dorothy Page Gary, Dorothy Markey, Dorothy Myra Page,
*   Myra Page*
D. of Benjamin Roscoe and Willie Alberta Barham Gray; m. John Markey

P.'s interest in writing was explicitly tied to her sense of art as social commentary. P.'s earliest memories are of accompanying her doctor father in his carriage as he made rounds. It was here that P. first recognized the severe extremes of class and race that characterized her town. When P. was told that her brother, not she, would be encouraged to pursue a career in medicine, her sense of social inequity deepened. Writing became her vehicle for social investigation and self-expression.

P. published her first poem at age nine in the Richmond *Times* and wrote fiction throughout high school. In 1918, she graduated from Westhampton College in Richmond, where she edited the yearbook and won an award for her short story, "Schuman's Why." After an unsatisfying year teaching literature and history in a local junior high school, P. went to Columbia University. She received her Master's degree in political science, writing a thesis on yellow journalism. During the months in New York City, P. also became familiar with the goals of the trade union movement and revolutionary socialism.

P. returned to Virginia as an industrial secretary for the YWCA. Her job was to organize women working in department stores and silk mills into cultural and educational clubs to prepare them for unionization, but

P. became disenchanted with the conservative attitude of the local YWCA leadership. She began to work with the Amalgamated Clothing-makers Union in Philadelphia, St. Louis, and Chicago. Her writing, primarily as a journalist covering labor issues, continued sporadically during this period.

In the late 1920s, P. received a teaching fellowship at the University of Minnesota. While in Minnesota she worked with the Minnesota Federation of Labor and the Farmers' Labor Party and married another graduate student. P. earned her Ph.D. in 1928, majoring in sociology and minoring in economics and psychology. Her dissertation was published as *Southern Cotton Mills and Labor* in 1929. Although she taught briefly at Wheaton College, most of P.'s time was given to her political work and her writing. She was a contributor to *Nation, New Masses, New Pioneer,* and *Labor Age* and a member of the Revolutionary Writers' Federation.

Gathering Storm (1932) is a fictional dramatization of several of the most significant events in the history of the American labor movement. The novel begins with an aging woman telling her spirited granddaughter about how the North Carolina hill people originally came to work in the cotton mills, and then traces the various characters through their involvement in and impressions of the 1910 shirtwaist makers' strike in New York City, the Russian Revolution, the political repression that accompanied patriotic zeal after World War I, the political debate between the Socialist Party and the IWW, the Chicago meatpackers' strike, and the formulation of an American Communist Party. The novel culminates with the cotton mill workers' strike in Gastonia, North Carolina, in 1929. Although heavily didactic, *Gathering Storm* is interesting because of P.'s attempts to make the problems of both women and black workers central to her discussion of the events and their possible resolution.

In the early 1930s, P. went to Europe to study and write about teachers' unions, and went from there to the Soviet Union. In the Soviet Union P. worked as a journalist and lived in a thriving artists' community. *Soviet Main Street* (1933) describes the changes which occur in Poldolsk, a small factory town outside of Moscow, as the residents adjust to the new life made possible by the revolution. *Moscow Yankee* (1935), a fictionalization of P.'s impressions of life in postrevolutionary Russia, is especially memorable for its portrayal of the personal dimensions of the conversion to Communism, most significantly the evolution of sexual relationships in a changing political climate.

With Sun in Our Blood (1950) is a fictionalized biography of Dolly

Hawkins, the daughter, wife, and mother of coal miners in the Cumberland Mountains of Tennessee. P.'s admirable blend of local-color realism, lyrical, often ballad-like descriptions, and astute social commentary make the novel one of lasting significance.

Blacklisted during the repressive literary and political climate of the 1950s, P. adopted her husband's name when she could not get work published under her own. As Dorothy Markey, she wrote two biographies of American scientists for adolescent readers: *The Little Giant of Schenectady* (1956), a biography of Charles Steinmetz, and *Explorer of Sound* (1964), a biography of Michael Pupin.

P. is currently working on the first two volumes of her fictionalized autobiography, *Soundings* and *Midstream*. She writes in her preface to *Soundings*: "A man's reach must exceed his grasp, what then about a woman's?"

WORKS: *Southern Cotton Mills and Labor* (1929). *Gathering Storm: A Story of the Black Belt* (1932). *Soviet Main Street* (1933). *Moscow Yankee* (1935). *It Happened on May First* (1940). "The March on Chumley Hollow," *100 Non-Royalty Plays* (Ed. W. Konzlenko, 1941). *With Sun in Our Blood* (1950; reprinted as *Daughter of the Hills: A Woman's Part in the Coal Miners' Struggle*, 1977). *The Little Giant of Schenectady* (1956). *Explorer of Sound* (1964).

BIBLIOGRAPHY: Blake, F., *The Strike in the American Novel* (1972). Hill, V., "Strategy and Breadth: The Socialist-Feminist in American Fiction" (Diss., SUNY at Buffalo, 1979). Rideout, W., *The Radical Novel in the United States, 1900–1954* (1956).

Other references: *In These Times* (May 1978). *Mountain Heritage* (May 1978). *Social Research* (1971). *Westchester Gannet* (23 Jan. 1978).

VICKI LYNN HILL

Grace Paley

B. *11 Dec. 1922, New York City*
D. *of Isaac and Mary Ridnyik Goodside; m. Jess Paley, 1942;*
m. Robert Nichols

Reared in New York City, P. studied at Hunter College (1938–39) and New York University. P. is the mother of two children. P. was active in radical, nonviolent anti-Vietnam war organizations. She has taught at Columbia and Syracuse University and currently teaches at Sarah Lawrence College.

Portraying the "irremediableness of modern life," P. nevertheless writes with the ironic vision of the joy and dirty diapers that an irrepressible tomorrow will bring. Her language leaps and somersaults, linking lofty abstractions with the colloquial, as in the titles of her two collections of short stories: *The Little Disturbances of Man* (1959) and *Enormous Changes at the Last Minute* (1974).

P. often uses ethnic first-person narrators who reveal the pathos or courage of their lives, often with unconscious and unsentimental hilarity. "Goodbye and Good Luck" describes the thirty-year affair of the warm-hearted Rose Lieber with Vlashkin, the Valentino of the Yiddish theater. Traditional Jewish sexual mores clash with Rosie's decision to "live for love" until Vlashkin's wife divorces him, and the fiftyish Rosie insists on marriage. In "The Loudest Voice," a young Jewish girl happily participates in the school Christmas play while her parents argue about religious freedom and assimilation. "An Interest in Life" and "Distance" tell about Mrs. Raftery and her married son John's affair with his old girlfriend Ginny (now deserted with her four children). In the former, Ginny finally takes John as her lover to keep him around helping her raise her family, although she dreams passionately of the (unlikely) return of her husband. In "Distance," Mrs. Raftery's monologue shows how she, wild and passionate in her youth like Ginny, pushed John toward respectability and away from Ginny, only to encourage the later liaison as a way of seeing her respectable suburbanite son. In such stories, P. achieves the goal articulated in "Debts": to tell stories "in order . . . to save a few lives."

In many of the stories about Faith, the plot is less important than P.'s insight into the emotional nature of women. Husbands and lovers are the transients—to be loved, tended, and mourned—but children are the comforters and inspirers. In "A Subject of Childhood," Faith's younger son comforts her after her lover leaves; her elder son's "heartfelt brains" and gesture of revolt guide Faith out of a child-infested, man-hunting playground into political activism in "Faith in a Tree."

Enormous Changes at the Last Minute epitomizes P.'s strengths and weaknesses. The author has protested in the autobiographical "A Conversation with My Father" against the well-plotted story: "because it takes all hope away. Everyone, real or invented, deserves the open destiny of life." The esthetic result of this theory, however, is abrupt, unlikely, and unsatisfying endings, as in "Enormous Changes." But the heart of the story is the characterization of Alexandra, a middle-aged, childless social worker caught between love for her ailing socialist-intellectual Jewish father and for Dennis, a young rock lyricist who gets her pregnant. The characters' reactions to Alexandra's pregnancy contradict their supposed credos but reveal their humanity. With a tremendous capacity for vulnerability, P.'s characters endure the glacial weight of "little disturbances," armed with love, humor, and acceptance.

WORKS: *The Little Disturbances of Man* (1959). *Enormous Changes at the Last Minute* (1974).

BIBLIOGRAPHY: Wisse, R., *The Schlemiel as Modern Hero* (1971).
Other references: *Commonweal* (25 Oct. 1968). *Esquire* (Nov. 1970). *Genesis West* (Fall 1963). *Ms.* (May 1974). *Nation* (11 May 1974). *NYT* (19 April 1959). *TLS* (14 Feb. 1975).

HELEN J. SCHWARTZ

Phoebe Worrall Palmer

B. *18 Dec. 1807, New York City; d. 2 Nov. 1874, New York City*
D. *of Henry and Dorothea Wade Worrall; m. Walter Clark Palmer, 1827*

Author and evangelist of the "Holiness" movement, P. was the fourth of ten children of an American Methodist mother and an English father. In 1827, P. married a doctor and fellow Methodist. Both were lifelong New Yorkers. The Palmers had six children, only three of whom survived infancy.

In the 1840s, P. distributed tracts in the slums and regularly visited the Tombs, the legendary New York prison. For eleven years she was corresponding secretary of the New York Female Assistance Society for the Relief and Religious Instruction of the Sick Poor. P.'s most lasting contribution was the founding of the Five Points Mission in 1850 in the city's worst slum. Supported by the Methodist Ladies' Home Missionary Society, it was the forerunner of later settlement houses.

P.'s sister Sarah Worrall Lankford (1806–1896, who became the second wife of Walter Palmer in 1876) experienced "entire sanctification" in 1835. Though the experience was one testified to by many early Methodists in response to John Wesley's teachings on Christian perfection, it had not been stressed by American Methodists. In August 1835, Sarah founded the Tuesday Meeting for the Promotion of Holiness, which met in the home the Palmers and Lankfords shared. This weekly meeting for prayer, Scripture reading, and testimony, which continued for more than sixty years, was widely copied and became the catalyst for the "Holiness" or "Lay" revival of 1857–58, which eventually led to the formation of such holiness denominations as the Church of the Nazarene and such Pentecostal groups as the Assemblies of God.

P. testified to the same experience in 1837. Her writing and speaking, as well as her leadership in the Tuesday Meeting, soon made P. the more prominent sister. For six months each year "Dr. and Mrs. Phoebe Palmer" spoke in churches and camp meetings throughout the eastern U.S. and Canada. In 1859, they took the revival to the British Isles. Magazine reports on this trip were published as a book, *Four Years in the Old World*, in 1865.

P. was also a frequent contributor to the *Guide to Christian Perfection*, founded in Boston in 1839. Rechristened the *Guide to Holiness* in 1843, it was merged with the *Beauty of Holiness* when the Palmers purchased both in 1864. P. became editor, a post she held until her death. P.'s series of articles, "Fragments from My Portfolio," were collected as *Faith and Its Effects* in 1849.

Revivalist Charles G. Finney and his colleague at Oberlin College, President Asa Mahan, began in 1836 and 1837 to develop what came to be known as "Oberlin Perfectionism." Finney had transformed the old Puritan notion of religious conversion as an agonizing process contingent on divine election into a simple decision of human free will, an act, and an event.

P. transformed Wesley's idea of perfection as a lifelong process into an act and an experience. In response to a Presbyterian elder's question as to whether "there is not a *shorter way* of getting into the way of holiness?" P. replied in the *Christian Advocate and Journal*, "THERE IS A SHORTER WAY!" Her articles became her most famous work, *The Way of Holiness* (1843). P. begins with the premise that "God requires *present* holiness." Using Finney's logic that God would not command something people cannot do, P. declares that a person must consecrate all to God. (For eighty descriptions of this by ministers who have experienced it, see P.'s *Pioneer Experiences*, 1868.) Using rather dubious biblical exegesis, P. termed this "laying all upon the altar." She declared that the altar was Christ and that "whatever *touched* the altar became holy, virtually the *Lord's property, sanctified to His use.*" Since God has declared this to be true, any person who consecrates everything to God can simply claim sanctification and testify to it publicly, whether or not he or she receives any inner confirmation from the Holy Spirit (as Wesley taught) or has any emotional experience. A person simply claims holiness on the basis of faith in God's promise.

P.'s other significant work was *Promise of the Father* (1859), in which she argued from Scripture, church history, and biographical example for the right of women to preach. Although P. never considered herself a "woman's rights" advocate or sought ordination for her own ministry, she strongly supported the right, and even Christian duty, of women to publicly testify to their religious experience and to become full-time preachers if they felt that to be God's call.

P.'s understanding of holiness, despite her very controversial "altar terminology," transformed the notion from one of process to one of experience. The movement P. helped give birth to left a lasting impact on American religious culture. P.'s defense of women's ministry was the first of many in the holiness-Pentecostal tradition, which led such churches to ordain women more than fifty years before "mainline" Protestantism.

WORKS: The Way of Holiness (1843). *Faith and Its Effects* (1849). *Present to My Christian Friend on Entire Devotion to God* (1853). *The Useful Disciple; or, A Narrative of Mrs. Mary Gardner* (1853). *Incidental Illustrations of the Economy of Salvation* (1855). *Promise of the Father* (1859). *Four Years in the Old World* (1865). *Pioneer Experiences* (1868). *A Mother's Gift* (1875).

BIBLIOGRAPHY: Wheatley, R., *The Life and Letters of Mrs. Phoebe Palmer* (1876). Hughes, G., *The Beloved Physician, Walter C. Palmer, M.D.* (1884). Hughes, G., *Fragrant Memories of the Tuesday Meeting* (1886). Roche, J., *The Life of Mrs. Sarah A. Lankford Palmer* (1898). Peters, J. L., *Christian Perfection and American Methodism* (1956). Smith, T., *Revivalism and Social Reform in Mid-Nineteenth Century America* (1957). Dayton, D. W., *Discovering an Evangelical Heritage* (1976).

For articles in reference works, see: *NAW* (article by W. J. McCutcheon).

NANCY A. HARDESTY

Helen Waite Papashvily

B. *19 Dec. 1906, Stockton, California*
Writes under: *Helen Papashvily, Helen Waite Papashvily*
D. *of Herbert and Isabella Findlay Lochhead Waite; m. George Papashvily,*
1933

P. was educated in public schools and at the University of California at Berkeley. She graduated in 1929, and then opened a bookstore. The next year she met her husband, an immigrant from Kobiankari in Soviet Georgia who had come to the U.S. in 1923. About the same time P. began her writing career with a variety of short pieces.

In 1933, the Papashvilys moved to New York City, where P. collected books for private libraries and wrote short stories, works for children, and articles. In 1935, they bought the Ertoba Farm in Bucks County, Pennsylvania, where P. still lives.

It was P.'s idea to set down her husband's accounts of his involved and colorful twenty-year Americanization. *Anything Can Happen* (1945) quickly sold 600,000 copies, was translated into fifteen languages, and was made into a film.

Anything Can Happen looks back to a period early in this century, just before the National Origins Act (1924) cut off the large wave of immigration from southern and eastern Europe. The book, told from a personal perspective, constitutes a "psychological case-study in the adjustment of the alien" (H. Fields). P. approaches the immigrant's quest for food, shelter, and matrimony with wit, enthusiasm, honesty, and gracious old-world manners. His story presents a version of the old theme of innocence encountering experience—with not all the innocence on the immigrant's side.

Part of the book's popularity originally stemmed from its optimistic portrayal of life in America, its tone being one of philosophic acceptance rather than rebellion against injustices. Consequently, the book lends credence to the vision of America as a melting pot. Its appeal, however, is also attributable to its vivid, charming, and often poetic use of language. This can be credited in part to P., who set out to capture the rhythm and flavor of her husband's English rather than his exact speech.

The Papashvilys' five joint works constitute total and perfect collaboration. Papashvily supplied the material; his wife, seeing its potential, transformed it from verbal anecdotes into written words. (Papashvily, coming from a rural, oral tradition, and involved in tactile rather than verbal pursuits, eventually learned to read English, but never to write it.) Moreover, as an American married to an immigrant, P. sensed how best to present her husband's material to an American audience. Perhaps because the collaboration was so successful, the extent of P.'s contribution to it is often glossed over.

Of the Papashvilys' other works the most important is *Yes and No Stories* (1946), one of the few books to render the folklore of Georgia, a country inaccessible both geographically and linguistically, into a language other than Russian. Because Georgian history involves recurrent invasions that resulted in the grafting of diverse ethnic cultures upon native materials, the tales, "though circumscribed in their locale, merge with the main stream of Indo-European folk matter" (H. Wedeck).

P.'s most important independent effort, *All the Happy Endings* (1956), was the first book to study in detail the enormous quantities of popular 19th-c. American fiction written by, for, and about women; to discuss its authors individually; and to assess the relationship of their work to feminism. Treating domestic fiction as a social and psychological phenomenon, P. concluded that while the suffragists of the period waged outright rebellion, the novelists engaged in surreptitious warfare "to destroy their common enemy, man." As Nancy Cott notes, P. thus found "the roots of feminism, in a shrewdly adapted form, in domesticity itself."

WORKS: *Anything Can Happen* (with G. Papashvily, 1945; film version, 1952). *Yes and No Stories: A Book of Georgian Folk Tales* (with G. Papashvily, 1946). *Thanks to Noah* (with G. Papashvily, 1951). *Dogs and People* (with G. Papashvily, 1954). *All the Happy Endings: A Study of the Domestic Novel in America, the Women Who Wrote It, the Women Who Read It, in the Nineteenth Century* (1956, 1972). *Louisa May Alcott* (1965). *Russian Cooking* (with G. Papashvily and the editors of Time-Life Books, 1969). *Home, and Home Again* (with G. Papashvily, 1973). *George Papashvily: Sculptor, A Retrospective Catalogue* (1979).

BIBLIOGRAPHY: Cott, N., *Bonds of Womanhood* (1977). Fields, H., in *Saturday Review* (13 Jan. 1945). Wedeck, H., in *NYTBR* (1 Dec. 1946).
   Other references: *Christian Science Monitor* (22 Oct. 1956; 4 Nov. 1965; 17 Oct. 1973). *New Republic* (15 Jan. 1945). *NYHTB* (5 April 1951; 21 Oct. 1956). *NYT* (21 Nov. 1954). *NYTBR* (31 Dec. 1944; 21 Oct. 1956). San Francisco *Chronicle* (8 Nov. 1946). *SatR* (9 Nov. 1946; 10 Nov. 1956).

JANET SHARISTANIAN

Charlotte Blair Parker

B. 1858, Oswego, New York; d. 5 Jan. 1937, Great Neck, New York
Wrote under: Lottie Blair Parker
D. of George and Emily Hitchcock Blair; m. Harry Doel Parker

P.'s earliest theatrical experience was as an actress. She studied for the
stage under Wyzeman Marshall in Boston, performed with the stock
company of the Boston Theatre, and later toured with such major figures
as the Czech tragic actress Mme Janauschek and American actor-
producer of poetic drama Lawrence Barrett. P. married a theatrical manager. She turned to playwriting when *White Roses,* a one-act play she
submitted to a New York *Herald* contest, received honorable mention.

P.'s most popular full-length play was *Way Down East,* which she
wrote in 1897. "Elaborated by Joseph R. Grismer," it opened at the Manhattan Theatre in 1898. Grismer's wife, Phoebe Davis, played the leading
role of Anna Moore in the original production and in the 1903 and 1905
revivals. In 1920, D. W. Griffith paid $175,000 for screen rights to the
melodrama, which was by then considered dated. His film version was
a popular success and an artistic triumph, largely because of the sweetly
expressive face of Lillian Gish.

Critics saw a strong resemblance between *Way Down East* and Steele
MacKaye's 1880 melodrama *Hazel Kirke,* in which P. had once played
the title role. Both plays feature an innocent girl who loves a man above
her station in life and is duped by a sham marriage ceremony. Upon
her learning of her dishonor, Hazel Kirke throws herself into the mill
race. In *Way Down East,* Anna Moore is sent out into a New England
blizzard. In both plays, the heroine is rescued at the last minute and a
reconciliation is effected. The originality of P.'s treatment lies in her use
of "Down East" atmosphere and such comic characters as Hi Holler,
Martha Perkins, and Reuben Whipple.

Under Southern Skies was set in Louisiana in 1875. It opened 12 November 1901, with Grace George in the leading role. True to its reviewer's prediction, the play was a popular success with "that large class of
playgoers who like their color on thick without too much delicacy of
shading, and with no great subtlety in the handling." This criticism was
intended metaphorically, but it might also be noted that several roles

were performed in blackface. As in *Way Down East*, the heroine is caught between a false-hearted cad and an honorable young suitor; again, virtue triumphs.

P.'s third full-length play to reach Broadway was *The Redemption of David Corson*, based upon the novel by Charles Frederic Goss. It opened 8 January 1906 and ran for only sixteen performances.

With the novel *Homespun* (1909), P. returned to a New England village milieu, Yankee characters, and rustic dialect. She used the formula of her stage melodramas—a conflict between a rich scoundrel and a poor-but-honest young man. A review of *Homespun* in the *New York Times* (14 Aug. 1909) sums up her characteristic manner: "It is as moral as a Sunday school tale, and at the end pleases if not surprises the reader by the tableau of virtue triumphant and vice in the dust."

WORKS: *Homespun* (1906).
None of P.'s plays was published, but the New York Public Library has *Way Down East* and *Under Southern Skies* in typescript.

BIBLIOGRAPHY: Parker, L. B., "The Writer's Thoughts concerning her Play," *Green Book Album* (Oct. 1911).
For articles in reference works, see: *NCAB*, 10 and 25.
Other references: New York *Dramatic Mirror* (27 Aug. 1901). *NYT* (8 Feb. 1898; 13 Nov. 1901; 9 Jan. 1906). *The Stage* (Jan. 1937; Aug. 1937).

FELICIA HARDISON LONDRÉ

Dorothy Rothschild Parker

B. *22 Aug. 1893, West End, New Jersey; d. 7 June 1967, New York City*
Wrote under: "Constant Reader," Dorothy Parker, Dorothy Rothschild
D. *of Henry and Eliza A. Marston Rothschild; m. Edwin Pond Parker, 1917;*
   m. Alan Campbell, 1933

P. was the only daughter of a Jewish father and a Scottish mother who died while P. was still an infant. After a very restricted youth and adolescence, P. entered the publishing world in a minor editorial position at *Vogue* in 1916. A year later, she became drama critic for *Vanity Fair* and married Parker, whose name she retained even after their divorce in 1928.

P. became the acknowledged leader of the (Hotel) "Algonquin Round Table," surrounded by such notables as Edna Ferber, Robert Benchley, and Alexander Woollcott. She left *Vanity Fair* in 1926, after her first volume of poetry, *Enough Rope*, became a bestseller.

The opening poems of *Enough Rope* are composed of love lamentations and reiterate the desire for death in a dismal, often dirgelike tone. However, the tender lovers and passive victims soon give way to the carefree adventuress and the jaundiced "flapper." The poems are characterized by regular lines of alternating rhyme and lapidary verse. Romance is often countered by a satiric thrust: "All of my days are gray with yearning. / (Nevertheless, a girl needs fun.)"

Sunset Gun (1928) achieves a solidarity through alternating voices of melancholy and seriousness. The cavalier tone often reveals the comic dimensions of sorrow, but various poems, such as those concerning Mary's pain at the loss of Jesus, touch on the universal nature of tragedy. *Death and Taxes* (1931) emphasizes the artistic integrity of the poetry by moving even further into the realm of the dramatic monologue. The usual caustic verse alternates with statements by various historical and literary figures. The contemplative verse shows a fine mastery of mood and tone and a manipulation of public myths, which places P. far above the level of light entertainer. Poems from all three volumes were collected in *Not So Deep as a Well* (1936).

In 1927, P. began writing stories and a book-review column signed "Constant Reader" for *The New Yorker*. P. wrote for many popular magazines, but her most sustained critical endeavor was the "Constant Reader" column. Like her play reviews of the same period, the forty-six pieces are characterized by an easy conversational tone that seems to effortlessly interweave epigrams, puns, and personal anecdotes. Notwithstanding the subjective mode of approach, sound literary commentary and insightful critical evaluations distinguish most of P.'s work.

P. published stories in *Laments for the Living* (1930) and *After Such Pleasures* and collected them in *Here Lies* (1939). The stories reveal her as a master of cutting, ironic fiction.

"Big Blond," won the O. Henry Prize for 1930. Hazel Morse works hard at being a "good sport." However, when near thirty, she marries Herbie and delights in being able to relax and give in to her moods. Unfortunately, he tires of her and leaves. The need to be a "good sport" again prevails. Hazel is provided for by a succession of men, but always in a mist of alcohol, depressed and longing for peace. The four-part presentation traces the progressive disintegration from contentment through despair over a number of years with an admirable unity of effect. The analogy made between the nonintrospective, passive victim and a "beaten driven, stumbling" horse struggling "to get a footing" is the heart of the narrative and is all the more vivid for the stark rendering of the background details.

"A Telephone Call" (1930) provides a striking example of P.'s proficiency in the modified stream-of-consciousness technique. As a woman futilely awaits a promised telephone call, the shifting phases of desperation and pain are revealed through a superb rhetorical display that encompasses rushing prayers, meandering introspections, and angry threats.

"Clothe the Naked" (1939) concerns Big Lannie, a stoic black laundress whose only surviving daughter dies in childbirth leaving her with a blind grandson. The distanced narrative tone imparts a sense of sustained suffering throughout.

Although P.'s reputation has suffered a sharp decline, the literary merit of her short stories and much of her poetry can scarcely be contested. The perennial concerns of alienation and loss of love are treated with an irony that only barely masks the sense of deep tragedy beneath. The economy of language, flawless dialogue, and sharp eye for detail that characterize the short stories is directly attributable to P.'s poetic sense. The crystalline, concise sentences set the tone and sum up the characters as aptly as the measured, polished verse.

WORKS: *Enough Rope* (1926). *Sunset Gun* (1928). *Laments for the Living* (1930). *Death and Taxes* (1931). *After Such Pleasures* (1933). *Not So Deep as a Well* (1936). *Here Lies* (1939). *Dorothy Parker* (1944).

BIBLIOGRAPHY: Keats, J., *You Might As Well Live: The Life and Times of Dorothy Parker* (1972). Wilson E., *Classics and Commercials* (1950).

Other references: *EJ* 23 (1934). *Esquire* 70 (1968). *Horizon* 4 (1962). *Paris Review* 13 (1956). *Poetry* (30, 1927; 33, 1928; 39, 1931). *Rendezvous* 3 (1968). *Revue de Paris* 54 (1947).

FRANCINE SHAPIRO PUK

Elsie Worthington Clews Parsons

B. 27 Nov. 1875, New York City; d. 19 Dec. 1971, New York City
Wrote under: John Main
D. of Henry and Lucy Madison Clews; m. Herbert Parsons, 1900

P. was the daughter of wealthy and socially prominent parents. She was educated in New York City, receiving from Columbia University a B.A. in 1896, M.A. in 1897, and Ph.D. in 1899. In 1900, she married a New York attorney who became a Congressman and a leader in the Republican Party. The marriage lasted until his death in 1925 and seems to have been unusual in the degree of autonomy P. achieved within it. There were six children born of this marriage, four of whom survived P.

Primarily a researcher and writer, P. taught only briefly, from 1899 to 1905 at Barnard College and then at the New School for Social Research in 1919. But her professional achievements were well recognized: She presided over the American Folklore Society (1918), the American Ethnological Association (1923–25), and the American Anthropological Association (1940–41); she was also associate editor of the *Journal of American Folklore* (1910–1941) and vice-president of the New York Academy of Sciences (1936).

P.'s career may be divided into two periods, the first beginning in 1899 when she undertook speculative work in sociology, committed to the belief that individuals have the right to self-development, and that civilized society must allow for and benefit from such development. Occasionally, P.'s objective observations of her own society made readers uncomfortable. For example, a college textbook titled *The Family* (1906) attracted unusual attention because it was directed at both students and "intelligent mothers" of daughters, and discussed not only the family but also the inequities of the double standard and the advantages of trial marriage.

P.'s next five books also dealt with social oppression, but from a broader perspective. *The Old-fashioned Woman* (1913) is a book written with wit and quiet irony. Here P. reviews attitudes and customs relating to women in so-called primitive societies and in her own society so that the limitations of her society are revealed as being painfully like the limitations of primitive societies. In *Social Freedom* (1915) P. explores the negative effects of such social categorization by age and sex on the development of individual personality. In *Social Rule* (1916) she argues that social categories are used as a way of controlling such groups as women, children, employees, and "backward peoples." Of special interest in this book is P.'s view of the ideal role of feminism.

The second stage of P.'s career began about 1915, when she became interested in the anthropological approach of Franz Boas. P. did not abandon her commitment to self-development, but turned from speculating about the way society functioned to collecting ethnographic data that could indicate how a specific culture functioned. After 1915, P. undertook at least one field trip a year to study various groups, though her chief work was done with American and West Indian blacks and with Indians of the southwest Pueblos. On occasion, she returned to her earlier speculations and her interest in feminist-related issues when she wrote journal articles.

Boas and other anthropologists cite two works of this period as having special significance—*Pueblo Indian Religion* (1939) and *Mitla: Town of the Souls, and Other Zapoteco-speaking Pueblos of Oaxaca, Mexico* (1936)—but these books are aimed at the specialist reader.

Vital to any assessment of P. is a consideration of her character, which was marked by an uncompromising commitment to her work and to living in accordance with her beliefs. She was, Boas wrote: "intolerant towards [herself], tolerant towards others, disdainful of selfish pettiness and truthful in thought and action." So strong was her personality that Robert Herrick, a novelist of the period, used it as the basis for several characterizations in *Wanderings* (1925), *Chimes* (1926), and *The End of Desire* (1932).

Since P.'s death, her work has attracted little general attention, though at the time of her death the value of her work and the significance of her support of the American Folklore Society and of the field work of other anthropologists were acknowledged by many.

WORKS: *Educational Legislation and Administration of the Colonial Governments* (1899). *The Family* (1906). *The Old-fashioned Woman* (1913). *Religious Chastity* (1913). *Fear and Conventionality* (1914). *Social Freedom: A Study of the Conflicts between Social Classifications and Personality* (1915). *Social Rule: A Study of the Will to Power* (1916). *Notes on Zuñi* (1917). *Folk-tales of Andros Island, Bahamas* (1918). *Notes on Ceremonialism at Laguna* (1920). *Winter and Summer Dance Series in Zuñi in 1918* (1922). *Folk-lore from the Cape Verde Islands* (1923). *Folk-lore of the Sea Islands, South Carolina* (1923). *Laguna Genealogies* (1923). *The Scalp Ceremonial of*

Zuñi (1924). *The Pueblo of Jemez* (1925). *Tewa Tales* (1926). *Kiowa Tales* (1929). *The Social Organization of the Tewa of New Mexico* (1929). *Isleta, New Mexico* (1932). *Folk-lore of the Antilles, French and English* (1933). *Hopi and Zuñi Ceremonialism* (1933). *Mitla: Town of the Souls, and Other Zapoteco-speaking Pueblos of Oaxaca, Mexico* (1936). *Taos Pueblo* (1936). *Pueblo Indian Religion* (2 vols, 1939). *Taos Tales* (1940). *Notes on the Caddo* (1941). *Pequche, Canton of Otavelo, Province of Imbabura Ecuador: A Study of Andean Indians* (1945).

BIBLIOGRAPHY: Boas, F., in *The Scientific Monthly* 54 (May 1942).

Other references: *American Anthropologist* 45 (1943). *Journal of American Folk-lore* 56 (1943). *Proceedings of the American Philosophical Society* 94 (1950).

PHYLLIS FRANKLIN

Frances Theodora Smith Dana Parsons

B. 5 Dec. 1861, New York City; d. 10 June 1952, Katonah, New York
Wrote under: Mrs. William Starr Dana, Frances Theodora Parsons
D. of N. Denton and Harriet Shelton Smith; m. William Starr Dana, 1884;
m. James Russell Parsons, Jr., 1896

P. was brought up and educated in New York City. During summers P. developed her lifelong love of the outdoors at her maternal grandparents' home at Newburgh. After the loss of her first husband, a naval officer many years her senior, P. turned to nature writing. She gave up writing after 1899 to devote herself to other interests. After the accidental death of her second husband, an educator, in 1905, P. became a campaign worker in the suffrage movement. With the success of the campaign, she moved into Republican politics. P. had two children, a son and a daughter.

P.'s most popular work was *How to Know the Wildflowers* (1893). Basically a guidebook, arranged by flower colors, it not only describes a plant and gives botanical data but also tells where to find it. P. was not an authority on flowers, but she saw that a guidebook was needed and proposed the project to her publishers. The 1890s saw the real beginnings of the conservation movement, which today dominates popular nature sentiment, and the book was the first of many such books published during that decade.

According to Season (1894) is a collection of essays about wildflowers that first appeared in the New York *Tribune*. This volume makes a nice supplement to the more scientific *How to Know the Wildflowers*, with informal descriptions of the flowers.

The study of botany by children was especially encouraged in the 19th c. *Plants and Their Children* (1896), a charming, informal volume, is P.'s contribution to this field. In a series of essays on topics like "Seed Sailboats," P. introduces the child to botany and nature study in an interesting and unpatronizing way.

During the early years of her second marriage, P.'s husband had financial problems, and so she wrote a companion volume to her wildflower guide, called *How to Know the Ferns* (1899). This volume was well received.

Perchance Some Day, P.'s privately printed autobiography, was published in 1951. This book gives insight into the life of a gifted, spirited woman of the eastern aristocracy, but does not dwell on P.'s personal life. Instead, P. portrays a way of life and tells inside stories of political intrigue. As an intimate of the Roosevelt family, P. was well placed to talk about the jockeying for position that went on in state Republican circles. Occasionally P. comments on the position of women or their interests, often seeming surprised at the lack of masculine support for women's rights.

P. was not a serious botanist or naturalist, but her organizing abilities, thoroughness, and common sense made her books successful. Politics and nature make an interesting combination in her writings.

WORKS: *How to Know the Wildflowers* (1893). *According to Season* (1894). *Plants and Their Children* (1896). *How to Know the Ferns* (1899). *Perchance Some Day* (1951).

BIBLIOGRAPHY: *NYT* (11 June 1952).

BEVERLY SEATON

Louella Oettinger Parsons

B. 6 Aug. 1893, Freeport, Illinois; d. 9 Dec. 1972, Beverly Hills, California
D. of Joshua and Helen Wilcox Oettinger; m. John Parsons, 1910;
m. Dr. Harry Martin, 1931

As a youngster, P. showed an interest in writing and had her first story published in the Freeport *Journal-Standard* before she reached high-school age. While in high school, P. acquired her first newspaper job, working as the dramatic editor and assistant to the city editor on the Dixon, Illinois, *Morning Star*. P. received most of her journalism education through such practical experiences.

In 1910, P. married a real-estate agent. The couple soon moved to Burlington, Iowa, where P. became frustrated and bored. After the birth of a daughter in 1911, P. left with the child to visit an uncle in Montana. From then on, P. and her husband drifted apart.

After the death of her husband in 1914, P. took her daughter to Chicago and worked as a reporter for the *Tribune*. P. soon became involved in the movie business and took a job with the Essanay Company reading scripts and writing scenarios.

P. was later able to convince the Chicago *Record-Herald* to run a series of her articles on how to write for the movies. These articles were well received, and P. realized that if people were interested in a behind-the-scenes look at films, they would also be interested in a more surface view—a look at the movie stars.

In 1918, P. moved with her daughter to New York City. She became the movie critic for the *Morning Telegraph*, where she remained until 1924. During her five years with the *Telegraph*, P. was made editor of the motion picture section and was presented with an all-female staff nicknamed the "Persian Garden of Cats."

P. started writing for the Hearst papers in 1924. In 1925, P. discovered that she had tuberculosis; she spent a year (on full salary) resting. After she recovered from the illness, Hearst sent P. to California, and she wrote her stories from Hollywood. At this time P.'s column became syndicated.

In 1931, P.'s work expanded to the broadcast field when she was hired by the Sunkist Orange Company to do a thirteen-week radio show. She began a second radio show in 1934, on which she interviewed movie stars. For four years, "Hollywood Hotel" was one of the leading radio programs.

Throughout the 1940s, P. continued to write her column, which was by then widely syndicated. Even at the age of sixty-four, P. was still doing a weekly radio show, writing her column, covering hard news events, writing stories for *Photoplay* and *Modern Screen*, and reviewing movies for *Cosmopolitan*. She retired in 1964.

Besides writing columns and doing radio shows, P. was also the author of three books. The first, *How to Write for the Movies*, was published in 1915 and used as a text in early film classes at Ohio State University. With the advent of the "talkie," however, the book became dated.

The Gay Illiterate (1944) is a delightful account of P.'s life until 1939. P.'s entertaining style of writing makes the book a pleasure to read even today.

Tell It to Louella (1961) is an account of some of P.'s more memorable celebrity interviews. Her quick and often acerbic wit provides greater insight into P.'s life and personality than into the personalities of the stars she covered.

P. was the first widely read gossip columnist in the U.S. She once wrote that she would "do almost anything" in order to get a scoop. Her columns were largely devoted to interviews with the most popular movie stars and reports on weddings, divorces, and births; she was most proud of "scooping" the divorces of famous stars. P. maintained a colorful reputation throughout her career.

WORKS: *How to Write for the Movies* (1915). *The Gay Illiterate* (1944). *Tell It to Louella* (1961).

BIBLIOGRAPHY: Eells, G., *Hedda and Louella* (1972).
For articles in reference works, see: *CA* 37 (1973). *CB* (1940).

SANDRA CARLIN

Sara Payson Willis Parton

B. 9 July 1811, Portland, Maine; d. 10 Oct. 1872, New York City
Wrote under: Olivia Branch, Fanny Fern
D. of Nathaniel and Hannah Parker Willis; m. Charles Eldredge, 1837;
m. Samuel Farrington, 1849; m. James Parton, 1856

P. preferred her talented mother to her harsh, narrowly religious father; she believed that her mother would have distinguished herself in literature had she not had such a large family. P. said her pen name, "Fanny Fern," was inspired by happy childhood memories of her mother picking sweet fern leaves.

When P. was a small child, her family moved to Boston, where her father established a religious newspaper. P. attended Boston schools and Catharine Beecher's famous seminary in Hartford, Connecticut, at the time when Harriet Beecher was a student teacher. Despite a lack of studiousness, P. wrote witty essays at the Beecher school and on her return to Boston contributed to her father's new publication, *Youth's Companion*.

In 1884, P.'s mother died, and in the next two years she lost the older of her three daughters and her first husband, a bank cashier. P. was reduced to relative poverty, with only grudging support from her father and in-laws. She tried marriage to a Boston merchant, but he soon left her. Although P. attempted to forget her second marriage, never directly referring to it, she later used Farrington as a model for one of her characters. In *Rose Clark* (1856), a "hypocrite" and "gross sensualist" tricks a reluctant widow into marriage and then slanders her and leaves her penniless.

When P. failed in her attempts to earn a living teaching and sewing, she appealed unsuccessfully to her brother, a successful poet and editor in New York, for help in launching a literary career. P. began to write short sketches, and by 1851 she was placing her work in small Boston magazines. Her magazine pieces were so popular that in 1853 J. C. Derby published a collection of them as *Fern Leaves from Fanny's Portfolio*. P. continued the next year with a second series and a juvenile, *Little Ferns for Fanny's Little Friends*. The three books sold an astonishing 180,000 copies in America and England, and P. was suddenly rich and famous.

Based very closely upon P.'s own experience, *Ruth Hall* (1855) recounts the struggles of a widow to support herself and her children. Ruth Hall finds few opportunities open to women and is treated shabbily by her relatives, who can tolerate neither a passive dependent nor the successful and assertive writer Ruth finally becomes. *Ruth Hall* caused a sensation in the literary world. P. had apparently thought herself protected by her pseudonym and neglected to disguise the characters, who were obviously based on P.'s relatives. P.'s true identity was discovered and the family quarrel aired in public.

Ruth Hall was admired by Hawthorne, and attacked by the critics for the same reasons he praised it—its lack of restraint and "female delicacy"; one critic referred to it as "Ruthless Hall." Soon after the publication of *Ruth Hall*, the anonymous *Life and Beauties of Fanny Fern* appeared, satirizing P. as a spendthrift, adventuress, and ingrate to her family.

In the meantime, P. moved to New York City and was engaged by Robert Bonner, publisher of the New York *Ledger*, to write a weekly column for the then outlandish sum of $100 a week. For the next twenty years, P. wrote weekly for the *Ledger*, never missing a column. P. lived a relatively quiet life with her third husband, James Parton, a well-known biographer eleven years her junior.

After *Ruth Hall*, P. wrote only one more novel, *Rose Clark* (1856), but her talent was not for fiction, and after *Rose Clark* she stuck with the form she was best at—the informal essay, sometimes lightly fictionalized but always short. She published several collections of these from her *Ledger* columns.

Because her early work is best known, P. has been mistakenly classified as a sentimentalist. However, P.'s writing changed and developed significantly after her initial success. In the first series of *Fern Leaves* there are two parts: the first, which comprises about three quarters of the book, is indeed lachrymose, but the remaining quarter consists of humorous and satirical pieces. In the second series of *Fern Leaves* the proportion is exactly reversed.

In *Folly as It Flies* (1859), P. adopted a new voice, which she would maintain for the rest of her career. Her sentimentality and heavy-handed satire give way to relaxed, humorous philosophizing. She abandons the artificiality and straining for effect of her earlier pieces, and writes more naturally and spontaneously. While P.'s staple continued to be everyday domestic topics, like child care and the annoying habits of husbands, she became conscious of social conditions in New York City and began to depict poverty, prostitution, exploitation of workers, and prison life.

P. also became more direct and outspoken in her championship of women. Women's estate and the relationship between the sexes had always been P.'s major subject, but in her early fiction she protested injustice to women by portraying them as passive victims of male brutality. By the end of the 1850s, P. came to support the women's rights movement and encourage her readers to seek suffrage, better education, and wider fields of endeavor.

WORKS: *Fern Leaves from Fanny's Portfolio* (English title, *Shadows and Sunbeams;* 1st series, 1853; 2nd series, 1854). *Little Ferns for Fanny's Little Friends* (1854). *Ruth Hall* (1855). *Rose Clark* (1856). *Fresh Leaves* (1857). *Play-Day Book* (1857). *Folly as It Flies* (1859). *A New Story Book for Children* (1864). *Ginger-Snaps* (1870). *Caper-Sauce* (1872). *Fanny Fern: A Memorial Volume* (Ed. J. Parton, 1873).

BIBLIOGRAPHY: Adams, F. B., *Fanny Fern* (1966). Derby, J. C., *Fifty Years Among Authors, Books and Publishers* (1884). *The Life and Beauties of Fanny Fern* (1855).

For articles in reference works, see: *NAW* (article by E. B. Schlesinger).

Other references: *AL* (Nov. 1957). *Biblion* (Spring 1969). *Colophon* (Sept. 1939). *NY Historical Society Quarterly* (Oct. 1954). *WS* 1 (1972).

BARBARA A. WHITE

Frances Gray Patton

B. *19 March 1906, Raleigh, North Carolina*
D. *of Robert Lilly and Mary S. MacRae Gray; m. Lewis Patton, 1927*

Doubtlessly influenced by her family's literary bent (her father and brothers were journalists, and her mother published occasional pieces), P. began writing for her high school newspaper and continued on through a play-writing fellowship at the University of North Carolina in Chapel Hill. She wrote the Carolina Playmakers' opening play in 1925, and another play published in a volume that also contains Thomas Wolfe's first known work. A fourth-generation North Carolinian, P. married a University of North Carolina English professor in 1927, had three children, and continues to reside in Durham.

During the 1940s and 1950s, P.'s short stories appeared in magazines such as *Harper's*, *The New Yorker*, and *McCall's*. Her first book, *The*

Finer Things in Life (1951), is composed of reprints of these simple stories of small-town southern life. Whether openly employing the first person or relating the problems of the Potter family—college professor, wife, and three children—these tales are primarily low-keyed autobiographical sketches lacking energy, substance, or depth of character. Only when P. places some distance between herself and the subject does she succeed in generating a feeling of involvement through a fine use of dialogue and local color. "A Nice Name" won a Society of Intercultural Education award for its fine portrayal of the reactions of a group of young southern matrons when they learn that the charming, intellectual "pen-pal" they had all thought "wonderful" and "bril-l-iant" is black. "The *Terrible* Miss Dove" is the seminal episode of the subsequent novel and is highly successful in characterization and tone.

P.'s second volume of short stories, *A Piece of Luck* (1955), shows a greater mastery of form and language. The autobiographical strain has been submerged, and the southern setting serves to illuminate rather than define the characters, as in the first volume. The various shifts of narrative perspective and the ironic detachment give this volume considerable substance. The masculine revenge of "The Homunculus" and the sorrow at the end of "The Game" of Maria, who has "nothing pure and beautiful left to love," are delicately depicted and sensitively rendered. The fine use of dialogue, gentle irony, and vivid delineation of character convey "a time when life, for all its troubles, had been sweet and juicy in the mouth."

P.'s greatest achievement is her only novel, *Good Morning, Miss Dove* (1954). Highly successful in both America and England, this work has been justly dubbed a minor classic. Although the story is overly sentimentalized, the great force of the general impression is sustained through the successful depiction of both small-town life and the monolithic character of the "terrible Miss Dove"—the sixth grade geography teacher who "caused children to flex their moral muscle." As "the public conscience of Liberty Hill," Miss Dove has placed her stamp on almost every person in town. Each of them has spent a period under her tutelage, "where no leeway was given to the personality"; and in her room one was "sustained by the classic simplicity of inflexible rights and wrongs." Miss Dove is a dedicated pedagogue who believes that each child's character is in her keeping. She attempts to prepare the children for the "inescapable perils of independent thinking" and to show them that "life demanded all the disciplined courage and more, that one could bring to it." Through the use of flashbacks, rhetorical questions, and multicharacter psychological intrusions, the personality of Miss Dove, her life, and the impact on her pupils are portrayed in a matter-of-fact tone with occasional ironic thrusts that balance the sentimental tendencies of the narrative.

Although P. seeks to illustrate the "vein-structure of human life" through a moment of illumination, most of her stories fall short through a lack of substance—the mundaneness of the insight or the inconsequence of the character. At her best, P. judiciously balances the simultaneous planes of humor and tragedy while ironically exposing the foibles and nobility of human nature. These successful moments in a half-dozen stories and her novel have secured P.'s place in American letters.

WORKS: *The Finer Things in Life* (1951). *Good Morning, Miss Dove* (1954; film version, 1955). *A Piece of Luck* (1955). *Twenty-Eight Stories* (1969).

BIBLIOGRAPHY: NYHT (9 Dec. 1951; 2 Oct. 1955; 31 Oct. 1954). *NYT* (16 Oct. 1955). *SatR* (6 Nov. 1954). San Francisco *Chronicle* (8 Nov. 1951).
                                                                    FRANCINE SHAPIRO PUK

Elizabeth Palmer Peabody

B. *16 May 1804, Billerica, Massachusetts; d. 3 Jan. 1894, Boston, Massachusetts*
D. *of Nathaniel and Elizabeth Palmer Peabody*

The oldest of seven children, P. was educated by her mother, whose school for local children in Salem, Massachusetts, was dedicated to the principle that every child should be treated as a genius. In 1822, P. opened her own school in Boston and established her friendship with Ralph Waldo Emerson, who tutored her in Greek. The school failed, and after two years as a private governess P. opened a school in Brookline, a Boston suburb.

Always responsive to "genius," P. soon established two more significant friendships. The first, with William Ellery Channing, whose daughter was enrolled in P.'s school, shaped P.'s views on education, philosophy, and religion. P. eventually became Channing's editor and prepared many of his sermons for the press. Friendship with Bronson Alcott, a leading Transcendental philosopher, led P. to give up her own school and become his assistant in an experimental school in Boston.

Record of a School (1835) suggests the idealistic philosophy she and Alcott shared. The second edition (1836) attempts to answer the popular outcry against Alcott's discussion of childbirth in a conversation with the school children. Although his concern was to account for the creation of the individual soul, Victorian Boston was outraged that he should have discussed childbirth at all. P. defended Alcott, but withdrew from his school and in July 1840 opened a bookshop in Boston, which soon became a center for the Transcendental movement. Here Margaret Fuller held her conversations with women, the so-called Transcendental Club met, and its journal—*The Dial*—was published. When *The Dial* failed, it was succeeded by P.'s short-lived journal, *Aesthetic Papers*. Though influential, the bookshop did not prosper, and closed in 1850.

P. taught for a time and through the 1850s campaigned for the adoption of Jozef Bem's chronological history charts in elementary and secondary schools. She also traveled widely to speak in favor of the abolition of slavery. In 1859, P. became acquainted with the system of kindergarten education developed by Friedrich Froebel in Germany. From then to the end of her life, often assisted by her sister Mary Tyler Peabody Mann, P. devoted herself to establishing kindergartens and recruiting kindergarten teachers throughout the U.S. In her eighties, still vigorous, P. lectured successfully at Bronson Alcott's Concord School of Philosophy.

Although she was learned and widely read, P. was not an effective writer. Pieces like her "Plan of the West Roxbury Community" (*The Dial*, March 1844) and "Language" (*Aesthetic Papers*, 1849) suffer from the vague, inflated diction often characteristic of Transcendental essays. *Record of a School* has historical significance as a journal of Alcott's attempt to elicit evidence of an awareness of the Soul from very young children. P.'s writings on kindergartens, especially *The Moral Culture of Infancy* (with her sister, 1863) indicate the connection between Transcendentalism and this significant movement in modern education. P.'s warm personal enthusiasms are reflected in her memoirs of Channing (*Reminiscences of William Ellery Channing, D.D.*, 1877) and the painter Washington Allston (*Last Evening with Allston*, 1886).

P. was "an intellectual spinster who lived to become a Boston institution," according to Perry Miller (*The Transcendentalists*, 1950). Stout and plain, P. was eccentric and careless of her appearance. In old age, she is said to have traveled with no luggage but a toothbrush in her pocket and a nightgown under her dress. She is assumed to be the model for Miss Birdseye in Henry James's *The Bostonians* (1886).

P. was a central figure in the Transcendental movement, the only woman other than Margaret Fuller to make a considerable intellectual contribution in this religious and philosophic forum. She was fortunate in her friendships with Jones Very, Horace Mann, and Nathaniel Hawthorne (who married her sister Sophia). P.'s lifelong interest in the development and education of young children stimulated others to contribute to this field.

WORKS: *First Steps to the Study of History* by J. M. Gerando (edited by Peabody, 1832). *Self-Education* (1832). *Key to History* (1833). *The Water-Spirit* (1833). *Record of a School* (1835). *Method of Spiritual Culture* (1836). *Aesthetic Papers* (edited by Peabody, 1849). *First Nursery Reading Book* (1849). *Blank Centuries Accompanying the Manual of the Polish-American System of Chronology* (1850). *Crimes of the House of Austria Against Mankind* (1852). *Chronological History of the United States* (1856). *A Sunday School Hymn Book* (1857). *Memorial of . . . Wesselhöft* (1859). *Universal History* (1859). *American Kindergarten* (with M. T. P. Mann, 1863). *The Moral Culture of Infancy* (with M. T. P. Mann, 1863). *A Plea for Froebel's Kindergartens* (1869). *Blank Centuries for Monographs of History* (1870). *The Kindergarten Messenger* (edited by Peabody, 1873–77). *Lectures on the Nursery and Kindergarten* (1874). *Record of Mr. Alcott's School* (1874). *Manual of Universal History* (1875). *Kindergartens* (1876). *Reminiscences of Rev. William Ellery Channing* (1877). *After Kindergarten—What?* (1878). *Female Education in Massachusetts* (1884). *Last Evening with Allston, and Other Papers* (1886). *Lectures in the Training Schools for Kindergarten* (1886). *Education in the Home, Kindergarten, and Primary School* (1887). *The Piutes* (1887). *Mother-Play and Nursery Songs* by F. W. Froebel (edited by Peabody, 1906).

BIBLIOGRAPHY: Baylor, R., "The Contribution of Elizabeth Palmer Peabody to Kindergarten Education in the United States," (Ph.D. diss., N. Y. Univ., 1960). Bilbo, Q. N., "Elizabeth Palmer Peabody, Transcendentalist," (Ph.D. diss., New York University, 1932). Gohdes, L. F., *The Periodicals of American Transcendentalism* (1931). Miller, P., *The Transcendentalists* (1950). Tharp, L. H., *The Peabody Sisters of Salem* (1950).
Other references: *New England Quarterly* (Sept. 1942).

JANE BENARDETE

Josephine Preston Peabody

B. 30 May 1874, Brooklyn, New York; d. 4 Dec. 1922, Cambridge,
 Massachusetts
D. of Charles and Susan Morrill Peabody; m. Lionel S. Marks, 1906

Both P.'s parents were from Massachusetts families. When P.'s father
died in 1884, she moved with her mother and elder sister to her maternal grandmother's house in Dorchester, Massachusetts. P. spent the remainder of her life, except for vacations and several trips abroad, in Dorchester and, later, Cambridge.

P.'s diary, kept from age sixteen until her death, describes a life
somewhat devoid of companionship and certainly of luxuries. P. early
learned to love the theater, literature, and music, however; as a young
woman, she saved for standing room at concerts and plays or for the
purchase of a long-desired book. P.'s health was not robust, and writing—
mainly poetry—was her greatest joy during a rather lonely girlhood.

P. left Girls' Latin School in Boston in her junior year, owing to ill
health. She attended Radcliffe College from 1894 to 1896, and lectured
on English Literature at Wellesley College from 1901 to 1903. In 1906, she
married a professor of engineering at Harvard.

P. began sending poems to magazines and journals during her school
years. In 1887 and 1888, several were published; and in successive years,
P.'s work appeared regularly in *Atlantic Monthly, Scribner's,* and other
periodicals. *Old Greek Folk Stories* was published in 1897, and *The Wayfarers,* P.'s first volume of poetry, in 1898. *Portrait of Mrs. W—* (1922),
a play about Mary Wollstonecraft and William Godwin, was published
the year of her death.

Despite household and maternal obligations (P. bore a daughter in
1908 and a son in 1910), and in the face of rapidly failing health, P. continued to write and work for causes she believed in. P. expressed her
conviction that peace and a more humane social order might be
achieved if women could have equality of influence and participation in
world affairs. Her last volume of poems, *Harvest Moon* (1916), expresses
despair at war's harvest: the blood shed by children women have borne,
reared, and loved.

P.'s writing reflects her deepest interests: the literature of the past and
especially of the English Renaissance, nature, and the rights of all men

and women to lead joyous, fulfilling lives. Her Greek tales and her poems for children—*The Book of the Little Past* (1908), for example—have a directness and simplicity that charms. P.'s verse dramas are credited with having revived interest in the traditional English blank-verse drama, but they are of concern chiefly to literary historians today. *Marlowe* (1901), an imaginative play about the Renaissance dramatist and poet, and *The Piper* (1909), an idealized version of the Pied Piper legend, are perhaps the most successful of these efforts. *The Piper* won the Stratford Play Competition in 1910, and was produced in both Stratford and London.

The vibrant idealism of P.'s personality finds expression in her work, but unfortunately this idealism is not supported by a down-to-earth grappling with reality or by the intellectual rigor of argument. As a result, there is a quality of immaturity to P.'s writing which deprives it of force and limits its appeal.

WORKS: *Old Greek Folk Stories* (1897). *The Wayfarers* (1898). *Fortune and Men's Eyes* (1900). *Marlowe* (1901; produced, 1905). *The Singing Leaves* (1903). *Pan* (1904). *The Wings* (1907; produced, 1912). *The Book of the Little Past* (1908). *The Piper* (1909; produced, 1910). *The Singing Man* (1911). *The Wolf of Gubbio* (1913). *Harvest Moon* (1916). *The Chameleon* (1917). *Portrait of Mrs. W—* (1922). *Diary and Letters of Josephine Preston Peabody* (Ed. C. Baker, 1925). *Collected Poems of Josephine Preston Peabody* (Ed. K. Bates, 1927).

BIBLIOGRAPHY: Baker C., *Diary and Letters of Josephine Preston Peabody* (1925). Bates, K., in *Collected Poems of Josephine Preston Peabody* (1927). Dickason, D., *The Daring Young Men* (1953). Gregory, H., and M. Zaturenska, *History of American Poetry, 1900–1940* (1942).

For articles in reference works, see: *NAW* (article by J. Baird, Jr.). *20thCAS.*

Other references: *Atlantic* (Dec. 1927). *SatR* (20 Mar. 1926). *NYT* (5 Dec. 1922).

ANN PRINGLE ELIASBERG

Elia Wilkinson Peattie

B. *1862, Kalamazoo, Michigan; d. 12 July 1935, Wellington, Vermont*
Wrote under: Elia W. Peattie, Sade Iverson
Given name: Elia Wilkinson
M. Robert Burns Peattie, 1883

P.'s family moved from Michigan to Chicago shortly after the 1871 fire. They built a comfortable house, in which P. and her husband later raised their own children.

In 1884, P. became the first "girl reporter" on the Chicago *Tribune*. After ten years in Omaha, where P. wrote pot-boiler histories and her best stories while her husband managed the *World-Herald*, P. returned to Chicago in 1898, when she bore their third son. A daughter died in childhood; all three sons survived their parents, two becoming writers who married writers.

From 1901 to 1917, P. was Chicago *Tribune* literary critic, while also publishing prolifically. Invitations to the Peatties' Sunday afternoon gatherings represented acceptance into the Chicago literary establishment.

P. left Chicago in 1917, when her husband joined the *New York Times*. They retired to Tryon, North Carolina, in 1920, where P. remained after his death in 1930.

Many of P.'s publications were primarily commercial ventures. *The Story of America* (1889) has neither original interpretation nor careful writing to recommend it, yet P. published several editions and adaptations. Similarly commercial were the two poetry anthologies that the *Tribune*'s influential literary critic edited in 1903.

P.'s other historical works reflect her involvement in Chicago's cultural "uplift" movement. Her early historical romances and romanticized histories promoted the cultural establishment's fascination with knighthood's European flowering. P.'s one-act costume pageant of women's changing status from mythological to modern times, *Times and Manners* (1918), was written specifically for a Chicago Woman's Club production.

P.'s involvement with club theatricals also inspired several fine one-act plays late in her career. The title piece of *The Wander Weed* (1923) is probably her best, dealing with a Blue Ridge mountain girl's encounter with a sphinxlike old woman who breaks silence to convince Lu Constant of the need to accept the pains and joys of ongoing family relationships.

Family settings and themes are the common denominators for P.'s girls' books. *Azalea* (1912) is representative; its young heroine forsakes nomadic circus adventures for the everyday continuities and domestic affections of small-town family life. Such small-town virtues also win out over artistic ambition and urban wealth in *Lotta Embury's Career* (1915) and *Sarah Brewster's Relatives* (1916).

The best of P.'s early magazine short stories, collected in *A Mountain Woman* (1896), call domestic sentimentality into question. In "Jim Lancy's Waterloo," newly married Annie Lancy confronts the hard facts of premature aging and madness among neighboring Nebraska wives and of infant death in her own home. Generally, the *Mountain Woman* stories embody a conviction that city and frontier pose irreconcilable cultures, engendering psychic disorientation for intercultural migrants.

Similarly critical of domestic sentimentality are P.'s two adult novels. An implicitly erotic relationship between father and daughter informs the violent action of *The Judge* (1890), while *The Precipice* (1914) exposes patriarchal tyranny and neighborly hypocrisy underlying small-town family life. Nonetheless, Kate Barrington's search for independence in *The Precipice* is undercut by her friends' dramatizations of feminine limitations and the joys of motherhood. Kate's own social-work activities—modeled on those of Julia Lathrop, first head of the U.S. Children's Bureau—remain in the novel's background. The organizing marriage-versus-career theme ultimately resolves itself ambiguously in Kate's decision to relinquish "prideful" independence for marital commitment, yet to subordinate "womanly" fulfillment to civic duty by living in Washington, D.C., apart from her husband.

A few of P.'s short stories and one-act plays are fully realized literary works, and *The Precipice* is fascinating in its treatment of feminist issues. However, P.'s career was ultimately compromised by easy commercial productions and thematic contradictions. As a critic and romancer, she upheld derivative genteel standards of "noble" thoughts and "classic" forms. Yet her best fictions and plays are realistic, and "The Milliner" (1914), a pseudonymous free verse poem for *The Little Review*, met with deserved acclaim.

WORKS: *The Story of America* (1889; rev. eds., 1892, 1896; reprinted as *America in Peace and War*, 1898). *A Journey through Wonderland* (1890). *The Judge* (1890). *With Scrip and Staff* (1891). *The American Peasant* (with T. Tibbles, 1892). *A Mountain Woman* (1896). *Our Chosen Land* (1896). *The Pictorial Story of America* (1896). *Pippins and Cheese* (1897). *The Love of a Calaban: A Romantic Opera* (1898; adapted by E. Freer as *Massimillano*, 1925). *The Shape of Fear, and Other Ghostly Stories* (1898). *Ickery Ann, and Other Boys and Girls* (1899). *The Beleaguered Forest* (1901). *How Jacques Came into the Forest of Arden* (1901). *Castle, Knight, and Troubador* (1903). *The Edges of Things* (1903). *Poems You Ought to Know* (edited by Peattie, 1903). *To Comfort You* (edited by Peattie, 1903). *Edda and the Oak* (1911). *Azalea* (1912). *Annie Laurie and Azalea* (1913). *Azalea at Sunset Gap* (1914). *The Precipice* (1914). *The Angel with a Broom* (1915). *Azalea's Silver Web* (1915). *Lotta Embury's Career* (1915). *Sarah Brewster's Relatives* (1916). *The Newcomers* (1917). *Painted Windows* (1918). *Times and Manners* (1918). *The Wander Weed, and Seven Other Little Theater Plays* (1923). *The Great Delusion* (1932). *The Book of the Fine Arts Building* (n.d.).

BIBLIOGRAPHY: *Atlantic* 83 (1899). *Bookman* (April 1914; Jan. 1916). Boston *Transcript* (18 Feb. 1914). *NYT* (24 Dec. 1916).

SIDNEY H. BREMER

Louise Redfield Peattie

B. *14 June 1900, Northern Illinois*
Writes under: Louise Redfield Peattie
D. *of Robert and Bertha Dreier Redfield; m. Donald Culross Peattie, 1923*

P.'s father was a prominent corporation lawyer, and her mother was the daughter of the Danish consul in Chicago. They gave P. a very happy childhood, much of it spent on the extensive farm where she was born—an estate that had been established by P.'s ancestors several generations back. P. was educated by tutors and in private schools in Chicago. P.'s marriage to the naturalist-writer Donald Culross Peattie has been a very happy one, although the couple's only daughter died young. There are three sons.

The family has lived in various places: Washington, D.C., Provence and the French Riviera, P.'s childhood home, and Tryon, North Carolina. They finally settled in Santa Barbara, California. All these places have given P. colorful settings for the fiction she began to write shortly after her marriage. With her husband's generous encouragement and cooperation, P. became a prolific author. At times they collaborated on books, but most of P.'s writing has been on her own.

P. sums up her life work in these words: "Grateful for the opportunity to combine a career with family life, it has been my endeavor that my family shall profit, never suffer, from my occupation with writing. My greatest pride is in the share I am privileged to have in my husband's writing; this is the first of my interests. All that I asked of life in the first hope of youth has been fulfilled; I ask now only the opportunity to complete fully what we have begun together."

P.'s fiction is almost invariably concerned with the problems of male-female relationships and those of parents and children. Reviewers have praised the breadth of P.'s insight into the inner lives of men and women and her sense of the comic as well as the pathetic. P.'s poetic prose has pleased many critics, and her delicate sentiment usually manages to escape sentimentality.

Not all readers agree that P.'s work is entirely devoid of oversweetness, and some critics have objected to the "thinness" of some of her stories. The style of P.'s later books often comes perilously close to being precious and affected.

A Child in Her Arms (1938) shows what happens when a beautiful, barren woman longing for a child meets a beautiful pregnant girl who eventually gives birth to a perfect baby. The first woman is wealthy and educated, with a husband who wants only her happiness; the second is the "earth mother" type, almost a symbol of maternity, with no family and no place to go. *Star at Noon* (1939) tells of the oddly assorted members of a family coming together, puzzled and wondering about their tangled relationships: a man and his second wife, his second wife's son, his first wife, and his daughter.

The problems of these plots are beautifully smoothed out to leave the reader satisfied that human affairs can always be resolved, although not without emotional turmoil and soul-searching. Of one of P.'s books a critic says, "It leaves the impact of a bigger and better story than it is, perhaps; but nevertheless it is a crisp, economical job of writing that makes for entertaining reading."

Although P.'s work can certainly not be called great realistic fiction, it cannot be considered mere "light romance." Serious purpose is at the core of each novel and story.

WORKS: *Bounty of Earth* (with D. C. Peattie, 1927). *Dagny* (1928). *Up Country* (with D. C. Peattie, 1928). *Down Wind* (with D. C. Peattie, 1929). *Pan's Parish* (1931). *Wine with a Stranger* (1932). *Wife to Caliban* (1934).

Fugitive (1935). *American Acres* (1936). *Tomorrow Is Ours* (1937). *A Child in Her Arms* (1938). *Lost Daughter* (1938). *Star at Noon* (1939). *The Californians* (1940). *Ring Finger* (1943).

BIBLIOGRAPHY: Boston *Evening Transcript* (13 April 1935). *NYT* (23 Aug. 1936; 20 March 1938; 26 March 1939; 10 March 1940).

ABIGAIL ANN HAMBLEN

Annie Smith Peck

B. *19 Oct. 1850, Providence, Rhode Island; d. 18 July 1935, New York City*
D. *of George Bacheler and Ann Power Smith Peck*

Not only a writer, P. was also an explorer, mountaineer, photographer, lecturer, and feminist. P. was a descendant of the first New England settlers. Her family was well educated, rather austere, orthodox Baptists, who encouraged P.'s education but did not condone her later mountaineering exploits. P.'s self-confidence, self-reliance, healthy physical development, and feminist attitudes originated in her relationship to her three older brothers—she became determined to outdo them in sports when they denied her equal participation.

P. was precocious in school, entering the University of Michigan when it was first opened to women; she graduated in 1878 with honors in diverse subjects. P. taught Latin at Purdue and Smith College for four years and studied in Europe, including a year as the first female student at the American School of Classical Studies in Athens, earning an M.A. in Greek. Upon her return to the U.S., she began giving parlor lectures on Greek and Roman archeology, showing her own stereopticon slides.

After seeing the Matterhorn in Europe, P.'s "allegiance, previously given to the sea, was transferred for all time to the mountains." Thus began her long and celebrated mountaineering career. She first climbed Mt. Shasta in California, in 1888; she scaled the Matterhorn in 1895, which brought her instant fame.

P. then ventured to South America, where she hoped to ascend the highest peak on that continent. After several harrowing attempts over six years, P. (at fifty-eight) succeeded in climbing Mt. Huascaran in Peru. For having climbed higher than any American in the Western hemisphere at that time, she received several awards, and the north peak of Huascaran was named "Cumbre Ana Peck" in her honor in 1908.

While in South America, P. explored and made first ascents of other mountains, planting a "Votes for Women" banner on the top of one. These expeditions were pitifully financed. P. was dependent upon contributions from a few friends, several articles for magazines (including *Harper's*), her stereopticon slide lectures on archeology and mountaineering, and the generosity of South American acquaintances.

A Search for the Apex of America (1911) was well received. This work, written in journal form, graphically relates P.'s incredible six years of mishaps and adventures in this quest. Many photographs are included, some from P.'s own collection.

The hospitality, assistance, and encouragement of many South Americans that P. encountered were responsible for her desire to promote trade and friendly relations between North and South America. This resulted in two books, both of which are now largely obsolete. *The South American Tour* (1913) is P.'s version of what was commonly known as the "Grand Tour of South America," including fares, routes, attractions, historical data, and photographs. *Industrial and Commercial South America* (1922) is a statistical handbook written mainly for the business person, describing the history, politics, and resources of South American countries, with little regard for human problems.

At age eighty, P. made an extensive air tour of South America, which was recounted in *Flying Over South America* (1932). Written the first year that air transportation was available in South America, the book was designed to promote air travel.

P. is remembered mainly for her outstanding accomplishments as one of the first women mountaineers, as a promoter of South American trade and tourism, and for her furthering of women's independence by living an outspoken and daringly unconventional life.

WORKS: *A Search for the Apex of America* (1911). *The South American Tour* (1913). *Industrial and Commercial South America* (1922). *Flying Over South America* (1932).

BIBLIOGRAPHY: McGuigan, D. G., *A Dangerous Experiment* (1970).
For articles in reference works, see: *AW. NAW* (article by B. N. Briggs). *Standard Encyclopedia of the World's Mountains*, Ed. A. Huxley (1962).

PATRICIA E. PENN

Ellen Peck

Wrote under: Cuyler Pine

No biographical information is available on P. Her early novels indicate that the pseudonym Cuyler Pine designates only the male editor of "memoirs" supposedly written by his sister and her friend.

P.'s earliest novels, *Mary Brandegee: An Autobiography* (1865) and *Renshawe* (1867), are fast-paced love stories which rather awkwardly form two parts of an unfinished "trilogy" about Southern society immediately before and during the Civil War. The viewpoint is Northern, but the second novel is prefaced by the editor's plea for mutual understanding between regions.

Mary Brandegee chronicles the erring ways of a Northern-educated Southern heiress who begins by reading "trashy" novels and ends up nearly fatally poisoning her rival for the rather uncertain affections of the handsome, arrogant Southerner George Berkeley, whom she finally rejects in favor of a dependable lover. Although serious questions about the relationship between masters and slaves are raised, the focus is on the tendency for men and women to misinterpret each other's characters.

Renshawe introduces a new heroine, the Northerner Louisa Renshawe, and delineates the disruptive effects of war on both Northern and Southern society; but the center of interest lies in the heroine's relationship with the unrepentant George Berkeley. While the Northern heroine tries to sort out spies from counterspies, she is allowed several major acts of physical courage but finally ends up paroled as a Union spy to her unacknowledged lover-enemy, the Confederate Colonel Berkeley. Although the thrust of the plot seems to be toward the eventual reconciliation of regional differences after the North and Louisa presumably humble the South and the proud Berkeley, no evidence exists that the promised third part of the trilogy (*Delaware*) ever saw print.

Ecce Femina (1874), republished as *Ecce Femina; or, The Woman Zoe* (1875), uses a highly economical style and well-motivated plot to satirize the worldly elitism of the Presbyterian church as revealed by the psychological struggles of the ambitious clergyman Mr. Bowen. He courts, marries, and then unjustly casts off his wife, Zoe, a reformed "Magdelene" and artist whose personal fate becomes the embodiment of her sculptured symbol of Woman—"the world's ignored and terrible sufferer" who does not want charity, but only the justice she is due. While P.'s assumptions are hardly feminist, this short novel is sharply critical of the church's short-sighted biases against women.

Although P.'s literary output was limited in volume and artistic merit, she managed to write entertaining popular fiction which included serious social themes and vivid character conflicts as well as fast-paced action and romantic adventure.

WORKS: *Mary Brandegee: An Autobiography* (1865). *Renshawe, A Novel* (1867). *Ecce Femina* (1874; republished as *Ecce Femina; or, The Woman Zoe*, 1875).

KATHLEEN L. NICHOLS

Phoebe Yates Pember

B. *18 Aug. 1823, Charleston, South Carolina; d. 4 March 1913, Pittsburgh, Pennsylvania*
D. *of Jacob and Fanny Yates Levy; m. Thomas Pember, 185?*

P. was the fourth of seven children. Little is known about her early life or education. The family moved to Savannah, Georgia, in 1850. A few years later, P. married. After her husband's death, P. returned to live with her parents first in Savannah, then in Marietta, where they were refugees.

In 1862, P. received and accepted an offer to become matron of Chimborazo Hospital in Richmond. She remained there until the occupation of Richmond by federal troops in April 1865. After the war, P. returned to Georgia and obscurity.

P.'s reminiscences of her life at Chimborazo were originally published in 1879. A modern edition of *A Southern Woman's Story*, including several letters from P. to her sister Eugenia, was prepared by historian Bell I. Wiley in 1959. Sometimes moving, sometimes humorous, these reminiscences are among the most revealing accounts of a woman's life and work during the Civil War. P. was unusual in that she received a salary for her nursing, and she had more responsibilities than volunteer nurses.

Chimborazo was the largest military hospital in the world at that time. Matrons like P. were assigned a number of wards for which they supervised the meals and the laundry, and oversaw the general welfare of their patients.

Even though the Confederate Congress had made provisions for the use of matrons in army hospitals, P. was not greeted with enthusiasm. Fear of "petticoat government" led one surgeon to remark in her presence that "one of them had come," and things would never be the same again. Under P.'s direction, care at Chimborazo's second ward improved dramatically. Food and medications were prepared properly and delivered to the patients on time. Slaves and civilian laundresses were hired to wash the wards and linens regularly. P. often went to great lengths or used her own money to prepare some special delicacy for a patient.

P.'s major conflict with members of the medical staff concerned the distribution of the whiskey ration. Believed to be both a stimulant and a narcotic, whiskey was a vital element in the treatment of disease. Almost immediately after her arrival at the hospital, P. learned that whiskey intended for the patients was being consumed by the male nurses and surgeons. P. decided to remove all temptation by locking the cabinet at night and keeping the key on her person. Resenting P.'s interference, the surgeons bombarded her with insulting and demeaning requests and even threatened her. Fortunately the chief surgeon supported P., and the harassment ceased.

A Southern Woman's Story helps strip the Confederacy of romantic myths. There was self-sacrifice and nobility of spirit, but P. records the selfishness and pettiness which also marked the Confederate experience. P. herself emerges as a strong vital woman, capable of great kindness and patience but certainly no saint. Its combination of wit and grim reality makes *A Southern Woman's Story* a classic in its field.

WORKS: *A Southern Woman's Story* (1879; rev. ed., Ed. B. I. Wiley, 1959).

BIBLIOGRAPHY: Adams, George W., "Confederate Medicine," *Journal of Southern History* (1940). Cunningham, H. H., *Doctors in Gray* (1958). Hume, E. E., "The Days Gone By: Chimborazo Hospital," *The Military Surgeon* (1934).

JANET E. KAUFMAN

Lucy Fitch Perkins

B. 1865, Maples, Indiana; d. 18 March 1937, Pasadena, California
Wrote under: Lucy Fitch Perkins
D. of Appleton Howe and Elizabeth Bennett Fitch; m. Dwight Heald
  Perkins, 1891

P. grew up in Maples, Indiana, and Kalamazoo, Michigan; her family also made frequent visits to Massachusetts, where both parents' roots were. P. attended school at the Museum of Fine Arts, Boston, graduating at age twenty-one. For a year she was employed by the Louis Prang Educational Company of Boston to do illustrations for school materials. The following four years, P. was on the faculty of the newly established art school at Pratt Institute, Brooklyn.

In 1891, she married and later had two children. The family made their home in Evanston, Illinois, and P. was employed by Prang's Chicago office.

By the time P. began her Twins series in 1911 (*The Dutch Twins*), she had become convinced of two things. One was that peace could come to the world only if the peoples of all nations could achieve "mutual respect and understanding," and the other was that children could grasp really big issues if they were made interesting to them. P. also had a strong conviction that American children should realize the labor, suffering, and inspiration that went into building the country. Utilizing both international and patriotic themes, P. produced the Geographical and Historical Twin series.

Because P. understood the fear of loneliness, she gave each book two protagonists—inseparable twins; because she knew that girls and boys love to laugh, she laced her text with puckish humor, but humor that never detracts from the serious themes. Plots are invariably full of action and suspense, with clever denouements that never seem contrived. P.'s delightful drawings illustrate the novels, but fully as delightful are the word pictures with which P. makes the reader familiar with faraway places and long-ago happenings.

The geographical books show vividly how life is lived in various foreign countries. Customs, festivals, and games are skillfully woven into the plots. Glossaries for pronunciation of unfamiliar names and some foreign words and phrases are supplied. One critic cites P. as "one of the rare pioneers in . . . foreign background story books." She shows "that the 'travel story book' could create sympathetic understanding of other people, that American children enjoyed the kinship they felt with her book children." The same might be said for the historical books, which depict various eras and episodes in the nation's life.

P. never regarded herself as a feminist, but her stories give glimpses of a strong feeling about the role of women in society. Her twins are, with one exception, a boy and a girl (the Spanish twins are both male); the sister shares all the adventures of the brother (except in *The American Twins of 1812*, 1925, in which the boy becomes involved in the war). More than one of P.'s little girls voices frustration with her feminine lot, disliking the idea of being forced into an acquiescent, passive way of life and prevented from questing the new, the strange, and the dangerous.

All the books have great charm, infused as they are with enthusiasm and cheerfulness. Few people of any age can read them without being captivated. But because they were aimed specifically at children, P. used to test each manuscript on a group of girls and boys she called "the poison squad," taking their comments and suggestions seriously. As a result, the Twin series had a devoted following, achieving great popularity through the years.

WORKS: *The Goose Girl* (1906). *A Book of Joy: A Story of a New England Summer* (1907). *The Dutch Twins* (1911). *The Japanese Twins* (1912). *The Irish Twins* (1913). *The Eskimo Twins* (1914). *The Mexican Twins* (1915). *The Cave Twins* (1916). *The Belgian Twins* (1917). *The French Twins* (1918). *The Spartan Twins* (1918). *The Scotch Twins* (1919). *The Italian Twins* (1920). *The Puritan Twins* (1921). *The Swiss Twins* (1922). *The Filipino Twins* (1923). *The Colonial Twins of Virginia* (1924). *The American Twins of 1812* (1925). *The American Twins of the Revolution* (1926). *The Pioneer Twins* (1927). *The Farm Twins* (1928). *Kit and Kat: More Adventures of the Dutch Twins* (1929). *The Indian Twins* (1930). *The Pickaninny Twins* (1931). *The Norwegian Twins* (1933). *The Spanish Twins* (1934). *The Chinese Twins* (1935). *The Dutch Twins and Little Brother* (1938). *Robin Hood* (n.d.). *Cornelia: The Story of a Benevolent Despot* (n.d.).

BIBLIOGRAPHY: Meigs, C., et al., *A Critical History of Children's Literature* (1953; rev. ed., 1969). Perkins, E. E., *Eve Among the Puritans* (1956). Perkins, E. E., "The Twins—Their Origin," *Elementary English Review* (May 1936).

For articles in reference works, see: *Junior Book of Authors*, Eds. S. Kunitz and H. Haycraft (1951). *NAW* (article by R. H. Viguers).

ABIGAIL ANN HAMBLEN

Rose Pesotta

B. 20 Nov. 1896, Derazhyna, Russia; d. 6 Dec. 1965, Miami, Florida
Given name: Rachelle Peisoty
D. of Masia and Issak Peisoty

While it is for her years as an able and often inspiring trade union organizer that P. is best known, she is also the author of two autobiographical books. *Bread Upon the Waters* (1944) concerns itself largely with
her eight years as a general organizer for the International Ladies' Garment Workers' Union (ILGWU); *Days of Our Lives* (1958) recalls her
youth in a Ukrainian village in the Jewish "Pale."

Days of Our Lives links some of P.'s childhood experiences with her
later calling. In recounting hearing of the revolts of the mujiks and the
"Peasants' Union" they formed, P. comments that that was "the first time
I ever heard two words that would mean so much to me later on—
organized and *union*." Vivid descriptions are given also of her activities
in the underground movement against the Czar, beginning at the age of
ten as a clandestine carrier of leaflets.

In 1913, P. emigrated to the U.S., joining an older sister working in a
New York shirtwaist factory. P. had left Russia, she wrote, because she
rebelled against a tradition in which she could "see no future for myself
except to marry . . . and be a housewife." She saw the new land as an
alternative, a place where "a decent middle class girl can work without
disgrace."

Soon after her arrival, P. joined the two social-political movements
to which she was to devote the rest of her life—trade unionism and an-
archism. By the 1920s she was taking an active role, as a public speaker,
in the drive to release the celebrated imprisoned Italian-American an-
archists, Sacco and Vanzetti. (It is noteworthy that in neither of P.'s
books does she describe her experiences in the anarchist movement, although her participation in it is well-documented and well-remembered
in interviews with her comrades still living today.)

In 1922, P. was elected to the executive board of ILGWU Local 22.
Over the next decade, P. served on various important strike committees,
and attended Bryn Mawr's Summer School for Women Workers, and
Brookwood Labor College. In 1933, she was appointed to a paid, full-time
position as a general organizer for the ILGWU. The following year she

was elected to serve as a vice-president on its General Executive Board—a post she held for ten years.

In *Bread upon the Waters*, P. describes organizing thousands of women (including Mexican-American, Puerto Rican, and French-Canadian women frequently alleged to be "unorganizable") into new ILGWU locals, and how she planned and conducted strikes and negotiations in cities from Los Angeles to Buffalo, in Puerto Rico and Montreal. The imaginative flair with which she conducted her campaigns gained her a reputation as a skilled organizer which soon spread beyond her own union.

P. was well aware that she distinguished herself in a field in which there were few women, and she understood the important role played by sexual discrimination in this dearth. Indeed, it was discrimination that was in large part responsible for her resignation, in 1942, of her position as a general organizer for the ILGWU. In a statement explaining her resignation to the ILGWU General Executive Board, P. cited the refusal of the union's leadership to recognize that she was as competent as any of the men on the ILGWU's staff, and its concomitant refusal to give her responsibilities commensurate with her experience. Interestingly, P. was publicly silent on the reasons surrounding her resignation. Like her participation in the anarchist movement, it is not discussed in either *Bread upon the Waters* or *Days of Our Lives*.

The importance of P.'s books is not their literary quality, which is marginal, but their historical value. *Bread upon the Waters* is almost certainly the first autobiography of a female labor union organizer ever published, and details the special challenges presented someone choosing this career. *Days of Our Lives* provides essential information on P.'s ethnic, family, and political background, as well as suggesting what experiences such a woman considered important or formative enough to record. Together, these works add to the scant store of knowledge available on the lives that were led by the small but significant number of women who became union organizers and worked with the most desperately exploited workers—women.

WORKS: *Bread upon the Waters* (1944). *Days of Our Lives* (1958).

The Rose Pesotta Collection at the New York Public Library includes diaries and letters. There are papers of Rose Pesotta at the Bund Archives of the Jewish Labor Movement, in New York. The Tamiment Library of New York University has early drafts of *Bread upon the Waters* in its John Beffel Papers.

BIBLIOGRAPHY: Kessler-Harris, A., "Organizing the Unorganizable: Three Jewish Women and Their Union," *Labor History* (Winter 1976).

ERIKA GOTTFRIED

Julia Mood Peterkin

B. 31 Oct. 1880, Laurens County, South Carolina; d. 10 Aug. 1961,
Fort Motte, South Carolina
D. of Julius Andrew and Alma Archer Mood; m. William Peterkin, 1903

The youngest of four children, P. spent several years with her grandparents in rural South Carolina after her mother's early death. Later, she lived in Sumter, South Carolina, with her father. After receiving her B.A. and M.A. degrees from Converse College, Spartanburg, South Carolina, P. taught at Fort Motte, a small, isolated community. She married the owner of Lang Syne plantation there. There were few whites and many blacks on the two-thousand-acre plantation. Because of her husband's ill health, P. took over most of the responsibilities of running Lang Syne until her son William was able to assume the actual management.

P. began writing in her early forties, and her work was centered around Fort Motte and Murrell's Inlet, a coastal village in South Carolina where she had a summer home.

Plantation stories were a popular genre from antebellum days until well into the 20th c., and it is one of P.'s contributions that she brought to this genre a sense of realism and dignity in her portrayal of the lives of black characters. In most of her work there is no stereotyped or affected local color, a common characteristic of plantation stories. P. also broke out of the southern pattern of sentimentality.

P.'s first works, which appeared in many magazines in the early 1920s, may be divided generally into two groups: Gullah-dialect sketches and more conventionally structured short stories. The former are usually dramatic monologues in the words of coastal South Carolina blacks, but the dialect at times becomes obtrusive. The larger group, in which P. departs from extended use of dialect but maintains the rhythm and syntax of the speech, are stark, powerful portrayals of the lives of these isolated people. The stories in *Green Thursday* (1924) continue in this vein, but there is more description of the land and the natural cycles, which always play an integral part in the lives of her characters. The stories may be read almost as a novel, centering on Killdee and his family.

Black April (1927), P.'s first novel, incorporates some of the incidents of the stories. The book is episodic rather than tightly plotted. It gives a convincing picture of the daily lives of the characters and a strong sense of community.

In *Scarlet Sister Mary* (1928), P.'s Pulitzer Prize–winning novel, P. creates a fully conceived heroine of modern fiction. Mary reveals a strong affirmation of life as she steers between the restrictive mores of the community and her sense of freedom and selfhood. Mary's guiding principle is, "Everybody has a selfness that makes the root of his life and being." Like many of Eudora Welty's women characters, Mary, intelligent but uneducated, frequently articulates her emotions through metaphorical identifications with the natural world.

Bright Skin (1932) is a sensitive portrayal of the developing relationship of a boy and girl as they mature.

Roll, Jordan Roll (1933) is P.'s commentary on photographs of blacks at Lang Syne. In this book, P. loses her artistic objectivity and becomes somewhat nostalgic. Interestingly, Doris Ullman's photographs capture much of the dignity and realism that is portrayed in P.'s fiction. In *A Plantation Christmas* (1934), P. seems overwhelmed by a sense of the past, and although there are fine descriptions, the total effect is local color for its own sake, nostalgic and sentimental. These two books are weakened by the presence of a white narrator; in P.'s best works, all the characters are black and events are viewed entirely through their eyes.

Though P. lived and wrote in isolation from the literary world, she was helped and encouraged by many literary figures who praised her economy of style, detachment, and compassion. P.'s characters live in an isolated but believable society in which folk beliefs and folk wisdom aid them in the struggle between personal responsibility and fate. Their lives reveal the drama and dignity of the ordinary events of life.

WORKS: *Green Thursday* (1924). *Black April* (1927). *Scarlet Sister Mary* (1928). *Bright Skin* (1932). *Roll, Jordan Roll* (with D. Ulmann, 1933). *A Plantation Christmas* (1934). *The Collected Short Stories of Julia Peterkin* (Ed. F. Durham, 1970).

BIBLIOGRAPHY: Clark, E., *Innocence Abroad* (1931). Davidson, D., in *The Spyglass: Views and Reviews, 1924–1930*, Ed. J. Fain (1963). Durham, F., Introduction to *The Collected Short Stories of Julia Peterkin* (1970). Landers, T. H., *Julia Peterkin* (1976).

Other references: *NYHT* (17 Jan. 1933).

ANNE NEWMAN

Maud Fuller Petersham

B. *1890, Kingston, New York; d. 5 Aug. 1971, Ravenna, Ohio*
M. *Miska Petersham*

The daughter of a Baptist minister, P. grew up in New York State, South Dakota, and Pennsylvania. P. faithfully attended church, listened to the stories told by visiting missionaries, and reveled in her Quaker grandfather's stories, which she heard while living with her aunt in the summers. P. graduated from Vassar College in 1912, and then attended the New York School of Fine and Applied Arts. While working at her first job with International Art Service, P. met a young commercial artist from Hungary. At first he was her tutor in art, but later when they were married, P.'s influence in their cooperative creative activities was as strong as his. After they turned to children's literature, P. usually wrote the major part of the text.

The Petershams' first picture book, *Miki* (1929), is about Miska's early experiences in Hungary. Their early books continued to draw from their own childhoods and from the childhood experiences of their son Miki. Although the early books received good reviews, critics called the final book of the series, *Get-a-way and Háry János* (1933), old-fashioned and quaint. The stories were episodic in nature. While cute, they were not significant in theme or writing style. Their major con-tributions to children's literature came from their effective use of foreign lands and strong female characters. In *Miki and Mary: Their Search for Treasures* (1934), Mary is equal to Miki in courage and intelligence. Be-cause of their quaint illustrations and overromanticized style, these early books are of little interest today.

Their strongest books were those based on the Bible or on early U.S. history. Designed with the youngster in mind, these stories contained humor, optimism, and realistic drama. Their first religious book, *The Ark of Father Noah and Mother Noah* (1930), gave Mother Noah a more distinctive role without detracting from the biblical story. *The Christ Child* (1931) was produced after the Petershams had spent three months in Palestine. It is a reverent retelling of the Christian epic.

In 1946, the Petershams won the Caldecott medal for their illustrations in *The Rooster Crows* (1945). The book, a compilation of American nursery rhymes, contains some of their finest art.

The Box with Red Wheels (1949) and *The Circus Baby* (1950) are valuable as examples of their literary talents. Both are slight fantasies designed for the preschooler. The writing is simple and smooth; it is not descriptive and is not detailed in plot. The themes reflect P.'s optimism. The plots contain an exciting drama and are resolved through positive actions.

The Petershams are also remembered for their many children's nonfiction books. Not creative in writing style, these books follow an established format. They were instructive and therefore useful to children, but they were not significant as literature.

As early author-artists in the field of children's literature, this husband-wife team created lively females relating to the world around them. Their biblical adaptations are significant, and their picture-book stories are charming. They were not trend-setters, but they successfully buoyed the expectations of children for quality writing and illustrating.

WORKS: *Miki* (1929). *The Ark of Father Noah and Mother Noah* (1930). *The Christ Child* (1931). *Auntie and Celia Jane and Miki* (1932). *Get-a-Way and Háry János* (1933). *The Story Book of Clothes* (1933). *The Story Book of Food* (1933). *The Story Book of Houses* (1933). *The Story Book of Things We Use* (1933). *Miki and Mary: Their Search for Treasures* (1934). *The Story Book of Earth's Treasures* (1935). *The Story Book of Gold* (1935). *The Story Book of Iron and Steel* (1935). *The Story Book of Oil* (1935). *The Story Book of Ships* (1935). *The Story Book of Wheels* (1935). *The Story Book of Trains* (1935). *The Story Book of Corn* (1936). *The Story Book of Foods from the Fields* (1936). *The Story Book of Rice* (1936). *The Story Book of Sugar* (1936). *The Story Book of Transportation* (1936). *The Story Book of Wheat* (1936). *David* (1938). *Joseph and His Brothers* (1938). *Moses* (1938). *Ruth* (1938). *Stories from the Old Testament* (1938). *The Story Book of Cotton* (1939). *The Story Book of Things We Wear* (1939). *An American ABC* (1941). *The Rooster Crows* (1945). *America's Stamps* (1947). *The Box With Red Wheels* (1949). *The Circus Baby* (1950). *A Bird in the Hand: Sayings from Poor Richard's Almanack* (1951). *The Silver Mace: A Story of Williamsburg* (1951). *Story of the Presidents of the United States of America* (1953). *Off to Bed: Seven Stories for Wide-Awakes* (1954). *The Peppernuts* (1958). *The Shepherd Psalm* (1962). *Let's Learn about Silk* (1967). *Let's Learn about Sugar* (1969).

BIBLIOGRAPHY: For articles in reference books, see: *Caldecott Medal Books, 1938–1957*, Eds. B. M. Miller and E. W. Field (1963). *Illustrators of Children's Books, 1946–1956*, Eds. R. H. Viguers, M. Dalphin, and B. M.

Miller (1958). *Junior Book of Authors*, Eds. S. J. Kunitz and H. Haycraft (1951).

Other references: *Horn Book* 22 (Sept./Oct. 1935).

JILL P. MAY

Ann Lane Petry

B. *12 Oct. 1908, Old Saybrook, Connecticut*
Writes under: Ann Petry
D. *of Peter Clark and Bertha James Lane; m. George D. Petry, 1938*

P. was born into a poor black family of Old Saybrook, Connecticut, a predominantly white New England community. Her father was the local druggist. After receiving her Ph.G. in 1931 from the University of Connecticut, P. returned home to work as a pharmacist in the family drugstores from 1931 to 1938. In 1938, she married Petry (they have one daughter) and moved to New York City, becoming an advertising sales-person and writer for the *Amsterdam News* (1938–41), and then re-porter and woman's-page editor for the rival *People's Voice* of Harlem (1941–44). P. was also a member of the American Negro Theater and wrote children's plays.

P. studied creative writing at Columbia University from 1944 to 1946 and published her first short stories in *The Crisis* and *Phylon*. In addition to writing, P. has lectured at Berkeley, Miami University, and Suffolk University, and was a visiting professor of English at the University of Hawaii (1974–75).

After P. had served her literary apprenticeship as a journalist, she began to publish short stories. "Like a Winding Sheet" was reprinted in *Foley's Best American Short Stories of 1946*, and another story led to a Houghton Mifflin Literary Fellowship, under which P. completed her first novel, *The Street* (1946). *The Street* is a naturalistic novel usually associated with the Wright school of protest fiction. The protagonist, Lutie Johnson, imbued with the American success ethic of Benjamin Franklin, is defeated in her attempts to improve her life by the detri-mental influences of Harlem. Critics see the novel as gripping yet simplistic.

Country Place (1947) is an "assimilationist" novel set in the small town of Lennox, Connecticut. The major characters are white, and are enmeshed in a plot and setting reminiscent of a cross between *Winesburg, Ohio* and *Peyton Place*, as an apocalyptic autumn storm brings out the true natures of the townspeople. *Country Place* is considered P.'s most successful novel in scope and use of symbol and metaphor to parallel action and evoke character. The plot is unified and the prose clear and powerful.

The Narrows (1953) demonstrates a return to the theme of race. The plot revolves around the classic love conflict between heroic black man and rich white woman. Link Williams, the protagonist, is a fine portrayal of a young black man, an orphan and possessor of a college degree who has chosen to tend bar in the hub of the Narrows, the black section of Monmouth, Connecticut, rather than become a member of the black bourgeoisie. *The Narrows* is simultaneously sophisticated and melodramatic, as brilliantly conceived characters outshine a standard plot.

The rest of P.'s opus consists of four juvenile books and a collection of short stories, *Miss Muriel, and Other Stories* (1971). "In Darkness and Confusion" concerns a poor black couple's way of coping with their son's mistreatment in a segregated army by participating in looting and property damage during the Harlem riot of August 1943. The well-wrought title story is semiautobiographical, told from the perspective of a twelve-year-old black girl. Set in the drugstore of a New England town, the story treats the loss of innocence that comes with a growing awareness of maturity.

P.'s fiction is of a fine quality. Her stories succeed better than her novels, although the novels certainly belong in the mainstream of American naturalism and realism. P.'s work has not yet received thorough treatment by literary critics.

WORKS: *The Street* (1947). *Country Place* (1947). *The Drugstore Cat* (1949). *The Narrows* (1953). *Harriet Tubman* (1955). *Tituba of Salem Village* (1964). *Legends of the Saints* (1970). *Miss Muriel, and Other Stories* (1971).

BIBLIOGRAPHY: Bone, R. A., *The Negro Novel in America* (1958; rev. ed., 1965). Royster, B. H., "The Ironic Vision of Four Black Women Novelists: A Study of the Novels of Jessie Fauset, Nella Larsen, Zora Neale Hurston, and Ann Petry" (Ph.D. diss., Emory Univ., 1975).

For articles in reference works, see: *CB* (March 1946). *Great Black Americans*, Eds. B. Richardson and W. A. Fahey (1976). *Twentieth Century Children's Writers*, Ed. D. L. Kirkpatrick (1978).

Other references: *Crisis* 53 (1946). *Crit* (Spring 1974). *NEQ* 47 (1974). *NYHT* (16 Aug. 1953). *Opportunity* 24 (1946). *SBL* (Fall 1975).

ANN RAYSON

Almira Hart Lincoln Phelps

B. *15 July 1793, Berlin, Connecticut; d. 15 July 1884, Baltimore, Maryland*
D. *of Samuel and Lydia Hensdale Hart; m. Samuel Lincoln, 1817;*
 m. John Phelps, 1832

P. and her elder sister, Emma Hart Willard, shared a love for study, an aptitude for teaching, and a desire to improve the intellectual status of women. Close association with the pioneering Troy, New York, Female Seminary has made Emma more celebrated than her equally productive but more eclectic sister. P.'s early schooling was in Berlin, and she later studied at Middlebury and Pittsfield, Massachusetts.

After teaching for several years, P. married a Federalist editor. Left a widow with two small daughters in 1823, she returned to teaching and to writing to earn a family income. After joining Emma at the Troy Female Seminary, she studied science with Amos Eaton, a professor of natural science at nearby Rensselaer Institute. In 1832, P. remarried. She continued to write, and in 1838 her husband urged her to accept the principalship of a promising new seminary in West Chester, Pennsylvania. After brief administrations in Pennsylvania and at the Rahway, New Jersey, Female Institute, P. headed the Patapsco Female Institute in Ellicott's Mills, Maryland, from 1841 to 1855.

An imaginative and successful educator, P. was also a prolific writer. Her first textbook, *Familiar Lectures on Botany* (1829), was her most original and useful. Botany was a popular subject, and P.'s text provided a middle ground between the conversational style of many books written for young ladies and the formal presentation of scientific principles designed for advanced students. Traditional in its reliance on the Linnean artificial classification system, the book provides diagrams and suggestions for study designed to engage the student's participation in learning; appendixes provide all necessary reference material, including a description of genera and species, a dictionary of terms, and a common-name index. Frequently revised and used widely in academies for boys and girls, the volume went through twenty-eight editions (275,000 copies) by 1872. There were eighteen editions of an abridged version, *Botany for Beginners* (1833). Moral observations, literary references, and history were combined with sound science in a text designed to develop specific skills while integrating student learning. The success of the botanical text led P. to write books on chemistry, natural philosophy, and geology; but these were more derivative in content and less popular. *Familiar Lectures on Chemistry*, for example, used similar teaching techniques, but a reliance on household examples circumscribed its audience, and borrowed material caused the book to lack cohesion.

Most of P.'s writing was intended to educate and elevate young women. P.'s stories were in the popular, melodramatic, and didactic mode of antebellum novels. *Caroline Westerley; or, The Young Traveler from Ohio* (1833) presents a series of letters from an older sister to a younger; it is a guide through the New England landscape, an educational commentary on topics from plant life to housing styles, and a moral analysis of people encountered. Sarah Josepha Hale's review found this story "a charming picture of a young girl, engaged in improvement, and finding happiness. . . ." P.'s two other novels held more drama but similar purposes. Both *Ida Norman; or, Trials and Their Uses* (1848) and *The Blue Ribbon Society; or, The School Girls' Rebellion* (1879) were presented chapter by chapter for evening discussion at Patapsco Institute and were later published.

As educator and writer, P. could not resist contemporary discussion about the purpose and nature of education for young women, whether in public addresses, journal articles, or books. Although a domestic feminist, P. did not advocate a curriculum to develop household skills, but stressed classical subjects as well as the sciences. Her *Lectures to Young Ladies* (1833) stressed the need to study widely and to discipline the mind. Discussions of morality became more common in later editions. *The Female Student* (1836) emphasized the value of study but also stressed the need for a good diet, proper exercise, and proper clothing. This volume, like *Lectures*, was published as part of the School Library series, under the sanction of the Massachusetts School Board. P. moved with the vanguard of women educational reformers of the mid–19th c.

After the Civil War, P. retired from teaching but continued to write for national journals. Some of her essays explored the fine arts. P. also dedicated her energy to opposing the woman suffrage movement, although she continued to advocate educational equality for women. P.'s ideas and leadership, so significant to her own generation, were often disregarded or even dismissed by the suffragists and co-educational reformers of the late 19th c. Herself the model of the self-determination she taught, P. helped establish the possibility for women's public and political roles.

WORKS: *Familiar Lectures on Botany* (1829). *Address on the Subject of Female Education in Greece and the General Extension of Christian Intercourse among Females* (1831). *The Child's Geology* (1832). *Botany for Beginners* (1833). *Caroline Westerley; or, The Young Traveler from Ohio* (1833). *Lectures to Young Ladies* (1833). *Chemistry for Beginners* (1834). *The Female Student; or, Lectures to Young Ladies on Female Education* (1836; republished as *The Fireside Friend*, 1840). *Familiar Lectures on Natural Philosophy* (1837). *Lectures in Chemistry for the Use of Schools, Families, and Private Students* (1838). *Natural Philosophy for Beginners* (1838). *Ida Norman; or, Trials and Their Uses* (1848). *Christian Households* (1858). *Hours with My Pupils* (1859; republished as *The Educator*, 1868). *Foreign Correspondence in Relation to the Rebellion in the United States* (1863). *Our Country, in Its Relations to the Past, Present, and Future* (edited by Phelps, 1864). *Reviews and Essays on Art, Literature, and Science* (1873). *Women's Duties and Rights, the Woman's Congress: An Address to the Women of America* (1876). *The Blue Ribbon Society; or, The School Girls' Rebellion* (1879).

BIBLIOGRAPHY: Bolzau, E. L., *Almira Hart Lincoln Phelps: Her Life and Work* (1936). Lutz, A., *Emma Willard: Daughter of Democracy* (1929). Woody, T., *A History of Women's Education in the United States* (2 vols., 1929).

For articles in reference works, see: *DAB*, VII, 2. *NAW* (article by F. Rudolph). *NCAB*, 11.

SALLY GREGORY KOHLSTEDT

Elizabeth Stuart Phelps

B. 13 Aug. 1815, Andover, Massachusetts; d. 29 Nov. 1852, Andover,
  Massachusetts
Wrote under: E. S. Phelps, H. Trusta
D. of Moses and Abigail Clark Stuart; m. Austin Phelps, 1842

P.'s mother was a long-term invalid and her father a clergyman and professor of Greek and Hebrew literature at Andover Theological Seminary.
At age ten, P. began to compose tales to amuse family and servants.

P. was educated at Abbot Academy in Andover. At age sixteen, she
went to live in Boston with the Reverend Jacob Abbott, author of the
juvenile Rollo series, and attended the Mount Vernon School. P.'s first
publications—brief articles written over the name "H. Trusta," an ana-
gram of "Stuart"—appeared in a religious magazine edited by Abbott.
According to P.'s husband, P.'s early literary ambition was to gain her
father's approval. By 1834, P. was beginning to suffer from a "cerebral
disease" characterized by headache, partial blindness, and temporary pa-
ralysis. When P. began to write, her health improved, although she was
never again "for any long time" without symptoms of disease.

P.'s daughter, who became a successful author writing under her
mother's name, was born in 1844. P.'s father died in January 1852. She
herself followed within eleven months, never fully recovering from the
birth in August of her second son.

P. wrote newspaper and magazine articles as well as children's books,
the latter published anonymously and later not identifiable even by P.
After her marriage, P. kept a "Family Journal" as well as journals of her
children's lives. She reviewed contemporary books and continued to
write for children as well as older readers. From the late 1840s until
her death in 1852, P. wrote five juvenile books, two collections of short
fiction, and two novels.

P.'s husband located one of the strong motivations for P.'s juvenile
writing in her childhood sleeplessness from a deep fear of death. Finding
in children's Sunday-school literature an association of "early piety with
the necessity of an early death," P. wished to provide a counter to such
association in the depiction of "religious principle as it is in life." From
1851 to 1853, P.'s four "Kitty Brown" books appeared. In Little Kitty

Brown and Her Bible Verses (1851), anecdotes demonstrate to a juvenile reader the behavioral correlates of various biblical dicta. These highly didactic tales present numerous realistic details from everyday living. *Little Mary; or, Talks and Tales for Children* (1854) was probably written for P.'s own children.

All of P.'s short writings point clear morals, but they demonstrate a literary advance over P.'s juvenilia, first by leaving morals implied and second by achieving greater realism from increased attention to the documentation of daily life. *The Angel over the Right Shoulder* (1852), one of P.'s best works, describes the daily round of duties expected of a mother, develops the mother's deep concern for the future of her daughter, and reveals the conflict existing between these expectations and a woman's need to "cultivate her own mind and heart." P.'s two posthumously published collections consider a range of topics. *The Tell-Tale* (1853) includes six sketches concerning marital relationships, and one each about the relationships between father and daughter and between older women and younger women, as well as a satiric view of celebrating July 4th.

P.'s two anonymous novels sold well. *The Sunny Side; or, The Country Minister's Wife* (1851) received international recognition and by P.'s death claimed 300,000 to 500,000 readers. *A Peep at "Number Five"; or, A Chapter in the Life of a City Pastor* (1852), a partially autobiographical fiction and P.s favorite, sold 20,000 copies in less than one year. *The Sunny Side* first brought to P. renown as an author. The book follows Emily Edwards from wedding through marriage and motherhood to funeral, detailing her domestic and familial trials and triumphs. Undoubtedly the popularity of this book comes from its sympathetic and realistic presentation of a woman's daily life. *A Peep at "Number Five"* delineates the burdened life of Lucy Holbrook, who for the six years of the novel must meet parishioners' expectations at the expense of her own needs, but who nonetheless is relieved that her husband declines a call to a more prestigious position in favor of their remaining within the city parish. In both novels, P. presents a detailed view of a 19th-c. minister's household as seen through the eyes of his wife, and thus demonstrates the wife's excessive burdens and need for relief.

In her best work, P. depended little upon imaginative fabrication and largely upon meticulous observation. P. must be counted among the earliest depicters of the New England scene, antedating the regional novels of her Andover neighbor, Harriet Beecher Stowe. P. wrote at the beginning of the transition in American women's writing from domestic sentimentality to regional realism.

WORKS: *Little Kitty Brown and Her Bible Verses* (1851). *The Sunny Side; or, The Country Minister's Wife* (1851). *The Angel over the Right Shoulder* (1852). *Kitty Brown and Her City Cousins* (1852). *Kitty Brown and Her Little School* (1852). *A Peep at "Number Five"; or, A Chapter in the Life of a City Pastor* (1852). *Kitty Brown Beginning to Think* (1853). *The Last Leaf from Sunny Side* (1853). *The Tell-Tale; or, Home Secrets Told by Old Travellers* (1853). *Little Mary; or, Talks and Tales for Children* (1854).

BIBLIOGRAPHY: Hart, J. D., *The Popular Book* (1950). Kessler, C. F., " 'The Woman's Hour': Life and Novels of Elizabeth Stuart Phelps, 1844–1911" (Ph.D. diss., Univ. of Pennsylvania, 1977). McKeen, P., and P. McKeen, *Annals of Fifty Years: A History of Abbot Academy* (1880). Phelps, A., "Memorial of the Author" in *The Last Leaf from Sunny Side* (1853). Robbins, S. S., *Old Andover Days: Memories of a Puritan Childhood* (1909). Ward, E. S. P., *Austin Phelps: A Memoir* (1891). Ward, E. S. P., *Chapters from a Life* (1896).

For articles in reference works, see: *AA. CAL. DAB*, X, 1. *NAW* (article by O. E. Winslow). *NCAB*, 9.

Other references: *Frontiers: A Journal of Women Studies*, 1 (1976).

CAROL FARLEY KESSLER

Irna Phillips

B. 1 July 1901, Chicago, Illinois; d. 23 Dec. 1973, Chicago, Illinois
D. of William and Betty Phillips

P. was the tenth and youngest child of a Chicago grocer. P.'s interest in dramatics began in childhood and continued through her years at the universities of Illinois and Wisconsin. P. taught school in Missouri and Ohio. With her mother as a sturdy model of single parenthood (her father died in 1910), P. adopted two children in 1941.

P. began her radio career as an unpaid actress on Chicago's WGN in 1930. She broadcast a daily program of poetry and philosophical commentary entitled "Thought for Today." P. was then asked to write a serial. The result was *Painted Dreams* (1930–32), the story of Mother

Monahan, a widow modeled after P.'s mother, and her daughter Irene. The central theme was the fulfillment of womanhood through marriage, love, and motherhood. All six female characters (and the sound effects) were played by P. and Irene Wicker.

P. later went to work for NBC. The daytime serial *Today's Children* (1932–38) was *Painted Dreams* with new names.

The Guiding Light (1937–) featured the male equivalent of Mother Monahan in Dr. Rutledge, pastor of the nonsectarian Little Church of Five Points. Dr. Rutledge's mission was to teach people how to live the good life. Scenes made up of long, slow discussions between two characters in sparse settings became a P. trademark. *The Guiding Light* went on television in 1952. Although P. eventually turned the television version over to Agnes Eckhardt Nixon, the program continues to bear the stamp of P.'s devotion to professionals as heroes.

The Road of Life (1937–59) gave the soap opera its first physician for a main character. The program's standard opening, "Dr. Brent, call surgery! Dr. Brent, call surgery!" was its most memorable aspect. *Woman in White* (1938–42) was notable for its relative independence in treating subjects usually taboo in radio programs of the period.

The Right to Happiness (1939–60) was the original program spinoff. The central characters were *The Guiding Light*'s most popular family, the Kranskys. In *The Right to Happiness*, they became the Kramers, each of whom was certain of a God-given right to happiness. An innovation in this program was the voice of "The Past," a haunting voice of conscience used regularly from 1941 to 1944, which P. later used in *Today's Children* and *The Guiding Light*.

In *The General Mills Hour* (1944–48), P. introduced a concept that has since been employed in television soap operas and prime-time series. Characters from *Today's Children*, *Woman in White*, and *The Guiding Light* interacted with one another.

In 1941, P. created television's first soap opera, *These Are My Children*. It was a resounding failure, but two later television serials remain highly successful. *As the World Turns* (1956–) carried several conventions of the daytime radio serial into television, including the use of organ music for mood enhancement and transitions, and the "glacier-like" progress of the plot.

In *Another World* (1964–), Ada Matthews McGowan wrestles regularly with the problem of how to guide her children's lives without seeming to interfere. *Another World* has dealt forthrightly with such issues as drugs, alcoholism, and rape.

P.'s penchant for philosophizing in her scripts grew out of her identification of three themes basic to successful daytime serials: appeals to self-preservation, sex, and family instinct. As a writer, P. saw herself as "part mechanic, part psychologist, and part dialogist." In the early 1940s, when she had five dramatic serials on radio at one time, she kept their sixty characters and multiple plots straight with elaborate charts. This "veteran script carpenter" disdained voice-over narration and flashbacks as "lazy devices." Rather, she built the review necessary to the serial form into the dialogue.

Technically speaking, P. did not write her scripts. She acted them before secretaries who recognized the characters by P.'s interpretation of their voices. When something elicited the wrong reaction, P. edited the script on the spot. The typed scripts were sent into production without her seeing them. In the interest of authenticity, P. retained a lawyer and two doctors for technical advice. She invited police officers, mail carriers, and icemen into her office as live models. P. once said, "Everybody is a serial story. We're reporters."

P. was radio's most prolific writer, at one point turning out 2 million words (the equivalent of forty novels) per year. To radio script technique, P. contributed the provocative "tease" ending, used to keep audiences interested from day to day, and the use of organ music to establish mood and to bridge breaks in the narrative. She also is credited with the introduction of amnesia as a plot device. P. was the only daytime radio dramatist to make a successful transition to television. In addition to the serials she created, P. regularly advised producers of other serials. She is recognized as the single most important influence on daytime television serials.

WORKS: *Painted Dreams* (1930–32). *Judy and Jane* (1932). *Today's Children* (1932–38). *The Guiding Light* (1937–47; 1947–56; 1952–). *The Road of Life* (1937–59). *Woman in White* (1939–40; 1940–42). *The Right to Happiness* (1939–60). *These Are My Children* (1941). *Lonely Women* (1941). *The General Mills Hour* (1944–48). *The Brighter Day* (1944–48). *As the World Turns* (1956–). *Another World* (1964–). *Love Is a Many Splendored Thing* (1967–73). *Bright Promise* (1969–71).

BIBLIOGRAPHY: Edmondson, M., and D. Rounds, *From Mary Noble to Mary Hartman: The Complete Soap Opera Book* (1976). Stedman, R., *The Serials: Suspense and Drama by Installment* (1971). Wakefield, D., *All Her Children* (1976).

For articles in reference works, see: Buxton, F., and B. Owen, *The Big Broadcast, 1920–1950* (1966). CB (1944). Dunning, J., *Tune Into Yesterday: The Ultimate Encyclopedia of Old Time Radio 1925–1976* (1976).

Other references: *Broadcasting* (6 Nov. 1972). *Fortune* (June 1938). *Newsweek* (13 July 1942; 11 May 1964). *NYT* (30 Dec. 1973). *SatEvePost* (25 June 1960). *Time* (10 June 1940). *Variety* (2 Jan. 1974).

CAREN J. DEMING

Sarah Morgan Bryan Piatt

B. 11 Aug. 1836, Lexington, Kentucky; d. 2 Dec. 1919, Caldwell, New Jersey
Wrote under: Sarah M. B. Piatt, "A Woman"
D. of Talbot and Mary Spiers Bryan; m. John James Piatt, 1861

P. was related through her mother to the earliest settlers of Kentucky, including Daniel Boone. At the age of three, P. moved to Versailles, Kentucky, where her mother died five years later. P. was raised by her maternal grandmother, a well-to-do slave-owner, and educated at the fashionable Henry Female College.

Soon after her marriage to a poet, P. moved to Georgetown, Virginia, where her husband was appointed to a clerkship which he held for the next six years. In 1867, they moved to North Bend, Ohio, where they built a house overlooking the Ohio River. In 1870, Piatt, appointed librarian to the House of Representatives, returned to Washington, where his family joined him each winter.

In 1882, P. went to live in Queenstown, Ireland, after her husband was appointed consul in Cork. During this sojourn, she became acquainted with a wide circle of literary people.

Soon after the Piatts' return from Ireland in 1894, their home was destroyed by fire. Though the house was later rebuilt, this misfortune signaled the onset of financial reverses from which they never recovered.

P. bore seven children, two of whom died tragically. Their deaths form the subject matter and references of many of P.'s poems, particularly those written during the earlier part of her career.

Thoroughly steeped in the traditional southern woman's role, she was devoted to domesticity and to the instruction of her children, and never spoke to anyone about her writing. It was only through the efforts of her husband, it seems, that P.'s work appeared in print.

Of P.'s eighteen volumes of poetry, the two earliest were written in collaboration with her husband. Later volumes focus on the death of children and others, on disillusion with life and living, and to some extent on nature and the Civil War. Poems for and about children form another grouping. P.'s interest in children elicited comment from many critics, especially Edmund Stedman, who pointed out that she had "a special gift for seeing into a child's heart." In addition to formal collections, P. contributed to many periodicals, among them the *Atlantic Monthly* and *Scribner's*.

If there is any difference between P.'s early and late poems, it is in the direction of greater formal flexibility and greater awareness of the world outside. As the deaths of her two children receded in time, P. became less introspective. Her stay in Europe no doubt helped turn her toward less subjective themes.

Some critics commented on P.'s simplicity and "daintiness," a term so often applied to women poets. Several critics, Howells among them, commented on the universality of subject matter of the poems in relation to women's lives; Emerson Venable called the poems "sometimes deeply tragic."

P.'s reputation was considerable, although much smaller than her husband's. Whittier quoted from her work; Stedman called her America's "best-known western poetess." Some English critics believed her "hard to surpass on either side of the Atlantic."

P.'s melancholy tone and modesty of scope were doubtless rooted in the female literary conventions of her time. Her poems express once again the unhappiness of a woman of talent and intelligence restricted by her role as the wife of another poet, who received acclaim and satisfaction that was denied her.

WORKS: *The Nests at Washington, and Other Poems* (with J. J. Piatt, 1864). *A Woman's Poems* (1871). *A Voyage to the Fortunate Isles, Etc.* (1874). *Poems in Company with Children* (1877). *That New World, and Other Poems* (1877). *Dramatic Persons and Moods, and Other New Poems* (1880). *An Irish Garland* (1884). *The Children Out-of-Doors* (with J. J. Piatt, 1885). *Selected Poems* (1885). *Child's World Ballads* (1886). *In Primrose Time: A New Irish Garland* (1886). *Child's World Ballads, Second Series* (1887). *The Witch in the Glass, and Other Poems* (1889). *An Irish Wildflower* (1891). *An Enchanted Castle, and Other Poems* (1893). *Pictures, Portraits, and People in Ireland* (1893). *Poems* (1894).

BIBLIOGRAPHY: Howells, M., *Life in Letters of William Dean Howells* (1928). Stoddard, R. H., et al., *Poet's Homes* (1877). Townsend, J. W., *Kentucky in American Letters* (1913). Tynan, K., *Twenty-Five Years: Reminiscences* (1913).

For articles in reference works, see: *AW. CAL. LSL. NAW. NCAB*, VIII. *The Part Taken by Women in American History*, M. S. Logan (1912). Other references: *Ohio State Archeological and Historical Quarterly* (Jan. 1936).

VIRGINIA R. TERRIS

Marge Piercy

B. 31 March 1936, Detroit, Michigan
D. of Robert and Bert Bunnin Piercy

P. grew up in a lower-class family and has remained committed to the common people. She was educated at the University of Michigan and Northwestern University. P. was a member of SDS and has for many years been intensely committed to the women's movement. She was briefly married, and now lives with a group of women in Cape Cod.

P.'s novels are richly peopled, strongly political works which have been attacked for their polemicism. Reviewers often suggest that literary integrity has been sacrificed to political convictions. Yet P. forcefully confronts the important social issues of our time, exposing sexual, economic, and political injustices.

P.'s first two novels are largely concerned with the New Left of the 1960s. *Going Down Fast* (1969) portrays the conversion of conscientious liberals from pacifism to militancy. *Dance the Eagle to Sleep* (1970) pictures the revolt of a group of student revolutionaries against a highly systematized and dehumanized American society of the near future.

With *Small Changes* (1973), P. moves to a stronger feminist theme. The opening traces the disillusionment of Beth, whose marriage simply trades a mother's domination for a husband's. Beth's flight leads to her friendship with Miriam, who is eventually trapped in an equally oppressive marriage. Meanwhile, Beth leaves for a women's commune and then a lesbian relationship in which, despite social persecution, she finds personal fulfillment. The novel's bias is obvious in the unrelentingly negative male characterizations and the idealization of Beth's lesbian relationship. Yet it is a powerful and popular novel, frequently used in women's courses.

Woman on the Edge of Time (1976) combines feminism with other social issues, particularly economic inequality. Its protagonist, an impoverished Chicana, is victimized by husbands, lovers, pimps, and male doctors at the institution where she is finally confined. She escapes from the asylum by imagining a utopian future with political and sexual freedom, and economic and social equality.

The High Cost of Living (1978) again combines economic and sexual inequality, showing the price working-class children must pay to get ahead. The male's attempt to dominate ends the brief heterosexual affair of the protagonist, who then returns to lesbian relationships and feminist ideals.

Vida (1980) traces, through flashbacks, the antiwar movement of the 1960s, the increasing activism of the radical left, the movement underground in the 1970s, and the eventual fragmentation of a once strong and optimistic political movement. P. realistically portrays the personal price, the loneliness and despair, that the characters pay for their political ideals. Vida is P.'s most powerful protagonist, and her lover, Joel, is one of the few sympathetic men in P.'s fiction.

Much of P.'s poetry contains the same anger and intensity. Whereas the novels are complex and often unfocused, the poetry is simply stated and often formally structured, sometimes employing brilliant metaphors. In "The Friend," the woman, eager to please, says, "I love you," and her lover responds, "Cut off your hands." Similarly, "Barbie Doll" presents a young woman whose attempts to conform to ideals of feminine beauty culminate in death when she cuts off her too-fat legs and nose.

P.'s poetic tone is impressively varied. It may achieve a mocking humor as in "To the Pay Toilet": "You strop my anger, especially / when I find you in a restaurant or bar / and pay for the same liquid, coming and going." Many poems deal with simple and homely pleasures—baking bread or planting gardens. There are nature poems, suffused with the Cape Cod environment, and sensual, sensitive love poems. P.'s poetic voice is always honest, never coy, avoiding word games and conveying moments of intensity with forthright feeling. While there has been some division of opinion concerning P.'s novels, most critics agree that she is an important and gifted poet.

WORKS: *Breaking Camp* (1968). *Going Down Fast* (1969). *Hard Loving* (1969). *Dance the Eagle to Sleep* (1970). *4-Telling* (with three other poets, 1971). *Small Changes* (1973). *To Be of Use* (1973). *Living in the Open* (1976). *Woman on the Edge of Time* (1976). *The High Cost of Living* (1978). *The*

Twelve-Spoken Wheel Flashing (1978). *Vida* (1980). *The Moon is Always Female.* (1980).

BIBLIOGRAPHY: *American Poetry Review* (July/Aug. 1974). *Nation* (10 Dec. 1970). *New Republic* (27 Oct. 1973). *NYTBR* (24 Feb. 1980). *Parnassus: Poetry in Review* (Fall/Winter 1979). *Poetry* (1971).

SUZANNE HENNING UPHAUS

Mary Hayden Green Pike

B. *30 Nov. 1824, Eastport, Maine; d. 15 Jan. 1908, Baltimore, Maryland*
Wrote under: Mary Langdon, Sydney A. Story
D. *of Elijah and Hannah Claflin Hayden Green; m. Frederick Augustus Pike, 1845*

A writer of sentimental antislavery novels, P. was descended from old New England Puritan stock; her father was a Baptist deacon, bank director, and militia officer in Calais, Maine. P. attended public schools and the Charleston, Massachusetts, Female Seminary. In 1845, she married Pike, a lawyer, who served in the U.S. Congress between 1861 and 1869 as a radical Republican. An adopted daughter was their only child.

The religious enthusiasm evident in P.'s early life was soon mingled with the cause of abolition. Her husband and his brother were also ardent abolitionists, yet both were dubious about allowing full citizenship to freed blacks. P. was more egalitarian; she believed that, given adequate education, blacks could be fully integrated, both politically and socially.

P.'s three acknowledged novels were published between 1854 and 1858 under the names "Mary Langdon" and "Sydney A. Story." She also made anonymous or pseudonymous contributions to newspapers and periodicals. In about 1860, P. turned from literature to landscape painting. Her last years were devoted to charitable and religious work.

Ida May (1854) was one of the more popular novels to follow in the wake of *Uncle Tom's Cabin*. Instead of requiring their readers to identify with black protagonists, most second-generation abolition novelists depended on the figure of the beautiful quadroon or octoroon. P. went one step further—Ida May is wholly white, kidnapped as a child, taken South, and sold into slavery. P. was probably attempting to make northern readers feel personally endangered. The repeal of the Missouri Compromise had made the expansion of slave territory a topical issue. In passages of authorial comment, P. notes the number of children, both black and white, who inexplicably disappear every year, and claims that poor whites have been known to sell their children as mulattoes. The chief evil of slavery in *Ida May* is that it destroys the family.

Caste (1856) was less popular, perhaps because the indictment was closer to home. Charles and Helen Dupré, a brother and sister, are discovered to have black blood. Helen immediately suffers a broken engagement and a bout of brain fever, but the effects are even more disastrous for Charles. His business associate dissolves their partnership, his father-in-law vows to have his marriage annulled, and his wife dies of distress in childbirth. The sudden alteration of attitudes toward Charles demonstrates the depth of prejudice; northerners cannot point to the black's brutishness, ignorance, and slavery-induced childishness to excuse their discrimination, since Charles's manners, morals, education, and tastes remain the same. P. explicitly argues that northern prejudice is more entrenched and will be harder to overcome than the institutionalized slave system of the South.

Agnes (1858) attempts to show Indians as human beings with thoughts, emotions, and desires which are neither noble nor savage, but simply like those of other members of the human race. This subject matter, however, occupies a secondary place in the novel. The main plot is a sentimental melodrama laid during the Revolutionary War and using nearly all the conventional figures and situations of the genre.

All three of P.'s novels are based on the staple element of 18th- and 19th-c. popular fiction: An innocent and unprotected woman is placed undeservedly—and repeatedly—in threatening situations. The melodrama is given social meaning by introducing race as an element increasing the threat. P. also made the analogy between race and sex as handicaps. P.'s characters sometimes verbalize feminine independence and aspirations but never realize them; the conventional plot situations require helplessness, victimization, and male rescue.

Despite the stereotyped plots, P.'s writing is vigorous and touched by moments of fine dramatic irony. She is able to make moral points clearly without sermonizing. P. is remembered as a committed woman who used the weapons of sentiment in the service of a cause she believed in.

WORKS: Ida May (1854). *Caste* (1856). *Agnes* (1858).

BIBLIOGRAPHY: For articles in reference works, see: *NAW*.
Other references: *Journal of Popular Culture*, 3 (1969).

SALLY MITCHELL

Josephine Lyons Scott Pinckney

B. *25 Jan. 1895, Charleston, South Carolina; d. 4 Oct. 1957, New York City*
Wrote under: Josephine Pinckney
D. of Thomas and Camilla Scott Pinckney

P.'s Charleston heritage is evident in most of her writing. During the 1920s, she was active in the Poetry Society of South Carolina, which she helped to found; she was also one of its leading poets. Some of P.'s work was published in *Poetry* before she gathered it together in *Sea-Drinking Cities* (1927).

P.'s poetry skillfully evokes scenes and moods of the Carolina Low Country; at times, however, it tends to be artificial and contrived. Realizing her limitations, P. soon turned to writing prose fiction. During the 1930s, P. published short stories in some of the better literary magazines.

Hilton Head (1941) is a fictionalized account of the life of Henry Woodward, one of the first English settlers of South Carolina. P.'s research into Woodward's life and into the Indian and Spanish, as well as early English, settlements of the period was painstaking. The prose style is at times marred by P.'s background as a poet of the imagist school, producing descriptions with the quality of stiff brocade. The major flaw is P.'s failure to dramatize the complex actions she presents. The novel's best passages are those which describe landscapes and personal interactions.

P. realized her inability to dramatize action, and in *Three O'Clock Dinner* (1945) she found a genuine fictional mode in the novel of manners, especially the manners of Charleston. A Literary Guild selection, this was the most popular of P.'s works and perhaps her best. Set in early 20th-c. Charleston, the story is of the inroads made by the daughter of a German immigrant family into one of the bastions of Charleston aristocracy, the Redcliff family. Although the girl fails to breech the family bulwark, she does shake and weaken its foundations. P.'s skillful description of Charleston manners displays both the charms and shortcomings of her characters; and she retains the ability to capture the scenery and moods of her native city.

Charleston is also the setting for *Great Mischief* (1948), but here it is the Charleston of the late 19th c. In addition to her careful research on the period, P. explores the superstitions of the time and includes a historically accurate account of 19th-c. witchcraft. These elements are woven together so skillfully that the line between fantasy and reality is blurred not only for the characters but also for the readers. The night of the witches' sabbath coincides with the great Charleston earthquake of 1886 so that both the main character and the reader are left to wonder if the witching was real or merely a dream.

In *My Son and Foe* (1952), P. abandons the Charleston setting to study the interactions of her characters in the crucible of a small, remote Caribbean island—interactions of love and jealousy, good and evil.

P. returned to a Charleston setting with *Splendid in Ashes* (1958). She chronicles the feelings of a generation of Charlestonians about the life and times of Augustus Grimshawe, recently deceased. Grimshawe's career and personality, as well as the personalities of those with whom he came into contact, are revealed as the characters react to the news of his death. P. ties the past to the present with a skillful combination of reminiscence and flashback.

P.'s first two books are the works of a literary novice. With her third book, P. found herself and became not only a writer with popular appeal but also a skillful delineator of the manners of the rigid Charlestonian society she knew so well. In her best novels, P. reveals the Charlestonian mind with wit and ironic humor.

WORKS: Sea-Drinking Cities (1927). *Hilton Head* (1941). *Three O'Clock Dinner* (1945). *Great Mischief* (1948). *My Son and Foe* (1952). *Splendid in Ashes* (1958).

BIBLIOGRAPHY: Davidson, D., *The Spyglass: Views and Reviews* (1963).
For articles in reference works, see: *American Novelists of Today*, H. R. Warfel (1951). *20thCAS.*
Other references: *NYHTBR* (20 Jan. 1952). *NYTBR* (23 Sept. 1945; 21 March 1948; 4 May 1958).

HARRIETTE CUTTINO BUCHANAN

Sylvia Plath

B. 27 Oct. 1932, Boston, Massachusetts; d. 11 Feb. 1963, London, England
Wrote under: Victoria Lucas, Sandra Peters, Sylvia Plath
D. of Otto Emil and Aurelia Schober Plath; m. Ted Hughes, 1956

P.'s father emigrated from the Polish corridor and became a biologist at Boston University; her mother, also a German immigrant, taught high-school English. P. was instilled with an achievement ethic which fueled her precocious talent for writing and drawing.

The facts of P.'s biography directly inform her writing, especially her idyllic yet menaced childhood by the sea, which ended abruptly with her father's death when P. was eight. His death, its dramatic circumstances, and the ensuing move inland to Wellesley affected P. profoundly. Writing poetry became "a new way of being happy." Sea, father, and childhood became a haunting amalgam of loss.

P.'s legend as superachiever began early. By the time she won a scholarship to Smith (1950), P. had drawings, poems, and stories in national publications, including *Seventeen*. Maintaining her momentum at Smith with school honors and steady publication, she won *Mademoiselle*'s College Fiction Contest, was named Guest Editor ("the literary woman's 'Miss America' "), and in June 1953 was initiated to "Mad"-ison Avenue.

Exhausted, demoralized, and at odds with her hard-won image as the all-American girl, P. had a mental breakdown and attempted suicide. After psychiatric treatment she returned to Smith, graduating summa cum laude (1955), again winning top awards and also a Fulbright to Cambridge for graduate work.

During her two years at Cambridge, P. married Hughes, a poet. Returning to Smith as English professor, she found the conflict between teaching and writing untenable. After another year attending Robert Lowell's poetry seminar and Yaddo, P. made her life in England, immersing herself in writing, Devon country life, and motherhood.

Worn down by competing pressures of motherhood and muse, chronic ill health, a cold winter, a failed marriage, and recurrent depression, P. gassed herself at the age of thirty-one.

P.'s middle-class, Unitarian upbringing induced no radical activism. Although a liberal conscience does plead for peace, and a mature P. fears the military-industrial complex and deplores "The Thin People," P.

reaches out from her "bell jar" for an image of her own experience as a woman and artist. Compulsively trying to come to terms with the meaning of her female sexuality as she tries to realize her ambitions, P. interprets global distress in terms of her personal conflicts. As a woman, P. frequently identifies with the underdog; in her art she is Jew to a Nazi paternity, "chuffed off" to Auschwitz, turning and burning in Holocaust ovens, even the bright oven of Hiroshima.

In her apprentice work, P. submerges her specific concerns about identity, creation, death, and muse beneath detached, synthetic, allusive pieces on nature and art. P.'s early poems attest to her control, not only over form but over the emotion it contains. Her middle poems are best represented by *The Colossus* (1960), which spans her college, breakdown, scholar, and marriage phases of development. Painstakingly wrought, word by well-chosen word, the clenched poems elicit admiration for their mature technical virtuosity, and criticism (shared by P.) for their elaborate "checks and courtesies," "maddening docility," and "deflections." The poems not only present the themes and images of the later *Ariel*-type poems (the baby/moon/mother/muse matrix and father/sea/suicide cluster), but introduce the exuberant passion and wit that distinguish P.'s greatest works.

Three Women: A Monologue for Three Voices (1962) is a transitional, formative work. Always obsessed by, and ambivalent about, female creativity, P. now presents her Darwinian value system: the mother is victor, for *she* produces, while the Girl and the Secretary are "empty," "restless and useless," creating "corpses." The three voices represent P.'s consciousness of her role conflict as artist, wife, and mother. The radio-play format opens up P.'s style. After this, P.'s poetry is dramatic rather than narrative or expository, written "all of one piece," to be read aloud; its imperfect cadences, careless-seeming rhymes, and impression of spontaneity and free association underlie P.'s new aesthetics, which demand of the poems that they be "possessed . . . as by the rhythms of their own breathing."

The poems in *Ariel* (1965), *Crossing the Water* (1971), and *Winter Trees* (1971) are the culmination of themes and images of P.'s previous works. They are different only in degree—"extremist" in their profound disillusionment in her idealized marriage and the "years of doubleness, smiles, and compromise." P. releases her long-suppressed rage and is, at the same time, disconcertingly gleeful and triumphant, gaily macabre, and erotically murderous. Vitality, not iambics, produces the rhythm, and the half, slanted rhymes sound like a drunk's.

While the poems appear autobiographical and private in imagery (the "toe" of "Daddy," one of P.'s best-known poems, refers to her father's amputated foot) and bare of artifice, years of practice with form and poetics underlie these outbursts, and the literal concrete metaphors universalize the meaning.

P.'s fiction contains the same preoccupation with her own experience, but it never loosens control as in her breakthrough poetry and hence never assumes the poetry's powerful voice. It was written throughout P.'s career, largely for the commercial market. Yet in these manufactured stories, with their studied moralistic formulas, P. gives candid expression to her own anxieties. In "The Fifty-ninth Bear," she projects a wife's canny hostility to her husband. "Den of Lions" reveals the Plathian voice at its best, where the persona is "game," wryly humorous, and self-deprecating about her traumas.

The engaging narrator of "Den of Lions" turns up again in *The Bell Jar* (1963), P.'s autobiographical novel about her mental breakdown. Again, disillusionment fuels the criticism P. now levels about growing up female in middle-class America. P.'s approach is satiric; the world's injustice is more absurd than evil. The heroine's summer on "Mad" Avenue is an initiation ritual into "the real world," which turns out to be a disillusioning joke. P.'s refusal to moralize and her naive insistence on the private nature of her vision effectively result in a moving book with tragic and universal overtones.

Her earnest effort to conform as woman and artist led to P.'s breakdown. As P. herself disengages the gagging mask of pleasing, pleased normalcy, her literature devolves from its disguised interest in landscapes and events to the subject of raw, terrifying self released from the pretense of objectivity: "Peel off the napkin / O my enemy. / Do I terrify?" ("Lady Lazarus"). Accompanying the unmasking of the subject is the conversion of duty-bound literary behavior to the exuberant anarchies of a released prisoner of style.

WORKS: *The Colossus* (1960). *A Winter Ship* (1960). *American Poetry Now* (edited by Plath, 1961). *The Bell Jar* (1963; film version, 1979). *Ariel* (1965). *Uncollected Poems* (1965). *Three Women: A Monologue for Three Voices* (1968; BBC television broadcast, 1962). *Crossing the Water* (1971). *Crystal Gazer* (1971). *Fiesta Melons* (1971). *Lyonesse* (1971). *Winter Trees* (1971). *Pursuit* (introduction by T. Hughes, 1973). *Letters Home: Correspondence 1950–1963* (edited by A. S. Plath, 1975). *The Bed Book* (1976). *Johnny Panic and the Bible of Dreams, and Other Prose Writings* (edited by T. Hughes, 1978).

The Sylvia Plath collection is at the Lilly Library, Bloomington, Indiana.

BIBLIOGRAPHY: Aird, E., *Sylvia Plath: Her Life and Work* (1973). Alvarez, A., *The Savage God* (1971). Butscher, E., *Sylvia Plath: Method and Madness* (1976). Butscher, E., ed., *Sylvia Plath, The Woman and Her Work* (1977). Gilbert, S. M., in *Shakespeare's Sisters,* Eds. Sandra M. Gilbert and Susan Gubar (1979). Howard, R., in *Alone With America: Essays on the Art of Poetry in the United Statest Since 1950* (1969). Kroll, J., *Chapters in a Mythology: The Poetry of Sylvia Plath* (1976). Lane, G., and M. Stevens, *Sylvia Plath: A Bibliography* (1978). Newman, C., ed., *The Art of Sylvia Plath: A Symposium* (1970). Rosenthal, M. C., "Confessional Poets" in *The New Poetry* (1975). Steiner, G., *Language and Silence* (1969).

For articles in reference works, see: Crowell's *Handbook of Contemporary American Poetry*, Ed. Karl Malkoff (1973). *WA.*

Other references: *London Magazine* (Feb. 1962). *Mademoiselle* (July 1975). *Ms.* (October 1975). *Southern Review* (Summer 1973).

BARBARA ANTONINA CLARKE MOSSBERG

Josephine Pollard

B. 1834, New York City; d. 1892, New York City

"A litterateur of New York City, whose work was mainly intended for juvenile readers," P. was a prolific and inventive writer. Her juvenile books include original fairy tales, verses, natural histories, Bible stories, biographies, and histories. P. also wrote several volumes of poetry, including *Coeducation* (1883), a rhymed tract promoting equal rights for women.

P.'s most inventive contribution to the field of juvenile literature was a series of books consisting almost entirely of words of one syllable. The few polysyllabic words are divided into syllables to help the young reader. The series includes *The History of the United States* (1884), *Our Hero, General U. S. Grant* (1885), *Bible Stories for Children* (1899), and many others.

P. uses simplified words, but she does not simplify her ideas or sacrifice accuracy and detail. P.'s rendition of the Sermon on the Mount, for example, loses none of the message of the biblical passage.

P.'s poetry for adults, as exemplified by *Vagrant Verses* (1886), tends to be of the Edgar A. Guest school of philosophy and versification.

"Don't Take It to Heart," a poem warning against nursing grudges, offers this insight: "There's many a sorrow would vanish tomorrow, / Were we not unwilling to furnish the wings; / So, daily intruding, and quietly brooding, / It hatches out all sorts of horrible things." "The Elder's Talk" is a dialect poem contrasting the pious wisdom of Nancy, the old country wife, with the cold, "college l'arnt" theology of the parson. "A Mother-Boy" is a paean to the youth who, despite his friends' scorn, remains tied to "the strong cable of mother's apron strings" for life. "A Commonplace Wooing" mocks the romantic and intellectual expectations of bluestocking maidens who want to be wooed with pages of "Emerson, Plato, Virgil and Cato." P.'s model female here is "An Every-day Girl," who is described as "womanly, gentle, and kind, the least little bit of a prude."

Coeducation, P.'s rhymed feminist tract, undercuts the conventional views of *Vagrant Verses* entirely. Divided into four chapters, the poem traces woman's history as a helpmate and slave, describes her present condition as a toy, and looks forward to her future as an equal. In biblical times, men and women worked together as partners. Woman was a respected part of early society: "Her wit was keen, her judgment clear, / And no one talked of woman's sphere." But woman was too keen and clever, and so envious man enslaved her through brute strength.

In modern times man uses woman as a toy, not a slave. Compliant to his wishes, woman dresses in velvet and silk and passes her time idly. Consequently, when her husband dies, the toy-woman, "upon her own resources thrown," cannot support herself.

Woman's future must lie in education and professional equality. Educated woman will have a career, and her husband will soon discover the cash benefit. The professional woman will have less time for her children, less leisure, and "an equal right to pay the bills." She will cleverly hide any disappointments from man, however, and will strive to remain equal.

P.'s primary talent lies in writing instructional and entertaining books for children. Her commercial poetry is rather trite. *Coeducation*, while it may be doggerel, raises interesting issues and predicts a future that has not yet fully arrived.

WORKS: *Wild Animals for Children* (185?). *Lydia's Duty* (1869). *The Open Door; or, Valera in Search of a Mission* (1872). *Gipsy in New York* (1873). *Gipsy's Early Days* (1873). *Gipsy's Travels* (1874). *Gipsy's Adventures* (1875). *Gipsy's Quest* (1876). *The Other Gipsy* (1876). *A Piece of Silver* (1876). *A Step, or a Mis-Step* (1877). *The Decorative Sisters, a Modern Ballad* (1881). *The Boston Tea Party* (1882). *The Burden Lifted* (1882). *Elfin*

Land (1882). *Gellivor: A Christmas Legend of the North Land* (1882). *The Brave Little Tailor* (1883). *Coeducation* (1883). *Good Manners: A Few Hints About Behavior* (1883). *Hours in Fairy Land* (1883). *Pantomime and Minstrel Scenes* (1883). *The Six Swans* (1883). *Snow White* (1883). *The Story of Bonnybelle* (1883). *Tales of the Fairy World* (1883). *Artistic Tableaux* (1884). *The History of the United States* (1884). *Our Hero, General U. S. Grant. When, Where, and How He Fought* (1885). *Songs of Bird Life* (1885). *Domestic Animals* (1886). *Large Birds* (1886). *Our Naval Heroes* (1886). *Pictures and Stories from Natural History* (1886). *Small Animals* (1886). *Small Birds* (1886). *Vagrant Verses* (1886). *Wild Animals* (1886). *Winter Sports* (1886). *Favorite Birds and What the Poets Sing of Them* (1888). *Flowers from Field and Woodland* (1888). *History of the Old Testament in Words of One Syllable* (1888). *Young Folk's Bible in Words of Easy Reading* (1888?). *The Bible and Its Story* (1889). *Boys and Girls Name A, B, C* (1889). *History of the Battles of America in Words of One Syllable* (1889). *Plays and Games for Little Folks* (1889). *Fireside Fun* (1890). *Little Pig Series* (1890). *Pleasewell Series* (1890). *Singing Games* (1890). *Sports of All Sorts* (1890). *Two Little Tots on Their Way Through the Year* (1890). *The Wonderful Story of Jesus* (1890). *Young Folks' Life of Jesus Christ* (1891). *The Life of George Washington* (1893). *Bible Stories for Children* (1899). *The Boyhood of Jesus* (1899). *God Made the World* (1899). *The Good Samaritan and Other Bible Stories* (1899). *Ruth, a Bible Heroine, and Other Stories* (1899). *The Story of Jesus; Told in Pictures* (1899). *Sweet Stories of God* (1899). *The Children's Bible Story Book* (1925). *Everyday Bible Stories* (1926). *A Child's Life of Our Lord* (1934).

BIBLIOGRAPHY: Allibone, S. A., *A Critical Dictionary of English Literature and American Authors Supplement* (1891).

ZOHARA BOYD

Eleanor Hodgman Porter

B. 1868, Littleton, New Hampshire; d. 23 May 1920
Wrote under: Eleanor Stewart
D. of Francis H. and Llewella Woolson Hodgman; m. John Lyman Porter, 1892

When P. died, the headline of her brief obituary in *The New York Times* read simply: "Author of *Pollyanna* dies." P. had written four volumes of short stories and fourteen novels, but it was the phenomenal success of *Pollyanna* that had made her famous.

P. dropped out of high school to lead a more robust outdoor life. Later she studied music at the New England Conservatory in Boston, going on to make public appearances as a singer and traveling with church choirs. In 1892, P. married a businessman. Switching her profession from music to writing, P. began to submit stories to magazines, at first with little success, but finally with the publication of her novel *Cross Currents* (1907) the tide began to turn. P. wrote a sequel in 1908 called *The Turn of the Tide*. An even more significant turning point was reached in 1913, when *Pollyanna* appeared, an event described by one commentator as "only less influential than the World War."

Pollyanna, that incredibly cheerful champion of the Glad Game, who could find in even the grimmest situation something to be glad about (if you break a leg, "be glad 'twasn't two"), stirred the hearts and hopes of people of all ages all over the world. After selling a million copies in this country, the book appeared in editions in France, Germany, Holland, Poland, Czechoslovakia, Norway, Sweden, Switzerland, Scotland, and Japan.

Critics sang *Pollyanna*'s praises: "It is a wholesome, charming book, moral but not preachy," said the popular *Literary Digest*. The *Bookman* earnestly agreed: "If the *Pollyanna* books are read with the sympathetic comprehension they deserve, many a child's life will be made happier. . . ." With this end in view, Glad Clubs sprang up everywhere—and not just for children. One branch, "The Pollyanna Glad Kids," was started by inmates of a penitentiary. Mary Pickford paid the then astronomical fee of $115,112 for the silent screen rights for *Pollyanna*.

Although P. won instant celebrity, she was not thereby admitted to the ranks of serious authors. A growing number of readers irked by the sentimental and simplistic outlook would join in Aunt Polly's exasperated demand that Pollyanna "stop using that everlasting word. . . . It's 'glad'—'glad'—'glad'—from morning till night until I think I shall go wild." In a recent survey of girl's fiction, the authors dismiss Pollyanna as hopelessly "puerile" and "intellectually debilitating," her "imbecile cheerfulness" issuing from stupidity and an infuriating tactlessness, especially when she tells a chronic invalid to be glad other folks aren't like her—"all sick, you know"; or when she tells the elderly gardener, bent with arthritis, to be glad he doesn't have to stoop so far to do his weeding.

Some critics claim that P.'s later writing was not as relentlessly cheerful as her earlier works, but evidence provided by the posthumously published *Hustler Joe, and Other Stories* (1970) indicates otherwise. In each of the stories a downbeat plot works itself miraculously into an upbeat ending. Hustler Joe, for instance, who shoots his father in the opening chapter, discovers in the closing chapter that the bullet didn't kill him after all.

When accused of being overly optimistic, P. was quoted as saying, "I have never believed that we ought to deny discomfort and pain and evil. I have merely thought that it is far better to greet the unknown with a cheer." That she did, and—despite her critics—there are readers of Pollyanna even today who are still cheering.

WORKS: Cross Currents (1907). The Turn of the Tide (1908). Miss Billy (1911). The Story of Marco (1911). Miss Billy's Decision (1912). Pollyanna (1913). Miss Billy Married (1914). Pollyanna Grows Up (1915). Just David (1916). The Road of Understanding (1917). Oh Money! Money! (1918). Dawn (1919). May-Marie (1919). Sister Sue (1921). The Tie that Binds: Tales of Love and Marriage (1924). Across the Years (1924). Money, Love, and Kate (1924). The Tangled Threads (1924). Hustler Joe, and Other Stories (1970).

BIBLIOGRAPHY: Cadogan, M., and P, Craig, You're a Brick, Angela! A New Look at Girls' Fiction from 1839–1975 (1976). Overton, G., The Women Who Make Our Novels (1918).

For articles in reference works, see: 20thCA.

Other references: Bookman (60, 1914; 61, 1915; 63, 1916). Good Housekeeping (July 1947). PW (19 July 1941). Woman's Home Companion (April 1920).

JACQUELINE BERKE

Katherine Anne Porter

B. 15 May 1890, Indian Creek, Texas; d. 18 Sept. 1980, Silver Spring, Maryland
D. of Harrison Boone and Mary Alice Jones Porter; m. ?, 1906; m. Eugene
Dove Pressly, 1933; m. Albert Russel Erskine, Jr., 1938

P. was the fourth of five children, a descendant of pioneers. Her mother died as a young woman, and P. was raised by her father and paternal grandmother.

Although P. is generally acknowledged to be a master stylist, she rarely earned her living directly through her writing. Instead, she supported herself through a variety of related activities: as a reporter, writer of screenplays in Hollywood, translator, hack writer, and most often, as a lecturer, writer-in-residence, and guest speaker. P. has received a number of honorary degrees and an impressive range of prestigious literary awards, including Guggenheim fellowships in 1931 and 1938, Fulbright and Ford Foundation grants in the 1950s, an O. Henry Award in 1962, and the Pulitzer Prize in 1966 for her *Collected Stories* (1965).

P. has traveled extensively, lived often in Europe and Mexico, been married three times, and involved herself in political events. Yet these activities are only peripherally reflected in her stories. P. makes a clear distinction between *adventure*, something you do to find an "illusion of being more alive than ordinarily," and *experience*, which is "what really happens to you in the long run; the truth that finally overtakes you." The latter is the subject of P.'s prose. She delights in revealing through microcosmic events truths about human nature.

"The Downward Path to Wisdom" (*The Leaning Tower, and Other Stories,* 1944) is a pivotal story in understanding the etiology of disillusionment in P.'s work. The protagonist, a child named Stephen, is shuffled from adult to adult in an awkward and futile attempt to keep him unaware of his parents' quarreling. P. emphasizes Stephen's genuineness by continually alluding to his sensual awareness of being warm, bare, embraced, sticky, scrubbed roughly, etc. In contrast, P. shows us, through the overheard dialogue of the parents, that they experience him simply as a reminder of their growing antipathy. She deftly controls the emergence of Stephen's final decision to set himself emotionally apart from these people who "love" him by juxtaposing the child's motives with the adults' harsh judgments of him. Stephen's final rejection of them seems healthy, yet P. manages to convey that the act of rejection forecasts Stephen's own inability to love as an adult.

Some of P.'s best stories reflect the deterioration of relationships, especially of marriages, which are corrupted by the bitterness and anger accompanying dependence. P. has said that one's spouse is a "necessary enemy," for whom we cannot help but feel both love and hate because we resent our need for him or her. P. characterizes one such marriage in "Rope" (*Flowering Judas, and Other Stories,* 1930). The husband and wife quarrel over his purchase of some unneeded rope, and their discussion evolves into a destructive verbal battle about the entire relationship and their disappointments in one another. P. conveys the tediously repetitive nature of these complaints by quoting them obliquely:

"She had her notion of what had kept him in town. Considerably more than a notion, if he wanted to know. So, she was going to bring all that up again, was she? Well, she could just think what she pleased." P.'s use of this intriguing narrative technique shows us the depth of sarcasm, bitterness, and emotional stinginess underlying this marriage and belies the appearance of reconciliation at the end of the story. In P.'s carefully crafted stories, narrative technique fuses with meaning in an almost perfect merging of form and content.

P.'s portraits of relationships ring true because she has a perfect eye for the tiny, telling domestic detail. Time and again, a single incident conveys the character of an entire relationship. In "Noon Wine" (*Pale Horse, Pale Rider*, 1939), Mr. Thompson affectionately yet cruelly pinches his wife Ellie, and we are introduced to those notions about himself, his intense, masculine pride, that will make Mr. Thompson capable of killing a man later in the story. "Noon Wine" is a study of sources of violence and self-betrayal in essentially good people.

The disappointments that grow between people are evident in both men and women in P.'s stories, but perhaps because her own awareness is based so firmly in feminine realities, P. is especially effective in depicting the limitations in relationships as women experience them, or rather, the limiting relationships that she saw as the only ones allowed to women. In stores based around the experiences of Miranda (the character who seems most similar to P.), Miranda's grandmother (based on P.'s grandmother), and others, P. implies that for a woman the rejection of close and demanding relationships is virtually the only means of finding autonomy.

In the three sections of "Old Mortality," we see Miranda (raised with her sister by a likeable, average father and a strong-willed grandmother) withdraw successively further from the family myths which have comprised her whole understanding of reality as a young child. Miranda cannot reconcile what adults tell her about the beautiful, romantic, exciting, and perfect past (especially Aunt Amy, around whom an entire legend has been built) with the shabby remnants of the past she finds around her. At eighteen, Miranda realizes that the unequivocally negative memories of Cousin Eva, a poor defeated relative of Amy, are just as distorted as the romantic, tragic account the family has always given her and, drawing back from this massive collusion of lies, tells herself, in "her hopefulness, her ignorance," that whatever else, she will live her life without illusions. P. knows that this is naive and that there are no easy answers.

For all of P.'s thoughtful characters, life involves introspection, disappointment, and moral dilemmas. If her characters (like her married couples) stay in their oppressive relationships, resentment eats away at them. If they break free, they are terribly alone. It is not surprising that P. projects onto her primitive characters—such as the eponymous Mexican Indian in the story "María Concepción" (*Flowering Judas*) and the Spanish dancers in *Ship of Fools* (1962)—the very strengths which she believes introspective people cannot achieve: a passionate, unselfconscious, unquestioning spontaneity that carries with it no moral complications.

Ship of Fools, P.'s long-awaited novel, appeared in 1962. P. was deeply shaken by the two world wars and by world events that for decades threatened the human race with catastrophe. She tells us that much of her energy in those years was given to an attempt "to grasp the meaning of those threats, to trace them to their sources and to understand the logic of this majestic and terrible failure of the life of man in the Western world." P.'s allegorical novel became an exploration into the possible sources of human evil and particularly into the states of mind which could account for such horrors as the Holocaust.

The story takes place on a German freighter-passenger ship traveling from Veracruz, Mexico, to Bremerhaven, Germany, in late summer of 1931, with a passenger list representing various nationalities. To the degree that the characters become stereotypes for particular countries, the novel seems a failure, for its ironies are heavy-handed and the notes of prophecy seem contrived, written as they were long after World War II. But on the level of individual human encounters, P.'s portrayals are meticulous, vivid, and often engrossing. In depicting a range of individuals preoccupied with their narrow personal concerns, she shows acute perception of how we tend to blind ourselves to external realities and become culpable in evil events.

Ultimately, the pleasures we find in reading P.'s stories prove to be subtle ones: the frequent perfection of her choice of words and details and commentary on a character's behavior; the telling scenes; the recognitions about human nature; the ironic narrative; and P.'s understanding of the pleasures of childhood (always being crushed by somber adult realities), of the stories we tell ourselves to make our lives make sense, of the self-delusions, self-betrayals, and ultimate isolation of each of us. Her perceptions are acute, and her prose is often superb. P. severely limited the number of stories she would allow to be published, yet her choices seem to have been wise ones, for they offer us a surprisingly consistent vitality in their revelation of human truths.

WORKS: Outline of Mexican Popular Arts and Crafts (1922). *Flowering Judas, and Other Stories* (1930; republished with added stories, 1935). *Katherine Anne Porter's French Song Book* (1933). *Hacienda: A Story of Mexico* (1934). *Noon Wine* (1937). *Pale Horse, Pale Rider: Three Short Novels* (1939). *The Itching Parrot* (1942). *The Leaning Tower, and Other Stories* (1944). *The Old Order: Stories of the South* (1944). *The Days Before* (1952). *A Defense of Circe* (1955). *Holiday* (1962). *Ship of Fools* (1962). *The Collected Stories of Katherine Anne Porter* (1965). *A Christmas Story* (1967). *The Collected Essays and Occasional Writings of Katherine Anne Porter* (1970).

BIBLIOGRAPHY: Auchincloss, L., *Pioneers and Caretakers: A Study of Nine American Women Writers* (1965). Emmons, W. S., *Katherine Anne Porter: The Regional Stories* (1967). Hardy, J. E., *Katherine Anne Porter* (1973). Hartley, L., and G. Core, eds., *Katherine Anne Porter: A Critical Symposium* (1969). Hendrick, G., *Katherine Anne Porter* (1965). Kiernan, R. F., *Katherine Anne Porter and Carson McCullers: A Reference Guide* (1976). Krishnamurthi, M. G., *Katherine Anne Porter: A Study* (1971). Liberman, M. M., *Katherine Anne Porter's Fiction* (1971). Mooney, H. J., Jr., *The Fiction and Criticism of Katherine Anne Porter* (1962). Nance, W. L., *Katherine Anne Porter and the Art of Rejection* (1964). Waldrip, L., and S. A. Bauer, eds., *A Bibliography of the Works of Katherine Anne Porter, and A Bibliography of the Criticism of the Works of Katherine Anne Porter* (1969). Wescott, G., "Katherine Anne Porter, Personally," *Images of Truth: Remembrances and Criticism* (1962). West, R. B., Jr., *Katherine Anne Porter* (1963).

GAIL MORTIMER

Rose Porter

B. 6 Dec. 1845, New York City; d. 10 Sept. 1906, New Haven, Connecticut
D. of David and Rose Anne Hardy Porter

The author or editor of more than seventy books on religious themes, P. was descended from New England clergymen. Her father was a prosperous businessman and her mother an upper-class Englishwoman. P. attended a New York City private school and spent time in England. After her parents' deaths, she became a semiinvalid and lived alone in New Haven.

Besides her fifteen novels and her volumes of religious essays, P. produced devotional exercises; anthologies of consolatory verse, such as *Hope Songs* (1885) and *Comfort for the Mothers of Angels* (1881);

prayer books for the sick, such as *In the Shadow of His Hand* (1892); and collections of texts from literature and scripture arranged on calendars or diaries. P. also edited selections from many poets.

Her first success was *Summer Driftwood for the Winter Fire* (1870). Presented as the diary of a nineteen-year-old girl, the book records a summer's travel, during which she falls in love and her lover dies. But most of the pages are occupied by the girl's meditations about Ruskin, heaven, her dead mother, and the beauties of nature. At the end, she is consoled in her single life because she has found work helping orphans.

Most of P.'s novels are similar: calm, retrospective, meditative, and told without suspense or emotional tension. P. seldom created a villain or even a character with whom the hero or heroine might have serious conflict. When she did attempt novels with more plot, P. used the conventions of sentimental melodrama.

In *Foundations; or, Castles in the Air* (1871), Alfred Merwin leaves his widowed mother in the country and goes off to be a city merchant's clerk. He falls into temptation—stays home from church, goes to "places of amusement" (unspecified), and gambles—and the farm is mortgaged to pay his debts. Ultimately, his mother's faith saves him; he prospers, gives to charity, returns to church, and marries his childhood sweetheart. The action is omitted; we do not see his debauchery or even his confession to his mother, but are told about both much later.

The masochistic elements of victory through suffering are most clearly visible in *Uplands and Lowlands* (1872). After an idealized relationship with his mother, orphaned Paul Foster goes to Rome and paints a magnificent holy picture. Because he will do no crass commercial work, he starves to death. His genius, of course, is recognized as soon as he has died.

The devotional books make P.'s basically conservative theology explicit. Her God is not human and domesticated but other and unfathomable. P. emphasizes faith rather than works. Most importantly, she extols weakness and submission and suffering, which subdue the individual will and open the mind to God, and which are also particularly suitable for women. In *Life's Everydayness* (1893), P. praises the daily annoyances and petty discouragements of the household because they enable one constantly to deny self and to exercise passivity and renunciation. Sympathy is woman's special vocation; many days may be well spent doing nothing but attending to the interests of others. P. also finds it important to fight discontent; a woman should daily count her blessings and be happy with the people and circumstances around her.

P.'s writing gave theological support to a conception of woman as domestic, virtuous, passive, weak, devoted to the trivial, inculcating morality by example, enforcing obedience by suffering, and utterly unfit for any sphere beyond house walls. Reviewers praised P.'s novels for their purity; they were often included in series for young readers; and, to judge from the sheer number of titles, they must have had a fairly steady sale.

WORKS (selected): Summer Driftwood for the Winter Fire (1870). Foundations; or, Castles in the Air (1871). Uplands and Lowlands (1872). The Winter Fire (1874). The Years That Are Told (1875). Christmas Evergreens (1876). A Song and a Sigh (1877). In the Mist (1879). Charity, Sweet Charity (1880). Comfort for the Mothers of Angels (1881). Our Saints: A Family Story (1881). The Story of a Flower (1883). Foregleams of Immortality (1884). Honoria; or, The Gospel of a Life (1885). Hope Songs (1885). A Modern Saint Christopher (1887). Driftings from Mid-Ocean (1889). Looking toward Sunrise (1890). Open Windows, a Heart-to-Heart Diary (1890). Saint Martin's Summer; or, The Romance of the Cliff (1891). Women's Thoughts for Women: A Calendar (1891). In the Shadow of His Hand (1892). Life's Everydayness: Papers for Women (1893). My Son's Wife (1895). One of the Sweet Old Chapters (1896). The Pilgrim's Staff (1897). A Daughter of Israel (1899). The Everlasting Harmony (1900).

BIBLIOGRAPHY: For articles in reference works, see: NCAB, 10. A Woman of the Century, Eds. F. Willard and M. Livermore (1893).
    Other references: Harper's (Sept. 1870; June 1871). NYT (11 July 1870).

SALLY MITCHELL

Sarah Porter

P. lived during the late 18th c. and probably the early 19th c. She was probably a resident of Plymouth, Massachusetts, and a member of either a Congregationalist or a Presbyterian church.

P.'s slender volume of published poetry, The Royal Penitent, in Three Parts, to Which Is Added David's Lamentation over Saul and Jonathan (1791), contains work of such quality and interest that it seems probable that she produced other works. This work reveals ambition and talent in its three hundred and fifty-two lines, which deal with David's guilt and repentance for his seduction of Bathsheba and betrayal of her husband, his loyal general, Uriah. P.'s handling of this subject includes not only religious but also political and social themes relevant to contemporary interests of late-18th-c. Americans. The structure and content indicate at least a passing familiarity with Dryden's *Absalom and Achitophel* and the American poet Timothy Dwight's epic, *The Conquest of Canaan*.

P.'s poem presents two major themes: the workings of divine providence and the necessity for morality in government. The poem particularly emphasizes the concept that a country is only as good (moral) as its leaders. A decadent ruling class subverts national morals. P.'s was not a very veiled criticism of the contemporary political situation in the U.S. in the decade after the revolutionary war. During those years, a major complaint of those who remained staunch republicans was that the government and the nation as a whole were being subverted from the high ideals of the revolutionary era. This "subversion" was a result of an influx of new wealth, followed by a vulgar taste for luxury. P. shows this type of moral decay through the example of King David as he remembers his humble beginnings, his rise to power, and his subsequent immoral behavior, the result of his lust for material possessions. Thus, David's downfall becomes a warning for P.'s compatriots about their politics.

P.'s poetic ambitions appear also in her choice of style and form. She exhibits a thorough understanding of neoclassical poetic techniques and evidently possessed the training and ability to employ them with success. P. produced a heroic poem in which characters of great personal and historical stature act against a background of national events as the supernatural and natural worlds mingle. The narrative alternates between descriptive passages and dialogue, producing an effective variety.

Published along with the successful *Royal Penitent* is a short work, a paraphrase of David's lament for Saul and Jonathan (2 Samuel 1:17). Taking full advantage of the substance of her biblical model, P. uses the elegy to convey both religious and political themes. Using the Puritan concept of America as the new Israel, P. draws an implied analogy between the dead Hebrew heroes and the dead American revolutionary heroes, stressing the recurrent theme of late-18th-c. American literature— the necessity for national political unity in the face of anarchic and external incursions.

P. made important contributions to the broadening thematic materials in the poetry of American women. She enlarged the scope of women's poetry to encompass current political and ideological interests through the device of the contemporaneously popular heroic verse form.

WORKS: *The Royal Penitent, in Three Parts, to Which is Added David's Lamentation over Saul and Jonathan* (1791).

JACQUELINE HORNSTEIN

Sylvia Field Porter

B. *18 June 1913, Patchogue, New York*
Writes under: *S. F. Porter, Sylvia Porter*
D. *of Louis and Rose Maisel Feldman; m. Reed Porter, 1931; m. G. Sumner Collins, 1943; m. James F. Fox, 1979*

P. was born to Jewish immigrants from Russia. Her father, a physician, had a fatal heart attack when P. was twelve. Four years later, the family lost everything in the stock market crash. P., a freshman at Hunter College, changed her major to economics in order to understand the causes of the Depression. She graduated magna cum laude in 1932 and went to work for a bond dealer at $15 per week.

For the next few years, P. learned her trade at several different Wall Street firms. At twenty-two, she started writing occasional financial columns for the *American Banker* and the New York *Post*. Ten years later, when the *Post* editors realized she had earned a large audience as well as recognition in her field, they published her picture and changed to the Sylvia Porter byline.

P. served on the Board of Editors of the World Book Encyclopedia Yearbook from 1961 through 1978, and wrote the annual economics survey for the publication. She is also a contributing editor of the *Ladies' Home Journal* and writes its monthly column, "Spending Your Money."

P. has received many awards as an outstanding financial writer, journalist, and woman of achievement. She holds fourteen honorary degrees from academic institutions such as Hood College, Bates College, Tufts University, and Smith College.

P. kept her first husband's name after their divorce in 1941. Her second marriage lasted until Collins's death in 1977. P. has a daughter and a step-son.

P.'s writing falls into two categories: newsletters on bonds and interest rates for professional bankers and financial analysts, and books and newspaper columns for the consumer. P. began a column on bonds for the *American Banker* soon after graduation. By 1944, this developed into *Reporting on Governments . . . Weekly Fixed Income Market Analysis,* a high-priced weekly newsletter for banks and other financial institutions. The weekly publication, reported to be the most widely distributed newsletter of its kind, provides clear and specific analysis of interest-rate trends, monetary and fiscal policies, and investment strategy in the bond market. The letter covers what is happening in money markets, why it is happening, and what will be the likely effect on interest rates.

P.'s daily column is syndicated by Field Newspaper Syndicate in more than four hundred newspapers, with a readership of over forty million. *Sylvia Porter's Money Book* (1975) was on the *New York Times* bestseller list for thirty-six weeks. The title is a good indication that P. has become a household word in the field of family finances. *Sylvia Porter's Money Book* is a compendium—more than one thousand pages long— of her syndicated newspaper columns, designed as a basic book in personal finance and consumers' rights.

P. has been successful in the field of personal finances because her information is reliable, her writing style is clear and concise, and her subject matter relates to every household. She admits to "often being superficial because of early deadlines and space limitations" but nevertheless believes that she has helped to educate millions of Americans in basic economics. P. has built up a reputation for sound advice that has gained the confidence of middle-class America. She does not pretend to be an economist, but as "Everyman's guide to the businessworld" she has no rivals.

WORKS: *How to Make Money in Government Bonds* (1939). *If War Comes to the American Home* (1941). *How to Live within Your Income* (with J. K. Lasser, 1948). *Managing Your Money* (1953; 1961). *Sylvia Porter's Money Book: How to Earn It, Spend It, Save It, Invest It, Borrow It—and Use It to Better Your Life* (1975). *Sylvia Porter's New Money Book for the 1980s* (1979).

BIBLIOGRAPHY: Bird, C., in *Enterprising Women* (1976). Diamonstein, B., in *Open Secrets* (1972).

For articles in reference works, see: *CB* (Oct. 1941).

Other references: *Across the Board* (July 1978). *Ladies' Home Journal* (Jan. 1976). *Time* (28 Nov. 1960). *Wall StJ* (24 March 1972).

JOAN M. McCREA

Emily Price Post

B. 3 Oct. 1873, Baltimore, Maryland; d. 25 Sept. 1960, New York City
Wrote under: Emily Post
D. of Bruce and Josephine Lee Price; m. Edwin Post, 1892

P. was a member of New York society, raised in the well-educated and proper atmosphere of Tuxedo Park. Her early career was prescribed by the conventions of upper-class leisure and manners: governesses, trips to Europe, private schooling, and debutante balls. After being divorced and then forced by economic stress to explore and expand upon her native talents, P. began her public life with interior decoration schemes. She wrote travelogues and a series of light novels of manners about Americans vacationing in Europe and associating with the Continental gentry. P. soon expanded her scope and wrote about American standards of manners, mores, and taste in manuals of etiquette and home decor.

The original dean of modern American decorum, P. was the first in a line of inventive women writers of handbooks on etiquette and manners. She remains a key figure in setting the tone for civil behavior in a rapidly changing world of styles, relationships, and attitudes—a kaleidoscopic social scene of shifting patterns in class, money, taste, and mobility, intensified by the departure from 19th- and early 20th-c. "laws" of social procedure, which had long been relied on as fixed and permanent. The need for more relaxed and flexible standards of behavior suited to the millions of upwardly mobile Americans after World War I made P.'s *Etiquette: The Blue Book of Social Usage* (1922) an immediate and long-lived success.

P.'s name quickly became a household word for "proper" manners, even if in a new key. Ironically, the conventions of formality and civility now associated so firmly with her were heartily opposed in all P.'s analysis and advice, her most famous aphorism being, "Nothing is less important than which fork you use."

P.'s *Blue Book* was the most popular and influential book of etiquette by a woman of social standing since Mary Sherwood's *Manners and Social Usages* (1884). P.'s easy readability and practical approach to the myriad problems of interpersonal relations posed by the unfamiliar contexts of changing times have made the *Blue Book* a perennial best-seller. In recent years, more progressive works by younger writers have supplanted the *Blue Book,* but P.'s emphasis on the spirit rather than the letter of the law of manners has made the *Blue Book* adaptable to change, assuring it a lasting place as a reference statement in the field. For example, in the 1940s, a supplementary edition was devised to deal with the special circumstances of wartime.

The book's success led to a newspaper column and a radio broadcast series, as well as many requests for P.'s endorsement of food, drink, and household products. The formulations P. established for diplomatic protocol were adopted by Washington offices as a uniform code, and *The Personality of a House* (1930), used as a text in courses about taste and decoration, is further evidence of her strong feeling for atmosphere and the quality of life. This feel for style informs such other works as *Children Are People* (1940).

To P., it was obvious that simplicity and grace are the fundamental precepts of manners, and that there is an urgent need to state this principle in detail, dramatizing its application in every conceivable setting and circumstance. Her writing ushered in a new era, which thought about etiquette not as a fixed system of gestures and words but as an ever-changing rule of thumb, based on a much more open, democratic, and classless view of society with an active sense of mobility and impermanence. P.'s interpretation of etiquette as a "science of living" sets the terms of discussion later taken up and developed in the contemporary scene by a core of women social arbiters including Jean Kerr, Peg Bracken, Amy Vanderbilt, Abigail Van Buren, and Ann Landers.

WORKS: *The Flight of a Moth* (1904). *Purple and Fine Linen* (1906). *Woven in the Tapestry* (1908). *The Title Market* (1909). *The Eagle's Feather* (1910). *By Motor to the Golden Gate* (1915). *Etiquette: The Blue Book of Social Usage* (1922; rev. ed., 1955). *Parade* (1925). *How to Behave Though a Debutante* (1928). *The Personality of a House* (1930; rev. ed., 1948). *Children Are People* (1940). *Emily Post Institute Cook Book* (with E. M. Post, Jr., 1949). *Motor Manners* (1950).

BIBLIOGRAPHY: For articles in reference works, see: *CB* (1941).
Other references: *AH* (April 1977). *NYT* (27 Sept. 1960).

MARGARET J. KING

Ella Farman Pratt

B. 1 Nov. 1837, Augusta, New York; d. 22 May 1907, Warner,
  New Hampshire
Given name: Eliza Anna Farman
Wrote under: Ella Farman, Ella Farman Pratt, Dorothea Alice Shepherd
D. of Tural Tufts and Hannah Burleson Farman; m. Charles Stuart Pratt,
  1887

Daughter of a Methodist minister, P. was educated in private schools. From her early years P. wrote for her own enjoyment, though she did not begin to publish in periodicals until about 1870. Her first books, *Anna Maylie* and *Grandma Crosby's Household*, appeared in 1873.

Like Mary Mapes Dodge, editor of *St. Nicholas* magazine, P. counted herself as one of the "new school" of writers who wished to change the balance between entertainment and instruction in children's literature. However, when P. was chosen to edit Lothrop and Co.'s *Wide Awake*, a competitor to *St. Nicholas*, her statement of editorial policy showed that the didactic still had a strong hold: "Stories, poems and sketches can be instructive and elevating, high in sentiment and pure in tone without being as solid as a sermon or as dull as ditchwater."

With her husband, P. edited *Wide Awake* from 1875 to 1892, when the magazine merged with *St. Nicholas*. The couple also edited several other juvenile periodicals, including *Babyland*, *Little Men and Women*, and *Little Folks*. P. also wrote more than twenty books, including one volume of poems, *Sugar Plums* (1877). Many of P.'s best stories for young children, such as *The Little Cave Dwellers* (1901), were episodic tales based on the adventures of her son and his friends.

P.'s greatest virtue as a writer is that her heroes and heroines are interesting, though idealized, mixtures of strengths and weaknesses. Lois Gladstone of *Mrs. Hurd's Niece* (1884), a novel for teenage girls, is an orphan; and "though quite a superior girl in many respects, she is unsophisticated in the ways of the great noisy selfish world. In some respects, she is not a modern girl at all." Luckily, Lois also has spirit and temper enough to resent mistreatment.

Despite the strengths of characterization, *Mrs. Hurd's Niece* is marred by two common faults of the era: a tendency to melodrama and a compulsion to have very young characters speak baby talk. The melodramatic tendencies generally surface in elucidations of theme: "Lois feels no longer quite alone. Near her is a member of the great Household of Faith to which she belongs. As he comes down past her door, she impulsively steps out." The baby talk, however, presents a more serious barrier to readability.

A critic for *The New Century* wrote of P. that she "has the very desirable knack of imparting valuable ideas under the guise of a pleasing story"; but, for the contemporary reader, P.'s work is chiefly interesting for what it reveals of the values and attitudes that an author and editor of widely read juvenile literature of the 19th c. wished to inculcate in her readers.

WORKS: *Anna Maylie* (1873). *Grandma Crosby's Household* (1873). *A Little Woman* (1873). *A Girl's Money* (1874). *A White Hand* (1874). *The Cooking Club of Tu-Whit Hollow* (1876). *The Doll Doctor, and Other Stories* (1877). *Good-for-Nothing Polly* (1877). *Lill's Travels* (with E. Towne, 1877). *Sugar Plums* (1877). *Little Miss Mischief and Her Happy Thoughts* (1878). *Prue's Pocket Book* (1878). *How Two Girls Tried Farming* (1879). *The Home Primer* (1882). *Bo-Peep's Stocking* (1883). *Mrs. Hurd's Niece* (1884). *A Dozen Darlings and Their Doings* (1898). *The Play Lady* (1900). *The Little Cave Dwellers* (1901). *Chicken Little* (1903). *The Little Owls at Red Gates* (1903). *Dear Little Sheila* (1905).

BIBLIOGRAPHY: For articles in reference works, see: *DAB*, VIII, 1.
Other references: *Wide Awake* (Sept. 1881; Sept. 1892).

KATHARYN F. CRABBE

Elizabeth Payson Prentiss

B. 26 Oct. 1818, Portland, Maine; d. 13 Aug. 1878, Dorset, Vermont
D. of Edward and Ann Louisa Shipman Payson; m. George Lewis Prentiss, 1845

P. was the fifth of eight children of a Congregational minister; both her theology and piety were deeply influenced by P.'s father. Sickly and intense even as a child, P. professed her faith in 1831 and joined the Bleecker Street Presbyterian Church in New York City. That same year her family returned to Portland, and P. opened a school there in 1838. From 1840 to 1843, P. taught in Richmond, Virginia.

P. married a recently ordained Congregational minister, and they moved first to New Bedford, Massachusetts, where they had two children, and later to New York City, where four more children were born.

P. began her writing career with the publication of children's books. In *Little Susy's Six Birthdays* (1853), *Little Susy's Six Teachers* (1856), and *Little Susy's Little Servants* (1856), P. teaches children by example and allegory. Her use of realistic accounts of children's high jinks and trials set a new trend in juvenile literature, and the Suzy books were printed in numerous domestic and foreign editions for the remainder of the century.

The Flower of the Family (1853) was written to show girls that "trivial home duty," when performed in the fear of God and love for Christ, leads "onward and upward through present self-denial, to the highest usefulness, peace and joy."

Similar themes mark P.'s adult fiction, including *Stepping Heavenward* (1869). In this semiautobiographical spiritual manual, the protagonist is Katherine Mortimer, who marries Dr. Ernest Elliott and has six children. Katy is spurred to spiritual growth by such misfortunes as the insensitivity of her husband, the death of a child, the never-ending drudgery of housewifery, and, finally, her own terminal seven-year illness.

For P., the path to Christian perfection—a very popular quest of the day—was through suffering endured and sorrow accepted. In all her novels the protagonists finally reach Christian maturity after their faith has been deepened, their spirituality refined by broken engagements, children's sickness and death, social alienation, unjust accusations, or the nearly fatal illness of a spouse. As P.'s husband and biographer writes, "she came to regard suffering, when sanctified by the word of God and by prayer, as the King's highway to Christian perfection."

Although P.'s books did not gain literary acclaim, they were a significant contribution to the "higher life" movement of the day. P.'s most enduring contribution was her poem "More Love to Thee, O Christ," still found in most hymnals.

WORKS: *The Flower of the Family* (1853). *Little Susy's Six Birthdays* (1853). *Henry and Bessie* (1855). *Little Susy's Little Servants* (1856). *Little Susy's Six Teachers* (1856). *Peterchen and Gretchen, Tales of Early Childhood* (translated by Prentiss, 1860). *The Little Preacher* (1867). *Fred, and Maria, and Me* (1868). *Little Threads* (1868). *Stepping Heavenward* (1869). *Aunt Jane's Hero* (1871). *Religious Poems; or, Golden Hours* (1873–74). *Urbane and His Friends* (1874). *The Home at Greylock* (1876). *Pemaquid* (1877). *Avis Benson* (1879).

BIBLIOGRAPHY: Douglas, A., *The Feminization of American Culture* (1977). Prentiss, G. L., *The Life and Letters of Elizabeth Prentiss* (1882). For articles in reference works, see: *AA. DAB*, VIII, 1. *NAW* (article by O. E. Winslow). *NCAB*, 7.

NANCY A. HARDESTY

Harriet Waters Preston

B. *6 Aug. 1836, Danvers, Massachusetts; d. 14 May 1911, Cambridge, Massachusetts*
D. *of Samuel and Lydia Proctor Preston*

P. received her education at home and later, during a prolonged residence in Europe, became an accomplished linguist. Her final years were spent in the New England area.

P. contributed reviews and critical articles to magazines such as the *Atlantic Monthly*, attempted several experimental fictions, and became a recognized scholar through her many excellent translations of Provençal literature and other subjects.

Although P.'s five novels about New England life and customs have been dismissed as negligible, as a whole they are competent fictions combining P.'s intellectual interests with a type of regionalism somewhat reminiscent, at times, of Sarah Orne Jewett's fictions.

Aspendale (1871) and *Love in the Nineteenth Century: A Fragment* (1873) might be called "essay-novels." *Aspendale* illustrates P.'s ideas on friendship between two women, and *Love in the Nineteenth Century* presents P.'s commonsensical program for establishing a workable love relationship. Liberally interspersed throughout these two novels are P.'s astute critical evaluations of numerous authors and her ideas on national types, tradition, "modern" music, marriage, and feminism. The second novel also includes a long discussion on the deficiencies of male writers' fictional portraits of women and a prediction that when women writers finally "dare" to speak their minds freely, a "new order of things in fiction" will result.

Much more conventional in plot and character development are P.'s later novels of manners. *Is That All?* (1876), a study of small-town

New England courtship and social rivalry, was one of the earlier selections published anonymously in the Robert Brothers' "No Name Series," an innovative publishing project designed to allow readers to judge fiction solely on its intrinsic merits rather than on an author's established reputation. Probably her best novel, although somewhat superficial in some respects, *Is That All?* seriously strives to develop a new kind of heroine—the older society matron as a viable, admirable type.

In *The Guardians* (1888), written with her niece Louise Preston Dodge, P. tried to bring a new, sensible realism to the well-worn genre of the 19th-c. women's novel. Using the conventional plot based on the erring ways of the orphaned heroine, P. seriously analyzes the deficiencies in the education of young women. She also explores the character-building effects of duty on the handsome but weak New England hero who must assume the responsibility of guardianship for the two orphaned sisters, undergo the horrors of the Civil War, and finally give up his claim on the affections of his grown-up ward.

P.'s highly regarded work as a translator and editor reflects her interest in the lives and writings of famous women. She made notable translations of Sainte-Beuve's *Portraits of Celebrated Women* (1868), *The Writings of Madame Swetchine* (edited by Count de Falloux, 1870), and *Memoirs of Madame Desbordes-Valmore* (edited by Sainte-Beuve, 1872); and she coedited *The Complete Poetical Works of Elizabeth Barrett Browning* (1900). P.'s scholarly reputation was ensured with her translations of Provençal literature, a subject she also wrote about in Charles Dudley Warner's *Library of the World's Best Literature* (1897). She also translated and wrote critical articles on Roman life and writers.

The recognition P. earned as a translator-critic has not been accorded to her novels. However, P.'s minor but quietly realistic fictions reveal a technical competence as well as some interesting experiments with and ideas about genre, women's roles and images, and New England life.

WORKS: *Portraits of Celebrated Women* by C. A. Sainte-Beuve (translated by Preston, 1868). *The Writings of Madame Swetchine*, Ed. Count de Falloux (translated by Preston, 1870). *Aspendale* (1871). *Memoirs of Madame Desbordes-Valmore*, Ed. C. A. Sainte-Beuve (translated by Preston, 1872). *Mireio: A Provencal Poem* by F. Mistral (translated by Preston, 1872). *Love in the Nineteenth Century: A Fragment* (1873). *Sea and Shore: A Collection of Poems* (edited by Preston, with M. Le Baron Goddard, 1874). *Is That All?* (1876). *Troubadours and Trouveres: New and Old* (translated by Preston, 1876). *Biography of Alfred de Musset* by P. de Musset (translated by Preston, 1877). *The Georgics of Virgil* (translated by Preston, 1881). *A Year in Eden* (1887). *The Guardians* (with L. Preston Dodge, 1888). *The Private*

Life of the Romans (with L. Preston Dodge, 1893). *The Complete Poetical Works of Elizabeth Barrett Browning* (edited by Preston, with M. Le Baron Goddard, 1900).

BIBLIOGRAPHY: Preston, C., *Descendants of Roger Preston of Ipswich and Salem Village* (1931).
For articles in reference works, see *DAB*, VIII, 1.
Other references: *Boston Transcript* (15 May 1911).

KATHLEEN L. NICHOLS

Margaret Junkin Preston

B. 19 May 1820, Milton, Pennsylvania; d. 28 March 1897, Baltimore, Maryland
D. of George and Julia Miller Junkin; m. John T. L. Preston, 1857

P.'s father, a Presbyterian minister and educator, headed several schools before coming in 1848 to Washington College in Lexington, Virginia, where P. lived until 1892. P. received a rigorous classical and biblical education overseen by her father at home. The deaths of a brother, a sister (Stonewall Jackson's first wife), and P.'s mother saddened the 1850s. In 1857 P. married a Virginia Military Institute professor nine years her senior and a widower with seven children. She bore two sons.

Excerpts from P.'s letters and journals published in Elizabeth Preston Allen's laudatory but sometimes inaccurate *Life and Letters of Margaret Junkin Preston* (1903) reflect P.'s reading taste, which while eclectic was conservative. Nevertheless, P. was a "woman of letters," numbering several important writers among a host of correspondents. P.'s prose and poetry contain allusions that establish her knowledge of numerous works, writers, artists, paintings—American, English, and Continental.

Known primarily as a poet, P. was prolific, publishing widely in newspapers and journals and bringing out six books of collected verse. The abundant output may account in part for the general mediocrity of P.'s poetry. P. herself frequently commented on the "excessive rapidity" with which she turned out a poem—"only a morning's work."

Responsive to requests for occasional verse, P. celebrated weddings, births, deaths, and agricultural fairs. Occasionally a poem enjoyed considerable popularity as did *Beechenbrook* (1865). Exonerating the South,

P. weaves a tale of brave suffering and death. Biblical imagery occurs frequently, classical allusions abound, and sentimental detail characterizes the lines. Yet P. uses a considerable number of verse patterns, from an eight-line stanza to tercets, providing variety and displaying some ingenuity. Dedicated to "every Southern woman widowed by the war" and centered on love, duty, and sacrifice for family and state, the poem was read widely.

In *Silverwood* (1856), a semiautobiographical novel, the protagonist Edith, shackled by genteel poverty, feels hampered by the restraints society imposes. Edith is P. herself, who noted in letters, journal entries, and her published work the conflict of being a mother, wife, and artist, of dividing time between the kitchen and the writing table. Whatever its slight virtues (the death scenes are moving and drawn from P.'s own experience, the countryside is convincingly described, and the suffering is real), *Silverwood* must be placed with its countless companions, the domestic-sentimental novels of the 1850s and 1860s—those trite, contrived, formula-ridden books.

Incapable of producing fiction of the first order, P. continued the nostalgic memories of the South's triumphs and trials while other American writers moved into the complex and realistic concerns of the 20th c. What redeems *Aunt Dorothy: An Old Virginia Plantation Story* (1890) from banality are comic scenes, the somewhat ambitious structure, and the mixture of black dialect with artificial and formal white speech.

Burdened with a large family, household duties, ill health, and requests from aspiring writers, P. could never devote her full energy to her literary abilities, but she was sincere and displayed an occasional spark of talent.

WORKS: *Silverwood: A Book of Memories* (1856). *Beechenbrook: A Rhyme of the War* (1865). *The Young Ruler's Question* (1869). *Old Songs and New* (1870). *Cartoons* (1875). *Centennial Poem* (1885). *A Handful of Monographs* (1886). *For Love's Sake* (1886). *Colonial Ballads, Sonnets, and Other Verse* (1887). *Chimes for Church Children* (1889). *Semi-Centennial Ode* (1889). *Aunt Dorothy: An Old Virginia Plantation Story* (1890).

BIBLIOGRAPHY: Allen, E. P., *Life and Letters of Margaret Junkin Preston* (1903).
For articles in reference works, see: *CAL. DAB*, VIII, 1. *NAW* (article by R. H. Land). *NCAB*, 7.
Other references: *Commonwealth* 18 (1950).

ELIZABETH EVANS

Olive Higgins Prouty

B. 10 Jan. 1882, Worcester, Massachusetts; d. 24 March 1974, Brookline,
Massachusetts
D. of Milton Prince and Katharine Elizabeth Chapin Higgins; m. Lewis Isaac
Prouty, 1907

P. was born into a loving New England family of comfortable means
but had a troubled childhood saddened by the death of a beloved nurse.
About the age of twelve, P. suffered a nervous breakdown that lasted
nearly two years. Excelling only in composition, P. graduated from Worcester Classical High School in 1900; she was graduated from Smith
College in 1904, with a Bachelor of Literature degree.

P.'s professional writing career began with the encouragement of Albert
Boyden, an editor at the *American Magazine* who published her first
story, "When Elsie Came" (1909). This story, narrated by a young girl
named Bobbie, was followed by some half dozen others about the same
family. At Witter Bynner's urging, P. transformed the Bobbie stories into
her first novel, *Bobbie, General Manager* (1913).

The Fifth Wheel (1916) takes up the story of Bobbie's younger sister Ruth, who first achieves and then abandons a successful career to
take temporary responsibility for several nieces and nephews. The experience of being needed by young children convinces Ruth that fulfillment lies in home and family, and she permanently renounces her
vocation for reunion with an early suitor. While the resolution to *The
Fifth Wheel* is sentimental and conventional, the conflict between the
desire for self-determination through a career and commitment to family life is still relevant. This conflict between career and home, so
neatly resolved in the novel, caused much stress in P.'s personal life and
was in part responsible for her second nervous collapse in 1925.

P.'s best-known novel, *Stella Dallas* (1923), received generally favorable reviews, although some critics complained of its sentimentality. It
concerns a mother who sacrifices herself to assure her daughter's social
position. The plot is moved along by a jarring series of coincidences
leading to a melodramatic climax, but the narrative style is smooth and
P.'s characters draw us into their world.

In 1931, P. began a series of novels about a wealthy Boston family,
the Vales. These novels deal with themes typical of P.: the propriety

of possible marriage partners and the obligations of social position. Two of the novels, however, include sympathetic treatments of psychological problems. *Now, Voyager* (1941) tells the story of Charlotte Vale, a woman unable to break away from the domination of her mother until early middle age. Charlotte's growth toward independence begins with several months of treatment in a psychiatric sanatorium and a liberating love affair with a married man. *Home Port* (1947) describes the inferiority complex of a quiet, younger son growing up in the shadow of his athletic and popular older brother. The other novels of the Vale series are *White Fawn* (1931), *Lisa Vale* (1938), and *Fabia* (1951).

P.'s psychological problems perhaps made her particularly sensitive to the demons of others. When the holder of the 1950 Olive H. Prouty Scholarship at Smith College, Sylvia Plath, attempted suicide in the summer of 1953, P. arranged to have her removed from the psychiatric ward of Massachusetts General Hospital and cared for at a private sanatorium near Boston. Plath's five-month stay there was paid for by P., who was rewarded for her generosity by the scathing caricature of herself as Philomena Guinea in Plath's *The Bell Jar*.

P.'s novels have been translated into many languages and have given pleasure to millions of readers. P.'s last book was a memoir, *Pencil Shavings* (1961). In it P. admits that she "was not as good a writer as [she] once thought [she] might be," and candidly describes herself as a writer of light fiction.

WORKS: *Bobbie, General Manager* (1913). *The Fifth Wheel* (1916). *The Star in the Window* (1918). *Good Sports* (1919). *Stella Dallas* (1923; dramatized, 1924; film versions, 1925 and 1937). *Conflict* (1927). *White Fawn* (1931). *Lisa Vale* (1938). *Now, Voyager* (1941; film version, 1942). *Home Port* (1947). *Fabia* (1951). *Pencil Shavings* (1961).

Olive Higgins Prouty's manuscripts are at the Robert Hutchins Goddard Library of Clark University, Worcester, Massachusetts.

BIBLIOGRAPHY: For articles in reference works, see: *American Novelists of Today*, H. R. Warfel (1951). NCAB, 57. 20thCA. 20thCAS.

Other references: *NYT* (26 March 1974). *NYTBR* (22 April 1923). *Washington Post* (28 March 1974).

HEDDY A. RICHTER

Sara Agnes Rice Pryor

B. *19 Feb. 1830, Halifax County, Virginia; d. 15 Feb. 1912, New York City*
D. *of Samuel Blair and Lucinda Walton Rice; m. Roger Atkinson Pryor, 1848*

P., the daughter of a Baptist minister, was educated primarily by tutors from the University of Virginia. At the age of eighteen, P. married a law student there. The early years of P.'s marriage were uneventful. While her husband practiced law and entered politics, P. occupied herself with her growing family and the duties of home. By the 1850s, Pryor had been elected to Congress as a southern-rights man; he resigned in March 1861 to work for the secession of Virginia. During the Civil War, Pryor served as a brigadier general in the army of northern Virginia. In her autobiography, P. recalled that period of her life as one of unremitting anxiety. Food and shelter were difficult to find at any price, and the enemy was never far away. Pryor was captured in November 1864 and held prisoner for several months.

After the war, Pryor joined a law firm in New York City. He gained a reputation as counsel in some of the most famous civil and criminal cases of the late 19th c., while P. became active in patriotic and philanthropic organizations.

In the 1880s, P. began to contribute occasional pieces to *Cosmopolitan* and the *Delineator*. In 1897, she wrote a chapter for a collective genealogy of the Robert E. Lee family compiled by Robert A. Brock. However, when her husband retired from the New York Supreme Court in 1899, P. began to write more regularly. Her first book, *The Mother of Washington and Her Times* (1903), was a popular history of colonial Virginia. P. returned to this theme in *The Birth of the Nation, Jamestown, 1607* (1907).

These popular histories are highly romanticized versions of the facts and catered to reader nostalgia for the antebellum South. *The Mother of Washington* is both a biography of Mary Ball Washington and a social history of Virginia's "Golden Age," the latter half of the 18th c. Mary Washington appears as the ideal of 19th-c. womanhood—modest, pious, and self-sacrificing—rather than a representative of the 18th c., which did not place such restrictions on women. Having had such a noble mother, George Washington could only be a great man, and P. spares no pains to embellish his accomplishments.

Both *The Mother of Washington* and *Jamestown* contain serious factual inaccuracies; even by the standards of amateur history at the time,
these works are inadequate. P. tends to superimpose her image of the
antebellum South on earlier periods so that her descriptions of life in
Colonial and Revolutionary Virginia do not convey the rough-hewn
frontier qualities of those times. Instead, we see them as earlier versions
of the slave South.

P. is best known for her two autobiographical works: *Reminiscences
of Peace and War* (1905) and *My Day: Reminiscences of a Long Life*
(1909). The first begins with the Pryors' life in Washington in the
1850s. P. takes the reader to the fancy dress balls and suppers. These
halcyon days were ended, however, with secession and war, and P. turns
to her precarious life in Petersburg, Virginia, where P. lived during the
Union siege of that city.

My Day is more fully autobiographical, containing P.'s recollections
of her childhood and encompassing her life in New York after the war.
In many ways, it is less interesting than *Reminiscences,* as P. focuses
more on her husband's career than on her own life and works. P.'s
observations of New York society during the Gilded Age and the position of southerners in it are valid. Like her other works, these two
autobiographies belong to the "moonlight and magnolias" school of
history.

WORKS: *The Mother of Washington and Her Times* (1903). *Reminiscences
of Peace and War* (1905). *The Birth of the Nation, Jamestown, 1607* (1907).
My Day: Reminiscences of a Long Life (1909). *The Colonel's Story* (1911).

BIBLIOGRAPHY: For articles in reference works, see: *LSL. NAW* (article
by M. L. Simkins).

JANET E. KAUFMAN

Eliza Lofton Phillips Pugh

B. 15 Dec. 1841, Lafourche Parish, Louisiana; d. 24 July 1889, Assumption
  Parish, Louisiana
Wrote under: Arria
D. of George Wythe and Sarah McRhea Phillips; m. William Whitmell
  Pugh, Jr., 1858

P.'s father, a successful politician and member of the Louisiana Legislature, died when P. was a child. Her mother raised P. on their plantation,
the Hermitage, near Bayou Lafourche, a rich farming region of south
Louisiana. P. grew up in relative isolation. Physically delicate, she is
said to have begun writing stories to amuse herself when she was ten.
In 1856, she matriculated at Miss Hull's Seminary in New Orleans, and
two years later, after graduating, she promptly married the son of a
wealthy planter in nearby Assumption Parish. They had one son.

Shortly before the Civil War, P. began to write professionally, beginning her first novel, and under her pen name, Arria, contributing
several literary and political sketches to the New York *World*, the New
Orleans *Times*, and other journals and papers. Later, she wrote an unpublished account of the battle of Georgia Landing and the Union invasion of the countryside near the Pugh plantation. P.'s husband died
shortly after the war, and she continued to live and write at Bayou
Lafourche until her death.

Unrequited and hopeless love is the theme of both of P.'s novels.
Not a Hero (1867) recounts the story of Rachel Grant, who, because
of emotional infidelity to her husband, is punished by exile from their
home and daughter, Judith. When Judith is fifteen, Rachel returns, begging her embittered husband to let her join the household anonymously.
Phillip consents reluctantly. Their daughter then proceeds to repeat her
mother's mistake: marrying one man but falling in love with another,
Stanley Powers, the very rake who had so unfortunately attracted her
mother. The situation is enlarged rather than complicated by Powers's
staunchly faithful mistress, Janet Somers—who is, interestingly enough,
a self-supporting artist in the French Quarter of New Orleans—and Elinor Grey, a Garden District matron. As a model of womanly virtue and
an understanding friend, Elinor eventually saves Judith from repeating
her mother's folly of alienating her husband. We conclude, finally, that

Powers, the catalyst of all the distress, is certainly not a hero, despite his battlefield death.

In a Crucible (1872) is a more complex novel, involving several unworthy loves, particularly between Parolet, a south Louisiana beauty with a mysterious past, and two brothers of a wealthy rural family, not unlike the distinguished Pugh clan of Bayou Lafourche. This second novel is far more controlled and direct than *Not a Hero*, which is heavily encumbered with Latinate structures and moralizing effusions. But even here, P. has difficulty telling a straight story. The plots of both novels tend to be obscured by circumventions and P.'s attempts to maintain suspense without resolving it adequately.

P. was not unable to imagine interesting characters and situations, or to capture the flavor of south Louisiana life-styles. Her efforts to probe the psychology of hopeless love have the ring of authenticity, but the dated inefficiency of her style keeps P.'s creations from springing to life and tends to obscure her thought.

WORKS: Not a Hero (1867; English title, *Judith Grant; or, the Tempted Wife*). *In a Crucible* (1872).

The papers of Eliza Lofton Phillips Pugh are at the Louisiana State University Library, Baton Rouge, Louisiana.

BIBLIOGRAPHY: Lathrop, B. F., "The Pugh Plantations: 1860–1865" (Ph.D. diss., Univ. of Texas, 1955).

For articles in reference works, see: *Appleton's Cyclopaedia of American Biography*, Eds. J. G. Wilson and J. Fiske (1888). *Dictionary of American Authors*, Ed. O. F. Adams (1904). *The Living Female Writers of the South*, M. T. Tardy (1872). *The Living Writers of the South*, J. W. Davidson (1869).

Other references: New Orleans *Picayune* (31 Dec. 1871; 25 Feb. 1872). [Biographical data furnished by Dorothy Pugh.]

BARBARA C. EWELL

Emily James Smith Putnam

B. 15 April 1865, Canandaigua, New York; d. 7 Sept. 1944, Kingston, Jamaica
D. of James Cosslett Smith and Emily Ward Adams Smith; m. George
  Haven Putnam, 1899

The daughter of a judge, P. was the youngest of five children. P.'s parents encouraged her intellectual curiosity, and gave her every educational opportunity. At an early age, P. became fascinated with ancient Greek history. She was a member of the first graduating class of Bryn Mawr College (1889).

P. became a pioneer in postgraduate education. She was among the first women to study at Girton College, Cambridge, England. P. taught at Packer Collegiate Institute in Brooklyn Heights, New York (1891–93) —where she published her first scholarly work, *Selections from Lucian* (1892)—and at the newly established University of Chicago (1893–94). In 1894, she accepted the challenging appointment of dean of Barnard College. P. believed that women should be educated to pursue their interests, whatever they might be, and that her job as dean was to make certain that the young women received an education equal to that of the young men at Columbia University. P. helped create an innovative relationship between the men's and women's colleges which was followed by administrators at other universities.

P. married a publisher and scholar in 1899, and when she became pregnant in 1900, she was forced to resign her position. Her only child, Palmer Cosslett Putnam, became a noted author of scientific and technical works. Although P. maintained her ties with Barnard as a member of the Board of Trustees (1901–05), she devoted the next fourteen years to her family and writing. During this period, P. published a variety of articles, ranging from "Americans at the English Universities" and "Preparation for College" to "Lucian the Sophist" and "Pagan Morals." These articles, in addition to short stories, appeared in the most noted journals of the day.

In 1914, P. returned to Barnard as a lecturer on Greek literature and history. In 1919, P., together with Columbia University professor James Harvey Robinson, helped found the New School for Social Research in New York City, an institution for the promotion of adult education. P. became a member of the New School's board of directors, and lectured there from 1920 until 1932. P. continued to write articles and short stories, and translated a number of works by French social theorists. *Candaules' Wife, and Other Old Stories* (1926) is devoted to interpreting and expanding upon certain stories of Herodotus.

After retiring from Barnard in 1929 and from the New School in 1932, and after the death of her husband in 1930, P. moved to Spain with her sister Alice, and lived there until the Spanish Civil War forced them to relocate in Kingston, Jamaica.

The Lady: Studies of Certain Significant Phases of Her History (1910), the volume for which P. is best known, combines P.'s interest in history and the educational development of women: woman "can hardly understand herself unless she knows her own history." *The Lady* contains essays on the role, education, and social life of the "female of the favored social classes" in ancient Rome and Greece, the Middle Ages, and the Renaissance. P. studies other life-styles in "The Lady Abbess," "The Lady of the Salon," and "The Lady of the Blue Stocking." Her work concludes with the chapter, "The Lady of the Slave States," because P. believed that the economic changes the world was undergoing at the turn of the century eliminated the distinctions between social classes which had been so prevalent in history. Her collection of historical sketches is as valuable now as it was in 1910.

A noted scholar, writer, historian, and educational administrator, P. provided an example for many women of her own and subsequent generations to follow in the quest for knowledge.

WORKS: *Selections from Lucian* (translated by Putnam, 1892). *The Lady: Studies of Certain Significant Phases of Her History* (1910). *The Dread of Responsibility* by E. Fauget (translated by Putnam, 1914). *The Secret of the Maine* by M. Berger (translated by Putnam, 1918). *The Illusion* by R. Escholier (translated by Putnam, 1921). *Candaules' Wife, and Other Old Stories* (1926).

BIBLIOGRAPHY: Mirskey, J., Foreword to *The Lady: Studies of Certain Significant Phases of Her History* (1972).
For articles in reference works, see: *AW. NAW* (article by A. K. Baxter).
Other references: *Harper's Bazaar* (April 1911). *PW* (14 Aug. 1944).
PAULA A. TRECKEL

Mary Traill Spence Lowell Putnam

B. 3 Dec. 1810, Boston, Massachusetts; d. 1898, Boston, Massachusetts
Wrote under: M. L. P., Mary Lowell Putnam
D. of Charles and Harriet Brackett Spence Lowell; m. Samuel R. Putnam

P.'s mother imbued her Christian rectitude and love of learning in her children. Her father, a minister at West Church in Boston, was descended from Judge John Lowell, who was a member of the Continental Congress and a district and circuit court judge. Judge Lowell's benevolence toward black people, the family's proud New England heritage, and a fervent Christian faith are all reflected in P.'s work.

P. is noted for translating Fredrika Bremer's play, *The Bondmaid*, from Swedish (1844). P.'s fluency in French, coupled with her voracious reading, allowed P. to take on the editor of the *North American Review*, Francis Bowen, who had sharply criticized Kossuth and the Magyars after their revolution. In two essays in the *Christian Examiner* P. shreds Bowen's articles, taking them line by line and proving their inaccuracy and bad logic.

P.'s four chief works, all published anonymously and centered on the issue of slavery, are told from the vantage point of Edward Colvil, a New England farmer-poet transplanted to the South. *Record of an Obscure Man* (1861) and *Fifteen Days: An Extract from Edward Colvil's Journal* (1866) are filled with exposition and speculation about black history and alternatives to slavery. *Tragedy of Errors* (1862) and *Tragedy of Success* (1862), both plays, embody some of P.'s theories about the beauty of black music, the eloquence of black preaching, and black people's special capacity for loyalty and revenge.

Record of an Obscure Man is narrated by a friend of Colvil's who listened to Colvil's discussion of African history and theories about slavery and, after Colvil's death, arranged for publication of his two verse plays, *Tragedy of Errors* and its sequel, *Tragedy of Success*. Written "in the dramatic form, but not intended for the stage," the plays form the core of P.'s series.

Their plot is overly complicated. The intrigue of a jilted mulatto woman, Dorcas, catapults a young white woman, Hecate, into slavery.

She has a child by her plantation owner, Stanley, switches her baby with that of his wife, and watches her illegitimate daughter, Helen, grow up as a generous, highly intelligent, free woman who endears herself with the slaves and longs to accomplish some great work but feels hampered by a weak-spirited husband. After the baby-switching comes to light, Helen takes her place as a slave, but escapes with her son when her husband tells her that he wants to keep her as his mistress. Just as he sees the light (encouraged by proof that Helen is white), Helen is captured and dies in jail from loss of hope (but not faith).

In contrast to P.'s very readable prose, the verse in the plays is only occasionally strong; but a few of the scenes have convincing dialogues: in one, Dorcas successfully confronts her remorseful accomplice, a slave trader, by skillfully reminding him of his self-doubts and mixed motivations. In another, Helen powerfully decries the severe limitations of woman's freedom to her sister-in-law Alice: "Restrained and cramped / In all her outward acts, she cannot know / The joys of self-possession, —man's great bliss; / She only claims those of renunciation." Despite her limits, however, woman is "man's second conscience," and must speak "the word God printed on her soul."

Fifteen Days is the most unified work in the series. The journal starts on Good Friday, 1844, and describes Colvil's meeting with a charismatic figure, Harry Dudley, a young visiting botanist from Massachusetts who tries to buy a slave so that he can free him. *Fifteen Days* balances the joy of deepening friendship between Colvil and Dudley against the sense of looming tragedy. Colvil seems excessively anxious to live up to Dudley's expectation, but his anxiety is interestingly confirmed when Dudley is killed at the end, ironically by a good friend who was also the slave's former owner.

The central victims in P.'s tragic series are all young, perceptive, and white, but her exposition of African history shows a sensitivity to the intelligence and culture of black people. P.'s writings on Hungary show her capable of imagining herself in other people's shoes. Although P.'s characters are scarce on flesh and blood, their sensibility is frequently compelling.

WORKS: *The Bondmaid* by Fredrika Bremer (translated by Putnam, 1844). *The North American Review on Hungary* (reprinted from the *Christian Examiner*, Nov. 1850; March 1851). *Record of an Obscure Man* (1861). *Tragedy of Errors* (1862). *Tragedy of Success* (1862). [*Memorial of William*] *Lowell Putnam* (1863). *Fifteen Days: An Extract from Edward Colvil's*

Journal (1866). *Guépin of Nantes: A French Republican* (1874). *Memoir of Rev. Charles Lowell, D.D.* (1885).

BIBLIOGRAPHY: Adelman, J., *Famous Women* (1926). Dorland, W. A. N., *The Sum of Feminine Achievement* (1917). *Homes of American Authors* (1857).

For articles in reference works, see: *American Authors, 1795–1895: A Bibliography*, Ed. P. K. Foley (1897). *American Fiction, 1851–1875*, Ed. L. H. Wright (1965). *A Critical Dictionary of English Literature and British and American Authors*, Ed. S. A. Allibone (1872). *A Dictionary of American Authors*, Ed. O. F. Adams (1897). *DAB* (article on James Russell Lowell) VI, 1. *Index to Women of the World, from Ancient to Modern Times: Biographies and Portraits*, Ed. N. O. Ireland (1970). *Women's Record*, Ed. S. J. Hale (1870).

Other references: *North American Review* (Jan. 1862; April 1862).

KAREN B. STEELE

Ruth Putnam

B. 18 July 1856, Yonkers, New York; d. 12 Feb. 1931, Geneva, Switzerland
D. of George Palmer Putnam and Victorine Haven Putnam

P. spent her youth in an exceptionally stimulating environment. Her father founded the publishing firm which bears his name; her brother George succeeded as head of the company; and her sister Mary Putnam Jacobi, about whom P. wrote in *Life and Letters of Mary Putnam Jacobi* (1925), was a pioneer in women's medical education. P.'s interest in language and literature became evident during her undergraduate years at Cornell University, from which she graduated in 1878. She also studied in Paris, Oxford, Leiden, Geneva, and London. Besides her writing, P. was actively involved in the woman suffrage movement.

P.'s first publication, *The Pearl Series* (1886), was a six-volume poetry anthology. In 1887, P. collaborated with Alfred Church on a historical novel entitled *The Count of the Saxon Shore*. Her first work indicating an interest in Dutch history is *William the Silent, Prince of Orange: The Moderate Man of the Sixteenth Century* (2 vols., 1895). P. attempts an unbiased biography, using an impressive number of primary sources, principally letters and documents signed by the Prince of Orange, which she describes as "authentic phrases of the subject-matter, though they may not be the whole truth." As with a number of her historical works, P. consulted French, English, Dutch, and German sources, traveling widely throughout Europe and the U.S. to obtain as complete and accurate a picture of the protagonist as possible.

In 1897 P. coedited the two-volume *Historic New York during Two Centuries*. The work, dealing with the days of New Amsterdam and early New York, contains P.'s own contribution on Annetje Jans' Farm, which she traces until 1897.

P.'s next work dealing with the history of the Netherlands was *A Mediaeval Princess: Jacqueline, Countess of Holland (1401–1436)* (1904). P. details Philip the Good's incursion into Holland, which until that time (1904) had received little attention among English historians. Jacqueline was a contemporary of Jeanne d'Arc, who fought against and was finally conquered by the same men with whom Jacqueline maintained her futile struggle.

P.'s second contribution to the Heroes of the Nations series was *Charles the Bold: Last Duke of Burgundy (1433–1477)* (1908). This biography is principally based on the materials of John Foster Kirk. As with all her historical works, P.'s wonderfully clear, readable prose makes these figures from remote history come alive.

With the eruption of World War I, P. published a short work, *Alsace and Lorraine from Caesar to Kaiser* (1915), followed in 1918 by a much longer volume entitled *Luxemburg and Her Neighbors*, in which she gives a precise history of Luxemburg from the 10th c. to the 20th. Both works deal with areas brought to the public attention because of the events of the war. In the meantime, P. collaborated with H. I. Priestley on a lengthy monograph, "California: The Name." P.'s extraordinary versatility is evident in the extensive use of Spanish historical and literary sources. She traces the name California to a 15th-c. Spanish romance.

P.'s most monumental historical work was the translation and adaptation of Petrus Blok's volumes, *The History of the Nederland People* (5 vols., 1898–1912). P. condensed a great deal of political detail in the Dutch original in order to emphasize the cultural aspects of Dutch history.

P.'s contribution to interest in the history of the Netherlands in the U.S. was substantial. Her personalization of important, though perhaps little-known, historical figures made her subject popular. Although her status as daughter of Putnam no doubt helped P., the research skills and great versatility evident throughout her work warrant P. a position among respected historical writers.

WORKS: *The Pearl Series: Selected English Poetry* (6 vols., edited by Putnam, 1886). *The Count of the Saxon Shore* (with A. Church, 1887). *William the Silent, Prince of Orange: The Moderate Man of the Sixteenth Century* (2 vols. 1895). *Historic New York during Two Centuries* (edited by Putnam, with M. W. Goodwin and A. C. Royce, 2 vols., 1897). *The History of the Nederland People* by P. Blok (translated by Putnam, 5 vols., 1898–1912). *A Mediaeval Princess: Jacqueline, Countess of Holland (1401–1436)* (1904). *Charles the Bold: Last Duke of Burgundy (1433–1477)* (1908). *William the Silent, Prince of Orange and the Revolt of the Netherlands* (1911). *Alsace and Lorraine from Caesar to Kaiser* (1915). *Luxemburg and Her Neighbors* (1918). *Life and Letters of Mary Putnam Jacobi* (edited by Putnam, 1925).

BIBLIOGRAPHY: For articles in reference works, see: *DAB*, VIII, 1.
　　Other references: *Education Review* (April 1908). *Literary Digest* (2 May 1908). *Nation* (13 Aug. 1908). *SatR* (5 Sept. 1908).

CAROLE M. SHAFFER-KOROS

Sallie A. Brock Putnam

B. 1828, Madison County, Virginia; d. 1911
Wrote under: Virginia Madison
D. of Ansalem and Elizabeth Beverly Brock; m. Richard Putnam, 1882

Little is known of P.'s early life except that she was educated by private tutors and by her father, who taught at the University of Virginia. After his death, P. and her mother moved to Richmond, Virginia, until the mother's death in 1865.

That summer, P. traveled to New York City and was persuaded to write an account of her life in the former Confederate capital, which was published in 1867 as *Richmond during the War*. *The Southern Amaranth* (1869) was a collection of Civil War poetry and included some of P.'s own verses. For ten years, P. was associated with *Frank Leslie's Lady's Journal* and also contributed pieces to other women's magazines. She married a New York City minister, and they traveled extensively.

Richmond during the War displays P.'s keen eye for detail. Filled with chatty gossip and shrewd observations of life in the beleaguered city, it is a fascinating account of civilians in a war zone. Historians have relied heavily on its descriptions of the inauguration of Jefferson Davis and the Richmond Bread Riot of 1863. P. evidently knew the city and its people well. Although P. wrote from hindsight, many of her conclusions are valid. She was correct in condemning the government's willingness to give President Davis total control of the army, a function more properly entrusted to the Secretary of War and the generals. Similarly, her criticisms of Richmond's defenses and food supply are justified. Striking a note of sectional reconciliation at the end of the memoir, P. has only praise for Lincoln's policy of Reconstruction and the conduct of the federal troops occupying Richmond in the last days of the war.

Kenneth, My King (1873) is a romance set in the prewar South. It is very much like *Jane Eyre*. The plot revolves around the love between a young governess, Harriet Royal, and her employer, Kenneth Darrow. Harriet learns the secret of Kenneth's wife Bertha's madness and the "shadow of a terrible living sorrow" which hangs over Kenneth. Both Kenneth and his brother Richard were in love with Bertha, and although she married Kenneth, Richard was the father of her child. The novel ends happily with the marriage of Kenneth and Harriet after Bertha dies of a brain hemorrhage, Richard commits suicide, and Harriet's fiancé is conveniently lost at sea.

Kenneth, My King is a standard 19th-c. romance, overlaid with Gothic trappings and a Pollyannish nostalgia for the Old South. What saves the novel from mere silliness is the character of Harriet. She is neither a clinging vine nor a flirt, but an independent, reasonable woman. Whereas Jane Eyre displayed the virtues of patience and self-sacrifice, Harriet was far stronger, choosing to work as a governess, rather than dutifully going where others sent her.

It is unfortunate that P. chose to try her hand at fiction. While *Kenneth, My King* may have pleased its audience, it does nothing to enhance P.'s reputation as a writer. It is difficult to understand how someone who displays such perception in her autobiographical works could write such an inane novel.

WORKS: *Richmond during the War: Four Years of Personal Observations* (1867). *The Southern Amaranth* (edited by Putnam, 1869). *Kenneth, My King: A Novel* (1873).

BIBLIOGRAPHY: M. T. Tardy, *Living Female Writers of the South* (1872).

JANET E. KAUFMAN

Martha Laurens Ramsay

B. 3 Nov. 1759, Charleston, South Carolina; d. 10 June, 1811, Charleston,
South Carolina
D. of Henry and Eleanor Ball Laurens; m. David Ramsay, 1787

R. was the daughter of a prominent South Carolina patriot leader and the wife of another Revolutionary patriot. She achieved posthumous recognition as a writer when her husband published *Memoirs of the Life of Martha Laurens Ramsay* (1811). The work included his memoir of R. as well as R.'s writings: extracts from her diary, letters, and religious meditations and exercises. R. had kept the writing secret until immediately before her death, and Ramsay published them as a testimonial and a guide to others.

Although R. began writing in childhood, only a few things remain from the early years, the significant one being the "Covenant with God" which she drew up at age fourteen. There are some religious meditations from the period 1775–85, when R. lived in England and France. These works reflect both the faith and the fear of "apostasy" on the part of a young woman first entering "gay, worldly, and even . . . profane company." R. did experience a decline of religious fervor at one point. What proved of more lasting significance was her encounter with the English evangelical movement, which helped confirm what Ramsay called R.'s "heart religion."

The central core of R.'s writings is the diary she kept after her return to Charleston and her marriage. The published extracts cover the period 1791 to 1808. Hers was a sporadically kept record of a life of faith, troubled by R.'s recurring sense of falling away from God. Throughout, R. underscores a "sense of being drawn to God through trials." These trials included the deaths of three of her eleven children and the family's troubled financial affairs.

R. did not give details of the experiences of trial but instead recorded her inner turmoil and anguished efforts to regain stability. R. felt the weight of "those sins which required this chastisement" and the fear lest her rebellions lead to "forfeiting all thy mercies." Throughout the diary R. stresses the importance of the sense of that grace "by which alone I stand." She utilizes hymns and religious poetry to sum up her faith and the struggles with doubt.

Almost all the writings were for R.'s own use, with the exception of the letters, a small number of which Ramsay included. The warmth of R.'s nature is more evident here. The letters to her children are instructive, supportive, and appreciative.

R. gives the impression of being at ease with the traditional role of women. Although she had read contemporary feminist writings, her husband maintained that R. preferred "the teachings of the Bible to human reasoning." She gives no indications of her feelings about the institution of slavery, which so troubled her fellow Charlestonian Sarah Grimké.

R.'s writing was essentially a private experience, a means of intensifying her religious life. One feels the intensity of R.'s religious struggles and her personal affection for her family, but she does not reveal herself as a rounded human being. For R., personal spirituality was at the heart of existence; it was also at the heart of her writing.

WORKS: *Memoirs of the Life of Martha Laurens Ramsay* by D. Ramsay (1811).

BIBLIOGRAPHY: Rogers, G. C., Jr., *Evolution of a Federalist: William Loughton Smith of Charleston* (1962). Spruill, J. C., *Women's Life and Work in the Southern Colonies* (1938). Wallace, D. D., *The Life of Henry Laurens* (1915).

For articles in reference works, see: *CAL. NAW* (article by G. C. Rogers, Jr.).

Other references: *South Carolina Historical and Genealogical Magazine* (Oct. 1935).

INZER BYERS

Vienna G. Morrell Ramsay

B. *1817 (?), Maine; d. after 1897*
Wrote under: Mrs. V. G. Ramsay, Mrs. Vienna G. Ramsay, Mrs. Vienna G. Morrell Ramsay (occasional variant spelling: Ramsay, Ramsey)

R. was both a religious writer and a children's writer, frequently merging the two. R.'s earliest available work, *Facts and Reflections on the Condition of the Heathen World* (1848), is a traditional treatise intended to awaken "in the hearts of Christians a deeper sympathy for those who are perishing in the darkness of Heathenism. . . ." In the often eccentric idiom of early-19th-c. evangelism, R. documents the importance of missions and conversion throughout "primitive" societies—Africa, Asia, South America.

Evenings with the Children; or, Travels in South America (1871) serves the multifold purpose of much early children's literature: to instill moral and religious values while instructing the young reader. R. dedicates the book to the children she has known, ". . . with the prayer that it may aid them in the acquisition of knowledge and that they may all be taught of Him whom to know is Eternal."

The twenty chapters—called "evenings"—find "Mrs. White" taking her two very eager children on an imaginary journey through South America. The trip is, of course, geographically and culturally instructive, and the boy and girl await each lesson excitedly.

The children are models for those reading the book. The young adventurers "study hard in order to get through their lessons early" and beg "their mother that they might continue their travels." Thus, R. places factual history within the fictional frame of a woman and her two children, discussing the animals, vegetation, and geography of Central and Latin America.

R.'s evangelistic writings remain conventional in purpose and execution. *Evenings with the Children*, although of great factual integrity, has aged poorly in its strict, unimaginative presentation of the "ideal child."

WORKS: *Facts and Reflections on the Condition of the Heathen World and the Importance of Missions* (1848). *Evenings with the Children; or, Travels in South America* (1871). *A Legend of the White Hills, and Other Poems* (n.d.).

DEBORAH H. HOLDSTEIN

Ayn Rand

B. 2 Feb. 1905, St. Petersburg, Russia
M. Frank O'Connor, 1929

R.'s early life of relative comfort was abruptly terminated when the family business was nationalized after the Russian Revolution. An excellent student whose far-ranging interests included mathematics, literature, philosophy, and engineering, R. graduated from the University of Leningrad with a degree in history. Not able to adjust to the Communist regime, she accepted an invitation to visit relatives in New York in 1926.

R. went to Hollywood to write screen scenarios and was given a job as an extra by Cecil B. de Mille. Though de Mille rejected her first five scenarios as too romantic, unrealistic, and improbable, R. did eventually work as a screenwriter.

We, the Living (1936) received a lukewarm critical reception. The themes are the sanctity of human life and the evil of collectivism in Russia. Written at the same time, *The Night of January 16th* (1936) is an effective dramatic piece. The play's originality derives from the gimmick of allowing each night's audience to serve as the jury in a murder trial.

The Fountainhead (1943) established R. as a popular writer and is considered her best work. The world of contemporary architecture serves as the backdrop for this battle between the forces of individualism and collectivisim, between creativity and derivativeness.

The plot follows protagonist Howard Roark's career from the day he is expelled from architectural school, through his difficulties in establishing a career, to his professional and personal victory and vindication. The book ends with the triumph of the virtuous and the creative. The heavy moralizing has drawn negative reactions from some commentators.

The philosophies set forth in *The Fountainhead* were amplified in *Atlas Shrugged* (1957), the fullest novelistic treatment of R.'s theories. *Atlas Shrugged* established R. as an intellectual cult figure. A novel which can be read to satisfy many different tastes, it has been categorized by various critics as a mystery story, science fiction, a philosophical diatribe, a female fantasy novel, and a justification of capitalism.

The protagonist, Dagny Taggart, whose attempts to run a transcontinental railroad are complicated by networks of bureaus, councils, and committees that strangle productive initiatives, fights a losing battle against a group that wants to "stop the motor of the world" in order to rebuild a society of free enterprise, devoid of government controls. She inadvertently finds a projection of this society, Galt's Gulch, a utopia in a hidden valley in Colorado. Galt's Gulch was born as a reaction against the collectivist maxim, "From each according to his ability, to each according to his need"; its motto is "I swear by my life and my love of it that I will never live for the sake of another man nor ask another man to live for mine."

R. is also known as a philosopher. All of her publications since *Atlas Shrugged* have been nonfiction. During the 1960s she was a popular campus lecturer. In conjunction with *The Objectivist*, a newsletter published to explain R.'s philosophy, courses in Objectivism were taught by the Nathaniel Branden Institute.

R.'s novels, though popular, have received little serious consideration as works of literature; she is something of a cultural phenomenon. Though R.'s politics are anathema to most feminists, her commitment to self-actualization both as a philosopher and as creator of one of the most positive female protagonists in American literature (Dagny Taggart) suggests that perhaps her works need to be reevaluated by women.

WORKS: We, the Living (1936). *The Night of January 16th* (1936). *Anthem* (1938; rev. ed., 1946). *The Fountainhead* (1943; film version, 1949). *Atlas Shrugged* (1957). *For the New Intellectual: The Philosophy of Ayn Rand* (1961). *The Virtue of Selfishness* (1964). *Capitalism: The Unknown Ideal* (1966). *Introduction to Objectivist Epistemology* (1967). *The Romantic Manifesto* (1969). *The Ayn Rand Letter* (1971). *The New Left: The Anti-Industrial Revolution* (1971).

BIBLIOGRAPHY: Branden, N., and B. Branden, *Who is Ayn Rand?* (1962). O'Neill, W., *With Charity toward None* (1971).

For articles in reference works, see: *CA*, 13–16 (1975). *20thCAS.*

Other references: *Commonweal* (8 Nov. 1957). *NY* (26 Oct. 1957). *NYTBR* (16 May 1943). *Playboy* (March 1964). *SatR* (12 Oct. 1957).

MIMI R. GLADSTEIN

Ruth Painter Randall

B. 1 Nov. 1892, Salem, Virginia; d. 22 Jan. 1971, Urbana, Illinois
D. of Franklin V. N. and Laura Trimble Shickel Painter; m. James G.
  Randall, 1917

R., whose father wrote books on American and English literature, grew up in an academic atmosphere. She received a B.A. from Roanoke College, Virginia, in 1913, and an M.A. from Indiana University in 1914. After marrying a well-known Lincoln historian, R. began writing. She shared her husband's research and collaborated with him on two chapters of his monumental biography of Lincoln. Although she was a southerner, her mature life was devoted to the study of Lincoln.

Just as this work caused historians to reevaluate Lincoln's presidency, R.'s *Mary Lincoln: Biography of a Marriage* (1953) altered the view of Mary Todd Lincoln that many detractors had shaped. This substantial work of historical research is scrupulous in its accuracy and original in presenting new materials. The result is a balanced judgment of the Lincolns' personalities and their private life.

After this first biography, R. avoided footnotes but always explained that her studies had been fully documented and provided long bibliographies. She continued her exploration of the family life of the Lincoln's in *Lincoln's Sons* (1956), which both follows the lives of Lincoln's heirs and considers the President's role as a father, and in *The Courtship of Mr. Lincoln* (1957). R. also wrote articles about Lincoln in *American Heritage, Saturday Review,* and the *New York Times Magazine,* and she contributed radio and television sketches for the American Story series and the Lincoln Story series. Her study of the Lincoln circle was extended with a biography of Colonel Elmer Elsworth (1960).

Several appealing books for children occupied R.'s last years. With *Lincoln's Animal Friends* (1958), R. reached an audience of young readers aged nine to twelve. *I, Mary* (1959) presents Mary Todd Lincolns in *Lincoln's Sons* (1956), which both follows the lives of Linvolume, telling the story of the wife of Jefferson Davis, president of the Confederacy. In these two volumes R. shows remarkable sympathy, understanding, and admiration for the First Ladies of the North and the South. R. shows how the personal lives of both women included great tragedy, inspiring determination, and deep love.

As a writer of children's literature, R. continued to choose as subjects women whose lives had been exciting and difficult, such as the daughter of the politician Thomas Hart Benton (*I, Jessie*, 1963) and the wife of General George Armstrong Custer (*I, Elizabeth*, 1966). *I, Ruth: Autobiography of a Marriage* (1968) reiterates the traditional virtues of American family life and the wife's supporting role; the sensibility is pre–World War I.

R. wrote with a clear sense of purpose. Clarity of style, meticulous attention to details, evocative descriptions of the historical moments and places, and sensitivity to emotions make R.'s history very readable. Thus R. not only reached specialist historians but had a wide public audience as well.

WORKS: *Mary Lincoln: Biography of a Marriage* (1953). *Lincoln's Sons* (1956). *The Courtship of Mr. Lincoln* (1957). *Lincoln's Animal Friends* (1958). *I, Mary* (1959). *Colonel Elmer Elsworth* (1960). *I, Varina* (1962). *I, Jessie* (1963). *I, Elizabeth* (1966). *I, Ruth: Autobiography of a Marriage* (1968).

BIBLIOGRAPHY: For articles in reference works, see: *CA*, 1–4 (1967). *CB* (1957).
Other references: *AHR* 58 (1953). *NYHTB* (5 June 1960). *NYTBR* (8 Feb. 1953; 3 Feb. 1957; 13 Oct. 1963). *SatR* (16 Feb. 1957).

VELMA BOURGEOIS RICHMOND

Fannie W. Rankin

Wrote under: F. W. R.

Biographical information on R. is not available. R.'s novel, *True to Him Ever* (1874), typified 19th-c. sentimentality. The action takes place in the Tremount family's country home. Through the vicissitudes of the final pairing of eight young men and women, R. deals just deserts to an indomitable woman and her determined lover, two childhood sweethearts, a flirt and a dandy, and lovers at first sight.

The women's perceptions, hopes, and acts are the novel's focus, while the men disappear to conduct their business in New York and return to the home sphere to cause anguish and delight again. Maude loves Harold, yet her earnest desire for liberty causes her to act capriciously. Bessie and Tom's youthful affection matures into conjugal love. And although Loo converses coquettishly with every young bachelor who visits the Tremount home, she eventually is attracted to the man most like herself—an opportunistic playboy. These couples play the social games of courtship throughout the novel.

Rather than pierce the surface of these drawing-room conversations and explore the deep and conflicting faces of love, R. developed conventional characters who conformed to the prescribed rounds of courtship. In the Tremount sisters' reflections on their personal identities as women and discussions of woman's role in society, R. explored the issue of women's rights. Yet Mrs. Tremount's assertion that woman "brightens and encourages" man "in his aspirations after fame" circumscribes the sphere into which her daughters settle.

Esther Tremount's singular notion of joining a woman's group is forgotten in her devotion to Cecil Graham. His untimely death does not diminish the strength of Esther's love but sanctifies it—she devotes her life to working with the poor. The commonplace twists of love in the other couples' courtships provide contrast to Esther's eternal love, which surmounts even death. The woman who ventured to think of social activism is transformed by love to a saintly provider for the poor.

R.'s characters come to their predictable ends; however, Esther's goodness is rewarded on a higher plane than a happy family of her own. She achieves a religious devotion in life and a sort of spiritual communion with her beloved. These moralistic outcomes and homely sentiment typical of the fiction of the day were criticized in a review in *Godey's Lady's Book* that faulted the constant concern with "love, jealousy, and engagements, as if they were the staples of existence."

WORKS: True to Him Ever (1874).

BIBLIOGRAPHY: For articles in reference works, see: *American Fiction 1851–1875*, Ed. L. H. Wright (1965). *A Supplement to Allibone's Critical Dictionary*, Ed. J. F. Kirk (1891).
    Other references: *Godey's* (Aug. 1874).

ELIZABETH ROBERTS

Dora Knowlton Thompson Ranous

B. 16 Aug. 1859, Ashfield, Massachusetts; d. 19 Jan. 1916, New York City
Wrote under: Dora Knowlton Ranous
D. of Alexander Hamilton and Augusta Comfort Knowlton Thompson;
m. William V. Ranous, 1881

An author, editor, and translator, R. was the younger of two daughters in a learned, affluent Massachusetts family. Their birthplace, the Knowlton Homestead, attracted such scholars as James Russell Lowell during the summer months, "lending to Mrs. Thompson's dinner table an air of scholarship." R. graduated from the Sanderson Academy in Ashfield, completing her formal education at the Packer Institute in New York City.

R.'s acting career was encouraged by her mother. In her journal, R. writes of the trials and tribulations of a young actress seeking her first engagement. These experiences were published in R.'s autobiographical *Diary of a Daly Debutante* (1910), an interesting period piece of theatrical life in the late 19th c. R. is unassuming but confident, describing numerous rehearsals and travels; her strength lies in vivid characterization of associates and friends.

Newspaper and magazine reviews of the book were almost unanimously enthusiastic. Public reaction was also strong; readers evidently asked that R. continue the story by documenting later experiences with the Kiralfy Theatre Co. R. continued writing a journal, but the manuscript remains unpublished.

R. might not have found her literary career had her marriage succeeded. While part of the Kiralfy group, R. met her husband and left the stage. But after the marriage dissolved, R. mastered stenography in order to earn a living for herself and her daughter. This led to work in rare books and editing. As a result, R. translated and edited works by authors such as de Maupassant, Flaubert, and D'Annunzio. In one of her early projects, R. initiated and completed (with Rossiter Johnson) a set of sixteen volumes on the literature of Italy (1907), including translations and biographical notes on authors from the time of Dante to the early 20th c.

R.'s last book, *Good English in Good Form* (1916), is a remarkably useful reference guide. A basic composition text, its topics include "The Art of Punctuation" and "Words and Sentences," although lengthy chapters on "Words Derived from Latin and Greek" are perhaps less useful.

R.'s literary contributions are remarkable in their diversity. It is difficult to ascertain R.'s place among American writers, but her works are examples of concise, lucid prose, and her translations are strong. R.'s co-editors and translators eulogized her as one "of brilliant intellect," with "great literary ability."

WORKS: *The Conquest of Rome* by M. Serao (translated by Ranous, 1906). *The Flame* by G. D'Annunzio (translated by Ranous, 1906). *An Anthology of Italian Authors from Cavalcanti to Fogazzaro (1270–1970)* (edited by Ranous, with R. Johnson; 16 vols., 1907). *The Complete Works of Guy de Maupassant* (translated by Ranous, 1910). *Diary of a Daly Debutante* (1910). *Zibeline* by P. de Massa (translated by Ranous, 1910). *Good English in Good Form* (1916). *Influence, and How to Exert It* by B. D. Blanchard (translated by Ranous, 1916). *Madame Bovary* by G. Flaubert (translated by Ranous, 1919). *Salammbo* by G. Flaubert (translated by Ranous, 1922). *Sentimental Education* by G. Flaubert (translated by Ranous, 1922). *The Temptation of Saint Antony, and the Legend of St. Julien the Hospitaler* by G. Flaubert (translated by Ranous, 1923).

BIBLIOGRAPHY: Johnson, R., *Dora Knowlton Ranous: A Simple Record of a Noble Life* (1916).
    For articles in reference works, see: *NCAB*, 17.

DEBORAH H. HOLDSTEIN

Marjorie Kinnan Rawlings

B. 8 Aug. 1896, Washington, D.C.; d. 14 Dec. 1953, Crescent Beach, Florida
D. of Arthur F. and Ida May Traphagen Kinnan; m. Charles A. Rawlings, 1919; m. Norton Sanford Baskin, 1941

Daughter of a U.S. patent examiner, R. graduated Phi Beta Kappa from the University of Wisconsin in 1918 with a major in English. R. wrote for the Louisville *Courier-Journal* and the Rochester *Journal-American* from 1920 to 1928. Needing solitude, she bought an orange grove in Hawthorn, Florida, near Cross Creek, where she farmed and wrote from

1928 to 1947. R. traveled in England, Alaska, and Bimini. Her marriage to a journalist ended in divorce (1933). R.'s second husband was a hotel owner in St. Augustine. Sued for libel, R. left Florida to buy a New York farm.

R.'s earliest published story was "Cracker Chidlings" (1930) in *Scribner's*. Her humorous sketches about local figures contained accounts of a squirrel feast at a church picnic, domestic squabbling, and an explanation of "Cracker" as the whip-cracking country cattle driver. In 1931, *Scribner's* published "Jacob's Ladder," a sensitive odyssey of a young Cracker pair through storm-ridden piney woods and scrub. These were R.'s continuing subjects: the human bond to the earth, and the Florida Crackers with their folklore, language, and struggles.

South Moon Under (1933) received critical acclaim. Three generations of a Cracker family subsist in the Florida scrub. Old Lantry, an irascible loner and moonshiner, moves his family into obscurity to elude the law for murdering a Prohibition official. He gives up moonshining and tries to farm. His grandson, Lant Jacklin, forced to early manhood by his father's death, labors at farming and trapping. Hardships finally compel Lant to moonshine. Betrayed, he repeats his grandfather's crime and kills a man, condemning himself to a life of restless fear and flight. The moon of the title symbolizes the powerful necessity laid upon all creatures, men and animals, forcing them to act against their will. Moon lore abounds. Deer feed in the moonlight. "South moon under" meant that the moon was directly under the earth, unseen, and yet "it reached through the earth" with a "power to move the owls and rabbits," and drive a man to kill. Despite R.'s descriptions of the earth's beauty, these dark lunar forces, the treachery of kin, the legacy of family violence, and the intractability of the wilderness, convey her somber vision of the human lot.

Golden Apples (1935) describes an uneasy idyll between a frail ignorant Cracker girl and a callous, hard-drinking young English planter who comes to the fertile hummock to reclaim his father's homestead. R. deals more frankly than elsewhere with sexuality: Desire seems to rise up out of the steamy Florida undergrowth. But the man's real view of the land is that it is a "damn rotten crawling place," and when the girl he seduces looks "all eyes and belly" as she wordlessly kneels to clean his boots, he looks at her with repugnance. The girl dies in premature labor. A strange reconciliation takes place between her brother and her lover, as they join together to plant an orange grove.

The Yearling (1938) won the 1939 Pulitzer Prize for fiction. R.'s editor, Maxwell Perkins, liked her hunt and river scenes, and urged her to do a boy's book. *The Yearling*'s theme is the passage from childhood to manhood for fourteen-year-old Jody Baxter. The plot is based on Jody's adopting a baby fawn when its mother is slain. After thirteen months, the fawn is no longer a baby but a yearling that destroys the family's crops and whose wild nature cannot be subdued. Jody is at first unable to obey his father's directive to kill the yearling, which has become a part of himself, but is forced to do so when his mother's faulty aim wounds the creature. His grief drives him from home to a river journey, and he wishes for the death of his gentle father, who, it seems, has betrayed him. Jody's homecoming shows him ready to put a child's happiness behind him and embrace the lonely hardships of manhood.

R. creates a Floridian earthly paradise. With all its loveliness, however, this wilderness reveals to the growing boy many signs of nature's cruelty. This sacrifice of the wild creature is a gesture implying that to attain maturity a man must quell his own rapturous, irresponsible, animal nature. Biblical echoes reinforce the end of innocence.

When the Whippoorwill (1940) collects R.'s best magazine stories. Noteworthy is "Gal Young Un," about a gaunt gray woman married for her wealth by a flashing opportunist. Several stories introduce R.'s fine comic narrator, Quincey Dover, "a woman with a tongue sharp enough to slice soft bacon." Others treat of moonshining, alligator hunting, and family life.

In 1942, R. published *Cross Creek*, chronicling her years in this chosen spot. R. describes the farmhouse, the tall old orange trees, the coral honeysuckle twisting on the wire fence. She gathers materials that will feed her fiction: scenes, animals, anecdotes, personalities. Her portraits of the neighbors whose lives she shared, notably of black women, are both humorous and painful, revealing R.'s sure grasp on human realities. In "Hyacinth Drift," two women, R. and a friend, navigate several hundred miles of river in an eighteen-foot boat. Beset with cares, R. had momentarily "lost touch with the Creek"; this is a journey of renewal that enables R. once again to long for home. "Because I had known intimately a river, the earth pulsed under me." *Cross Creek* ranks as a classic of the American pastoral scene.

Although she was admired as a regional writer, R.'s ambivalence about this designation led her to approach new subjects. R. believed that a "great" writer could write anywhere, and she broke from Cross Creek. R.'s last novel, *The Sojourner* (1953), about a Hudson Valley farm after the Civil War, shows the strain. It spins a vision of mythic rural America.

This dream of plenty is dissipated in the reality of family bitterness: the cheerful wife does not adore her husband; a brother abandons home on a doomed quest of silver and diamonds; a mad and treacherous mother-in-law allows a child to die in a snowstorm; a corrupt son drives a red Cadillac; stale apple pies fester uneaten and the wife bakes yet another. Romantic figures—an Indian, a gypsy queen—whose earthly vitality might be redemptive perish obscurely. The main character dies in an airplane, significantly separated from the earth, which he sees below him as a "battered planet." R. seeks to depict broad movements: the American rural dream shattered by the rise of a money economy, westward expansion, "progress," and foreign war. However, the novel lacks the power of R.'s earlier writing.

R. belongs to the tradition of Thoreau and Whitman. Nature for R. is cruel as well as beneficent, and she accepts the savagery as part of the cycle of living and dying. R.'s witty revelation of regional character and language places her in the mainstream of writers from Mark Twain on. R.'s typical fictional perspective is that of a male, usually naive, forced to acknowledge the sinister side of a seductive pastoral world.

WORKS: *South Moon Under* (1933). *Golden Apples* (1935). *The Yearling* (1938; film version, 1945). *When the Whippoorwill* (1941). *Cross Creek Cookery* (1942). *The Sojourner* (1953). *The Secret River* (1955).

BIBLIOGRAPHY: Bellman, S., *Marjorie Kinnan Rawlings* (1974). Berg, A. S., *Max Perkins, Editor of Genius* (1978). Bigelow, G. E., *Frontier Eden: The Literary Career of Marjorie Kinnan Rawlings* (1966). Bigham, J. S., Introduction to *The Marjorie Rawlings Reader* (1956).

Other references: *Collier's* 116 (29 Sept. 1945). *EJ* 64 (1975). *Family Circle* (7 May 1943). *NYT* Sunday Travel Section (27 Jan. 1980). *SLJ* 9 (1977).

MARCELLE THIÉBAUX

Harriette Fanning Read

B. Jamaica Plain, Massachusetts

R. was born to a family whose Irish ancestors came to the U.S. during the time of Cromwell's government in England. Both parents wanted their daughter to be a "literary woman." R.'s father, a publisher and bookseller, died when she was very young. After attending school briefly in Boston, R. went with her mother to Washington, D.C., where they joined the household of an uncle, Colonel Fanning. Because of his career, they moved from one military post to another for a time, then returned to the Washington area, where they resided until Fanning's death.

In 1847, R. published *Dramatic Poems* (dated 1848), a collection of three plays, *Medea, Erminia,* and *The New World.* In 1848, R. made her acting debut at the Boston Theater. Her novel, *The Haunted Student: A Romance of the Fourteenth Century,* appeared in 1860. By 1865, R. was living in New York City.

Medea stands out as the least typical and most interesting of R.'s three romantic tragedies, all written in blank verse and modeled after Shakespeare's poetic diction and five-act structure. Perhaps because the classical myth imposes a simplicity of plot and unified tone, *Medea* has a powerful, elemental quality that usually avoids the declamatory bombast and sentimental clichés that mar *Erminia* and *The New World.*

R. follows Euripides' version of the Greek myth, frequently quoting from his *Medea,* but she rearranges the story to emphasize the themes of blind passionate love and defiant individual freedom. The author's choice of this particular Greek myth suggests an awareness of women's frustrations over their limited roles in 19th-c. American society. When Medea's younger brother asks, "When shall I be a man?" we are reminded that the play raises questions about how we define man, woman, father, and mother in a society ruled by Creons and Jasons, who leave little choice between passive submission and extreme action in response to their inflexible and arbitrary dictates. As a prototype of what a talented, strong, and independent woman can do in a male-dominated society, Medea offers little hope besides self-destructive defiance.

Erminia: A Tale of Florence enacts a brittle, banal tragedy of love and intrigue. After rousing family and friends to revenge her honor after she is jilted by her fiancé, Erminia regrets her action when it is too late to save her lover from execution, and she dies of remorse and love for him. Like Medea, Erminia squanders her love on a man of power and ambition but little moral integrity.

The New World takes place in Haiti against a background of native resentment of Spanish colonial exploitation. Two lovers, the Spanish noble Guevara, and Alana, the daughter of the local chief, commit suicide to cheat the island's corrupt Spanish governor of his planned marriage with Alana.

The Haunted Student is a romantic novel with a gothic setting, complete with chivalrous knights and corrupt priests, convents and castles, and secret passages, dungeons, and torture chambers. But love rather than brooding darkness and evil forms the center of the story, set in 14th-c. Germany during the struggle between the feudal nobility and the emerging free cities of the Hanseatic League. The beautiful Countess Ludmila plans to "haunt" her betrothed, Albert of Rabenstein, in order to win his love and secure him from the influence of his mentor, Father Cyrillus, who intends to make Albert a monk so that his father, the Baron of Rabenstein, will have no heir.

The characters rather than the elaborate plot provide unity and interest, particularly Ludmila and Father Cyrillus. Ludmila's energetic impulsiveness wins our affection, and her imaginative intelligence, outspokenness, and refusal to wait passively upon events win our respect. The complex Father Cyrillus, a good man corrupted by a justified desire for revenge, confounds our impulse to wholly like or dislike him, a tension increased because R. withholds his motives for revenge until late in the novel.

Ludmila's stubborn insistence upon doing whatever she believes is necessary and right exemplifies the novel's main theme of individual freedom, whereas her actions illustrate the theme that although the methods may vary, woman's strength, intelligence, and courage equal that of a man in achieving a desired goal.

The Haunted Student is a competently written and pleasantly readable example of the romantic novel, but R.'s powerful tragedy *Medea* stands out as her greatest achievement.

WORKS: *Dramatic Poems* (1848). *The Haunted Student: A Romance of the Fourteenth Century* (1860).

BIBLIOGRAPHY: Watts, E. S., *The Poetry of American Women from 1632 to 1945* (1977).
For articles in reference works, see: *American Female Poets*, C. May (1853). *Critical Dictionary of English and American Authors Living and Deceased*, S. A. Allibone (1900).

MELANIE YOUNG

Martha Read

R.'s only work, *Monima; or, The Beggar Girl: A Novel* (1802), reveals the author's conscious control of plot and structure. In her dedication and preface to this long narrative, R. offers the conventional apology for the work's defects and places a conventional stress on the novel's foundation on fact. But she also hints at a developed aesthetic that her story will illustrate—adherence to truth and to nature, R. feels, determines a novel's artistic success.

The plot is thus simpler than those of many of the novels of late-18th-, early-19th-c. America and the principal characters are fewer. Set in Philadelphia in the early 1790s, the novel immediately focuses on Monima Fontanbleu, a beautiful seamstress of sixteen, and her old father, who have fallen upon hard times. Monima has lost her position with Madame Ursala Sontine, a selfish woman who fears her virtuous husband's attraction to the young woman. The narrative grows naturally out of this situation as Madame Sontine repeatedly tries to remove Monima—by confinement to the workhouse, to her own country estate, and to a hospital for the insane—from possible contact with her husband. Ursala is abetted in her machinations first by her pliable maid, by her unscrupulous brother, and later by Pierre De Noix, an acquaintance of Sontine's who becomes Ursala's lover and who soon himself develops lecherous designs on Monima. Monima escapes from all these incarcerations, and even gains small sums through infrequent employment and occasional begging. Monsieur Sontine is attracted to Monima—but merely as a brotherly benefactor—and seeks to aid her, only sometimes succeeding because of his wife's elaborate plotting.

R.'s aesthetic principles seem clear. Actions are motivated by character, and the author emphasizes the historicity of her material. R. does not avoid unpleasant details despite the novel's many sentimental scenes (primarily concerning Monima's begging). The novel also contains sharply observed humor as R. exploits American prejudices against the French and satirizes the romantic plots of many of her contemporaries.

R.'s themes are not original—American purity and innocence will triumph, and a happy marriage is the just reward for female virtue—but her technique and conscious attempt to realize aesthetic principles distinguish *Monima* from other novels of the period.

WORKS: *Monima; or, The Beggar Girl: A Novel* (1802).

BIBLIOGRAPHY: Brown, H. R., *The Sentimental Novel in America: 1789–1860* (1940). Petter, H., *The Early American Novel* (1971).
Other references: *American Review and Literary Journal* 2 (1802).

CAROLINE ZILBOORG

Myrtle Reed

B. 27 Sept. 1874, Norwood Park, Illinois; d. 17 Aug. 1911, Chicago, Illinois
Wrote under: Olive Green, Katherine LaFarge Norton, Myrtle Reed
D. of Hiram Von and Elizabeth Armstrong Reed; m. James Sydney
  McCullough, 1906

R. was born of distinguished parents. Her father, a preacher, established Chicago's first literary magazine, the *Lakeside Monthly*, and her mother was a scholar of oriental literature and comparative religion. R.'s parents encouraged her to be a writer, and she began her literary apprenticeship with her high school paper, advancing to free-lance writing upon her graduation. R.'s first novel, *Love Letters of a Musician* (1899), was an immense success and established R. as a romantic writer. R.'s marriage did not live up to her romantic ideals, and her separation precipitated her suicide.

In addition to her poetry and fiction, R. also wrote cookbooks under the pseudonym of Olive Green and domestic articles under the pseudonym of Katherine LaFarge Norton. She is best known, however, for her many popular novels. Joseph Kesselring transformed her second novel, *Lavender and Old Lace* (1902), into the popular play *Arsenic and Old Lace* (1941).

R.'s novels are formulaic at best. Each contains at least one Dickensian caricature. There are always two heroines, generally competing for the same man. When a middle-aged woman is involved, she has invariably been separated from her "one true love" and is of course reunited with him by the novel's end. Each novel is interrupted at least once by "philosophical" commentary on the nature of love and destiny. The later novels even include a smattering of telepathic communication and precognitive dreams.

Typical of R.'s novels is *A Spinner in the Sun* (1906), in which the heroine Evelina Grey had supposedly been disfigured when she saved her fiancé from injury in an explosion in his lab. The fiancé leaves Evelina and marries someone else, while for the next twenty-five years Evelina keeps a chiffon veil over her face. However, Evelina's face was not disfigured, only her shoulder and arms; she wears the veil to hide the beauty that has caused her so much sorrow. Eventually, Evelina forgives the ex-fiancé (after his suicide), discovers that she loves a man far more worthy of her, and casts off the veil forever.

R.'s most interesting novel is her last, *A Weaver of Dreams* (1911), which concerns Judith and Margery and their love for the same man, Carter Keith. Although initially engaged to Judith, Carter discovers that Margery is the woman fate intended for him. Upon discovering the truth, Judith graciously releases him. What makes the novel an oddity is that R. does not conjure up another man for Judith. As the novel ends, Judith is alone and bereft but determined to face the future with courage and dignity. Completed shortly before R.'s suicide, this conclusion serves as an ironic epitaph for the author.

WORKS: *Love Letters of a Musician* (1899). *Later Love Letters of a Musician* (1900). *The Spinster Book* (1901). *Lavender and Old Lace* (1902; dramatization by J. Kesselring, *Arsenic and Old Lace*, 1941; film version, 1944). *White Shield* (1902). *Pickaback Songs* (1903). *The Shadow of Victory* (1903). *The Book of Clever Beasts* (1904). *The Master's Violin* (1904). *At the Sign of the Jack o' Lantern* (1905). *Everyday Luncheons* (1906). *A Spinner in the Sun* (1906). *What to Have for Breakfast* (1906). *How to Cook Shell-Fish* (1907). *Love Affairs of Literary Men* (1907). *One Thousand Simple Soups* (1907). *Flower of the Dusk* (1908). *How to Cook Fish* (1908). *How to Cook Meat and Poultry* (1908). *How to Cook Vegetables* (1909). *Old Rose and Silver* (1909). *Master of the Vineyard* (1910). *Sonnets to a Lover* (1910). *Everyday Desserts* (1911). *Everyday Dinners* (1911). *The Myrtle Reed Year Book* (1911). *A Weaver of Dreams* (1911). *The White Shield* (1912). *Happy Women* (1913). *Threads of Grey and Gold* (1913). *A Woman's Career* (1914). *The Myrtle Reed Cook Book* (1916).

BIBLIOGRAPHY: Colson, E. S., and N. B. Carson, *Myrtle Reed* (1911). Powell, M. B., Foreword to *The Myrtle Reed Year Book* (1911).
Other references: *DAB*, VIII, 1. *NAW* (article by H. B. Christenson). *NCAB*, 15.

CYNTHIA L. WALKER

Lizette Woodworth Reese

B. 9 Jan. 1856, Waverly, Maryland; d. 17 Dec. 1935, Baltimore, Maryland
D. of David and Louisa Reese

R.'s life as a child and young woman in Waverly, a suburban village of Baltimore, provided the material for most of her writing, both poetry and prose. In R.'s poems and reminiscences, Waverly becomes the symbol for a time and a value system more stable than those of the present. R. not only grew up in Waverly but began her long teaching career in the local parish school. Her first poem, "The Deserted House," appeared in the *Southern Magazine* in June 1874. From that time until her death, R. continued to write lyric poetry that was of fairly consistent quality.

R.'s first volume of poetry, *A Branch of May* (1887), was privately printed through subscriptions from friends. This volume of thirty-three poems was sent to several of the leading critics of the day, all of whom received it favorably. R.'s reputation grew with *A Handful of Lavendar* (1891), which was published by a national publisher.

The subject matter and style of R.'s poetry remained constant through her subsequent volumes. R.'s subjects are the eternal truths of life and death—joy and sorrow, expressed in images drawn from R.'s childhood experiences in the Maryland countryside and readings in English literature. Her best poems make arrestingly fresh use of images from ordinary experience. R.'s central images are of village and orchard. The orchard becomes a primary image, for, as R. says, "although not so open as the lane, or so secret as the wood, it keeps the free heart of the one, and somewhat of the privileged quiet of the other."

R. was generally praised for the freshness of her images in a time when most lyric poetry was marked by the tired conventions of excessive and archaic expression. R.'s forte was the short lyric, but she was also an accomplished sonneteer. Her best-known poem was the sonnet "Tears," which first appeared in *Scribner's* magazine in 1899 and was repeatedly anthologized. The poem presents a series of arresting metaphors about the futility of grieving over the fugitive cares of life.

Although primarily a lyric poet, R. published one successful long narrative poem, *Little Henrietta* (1927), and was at the time of her death working on another, which was published posthumously as *The Old House in the Country* (1936). *Little Henrietta* probes the grief and eventual reconciliation over the death of a young child, and *The Old House* is an attempt to unify the diverse recollections of childhood memories.

Childhood memories form the substance of two volumes of auto-biographical reminiscence, *A Victorian Village* (1929) and *The York Road* (1931). These prose works poetically present the recollections and associations brought to R.'s mind by people, places, and events from her childhood and young adulthood. At the time of her death, R. was re-working these experiences into an autobiographical novel, published post-humously as *Worleys* (1936).

R. is neglected today, although she was one of the finest poets writing during the last decade of the 19th c. and the first decade of the 20th. She is a transition figure between the stylized conventions of the Victorian poets and the free form and subject matter of the moderns. At its best, R.'s poetry is characterized by a striking intensity and freshness of image.

WORKS: *A Branch of May* (1887). *A Handful of Lavender* (1891). *A Quiet Road* (1896). *A Wayside Lute* (1909). *Spicewood* (1920). *Wild Cherry* (1923). *The Selected Poems* (1926). *Little Henrietta* (1927). *A Victorian Village* (1929). *White April, and Other Poems* (1930). *The York Road* (1931). *Pastures, and Other Poems* (1933). *The Old House in the Country* (1936). *Worleys* (1936).

BIBLIOGRAPHY: Gregory, H., and M. Zaturenska, *A History of American Poetry, 1900–1940* (1946). Klein, L. R. M., "Lizette Woodworth Reese" (Ph.D. diss., Univ. of Pennsylvania, 1943). Rittenhouse, J. B., in *The Younger American Poets* (1906).

Other references: *Personalist* 31 (1900). *SAQ* (April 1930; Jan. 1957). *SUS* 8 (1969).

HARRIETTE CUTTINO BUCHANAN

Martha Remick

B. 11 June 1832, Kittery, Maine; d. 11 April 1906, Everett, Massachusetts
D. of Rufus and Sally Cram Remick

The youngest daughter of a shipwright and farmer who had earned a lieutenancy in the War of 1812, R. never married, dedicating her life

to writing. A family genealogy, the only source of biographical information on R., describes her as "unmarried, authoress and poetess."

In the preface to *Agnes Stanhope* (1862), R. declares that it is her purpose to show the "ever-present providence of God," but the novel is
a romantic thriller that entertains far more than it elevates. Agnes, a
heedless young girl, elopes with her sister Bertha's fiancé Howard.
Howard soon turns to cards, whiskey, and evil companions. One of
these takes Howard to visit his soon-to-be-discarded mistress Helen, who
has planned to poison her faithless lover with arsenic-laced champagne.
Howard accidentally drinks the potion, then staggers home to die. Accused of Howard's murder and condemned to die, Agnes escapes to
Italy, where she meets and marries De Lacey, Helen's brother, who
knows nothing of his sister's fallen life. They return to England, where
Agnes is hard-pressed to conceal her identity. The conscience-stricken
Helen does finally confess, and Agnes and De Lacey's happiness is assured.

Millicent Halford (1865), the story of a Massachusetts girl who goes to
live with her slave-owning relatives in Kentucky, is a pro-North Civil
War romance. Millicent is appalled by her first exposure to whippings
and slave sales. Fred, one of Millicent's Kentucky cousins, agrees with
her and joins the Union army; his brother, James, is a supporter of
the Confederacy. Fred survives the war and marries Millicent. Using the
brothers as symbols of North and South, R. deliberately leaves James's
fate in question, just as the fate of the defeated South was in question
when the book was written.

Richard Ireton (1875), purporting to be a tale of early American
Puritans and Quakers, is actually another romantic thriller. R.'s few
forays into New England history here produce dancing, party-going
Puritans, gaudily clad Quakers, and battle scenes from the French and
Indian War that are set in 1681.

R.'s heroines tend to be impossibly virtuous and pallid. To move her
somewhat creaky plots forward, R. relies heavily on the overworked
device of "had she but known the tragedies that would befall her." Despite these flaws, R. is a talented writer whose heroes and villains alike
are flawed, realistic, and sympathetic characters. Her villains have elements of kindness, gentleness, and even nobility, while her heroes have
streaks of pride and selfishness. R. also offers no simple, moralistic solutions to life's tragedies. The modern reader would still find these books
entertaining and worthwhile.

WORKS: *Agnes Stanhope: A Tale of English Life* (1862). *Millicent Halford:
A Tale of the Dark Days of Kentucky in the Year 1861* (1865). *Richard*

Ireton: A Legend of the Early Settlement of New England (1875). *Miscellaneous Poems* (1901).

Miscellaneous Poems is available only at the libraries of Brown University and the University of Chicago.

BIBLIOGRAPHY: Remick, O. P., *Geneaology of the Remick Family* (1893).

For articles in reference works, see: *A Critical Dictionary of English and American Authors*, S. A. Allibone (1891).

ZOHARA BOYD

Itti Kinney Reno

B. 17 May 1862, Nashville, Tennessee
Wrote under: "A Nashville Pen," Itti Kinney Reno
D. of Colonel George S. Kinney; m. Robert Ross Reno, 1885

Described in a biographical reference as a "high-strung, imaginative child, remarkably bright and precocious," R. was known as a novelist and social leader, "marked by the brilliance that wealth and social influence confer."

R. attended a convent in Kentucky, later marrying after a successful social debut. R. began writing "for amusement," and through family connections published *Miss Breckenridge: A Daughter of Dixie* in 1890.

In this novel, R. seems determined to show the extent of her learning and good breeding; she "name-drops," citing authors even when they are irrelevant to the narrative. Complete with a sympathetic "Mammy" whose dialogue is conveyed in dialect, the novel is a wholly conventional tale of a southern belle (of great athletic skill and personal charm) torn between two lovers. The story is predictably simple: In one episode, the heroine Cleo lapses into hysteria when the man she loves is called away to his ill mother; in another, "an unknown woman" arrives to tell Cleo that her lover has fathered a child. The expected complications, of course, are resolved through the noble efforts of the rejected suitor, and Cleo is reunited with her love.

An Exceptional Case (1891) is more than a narrative of conventional southern manners. It begins within the idiom of social-romantic banter, as "lips silenced their music in the lover's smile that came to him at the sight of the beautiful girl"; and R.'s name-dropping continues. Yet while R. stresses "that nameless charm . . . the signet that Refinement gives to the children of Birth and Breeding," the novel marks an early attempt at feminism.

"Surely you are not so unprogressive to think woman's career limited to the needle and the nursery?" asks Miss Hampton, an aspiring painter, of her admirer. Although the novel is uneven, marred by emotional traumas unrelated to R.'s purpose, the heroine does realize, after her marriage has settled into sameness, that she is indeed culturally and intellectually starved. The novel ends with a compromise: She will stay with her husband (who had earlier forbidden her interest in art), but her days will be devoted to painting, his to his business—and their evenings to each other. Considering the expectations of R.'s social class, the modern solution for her heroine's predicament is quite admirable.

R.'s novels are conventional and unremarkable, adhering to the directives of social manner and breeding. But *An Exceptional Case* is precisely that for its faint glimmer of feminism, especially in light of the highly structured milieu in which it was written.

WORKS: *Miss Breckenridge: A Daughter of Dixie* (1890). *An Exceptional Case* (1891).

BIBLIOGRAPHY: For articles in reference works, see: *AW. A Dictionary of American Authors*, O. F. Adams (1904).

DEBORAH H. HOLDSTEIN

Agnes Repplier

B. *1 April 1855, Philadelphia, Pennsylvania; d. 16 Dec. 1950, Philadelphia, Pennsylvania*
D. *of John George and Agnes Mathias Repplier*

R. did not learn to read until she was almost ten. Her formal education was limited to two years at the Convent of the Sacred Heart and three terms at Miss Irwin's School in Philadelphia. Both schools dismissed her because of independent behavior, so that R. was entirely self-educated after the age of sixteen. Her intensive reading was augmented by numerous trips (the first in 1890) and long periods of residence in Europe.

Urged by her mother, R. began publishing at sixteen to increase the family's income when her father's fortune collapsed, and throughout her life she loyally supported her family. R.'s first writings were stories and sketches for Philadelphia newspapers. After publishing "In Arcady" in *Catholic World* (1881), the editor urged R. to write essays, since she knew a great deal about books and not much about life. This set the direction of R.'s career, for she made the familiar essay distinctively her own form—witty, graceful, and richly textured with allusions from her vast reading.

In 1886, R. was accepted by the American literary establishment. "Children, Past and Present" appeared in the *Atlantic Monthly*. Here she continued to publish frequently—ninety essays in all, the last in 1940. A highly disciplined writer, R. was determined from the start that her work would have permanence. In 1888, R. arranged the first of many collections, *Books and Men*, which included the first seven essays from *Atlantic Monthly*. Similar volumes appeared throughout the years. R. was a popular public lecturer, noted for her sharp perceptions, lively manner, and witty expression.

A plain child and woman with an incisive mind and quick wit, R. never married. She thought the feminist cause a just one and opposed any kind of discrimination. She had, however, no use for reformers in any area because of their excessive claims and simplistic and sentimental solutions. "Woman Enthroned" presents her case, as do "The Strayed Prohibitionist" and "Consolations of the Conservative." For R., happiness was fleeting and lay in "the development of individual tastes and acquirements."

The urbane stance is typical of R. However, before U.S. involvement in World War I, R. argued passionately for several years against neutrality, collaborating with Dr. J. W. White on a pamphlet, *Germany and Democracy* (1914), and writing many essays, collected in *Counter-Currents* (1916).

A lifelong and devout Roman Catholic, R. wrote from a strong ethical code that provided a firm base for her relentlessly skeptical view of human performance. R.'s specifically Catholic writings are among her most successful and include a merry autobiography, *In Our Convent Days* (1905), and three distinguished biographies of American religious leaders: *Père Marquette* (1929), *Mère Marie of the Ursulines* (1931), and *Junipero Serra* (1933).

Addressing herself to a wide range of literary subjects and social change for more than half a century, R. was usually provocative but rarely inelegant in her commentary. Her familiar essays provide a distinctive and pleasing alternative to the prevailing realism of American literature. Perhaps R.'s most characteristic mode is epitomized by two collections separated by half her writing career, *A Happy Half-Century* (1908) and *In Pursuit of Laughter* (1936). R.'s range is broad, but her audience was always a select and patrician one.

WORKS: *Books and Men* (1888). *Points of View* (1889). *A Book of Famous Verse* (edited by Repplier, 1892). *Essays in Miniature* (1892). *Essays in Idleness* (1893). *In the Dozy Hours, and Other Papers* (1894). *Varia* (1897). *Philadelphia: The Place and the People* (1898). *The Fireside Sphinx* (1901). *Compromises* (1904). *In Our Convent Days* (1905). *A Happy Half-Century* (1908). *Americans and Others* (1912). *The Cat, being a Record of the Endearments and Invectives Lavished by Many Writers* (1912). *Germany and Democracy, the Real Issue* (with J. W. White, 1914). *Counter-Currents* (1916). *J. William White, M. D.: A Biography* (1919). *Points of Friction* (1920). *Under Dispute* (1924). *Père Marquette* (1929). *Mère Marie of the Ursulines* (1931). *Times and Tendencies* (1931). *To Think of Tea!* (1932). *Junipero Serra* (1933). *Agnes Irwin* (1934). *In Pursuit of Laughter* (1936). *Eight Decades* (1937).

BIBLIOGRAPHY: Repplier, E., *Agnes Repplier: A Memoir by Her Niece* (1957). Stokes, G. S., *Agnes Repplier: Lady of Letters* (1949).

For articles in reference works, see: *Catholic Authors: Contemporary Biographical Sketches, 1930–1947*, Ed. M. Hoehn (1948). *DAB*, Suppl. 4. *NAW* (article by G. S. Stokes). *NCAB*, 9.

Other references: *Nation* (29 Nov. 1933). *NYHTB* (13 Jan. 1929; 29 Nov. 1931). *SatR* (23 Dec. 1933). *YR* (March 1937).

VELMA BOURGEOIS RICHMOND

Alice Caldwell Hegan Rice

B. *11 Jan. 1870, Shelbyville, Kentucky; d. 10 Feb. 1942, Louisville, Kentucky*
Wrote under: Alice Caldwell Hegan, Alice Hegan Rice
D. *of Samuel Watson and Sallie Caldwell Hegan; m. Cale Young Rice, 1902*

R. was born and raised in Kentucky, the setting for most of her fiction. She married Rice shortly after the publication of her first book. They traveled widely in Asia and Europe, associating with many of the most prominent literary figures of the 20th c. Their permanent home was

Louisville. Though Rice was primarily a poet and R. a writer of fiction, they worked closely together, publishing short stories by each of them in three collections (*Turn About Tales*, 1920; *Winners and Losers*, 1925; and *Passionate Follies*, 1936). R. also published an autobiography (*The Inky Way*, 1940) and two collections of religious meditations (*My Pillow Book*, 1937, and *Happiness Road*, completed by her husband in 1942).

R.'s best works are set among Kentucky's poor, particularly the urban poor whom she came to know as a volunteer settlement worker. *Mrs. Wiggs of the Cabbage Patch* (1901), inspired by a real person and a slum area in Louisville, is noteworthy both for its fidelity to the facts of the lives of poor urban whites and for the gentle humor with which it depicts their characters. These are the "deserving poor," honest and willing to work. Mrs. Wiggs, a widow with five children, is poor and illiterate but wise and proud; she straightens out the personal lives of the wealthy young woman and man who, in turn, give her surviving children a chance to make something of themselves. The novel's humor comes from its use of dialect, from Mrs. Wiggs's malapropisms, and from the children's pranks and mishaps. *Lovey Mary* (1903) is a sequel about an orphan girl who flees the orphanage and is taken in by Mrs. Wiggs and her friends. Both novels are trite and sentimental in plot, but their restraint and gently comic tone keep them from becoming mawkish.

Four other novels center on poor but meritorious characters trying to make their way in a hostile world. *Sandy* (1905), loosely based on the experiences of the magazine editor S. S. McClure, tells of a Scottish waif finally lucky enough to be taken in by a wealthy Kentuckian. Also dealing with an adolescent boy is *Our Ernie* (1939), whose title character quits school at fourteen to support his loving but feckless family. He rises in the business world, becoming entangled with the daughter of his employer, but in a reversal of the Horatio Alger motif, frees himself from her while retaining his position. A rather melodramatic subplot concerns German spies. R.'s dedication describes it as "a happy book about funny people," a valid description for most of her novels.

Mr. Pete & Co. (1933) tells of a middle-aged derelict who returns home to Louisville when he inherits a riverfront tenement. The unaccustomed responsibility for the building and its inhabitants regenerates him, and by novel's end he has instigated an urban-renewal project and transformed the lives of his tenants.

R.'s most ambitious attempt to depict urban poverty and inspire reform is *Calvary Alley* (1917), which recounts the life of Nance Molloy, at eleven a mistress of gang-fighting techniques, later a reform-school inmate, and then a factory worker. Through much of the novel her prime goal is to escape the slum, but she matures and through hard work and good luck becomes a nurse in a clinic serving her people. R. was disappointed that this book was generally received as another comic novel rather than as the serious indictment of slum conditions she intended.

Most of R.'s other novels concern family situations, the central characters bearing responsibility for unworldly and eccentric relatives. Particularly interesting is *The Buffer* (1929), which centers on Cynthia Freer, an aspiring writer who is strong and self-sacrificing but has a sense of humor. At the novel's conventional happy ending, she seems to be ready to subordinate her literary ambitions to marriage—but she takes the manuscript of her novel with her.

R.'s novels are readable and amusing, though lacking in roundness of characterization or thematic depth. Compared to the works of her naturalistic contemporaries, who used many similar materials, R.'s treatments seem shallowly optimistic. She had few pretensions, however, always considering her husband's serious poetry more important than her own light fiction. But his work is largely forgotten today, while at least one of her characters, Mrs. Wiggs, still lives.

WORKS: *Mrs. Wiggs of the Cabbage Patch* (1901; film version, 1934). *Lovey Mary* (1903). *Sandy* (1905). *Captain June* (1907). *Mr. Opp* (1909). *A Romance of Billy-Goat Hill* (1912). *The Honorable Percival* (1914). *Calvary Alley* (1917). *Miss Mink's Soldier, and Other Stories* (1918). *Turn About Tales* (with C. Y. Rice, 1920). *Quinn* (1921). *Winners and Losers* (with C. Y. Rice, 1925). *The Buffer: A Novel* (1929). *Mr. Pete & Co.* (1933). *The Lark Legacy* (1935). *Passionate Follies: Alternate Tales* (with C. Y. Rice, 1936). *My Pillow Book* (1937). *Our Ernie* (1939). *The Inky Way* (1940). *Happiness Road* (1942).

BIBLIOGRAPHY: Overton, G., *The Women Who Make Our Novels* (1919).
Other references: *Book News Monthly* (Oct. 1909). *Boston Transcript* (31 Oct. 1917; 14 Sept. 1921; 23 Sept. 1933). *NYHTB* (10 Nov. 1940).

MARY JEAN DeMARR

Adrienne Cecile Rich

B. 16 May 1929, Baltimore, Maryland
D. of Arnold and Helen Rich; m. Alfred H. Conrad, 1953

R. was brought up in a southern, Jewish household which she has described as "white and middle-class . . . full of books, with a father who encouraged me to read and write." From her father's library R. read such writers as Rosetti, Swinburne, Tennyson, Keats, Blake, Arnold, Carlyle, and Pater, and as a child she was already writing poetry. Neither she nor her younger sister was sent to school until fourth grade: Dr. Rich, a professor of medicine, and Helen Rich, a trained composer and pianist, believed that they could educate their own children in a more enlightened, albeit unorthodox, way. In fact, most of the responsibility fell to the mother; she carried out the practical task of teaching them all their lessons, including music.

R.'s remaining education progressed conventionally enough, and she graduated Phi Beta Kappa from Radcliffe College in 1951. That same year she enjoyed success with the publication of her first book of poems, *A Change of World*, chosen by W. H. Auden for the Yale Younger Poets Award. Although Auden's tone in the preface has been criticized as condescending, he focused immediately on R.'s careful handling of form and clarity of thought: "The poems a reader will encounter in this book are neatly and modestly dressed, speak quietly but do not mumble, respect their elders but are not cowed by them, and do not tell fibs: that for a first volume is a good deal." Indeed, critic after critic has noted R.'s stylistic control and elegance as the hallmark of her early achievement.

This restrained style was to continue through the 1950s and be perfected in her second volume, *The Diamond Cutters* (1955). In a review of that volume, Randall Jarrell called her an "enchanting poet," an "endearing and delightful poet." But in the early 1960s, R. startled her critical audience with a shift to more political and feminist themes and an increasingly experimental style. Of her early experience, she has said, "In those years formalism was part of the strategy—like asbestos gloves, it allowed me to handle materials I couldn't pick up bare-handed . . . In the late Fifties I was able to write, for the first time, directly about experiencing myself as a woman."

From 1953 to 1966, R. resided in Cambridge, Massachusetts, with her three sons and her husband. These were years of personal and political growth and crisis for R. Her teaching career reflected her political commitment as she became involved in the SEEK and Open Admissions Programs of City College in New York City, where she took up residence after 1966. Her husband died tragically in 1970. R. continued teaching in the New York area until 1979, when she gave up her professorship at Rutgers University and settled in western Massachusetts with "the woman who shares my life."

R.'s early poetry is marked by a detached and objective formalism. The poems from her first two volumes reveal those qualities so dear to the critics: the skillful use of meter and rhyme and the simple and precise phrasing that serves equally abstract thought and concrete description. "The Ultimate Act," a meditative sonnet in octosyllabics, begins in the tones and syntax of Shakespeare, yet concludes with a line that is full of the elegiac ambiguities of Wallace Stevens. Other poems, such as "Pictures by Vuillard" and "The Celebration in the Plaza," captivate the reader by means of the occasional exotic adjective and an evocation of place. There are also poems here that anticipate R.'s later commitment to exploring feminine experience.

R. wrote the title poem of Snapshots of a Daughter-in-Law (1963) "in a longer and looser mode than I'd ever trusted myself with before. It was an extraordinary relief to write that poem." This and other poems here, composed of irregular stanzas, are about madness, anger, waste, and failure in women's lives. "A Marriage in the 'Sixties," "End of an Era," "Novella," and "Readings of History" explore the self in relation to society, intimacy, war, violence, and pacifism. In "From Morning-Glory to Petersburg," R. says, ". . . Now knowledge finds me out; / in all its risible untidiness / it traces me to each address, / dragging in things I never thought about."

R.'s next three books, The Necessities of Life (1966), Leaflets (1969), and The Will to Change (1971) carry her further into this new knowledge. R. goes beyond the cadences of Frost, Auden, and Yeats, the tones of a mainstream tradition that modulates her voice in the early poems. Instead she draws upon diverse material—translating from Dutch, adapting poems from Yiddish and Russian, and experimenting with the ghazal-like forms inspired by the Urdu poet Mirza Ghalib.

In the 1970s, R.'s poetry revealed an urgent and driving tone that was expressive of her militant feminism. Critics worried that politics and ideology were undermining the poetry, but R. made no such distinction between politics and poetry. *Diving into the Wreck* (1973) is an attempt to start from the bottom, speaking of matters as yet unspoken in words as yet undefined. There are disturbing poems of pain, anger, and violence. Yet coexistent with this anger is a deep sorrow over our vulnerabilities and our frustrated ideals.

In *The Dream of a Common Language* (1978), R. begins to rebuild and to document the difficult process of re-vision. Expanding on an earlier method, she draws some of her material from historical figures: Marie Curie, Clara Westhoff (who married the poet Rainer Maria Rilke), and Elvira Shatayev (the leader of a women's mountain-climbing team). But her primary concern seems to be to provide mythic structures that will confirm and nourish the vital hopes and experiences of women. Thus in her latest phase R. has not abandoned form and restraint; rather she is searching for a new poetics defined by and for women.

R.'s concern with myth has also appeared in her prose. *Of Woman Born: Motherhood as Experience and Institution* (1976) is a carefully documented attempt to demystify motherhood as a patriarchal institution. She has also published widely on poetry, feminism, and lesbianism.

Among contemporary poets, R. is regarded highly. The integrity of her craft and the timeliness of her themes have earned her not only an academic audience but also a popular one. Above all her voice is directed towards other women, sharing her perceptions and partaking of a common experience.

WORKS: *A Change of World* (1951). *The Diamond Cutters* (1955). *Snapshots of a Daughter-in-Law* (1963). *Necessities of Life* (1966). *Selected Poems* (1967). *Leaflets* (1969). *The Will to Change* (1971). *Diving into the Wreck* (1973). *Poems: Selected and New* (1975). *Twenty-One Love Poems* (1975). *Of Woman Born: Motherhood as Experience and Institution* (1976). *The Dream of A Common Language: Poems 1974–1977* (1978). *On Lies, Secrets, and Silence: Selected Prose, 1966–1978* (1979).

BIBLIOGRAPHY: Gelpi, B. C., and A. Gelpi, *Adrienne Rich's Poetry: The Texts of the Poems, the Poet on Her Work, Reviews and Criticism* (1975). Juhasz, S., *Naked and Fiery Forms: Modern American Poetry by Women* (1976). Karp, S. H., "Beginning Here: A Reading of Adrienne Rich's *The Dream of a Common Language* as Feminist Manifesto and Myth," in *The Proceedings of the Second CUNY English Forum* (1981).

Other references: *Anonymous* 2 (1975). *Hollins Critic* (Oct. 1974). *The Island* 1 (May 1966). *Ms.* (July 1973). *Newsweek* (24 Dec. 1973). *NYT* (3 Feb. 1980). *The Ohio Review* 13 (1971). *Parnassus* (2, 1973; 4, 1975). *Poetry* 109 (Jan. 1967). *Salmagundi* 22–23 (1973). *SatR* (22 April 1972). *Southwest Review* 60 (Autumn 1975).

SHEEMA HAMDANI KARP

Louise Dickinson Rich

B. *14 June 1903, Huntington, Massachusetts*
M. *Ralph Eugene Rich, 1934*

R. began writing about her life after her marriage. The couple settled in the Unorganized Territory of northwestern Maine. *We Took to the Woods* (1942) tells of their primitive housing, woods lore, various pets, and the birth of their first child without the aid of a midwife. The book was popular and successful in those discouraging war years. R. retained her chatty personal narrative style in later books, including *Only Parent* (1953), which describes her trials and adventures as a single parent (her husband died in 1944).

R.'s descriptions of nature are always incidental to the central personal narrative. Only in *The Natural World of Louise Dickinson Rich* (1962) does R. attempt to write a "natural history" of New England. Even here the writing is personal, anecdotal, and humorous. R. describes the creatures she has found and domesticated in each of New England's three geographical areas; the typical flora, with appropriate stories about their names and uses; and the contradictory nature of New England climate and geological history. R.'s more usual attitude toward nature is summed up in her "50-Year Bird Plan," enunciated in *My Neck of the Woods* (1950): she will learn to recognize one bird species a year, then tell all the resort guests that year that the small birds are yellow-bellied sapsuckers and the large ones ospreys.

A large portion of R.'s work was written for young people. She has seven books in a First Book series, as well as many short stories and juvenile novels. In *The First Book of New England* (1957), each chapter has a fictionalized account of one or two children growing up in a region with a very distinct ethnic background. Through this format R. manages to convey much history and economics. Sex-role stereotyping is thoroughgoing: Boys grow up to be tobacco farmers, lawyers, doctors, or scientists; girls aim to be teachers, wives, or even Olympic skiers.

An adventure series for young people about a young Maine guide, Bill Gordon, was abandoned after two volumes (*Start of the Trail*, 1949, and *Trail to the North*, 1952), but R.'s later juvenile fiction continues the genre. Somehow the clichéd writing is not so annoying when it comes through the consciousness of a twelve year old, but again the stereotyping is disturbing. R.'s boys must not show emotion or worry the women, while girls get hysterical over skunks and worms.

Perhaps the most satisfactory of all her works are R.'s informal guides to Maine: *The Coast of Maine* (1956), *The Peninsula* (1958), *State o' Maine* (1964), and *The Kennebec River* (1967). R. relates anecdotes well, and she obviously appreciates the unique down-east personality. Local history, geography, and lore are all told with great good humor. Describing the land, people, and creatures of the shore and sea around Maine's Gouldsboro Peninsula, *The Peninsula* includes chapters on lobstering, local speech, community customs, regional cooking, and the strong independent women of the peninsula.

At her best R. can be humorous, fascinating, evocative of place, and very readable. At her worst she is clichéd, historically inaccurate, and full of unsubstantiated generalizations; her style is neither creative nor economical.

R.'s works betray an intense desire for acceptability, for strengthening the image of the scatterbrained, flighty-but-responsible, cowed-by-men-and-tools, warmhearted American "mom." Every unconventional action or comment is followed with some kind of apology. If R. was forced into this pose by her popular audience, we can be thankful for the slightly heightened awareness of the 1970s.

WORKS: *We Took to the Woods* (1942). *Happy the Land* (1946). *Start of the Trail* (1949). *My Neck of the Woods* (1950). *Trail to the North* (1952). *Only Parent* (1953). *Innocence under the Elms* (1955). *The Coast of Maine* (1956). *The First Book of New England* (1957). *The Peninsula* (1958). *The First Book of the Early Settlers* (1959). *Mindy* (1959). *The First Book of New World Explorers* (1960). *The First Book of the China Clippers* (1962). *The First Book of the Vikings* (1962). *The Natural World of Louise Dickinson Rich* (1962). *State o' Maine* (1964). *The First Book of the Fur Trade* (1965). *The First Book of Lumbering* (1967). *The Kennebec River* (1967). *Star Island Boy* (1968). *Three of a Kind* (1970). *King Phillip's War, 1675-76* (1972). *Summer at High Kingdom* (1975).

BIBLIOGRAPHY: For articles in reference works, see: *CB* (May 1943). *20thCAS.*

MARGARET McFADDEN-GERBER

Laura Elizabeth Howe Richards

B. 27 Feb. 1850, Boston, Massachusetts; d. 14 Jan. 1943, Gardiner, Maine
Wrote under: "L. E. R."
D. of Samuel Gridley and Julia Ward Howe; m. Henry Richards, 1871

As a child, R. lived in her father's Perkins Institute for the Blind. Her early education was varied, with wide independent reading.

R. married an architect in 1871. When his business failed to support his growing family, Richards moved R. and their two children to Gardiner, Maine, in 1876 so that he could help with the family mill there.

R. was active in the life of Gardiner, founding the first American Red Cross chapter in Maine, the Gardiner Public Library (1884), the Women's Philanthropic Union (1895), and the Howe Club (1875) to encourage the appreciation of literature in young boys.

R. began her writing career with stories and verses taken from the amusements she invented for her own children, but she soon turned to longer children's stories and to adult novels as well. Her first book, *Five Little Mice in a Mouse Trap* (1880), was a group of stories about a family of boys and girls in a setting quite like R.'s own childhood home. *Sketches and Scraps* (1881), illustrated by her husband, was the first volume of nonsense rhymes written by an American and printed in the U.S.

Captain January (1890) tells of Star Bright and her guardian, the Maine lighthousekeeper who had rescued the infant from a shipwreck. Now ten years old, Star Bright is lively, and the joy of January's life. Star Bright epitomizes R.'s heroines: She is lively, sensitive to the feelings of others, bright, and generous, and has a sense of humor. Never wealthy, the R. heroines value their happiness above wealth.

The Margaret series develops the R. heroine by presenting an older girl with more opportunity for both mischief and woe. In *Three Margarets* (1897), three cousins, all named for their paternal grandmother, meet when their uncle invites them to spend the summer at Fernley House. Peggy is from a western ranch; impulsive and rough, she is the source of amusement and scorn for her worldly Cuban cousin, Rita. It is Margaret the orphan who achieves harmony and good will with her calm temperament ٭d soothing manner. By the end of the summer the three girls are fast friends. The next three books in the series each examine one of the Margarets.

R.'s first autobiography, *When I Was Your Age* (1893), was written for children. The second, *Stepping Westward*, appeared almost forty years later, in 1931. R. wrote several biographies for children. *Laura E. Bridgman* (1906) is about her father's famous pupil, for whom R. was named. R. also wrote biographies of her parents and edited their papers. *Life and Letters of Julia Ward Howe* (1910), which R. wrote with her sister Maude Howe Elliott, was awarded the first Pulitzer Prize for biography. R. also edited her mother's journals, *Walk with God* (1919).

R. wrote over eighty books. Her stories and novels offer neither profound nor unique glimpses into American life; but as the statements of the ideal nature of children and of young women, the tales are of great interest. By giving us competent young women who are kind and good and at the same time fallible and given to mischief, R. provides a model for young women, and offers some important clues to the social historian. Only slightly too good to be true, R.'s heroines are real people with real failings.

WORKS: *Five Little Mice in a Mouse Trap* (1880). *Sketches and Scraps* (1881). *Four Feet, Two Feet, and No Feet* (1884). *The Joyous Story of Toto* (1884). *Toto's Merry Winter* (1885). *Queen Hildegarde* (1889). *Captain January* (1890). *In My Nursery* (1890). *Hildegarde's Holiday* (1891). *Hildegarde's Home* (1892). *Glimpses of the French Court* (1893). *Melody: The Story of a Child* (1893). *When I Was Your Age* (1893). *Marie* (1894). *Nautilus* (1894). *Five Minute Stories* (1895). *Hildegarde's Neighbors* (1895). *Jim of Hellas* (1895). *Isla of Heron* (1896). *Narcissa* (1896). *Some Say* (1896). *Three Margarets* (1897). *Love and Rocks* (1898). *Rosin the Beau* (1898). *Peggy* (1899). *For Tommy* (1900). *Rita* (1900). *Snow White* (1900). *Fernley House* (1901). *Goeffry Strong* (1901). *The Hurdy Gurdy* (1902). *Mrs. Tree* (1902). *The Golden Windows* (1903). *The Green Satin Gown* (1903). *More Five Minute Stories* (1903). *The Merryweathers* (1904). *The Armstrongs* (1905). *Mrs. Tree's Will* (1905). *The Greek Revolution* (edited by Richards, 1906). *Laura E. Bridgman* (1906). *Letters and Journals of Samuel Gridley Howe* (2 vols.; edited by Richards, 1906 and 1909). *The Piccolo* (1906). *The Silver Crown* (1906). *Grandmother* (1907). *The Wooing of Calvin Parks* (1908). *Life of Florence Nightingale for Young People* (1909). *A Happy Little Time* (1910). *Up to Calvin's* (1910). *Aboard the Mary Sands* (1911). *The Story of Two Noble Lives* (1911). *Miss Jimmy* (1912). *The Little Master* (1913). *Three Minute Stories* (1914). *The Big Brother Play Book* (1915). *Fairy Operettas* (1916). *Life of Elizabeth Fry* (1916). *Life of Julia Ward Howe* (with M. H. Elliott, 1916). *Abigail Adams and Her Times* (1917). *Pippin* (1917). *To Arms!* (1917). *A Daughter of Jehu* (1918). *Life of Joan of Arc* (1919). *Walk with God* (1919). *Honor Bright* (1920). *In Blessed Cyprus* (1921). *The Squire* (1923). *Oriental Operettas* (1924). *Acting Charades* (1927). *Honor's New Adventure* (1925). *Star Bright* (1927). *Stepping Westward*

(1931). *Tirra Lirra* (1932). *Samuel Gridley Howe* (1935). *Edward Arlington Robinson* (1936). *Harry in England* (1937). *I Have a Song to Sing You* (1938). *What Shall the Children Read?* (1939). *The Hottentot, and Other Ditties* (1939).

BIBLIOGRAPHY: Gardiner, Maine, Public Lib. Assoc., *Laura E. Richards and Gardiner* (1940).
For articles in reference works, see: *NAW* (article by E. D. H. Johnson). *NCAB*, 39. *20thCA.*
Other references: *Horn Book* (17, 1941; 19, 1943; 30, 1956).

VIRGINIA GRANT DARNEY

Louisa Lula Greene Richards

B. 8 April 1849, Kanesville, Iowa; d. 9 Sept. 1944, Salt Lake City, Utah
Wrote under: Lula, Lulu, Louisa L. Greene Richards, Lula Greene Richards
D. of Evan Molbourne and Susan Kent Greene; m. Levi Willard Richards, 1873

R. was the eighth of thirteen children born in a temporary settlement of the Mormon church. After leaving Iowa in 1852, R.'s family lived in several Utah communities before settling permanently in Smithfield. Educated primarily by her father, a respected schoolteacher, R. later enrolled for a term at the University of Deseret, Utah. She taught school briefly before moving to Salt Lake City in 1872. She married in 1873 and bore seven children, three of whom died in infancy.

Contributing poems to local newspapers as early as age fifteen, R. was appointed editor of the *Smithfield Sunday School Gazette*, a handwritten weekly paper devoted to moral admonitions and homilies reflecting conventional sentiments. R.'s early poetic efforts led to an invitation to become founding editor of the *Woman's Exponent*, a Mormon women's newspaper published in Salt Lake City. In five years as editor, R. established the tone and format of the paper that would play an influential role in the activities of Mormon women for forty-two years (1872–1914).

R. was sympathetic to the women's movement of her time and editorialized frequently in the *Exponent* on its developments. Despite disclaimers by the paper's prospectus, woman suffrage became an issue treated extensively by R. Her editorials were perceptive, forthright, and unequivocating, especially when defending the practices of the Mormon faith.

After leaving the *Exponent*, R. became editor of the "Little Folks" department of the *Juvenile Instructor*, a Mormon Sunday-school periodical. She also contributed poems and stories to other local and church publications while serving for over twenty-five years on the general board of the Primary Association, a church-sponsored organization for young children.

R. belonged to a coterie of local literary women who wrote typically unrestrained romantic celebrations in verse and prose of life, virtue, and faith in a divine creator. R. compiled her writings under the title *Branches That Run over the Wall* (1904), a collection in three parts. The first part is a poetic rendering of selected Mormon scriptures; the second, a group of poems and stories based on the author's personal experiences and reflections; and the third, a group of children's pieces. Many of the poems were composed for musical settings. Domestic life and virtuous living are the dominant themes.

R. cannot be characterized as more than a pleasing versifier. Her images are predictable and her verses often rhythm-bound, the whole suffering from the sentimental effusiveness of the period.

As part of a large number of parlor poets produced by Victorian acceptance of the propriety of "scribbling women," R. and her peers represent a substantial facet of the 19th-c. literary world. Their significance derives not from the quality of their contribution, which is decidedly uneven, but from the strength of their broad commonality, distinguished less by regional characteristics than by common themes and style. That R. possessed another literary dimension as a journalist, more substantial and durable than her poetic efforts, attaches a specific importance to her place among popular Utah women writers.

WORKS: *Branches That Run over the Wall* (1904).

BIBLIOGRAPHY: Arrington, L., "Woman Journalist of the Early West," in *The Improvement Era* (1969). Gardner, H. R., *Life of Levi Richards, 1799–1876, Some of his Ancestors and Descendants* (1973). Greene, G. K., *Daniel Kent Greene, His Life and Times, 1858–1921* (1960). Madsen, C. C., "Remember the Women of Zion: A Study of the Editorial Content of the *Woman's Exponent*, a Mormon Woman's Journal," (M.A. thesis, Univ. of Utah, 1977). Richards, L. G., "How the *Exponent* Was Started," in *The Relief Society Magazine* (1928). Richards, L. G., "Pioneer Woman Editor of the Church," in *The Relief Society Magazine* (1925).

For articles in reference works, see: *Latter-Day Saint Biographical Encyclopedia, 1830–1936*, Ed. A. Jenson (1936).

Other references: *The Juvenile Instructor* (1931; 1950). *The Young Woman's Journal* (1891).

CAROL CORNWALL MADSEN

Grace Smith Richmond

B. 31 March 1866, Pawtucket, Rhode Island; d. 26 Nov. 1959, Dunkirk, New York
Wrote under: Grace Richmond
D. of Charles and Catherine Kimball Smith; m. Nelson Guernsey Richmond, 1887

The only child of a Baptist clergyman, R. was educated at Syracuse High School, New York, and took college work under tutors. Her father published several books on religious themes. After marriage to a physician, R. moved to Fredonia, New York, and had four children. In 1924, she was awarded a Doctor of Letters degree from Colby College, Maine.

R. began her writing career in the 1890s with short stories in women's magazines. Many of her novels were published in serial form in these magazines, especially *The Ladies' Home Journal*. R.'s novels upheld current popular ideals; she wrote patriotic war stories when needed, turned out several heartwarming Christmas books, and criticized nothing except dissipation (alcohol, nightclubs, drugs, aimless travel, and social climbing).

The Indifference of Juliet (1905) set the tone for many of R.'s stories. Juliet Macy, a rich young woman, cannot agree to marry Anthony Robeson, a young man of good family who has to make his own way in the world. He tricks her into marriage by asking her to furnish a little old house he has bought for his California fiancée (nonexistent). Juliet does so, falls in love with the house, and then realizes that she wants to marry Anthony herself. They are an example to other couples: very happy in their charming, inexpensive home, they have a son and, at the end of five years of marriage, are ready to remodel the house. The home itself is at the heart of many of R.'s novels.

In 1910, R. introduced her most popular character, Dr. Red Pepper

Burns, the hero of six novels. A surgeon in a small city, Dr. Burns is a redhead with a hot temper and a warm heart. His wife Ellen is the "perfect" woman—motherly, womanly, ladylike, and beautiful. The couple have children, although they play little part in the stories and their sex and number is not consistent from book to book. As R. describes this ideal couple, ". . . no wonder everybody knew or wanted to know the Burnses; their position was of the best, everywhere" (*Red of the Redfields*, 1924). Red is the manliest of men, capable of sitting up night after night holding the hand of a dying patient.

The plots of most of these books concern some philanthropy or other of his. However, the last of the series, *Red Pepper Returns* (1931), focuses on the hopeless love of Dr. Max Buller, Red's longtime associate, for Ellen and that of Amy Mathewson, Red's nurse, for Red. Max creeps off to Arizona to die (apparently of exhaustion) while Amy, going blind, confesses her love to Red and is allowed to examine his handsome countenance for the last time under his surgical spotlight. He kisses her good-bye.

The most prevalent theme in R.'s novels is the making of manly men and womanly women. There are novels with young heroines who think they want to be independent women, until they meet Mr. Right and are content to be homemakers. There are novels in which rich, spoiled young men make something of themselves by getting involved in real work. The making of a home and the raising of a family are the most important goals in life, and R.'s men and women are in complete agreement on this.

To a reader of R.'s work today, with some knowledge of American life and culture during the period in which she was writing, R. must seem like a woman who has made her daydreams public. But in a spirit of charity, let's say that perhaps R.'s happy life did seem to her a pattern for others. One can't help but point out, though, that the typical R. heroine does *not* write novels.

WORKS: *The Indifference of Juliet* (1905). *The Second Violin* (1906). *With Juliet in England* (1907). *Around the Corner in Gay Street* (1908). *On Christmas Day in the Morning* (1908). *A Court of Inquiry* (1909). *On Christmas Day in the Evening* (1910). *Red Pepper Burns* (1910). *Strawberry Acres* (1911). *Brotherly House* (1912). *Mrs. Red Pepper* (1913). *Under the Christmas Stars* (1913). *The Twenty-Fourth of June* (1914). *Under the Country Sky* (1916). *The Brown Study* (1917). *Red Pepper's Patients* (1917). *The Whistling Mother* (1917). *The Enlisting Wife* (1918). *Red and Black* (1919). *The Bells of St. John's* (1920). *Foursquare* (1922). *Rufus* (1923). *Red of the Redfields* (1924). *Cherry Square* (1926). *Lights Up* (1927). *At the*

South Gate (1928). *The Listening Post* (1929). *High Fences* (1930). *Red Pepper Returns* (1931). *Bachelor's Bounty* (1932).

BIBLIOGRAPHY: Overton, G., *The Women Who Make Our Novels* (1922).

BEVERLY SEATON

Marilla M. Ricker

B. *18 March 1840, New Durham, New Hampshire; d. 12 Nov. 1920, Dover, New Hampshire*
D. *of Jonathan and Hannah Stevens Young; m. John Ricker, 1863*

R.'s mother was an educated woman who taught R. to read; her father was a prosperous farmer who was an early suffragist and freethinker. R.'s husband, whom she married when she was twenty-three and he fifty-six, was a wealthy realtor who believed in equality for women. When he died five years after their marriage, he left R. a substantial fortune. In her writings, R. often remarks on the legal advantages of a widow's position in contrast to a wife's, and the value of financial independence.

After her husband's death, R. studied languages in Europe and then settled in Washington, D.C., where she read law in a private office. In 1882, she was admitted to the bar of the Washington, D.C., Supreme Court, having outscored all the men in her examination class. R. was later appointed a U.S. commissioner and examiner in chancery and was one of the first women admitted to the bar of the U.S. Supreme Court.

R. pleaded several important test cases in Washington. Although her challenge of the Sunday closing law failed, she succeeded in ending Washington's "poor convicts law," under which convicts were jailed indefinitely for inability to pay fines. For her work in prison reform and legal and financial aid to prisoners and prostitutes, R. became known as "the prisoners' friend."

R.'s activities in the women's rights movement began in 1869, when she attended the first National Woman's Suffrage Association convention in Washington. Years later, R. wrote that she was so stimulated that she "hurried home" to New Hampshire and tried to vote. Although her ballot was refused, she actually succeeded in voting in 1871, becoming the first woman to cast a vote in a state election on the basis of the Fourteenth Amendment.

In addition to suffrage work, R. lectured on feminist issues, employed her legal skills on women's behalf, and tried to open positions previously barred to women. In 1890, she gained the right for women to practice law in New Hampshire, and in 1910, at the age of seventy, she attempted to run for governor. R. was the first woman to seek a major diplomatic post in the U.S. foreign service, applying unsuccessfully for appointment as minister to Colombia.

The Four Gospels (1911) contrasts R.'s idols, Thomas Paine and Robert Ingersoll, with Jonathan Edwards and John Calvin. In other freethought essays, R. attacks the Bible, the clergy, and missionaries, along with the efficacy of prayer, the immortality of the soul, and other points of Christian doctrine and practice.

In her writings on women's rights, R.'s various interests converge. Her legal training and lifelong interest in language are evident in her arguments; a frequent theme is the injustice of the use of the pronoun "he" to include women in laws imposing penalties and to exclude them in laws conferring privileges. R.'s antireligious views are also prominent in her writings on women. In fact, she never separated the two subjects in her thinking and seldom discusses one issue without mentioning the other. R.'s basic position is revealed in her statement that "the church has done more to degrade woman than all other adverse influences put together."

R.'s style is direct and colorful. There are few smooth transitions in her writings, and she is given to strong statements, even assigning her essays titles like "I Believe in Neither God Nor the Devil and I Am Not Afraid." She is often intemperate, as in her pamphlet attacking Theodore Roosevelt when he was running for president in 1912; she calls him "coarse, vulgar and obscene," an "unmitigated liar and traitor." As a contemporary osberved, "It is her custom to call a spade a spade, and not to beat about the bush in search of euphemistic expressions to gild the edge of criticism."

WORKS: *The Four Gospels* (1911). *I Don't Know, Do You?* (1916). *I Am Not Afraid, Are You?* (1917).

BIBLIOGRAPHY: Scales, J., *History of Strafford County, New Hampshire* (1914).
Other references: (Dover, N.H.) *Foster's Daily Democrat* (23 June 1976; 25 June 1976). *Granite Monthly* (June 1910). *New Hampshire Profiles* (Sept. 1958). *Prologue: The Journal of the National Archives* (Winter 1973).

BARBARA A. WHITE

Lola Ridge

B. *12 Dec. 1873, Dublin, Ireland; d. 19 May 1941, Brooklyn, New York*
Given name: Rose Emily Ridge
Wrote under: Lola, L. R. Ridge, Lola Ridge
D. of Joseph Henry and Emma Reilly Ridge; m. Peter Webster, 1895; m.
  David Lawson, 1919

R. lived with her mother in Australia and New Zealand as a child. R.'s early interests included art and music, and when her marriage to the manager of a New Zealand gold mine proved unhappy, she moved to Sydney to study painting under Julian Ashton. R. later regretted having destroyed poems she wrote during this period, but a collection of her work has recently been discovered at the Mitchell Library in Sydney.

R. emigrated to San Francisco in 1907, and moved to New York City in 1908. She supported herself as a writer of fiction and poetry for popular magazines. At meetings of the Ferrer Association she met her second husband.

The Ghetto (1918), written during a five-year absence from New York City, was hailed as a book that seemed destined for greatness. Revolutionary in spirit and written in free verse, the title poem dwells on life among the Jewish immigrants of New York's Lower East Side and illustrates themes that recur throughout R.'s work—the moral courage of ordinary men and women, the paramount importance of liberty in human lives, and faith in the possibilities that America holds.

After the success of *The Ghetto*, R. edited a number of issues of *Others* and served as the American editor of *Broom*. She also toured the Midwest, speaking on subjects such as "Individualism and American Poetry" and "Woman and the Creative Will."

Sun-Up (1920) contains both personal and public poems. The title poem draws heavily on the author's own childhood. Technically, its flashing pictures resemble those of the Imagists; psychologically, it shares ground with the experiments of James Joyce. The public poems "Sons of Belial" and "Reveille" demonstrate R.'s sympathy with an exploited working class and affirm her function as a poet "[blowing] upon [their] hearts / kindling the slow fire."

Red Flag (1927) also includes poems saluting those who have fallen in the cause of freedom. "Red Flag" focuses on Russia and figures in the

Russian revolution, and "Under the Sun" commemorates martyrs of other struggles. Most of the poems in this volume, however, are poems about natural and spiritual beauty and imagistic portraits of R.'s contemporaries.

R.'s last two books are characterized by an increasingly stylized language and growing mysticism. *Firehead* (1929), R.'s response to the executions of Sacco and Vanzetti in 1927, retells the story of the Crucifixion. The nine sections view the Crucifixion from a variety of points of view, including those of Judas, the two Marys, and Jesus himself; the Christ of the poem is viewed as "one who had proclaimed men equal— aye / Even unto slaves and women . . . / And babbled of some communal bright heaven." During her lifetime, *Firehead* was widely acclaimed as R.'s masterpiece.

On a visit to Yaddo in 1930, R. outlined a poem cycle, "Lightwheel," which was to occupy the greatest portion of her creative energies in her last years. "Lightwheel" was to include *Firehead* and five other books treating ancient Babylon, Florence during the Renaissance, Mexico at the time of Cortez and Montezuma, France during the revolution, and Manhattan after World War I. R. traveled to the Near East (1931–32) and to Mexico (1935–37) to research her epic work, but the cycle remained unfinished at her death.

R.'s theory of history also shapes a sonnet sequence called "Via Ignis," the central poem in *Dance of Fire* (1935). But despite the poem's large theme—that we are at a crucial stage in history, but "may come forth, for a period, into a time of light"—its language is essentially private.

Though plagued by illness during much of her life, R. is remembered as an energizing person. Her work attests to the continuous if not special concern that American women poets have had with social issues.

WORKS: *The Ghetto* (1918). *Sun-Up* (1920). *Red Flag* (1927). *Firehead* (1929). *Dance of Fire* (1935).

BIBLIOGRAPHY: Gregory, H., and M. Zaturenska, *A History of Modern Poetry: 1900–1940* (1946). Perkins, D., *A History of Modern Poetry: From the 1890s to the High Modernist Mode* (1976). Untermeyer, L., *The New Era in American Poetry* (1919).

For articles in reference works, see: *Living Authors: A Book of Biographies*, Ed. S. J. Kunitz (1931). *NAW* (article by A. Guttmann).

Other references: *SatR* (31 May 1941).

ELAINE SPROAT

Mary Roberts Rinehart

B. *12 Aug. 1876, Allegheny, Pennsylvania; d. 22 Sept. 1958, New York City*
D. *of Thomas Beveridge and Cornelia Gilleland Roberts; m. Dr. Stanley Marshall Rinehart, 1896*

R. began her career in 1903, publishing short stories in magazines like *All-Story* and *Munsey's.* In three or four weeks in 1905, R. wrote *The Man in Lower 10* for serialization in *All-Story,* and she followed that the next year with *The Circular Staircase.* When Bobbs-Merrill published the *Circular Staircase* in 1908, R.'s long period of success began. These mysteries fleshed out the novel of deduction with fuller if somewhat stereotyped characters, a second, romantic plot line, a good deal of Gothic atmosphere, and frequently comic elements.

R. essentially stopped writing mystery novels after 1914, returning to the form in 1930 with *The Door,* her first novel to be published by her sons' new publishing house, Farrar and Rinehart. In the next twenty-three years, R. published eleven full-length mysteries in which she exploited fully the "buried story"—a sequence of events never narrated in the novel and emerging only as "outcroppings," places at which material about the past of the characters supplies clues to the solution of the mystery. R.'s "buried stories" most often center on errors of passion leading to sexual alliances across class lines and leading inexorably to crime some years later.

The villains in R.'s mysteries are frequently lower-class women who have ensnared richer, more aristocratic men. The heroines most often are unmarried young women with little money but of good family, who serve as the center of the romantic plot as well as the focus of the murder story. R.'s intention in establishing the young female narrator was to link her mystery plot as closely as possible with her romantic plot; however, the use of this central character type has had the effect of placing her work, erroneously, in the class of Gothics.

Although R. is remembered today as a writer of mysteries, she was more popular in her own time for her serious novels. Beginning with *The Street of Seven Stars* (1914) and *"K"* (1915), R. produced romances with some attention to contemporary problems. This emphasis became stronger with World War I; R. depicted life near the western front in *The Amazing Interlude* (1918) and sabotage and attempted insurrection on the home front in *Dangerous Days* (1919) and *A Poor Wise Man* (1920). Both critical and popular success eluded R. in her most serious attempt at fiction, *This Strange Adventure* (1929), a dark look at the life of a fairly typical married woman. R. recouped in 1931 with her fine autobiography, *My Story*.

R.'s humor was not restricted to isolated episodes in mystery novels. With the creation in 1910 of Letitia Carberry, "Tish," R. produced a character who would remain a staple of *The Saturday Evening Post* and a favorite of American readers for nearly thirty years. Tish is an undaunted spinster of about fifty who with her two companions travels America and Europe, resolving lovers' problems, rounding up bandits and kidnappers, once capturing an entire German company, and maintaining throughout her own slightly askew brand of absolute moral rectitude.

R. also achieved considerable success in the theater. In collaboration with Avery Hopwood, she wrote *Seven Days* (1909), with nearly four hundred performances, and *The Bat* (1920), with 878 performances and six road companies. *The Bat*, with close affinities to *The Circular Staircase*, mixes murder, romance, and comedy.

From 1910 to 1940, R. was America's most successful popular writer. Eleven of R.'s novels were among the ten top bestsellers of the year they were published, and in the 1930s mass-circulation magazines paid as much as $65,000 to serialize her novels. From its infancy the movie industry sought her work, and later radio and television used her material. Today, R.'s serious novels are dated by her cautious attitude toward popular morality; she was careful to offend neither editors nor audience. R.'s mystery novels have fared better with time, continuing to sell well in reissue. *The Circular Staircase* has achieved the status of a classic in the genre.

WORKS: *The Circular Staircase* (1908). *The Man in Lower 10* (1909). *When a Man Marries* (1909). *The Window at the White Cat* (1910). *The Amazing Adventures of Letitia Carberry* (1911). *Where There's a Will* (1912). *The Case of Jennie Brice* (1913). *The After House* (1914). *The Street of Seven Stars* (1914). *"K"* (1915). *Kings, Queens, and Pawns* (1915). *Through Glacier Park* (1916). *Tish* (1916). *The Altar of Freedom* (1917). *Bab: A Sub-Deb* (1917). *Long Live the King* (1917). *The Amazing Interlude* (1918). *Tenting Tonight* (1918). *Twenty Three and a Half Hours Leave* (1918). *Dangerous Days* (1919). *Love Stories* (1919). *Affinities* (1920). *Isn't That Just Like a Man? Well! You Know How Women Are!* (with I. S. Cobb, 1920). *A Poor Wise Man* (1920). *The Truce of God* (1920). *The Breaking Point* (1921). *More Tish* (1921). *Sight Unseen and the Confession* (1921).

The Out Trail (1922). *Temperamental People* (1924). *The Red Lamp* (1925). *Nomad's Land* (1926). *Tish Plays the Game* (1926). *Two Flights Up* (1926). *Lost Ecstasy* (1927). *The Trumpet Sounds* (1927). *The Romantics* (1929). *This Strange Adventure* (1929). *The Door* (1930). *Mary Roberts Rinehart's Mystery Book* (1930). *The Book of Tish* (1931). *Mary Roberts Rinehart's Romance Book* (1931). *My Story* (1931; rev. ed., 1948). *Miss Pinkerton* (1932). *The Album* (1933). *The Crime Book* (1933). *The State Versus Elinor Norton* (1933). *Mr. Cohen Takes a Walk* (1934). *The Doctor* (1936). *Married People* (1937). *Tish Marches On* (1937). *The Wall* (1938). *Writing Is Work* (1939). *The Great Mistake* (1940). *Familiar Faces* (1941). *Haunted Lady* (1942). *Alibi for Isabel, and Other Stories* (1944). *The Yellow Room* (1945). *A Light in the Window* (1948). *Episode of the Wandering Knife* (1950). *The Swimming Pool* (1952). *The Frightened Wife, and Other Murder Stories* (1953). *The Best of Tish* (1955). *The Mary Roberts Rinehart Crime Book* (1957).

BIBLIOGRAPHY: Cohn, J., *Improbable Fiction: The Life of Mary Roberts Rinehart* (1980). Disney, D. C., and M. Mackaye, *Mary Roberts Rinehart* (1948). Doran, G. H., in *Chronicles of Barrabas* (1935). Overton, G., et al., *Mary Roberts Rinehart: A Sketch of the Woman and Her Work* (1921?). Overton, G., in *When Winter Came to Main Street* (1922).

Other references: *American Magazine* (Oct. 1917). Boston *Evening Transcript* (12 June 1926). *Good Housekeeping* (April 1917). *Life* (25 Feb. 1946). *Writer* (Nov. 1932).

JAN COHN

Eliza Moore Chinn McHatton Ripley

B. *1 Feb. 1832, Lexington, Kentucky; d. 13 July 1912*
Wrote under: Eliza M. Ripley
D. of Richard Henry and Betsy Holmes Chinn; m. James Alexander McHatton, 1852; m. M. Dwight Ripley, 1873

R. was the tenth child of a judge. R. grew up in New Orleans and lived at Arlington Plantation on the Mississippi River below Baton Rouge after her marriage. After the fall of that city in June 1862, the McHattons began a nomadic existence, living out of an ambulance while carrying Confederate cotton from Louisiana to Mexico to be sold. Six weeks before the fall of the Confederacy, the McHattons joined a growing number of southern exiles in Cuba. Using Cuban and Chinese coolie labor, they attempted to run a sugar plantation on the southern model. James McHatton died in Cuba and R. returned to the U.S.

From Flag to Flag: A Woman's Adventures in Wartime (1889) is autobiographical, dealing with R.'s flight from Louisiana and life in Cuba. Although R. and her husband spoke little Spanish, they were welcomed on the island and soon moved in the highest social circles. For the most part, life in Cuba was pleasant and the exiles adapted quickly. R. notes but does not condemn the arrogance and extravagance of the plantation owners and shares their fears of reprisal by the peasants.

Social Life in Old New Orleans (1912) is a combination of personal reminiscences and social commentary. It is R.'s attempt to preserve a vanishing past as a standard for future generations. Written in the "Moonlight and Magnolias" tradition of southern history, *Social Life in Old New Orleans* deals in great detail with the life of southern women before the Civil War. These were easy, carefree days, when life moved slowly and conventions governed social relationships.

R. did not claim to be an apologist for slavery but was, in fact, a firm supporter of the institution. Although she states that "the whites suffered more from its demoralizing influence than the blacks," this is not substantiated in the text. R. gives us an idyllic picture of life on a southern plantation, with happy, well-cared-for slaves and kindly masters. She entitles one chapter "A Monument to Mammies," and paints an affectionate portrait of those hefty black women of indeterminate age who governed both white and black with an iron hand. Yet R. is reconciled to the changes undergone since the halcyon days of the antebellum South. "We lived," she concludes, "a life never to be lived again."

Taken together, R.'s works provide a wealth of information on manners and customs of the prewar South. Her descriptions of fashions and entertainments, although rose colored by memory, are unequaled.

WORKS: *From Flag to Flag: A Woman's Adventures in Wartime* (1889). *Social Life in Old New Orleans* (1912).

BIBLIOGRAPHY: Eaton, C., *The Growth of Southern Civilization* (1961).

JANET E. KAUFMAN

Anna Cora Mowatt Ritchie

B. 5 March 1819, Bordeaux, France; d. 21 July 1870, Twickenham, England
Wrote under: Helen Berkeley, Henry C. Browning, Cora, Isabel, Charles A.
  Lee, M. D., Anna Cora Mowatt, Anna Ritchie
D. of Samuel Gouvernour and Eliza Lewis Ogden; m. James Mowatt, 1834;
  m. William Fouchee Ritchie, 1854

The ninth of fourteen children, R. was descended from old colonial
families. Her early years were spent in France, but when she was seven
the family moved to New York, where R. was educated in private
girls' schools. Although "Lily," as she was called, was not outstanding
at her studies, she was considered precocious by her family because of
her ability to write and act in home theatricals.

At fifteen she eloped with Mowatt, a wealthy young lawyer, and
moved to Melrose, his estate on Long Island. Here she wrote *Pelayo*
(1836), a romantic poem in six cantos "founded strictly upon historical
facts." R.'s preface to this poem reveals an extensive acquaintance with
literature. It was not well received, however, and R. retaliated with
Reviewers Reviewed (1837), a satiric essay on criticism.

An attack of tuberculosis, her constant enemy, led R. to visit Europe
in 1838. Ironically, as her health improved that of her husband began
to fail. Nonetheless, they returned to the U.S. and celebrated his "cure"
with a ball at which R.'s blank verse melodrama in five acts, *Gulzara;
or, The Persian Slave*, was presented with R. in the title role. The play
attracted much favorable attention from critics when it was published
in the *New World* in 1841.

Her husband's fragile health and the loss of his fortune led R. to give
public poetry readings. When she became too ill to perform, she began
to write articles for *Godey's Lady's Book, Graham's Magazine, The Democratic Review*, and other magazines. Under the pseudonym "Henry
C. Browning," she wrote a life of Goethe, and as "Charles A. Lee, M.D."
compiled *Management of the Sickroom* (1844). In 1842, R. won a hun-
dred-dollar prize from *New World* for her novel *The Fortune Hunter*
(1842). R.'s play *Fashion* (1845) had an unprecedented three-week run,
and was long a favorite of audiences in England and America. The
money she earned not only supported her and James, but three orphans
she had taken into her childless home.

Even more profitable than writing was R.'s career as an actress. Starting as a star, she remained one for eight years of touring the U.S. and Great Britain.

After Mowatt's death in 1851, R. returned to New York. Again she turned to writing to supplement her income, and her lively *Autobiography of an Actress* (1854) was an immediate success.

In 1854, R. married a prominent Virginian and editor of *The Richmond Enquirer*. In 1861 R. left her husband because of irreconcilable political and personal differences. She went to Florence, where she supported herself by writing novels and sketches. In 1865, R. visited England, became too ill to travel back to Italy, and took a small house in Twickenham, where she died five years later.

Fashion (1845), R.'s most important work, is a bright, witty satire of 19th-c. New York society. The basic plot line is a standard love story with melodramatic elements; but the sharp comedy has kept its freshness. The play reveals a remarkable sense of theater and a grasp of dramaturgy rare in a first effort. The action moves rapidly, the plot turns are cleverly planned, and the climax satisfies the comedic expectations. The first American social comedy, *Fashion* was successfully revived in 1924 and again in 1959.

R.'s early novels, *The Fortune Hunter* (1842) and *Evelyn* (1845), are also contemporary views of New York life; R. draws upon her own experience as a member of upper-class society, giving these works more substance than is usual in such tales. She paints the evils of money marriages and juxtaposes them with marriages based on honesty in values and actions. *Autobiography of an Actress* (1854) is an amusingly frank account of R.'s years on the stage, distinguished by unusual modesty concerning herself and generosity toward others.

Most of R.'s later stories make use of her theatrical experiences in setting and characters; both background and types are recognizable and timeless. Her plots are traditional romantic love stories, and her characters are often embodiments of the sentimentality so prevalent in that time. They are seasoned, however, with humor and a Dickensian awareness of the ridiculous.

R.'s reliance upon action precludes the development of profound characters, but her use of detailed description removes them from the stock types in most popular novels of the time. She also differs from her contemporaries in her treatment of women, for she places a high value on independence. Dependent females in her stories invariably fall victim to circumstances or villains, whereas the heroines not only think for themselves but are usually self-supporting. R. believed women should be wives and mothers, but she contemplated, and in some cases endorsed, the single life. A unique author, combining a European elegance with an American admiration for practical labor, she is, in the truest sense, the first transatlantic writer.

WORKS: *Pelayo; or, The Cavern of Covadongo* (1836). *Reviewers Reviewed* (1837). *The Fortune Hunter* (1842). *Evelyn; or, A Heart Unmasked* (1845). *Fashion; or, Life in New York* (1845). *Armand; or, The Peer and the Peasant* (1847). *The Autobiography of an Actress* (1854). *Mimic Life* (1856). *Twin Roses* (1858). *Fairy Fingers* (1865). *The Mute Singer* (1866). *The Clergyman's Wife, and Other Selections* (1867). *Italian Life and Legends* (1870).

BIBLIOGRAPHY: Barnes, E. W., *The Lady of Fashion* (1954). Bernard, B., *Tallis's Drawing Room Table Book* (1851). Blesi, M., *The Life and Letters of Anna Cora Mowatt* (1938). Harland, Mr., "Recollections of a Christian Actress," in *Our Continent* (1882). Howitt, M., "Memoirs of Anna Cora Mowatt," in *Howitt's Journal* (1848). McCarthy, I., *Anna Cora Mowatt and Her American Audience* (1952).

HELENE KOON

Jessie Belle Rittenhouse

B. 8 Dec. 1869, Mount Morris, New York; d. 28 Sept. 1948, Detroit, Michigan
Wrote under: Jessie B. Rittenhouse
D. of John E. and Mary J. MacArthur Rittenhouse; m. Clinton Scollard, 1924

R. was the fifth of seven children. R.'s early years were spent within the circle of a large and prosperous farm family in New York's Genesee Valley. She attended Nunda Academy, New York, and went on to the Genesee Wesleyan Seminary at Lima, New York, where she became absorbed in reading the poetry of Tennyson and Browning. R.'s schooling was interrupted when financial misfortunes caused the family to move to Cheboygan, Michigan.

Having to support herself, R. reluctantly chose to teach Latin and English. An aunt, seeing her anguish, suggested R. write a poem. Instead, R. wrote an article on St. Augustine, Florida, which she sold to the Rochester *Union and Advertiser*.

Stimulated by her success, R. moved to Rochester to work for the *Democrat and Chronicle*. Between 1905 and 1915, R. served as a reviewer for the *New York Times Review of Books* and *The Bookman* and lectured widely on modern poetry.

Throughout her career, R. was acquainted with many literary figures. In 1901, she helped found the Poetry Society of America, which she served as secretary for ten years. In 1930, she shared the society's bronze medal for distinguished service with her husband, the poet Clinton Scollard.

R.'s first book of poems, *The Door of Dreams*, did not appear until 1918. Her fourth and last volume, *The Moving Tide: New and Selected Poems* (1939), was awarded a gold medal by the National Poetry Center.

After her husband's death in 1932, R. moved to Grosse Point, Michigan, and wrote her autobiography, *My House of Life* (1934).

The publication of *The Younger American Poets* in 1904 advanced R. into the front rank of literary critics. Keenly aware of the neglect of American poetry, and of young American poets in particular, R. focuses her discussions on the work of eighteen relatively unknown poets. But it was R.'s "instinct for the popular and salable anthology" that produced *The Little Book of Modern Verse* in 1913, with new versions in 1919 and 1923, and brought R.'s name before a wide reading public. Represented in these anthologies are the best-known poets of the earlier part of the 20th c.

R.'s poems appeared in many periodicals. Focusing on love and loss, with nature and war as secondary themes, the poems were characterized as "slight," "gentle," and "graceful." One critic viewed her work as "more distinguished for grace and perfection than warmth of imagination."

R. had no illusions about the worth of her own poetry, nor did she, as anthologist, fail to recognize clearly the difficulties of keeping her perspective in regard to her contemporaries. The style of R.'s compilations was innovative in that she abandoned the conventional chronological method of arrangement in favor of one along thematic lines.

R. was an important moving force in American poetry in the earlier part of this century—she built morale and established a sense of community among poets and also awakened the reading public to the new directions poetry was taking. As we consider the scope and variety of her contributions, it is safe to say that her services to American poetry have been greatly undervalued.

WORKS: The Rubáiyát of Omar Khayyam; Comprising the Metrical Trans-lations of Edward Fitzgerald and E. H. Whinfield and the Prose Version of Justin Hartley McCarthy, with an Appendix Showing the Variations with the First and Second Editions of Fitzgerald's Rendering (edited by Ritten-house, 1900). *The Lovers' Rubáiyát* (edited by Rittenhouse, 1904). *The Younger American Poets* (edited by Rittenhouse, 1904). *The Poetry of Thomas S. Jones, Jr.* (edited by Rittenhouse, with W. S. Braithwaite and E. J. O'Brien, 1910). *The Poetry of Clinton Scollard* (edited by Rittenhouse, 1911). *The Little Book of Modern Verse: A Selection from the Works of Contemporaneous American Poets* (edited by Rittenhouse, 1913). *The Little Book of American Poets, 1787–1900* (edited by Rittenhouse, 1915). *The Door of Dreams* (1918). *The Second Book of Modern Verse* (edited by Ritten-house, 1919). *The Secret Bird* (1919). *The Lifted Cup* (1924). *The Little Book of Modern British Verse: One Hundred Poets Since Henley* (edited by Rit-tenhouse, 1924). *The Third Book of Modern Verse* (edited by Rittenhouse, 1925). *Selected Poems of Edith M. Thomas . . . with a Memoir* (edited by Rittenhouse, 1926). *The Rollins Books of Verse* (edited by Rittenhouse, 1929). *The Bird Lovers' Anthology* (edited by Rittenhouse, with Clinton Scollard, 1930). *Leonardo da Vinci, and Other Sonnets by Thomas S. Jones, Jr.* (edited by Rittenhouse, 1930). *The Image, and Other Sonnets by Thomas S. Jones, Jr.* (edited by Rittenhouse, 1932). *Patrician Rhymes: A Résumé of American Society Verse from Philip Freneau to the Present Day* (edited by Rittenhouse, with Clinton Scollard, 1932). *My House of Life* (1934). *The Singing Heart: Selected Lyrics and Other Poems by Clinton Scollard* (edited by Rittenhouse, 1934). *The Moving Tide: New and Selected Lyrics* (1939).

BIBLIOGRAPHY: Cook, W. H., *Our Poets of Today* (1918). Davidson, G., *In Fealty to Apollo* (1950). Untermeyer, L., *The New Era in American Poetry* (1919). Widdemer, Margaret, *Jessie Rittenhouse: A Centenary Memoir-Anthology* (1969).

For articles in reference works, see: *DAB*, Suppl. 4. *NAW* (article by G. S. Nutley). *20thCA*. *20thCAS*.

Other references: Detroit *News* (29 Sept. 1948). *NYT* (30 Sept. 1948). *SatR* (30 Oct. 1948).

VIRGINIA R. TERRIS

Elizabeth Madox Roberts

B. 30 Oct. 1881, Perryville, Kentucky; d. 13 March 1941, Orlando, Florida
D. of Simpson and Mary Elizabeth Brent Roberts

About 1884, R. moved with her family to Springfield, Kentucky, the town which would become the center of her stories and novels. As a child, R. listened to her father's storytelling. An equally important influence on R. as a child were family legends, including the tale of a great-grandmother who had come to Kentucky by the Wilderness Road.

R. attended a private academy in Springfield and later graduated from high school in nearby Covington, Kentucky. In 1900, she entered the State College of Kentucky but withdrew from school, probably because of ill health and financial problems. In 1917, R. registered at the University of Chicago—a college freshman at the age of thirty-six. R. wrote poetry while at Chicago and took part in a group—including such talented friends as Yvor Winters and Glenway Westcott—which met frequently to discuss one another's work. R. graduated in 1921 with honors in English.

In 1922, R. returned to Springfield, where she was to spend most of her life and devoted herself to writing, even after she learned in 1936 that she had Hodgkin's disease.

The quality of R.'s work is uneven. Few people would claim greatness for *Jingling in the Wind* (1928), an allegorical novel of the courtship of two rainmakers, or *He Sent Forth a Raven* (1935), a highly artificial and contrived novel, but other novels are more successful.

The Time of Man (1926) chronicles the life of Ellen Chesser, a poor white girl who is a descendant of Kentucky pioneers. Ellen is fourteen at the opening of the novel. R. portrays Ellen's early love affair, her marriage to Jasper Kent, and the hardships she suffers as wife and mother. The real strengths of the novel lie in R.'s use of Ellen's consciousness as we see her transcend the bleakness of her life and in the poetic quality of the narrative.

My Heart and My Flesh (1927) traces Theodosia Bell's initial rejection and ultimate acceptance of life. Theodosia, with a good family, wealth, and pride, loses her lover, her friends, her home, and her health. She is driven to suicide, but at last reaffirms her love for life.

The power of the self to transcend external forces is the controlling thesis of *The Great Meadow* (1930), set during the revolutionary-war period in Virginia and Kentucky. R.'s central characters are Berkeleian idealists whose lives appear as spiritual dramas deriving their substance from the mind of God. The protagonist, Diony Hall, chooses to leave the order and safety of her family's farm to enter the wilderness of the frontier. The most notable element of the novel is the mental or spiritual ordering Diony exerts over the chaos of her life and her surroundings.

R. wrote poetry throughout her life—her first important volume, *Under the Tree* (1922), was poetry—and, although her output in verse is slim in comparison with her prose, she wrote several first-rate poems, including "Love in the Harvest" and "Sonnet of Jack." R. also published two volumes of short stories—*The Haunted Mirror* (1932) and *Not by Strange Gods* (1941)—but they are less successful than her novels.

R. deserves further study and analysis. A fine prose writer whose experiments in stream-of-consciousness narration and feminine characterization seem far ahead of her time, she is of especial interest today for her penetrating analysis of the female consciousness.

WORKS: *In the Great Steep's Garden* (1915). *Under the Tree* (1922). *The Time of Man* (1926). *My Heart and My Flesh* (1927). *Jingling in the Wind* (1928). *The Great Meadow* (1930). *A Buried Treasure* (1931). *The Haunted Mirror* (1932). *He Sent Forth a Raven* (1935). *Black Is My Truelove's Hair* (1938). *Song in the Meadow* (1940). *Not by Strange Gods* (1941).

BIBLIOGRAPHY: Auchincloss, L., *Pioneers and Caretakers: A Study of Nine Women Writers* (1965). Campbell, H. M., and R. Foster, *Elizabeth Madox Roberts: American Novelist* (1956). McDowell, F. P. W., *Elizabeth Madox Roberts* (1963). Rovit, E. H., *Herald to Chaos: The Novels of Elizabeth Madox Roberts* (1960).

Other references: *Kentucky Historical Society Review* (April 1966). SatR (2 March 1963).

ANNE ROWE

Jane Roberts

B. 8 May 1929, Albany, New York
D. of Delmar and Marie Burdo Roberts; m. Robert F. Butts, Jr., 1954

R. dedicated herself early to writing, beginning with poetry in her teens and later writing fiction. Nothing in R.'s life, however, foreshadowed the development of her mediumistic abilities or the messages from Seth— "an energy personality essence no longer focused in physical reality"— which form the backbone of her literary production.

R.'s first novel, *Bundu*, was published in 1958 and her second, *The Rebellers*, in 1963. In September 1963, R. had her first psychic experience, during which she wrote almost automatically while simultaneously feeling the conditions about which she was writing. Shortly after this event, R. and her painter husband began research for *How to Develop Your ESP Power* (1966), using a Ouija board. In 1963, Seth introduced himself via the Ouija board and soon afterward R. started speaking as Seth's voice. Since then, more than one thousand similar sessions have taken place, providing the material for R.'s five Seth-dictated books and for seven books associated with the Seth communications. Virtually all the Seth dictations have been recorded in shorthand by Butts. Butts is also author of the running commentary which provides background and framework for the Seth-dictated material in the Seth books.

The cosmology voiced through R. by Seth is vastly different from the usual "spirit messages." Seth depicts a monist creation of which this universe is only a small fraction. Everything has consciousness. God is "All That Is" and, as a whole and in all Its parts, is constantly evolving.

As well as being parts of All That Is, humans are also parts of entities greater than themselves; humans have free will nonetheless. They have existed before birth as individuals and, after death, will continue to do so. The Seth teachings emphasize the power and potential of the individual human. "You create your own reality" is a basic tenet of his message.

Since Seth's advent, R. has not limited herself to material dictated by him. R.'s books depicting her own experiences in attempting to understand and apply Seth's philosophy add a poignantly personal dimension to the Seth communications. R. has also written two fast-paced novels about Oversoul 7, which embody and vivify Seth's teachings. A more recent development in R.'s career is her work on the "after-death journal." Two of these have been published, one received from the painter Paul Cézanne, and the other from the psychologist William James (*The Afterdeath Journal of an American Philosopher*, 1978).

The Seth teachings are complex, intellectually demanding, and not for everyone. Readers of like mind will find R.'s Seth books uniquely challenging, expanding, and—if fortune smiles—deeply satisfying.

WORKS: *Bundu* (1958). *The Rebellers* (1963). *How to Develop Your ESP Power* (1966; reissued as, *The Coming Of Seth*, 1976). *The Seth Material* (1970). *Seth Speaks: The Eternal Validity of the Soul* (1972). *The Education of Oversoul 7* (1973). *The Nature of Personal Reality: A Seth Book* (1974). *Adventures in Consciousness: An Introduction to Aspect Psychology* (1975). *Dialogues of the Soul and Mortal Self in Time* (1975). *Psychic Politics* (1976). *The Unknown Reality: Volume One of a Seth Book* (1977). *The World View of Paul Cézanne* (1977). *The Afterdeath Journal of an American Philosopher* (1978). *The Unknown Reality: Volume Two of a Seth Book* (1979). *The Further Education of Oversoul 7* (1979). *Emir's Education in the Proper Use of Magical Powers; The Nature of the Psyche: Its Human Expression (a Seth Book).* (1979).

BIBLIOGRAPHY: Andreae, C., *Seances and Spiritualists* (1974). Bentov, I., *Stalking the Wild Pendulum* (1977).
Other references: *New Realities* 1 (1977). *VV* (9 Oct. 1978; 16 Oct. 1978).

LUCY MENGER

Maggie Roberts

Wrote under: Eiggam Strebor

There is no biographical information available for R. She wrote in the late 1870s and was greatly influenced by the Civil War.

In the introduction to her first book, *Home Scenes during the Rebellion* (1875), R. disclaims any attempt to paint the "brilliant hues of fiction," instead confining herself to "incidents that actually occurred during the Rebellion." These episodic stories of the end of the war and the years afterward are peopled with struggling young widows, families and friends torn apart by opposing loyalties, illiterate blacks confused by their new status, and brave men in uniform. In scenes set in New

York, Washington, and New Orleans, R. relates the circumstances of young lovers bridging the Mason-Dixon line. Goodwill is established between North and South through the marriages of a "little rebel" and a Yankee captain, a southern heiress and a Union soldier, among others.

Although herself a southern sympathizer, R. respects the motivations on both sides of the conflict and surveyed the devastating results of the battles. R. chronicles these effects in the "home scenes" in which Americans beset by suffering carried on with unbeaten determination. Bravery tempered by faith and fierce loyalty to liberty were the noble principles of both Union and Confederacy, as R. paints them.

R. takes up the theme of war again in *Shadows and Silver Sprays* (1875). A majority of these poems are inspired by the events of the Civil War. The frightening spectacle of battle, the death of a young dragoon, the stirring parade of troops, and a sad tribute to the assassinated President are recorded in this collection. R. commemorates holidays with rhymed verses and wrote acrostics and whimsical songs. Her prosody relies on a regular rhyme scheme and recurring meter that overwhelms the subject at times.

The Shot Heard Round the World (1876) is a series of poems, from "Britannia's Insult to Columbia" to "America's Centennial," tracing America's history. Famous American victories are depicted as triumphs in the "dread name of Jehovah." R. attempts epic scope in this volume, with revolutionary generals Washington and Lafayette as "god-like heroes," and the allegorical figure of America, girded by truth and justice, rising up from under England's dominion.

Patriotic, religious, and sentimental, R.'s poetry and fiction are typical of the 19th c. She captured feelings stirred by the strife of Civil War, but often her sentiments and observations were optimistic and simplistic.

WORKS: *Home Scenes during the Rebellion* (1875). *Shadows and Silver Sprays* (1875). *Ambition; or, The Launch of a Skiff upon the Sea of Life* (1876). *Gem of Youth; or, Fireside Tales* (1876). *The Shot Heard Round the World* (1876).

BIBLIOGRAPHY: For articles in reference works, see: *American Fiction 1851–1875*, Ed. L. H. Wright (1965). *American Fiction 1876–1900*, Ed. L. H. Wright (1966). *A Dictionary of North American Authors Deceased Before 1950*, Ed. W. S. Wallace (1951). *Famous Women of History*, Ed. W. H. Browne (1895). *A Supplement to Allibone's Critical Dictionary*, Ed. J. F. Kirk (1891).

ELIZABETH ROBERTS

Elizabeth Robins

B. 1862, Louisville, Kentucky; d. 1952, Sussex, England
Wrote under: C. E. Raimond, Elizabeth Robins
D. of Charles E. Robins; m. George Richmond Parks, 1881

R. was one of eight children of a prosperous banker. She spent her early childhood in Staten Island, New York, but received formal education at the exclusive Putnam Seminary for Young Ladies in Zanesville, Ohio.

At the age of sixteen, R. left school for the stage. She began acting under an assumed name in the Boston Museum Company and then went on tour.

Married briefly to an actor, R. was widowed when he met a violent death. R. continued to act and developed an early and comprehensive interest in Ibsen's work.

R. visited Norway and, on her return, stopped in England and was soon on good terms with London producers, playing leading roles. She became a close friend of Henry James and later published their lengthy correspondence in *Theatre and Friendship* (1930).

R. created most of the Ibsen heroines in London productions of his plays during the 1890s. These were generally poorly received because of the antipathy to Ibsen's subjects, but R. gained acclaim.

An ardent suffragist, R. was deeply involved in the early women's rights movement, and a number of her books reflect this interest. *Woman's Secret* (1905) is an illuminating and thoughtful historical examination of woman's traditional place in Western culture. *Votes for Women* (1906), which gave English suffragists their slogan, is one of the few plays to deal directly with the question in an overt attempt to enlighten the public at large, as is R.'s novel, *The Convert* (1907). *Way Stations* (1913) is one of clearest and most concise histories of the women's rights movement of that time.

In the early 1900s, R. visited the western U.S. and the Alaskan Klondike during the gold rush, and the result was two novels set in that area. *Magnetic North* (1904) is perhaps the best known of all R.'s works, but *Come and Find Me* (1908) is equally well written.

R. lived in England for the rest of her life, although she made frequent visits to the U.S. After 1920, R. made her home in Henfield, Sussex, where she was considered the most important literary figure of the area.

Most of R.'s novels are about love and marriage; but unlike many of her contemporaries, R. is not sentimental about these subjects. She is primarily concerned with the relationships between men and women, and breaks away from the conventional view of romantic love and idyllic marriage as the only possible state. Indeed, she demonstrates the possibility of genuine friendship between the sexes.

R.'s writing is intelligent and lucid, her style clear and uncomplicated. Her descriptions are precisely visualized, her dialogue rings true, and she builds her characters, especially the women, fully. R.'s plots sometimes seem laborious and rambling when set beside a modern novel; but compared to contemporary novels, they are models of restraint.

Perhaps because R. spent so much of her life in England and published the majority of her work there, she has not been as well known in her native country. Nevertheless, R.'s stories bear a distinctively American stamp in the independence of her women and in the emphasis on their innate dignity and individuality.

WORKS: *George Mandeville's Husband* (1894). *The New Moon* (1895). *The Fatal Gift of Beauty, and Other Stories* (1896). *The Open Question* (1899). *Below the Salt* (1900). *Magnetic North* (1904). *The Dark Lantern* (1905). *Woman's Secret* (1905). *Votes for Women* (1906). *The Convert* (1907). *Under the Southern Cross* (1907). *Come and Find Me* (1908). *Ibsen and the Actress* (1908). *The Mills of the Gods* (1908). *The Florentine Frame* (1909). *Under His Roof* (1910). *Why?* (1912). *My Little Sister* (1913). *Way Stations* (1913). *The Messenger* (1919). *Time Is Whispering* (1923). *The Secret That Was Kept* (1926). *Theatre and Friendship* (1930). *Both Sides the Curtain* (1940).

BIBLIOGRAPHY: For articles in reference works, see: *Ohio Authors and Their Books*, Ed. W. Coyle (1962). *20thCA*.

Other references: *Athenaeum* (1887, 1888, 1909). *Atlantic* (1895, 1906). *Bookman* (1904, 1907, 1908, 1909). *Nation* (1899, 1905, 1908). *North American Review* (1910). *SatR* (1894, 1895, 1904, 1907, 1908, 1909).

HELENE KOON

Harriet Jane Hanson Robinson

B. 8 Feb. 1825, Boston, Massachusetts; d. 22 Dec. 1911, Malden, Massachusetts
Wrote under: Harriet J. Hanson, Harriet H. Robinson, Mrs. W. S. Robinson
D. of William and Harriet Browne Hanson; m. William Stevens Robinson,
1848

R.'s father, a carpenter, died in 1831, and her mother took her four
children to Lowell, where she managed a factory boardinghouse. R.
began working as a bobbin-doffer at ten. After working a fourteen-
hour day, she went to evening schools until she was able to attend Lowell
High School for two years. At fifteen her regular formal education
ceased. She tended a spinning frame and then became a "drawing-in
girl"—one of the most skilled jobs in the mill. Taking private lessons in
German, drawing, and dancing, R. read widely and began publishing
poetry in newspapers, annuals, and The Lowell Offering.

One of her verses caught the attention of William Stevens Robinson,
assistant editor of the Lowell Courier; after a two-year courtship, in
which R. was torn between love and literary ambition, they were married. W. S. Robinson published The Lowell American, one of the first
free-soil papers, from 1849 to 1854. R. joined him in his support of
abolition and worked as editorial assistant while becoming the mother
of four children. (Her elder girl became the second woman admitted
to the bar in Massachusetts.) After the Civil War, R. and her husband
worked for woman suffrage until his death in 1876. R. became the
Massachusetts leader of Susan B. Anthony's National Woman Suffrage
Association and a strong organizer and supporter of women's clubs.

All of R.'s books were published after her husband's death. Her first
is "Warrington" Pen-Portraits (1877), which combines her memoir of
her husband with a collection of his works. (The title refers to the
name under which his militant abolitionist writings had been published.)
It gives valuable pictures of abolitionist circles of the 1850s and of two
eras in Concord, Massachusetts, where W. S. Robinson grew up and the
couple lived from 1854 to 1857. "Among his schoolmates were John
and Henry D. Thoreau; 'David Henry,' as he was then called. Of the
elder, John, Mr. Robinson was very fond. He was a genial and pleasant
youth, and much more popular with his schoolmates than his more celebrated brother. Mr. Robinson had a high opinion of his talents and said

that he was then quite as promising as Henry D." *Pen-Portraits* also records impressions of John Thoreau, Sr., as "the most silent of men, particularly in the presence of his wife and gifted son," and of Cynthia Dunbar Thoreau as "one of the most graphic talkers imaginable, [who] held her listeners dumb."

In *The New Pandora* (1889), a verse drama, R. writes, "A woman should no more obey a man / Than should a man a woman. . . . My mate's no more my slave than I am hers;" and "Sex cannot limit the immortal mind. / We are ourselves, with individual souls, / Still struggling onward toward the infinite." Her pleas for equality of the sexes and the equal representation of women in councils of state, however, bog down in archaic verbs and verb forms and poetic diction.

Loom and Spindle (1898), R.'s most important work, adds personal history, anecdotes, and detail to the account she already had given in *Early Factory Labor in New England* (1883) of life in the cotton mills and corporation boardinghouses. *Loom and Spindle* provides analyses of the social hierarchy of Lowell and unforgettable vignettes, such as that of backwoods Yankee farm girls arriving to work in the city. R. also provides a full account of *The Lowell Offering* and biographical sketches of its chief contributors, carried through to 1898 whenever possible. R. admits that her account of "the life of every-day workinggirls" may omit a darker side of their existence, but says, "I give the side I knew best—the bright side!"

R.'s play may be only a relic of feminist propaganda, but her lucid first-person accounts of Lowell life in the 1830s and 40s, of *The Lowell Offering*, and of Concord will always be valuable to literary and social historians as well as enjoyable reading.

WORKS: *"Warrington" Pen-Portraits* (edited by Robinson, 1877). *Massachusetts in the Woman Suffrage Movement* (1881). *Early Factory Labor in New England* (1883). *Captain Mary Miller* (1887). *The New Pandora* (1889). *Loom and Spindle; or, Life among the Early Mill Girls* (1898).

BIBLIOGRAPHY: Eisler, B., ed., *The Lowell Offering: Writings by New England Mill Women* (1977). Foner, P. S., *The Factory Girls* (1977). Josephson, H. G., *The Golden Threads: New England's Mill Girls and Magnates* (1949). Merk, L., "Massachusetts and the Woman-Suffrage Movement" (Ph.D. diss., Radcliffe College, 1961). Rothman, E., "Harriet Hanson Robinson: A Search for Satisfaction in the Nineteenth Century Woman Suffrage Movement" (Ph.D. diss., Radcliffe College, 1973).

For articles in reference works, see: *American Literary Manuscripts*, Ed. J. A. Robbins (1977). *NAW* (article by G. Blodgett).

SUSAN SUTTON SMITH

Martha Harrison Robinson

Nothing is known about R.'s life. *Helen Erskine* (1870), R.'s only book, is a good example of conventional 19th-c. feminine fiction. It is escapist in nature, approaching the Gothic at times, and contains that staple of ladies' fiction, the ward and her wealthy guardian.

Helen Erskine is written in the American anglophile tradition; it curls up happily in a fantasy projection of English aristocracy. The main plot concerns the dutiful and stalwart Hugh Bolton's pursuit of the remarkable and equally honorable Helen Erskine. Hugh, in his late twenties, is legally related to Helen, a lass in her mid-twenties, but there is no blood connection. Helen's mother had been married to Hugh's uncle, but Helen was the result of her mother's first marriage. When Helen's stepfather, a Scottish laird, dies, he leaves his enormous holdings to Hugh. Hugh then becomes a variety of guardian to Helen's mother, Helen, and Helen's half-sister, Janet, the offspring of her mother's marriage to Hugh's uncle.

Hugh falls in love with Helen's stern rigorousness, but Helen cannot see the real motive for his offer to share his wealth and insists on working as a teacher to provide for herself. It is only after Hugh's attempted suicide (he throws himself from a cliff) that Helen agrees to marry him.

R. writes with a prodigious range of vocabulary. Her prose plays over a richly colored rainbow of words and allusions. On occasion, R. uses interesting images; a particularly arresting sexual metaphor has an unknown masked cavalier getting his parier tangled in the lace bedecking a luscious masked lady.

R. uses rather modern techniques to introduce the novel. She opens with an unmediated, entirely dramatized discussion of Hugh's virtues by two relatively minor characters. Without a word of direct commentary from the narrator, the main character is introduced and the moral tone of the novel is set.

Perhaps R.'s most interesting achievement is the creation of a strong, independent heroine who is chosen by the ideal man from among a bevy of passive conventional heroines. Helen exhibits, at least initially, the characteristics of the ideal liberated woman. She is intelligent, energetic, compassionate, dutiful, and courageous. After she has struggled to make her own way, however, Hugh nearly dies for her, and Helen admits that her independence was really the sin of pride. In a larger way, the passivity of the privileged is also lionized—work, in this novel, is quite hateful.

R. leaves us a novel highly charged with aristocratic romanticism and a subterranean streak of feminism.

WORKS: *Helen Erskine* (1870).

MARTHA NOCHIMSON

Katharine M. Rogers

B. 6 June 1932, New York City
D. of Martin and Jean Thompson Munzer; m. Kenneth C. Rogers, 1956

The daughter of a business executive and a psychiatrist, R. was educated at Barnard College (B.A. 1952) and Columbia University (Ph.D. 1957). After instructorships at Skidmore College and Cornell University, she joined the English department at Brooklyn College in 1958, becoming a full professor in 1974. R.'s major fields are Restoration and 18th-c. literature and 19th-c. fiction; her special interest is the status of women as subjects and as writers in these periods. A "committed but not extreme feminist," her view is that courses on women and literature should "never . . . reduce their texts to mere springboards for political theorizing or proselytizing."

The Troublesome Helpmate: A Study of Misogyny in Literature (1966) was inspired by the events of R.'s life. During the 1960s, regulations at Brooklyn College forced pregnant women to take leaves of absence. Since uninterrupted years of teaching were required for tenure, these regulations prevented R. from obtaining tenure at the end of the usual period of probationary service. She writes: "I managed to sublimate my indignation by applying my mind to a scholarly study of misogyny."

The Troublesome Helpmate defines misogyny not as the almost universal view that women are inferior to men and should therefore be subordinated to them, but as the fear, dislike, or contempt expressed by a writer who "insists on this view to an extent unusually harsh for his period." R. traces misogyny back to its origins in Greco-Roman and

Judeo-Christian cultures. She then proceeds in an encyclopedic fashion through English literature, concentrating on historical variations in the literary expression of misogyny and on several important authors. R. offers various social, historical, and psychological causes of misogyny, suggesting that the most basic of these is the need to rationalize "the wish to keep women subject to men."

R. has continued her analysis of male writers in *William Wycherley* (1972) and in essays on Richardson, Fielding, Thackeray, Ibsen, and others. In "The Feminism of Daniel Defoe" (in *Woman in the 18th Century, and Other Essays,* Eds. P. Fritz and R. Morton, 1976), R. analyzes carefully Defoe's treatment of marriage, love, sex, adultery, economic survival, and female psychology in both his journalism and fiction. Of Arnold's plea for birth control in *Culture and Anarchy,* she suggests that its motivation was social progress rather than sexual freedom (*Dalhousie Review,* Winter 1971–72).

Like other feminist critics, R. has gradually moved from images of women in literature by men to women writers, some once well known but now forgotten. She shows that late-18th-c. conventions of "feminine" writing inhibited Charlotte Smith, who centered her novels on insipid heroines, although her real skill lay in revealing political abuses and social pretensions, and Elizabeth Inchbald, who ignored conventions in the first half of her best novel but followed them "to the destruction of interest and plausibility in the second part" (*Eighteenth-Century Studies,* 1977). In a forthcoming book on 18th-c. England, R. continues analyzing the historical circumstances of women's lives, their subjective position as defined by ideology, the literary developments that helped to encourage the feminism of the period, and the influence of that feminism on the work of women writers in various genres.

WORKS: *The Troublesome Helpmate: A Study of Misogyny in Literature* (1966). *William Wycherley* (1972). *Before Their Time: Six Women Writers of the Eighteenth Century* (edited by Rogers, 1979). *Selected Poems of Anne Finch, Countess of Winchilsea* (1979).

BIBLIOGRAPHY: *Books Abroad* (Autumn 1967). *Johnsonian News Letter* (Dec. 1966). *Journal of Marriage and the Family* (May 1972). *PQ* (July 1973). *The Year's Work in English Studies* (1967).

JANET SHARISTANIAN

Anna Katharine Green Rohlfs

B. 11 Nov. 1846, Brooklyn, New York; d. 11 April 1935, Buffalo, New York
Wrote under: Anna Katharine Green
D. of James Wilson and Catherine A. Whitney Green; m. Charles Rohlfs, 1884

R. was the youngest child of a lawyer father and a mother who died when R. was three. R. received a B.A. from the Ripley Female Seminary in Poultney, Vermont, and began publishing poetry in *Scribner's*, *Lippincott's*, and other journals.

Although not the first American detective novel, *The Leavenworth Case* (1878) has been our most famous early mystery. Because of the decided success of *The Leavenworth Case*, R. gradually turned away from poetry writing. Only two of her forty books are not mysteries: a volume of verse, *The Defense of the Bride, and Other Poems* (1882), and a verse drama, *Risifi's Daughter* (1887).

In 1884, R. married a tragedian turned furniture designer. They made their home in Buffalo, New York. Over the next eight years, R. produced three children and eight books. The last two decades of the century were her most fertile writing years. She produced twenty-two published volumes between 1880 and 1900—for an ever-widening audience.

R.'s popularity grew with each new published thriller. She soon became the grande dame of the American mystery novel. R.'s international fame made her an effective lobbyist for international copyright.

The Leavenworth Case was, for many years, considered both the first American detective novel and the first detective novel by a woman, although it is neither. It is, however, a well-plotted, vastly entertaining murder puzzle of a type now classic. The rich Mr. Leavenworth is found murdered in his locked study. The suspects include his servants, employees, and two nieces. The sleuth is Ebenezer Gryce—a kind, rheumatic man and G.'s most frequently used detective. *The Leavenworth Case* was very popular. The Pennsylvania legislature even debated its authorship, consensus being that "the story was manifestly beyond a woman's powers."

Miss Hurd: An Enigma (1894) is a powerful mystery-melodrama in which the woman is the mystery to be solved. Vashti Hurd had wanted a "broad, free life." Instead, she was forced to marry the rich Mr. Murdoch. The murder puzzle that eventually develops is a subplot to the greater problem of Vashti's hatred for her husband and her need for freedom. Contemporary male critics found Miss Hurd an unsympathetic character. But feminist readers will find Vashti both sympathetic and heroic. Despite its rather sensational plot elements, the novel transcends its identity as a mystery novel and becomes a women's novel.

That Affair Next Door (1897) introduces R.'s prototype spinster sleuth, Miss Amelia Butterworth. A sharp, independent woman, Miss Butterworth works both with and against the police, as personified by the now-elderly Mr. Gryce. Amelia's own, rather satirical, narration makes the book a delight. It is also one of R.'s most challenging mysteries. Miss Butterworth would make two more appearances: a starring role in *Lost Man's Lane* (1898) and a cameo appearance in *The Circular Study* (1900).

The Golden Slipper, and Other Problems for Violet Strange (1915) is a short-story collection featuring a professional woman detective. Violet Strange is worthy of respect both as an investigator specializing in women's "problems" and for her motivation in becoming an investigator—to support a dearly loved but disinherited older sister.

R. brought detective fiction to a more "cultured" reading public. She frankly and proudly wrote for a popular audience, but her books were published in hardbound editions by respected houses. No longer was the American mystery relegated to dime-novel status. Prime ministers, presidents, and honored writers were avowed fans.

R.'s long and prolific career spanned from the infancy of the genre to its "golden age." But changing tastes within this fast-growing fiction formula dealt harshly with R. at the end of her career. Soon her poetic touches, her fondness for melodrama, her Victorian verbiage, were judged worthless by the jaundiced eye of the interwar reading public. The genre became rigidly formularized, lean, and cynical. By the 1940s, R.'s work was forgotten, or remembered only to ridicule.

R. is worthy of reexamination, both as a female forerunner in a largely female genre and as a writer with a real respect for women. R.'s female characters are strong, brave, and resolute against evil and largely male violence. There is a recurrent theme of sisterhood in R.'s works among women who pool their energies for survival. R. gave us some of the first female sleuths, both amateur and professional. Unlike many 20th-c. mystery writers who think of women only as victims or secondary characters, R. portrayed women as characters of primary importance who refused to be victimized.

WORKS: *The Leavenworth Case* (1878). *A Strange Disappearance* (1880). *The Sword of Damocles* (1881). *The Defense of the Bride, and Other Poems* (1882). *Hand and Ring* (1883). *X.Y.Z.* (1883). *The Mill Mystery* (1886). *Risifi's Daughter* (1887). *7 to 12: A Detective Story* (1887). *Behind Closed Doors* (1888). *The Forsaken Inn* (1890). *A Matter of Millions* (1890). *The Old Stone House* (1891). *Cynthia Wakeham's Money* (1892). *Marked 'Personal'* (1893). *Miss Hurd: An Enigma* (1894). *The Doctor, His Wife, and the Clock* (1895). *Dr. Izard* (1895). *That Affair Next Door* (1897). *Lost Man's Lane* (1898). *Agatha Webb* (1899). *The Circular Study* (1900). *A Difficult Problem* (1900). *One of My Sons* (1901). *Three Women and a Mystery* (1902). *The Filigree Ball* (1903). *The Amethyst Box* (1905). *The House in the Mist* (1905). *The Millionaire Baby* (1905). *The Woman in the Alcove* (1906). *The Chief Legatee* (1906). *The Mayor's Wife* (1907). *The House of Whispering Pines* (1910). *Three Thousand Dollars* (1910). *Initials Only* (1911). *Dark Hollow* (1914). *The Golden Slipper, and Other Problems for Violet Strange* (1915). *To the Minute / Scarlet and Black* (1916). *The Mystery of the Hasty Arrow* (1917). *The Step on the Stair* (1923).

BIBLIOGRAPHY: Harkins, E. F., and C. H. L. Johnson, *Little Pilgrimages among the Women Who Have Written Famous Books* (1901). Overton, G., *The Women Who Make Our Novels* (1928).

Other references: *Bookman* 70 (1929). *Reading and Collecting* 2 (1938). *The Writer* 2 (1888).

KATHLEEN L. MAIO

Klara Goldzieher Roman

B. *1881, Budapest, Hungary; d. 9 Aug. 1962, Zurich, Switzerland*
D. *of William Goldzieher; m. ? Roman, 1900*

Born in Hungary to a medical, tradition-bound family that disapproved of a medical career for women, R. secretly studied handwriting. Given her familial background and thwarted ambitions, R. naturally focused on physiological-neurological aspects in handwriting. However, only after her marriage, at nineteen, with her husband's reluctant consent, did R. study and experiment in Berlin. She became Kurt Lewin's research assistant. Recognition and honors soon accumulated: R. graduated from the Hungarian Royal State Institute for Abnormal Psychology; she was elected member of the Hungarian Society of Psychology; she founded the Hungarian Institute for Handwriting Research; and she became the official forensic handwriting expert for juvenile delinquents and later for adult criminal courts.

Although R. by no means overlooked characterological indications in handwriting, her emphasis was physiological, resulting in her invention of the graphodyne, a stylus for measuring tension. R. was best known for this invention and its use in her inquiries into handedness and children's mental development and maturation. Her inquiries resulted in the conclusion that writing speed is based on genetic factors, and writing pressure chiefly on special conditions and environmental influences.

When R. came to the U.S. in 1947, her work was met with scepticism and indifference. In 1948, R. won a unique prize: an appointment to teach graphology, as a staff member of the New School of Social Research. It was the first time that a recognized American college offered graphological courses for credit. In 1952, *Handwriting: A Key to Personality* was published and launched R.'s graphological method in print.

In the U.S., as in Europe, R. won recognition for her astute findings concerning speech disorders, criminality, and personality. Additionally, she did research in arthritis, child disturbances, and differential diagnosis in speech and hearing deficiencies. Invitations to lectures and assignments as teacher-in-residence and research collaborator took R. to many parts of the U.S. However, perhaps her most influential, far-reaching work, *Encyclopedia of the Written Word* (1968), treated graphology as only one aspect of what R. considered man's greatest achievement: the written word.

R.'s most valuable contributions to graphology relate to the proven link between children's handwriting variability and age, differential diagnosis in speech and hearing disturbances, and the psychogram ("the-profile-in-the-round"), devised in collaboration with S. W. Staemfli. The psychogram introduced a pictorial concept of personality structure and functioning that more easily dovetailed with personality theories of overlapping functions.

Three years before her death, eager to devote more time to the encyclopedia, R. resigned from the New School, but not without certainty that the graphological courses would continue under the able teaching of her long-time assistant.

WORKS: *Handwriting: A Key to Personality* (1952). *Encyclopedia of the Written Word* (Eds. R. Wolfson and M. Edwards, 1968).

BIBLIOGRAPHY: Vernon, P. E. and G. W., *Studies in Expressive Movement* (1933). Wolfson, R., Introduction to *Encyclopedia of the Written Word* (1968).

ROSE WOLFSON

Irma von Starkloff Rombauer

B. 30 Oct. 1877, St. Louis, Missouri; d. 14 Oct. 1962, St. Louis, Missouri
D. of H. Max-Starkloff and Clara Kuhlmann; m. Edgar R. Rombauer, 1899

R. once said of herself, "Although I have been modernized by life and my children, my roots are Victorian." R. was born into the social and cultural milieu of upper-class St. Louis. Her father was a physician and also served for several years as American consul in Bremen, Germany. Travel in Europe with her family during her adolescence formed R.'s taste in the traditional values of European society. R.'s mother had originally emigrated to St. Louis from Germany in order to found, with others, the first kindergarten there. Ironically, she educated R. in the traditional attributes of being "a lady."

In 1899, when she married a young attorney, R. was surprised to discover that her education had not prepared her for housekeeping and cooking. In self-defense, R. slowly learned to cook; she became a student of Mrs. Nannie Talbot Johnson of Paris, Kentucky, a well-known teacher and lecturer on cookery. Simultaneously, she acquired recipes from members of her well-connected German family as well as from friends and newspapers in St. Louis. During her married life, R. was actively involved with organizations in the cultural life of St. Louis. When her husband died, R. wrote her best-selling cookbook "chiefly to distract her keen unhappiness."

Privately printed in 1931, in an edition of 3,000 copies, *The Joy of Cooking* was quickly bought out by St. Louis hostesses. Despite the great number of other cookbooks on the market, increasing requests for a copy of the book prompted R. to work on a greatly enlarged edition, published in 1936. Since then it has gone through five hard-cover editions and sold more than six million copies.

The format that R. developed to unite the exact, scientifically measured ingredients with crystal-clear procedural instructions was unique for that era. Instead of listing ingredients at the beginning of each recipe or burying them in the text as many "lady" writers did, R. reduced her recipes to a step-by-step method of listing ingredients along with the mixing process.

R.'s daughter, Marion Rombauer Becker, tested recipes for the first edition and created simple illustrations for subsequent editions; her contributions help enliven the text. She became a full-fledged co-author in the 1940s.

R. published two additional cookbooks: *Streamlined Cooking* (1939) and *Cooking for Girls and Boys* (1946).

R.'s great accomplishment was to have written the perfect cookbook, a how-to-do-it manual at a time when servants were disappearing from middle-class homes because of a changing work force at the beginning of World War II. R.'s book bridged the gap between the remembered elegance and richness of the 19th c. and the more austere life of servantless homes of the 20th c. Her witty style, cultivated taste in multinational cuisines, and firsthand knowledge of the needs of American households provided America with its culinary classic.

WORKS: *The Joy of Cooking: A Compilation of Reliable Recipes with an Occasional Culinary Chat* (with M. Rombauer Becker, 1931; rev. and enlarged ed., 1936). *Streamlined Cooking* (1939). *Cooking for Girls and Boys* (1946).

BIBLIOGRAPHY: For articles in reference works, see: *CB* (Dec. 1953; Dec. 1962). Other references: *Coronet* (Oct. 1950). *NYTBR* (12 Aug. 1951). St. Louis *Post-Dispatch* (3 Dec. 1931; 29 June 1952). *Time* (26 Oct. 1962).

DOROTHEA MOSLEY THOMPSON

Eleanor Roosevelt Roosevelt

B. *11 Oct. 1884, New York City; d. 7 Nov. 1962, New York City*
Wrote under: Eleanor Roosevelt
D. *of Elliot and Anna Hall Roosevelt; m. Franklin D. Roosevelt, 1905*

R.'s writing always expresses an undying hatred of war, a personal method of fighting injustice, and a strong sense of duty to her husband, family, and country, as well as to world peace. Woven throughout is her unique sense of humor.

The Autobiography of Eleanor Roosevelt (1937) shows R.'s growth from an unhappy childhood to the wife of a president, her deep interest in world politics, and her own increasing independence.

Part III of the autobiography, "On My Own," speaks of R. as a woman alone after the death of her husband. It is an end and a beginning. She learns the ropes in the United Nations, travels widely, and campaigns vigorously for presidential candidate Adlai E. Stevenson. She writes of a visit to Russia, her vision of "The American Dream," and the Democratic Convention of 1960.

You Learn by Living (1960) is dedicated to R.'s grandchildren and great-grandchildren. It deals with the uses of time, the difficult art of maturity, endless readjustments, the right to be an individual, facing responsibilities, and how everyone can take part in politics and become a public servant. In *India and the Awakening East* (1953), R. tells of her journey to India and of the political climate she found. Her simplicity of style is effective in giving the reader an intelligent and coherent description of the country at that time.

"It is today that we must create the world of the future" is the message of *Tomorrow Is Now* (1963). Essentially it is the story of America: "How we started from scratch and America the unready. Today—the world revolution and the economic revolution, the social revolution, the revolution in Education, the machinery for peace, and the individual in the revolution."

R.'s writings bring to life her youthful shyness and fear of criticism, her growing independence, her triumph over sorrow and adversity brought about by her husband's illness, and finally her strength and courage. Although R. has been criticized for her "naive tone and use of clichés," she speaks to the reader in a warm, direct, thoughtful, and sincere fashion, and her candid style reveals the ability to laugh at herself.

WORKS: *When You Grow Up to Vote* (1932). *It's Up to the Women* (1933). *The Autobiography of Eleanor Roosevelt* (1937). *My Days* (1938). *The Moral Basis of Democracy* (1940). *If You Ask Me* (1946). *India and the Awakening East* (1953). *This I Remember* (1949). *UN Today and Tomorrow* (1953). *On My Own* (1958). *You Learn by Living* (1960). *Tomorrow Is Now* (1963).

BIBLIOGRAPHY: Hershan, S. K., *A Woman of Quality* (1970). Kearny, J. R., *Anna Eleanor Roosevelt: An American Conscience* (1968). Lash, J. P.,

Eleanor and Franklin (1971). Lash, J. P., *Eleanor: The Years Alone* (1972). For articles in reference works, see: *CB* (1949).

STELLA K. HERSHAN

Lillian Ross

B. 8 June 1917 (1927?), Syracuse, New York
D. of Louis R. and Edna Rosenberg Ross

R. comes from a middle-class Jewish background. She attended Hunter College in New York City, and in 1946 began writing for *The New Yorker*. R. became a staff writer in 1948 under founding editor Harold Ross, and most of the material in her books appeared first in *The New Yorker*. She has a son, Erik Jeremy. Details of R.'s private life are not available since she believes that "a reporter's most valuable asset is his anonymity."

In the course of gathering material for her first *New Yorker* profile in 1947 (on Brooklyn-born bullfighter Sidney Franklin, reprinted in *Reporting* as "El Unico Matador"), R. met Ernest Hemingway. When Hemingway visited New York for a few days in 1949, R. was invited to accompany him. The resulting profile (*New Yorker*, 13 May 1950) aroused both admiration and protest, a furor which surfaced again when the article appeared in book form as *Portrait of Hemingway* (1961). R. explained and defended the work, of which Hemingway himself approved, in a letter to the editors of *New Republic* (7 August 1961).

The Hemingway profile gave R. a certain cachet when R. went to Hollywood for eighteen months to cover the entire process of making a motion picture, from original conception to stockholders' box office report. The picture was MGM's *The Red Badge of Courage*, directed by John Huston, and *The New Yorker* articles became the book *Picture* (1952). *Picture* was considered a literary innovation because it told a factual story in fictional form. Many objected to the ingenuous exposé of Hollywood's preference for making money over making art, but the book remains, after twenty-five years, as instructive as it is entertaining.

The Player: Profile of an Art (1962) is a collection of self-portraits of fifty-five actors and actresses. Over a four-year period, R. and her sister Helen interviewed their subjects, taking copious notes and then arranging the material in the form of monologues, each prefaced by a "natural, unretouched" photograph taken by R.

Vertical and Horizontal (1963) is a collection of stories which, taken together, chronicle with wry humor and a touch of pathos the activities of a would-be upwardly mobile New York bachelor physician in his relationships with his less-than-competent psychiatrist, his patients, and the women he regards as "wife material."

Reporting (1964) contains five *New Yorker* articles, "Portrait of Hemingway," and "Picture." Although both "The Big Stone" and "Terrific" cover events which occurred over a period of a year, R. would seem to have been invisibly present at every moment of decision, every casual but crucial encounter of personalities. That sixth sense for striking chords of interest from an array of random notes reappears in *Talk Stories* (1966), a collection of sixty short pieces originally written for the unsigned "Talk of the Town" section of *The New Yorker*. R.'s preoccupations are reflected in the number of articles on Adlai Stevenson, theater people, and the United Nations. Occasionally she assumes the persona of "our man Stanley" (whose style is parodied in a review in *The Reporter*, 16 May 1966) or of the "wild-haired typist Miss Rogers."

Anonymity is the distinguishing feature of R.'s reporting as well as of her private life. She rarely allows herself to interpret or comment upon what she observes. Her artistry lies in the sensitive selection of detail and the ability to suggest more than she says. By documenting the objects that surround her subject or the subject's gestures, facial expressions, tone of voice, and interpersonal relationships, R. is able to evoke the essence of a particular personality, an entire corporate hierarchy, or a universal human foible.

Asked for her advice to young writers, R. tells them to "try to find the strongest and most direct line from your feelings and ideas to what you write. Hold to what you know is true, no matter what is offered to you in the way of distraction."

WORKS: *Picture* (1952). *Portrait of Hemingway* (1961). *The Player: Profile of an Art* (with H. Ross, 1962). *Vertical and Horizontal* (1963). *Reporting* (1964). *Adlai Stevenson* (1966). *Talk Stories* (1966). *Maine Lingo: Boiled Owls, Billdads, and Wazzats* (with J. Gould, 1975). *Moments with Chaplin* (1980).

BIBLIOGRAPHY: *Counterpoint* (1964). *NewR* (7 Aug. 1961). *Newsweek* (18 Dec. 1961). *NYTBR* (15 May 1966). *SatR* (14 March 1964). *Time* (1 May 1964).

FELICIA HARDISON LONDRÉ

Constance Mayfield Rourke

B. 14 Nov. 1885, Cleveland, Ohio; d. 23 March 1941, Grand Rapids, Michigan
D. of Henry Button and Constance E. Davis Rourke

R. was an only child; her father was a lawyer, her mother a kindergarten teacher. R. moved to Grand Rapids, Michigan, at age seven when her father died. Her close relationship with her mother, who passed on to R. an appreciation for painting and handicrafts, probably encouraged R.'s later concern for native American folk arts. In addition, R.'s professional interest in the details of ordinary life may have been a midwestern inheritance. This regard for the near-at-hand was never mere provincialism, however; for R. understood, as have all the best midwestern writers and critics, the profound relationship between local details and national myth, between particular experience and its more universal implications.

R. attended Vassar College (B.A. 1907); her primary interests were aesthetics and literary criticism. From 1908 to 1910, R. was a researcher at the Bibliothèque Nationale in Paris and the British Museum in London. She became an English instructor at Vassar in 1910, but in 1915 resigned from Vassar to live with her mother in Grand Rapids, and to do freelance research and writing on American history and culture.

R. is best known for her advocacy of a native American culture, her use of popular culture and other "living research" sources and methods, and her popular, highly readable prose style. R. argued from a social and anthropological view of history against a belief that the quality of American society made it difficult for "culture" to live and prosper in the U.S. She saw a significant relationship between low and high cultures, and believed that America had a robust cultural tradition wherein unique native arts grew and flourished. R. proposed that American culture, woven from a great number of low- and high-culture strands, was more unified and vigorous than some scholars had believed.

Implicit in R.'s work, especially in *American Humor: A Study of the American Character* (1931), is the belief that American culture need not be judged against European models. Rather, it has its own characteristics, resulting from the particular conditions of the national history that produced it. The first part of *American Humor* recreates the rich climate in which this culture arose. R. traveled widely and used personal interviews, oral history, and popular culture documents as well as traditional historical materials to present a vivid picture of the rise of American humor. She saw this humor as an essential element in the definition of American character and culture. The second part of the book analyzes mainstream- or high-culture American writers in relationship to their antecedents in native American humor.

In *American Humor*, R. demonstrates a remarkable harmony between style and thematic approach. She writes in a lively, unacademic prose, often using fictional narration and the present tense, which makes history come alive and which celebrates ordinary American experiences and the common man.

Although *American Humor* and *The Roots of American Culture* (1942) include the most explicit statements of R.'s ideas, *Charles Sheeler: Artist in the American Tradition* (1938) is also a convincing application of R.'s theories about the interrelations between the popular American cultural experience and the mainstream art it produces. Similarly, *Troupers of the Gold Coast; or, the Rise of Lotta Crabtree* (1928) exemplifies R.'s approach. This is the lively biography of two women: Mary Ann Crabtree and her actress-comedienne daughter, Lotta. Like all of R.'s social histories, it provides a myriad of everyday details from America's past. Lotta Crabtree's story is not only the chronicle of an important life, but the vital dramatization of San Francisco in the later days of the gold rush, and of the popular theater and American humor on the Gold Coast.

Critics have attacked R. for overstating her case on behalf of American culture and the interdependence of popular and so-called "high" arts; however, R.'s reputation has been sustained not only by later studies that support her views, but by the increased use of R.'s popular-culture research methods and by the continuing influence of her readable, scholarly books.

WORKS: *Trumpets of Jubilee* (1927). *Troupers of the Gold Coast; or, The Rise of Lotta Crabtree* (1928). *American Humor: A Study of the American*

Character (1931). *Davy Crockett* (1934). *Audubon* (1936). *Charles Sheeler: Artist in the American Tradition* (1938). *The Roots of American Culture* (Ed. V. W. Brooks, 1942).

BIBLIOGRAPHY: Brooks, V. W., Preface to *The Roots of American Culture* (1942). Hyman, S. E., *The Armed Vision* (1948). Rubin, J. S., "A World out of a Wilderness: Constance Rourke and the Search for a Useable Past" (Ph.D. diss., Yale Univ., 1974).

For articles in reference works, see: *CB* (May 1941). *Contemporary American Authors*, F. B. Millett (1940). *DAB*, Suppl. 3. *NAW* (article by K. S. Lynn). *NCAB*, 32.

Other references: *Nation* (17 Sept. 1938; 24 Oct. 1942). *NewR* (31 Aug. 1942). *WF* (April 1967).

NANCY POGEL

Anne Newport Royall

B. 11 June 1769, near Baltimore, Maryland; d. 1 Oct. 1854, Washington, D.C.
D. of William and Mary Newport; m. William Royall, 1797

R. began her long and colorful life in Maryland, but moved with her family to Westmoreland County, Pennsylvania, when she was three. The family lived in a rude cabin where William Newport taught his daughter to read and write. Newport, a Tory in those prerevolutionary days, died a few years later, and Mary Newport remarried. After the death of her second husband, she and R. moved to Sweet Springs, now in West Virginia. A planter, Major William Royall, took them in and gave Mary domestic work. R., then eighteen years old, had access to the gentleman's ample library and to his tutelage. Ten years later Anne married her benefactor and mentor, who was then in his mid-fifties. When he died in 1812, he left Anne wealthy, and she began to travel.

If a nephew had not broken Royall's will, charging R. with forgery and "barbarous treatment" of her husband, the world probably would not have heard of this strong-minded woman. Because she was without income, R. turned to writing as a livelihood. *Sketches of History: Life and Manners in the United States by a Traveller* (1826) is the product of R.'s trip from Alabama to New England in 1823, containing sketches of well-known and unknown people, descriptions of landscape and cities, and personal reflections. R.'s blend of documentary material with gossipy tidbits fulfills the promise of the book's subtitle. Although R.'s books have limited literary value, they contribute to our knowledge of the social history of America.

In spring 1824, R. arrived in the District of Columbia, a sprawling community that would eventually become her home. Her first activity there was to lobby Congress for a commutation-of-pay resolution that would give her an income from her husband's military service in the Revolutionary War. R., in near-rags, solicited political, literary, and financial support from whomever she could interview, including Secretary of State John Quincy Adams. During the next seven years, R. continued to crusade, travel, write, and interview influential people.

When age forced R. to stop traveling in 1831, she settled in Washington, where she founded and printed, in her kitchen, a weekly newspaper, *Paul Pry*. R. served not only as editor and printer but also as reporter, writer, and solicitor of subscriptions. For years R. had been attacking anti-Masons and fundamentalists, and she continued her propaganda against them in *Paul Pry*. One of her best-known conflicts with the "Holy Willies," as she called evangelicals, resulted in her conviction as a "common scold." R. was fined ten dollars.

Deciding that *Paul Pry* sounded too much like a gossip sheet, R. changed the name to *The Huntress* in 1836. In the prospectus for the new paper, R. vowed to "expose corruption, hypocrisy and usurpation, without favor or affection." Among the causes R. championed were states' rights on the issue of slavery, justice for the American Indian, separation of church and state, tolerance for foreigners and Roman Catholics, and abolition of the United States Bank monopoly. She interspersed editorials and diatribes against Congress with gossip and with stories and poems written by others. R.'s crusading journalism continued in *The Huntress* for eighteen years.

WORKS: *Sketches of History: Life and Manners in the United States by a Traveller* (1826). *The Tennessean: A Novel Founded on Facts* (1827). *The Black Book: A Continuation of Travels in the United States* (3 vols., 1828–29). *Mrs. Royall's Pennsylvania* (2 vols., 1829). *Mrs Royall's Southern Tour* (3 vols., 1830–31). *Letters from Alabama* (1830).

BIBLIOGRAPHY: Dodd, D., and B. Williams, "'A Common Scold': Anne Royall," *American History Illustrated* 10 (1976). Griffith, L., Introduction to *Letters from Alabama, 1817–22* (1969). Jackson, G. S., *Uncommon Scold: The Story of Anne Royall* (1937). James, B. R., *Anne Royall's U.S.A.* (1972). Porter, S. H., *The Life and Times of Anne Royall* (1909).

LYNDA W. BROWN

Sarah Bayliss Royce

B. 2 March 1819, Stratford-on-Avon, England; d. 23 Nov. 1891, San Jose,
   California
Wrote under: Sarah Royce
D. of Benjamin and Mary Bayliss; m. Josiah Royce, 1845

The Bayliss family immigrated to New York when Sarah was six weeks
old. She was raised and educated in Rochester, New York, in true Victorian style with a reverence for religion, family, and education. R. met
and married Josiah Royce (born in England, brought up in Dundas,
Canada) in Rochester, and in 1848, with their first daughter Mary, they
traveled to Iowa; in the spring of the following year they joined the
other hopeful migrants on the overland trek to the California gold
fields.

During that grueling journey and in her early years in California, R.
wrote intermittently in her "Pilgrimage Diary" of the hardships, events,
and impressions she experienced. Nearly thirty years later she would use
the diary to write a narrative account of the "family odyssey" at the re-
quest of her son Josiah, Jr. (Harvard professor of philosophy) for his
history of the early American period in California. The manuscript of
A Frontier Lady: Recollections of the Gold Rush and Early California
(1932) was prepared not for publication but for her son's interest and
instruction and quite probably as a defense of religious faith, which the
philosopher was questioning.

R.'s book is one of the more literate personal narratives we have of a
pioneer woman's experiences, but it is also a sensitive record of personal
growth. The first night on the trail she silently faced the "chilling
prospect" of months without house or home. In the morning she felt
"mildly exultant" at having "kept silent through a cowardly fit, and
finding the fit gone off."

The desire for and importance of a home are ideas that recur frequently in R.'s narrative. Her uncomplaining acceptance of keeping
house in tents, half-built cabins, and boardinghouse rooms (briefly described), offers a clearer picture of the deprivations and fears a pioneer
woman faced than most works on the subject. Male accounts of the gold
fields often stress the excitement, freedom, or camaraderie of the day;
R.'s view "etches in a few strong lines the sordidness of the mining

camps," so unlike anything a gently bred woman of the period could even imagine.

True to her Victorian upbringing, R.'s work is permeated with prescriptive and descriptive moral messages; it gives today's reader valuable insight into Victorian values. R. relinquished the necessary trappings of what was considered a civilized society, but she refused to compromise even minimally society's moral codes for herself or her fellow pioneers.

WORKS: *A Frontier Lady: Recollections of the Gold Rush and Early California* (Ed. R. H. Gabriel, 1932).

BIBLIOGRAPHY: Glendenning, J., *Letters of Josiah Royce* (1970).
For articles in reference works, see: *NAW* (article by R. W. Paul).

JACQUELINE BAKER BARNHART

Ella Giles Ruddy

B. *1851, near Jefferson, Wisconsin; d. 26 June 1917, Los Angeles, California*
Wrote under: Ella Giles, Ella Giles Ruddy
D. of H. H. and Augusta Giles; m. George Drake Ruddy, 1895

R.'s father was a railroad representative and politician. R. studied at the University of Wisconsin and at Medford Theological College. R. was an active clubwoman. She was a member of the Unitarian Church and was a city librarian for many years.

After her marriage, R. moved to Los Angeles and later to Venice, California. She attended the Friday Morning Club and founded the Los Angeles Political Equality League for woman suffrage, in which she was an officer until 1910.

Out from the Shadows; or, Trial and Triumph (1876) catalogues the diverse types of American womanhood. Helen Lowell personifies the perfect woman. She endures a sour marriage to a drunkard and keeps the family alive by running a boardinghouse. Unjustly accused of poisoning her husband, Helen even endures prison with patience. Melinda Corson is the villain. A jealous, devious female of the worst sort, she incites Mr. Lowell to poison himself and lets Helen undergo a jury trial and loss of reputation rather than explain her own role in the tragedy. Finally, however, the natural goodness of womanhood prevails and even Melinda tells the truth and takes her just punishment.

Maiden Rachel (1879) is a testimony to spinsterhood. Written when the author was aged twenty-eight and unmarried, it is an endorsement of Mary A. Livermore's remarks on the merits of single women at the 1875 meeting of the Association for the Advancement for Women. Instead of being pitied for her inability to create a wholesome environment for a husband and children, Rachel is lauded for the good works she does for all of society. R. insists that all women, regardless of their marital status, possess an intrinsic sensitivity and moral superiority that will bring love and service to the world.

For Ella Wheeler Wilcox, another Wisconsin writer, R. compiled a date book, with quotations from Wilcox's poems and blank pages for the diarist's entries. *The Story of a Literary Career, by Ella Wheeler Wilcox* (1905) contains an account of Wilcox's early life and a description of her summer home near New Haven and its furnishings.

The Mother of Clubs (1906) is a laudatory biography of Caroline Severance, which claimed that Severance founded the New England Woman's Club before Jane Croly founded Sorosis in New York City, thereby winning national acclaim for Severance's farsightedness in "mothering" the widespread club movement for women. It is rich in quotations from letters to Severance, her speeches and writings, and reminiscences by prominent reformers of the 19th c.

Club Etiquette (1902) attempts to be a witty attack on club members' habits. It deals with the problems of women hyphenating their last names to retain their maiden names, their difficulties in calling on social superiors at home, and the discourtesy of club officers who complain of the time, tact, and money required by their station.

WORKS: *Bachelor Ben* (1875). *Out from the Shadows; or, Trial and Triumph* (1876). *Maiden Rachel* (1879). *Amerikas Forste Opdagelse* by R. B. Anderson (translated by Ruddy, 1886). *Flowers of the Spirit* (1891). *Club Etiquette: A Conversation between a Club Woman and a Nonmember Who Answer the Calling Question Over the Tea Cups* (1902). *Around the Year with Ella Wheeler Wilcox* (edited by Ruddy, 1904). *The Story of a Literary Career, by Ella Wheeler Wilcox. With Description of Mrs. Wilcox's Home and Life, by Ella Giles Ruddy* (1905). *Lace o' Me Life* (1906). *The Mother of Clubs: Caroline M. Seymour Severance, an Estimate and an Appreciation* (1906).

The Caroline Severance papers are at the Huntington Library, San Marino, California, and the Ella Giles Ruddy papers are in the State Historical Society of Wisconsin.

BIBLIOGRAPHY: Los Angeles *Examiner* (14 Oct. 1904). *Madison Democrat* (27 June 1917).

KAREN J. BLAIR

Rosemary Radford Ruether

B. 2 Nov. 1936, St. Paul, Minnesota

An educator, theologian, author, and lecturer, R. holds degrees from Scripts College (B.A., 1958) and Claremont Graduate School (M.A., 1960; Ph. D., 1965). R.'s academic appointments have included positions at Howard University in theology and church history; Harvard Divinity School as lecturer in Roman Catholic studies; and Yale Divinity School. R. is currently on the faculty of Garrett Evangelical Theological Seminary, Evanston, Illinois, where she is Georgia Harkness Professor of Theology. R. is also on the editorial board of *Christianity and Crisis*.

R.'s written work explores the multifaceted area of theology and its relationship to contemporary society. Whether she is writing about sexist ideologies, the radical kingdom, anti-Semitism, or the eschatological community, R. attempts to destroy restrictive theological attitudes and reconstruct more liberating ones.

In *The Church against Itself: An Inquiry into the Conditions of Historical Existence for the Eschatological Community* (1967), R. asserts the importance of the pilgrim nature of the Catholic Church. The dialectic she poses examines the unresolved and timeless themes of institution and person, being and becoming, and receiving and giving in the context of the theological challenge presented by Vatican II.

Similarly, *Faith and Fratricide: The Theological Roots of Anti-Semitism* (1974) calls for a complete rethinking of Christian theology vis-à-vis the Jews. Beginning with the pre-Christian classical world, R. traces the Jewish experience with the gentile world to the Holocaust of the 20th c. Her thesis, a critique of the "Christian Anti-Jewish Myth," looks to a Judeo-Christian tradition exorcised of the "Christian imperialist myth." *Faith and Fratricide* repeats R.'s basic argument for an intellectual and human environment that encourages a radical approach to theological study.

New Woman/New Earth: Sexist Ideologies and Human Liberation (1975) explores the ideologies that support sexist behavior and the companion social structures (class and race) that are tending to the "denouement of the entire human project." This series of essays reveals the realism that is another quality of R.'s work. R. addresses a wide range of complex and varied topics and appeals for a shared search for needed solutions.

Women of Spirit: Female Leadership in the Jewish and Christian Traditions (1979) is a collection of essays coedited with Eleanor Mc-Laughlin. R. again asks for the destruction of false mythologies and the creation of new realities. By examining periods and figures in history to show that women have made their mark in the male world, the book corrects the notion that women have always been denied leadership positions in churches and synagogues because of sex. As R. points out in the introduction, most people have been ignorant of the responsible roles of women in churches because of the "reconstruction of early church history from the point of view of male dominance . . . a social and theological mythology . . . that justifies the present ecclesiastic structures of male power."

R.'s contributions to theological thought have been considerable and far-reaching. Her breadth of interests is paralleled by an equally impressive depth and sensitivity. Although a prolific writer, R. does not resort to "pop" theology, but rather focuses upon timely major questions that transcend the moment.

WORKS: *The Church against Itself: An Inquiry into the Conditions of Historical Existence for the Eschatological Community* (1969). *Gregory of Nazianzus, Rhetor and Philosopher* (1969). *The Radical Kingdom: The Western Experience of Messianic Hope* (1970). *Liberation Theology: Human Hope Confronts Christian History and American Power* (1972). *Faith and Fratricide: The Theological Roots of Anti-Semitism* (1974). *Religion and Sexism: Images of Women in the Jewish and Christian Traditions* (edited by Ruether, 1974). *New Woman/New Earth: Sexist Ideologies and Human Liberation* (with E. Bianchi, 1975). *Mary: The Feminine Face of the Church* (1977). *From Machismo to Mutuality: Essays on Sexism and Woman-Man Liberation* (edited by Ruether, with E. Bianchi, 1976). *Women of Spirit: Female Leadership in the Jewish and Christian Tradition* (edited by Ruether, with E. McLaughlin, 1979).

ANN THOMPSON

Muriel Rukeyser

B. 15 Dec. 1913, New York City; d. 12 Feb. 1980, New York City
D. of Lawrence B. and Myra Lyons Rukeyser

R. was educated at the Fieldston schools, Vassar College, and Columbia University. She was vice-president of the House of Photography, New York (1946–60), taught at Sarah Lawrence College (1946, 1956–60), and later served as a member of the Board of Directors of the Teachers-Writers Collaborative in New York, a member of the National Institute of Arts and Letters, and president of PEN.

R. wrote and published a play, TV scripts, a novel, juveniles, biographies, criticism, translations, and fourteen volumes of poetry. R.'s poems have been translated into European and Asian languages, and her readings from *Waterlily Fire* (1962) have been recorded for the Library of Congress. R.'s first book of poems, *Theory of Flight* (1935), won the Yale Series of Younger Poets competition in 1935.

From R.'s poems we can study much that has happened in modernist and postmodernist poetry in the last fifty years—from distance to confession, social protest, and feminism; from Yeats and Eliot to Ginsberg, Bly, and Levertov.

R.'s personality is manifest in the exuberant, hyperbolic, and generally optimistic tone that dominates her work. R. insists on experiencing and feeling *everything*, private or social, from the smallest physical sensation to transcendence of the physical. She treats sex, a cockroach, social injustice, and mystical self-dissolution with equal exuberance; *being* is its own excuse.

The result is that R.'s poetry, but not the individual poems, is multidimensional. Some poems are almost pure sensation ("Stroking Songs"); some are explanation ("Written on a Plane"); some are vituperation ("Despisals"); and some are pure fun ("From a Play: Publisher's Song"). Both her personal and artistic credos are expressed in the poem "Whatever."

For each mood or concept, R. selects or creates a perfectly suitable form. She is skillful enough so that her forms embody rather than contain their meanings: "Afterwards" is a poem that reaches into the unconscious for a "deep-image" ("We are the antlers of that white animal") expressed in breath rhythm. "Flying There: Hanoi" uses the incremental repetition and the rhythm of nursery rhyme to rededicate a poet. "Two Years" uses three terse stream-of-consciousness lines to express the dislocation of grief. "Rational Man" is a list of man's tortures of his kind in the rhythm of a dirge, ending in a prayer.

R.'s temperament and talent are best suited for writing the Dionysian sort of poems written by Bly and Levertov at their best—sensation, the concrete and physical, in ecstasy, rage, or prayer. R. weakens when she philosophizes and explains, and she frequently explains more than is necessary.

For a poet whose published volumes of poetry spanned more than forty years, R.'s range and energy were remarkable. Her changes were toward greater variety and flexibility and personal involvement.

WORKS: *Theory of Flight* (1935). *Mediterranean* (1938). *U.S. 1* (1938). *A Turning Wind: Poems* (1939). *The Soul and Body of John Brown* (1940). *Wake Island* (1942). *Willard Gibbs* (1942). *Beast in View* (1944). *The Children's Orchard* (1947). *The Green Wave* (1948). *Elegies* (1949). *The Life of Poetry* (1949). *Orpheus* (1949). *Selected Poems* (1951). *Come Back Paul* (1955). *One Life* (1957). *Body of Waking* (1958). *I Go Out* (1961). *Waterlily Fire: Poems 1932–1962* (1962). *Selected Poems of Octavio Paz* (translated by Rukeyser, 1963). *Sun Stone* by O. Paz (translated by Rukeyser, 1963). *The Orgy* (1966). *Bubbles* (1967). *The Outer Banks* (1967). *Selected Poems of Gunnar Ekelöf* (translated by Rukeyser, with L. Sjöberg, 1967). *Three Poems by Gunnar Ekelöf* (translated by Rukeyser, 1967). *Poetry and Unverifiable Fact: The Clark Lectures* (1968). *The Speed of Darkness* (1968). *Mayes* (1970). *Twenty-nine Poems* (1970). *The Traces of Thomas Hariot* (1971). *Breaking Open* (1973). *Brecht's Uncle Eddie's Moustache* (translated by Rukeyser, 1974). *The Gates* (1976). *The Collected Poems of Muriel Rukeyser* (1978).

BIBLIOGRAPHY: Jarrell, R., *Poetry and the Age* (1953). Kertesz, L., *The Poetic Vision of Muriel Rukeyser* (1979). Rexroth, K., *American Poetry in the Twentieth Century* (1971).

For articles in reference works, see: *Contemporary Poets*, Eds. J. Venison and D. L. Kirkpatrick (1975).

Other references: *Carolina Quarterly* (Spring 1974). *Christian Century* (21 May 1980). *LJ* (1 Oct. 1976). *Ms.* (April 1974). *Nation* (19 March 1977; 8 March 1980). *NR* (24 Nov. 1973). *NYTBR* (25 Sept. 1977). *Poetry* (Oct. 1974).

ALBERTA TURNER

Caroline E. Rush

R.'s first novel appeared in 1850. In a preface, she wrote that "the circumstances which have left me, at an early age, a widow, with two orphan boys to educate" forced R. to write to support herself. However, her books, which were probably published by subscription, "awakened in the hearts of a generous and sympathizing public, a deep and noble interest."

R., a native of New York, was able to travel to a number of American cities, and especially to the South—a region whose beauty, climate, and customs she praised highly in nearly all her works. R.'s fiction is characterized by moral and didactic purpose and by religious and sentimental subject matter, which, the author claimed, was founded strictly on fact.

Robert Morton; or, The Step-Mother (1850) is a collection of three short stories. "Edmund and Ione" describes the moral and spiritual regeneration of a wealthy young New York City bachelor whose adoption of two starving orphans leads him to devote his life to helping the needy. "Letters from the South" records a northern girl's delighted impressions of the scenery, people, and customs of the South. "The Step-Mother" shows how the influence of a cruel and negligent stepmother cancels the teachings of a child's mother, blights his childhood, and ruins his future.

The Dew Drop of the Sunny South (1851) describes the short but pious life of Kate Herford, a wealthy southern belle. Jilted by a dissipated fiancé, Kate resigns herself to remaining single, doing good, and spreading Christ's teachings. After converting Caroline, a schoolgirl, Kate quietly dies of consumption.

The North and the South; or, Slavery and Its Contrasts (1852) develops the proslavery argument that black southern slaves were better off than poor whites of northern cities by telling the sad tale of the Harleys, a wealthy New York family impoverished by drink, separated by work, and ruined by starvation, exposure, and the indifference of the well-to-do. Only one of the seven Harley children prospers; she is adopted by an affectionate and generous plantation family. The others —those who survive—are ground down by toil and hardship. The death of the Harleys' pure and lovely eldest daughter, her Christian resignation to starvation and disease, is R.'s strongest statement against wealthy northerners who feel no Christian charity for the poor.

Way-Marks in the Life of a Wanderer (1855) describes the edifying life of Marcia Walton, a beautiful and devout northern governess employed on a Georgia plantation. Although Marcia's gentle nature and piety endear her to the family for whom she works, she is poisoned by the jealous mulatto mistress of the planter's son. Her health is impaired. Adopted into the planter's family, she spends her remaining days traveling throughout the South—spreading love, ending misunderstandings, and practicing Christian teachings. She dies happy, surrounded by the people she loves.

Shallow and inconsistent characterization, frequent digressions, authorial intrusions, and shifts in point of view indicate that R.'s fiction is the work of an amateur. Even so, R.'s books illustrate one of the major concepts of the popular domestic fiction of her day: woman as moral teacher. R.'s heroines are all pious and resigned to low status, poor health, and oppressive circumstances; all are actively involved in spreading the gospel of Christian submission. Their beauty is moral as well as physical; they die young, pure, and certain of eternal life, providing the reader with both pleasurable tears and edifying Christian examples.

WORKS: *Robert Morton; or, The Step-Mother: A Book Founded on Fact* (1850). *The Dew Drop of the Sunny South: A Story Written from Every Day Life* (1851). *The North and South; or, Slavery and Its Contrasts: A Tale of Real Life* (1852). *Way-Marks in the Life of a Wanderer: The Incidents Taken from Real Life* (1855).

KATHERINE STAPLES

Rebecca Rush

Wrote under: A Lady of Pennsylvania
D. of Jacob Rush

The daughter of a judge of Philadelphia and the niece of Dr. Benjamin Rush, R. was the child of a prominent, wealthy, and well-educated family. She probably had access to the best education available to young women at that time, and must have moved in the highest social circles.

Kelroy, R.'s only known work, was published in 1812. The eponymous hero does not appear until the fourth chapter, and the novel is more the story of Mrs. Hammond and her daughters Lucy and Emily. Having been left moderately well off by the death of her husband, Mrs. Hammond takes her daughters to the country for five years to train them to make advantageous matches when they return to Philadelphia. The elder daughter thinks like her mother; Emily, however, has "a mind of the highest order" and "keen perceptions" and is not interested in her mother's schemes. She falls in love with the impecunious poet Kelroy. Mrs. Hammond forges letters and bribes people to ruin Emily's relationship with Kelroy. Emily does not learn the truth until after she has married someone else; devastated, she wastes away and dies. When Kelroy learns the truth, he almost loses his reason. Half mad, he travels aimlessly, eventually dying in a shipwreck.

Although R. uses melodrama and improbable events to move the story, neither is a fatal flaw. The chief virtues of the novel lie in its use of language and in its characters. R. calls this a "narrative of love," but the emphasis is on clear, rather spare narrative, not on sentimentality. The major characters are often provided with complex personalities, rendering them lively and interesting.

R.'s greatest success is with her "minor" characters. Mrs. Hammond is "a woman of fascinating manners, strong prejudices and boundless ambition," and her singleminded pursuit of financial security so enlivens the book that the reader almost ends up on her side. What is most striking about even very minor characters is that they all behave in manners consistent with their motivations and believable to the reader.

Kelroy is also noteworthy for its very "American" qualities. Most of the characters are strongly individualistic. The ease with which people, especially men and women, meet and talk, and the casual and joking nature of many of their conversations also seem very American. *Kelroy's* value lies in the fact that it embodies the best in an emerging national literature in a fairly polished work of art.

WORKS: Kelroy (1812).

BIBLIOGRAPHY: Allibone, S. A., *A Critical Dictionary of English Literature and British and American Authors* (1870).

JULIA ROSENBERG

Joanna Russ

B. 22 Feb. 1937, Bronx, New York
D. of Evarett I. and Bertha Zinner Russ

R. spent half her childhood "in the Bronx Zoo and half in the Botanical Gardens." A gifted student, R. went to Cornell University and received a B.A. in English in 1957. She later attended Yale University School of Drama, from which she received an M.F.A. in play writing and dramatic literature in 1960. Since her graduation, R. has worked as an assistant professor of English at Cornell and as an associate professor at the University of Washington at Seattle.

Although she is best known for science fiction, R. has written other kinds of fiction as well. "Nor Custom Stale," R.'s first science-fiction story, was published in the *Magazine of Fantasy and Science Fiction* (1959); since then, her stories have appeared in a variety of periodicals, including *Orbit, Epoch, Quark, Cimarron Review*, and *Galaxy*.

R. is a feminist. Although her belief in feminism came gradually, its impact on her writing came early and was accompanied by difficulties. Despite her fears and an occasional unsympathetic review, the critical reception of R.'s work has been positive. In 1972, she received the Nebula Award for "When It Changed," which has an overtly feminist theme.

"When It Changed" (1972) is one of R.'s most widely known short stories. The story's action occurs on Whileaway, a planet with no men on it since a plague killed them all six centuries earlier. In those six centuries, a society of women has evolved a new system of government, fair methods of distributing work and wealth, and a method of reproduction involving the merging of two ova and resulting in girl children with a mixture of genes from both mothers.

The story deals with the day Earthmen arrive on Whileaway and with the dreadful and inevitable changes that their arrival prefigures. After learning about the plague, the men extend their sympathy to the women for having lived so long without them. They take no notice of the women's happiness or accomplishments.

For Janet, the narrator, the moment is poignant. Her life and work are devalued, and her lifelong and loving marriage is demeaned. Janet realizes that all that is precious to her and to the other women of Whileaway will be destroyed, and she laments that the coming of men will cheat all women's daughters of "their full humanity."

The Female Man (1975) is a funny, angry, intelligent, and visionary novel about women's fantasies of power. Four women—each a version of the same person—come from four different worlds and tell their interlocking stories. There is Janet from Whileaway, and Jeannine who lives on a kind of 1950s Earth where World War II never happened and the Depression continues. The narrator is Joanna, whose world is much like our Earth. The fourth woman is Jael, from a possible futuristic Earth on which men and women are openly at war. She has been genetically altered to deal with warfare and has, among other qualities, ten retractable claws.

Janet's world on Whileaway is contrasted to the other three worlds, and the contrast results in an undercurrent of rage at how women have been devalued. The action provides women with a kind of revenge: Janet calmly breaks the arm of an obnoxious man at a cocktail party; Jael kills a man during the war on her world; and Joanna belittles the belittling critics and turns into the female man.

R. is a significant writer because she brings to science fiction truly innovative themes, perceptions, and subjects. Many of her works have a visionary quality, especially those which postulate worlds in which the exceptional woman is no exception. R. is one of the few science-fiction writers to have looked thoughtfully and innovatively at childbirth and mothering. She also has written seriously about homosexuality and the homosexual family. R. has brought a freshness, intensity, and rigor to science fiction.

WORKS: *Picnic on Paradise* (1968). *And Chaos Died* (1970). *Window Dressing* (1973). *The Female Man* (1975). *We Who Are About To* (1977). *Kittatinny: A Tale of Magic* (1978). *The Two of Them* (1978).

BIBLIOGRAPHY: Calkins, E., and B. McGhan, *Teaching Tomorrow: A Handbook of Science Fiction for Teachers* (1972). Delany, S., Introduction to *Alyx* (1976). Scholls, J., and E. Rabkin, *Science Fiction: History, Science, Vision* (1977). Sargent, P., *Women of Wonder* (1974). Sargent, P., *More Women of Wonder* (1976).

For articles in reference works, see: *CA*, 25–28 (1971).

BILLIE J. WAHLSTROM